T0183239

Lecture Notes in Computer Science 10065

Commenced Publication in 1973
Founding and Former Series Editors:
Gerhard Goos, Juris Hartmanis, and Jan van Leeuwen

Editorial Board

More information about this series at http://www.springer.com/series/7409

Guojun Wang · Yanbo Han
Gregorio Martínez Pérez (Eds.)

Advances in Services Computing

10th Asia-Pacific Services Computing Conference, APSCC 2016
Zhangjiajie, China, November 16–18, 2016
Proceedings

 Springer

Editors
Guojun Wang
Guangzhou University
Guangzhou
China

Gregorio Martínez Pérez
University of Murcia
Murcia
Spain

Yanbo Han
North China University of Technology
Beijing
China

ISSN 0302-9743   ISSN 1611-3349   (electronic)
Lecture Notes in Computer Science
ISBN 978-3-319-49177-6   ISBN 978-3-319-49178-3   (eBook)
DOI 10.1007/978-3-319-49178-3

Library of Congress Control Number: 2016956497

LNCS Sublibrary: SL3 – Information Systems and Applications, incl. Internet/Web, and HCI

Printed on acid-free paper

This Springer imprint is published by Springer Nature
The registered company is Springer International Publishing AG
The registered company address is: Gewerbestrasse 11, 6330 Cham, Switzerland

Preface

Welcome to the proceedings of the 10th International Conference on Asia-Pacific Services Computing (APSCC 2016), which was jointly organized by Central South University, Guangzhou University, Jishou University, and North China University of Technology.

APSCC 2016 was held in Zhangjiajie, China, during November 16–18, 2016. The conference aims at bringing together researchers and practitioners from both academia and industry who are working on services computing, cloud computing, big data, and social/peer-to-peer/mobile/ubiquitous/pervasive computing. APSCC is an important forum in which to exchange information regarding advances in the state of the art and practice of IT/telecommunication-driven business services and application services, as well as to identify emerging research topics and define the future directions of services computing. Previous APSCC conferences were held in Guangzhou, China (2006), Tsukuba Science City, Japan (2007), Yilan, Taiwan, China (2008), Biopolis, Singapore (2009), Hangzhou, China (2010), Jeju, Korea (2011), Guilin, China (2012), Fuzhou, China (2014), and Bangkok, Thailand (2015).

As a premier conference on services computing, APSCC 2016 received research papers on related research areas from all around the world. This year we received 107 submissions for the main conference. These manuscripts underwent a rigorous peer-review process with at least three reviewers per paper. According to the review results, 38 papers were selected for oral presentation at the conference, giving an acceptance rate of 35.5 %.

We would like to offer our gratitude to Prof. Hai Jin from Huazhong University of Science and Technology, China, and Dr. Liang-Jie Zhang from Kingdee International Software Group Company Limited, China, the Steering Committee chairs, for leading the conference and guiding its course. We are also indebted to the Program Committee members and the external reviewers, who contributed their valuable time and expertise to provide professional reviews working under a very tight schedule. Thanks also go to the conference secretariat, Dr. Chen Liu from North China University of Technology, for assembling an excellent Program Committee to expertly manage the paper reviewing and selection process.

Thanks also go to: the publicity chairs, Dr. Peter Mueller, Dr. Md. Zakirul Alam Bhuiyan, and Dr. Wenbin Jiang; the publication chair, Dr. Wenjun Jiang; the organization chairs, Prof. Fang Qi, Dr. Xiaofei Xing, Prof. Qingping Zhou; the registration Chair, Ms. Pin Liu; the conference secretariat, Dr. Chen Liu; and our Webmaster, Ms. Shan Peng.

We also take this opportunity to thank all the authors, participants, and session chairs for their efforts, many of whom traveled long distances to attend this conference and make their valuable contributions. Last but not least, we are very grateful to our keynote speakers who kindly accepted our invitation to give insightful talks.

Finally, we sincerely hope that the conference provided a very good opportunity for attendees to learn from each other. Enjoy the conference proceedings.

October 2016

Guojun Wang
Rasmus Hjorth Nielsen
Rongbo Lu
Yanbo Han
Gregorio Martínez Pérez

Organization

General Chairs

Guojun Wang	Guangzhou University, China
Rasmus Hjorth Nielsen	Movimento Group, California, USA
Rongbo Lu	Jishou University, China

Program Chairs

Yanbo Han	North China University of Technology, China
Gregorio Martinez	University of Murcia, Spain

Steering Committee Chairs

Hai Jin	Huazhong University of Science and Technology, China
Liang-Jie Zhang	Kingdee International Software Group Company Limited, China

Workshop Chairs

Jemal H. Abawajy	Deakin University, Australia
Tommaso Pecorella	Università di Firenze, Italy
Qin Liu	Hunan University, China

Publicity Chairs

Peter Mueller	IBM Zurich Research Laboratory, Switzerland
Md. Zakirul Alam Bhuiyan	Temple University, USA
Wenbin Jiang	Huazhong University of Science and Technology, China

Publication Chair

Wenjun Jiang	Hunan University, China

Registration Chair

Pin Liu	Central South University, China

Local Arrangements Chairs

Fang Qi	Central South University, China
Xiaofei Xing	Guangzhou University, China
Qingping Zhou	Jishou University, China

Program Committee

Baokang Zhao	The Hong Kong Polytechnic University, China
Bin Cheng	NEC Laboratories Europe, Germany
Bin Guo	Institut Telecom SudParis, France
Bo Cheng	Beijing University of Posts and Telecommunications, China
Cheng Wang	Tongji University, China
Chunming Hu	Beihang University, China
ChunYuan Lin	Chang Gung University, Taiwan
Deke Guo	National University of Defense Technology, China
Eduard Babulak	Sungkyunkwan University, Korea
Fei Li	Vienna University of Technology, Austria
Fu Chen	Beijing Foreign Studies University, China
Guanying Wu	Tennessee Technological University, USA
Hailong Sun	Beihang University, China
Hongbing Wang	Southeast University, China
Hongzhi Wang	Harbin Institute of Technology, China
Jian Wang	Wuhan University, China
Jianwu Wang	University of Maryland, USA
Jian Yu	Auckland University of Technology, New Zealand
Jiliang Wang	Tsinghua University, China
Kaijun Ren	National University of Defense Technology, China
Lai Xu	Bournemouth University, UK
Lei Wang	Southeast University, China
Liang Chen	Zhejiang University, China
Lizhen Cui	Shandong University, China
Nuno Laranjeiro	University of Coimbra, Portugal
Pengcheng Zhang	Hohai University, China
Qing Liu	Commonwealth Scientific and Industrial Research Organization, Australia
Qi Yu	Rochester Institute of Technology, USA
Quan Z. Sheng	The University of Adelaide, Australia
Shangguang Wang	Beijing University of Posts and Telecommunications, China
Shiping Chen	Commonwealth Scientific and Industrial Research Organization, Australia
Shizhan Chen	Tianjin University, China
Shuiguang Deng	Zhejiang University, China
Tadashi Dohi	Hiroshima University, Japan

Wei Dong	Zhejiang University, China
Weigang Wu	Sun Yat-sen University, China
Wei Song	Nanjing University of Science and Technology, China
Wei Tan	IBM, USA
Wenjun Wu	University of Chicago, USA
Xiang Lian	University of Texas — Pan American, USA
Xianzhi Wang	The University of Adelaide, Australia
Xiaofeng Gao	Shanghai Jiao Tong University, China
Xiapu Luo	The Hong Kong Polytechnic University, China
Xiwei Xu	National ICT Australia, Australia
Yanmin Zhu	Shanghai Jiao Tong University, China
Ye Yuan	Northeastern Universtiy, China
Ye Zhang	Pennsylvania State University, USA
Yi Cai	South China University of Technology, China
Yong Xia	Northwestern Polytechnical University, China
Yu Hua	Huazhong University of Science and Technology, China
Yungang Bao	Institute of Computing Technology, Chinese Academy of Science, China
Yutao Ma	Wuhan University, China
Zaiwen Feng	Wuhan University, China
Zhengwei Qi	Shanghai Jiao Tong University, China
Zhenhua Li	Tsinghua University, China
Zhuofeng Zhao	North China University of Technology, China

Secretariat

Chen Liu	North China University of Technology, China

Webmaster

Shan Peng	Central South University, China

APSCC 2016 Sponsors

Contents

COPO: A Novel Position-Adaptive Method for Smartphone-Based Human Activity Recognition

Changhai Wang, Yuwei Xu$^{(\boxtimes)}$, Jianzhong Zhang$^{(\boxtimes)}$, and Wenping Yu

Department of Computer and Control Engineering, Nankai University,
Tianjin 300350, China
{storm_xp2008,yuwenping}@mail.nankai.edu.cn, {xuyw,zhangjz}@nankai.edu.cn

Abstract. In recent years, smartphone-based human activity recognition has become a promising research field of mobile computing, and is widely applied in inertial positioning, fall detection, and personalized recommendation. In practical scenario, smartphone can be placed at several body positions, such as trouser pocket, jacket pocket and so on. Since data is collected from the accelerometer embedded in smartphone, different body locations cannot generate consistent data for the same activity. As a result, the samples at a new position usually obtains low recognition rate from the classifier trained by the original data collected from other positions. In this paper, we propose a COntinuity-based POsition-adaptive recognition method, abbreviated COPO, for dealing with this problem. Considering the continuous results with high probability of correct recognition, we select them as the retraining data in COPO for updating the initial classifier. To prove the effectiveness of retraining data selecting method theoretically, we use Hidden Markov Model (HMM) to calculate the probability that the continuous recognition results are correctly recognized. Finally, a number of experiments are designed to verify our COPO, including data collection, performance comparison, and parameter analysis. The results show that the recognition rate of COPO is 2.62 % higher than other common methods.

Keywords: Accelerometer · Activity recognition · Phone location independent · Hidden markov model · Activity duration

1 Introduction

In the past decades, accelerometer-based human activity recognition has been a research focus of industry and academia all over the world [1,6]. A lot of works have been put forward in the target of recognizing human activities(such as walking, running, going upstairs and so on) by the sensing data which is generated by accelerometer, and the research results have been widely applied in elderly health monitoring [11], human behavior tracking [10] and other commercial ways.

With the popularity of smartphone, PDA, and other kinds of mobile terminals, the mobile internet era comes. Since the accelerometer can be embedded in each smartphone, the smartphone-based human activity recognition is now becoming a novel hotspot in the research field of mobile computing. If obtaining

G. Wang et al. (Eds.): APSCC 2016, LNCS 10065, pp. 1–14, 2016.
DOI: 10.1007/978-3-319-49178-3_1

a user's daily body activities, we are able to analyze his behavior, learn much about personal information, and even speculate the surrounding environment. All of those information is useful for application development [6], personalized recommendation, and advertising targeted delivery. Overall, the smartphone-based human activity recognition is a promising research direction with great potential.

However, every coin has two sides. When enjoying the convenience, we have to face a new problem brought by smartphones. Different from traditional methods binding the accelerometer to a fixed position, a smartphone is usually placed at various positions of the human body, such as trouser pocket, jacket pocket and so on. For the same activity, those positions make accelerometer generate inconsistent data. As a result, it is difficult to use the classifier which is trained by original data to recognize the samples collected at a new position. In this case, the recognition rate of new samples is much lower than usual. In order to maintain the performance, a position-independent method should be further studied.

In this paper, we propose a COntinuity-based POsition-adaptive recognition method, abbreviated COPO, for dealing with the above problem. The contributions of our work are summarized as follows.

- We propose COPO to update the classifier by the continuous results, which is able to maintain high recognition rate for the samples collected from a new location.
- We use Hidden Markov Model (HMM) to theoretically analysis the probability that the continuous recognition results are correctly recognized in order to select the beneficial results for COPO.
- We prove the feasibility of COPO by the experiments on real dataset, compare it with the traditional methods, and also analyze its affecting factors.

This paper focuses on the issue of smartphone position adaptive activity recognition method. The paper is organized as follows. Section 2 will give the related research on human activity recognition. Section 3 will describe the overview of our method. Section 4 will analyze the retraining data selecting method theoretically. Section 5 will introduce the experiments, including the performance of different methods, influence of different parameters and so on. Section 6 presents the conclusions of this work.

2   Related Work

In recent years, a growing number of smartphones are embedded with accelerometers, gyroscopes and other sensors. These sensors can collect user's personal information and environment information. Rui W. et al. [16] leveraged smartphones to aware human's mental problem through analyzing user's habits including daily activities. Anshul R. et al. [13] applied human activity recognition to indoor localization. Hoseini-Tabatabaei S. et al. [6] and Bulling A. et al. [1] summarized the current situation of smartphone based activity recognition.

In order to improve the recognition rate when the phone's position is unfixed, several position independent feature extraction methods [2,14,15] were proposed. Chen et al. [2] proposed principal component analysis (PCA) dimension based feature extraction algorithm. This method could extract robust features for activity recognition. We proposed frequency domain features [15] and angle features [14] to improve activity recognition rate. However, position independent feature extraction methods can just reduce the impact of phone position. Due to the diversity of the phone positions, this problem can't be thoroughly solved through improving feature extraction algorithm.

Another method to solve this problem is using the new position's activities samples to update the original classifier. The updated classifier will significantly improve the recognition rate. In these methods, selecting the retraining data from unlabeled new positions' activities samples is a key issue should be settled. [2] proposed the concept of confidence which is calculated using extreme learning machine (ELM) [7] outputs. High confidence results were chosen as the retraining data in the updating. This method improved the recognition rate effectively. [3] employed the same confidence method to cross-people activity recognition. But, this confidence method has some limitation. The confidence which is calculated using the ELM outputs relates to samples' distribution. This correlation makes high confidence results are not conducive to improving the performance of the retrained classifier. The method of selecting retraining data has a large room for improvement.

HMM is a statistical model that is used to describe the Markov Model with hidden state. In recent decades, it has been widely used in speech recognition [8], bioinformatics [5] and other fields. In video based activity recognition, the HMM was used to recognize human activity [12] and detect abnormal activities [4]. The HMM was also used in human abnormal activities detection [9] based on accelerometer. These studies have shown that it can achieve good performance leveraging HMM to solve problems on human activity recognition.

This paper proposes COPO which is an improved method based on [2]. Compared with [2] which selects high confidence results as the retraining data, this method selects continuous results instead. In order to analyze the correctness and limitation of this method, this paper introduces the HMM of activity recognition and its parameters. The analysis result shows that the correct probability of continuous activities is significantly larger than single activities. Finally, the experiments show the advantages of this method.

3   Overview of COPO

3.1   Framework of COPO

Suppose that we have some labeled samples which are collected when the phone is placed on several known body positions. These samples are the original training set which are used to train an initial classifier. The initial classifier can effectively recognize user's activity when the phone is placed on these known body positions.

In online activity recognition, the phone is placed on a new body position. In this case, the recognition rate is low.

To improve the recognition rate, we want to label these unlabeled samples using the recognition results, and select some correctly recognized samples to update the initial classifier. After that, the recognition rate will significantly enhance when the phone is placed on this new position. The framework of phone position adaptive activity recognition is shown as Fig. 1.

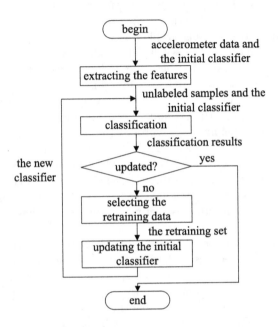

Fig. 1. The framework of phone position adaptive activity recognition

In this framework, selecting the samples which are correctly recognized is the most important step, and evaluating the correctness of recognition results is the key issue of this step [2].

3.2 Retraining Data Selection

Consider the activity recognition in actual application. As human's activities are continuous, there is correlation between two adjacent activities. For example, if the current activity is walking, the previous and the succeeding activities hold high probability of walking, and the probability of activity conversion is low. Taking this thought to the recognition results. In the recognition results sequence, if the recognized label of a sample is different from its previous and succeeding samples, this sample holds high probability of incorrectly recognized. If several adjacent samples are recognized as the same label, the probability that these samples are incorrectly recognized is relatively low. Thus, we define three basic concepts.

Definition 1. *In actual applications, as an activity appears, the mean sample number of this activity maintains is defined as activity duration.*

For example, when the activity upstairs appears, it always lasts 10 samples. The activity duration of upstairs is 10. This concept is used to calculated the transfer matrix shown as Eq. 2 in Sect. 4.2.

Definition 2. *Given a sequence of recognized labels, the labels who are different with their adjacent labels are defined as the single labels, and the rests are named continuous labels.*

Definition 3. *In the recognized labels sequence, if a label is the same with its n adjacent labels, the continuous number of this label is n.*

For example, if the results sequence is (w,r,r,r,w,r), the first, the fifth and the sixth are single labels, the second to the fourth are continuous labels. The continuous numbers of the second to the fourth are 3, and the rests are 1.

Based on these three definitions, we can evaluate the correctness of a recognition result by observing its continuous number. If the continuous number is one, the probability that the corresponding sample is correctly recognized is low. Otherwise, the probability is relatively high. Thus, in the framework of phone position adaptive activity recognition, we can choose the labels whose continuous number is higher than a predefined threshold and their corresponding samples as the retraining data.

3.3   Activity Recognition Algorithm

The detailed phone position adaptive activity recognition is shown as Algorithm 1.

As shown in Algorithm 1, the inputs are the initial classifier C_0, the predefined continuous number threshold τ, and the unlabeled samples sequence W. The outputs are the new classifier C_1 and the recognition results sequence L. In Algorithm 1, the first step is classifying the unlabeled samples using the initial classifier. After this step, we can get a temporary labels sequence of W, denoted by L. As the recognition rate which the W is classified by C_0 is low, there are many incorrectly recognized labels in L. Step 3 to Step 13 devote to selecting the correctly recognized labels from L, and adding these labels and their corresponding samples to the retraining set which is denoted by D. The method of selecting retraining set is detecting the continuous number of each recognition label. If the continuous number of a recognition label is higher than the threshold τ, this label and its corresponding sample are added to D.

After that, the selected retraining set is used to update the initial classifier, and the new classifier is denoted by C_1. As the new classifier is updated using samples collected from new phone position, the recognition rate which W is classified by C_1 is relatively higher than C_0. In the last step of Algorithm 1, C_1 is used to classify W, and the finally recognition labels sequence is obtained.

Algorithm 1. COntinuity-based POsition-adaptive recognition method (COPO)

Input:

    The initial classifier C_0;

    The predefined continuous number threshold τ;

    The unlabeled samples sequence collected from new phone positions $\boldsymbol{W} = (w_1, w_2, \cdots w_m)$;

Output:

    The updated classifier C_1;

    The recognition results of $\boldsymbol{W}$, $\boldsymbol{L} = (l_1, l_2, \cdots l_m)$;

1: $\boldsymbol{L} = \text{classification}(C_0, \boldsymbol{W})$;

2: $\boldsymbol{D} = \emptyset, len = 1, beg = 1$; //Initialise the parameters

3: **for** $i = 2 : m$

4:     **if** $l_{beg} \neq l_i \| i == m$

5:         **if** $len >= \tau$

6:             $\boldsymbol{D} = \boldsymbol{D} \cup \{(w_j, l_j) \, | \, beg \leq j < i\}$;

7:         **end**

8:         $first = first + len$;

9:         $len = 1$;

10:     **else**

11:         $len + +$;

12:     **end**

13: **end**

14: $C_1 = \text{update}(C_0, \boldsymbol{D})$;

15: $\boldsymbol{L} = \text{classification}(C_1, \boldsymbol{W})$;

---

4   Analysis of Retraining Data Selecting Method

4.1   Definition of $\mathcal{P}_m$

As shown in Fig. 1, selecting the retraining data from the unlabeled samples is the most important step in this framework. The correctness of these retraining data is directly related to the recognition rate of the updated classifier. In Algorithm 1, we suppose the recognized labels whose continuous numbers are larger than τ hold high probability of correctly recognized, and the corresponding samples are added to the retraining set. This section will analysis the correctness of our retraining data selecting method theoretically. Generally, we define the $\mathcal{P}_m$.

Definition 4. *Given a subsequence containing m same labels, the probability that this subsequence is correctly recognized is denoted by $\mathcal{P}_m$.*

In this definition, the m is the continuous number which defined in Definition 3. The relationship between $\mathcal{P}_m$ and m will be analyzed through building the hidden Markov Model.

As the definition, $\mathcal{P}_m$ is the probability that the actual label of this sequence is k on the condition that the recognized label is k. Here, we define two events. The event A is defined as the actual label of this subsequence is k. The event B is defined as the recognized label is k. Thus, the $\mathcal{P}_m$ can be calculated using Eq. 1.

$$\mathcal{P}_m = P(A|B) = \frac{P(A)P(B|A)}{P(B)} \tag{1}$$

In Eq. 1, $\mathcal{P}_m$ is defined as the conditional probability which is the probability that the event A occurs on the condition that the event B occurs. Using the Bayes formula, it can be converted into three probabilities which are easy to calculate. The $P(A)$ is the probability that the actual label of this sequence is k. The $P(B|A)$ is the probability that the recognized label of this sequence is k on the condition that the actual label is k, which is the probability that this subsequence is correctly recognized. The $P(B)$ is the probability that the recognized label is k without considering the actual label of this subsequence. To calculating the three probabilities, HMM should be used. Section 4.2 will introduce the HMM of activity recognition and its parameters. Section 4.3 will give the detailed derivation of $\mathcal{P}_m$. Section 4.4 will focus on the analysis of $\mathcal{P}_m$.

4.2   HMM Parameters

The HMM includes two states. One is hidden state while the other one is visible state. In activity recognition, the hidden states correspond to human's actual activities, while the visible states are recognized results. The state set is written as $\boldsymbol{S} = \{S_1, S_2, \cdots, S_n\}$, which includes all the possible activities. The HMM of activity is shown in Fig. 2.

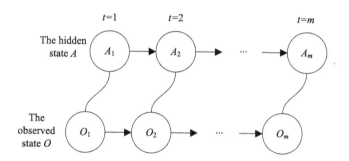

Fig. 2. The Hidden Markov Model of activity recognition

In Fig. 2, state A is the actual activity sequence, and the state O is the recognized activity sequence. When $t = i$, the hidden state is A_i, and $A_i \in \boldsymbol{S}$. With the changes of t, the human body may maintain the current activity, or change to another. The probability that one activity turn to another is called transfer probability. All transfer probabilities compose the transfer matrix, which describes the conversion relationship between different activities. In this paper, the transfer matrix is described as $|q_{ij}|_{n \times n}$. Where $0 \leq q_{ij} \leq 1$, and $\sum_{j=1}^{n} q_{ij} = 1$. q_{ij} indicates the probability that the current activity is S_i, and the succeeding activity is S_j.

In actual applications, this parameter is related to the duration of activity S_i. If the activity duration is l_i, q_{ij} can be calculated using the Eq. 2.

$$q_{ij} = \begin{cases} \frac{l_i - 1}{l_i}, & i = j \\ \frac{1}{l_i(n-1)}, & i \neq j \end{cases} \tag{2}$$

Corresponding with A_i, the observable state O_i is the recognized activity at $t = i$, and $O_i \in S$. The purpose of the activity recognition algorithm is making the recognized activity the same with the actual activity. But in practical application scenarios, not all the activities can be recognized correctly. In this model, the probability that activity S_i is recognized as activity S_j is called confusion probability. All the confusion probabilities compose confusion matrix. The confusion matrix in this paper is described as $|p_{ij}|_{n \times n}$. Where $0 \leq p_{ij} \leq 1$, and $\sum_{j=1}^{n} p_{ij} = 1$. p_{ij} indicates the probability that the activity S_i is recognized as the activity is S_j.

Another important parameter of HMM is the initial state vector, which describes each activity's probability in the state A_1. The initial state vector is written as $[\beta_1, \beta_2, \cdots, \beta_n]$. Where $0 \leq \beta_i \leq 1$, and $\sum_{i=1}^{n} \beta_i = 1$. β_i means the activity S_i's probability is β_i in the state A_1.

4.3 Derivation of $\mathcal{P}_m$

In Sect. 4.1, we introduced $\mathcal{P}_m$. In the equation, three probabilities should be calculated, that is $P(A)$, $P(B|A)$ and $P(B)$, which will be given in this section.

According to Sect. 4.2, the probability that the first activity is k is β_k. In the following $m - 1$ states, the human maintains this activity. Thus, $P(A)$ can be calculated using the Eq. 3.

$$P(A) = \beta_k q_{kk}^{m-1} \tag{3}$$

When the actual activity sequence is continuous and the activity label is k, $P(B|A)$ is the probability that this sequence is correctly recognized. For each activity, the correctly recognized probability is p_{kk}. Thus, $P(B|A)$ can be calculated using the Eq. 4.

$$P(B|A) = p_{kk}^{m} \tag{4}$$

When the model parameters are given, the $P(B)$ is the probability that the recognized sequence is continuous and the label is k. In HMM, it is a classical issue which has been solved by the Forward algorithm [8]. Based on the Eqs. 3, 4 and the Forward algorithm, the $\mathcal{P}_m$ can be calculated using Eq. 5.

$$\mathcal{P}_m = \frac{\beta_k q_{kk}^{m-1} p_{kk}^{m}}{\sum_{i=1}^{n} \alpha_m(i)} \tag{5}$$

Where, $\sum_{i=1}^{n} \alpha_m(i)$ is $P(B)$, and

$$\alpha_m(i) = \begin{cases} \beta_i p_{ik}, & m = 1 \\ p_{ik} \sum_{j=1}^{n} \alpha_{m-1}(j) q_{ji}, & m > 1 \end{cases} \tag{6}$$

As shown in Eqs. 5 and 6, $\mathcal{P}_m$ is affected by the initial state vector, the transfer matrix and the confusion matrix, where the transfer matrix is directly related to the activity duration. As the Eq. 6 is a recursion formula, we should analyze the $\mathcal{P}_m$ through simulation. In the simulation, these parameters are set to different values, and the $\mathcal{P}_m$ is calculated. It will be introduced in the following section.

4.4 Simulation of $\mathcal{P}_m$

In this section, HMM parameters are set to different values and $\mathcal{P}_m$ is calculated according to Eqs. 5 and 6. These parameters include the initial probability β_k, the correctly recognized probability p_{kk}, and the activity duration l_k.

For the initial probability, we assume other activities except activity k have the same initial probability. Thus, $\beta_i = \frac{1-\beta_k}{n-1}$ when $i \neq k$. For the confusion matrix, the probability that activity k is recognized by other activities is assumed has the same value. Thus, $p_{ik} = \frac{1-p_{kk}}{n-1}$ when $i \neq k$. Figure 3 shows the curves of $\mathcal{P}_m$ as these three parameters are set to different values.

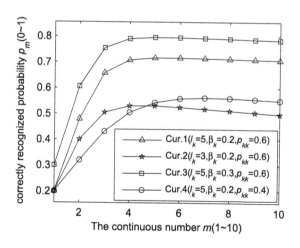

Fig. 3. The $\mathcal{P}_m$ of different parameters

In Fig. 3, there are four curves which represent different groups of parameters. For the Cur.1, the initial probability is 0.2, the correctly recognized probability is 0.6, and the activity duration is 5. As shown in Cur.1, when $m = 1$, $\mathcal{P}_m = \beta_k$.

With the increase of m, $\mathcal{P}_m$ is significantly increased. Compared to the Cur.1, the activity duration of Cur.2 reduces to 3. Comparing these two curves, it can be found that the $\mathcal{P}_m$ of Cur.2 is smaller than Cur.1. But the correctly recognized probabilities of continuous labels are still larger than single labels.

Compared to the Cur.1, the initial probability of Cur.3 increases to 0.3. But the tendencies of these two curves are substantially the same. It reveals that the initial probability doesn't affect the correctness of this assumption which the correctly recognized probabilities of continuous labels are larger than single ones. Compared to the Cur.1, the Cur.4 decreases the recognition rate from 0.6 to 0.4. Although the $\mathcal{P}_m$ becomes smaller, the correctly recognized probabilities of continuous labels are still larger than single ones.

Through the analysis of Fig. 3, we can know that the correctly recognized probabilities of continuous labels are much larger than single labels. The next section will evaluate our activity recognition method through experiments.

5   Experiments

While the COPO is introduced in Sect. 3 and the effectiveness of this method is analyzed in Sect. 4, this section will focus on the experimental evaluations. In Sect. 5.1, it will introduce the data collection and experimental approach. Section 5.2 will give the performance of different methods. Section 5.3 will analyze the impact of activity duration.

5.1   Data Collection and Feature Extraction

Before the experiments, the activities data were collected. The activities include standing still, walking, running, going upstairs and going downstairs. The data collecting device was MI 2S smartphone which embedded with a tri-axial accelerometer. The sampling frequency was 100 Hz. In the collecting, the smartphone was fixed on a specified body position while the participant performs these activities. Phone positions are shown in Fig. 4.

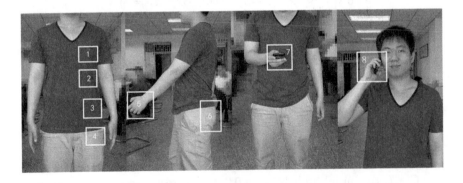

Fig. 4. Phone positions of data collection

As shown in Fig. 4, the positions of smartphone are front pockets (e.g. 1,2,3,4), hands (e.g. 5,7), rear pant pockets (e.g. 6) and next to the ears (e.g. 8). In the collecting, the collected data were automatically saved in the smartphone. After data collecting, we copied these data to PC for simulation. Before run the COPO, half-overlapping sliding window was used to divide these raw data to windows. Each window contains 256 raw data. Window numbers of each activity and each position are shown in Table 1.

Table 1. Window numbers of activities

	Running	Upstairs	Downstairs	Standing	Walking	Total
Loc.1	230	176	162	176	185	929
Loc.2	178	180	175	150	180	863
Loc.3	195	184	177	157	176	889
Loc.4	195	166	161	166	180	868
Loc.5	186	168	163	169	176	862
Loc.6	195	170	174	151	172	862
Loc.7	215	162	162	172	186	897
Loc.8	179	175	170	149	172	845
Total	1573	1381	1344	1290	1427	7015

After window division, frequency domain [15] and angle feature [14] were extracted from each window. Each window's features compose a vector which was called a sample. In the experiments, samples collected from 7 positions were used to train the initial classifier, while samples collected from the rest position were used to apply the COPO and test the performance of the updated classifier. The classifier in our experiment is ELM [2]. The following section will give the performance of different methods.

5.2   Performance Comparison

In the simulation, the initial classifier was trained using the training set first. Then, the testing set was used to perform the COPO. After classification, we recorded the number of samples which were correctly recognized, and the ratio between this number and total testing samples number was regarded as the recognition rate. The simulation repeated 1000 times for each position. The mean value of the 1000 times was regarded as the finally recognition rate.

The current popular phone position independent activity recognition method is TransELM which was proposed in [2]. Table 2 shows the performance of TransELM and our method. In TransELM, the confidence threshold was set to 0.6, in which the TransELM can achieve the best performance. In our method, the activity duration of testing set was set to 10 and the continuous number threshold τ was set to 3. Moreover, the None is the performance of the initial

Table 2. The performance of different methods

	None(%)	TransELM(%)	COPO(%)	Best(%)	Improved(%)
Loc.1	94.73	96.27	96.53	97.51	0.26
Loc.2	93.60	93.71	93.79	94.52	0.08
Loc.3	97.77	97.66	98.12	98.47	0.46
Loc.4	83.06	81.76	88.93	98.99	7.17
Loc.5	71.51	75.74	82.44	95.55	6.70
Loc.6	83.34	89.13	90.12	92.27	0.99
Loc.7	82.88	84.41	85.88	87.22	1.47
Loc.8	80.15	86.04	89.90	89.18	3.86
Aver	85.88	88.09	90.71	94.21	2.62

classifier which is not updated. The Best is the performance that the classifier was trained using samples collected from 8 positions. The Improved is the value of COPO minus TransELM.

In Table 2, the first row is the recognition rate which samples collected from Loc.1 are the testing set. The same goes for other rows. Comparing TransELM and COPO in Table 2, it can find that the COPO performs better than TransELM. In addition to Loc.2 whose recognition rate is approximately equal, other positions are all improved. The recognition rate of Loc.4 improves most, about 7.17 %. Overall, COPO can improve the recognition rate about 2.62 %.

5.3   Impact of Activity Duration

This section will focus on the impact of activity duration which is another important parameter in HMM of activity recognition. As the activity duration is different from scene to scene, the performance of COPO will be different. To analyze the impact of activity duration, the testing samples sequence are randomly restructured in this section. In the restructuring, the duration of each activity is set to a specified value, and the conversion between different activities is randomly appointed. After restructuring, we can get a new activity sequence. It could simulate different scenarios by simply changing the activity duration. Figure 5 depicts activity recognition rate as activity duration changes when the phone is on Loc.7. Substantially the same goes for other positions.

Figure 5 depicts the recognition rate as the activity duration changes from 2 to 15[1]. Analyzing the COPO individually, when the activity duration is 2 and 3, the recognition rate is relatively lower than other values. The main reason is that, as the activity duration is small, the number of incorrect recognized labels in continuous recognized results is large (see Cur.2 in Fig. 3). Incorrect recognized labels and their corresponding samples can reduce the recognition

---

[1] When the activity duration is 2, the continuous number threshold is set to 2.

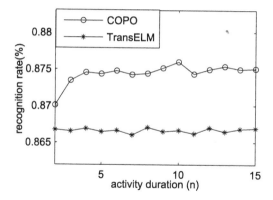

Fig. 5. The impact of activity duration

rate of updated classifier. As the activity duration is larger than 4, the number of incorrectly recognized samples is significantly reduced. Thus, the recognition rate floats near the highest value. But the performance of COPO is better than TransELM for all activity durations.

6   Conclusion

Smartphone based activity recognition is widely applied in inertial positioning, health monitoring. As the smartphone is always placed on different body positions, position adaptive activity recognition algorithm is badly needed. This paper proposed COPO which improved the most popular method TransELM. First, this paper gave the overview of COPO which selects continuous recognized results as the retraining data to update the initial classifier. Then, HMM of activity recognition is built in order to verify the correctness of retraining data selecting method. Finally, experiments show that compared with TransELM, TranCon improves the recognition rate about 2.62 %.

There are still plenty of advanced issues worth research in the further work. Comparing the COPO and the Best in Table 2, we can know that there is a gap between current method and the best situation. The issue of selecting retraining data still should be improved in the future work.

Acknowledgments. This work was supported by The Natural Science Foundation of Tianjin(No. 16JCQNJC00700).

References

1. Bulling, A., Blanke, U., Schiele, B.: A tutorial on human activity recognition using body-worn inertial sensors. ACM Comput. Surv. (CSUR) **46**(3), 33 (2014)
2. Chen, Y., Zhao, Z., Wang, S., Chen, Z.: Extreme learning machine-based device displacement free activity recognition model. Soft Comput. **16**(9), 1617–1625 (2012)

3. Deng, W.Y., Zheng, Q.H., Wang, Z.M.: Cross-person activity recognition using reduced kernel extreme learning machine. Neural Netw. **53**, 1–7 (2014)
4. Duong, T.V., Bui, H.H., Phung, D.Q., Venkatesh, S.: Activity recognition and abnormality detection with the switching hidden semi-markov model. In: IEEE Computer Society Conference on Computer Vision and Pattern Recognition, CVPR 2005, vol. 1, pp. 838–845. IEEE (2005)
5. Durbin, R., Eddy, S.R., Krogh, A., Mitchison, G.: Biological Sequence Analysis: Probabilistic Models of Proteins and Nucleic Acids. Cambridge University Press, Cambridge (1998)
6. Hoseini-Tabatabaei, S.A., Gluhak, A., Tafazolli, R.: A survey on smartphone-based systems for opportunistic user context recognition. ACM Comput. Surv. (CSUR) **45**(3), 27 (2013)
7. Huang, G., Huang, G.B., Song, S., You, K.: Trends in extreme learning machines: a review. Neural Netw. **61**, 32–48 (2015)
8. Jelinek, F.: Statistical Methods for Speech Recognition. MIT Press, Cambridge (1997)
9. Khan, S.S., Karg, M.E., Hoey, J., Kulic, D.: Towards the detection of unusual temporal events during activities using HMMs. In: Proceedings of the 2012 ACM Conference on Ubiquitous Computing, pp. 1075–1084. ACM (2012)
10. Lin, S.J., Chang, C., Hsu, M.F.: Multiple extreme learning machines for a two-class imbalance corporate life cycle prediction. Knowl.-Based Syst. **39**, 214–223 (2013)
11. Mazilu, S., Blanke, U., Dorfman, M., Gazit, E., Mirelman, A., Hausdorff, J.M., Tröster, G.: A wearable assistant for gait training for parkinsons disease with freezing of gait in out-of-the-lab environments. ACM Trans. Interact. Intell. Syst. (TiiS) **5**(1), 5 (2015)
12. Nguyen, N.T., Phung, D.Q., Venkatesh, S., Bui, H.: Learning and detecting activities from movement trajectories using the hierarchical hidden markov model. In: IEEE Computer Society Conference on Computer Vision and Pattern Recognition, CVPR 2005, vol. 2, pp. 955–960. IEEE (2005)
13. Rai, A., Chintalapudi, K.K., Padmanabhan, V.N., Sen, R.: Zee: zero-effort crowd-sourcing for indoor localization. In: Proceedings of the 18th Annual International Conference on Mobile Computing and Networking, pp. 293–304. ACM (2012)
14. Wang, C., Zhang, J., Li, M., Yuan, Y., Xu, Y.: A smartphone location independent activity recognition method based on the angle feature. In: Sun, X., et al. (eds.) ICA3PP 2014. LNCS, vol. 8630, pp. 179–191. Springer, Heidelberg (2014). doi:10. 1007/978-3-319-11197-1_14
15. Wang, C., Zhang, J., Wang, Z., Wang, J.: Position-independent activity recognition model for smartphone based on frequency domain algorithm. In: 2013 3rd International Conference on Computer Science and Network Technology (ICCSNT), pp. 396–399. IEEE (2013)
16. Wang, R., Chen, F., Chen, Z., Li, T., Harari, G., Tignor, S., Zhou, X., Ben-Zeev, D., Campbell, A.T.: Studentlife: assessing mental health, academic performance and behavioral trends of college students using smartphones. In: Proceedings of the 2014 ACM International Joint Conference on Pervasive and Ubiquitous Computing, pp. 3–14. ACM (2014)

Multi-relation Based Manifold Ranking Algorithm for API Recommendation

Fenfang Xie$^{(\boxtimes)}$, Jianxun Liu, Mingdong Tang, Dong Zhou,
Buqing Cao, and Min Shi

Key Laboratory of Knowledge Processing and Networked Manufacturing,
Hunan University of Science and Technology, Xiangtan 411201, China
`xiefragrance@gmail.com`, `ljx529@gmail.com`,
`tangmingdong@gmail.com`, `zdbloom@gmail.com`,
`buqingcao@gmail.com`, `toshimin132@gmail.com`

Abstract. The number of APIs on the Web has increased rapidly in recent years. It becomes quite popular for developers to combine different APIs to build innovative Mashup applications. However, it is challenging to discover the appropriate ones from enormous APIs for Mashup developers (i.e., API users). In order to recommend a set of APIs that most satisfy the users' requirements, we propose a multi-relation based manifold ranking approach. The approach exploits the textual descriptions of existing Mashups and APIs, as well as their composition relationships. It firstly groups Mashups into different clusters according to their textual descriptions, then explores multiple relations between Mashup clusters and between APIs. Finally, it employs a manifold ranking algorithm to recommend appropriate APIs to the user. Experiments on a real-world dataset crawled from ProgrammableWeb.com validate the effectiveness of the proposed approach.

Keywords: Mashup clustering · Web API · Multi-relation · Manifold ranking · API recommendation

1 Introduction

Mashup, as an emerging Web development mode, enables a developer easily combining the content from more than one source on the Web to create new applications for end-users. For example, a developer can combine the addresses and photographs of their library branches with a Google map to create a map Mashup [1]. With the spread of service computing and cloud computing, the past decade has witnesses a tremendous growth in the Application Programming Interfaces (APIs) published on the Web, which provide a variety of services such as data, storage, computing, and communication. How to Mashup APIs to create new applications thus has attracted great attention from both industry and academia. Although a user can occasionally employ a single API to meet his/her needs in Mashup creation, more often than not, the fulfilment of his/her needs relies on a combination of APIs. Therefore, to develop a Mashup, identifying a set of related APIs rather than a single specific one, becomes a key task.

According to latest statistics, the number of APIs and Mashup applications has been growing exponentially in recent years [2]. This observation indicates that finding

© Springer International Publishing AG 2016
G. Wang et al. (Eds.): APSCC 2016, LNCS 10065, pp. 15–32, 2016.
DOI: 10.1007/978-3-319-49178-3_2

appropriate APIs for Mashup developers become increasingly difficult, even for an experienced developer. For one thing, most APIs only provide a single functionality, which may not satisfy users' comprehensive needs. Therefore, APIs are often composed together to build a single application. How to discover and choose the appropriate APIs to compose for users' requirement is critical [3]. For another, only a few APIs were ever used by the users and the reuse rate of most services is rather low [4]. How to improve the usage rate of the existing APIs is also an important issue.

In order to solve the two problems mentioned above, we propose a multi-relation based manifold ranking algorithm to assist Mashup developers discovering a list of suitable APIs. Firstly, we cluster existing Mashups into groups according to their textual descriptions so that the Mashups within a cluster are similar in functionality. When a user proposes his/her requirement, we can measure the similarities between the user's requirement and the Mashup clusters to identify which cluster matches the best with the user's requirement. This can save more time than matching the user's requirement with the description of every single Mashup. Secondly, we measure the similarity relations between Mashup clusters by exploiting cosine similarity according to TF-IDF (Term Frequency–Inverse Document Frequency) vectors of them so that the Mashup clusters can associate with each other in a way of similar functionality. Thirdly, we measure the similarity relation, composition relation and potential composition relation between existing APIs so that a set of APIs relevant to the user's requirement can be identified. Finally, by integrating the different relations and the popularity of APIs, we employ a manifold ranking algorithm to recommend top-K most appropriate APIs to the user. Our approach can not only recommend APIs that are popular in the Mashups, but also recommend APIs that have similarity relations, composition relations, and potential composition relations with each other.

The main contributions of this paper are outlined below:

- We propose a multi-relation based manifold ranking algorithm to recommend APIs for Mashup creation according to the user's requirement.
- We define several relations between Mashups and between APIs, and present a set of algorithms to mine the relations.
- We conduct a set of experiments on a real-world dataset, experimental results validate the effectiveness of the proposed approach and show that our approach outperforms baseline approaches.

The remainder of the paper is organized as follows: Sect. 2 presents the framework of our approach. Section 3 gives a detailed description of our multi-relation based manifold ranking algorithm for API recommendation. Section 4 describes the experiments and discusses the results. Section 5 surveys the related work. Section 6 concludes the paper.

2 Framework

In this section, we describe the framework of our approach. The framework contains two parts: offline part and online part, which is shown in Fig. 1. The offline part includes the following main steps:

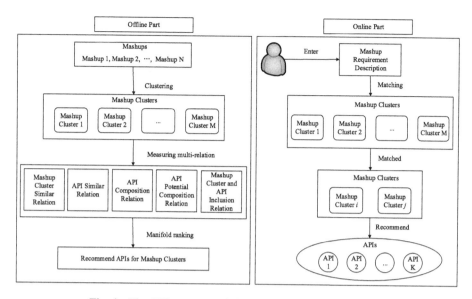

Fig. 1. The API recommendation framework of our approach

- Cluster Mashups into groups so that Mashups within a cluster are closely connected based on the similarities of their textual descriptions.
- Measure the similarity relations between Mashup clusters by using TF-IDF vectors generated from their textual descriptions.
- Measure the similarity relation, composition relation, and potential composition relation between APIs.
- Measure the inclusion relation between Mashup clusters and APIs according to the number of times that an API included in a Mashup cluster.
- Aggregate the above similarity relation, composition relation, potential composition relation and apply a manifold ranking algorithm to recommend APIs for every Mashup clusters.

The online part includes four main steps:

- Input requirement for Mashup creation. The user specifies his/her requirement of functions that he/she would like to develop for a Mashup creation.
- Match the input requirement with Mashup clusters. We calculate the similarities between the user's requirement description and every single Mashup cluster.
- Identify the matched clusters. On the basis of the similarities between Mashup clusters and the user's requirement, we choose two most similar clusters.
- Recommend APIs for Mashup creation. After identifying the similar Mashup clusters, we recommend the user with those APIs that are not only popular in the Mashups, but also have similarity relation, composition relation and potential composition relation with each other.

It is worth noting that we choose two most similar Mashup clusters instead of one single cluster in our approach. This is because the user's requirement may be complicated and needs more than one API to implement. Only one Mashup cluster may not be able to fulfill the user's requirement. For example, if a Mashup developer wants to create a Mashup that has the functions of location and sending messages, both the map cluster and the message cluster of Mashups may be needed. One can also choose three or more similar Mashup clusters to cover even more APIs. However, this may increase the algorithm complexity and reduce the precision of API recommendation.

3   Approach

In this section, we first describe the Mashup clustering algorithm, then introduce how to mine the relations between Mashup clusters and between APIs. At last, we present our proposed multi-relation based manifold ranking algorithm for API recommendation.

3.1   Mashup Clustering

Firstly, we collect the textual information of all Mashups. Secondly, we preprocess the Mashup description data, such as filtering stop words; extracting stem of words, and so on. Thirdly, we convert the preprocessed textual description of each Mashup into a TF-IDF vector. Finally, we use the *K-Medoids* algorithm [5] to cluster Mashups into similar groups in functionality. Specially, in order to measure the similarity relations between Mashup clusters, each Mashup cluster is also represented by a TF-IDF vector, which is computed by simply aggregating the description of each Mashup in it.

K-Medoids is a classical partitioning technique of clustering that clusters the data set of n objects into k clusters known a prior. A medoid can be defined as the object of a cluster whose average dissimilarity to all the objects in the cluster is minimal, i.e. it is a most centrally located point in the cluster. It is more robust to noises and outliers as compared to *K-Means* because it minimizes a sum of pair-wise dissimilarities instead of a sum of squared Euclidean distances [6].

3.2   Relation Definition and Mining

In this section, we define several relations: similarity relation between Mashup clusters and between APIs, composition & potential composition relations between APIs, and inclusion relation between Mashup clusters and APIs. We measure the similarity relations between Mashup clusters so that the similar Mashup clusters can be associated with each other. We measure the similarity, composition and potential composition relations between existing APIs so that a set of APIs relevant to a user's requirement can be identified. We measure the inclusion relation between Mashup clusters and APIs so that it will be conducive to recommend APIs that are popular in the Mashups.

Definition 1 (Similarity relation): Both the similarity relation between Mashup clusters and between APIs are exploited in this work. Let m be the number of Mashup clusters, n be the number of APIs. Let M be an $m \times m$ matrix representing the similarity relation between Mashup clusters. Let A^{sim} be an $n \times n$ matrix representing the similarity relation between APIs. Let V_i and V_j be the TF-IDF vectors of Mashup clusters or APIs.

The cosine similarity of two vectors can be calculated by using the following formula:

$$Sim(v_i, v_j) = \frac{V_i \cdot V_j}{|V_i| \cdot |V_j|} \tag{1}$$

Thus, $M_{ij} = Sim(m_i, m_j)$ and $A_{ij}^{sim} = Sim(a_i, a_j)$.

Definition 2 (Composition relation): The composition relation between two APIs represents that the two APIs have been jointly used by at least one Mashup, i.e., have been composed for creating at least one Mashup. Let A^{com} be an $n \times n$ matrix representing the composition relation between APIs. $\Psi(a_i)$ be a set of Mashups that invokes API a_i. We employed the idea of resource allocation [7, 8] to measure the composition relation in this paper.

Given a pair of API a_i and a_j, which can be used by different Mashups, among these Mashups, some Mashups may invoke both of the APIs. These Mashups can be regarded as resources allocated to a_i and a_j. If a_i and a_j have common Mashups, they are considered to have a composition relation between them. In this regard, the composition relation between API a_i and a_j can be calculated with the following formula:

$$\ell(a_i, a_j) = \sum_{c \in \Psi(a_i) \cap \Psi(a_j)} \frac{1}{k(c)} \tag{2}$$

where c is the common Mashup that invokes both a_i and a_j, and $k(c)$ is the number of APIs that c has used.

The values of $\ell(a_i, a_j)$ are likely to be greater than 1. So, we normalize the values of $\ell(a_i, a_j)$ into range [0, 1] using the following formula:

$$Com(a_i, a_j) = 1 - e^{-\ell(a_i, a_j)} \tag{3}$$

where $Com(a_i, a_j)$ represents the normalized composition relation, $A_{ij}^{com} = Com(a_i, a_j)$. Obviously, the larger of $\ell(a_i, a_j)$, the larger $Com(a_i, a_j)$ will be, i.e., the stronger is the composition relation between API a_i and a_j.

Definition 3 (Potential Composition relation): The composition relation between two APIs means that the two APIs have not been composed for Mashup creation, but have potential to be composed. Let A^{pcom} be an $n \times n$ matrix representing the potential composition relation between APIs. Based on the previously calculated similarity relation and composition relation, we measure the potential composition relation between APIs through a link prediction ideology.

To infer potential composition relation, we develop two heuristic rules based on our observations:

- Heuristics 1: If API a_i has a composition relation with API a_k, and API a_k has a composition relation with API a_j, then a_i and a_j are likely to be composed for Mashup creation. To verify this statement, we analysed the API network based on the composition relationship and found that the clustering coefficient of the network is 0.618, which is quite high, indicating there are many triangle-like structures in the network. Therefore, Heuristics 1 is reasonable.

- Heuristics 2: If API a_i has a composition relation with API a_k, and API a_k is very similar (or equivalent) to API a_j, then a_i and a_j are likely to be composed for Mashup creation. Because API a_k and API a_j are very similar, a_j can be considered as an alternative of a_k. This Heuristics is also reasonable due to our intuition.

The potential composition relations between APIs based on Heuristics 1 can be formulated as:

$$P^{H1}com(a_i, a_j) = (A^{com}A^{com})_{ij} = \sum_{k \in \Gamma(a_i) \cap \Gamma(a_j)} Com(a_i, a_k) \times Com(a_k, a_j) \quad (4)$$

where $\Gamma(a_i)$ and $\Gamma(a_j)$ are neighbor set of API a_i and a_j respectively. The more APIs acting as the role of a_k, the greater is the value of $P^{H1}com(a_i, a_j)$.

In a similar manner, to calculate the potential composition relation between APIs based on Heuristics 2, we adopt the following formula:

$$P^{H2}com(a_i, a_j) = (A^{com}A^{sim})_{ij} = \sum_{k \in \Gamma(a_i) \cap \Gamma(a_j)} Com(a_i, a_k) \times Sim(a_k, a_j) \quad (5)$$

Finally, we combine both Heuristics 1 and Heuristics 2 to infer the potential composition relation between APIs. The computation formula is:

$$Pcom(a_i, a_j) = \rho P^{H2}com(a_i, a_j) + (1 - \rho)P^{H1}com(a_i, a_j) \quad (6)$$

where $Pcom(a_i, a_j)$ represents the final potential composition relation between APIs a_i and a_j, and ρ is a real number in range [0,1] which can be customized according to specific application scenarios, $A_{ij}^{pcom} = Pcom(a_i, a_j)$.

Definition 4 (Inclusion relation): The inclusion relation between a Mashup cluster and an API means that the API has been used by at least one Mashup in the Mashup cluster. We use an $m \times n$ matrix P to represent the inclusion relation between Mashup clusters and APIs, where each entry denotes the number of times an API was included in a Mashup cluster. We can also model the inclusion relations between Mashup clusters and APIs as a heterogeneous bipartite graph.

3.3   Multi-relation Based Manifold Ranking Algorithm

Manifold ranking, a semi-supervised graph based ranking algorithm, has been widely applied in information retrieval (such as image retrieval), and shown to have excellent performance and feasibility on a variety of data types. The core idea of manifold ranking is to rank the data with respect to the intrinsic structure collectively revealed by a large number of data [9–11].

1. Original manifold ranking algorithm description

Given a set of data $X = \{x_1, x_2, \ldots, x_n\} \subset R^m$ and build a graph on the data. Let $W \in R^{n \times n}$ be the adjacency matrix wherein each entry w_{ij} represents the weight of the edge between point i and j. Let $F : X \rightarrow R$ be a ranking function which assigns to each point x_i via a ranking score F_i. Finally, we define an initial vector $q = [q_1, \ldots, q_n]^T$, in which $q_i = 1$ if x_i is a query and $q_i = 0$ otherwise.

The cost function associated with F is defined to be

$$
O(F) = \frac{1}{2} \left(\sum_{i,j=1}^{n} w_{ij} \left\| \frac{1}{\sqrt{D_{ii}}} F_i - \frac{1}{\sqrt{D_{jj}}} F_j \right\|^2 + v \sum_{i=1}^{n} \| F_i - q_i \| \right)^2 \tag{7}
$$

where $v > 0$ is the regularization parameter and D is a diagonal matrix with $D_{ii} = \sum_{j=1}^{n} w_{ij}$. The first term in the cost function is a smoothness constraint, which makes the nearby points in the space have close ranking scores. The second term is a fitting constraint, which means the ranking result should fit to the initial label assignment.

2. Our manifold ranking algorithm

In our application scenario, let $M_R = [M_{R1}, \ldots, M_{Rm}]^T$ and $A_R = [A_{R1}, \ldots, A_{Rn}]^T$ be ranking results of Mashup clusters and APIs respectively. Since we are trying to rank APIs for a given Mashup, we set $M_Q = [M_{Q1}, \ldots, M_{Qm}]^T$ in which query Mashup clusters are set to 1 and others are set to 0, and $A_Q = [A_{Q1}, \ldots, A_{Qn}]^T$ in which the corresponding APIs for the query Mashup cluster are set to 1.

After obtained the above five matrices, namely, M, A^{sim}, A^{com}, A^{pcom}, P, we employ our multi-relation based manifold ranking algorithm to recommend APIs.

By integrating multiple relations (i.e. the similarity relation between Mashup clusters and between APIs, the composition and potential composition relations between APIs, and the inclusion relation between Mashup clusters and APIs) into the original manifold ranking algorithm, our multi-relation based manifold ranking algorithm consists of seven terms, the first five terms are smoothness constraints, and the last two terms are fitting constraints. Details are as follows:

- The similarity relation between Mashup clusters

$$
\chi_1 = \frac{1}{2} \alpha \sum_{i,j=1}^{m} M_{ij} \left(\frac{1}{\sqrt{D_{M_{ii}}}} M_{Ri} - \frac{1}{\sqrt{D_{M_{jj}}}} M_{Rj} \right)^2 \tag{8}
$$

This term makes the similar Mashup clusters have close ranking scores.

- The similarity relation between APIs

$$\chi_2 = \frac{1}{2}\beta \sum_{i,j=1}^{n} A_{ij}^{sim} \left(\frac{1}{\sqrt{D_{A_{ii}^{sim}}}} A_{Ri} - \frac{1}{\sqrt{D_{A_{jj}^{sim}}}} A_{Rj} \right)^2 \tag{9}$$

This term makes the similar APIs have close ranking scores.

- The composition relation between APIs

$$\chi_3 = \frac{1}{2}\theta \sum_{i,j=1}^{n} A_{ij}^{com} \left(\frac{1}{\sqrt{D_{A_{ii}^{com}}}} A_{Ri} - \frac{1}{\sqrt{D_{A_{jj}^{com}}}} A_{Rj} \right)^2 \tag{10}$$

This term makes the composable APIs have close ranking scores.

- The potential composition relation between APIs

$$\chi_4 = \frac{1}{2}\lambda \sum_{i,j=1}^{n} A_{ij}^{pcom} \left(\frac{1}{\sqrt{D_{A_{ii}^{pcom}}}} A_{Ri} - \frac{1}{\sqrt{D_{A_{jj}^{pcom}}}} A_{Rj} \right)^2 \tag{11}$$

This term makes the potential composable APIs have close ranking scores.

- The inclusion relations between Mashup clusters and APIs

$$\chi_5 = \gamma \sum_{i=1}^{m} \sum_{j=1}^{n} P_{ij} \left(\frac{1}{\sqrt{D_{PM_{ii}}}} M_{Ri} - \frac{1}{\sqrt{D_{PA_{jj}}}} A_{Rj} \right)^2 \tag{12}$$

This term makes the popular APIs in a certain Mashup cluster have close ranking scores.

- The fitting constraint

$$\chi_6 = \mu \sum_{i=1}^{m} (M_{Ri} - M_{Qi})^2 + \eta \sum_{i=1}^{n} (A_{Ri} - A_{Qi})^2 \tag{13}$$

These two terms make the APIs' ranking results be consistent with the queried Mashup cluster.

In the above seven terms, $0 < \alpha, \beta, \theta, \lambda, \gamma, \mu, \eta < 1$ are the regularization parameters and we set $\alpha + \beta + \theta + \lambda + \gamma + \mu + \eta = 1$. Wherein, α controls the similarity relation between Mashup clusters, β controls the similarity relation between APIs, θ controls the composition relation between APIs, λ controls the potential composition relation between APIs, γ controls the inclusion relation between Mashup clusters and APIs.

Based on the above seven terms, we model our objective function as follows:

$$\Phi(M_R, A_R) = \sum_{t=1}^{6} \chi_t \tag{14}$$

Our goal is to minimize the objective function and infer A_R from M, A^{sim}, A^{com}, A^{pcom}, P, M_Q, A_Q. By minimizing it, we can get the ranking of Mashup clusters and APIs as close as possible to the given training data.

In order to simplify the objection function, we symmetrically normalize M, A^{sim}, A^{com}, A^{pcom}, P by the form like $S = D^{-1/2} W D^{-1/2}$ [12]. With simple derivations, each part can be transformed to vector representation form as $M_R^T(I - S_M)M_R, A_R^T(I - S_A^{sim})A_R$, $A_R^T(I - S_A^{com})A_R, A_R^T(I - S_A^{pcom})A_R, M_R^TM_R + A_R^TA_R - 2M_R^TS_PA_R$ [13].

Then we can rewrite the objective function in the equivalent matrix-vector form:

$$\begin{aligned}\Phi(M_R, A_R) = {} & \alpha M_R^T(I - S_M)M_R + \beta A_R^T(I - S_A^{sim})A_R + \theta A_R^T(I - S_A^{com})A_R + \lambda A_R^T(I - S_A^{pcom})A_R \\ & + \gamma(M_R^TM_R + A_R^TA_R - 2M_R^TS_PA_R) + \mu(M_R - M_Q)^T(M_R - M_Q) + \eta(A_R - A_Q)^T(A_R - A_Q)\end{aligned} \tag{15}$$

Where I is the corresponding identity matrix.

We minimize the objective function with respect to M_R and A_R by differentiating it and set the corresponding derivatives to 0. Namely,

$$\frac{\partial \Phi}{\partial M_R} = [(1 - \beta - \theta - \lambda - \eta)I - \alpha S_M]M_R - \gamma S_R A_R - \mu M_Q = 0 \tag{16}$$

$$\frac{\partial \Phi}{\partial A_R} = [(1 - \alpha - \mu)I - \beta S_A^{sim} - \theta S_A^{com} - \lambda S_A^{pcom}]A_R - \gamma S_P^T M_R - \eta A_Q = 0 \tag{17}$$

Let $\varphi = (1 - \alpha - \mu)I - \beta S_A^{sim} - \theta S_A^{com} - \lambda S_A^{pcom}$ and $\phi = (1 - \beta - \theta - \lambda - \eta)I - \alpha S_M$, then we can obtain A_R.

$$A_R = \varphi^{-1}\left[\gamma S_P^T(\phi - \gamma^2 S_P\varphi^{-1}S_P^T)^{-1}(uM_Q + \gamma S_P\varphi^{-1}\eta A_Q) + \eta A_Q\right] \tag{18}$$

After computing A_R, we can employ it to recommend APIs for mashup clusters.

3. Recommend APIs for Mashup creation

Through our multi-relation based manifold ranking algorithm, we can obtain the recommended APIs for Mashup clusters. Now we can recommend APIs for Mashup developers according to his/her requirement specification. Firstly, we calculate the cosine similarities between the user's requirement and the Mashup clusters to identify which clusters match best with the user's requirement. Secondly, we choose two most similar Mashup clusters, because the developer may have a variety of requirements. Thirdly, after matching the two Mashup cluster, we recommend top-K APIs for Mashup creation. What's more, we can recommend APIs are not only popular in the mashups, but also have similarity relation, composition relation, and potential composition relation with each other.

4. General expression

For the ease of understanding, we use pseudo code to describe our multi-relation based manifold ranking algorithm in Table 1. Line 00 clusters Mashups into groups according to their textual description and aggregates the Mashup descriptions of each clusters as the whole description of the Mashup cluster; Lines 01–05 compute the similarity relation between Mashup clusters; Lines 06–11 compute the similarity and composition relations between APIs; Lines 15–23 compute the potential composition relation between APIs; Line 25 builds the bipartite graph between Mashup clusters and APIs which is based on the number of times APIs are invoked by Mashups in a certain Mashup cluster; Line 26 integrates M, A^{sim}, A^{com}, A^{pcom}, P, M_Q, A_Q and employs the manifold ranking algorithm to recommend APIs for Mashup clusters; Line 27 obtains the top-K APIs recommendation list for Mashup clusters.

Table 1. The multi-relation based manifold ranking algorithm

Algorithm: multi-relation based manifold ranking
Input:
A set of APIs a_1, a_2,...,a_n; a set of Mashups $M_1, M_2,...,M_n$; the textual descriptions of Mashups and APIs; the user's requirement for Mashup creation.
Output:
A set of APIs to a Mashup user's specific requirement description.
00:Cluster all Mashups into groups according to their textual description
01:For each Mashup cluster m_i do
02:   For each Mashup cluster m_j do
03:$Sim(m_i,m_j)\leftarrow$ similarity degree between m_i and m_j
04:   End for
05:End for
06:For each API a_i do
07:   For each API a_j do
08:$Sim(a_i,a_j)\leftarrow$ similarity degree between a_i and a_j
09:$Com(a_i,a_j)\leftarrow$ composition ability between a_i and a_j
10:   End for
11:End for
12:$M_{ij}\leftarrow$ store $Sim(m_i,m_j)$ to similarity relation matrix
13: $A_{ij}^{sim}\leftarrow$ store $Sim(a_i,a_j)$ to similarity relation matrix
14: $A_{ij}^{com}\leftarrow$ store $Com(a_i,a_j)$ to composition relation matrix
15:For each element A_{ij}^{com} do
16:   For each element A_{ij}^{com} do
17:$P^{H1}com(a_i,a_j)\leftarrow$ multiply A_{ij}^{com} by A_{ij}^{com}
18:   End for
19:   For each element A_{ij}^{sim} do
20:$P^{H2}com(a_i,a_j)\leftarrow$ multiply A_{ij}^{com} by A_{ij}^{sim}
21:   End for
22:End for
23: $Pcom(a_i,a_j)\leftarrow$ combine $P^{H1}com(a_i,a_j)$ and $P^{H2}com(a_i,a_j)$
24: $A_{ij}^{pcom}\leftarrow$ store $Pcom(a_i,a_j)$ to potential composition relation matrix
25:Build the inclusion relation P between mashup clusters and APIs according to the popularity of APIs
26:Assemble M, A^{sim}, A^{com}, A^{pcom}, P, M_Q, A_Q to recommend APIs for Mashup clusters by using (18).
27:For each Mashup cluster save top-K ranking APIs in A_R

4   Experiment

In this section, we present a set of experiments to validate our approach on a real dataset and give an analysis of experimental results.

4.1   Dataset Description

In our experiments, the dataset used is crawled from ProgrammableWeb.com website in the range from June 2005 to December 2013. We remove Mashups that are of the same name and contain no more information except its name. After manually pre-processing the dataset, we obtain a collection of 5955 Mashups and 1069 APIs. An overview of the APIs information and Mashups information are shown in Tables 2 and 3 respectively. Moreover, an overview of the dataset is shown in Table 4. We use this dataset to recommend APIs for Mashup developers. All of the experiments are conducted on computer with Intel(R) Core(TM) i3 CPU(3.2 GHz and 6.0 GB RAM) and all algorithms are implemented in Matlab 2014.

Table 2. The information of APIs

APIID	APIName	APIDescription
1	Cloudmade Leaflet	CloudMade provides application developers with tools and APIs for creating unique location based applications across all major web and mobile platforms. Leaflet is a modern, lightweight BSD-licensed JavaScript library for making tile-based interactive map
2	Acapela	Acapela is a Voice as a Service provider. The service offers text to speech solutions to give voice to content in up to 25 languages and up to 50 voices. The Acapela API lets developers integrate speech into their application and control the voice generat
3	Cohuman	Cohuman is a task-centric, team productivity tool that helps users coordinate and plan their daily tasks to effectively complete projects on time. The Cohuman API allows anyone to develop applications for the web, mobile devices and the desktop. With the API users can make a new task, assign the task to a person or to a team of people, and add content to the task by starting a conversation thread, attaching a file, or scheduling a due date. The API uses RESTful protocol and responses are formatted in XML and JSON.

4.2   Determination of the Number of Clusters

Because the number of Mashup categories is unknown in our dataset, we firstly conduct an experiment to determine the number of clusters, which is necessary in the following experiments.

Table 3. The information of Mashups

MashupID	Name	APIs	Tags	Description
1	5th Bar Phone Reviews	Amazon Product Advertising, CNET, eBay, YouTube	auction, mobile, shopping, video	5th Bar is a new way to avoid getting the wrong phone again. Find and share reviews and information about mobile phones, cell phone carriers, and accessories. Mashup content from YouTube, eBay, Amazon, and CNET.
2	A World of Nirvana	Google Maps, YouTube	mapping, music, nirvana, video	Dynamic tribute to Kurt Cobain, showing Nirvana live concerts on a Google map by year. Search for videos directly by keywords.
3	a.placebetween. us	Google Maps	events, mapping, social, travel	a.placebetween.us aims to simplify the task of finding a place to meet your friends. Provide your addresses and the type of place you want to meet at, such as coffee, diner, or movie and a.placebetween.us does the rest.

Table 4. Overview of the dataset

The total number of Mashups	5955
The total number of APIs used by Mashups	1069
The average number of APIs invoked by per Mashup	2.017
The minimum number of APIs in a Mashup	1
The maximum number of APIs in a Mashup	17

We select 85 % Mashups as training data and the rest as testing data. We then cluster these Mashups into multiple Mashup clusters with a number from 10 to 100 at a step 10 and employ the manifold ranking algorithm to recommend APIs. Finally, we evaluate the performance of the recommendation list using F-measure. The result is shown in Fig. 2.

Figure 2 shows a trend of decrease after an initial increase. When the cluster number reaches 40, F-measure obtains the maximal value. Therefore, in the following experiments, we set the number of clusters to be 40.

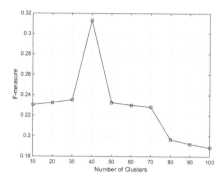

Fig. 2. Impact of number of Mashup clusters

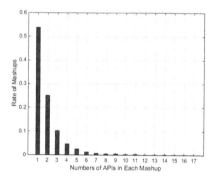

Fig. 3. Statistical analysis of the dataset

4.3 Evaluation Metrics

Before evaluating the quality of our approach, we make some statistical analysis on the dataset that we use. Figure 3 presents the relationship between the number of APIs in each Mashup and the rate of Mashups.

As we can see, over 88.9 % Mashups invoke few than 3 APIs. In the whole dataset, the average number of API used by Mashups is 2. It turns out that the usage of APIs is considerable low. Therefore, it is essential to recommend a list of APIs for Mashup developers.

Herein, we use the three measures of precision, recall, F-measure to evaluate the performance of our approach. The evaluation metrics are defined as follows.

- Precision:

$$p = \frac{T_A \cap E_A}{|T_A|} \tag{19}$$

where, T_A is the API recommendation result list, E_A is the testing Mashup actually used APIs, $|T_A|$ is the size of the API recommendation result list.

- Recall:

$$r = \frac{T_A \cap E_A}{|E_A|} \tag{20}$$

where, $|E_A|$ is the number of APIs the testing Mashup actually used.

- F-measure:

$$F = \frac{2 * p * r}{p + r} \tag{21}$$

It is a comprehensive evaluation on the precision and recall.

4.4 Performance of Our Approach

The API recommendation performance is likely to be influenced by data density. Data density means how many records in the matrix can be employed. In order to study the impact of training data density, in this experiment, we randomly remove 10 % to 90 % data from the original data as the training dataset, and use the rest data as testing dataset. There are a few parameters in our multi-relation based manifold ranking algorithm (i.e. DMRrank). These parameters control the weight of different terms in the manifold ranking formula. By adjusting these parameters, the approach can generate different recommendation lists. In our approach, we set $\rho = 0.1$, $\alpha = 0.1$; $\beta = 0.1$; $\theta = 0.1$; $\lambda = 0.2$; $\gamma = 0.3$; $\mu = 0.1$; $\eta = 0.1$. With these settings, our approach can perform better than other settings. We compare our approach with one of the state-of-the-art approaches, i.e. GMrank [13], which used manifold learning as well. We set the parameters of GMrank as $\alpha = 0.4$, $\beta = 0.1$, $\gamma = 0.1$, $\mu = 0.1$, $\eta = 0.3$, so that GMrank can get the best performance on our dataset. Moreover, in order to compare the impact on the number of selected Mashup clusters, we compare DMRrank with another approach (i.e. MRrank) which is just like DMRrank but simply selects the most similar Mashup cluster according to the user's requirement. Namely, DMRrank chooses one more similar Mashup cluster than MRrank and other settings are just keeping the same.

Figures 4, 5 and 6 present the precision, recall and F-measure comparisons on the training data with different density. As we can see, with the increasing density of training data, the precision, recall and F-measure values also grow. This observation means that larger density data is better for recommending APIs. Moreover, our approach outperforms the Gmrank and MRrank approach in all cases. The results also show, DMRrank is better than MRrank, and MRrank is better than GMrank. It means that considering the composition and potential composition relations between APIs and selecting the two most similar Mashup clusters is indeed helpful for recommending APIs.

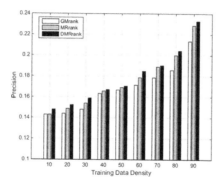

Fig. 4. Precision comparison

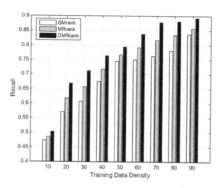

Fig. 5. Recall comparison

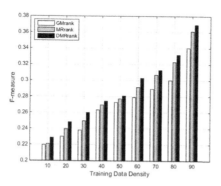

Fig. 6. F-measure comparison

5   Related Work

In this section, we survey related work on service ranking and recommendation.

There are several research work focusing on service ranking. Almulla et al. [14] presented a new Web services selection model based on fuzzy logic and proposed a new fuzzy ranking algorithm based on the dependencies between proposed qualities attributes. Jeh and Widom [15] designed a general similarity measure called SimRank, which is based on a simple and intuitive graph-theoretic model and defines the similarity between two vertices in a graph by their neighbourhood similarity. Mei et al. [16] proposed a ranking approach called DivRank, which is based on a reinforced random walk in an information network. It can automatically balance the prestige and the diversity of the top ranked vertices in a principled way. Tong et al. [17] proposed a goodness measure for a given top-K ranking list. It can capture both the relevance and the diversity for a given ranking list. Zhou et al. [18] proposed a unified neighborhood random walk distance measure called ServiceRank, which integrates various types of links and vertex attributes by a local optimal weight assignment to tightly integrate ranking and clustering by mutually and simultaneously enhancing each other.

With the increasing number of services in the Internet, service recommendation has become a hot topic in recent years. Li et al. [19] proposed a relational topic model to characterize the relationship among Mashups, APIs and their links to assist Mashup creators by recommending a list of APIs that may be used to compose a required Mashup given descriptions of the Mashup. Gao et al. [13] designed a manifold ranking framework for API recommendation. They recommend APIs for each Mashup cluster using manifold ranking algorithm which incorporates the relationships between Mashups, between APIs and between Mashups and APIs. Huang et al. [20] developed a novel approach for recommending developers in terms of navigation and completion of Mashup components with a large-scale components repository. They model the relationships between Mashup components by a generic layered-graph model. Huang et al. [21] presented a service recommendation method that suggests both services and their compositions, in a time-sensitive manner. Xu et al. [22] proposed a novel social-aware service recommendation approach, where multi-dimensional social relationships among potential users, topics, Mashups, and services are described by a coupled matrix model. Zheng et al. [23] presented a collaborative filtering approach for predicting QoS values of Web services and making Web service recommendation by taking advantages of past usage experiences of service users.

6   Conclusion

In this paper, we study the problem of recommending suitable APIs satisfying users' need for Mashup creation. We present a multi-relation based manifold ranking algorithm to assist Mashup developers by recommending a list of APIs that may be used to compose a required Mashup by giving a description of a Mashup. We firstly cluster existing Mashups into groups according to their textual descriptions. Then, we consider multiple relations between Mashup clusters and between APIs. Next, we associate Mashup clusters with APIs based on the popularity of APIs. Finally, we employ manifold ranking algorithm to recommend APIs that the user may be need for Mashup creation and perform a set of experiments to validate our approach on a realistic dataset. Experimental results validate the effectiveness of the proposed approach in terms of precision, recall, and F-measure and show that our approach outperformed the baseline approach for this particular dataset.

In future work, we would like to take the information of services providers and services users into consideration, and along with their potential relationships. Matrix factorization is a well-known service recommend method, so we will incorporate matrix factorization to our manifold ranking algorithm to get better recommendation performance.

Acknowledgments. The work described in this paper was supported by the National Natural Science Foundation of China under grant No. 61572186, 61572187, 61402168 and 61300129, Scientific Research Fund of Hunan Provincial Education Department of China under grant 15K043, 16K030, Hunan Provincial University Innovation Platform Open Fund Project of China under grant No. 14K037.

References

1. Fichter, D.: What Is a Mashup? http://books.infotoday.com/books/Engard/Engard-Sample-Chapter.pdf. Accessed 12 August 2013
2. Greenshpan, O., Milo, T., Polyzotis, N.: Autocompletion for Mashups. In: Proceedings of VLDB Endowment, Lyon, France, pp. 538–549 (2009)
3. Chen, L., Wu, J., Jian, H., et al.: Instant recommendation for web services composition. IEEE Trans. Serv. Comput. 7(4), 586–598 (2014)
4. Huang, K., Fan, Y., Tan, W.: An empirical study of ProgrammableWeb: a network analysis on a Service-Mashup system. In: Proceedings of IEEE 19th International Conference on Web Services (ICWS), Honolulu, HI, pp. 552–559 (2012)
5. Kaufman, L., Rousseeuw, P.: Clustering by means of medoids. In: Dodge, Y. (ed.) Statistical Data Analysis Based on the L1–Norm and Related Methods, pp. 405–416. North-Holland (1987)
6. Singh, S.S., Chauhan, N.C.: K-means v/s K-medoids: a comparative study. In: Proceedings of National Conference on Recent Trends in Engineering & Technology, vol. 13 (2011)
7. Lü, L., Jin, C., Zhou, T.: Similarity index based on local paths for link prediction of complex networks. Phys. Rev. E 80(4), 046122 (2009)
8. Zhou, T., Lü, L., Zhang, Y.: Predicting missing links via local information. Eur. Phys. J. B Condens. Matter Complex Syst. 71(4), 623–630 (2009)
9. Breitenbach, M., Grudic, G.Z.: Clustering through ranking on manifolds. In: Proceedings of the 22nd International Conference on Machine Learning, pp. 73–80. ACM (2005)
10. Xu, B., Bu, J., Chen, C., et al.: Efficient manifold ranking for image retrieval. In: Proceedings of the 34th International ACM SIGIR Conference on Research and Development in Information Retrieval, pp. 525–534. ACM (2011)
11. He, J., Li, M., Zhang, H.J., et al.: Manifold-ranking based image retrieval. In: Proceedings of the 12th Annual ACM International Conference on Multimedia, pp. 9–16. ACM (2004)
12. Zhou, D., Weston, J., Gretton, A., et al.: Ranking on data manifolds. In: Advances in Neural Information Processing Systems, vol. 16, pp. 169–176 (2004)

13. Gao, W., Chen, L., Wu, J., et al.: Manifold-learning based API recommendation for mashup creation. In: Proceedings of IEEE 22nd International Conference on Web Services (ICWS), pp. 432–439 (2015)
14. Almulla, M., Almatori, K., Yahyaoui, H.: A qos-based fuzzy model for ranking real world web services. In: Proceedings of IEEE 21st International Conference on Web Services (ICWS), pp. 203–210 (2011)
15. Jeh, G., Widom, J.: SimRank: a measure of structural-context similarity. In: Proceedings of the Eighth ACM SIGKDD International Conference on Knowledge Discovery and Data Mining, pp. 538–543. ACM (2002)
16. Mei, Q., Guo, J., Radev, D.: Divrank: the interplay of prestige and diversity in information networks. In: Proceedings of the 16th ACM SIGKDD International Conference on Knowledge Discovery and Data Mining, pp. 1009–1018. ACM (2010)
17. Tong, H., He, J., Wen, Z., et al.: Diversified ranking on large graphs: an optimization viewpoint. In: Proceedings of the 17th ACM SIGKDD International Conference on Knowledge Discovery and Data Mining, pp. 1028–1036. ACM (2011)
18. Zhou, Y., Liu, L., Perng, C.S., et al.: Ranking services by service network structure and service attributes. In: Proceedings of IEEE 20th International Conference on Web Services (ICWS), pp. 26–33 (2013)
19. Li, C., Zhang, R., Huai, J., et al.: A novel approach for API recommendation in Mashup development. In: Proceedings of IEEE 21st International Conference on Web Services (ICWS), pp. 289–296 (2014)
20. Huang, G., Ma, Y., Liu, X., et al.: Model-based automated navigation and composition of complex service Mashups. IEEE Trans. Serv. Comput. 8(3), 494–506 (2015)
21. Huang, K., Fan, Y., Tan, W., et al.: Service recommendation in an evolving ecosystem: a link prediction approach. In: Proceedings of IEEE 20th International Conference on Web Services (ICWS), pp. 507–514 (2013)
22. Xu, W., Cao, J., Hu, L., et al.: A social-aware service recommendation approach for Mashup creation. In: Proceedings of IEEE 20th International Conference on Web Services (ICWS), pp. 107–114 (2013)
23. Zheng, Z., Ma, H., Lyu, M.R., King, I.: QoS-aware web service recommendation by collaborative filtering. IEEE Trans. Serv. Comput. 4(2), 140–152 (2011)

A Novel Multi-granularity Service Composition Model

Yanmei Zhang, Yu Qiao$^{(\boxtimes)}$, Zhao Liu, Xiao Geng, and Hengyue Jia

Information School, Central University of Finance and Economics,
Beijing 100081, China
qiaoyu@email.cufe.edu.cn

Abstract. The number of services is proliferating dramatically and the rate of services' evolution has also been increasingly fluctuating in recent years. The demands of service composition also show the characteristics of individuation and diversification at the same time. The traditional methods of service composition are difficult to meet the multiple granularity demands of users. This paper proposes a novel multiple granular service composition model based on services granular space. The model firstly constructs service granularity by service clustering. And then constructs the service granularity space according to the relationships between service granularities. So the process of getting appropriate service compositions can be transformed into getting service compositions from different granularity layers. Through experimental analysis, we can demonstrate that this model can provide users with different granularity service compositions which meet the multiple granularity demands of users. And can also decrease the response time of service composition at the same time.

Keywords: Service computing · Service composition · Service recommendation · Granular computing · Services granular space

1 Introduction

With the development of new concepts of service computing such as pervasive computing and cloud computing, applications and data were available to the users in the form of Web services(or network interfaces), the concept of Services Computing came into being. Through the technology of services composition, users (cooperation or individuals) can build a new application of complex functions according to their needs utilizing the basic services which has existed on the Internet. As a new software development paradigm, service composition can improve the efficiency of software development and reduce costs of software development. At the same time, service composition has an important impact on the service customization and value-added.

However, since the user's own background and needs are different, services needs are often different, too, which show the characteristics of multi-granularity. On the one hand, the user needs for business construction have different granularity. For example, some users need a series of services including "Ticket booking-hotel booking-Car booking-Paying", and some users only need one service "Ticket booking". On the other hand, even if the needs are the same, the description from different users varies widely.

© Springer International Publishing AG 2016
G. Wang et al. (Eds.): APSCC 2016, LNCS 10065, pp. 33–51, 2016.
DOI: 10.1007/978-3-319-49178-3_3

Some descriptions are abstract while some are specific. For example, services "tour" can be specifically described as "Ticket booking-hotel booking-Car booking-Paying", which can also be described as "tourism" abstractly. Therefore, how to find the appropriate service compositions quickly which meet the multi-granular and complex needs of users are the major challenge in services composition filed.

Users usually seek service composition from coarse to fine. For example: the user wants to make a travel plan (Fig. 1), which may involve bank payments, transportation, hotel selection and so on. Each part here has a variety of options. For instance, in the payment part, users can choose to pay by ICBC, China Construction Bank or Bank of Communications. The user's final choice may be like this: pay by Bank of Communications → take the Air China aircraft → live in the Home Inns hotel.

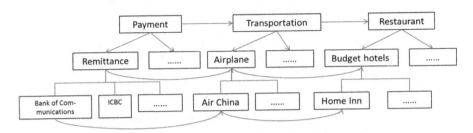

Fig. 1. An example of service composition

Granular computing originated from the 1970 is a simulation of solving problems in a human way. As Prof. Zhang Ling and Zhang Bo said: "The common characteristic of human intelligence is that individuals can observe and analyze the same problem in different granular. People can not only solve the problem in different granular worlds but also jump from one world to another without any difficulties." So the theory of granular computing is considered to achieve the goal of getting multi-granularity service composition. Granular computing, as one of the new concepts and methods in the field of artificial intelligence, is an effective tool to deal with uncertain problems. The feasibility of using granular computing theory to build the multi-granularity services space is as follows: Build the services which have same or similar functions into service grains. Build the multi-granularity service space by the relationships between services. The advantages are that service composition can be sought and transformed in different granular layers, which will not only meeting the complex user needs but also assist the user who lack expertise knowledge to service composition.

Therefore, a hierarchical Service Granular Space (SGS) is constructed based on granular computing: First, cluster services and mine service correlation to get related and hierarchical service grains. Then, do service composition in SGS. This model can be expected not only to provide users with multi-granularity service compositions but also improve the efficiency of service composition.

The structure of this paper is as following: Sect. 2 presents related work. Section 3 introduces our research. Section 4 details the SGS. Section 5 describes algorithm based on SGS. Section 6 evaluates the performance of the SGS algorithm. Section 7 concludes this work.

2 Related Work

The way of organization and management of services have a significant impact on the efficiency of the service composition, while service correlation mining is the premise of an effective organization for services. Many studies such as paper [1, 2] propose that the co-occurrence relationship can be used to represent the composite relationship between services, which can also be based on to do service recommendation. Co-occurrence frequency can represents the combined strength of service composition, but this co-occurrence relationship cannot express the relations of true predecessor-successor (such as interface matching), which means it cannot accurately express the potential composite relationship between services. Different with the ideas above, Guiling [3] takes the precursor - successor relations into account and then recommended successor services. The method firstly uses the input-output interface matching information to build a model of service network, and then uses context tag of user selections to do service recommendation based on the service network model. Xiao Lei [4] uses the example of Geospatial Information Systems to study the recommendation for service chains. By using the service description information and semantic information of input-output interfaces to build a model of service network, users only need to give the start and end information, with which the system can search for matched chains from service network model and then rank and recommend them. Paper [5, 6] consider that the API (services) and their Mushup (service composition) have the characteristics of evolving with time (such as publishing, demise and update), putting forward that the quality of service recommendation can be improved by the method of service ecosystem. Paper [5] uses LDA model and time series prediction to extract services evolutionary patterns, proposing a service recommendation for Mashup under the basis of combining with the evolution of services, collaborative filtering and matching method for content. Paper [6] introduced a Network Series Model, to represent the evolved service system, which can recommend the Top-K services and service chains according to network evolution forecast. Current researches on the service correlation mining, the construction of service network and service network evolution are all based on the services organization to improve the validity of service recommendation. However, limitations are: Firstly, the descriptions of correlation between service precursor and service successor are inaccurate. On the one hand, many researches utilise the co-occurrence relation to describe service correlation. Compared with precursor-successor relation, co-occurrence relation lacks accuracy. On the other hand, in terms of extraction of metrics related to service correlation, the existing studies only takes the strength of service correlation into consideration, while ignoring an important information that the structure of service correlation (such as sequential, parallel). Secondly, the granularity of service recommendation is inflexible, which precludes multi-granular service recommendations. Existing recommendation techniques mainly provide recommendation for specific service (service-level) [1, 3] or service chain (chain-level) [5]. Recommendations with service-level granularity are commonly less informative, whereas chain-level service recommendations are highly assertive. Neither of both is able to meet the complicated and diverse users demands. The multi-granularity (service level, the relationship level and the chain level) service recommendation will be better able to meet the diverse and complex needs of users. The "relationship level" means combined several services which have logical relations based on the relationship between predecessor and successor service and the correlation structures (such as sequential, parallel) information.

In recent years, the research on granular computing [7, 8] the field of artificial intelligence has laid a theoretical foundation for us to study multiple granular of service composition and service recommendation. For example, Swaroop [9] set the service as a node in graph model. It is determined whether the semantic relationship between the input and output of any two services according to the semantic description of the service input and output. The relations between all the services will be able to describe as a graph after setting the semantic relationships between the two services as the edge in graph model. Shen [10] proposes a service composition algorithm based on hierarchical quotient space by quotient space theory, by which build a user-oriented service composition model: Use owl-s semantic to describe services and domain ontology as the basis for semantic description. Then build hierarchical ontology concept tree and a quotient space based on service equivalence relation, true preserving principle and false preserving principle. Finally validate the algorithm through the analog service without actual semantics. Also, the efficiency of the algorithm is analyzed along with the average width level and the depth of the space. Experimental results show that the smaller the width of the ontology concept tree and the greater the depth of ontology concept hierarchy tree, the better the service grain structure. In order to deal with the challenges of service compositions of multi-granular users demands under the environment of cloud computing, Cai Huihui [11] proposes a service granularity space model and a concrete construction method of service space, but how to select the optimal service composition has yet to be perfected.

Other studies include: Romano [12] clustered the services into a service granularity and design the corresponding genetic algorithm to find these services cluster in order to reduce the number of service calls according to the user common service composition mode. Chen [13] discusses the reusing issues in the field of service composition. The traditional method is limited to reuse a single service or an entire packaged service module, so that efficiency of reusing is low. A concept of variable granularity index (VGI) based SSM-Tree is proposed, which can maximize the efficiency of reusing to meet the needs of the complex invokes of user.

3 Identifiers and Definitions Involved

The identifiers are used as shown in Table 1 for better describing.

Some Core concepts are defined as follows:

Definition 1. Services: services can be abstract described as a four-tuple S = (Fun, QoS, Input, Output). Respectively represent as services, quality of service, input and output parameters.

Definition 2. Service grain: Services grain also has the properties of service. As more focus should be laid on services' level of construction, each of them is described as a

Table 1. Identifiers and its definition

Identifiers	Definition
$S = \{s_1, s_2, \ldots s_n\}$	Service set
$SG = \{sg_1, sg_2, \ldots, sg_n\}$	Service Granularity set
sg_{in}	the Input of user need
sg_{out}	the Output of user need
SGS	Service Granularity Space
Fun	Function of Service or Service Granularity
$Goal$	User demand
$Input = \{in_1, in_2, \ldots, in_n\}$	Input of service or service granularity
$Output = \{out_1, out_2, \ldots, out_n\}$	Output of service or service granularity
$Similar$	Semantic similarity
CD	Correlation of service granularity
$AveCD$	Correlation between service granularity and service granularity set
AGD	Degree of Polymerization between service granularity
AveAGD	Degree of Polymerization between service granularity set
Rc	Correlation between service grains
Rh	Hierarchy relationship between service grains

triple SG = (Fun, Input, Output), sg_i.Input = A represents a sgi is a service grain and its input is A.

Definition 3. Relationship can be combined: For two service grains: sgi = (Funi, Inputi, Outputi) and sgj = (Funj, Inputj, Outputj), if Inputj $\subseteq$ Outputi, then sgi and sgj service grains are combined, and donated as $sg_i \rightarrow sg_j$.

Definition 4. User needs: user needs can be expressed as two virtual services grain: sg_{in} = (null, null, Outputin) and sg_{out} (null, Inputout, null), namely that sg_{in} only have output (user input), sg_{out} only have input (user output).

Definition 5. Service composition: service composition means that for a particular user needs (sg_{in}, sg_{out}), if there is a sequence of service grains set to meet the following three conditions: (1) $sg_{in} \rightarrow sg_1$; (2) $sg_n \rightarrow sg_{out}$; (3) $sg_i \rightarrow sg_i + 1$; $i = 1, 2 \ldots, n - 1$, then we think the service composition to meet user demand is found.

    Based on the above definitions, the service node is adopted to represent service grains and the straight line is adopted to represent the input-output relationship between service grains. So the relationship between service composition and user needs is shown in Fig. 2.

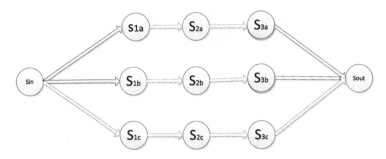

Fig. 2. Relationship between service composition and user needs

4   Construction of Hierarchical Service Granular Space SGS

The SGS's construction consists of three stages: ① Get service grains. Cluster the services which are similar to each other but not related into one cluster and then get service grain from the cluster. ② Service grains correlation mining. Discover the correlation between service grains by calculating the degree of correlation between service grains. The correlation can help users discover the composite relationship between service grains. And the service grains correlation mining includes the correlation between two service grains and correlation between a service grain and a set of service grains. ③ Construction of SGS. Service grains are fine or coarse, which can be a hierarchical structure. Having a hierarchical relationship between service grains means that the degree of polymerization of service grains in the same layer are higher and lower in different layers. The degree of polymerization can be calculated and used to construct SGS. The details are as follows:

4.1   Service Grains

The semantic similarity of concepts refers to how closely the semantic association between concepts, which can be expressed as the semantic distance between concepts in semantic tree. After all, the essence of the semantic similarity of concepts is the measurement of the distance between the concepts. The degree of similarity becomes lower with the longer of the distance between the two concepts. On the contrary, the degree of similarity becomes larger with the nearer of the distance between the two concepts. If the distance between the concepts is zero, their similarity is one. The distance between the concepts is infinity, its similarity is 0. Our definition of semantic similarity between the concept C_i and C_j is:

$$\text{Similar}(C_i, C_j) = \frac{1}{\text{dis}(C_i, C_j)} \tag{1}$$

We use $\text{dis}(C_i, C_j)$ to express the semantic distance between concept C_i and C_j in the semantic tree. These concepts will correspond to the services as follows:

For two service s_i and s_j, their input and output are composed of a set of message components and each message component corresponds to a concept in semantic tree. The definitions of the input and output of services are as follows:

$$\text{Input}_i \, (in_1, in_2, \ldots, in_m), \; \text{Output}_i = (out_1, out_2, \ldots, out_s);$$
$$\text{Input}_j \, (in_1, in_2, \ldots, in_n), \; \text{Output}_j = (out_1, out_2, \ldots, out_t).$$

(1) For service S_i, similarity to the input of S_j is calculated as follows $\text{Sim}(\text{Input}_i, \text{Input}_j)$:

$$\text{Sim}\left(\text{Input}_i, \text{Input}_j\right) = \frac{\sum\limits_{i=1}^{m} \underset{j=1}{\overset{n}{\text{Max}}} \; \text{Similar}\left(in_i, in_j\right)}{m} \tag{2}$$

Similarly, for service S_j, the similarity to the input of S_i is $\text{Sim}\left(\text{Input}_j, \text{Input}_i\right)$.

(2) The similarity of input messages of S_i and S_j:

$$\text{Similar}\left(\text{Input}_i, \text{Input}_j\right) = \frac{1}{2} \times \left(Sim\left(Input_i, Input_j\right) + Sim\left(Input_j, Input_i\right)\right) \tag{3}$$

Similarly, the similarity of output messages of S_i and S_j is $\text{Similar}\left(\text{Output}_i, \text{Output}_j\right)$

(3) semantic similarity of service S_i and S_j is

$$\text{Similar}\left(s_i, s_j\right) = w_1 \times \left(Similar\left(Input_i, Input_j\right) + w_2 \times Similar\left(Output_i, Output_j\right)\right) \tag{4}$$

The weight of the input and output messages of the service is respectively w_1 and w_2, and $0 \leq w_1, w_2 \leq 1$. We put the services which meet the threshold of similarity into one cluster and extract service grains from the clusters base on the formula (4).

4.2   Service Correlation Mining

Service Correlation reflects the closeness of two related services. Service Correlation between sg_i and sg_j can be expressed as:

$$CD\left(sg_i, sg_j\right) = Similar\left(Output_i, Input_j\right) = \frac{1}{2} \times \left(Sim\left(output_i, Input_j\right) + Sim\left(Input_j, Output_i\right)\right) \tag{5}$$

For Services grain set $SG = \{sg_1, sg_2, \ldots \ldots, sg_n\}$ and service grain sg_j, if output of SG can be met by the input of the sg_j, the correlation between SG and sg_j can be expressed as follows:

$$AveCD\left(sg_1, sg_2, \ldots \ldots, sg_n, sg_j\right) = \frac{\sum\limits_{i=1}^{n} CD\left(sg_i, sg_j\right)}{n} \tag{6}$$

The identifier "n" is the number of service grains. Based on the formula (5) and (6), a correlation matrix SGCM can be formed after service correlation mining. The value 1 and 0 of the matrix respectively indicated whether has a correlation or not.

4.3   Construction of Hierarchical Service Granular Space SGS

After the service correlation mining, whether there exists a coarse service grain can be checked that can accomplish the functions which should be completed by several service grains. Once the service grain existed, we can build a hierarchical relationship between them (Fig. 4).

For service grains sg_k, sg_i and sg_j, $sg_i \xrightarrow{R_c} sg_j$, if sg_i, $sg_j \xrightarrow{Rh} sg_k$, the degree of polymerization of service grain sg_k and sg_i, sg_j can be expressed as:

$$AGD(s_i, s_j) = w_1 \times Similar(Input_k, Input_i) + w_2 \times Similar(Output_k, Output_j) \tag{7}$$

For $SG = \{sg_1, sg_2, \ldots \ldots, sg_n\}$, sg_j and sg_k, $sg_1 \cup sg_2 \cup \ldots \cup sg_n \xrightarrow{R_c} sg_j$, if sg_1, $sg_2, \ldots \ldots, sg_n, sg_j \xrightarrow{Rh} sg_k$, the degree of polymerization between service grain sg_k and SG, sg_j can be expressed as:

$$AveAGD\left(sg_1, sg_2, \ldots \ldots, sg_n, sg_j, sg_k\right)$$
$$= w_1 \times \frac{\sum\limits_{i=1}^{n} similar(sg_k.Input, sg_i.Input)}{n} + w_2 \times Similar\left(sg_k.Output, sg_j.Output\right) \tag{8}$$

Based on the degree of polymerization calculated by the formula (7) and (8), a coarse service grain can be found which is functionally equivalent to two or a set of service grains, and build a hierarchical relationship between them.

The pseudo-code and flow charts are as follows:

Algorithm 1. Get the sg(service granularity)
Description: ServiceCluster$_i$ is the cluster of service,and
    ServiceCluster is the cluster of ServiceCluster$_i$.
Input: S(Service cluster), ts(threshold of similarity)
Output: SG (Service granularity cluster)
Steps:
(1)ServiceCluster$_i$={s$_i$},ServiceCluster={ServiceCluster$_i$}
(2)If Similar(s$_i$,s$_j$)>ts,ServiceCluster$_i$.add(s$_j$),else go to
    step(3)。
(3)If Similar(ServiceCluster$_x$.get(x),s$_j$)>ts, ServiceClus-
    ter$_x$.add(s$_j$),else go to step(4)。
(4)If ServiceCluster$_x$.get(x)!=sj,then new ServiceClus-
    ter$_j$={s$_j$}
(5)For s$_x$ S,go to step(2),until s$_x$ ServiceCluster$_x$,then
    ServiceCluster={……,ServiceCluster, ServiceCluster$_j$……}。
(6)sg$_i$ = (same input of every service in ServiceCluster$_i$,
    same output of every service in ServiceClus-
    ter$_i$) ,SG={sg$_1$,sg$_2$,……,sg$_i$……,sg$_{nc}$}

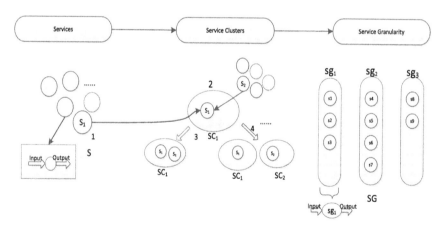

Fig. 3. The illustration of Algorithm 1

Algorithm 2. Get SGCM(correlation matrix of service granularities)

Description: tempSG is the clone cluster of SG, and comSG is the cluster of any number of sg.

Input: SG (Service granularity cluster), tc(threshold of correlation)

Output: SGCM(correlation matrix of service granularities)

Steps:

(1) tempSG=SG, SGCM={}

(2) If CD(sg_i,sg_j)>tc,SGCM[sg_i][sg_j]=1, tempSG.remove(sg_j)

(3) comSG={$sg_1,sg_2,……,sg_k$}, If CD($sg_{1/2/……/k}, sg_j$)>tc, SGCM[$sg_{1/2/…/k}$][sg_j]=1, tempSG.remove($sg_{1/2/…/k}$)

(4) Repeat step(1)to(3) until tempSG.size<k,return SGCM

Algorithm 3. Establishment of SGS(service granular space)

Description: Predecessor is the Predecessor sg of sgi, getPredecessor is the function of finding predecessor.

Input: SG (Service granularity cluster), SGCM(correlation matrix of service granularities), tp(threshold of polymerization degree)

Output:SGS(Service granular Space)

Steps:

(1) for each sgi SG, Predecessor = getPredecessor(sgi,SGCM), if AGD(sgi, Predecessor,sgk)>tp,then build Rh(sgi, Predecessor,sgk),so we get the current layer of SGS,else go to step (2)

(2) new sg,build Rh(sgi, Predecessor,sg)

(3) for each sgm in the current layer of SGS, then repeat step(1),we can get the next layer of SGS

(4) Repeat step(1)to(3) until there is no sg in the current layer ,return SGS.

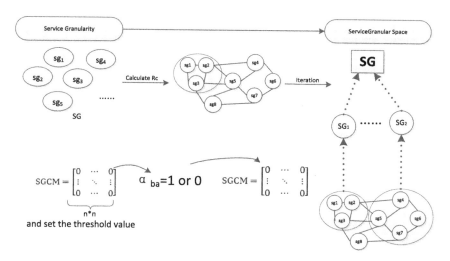

Fig. 4. The illustration of Algorithms 2 and 3

5 Service Composition Algorithm Based on the Hierarchical Service Granular Space SGS

First, get service composition list based on SGS. Then use the skyline [14, 15] algorithm to filter them to obtain non-dominated service composition list, so that the efficiency will be improve and the redundancy of service composition will be reduced.

Definition 6. Non-dominated service composition list: Suppose that in a n-dimensional space, there is a service $S_1(p_1, \ldots, p_n)$ and $S_2(q_1, \ldots, q_n)$, if the quality of service on any dimension $p_i \geq q_i$, $i \in [1, n]$, and $\exists_i \in [1, n]$ make that $p_i > q_i$, then we say S_1 disposal S_2. Non-dominated service composition list consisted by all the service compositions which are not dominated by all the others.

The algorithm process is as follows:

(1) First, Add the needs(services) of the target user to the service composition list. If the needs(services)can be decomposed into a sequence of fine-grained services composition, continue to decompose, otherwise return the list of service composition.

(2) If a service has a business process and can be decomposed continuously, check that whether each sub-grain of this service can be decomposed. If so, the service grain is considered can be replaced by its sub-grain services which means a new service composition can be get. Then add it to the list of service composition.

(3) For the new service composition list, decompose all the service grains which has a business processes iterative, and return a series of different granular service compositions, until all the service grains in the service composition we got are atomic.

(4) For service composition list we got, if there exists any parent service grains that contains service grains customized, substitute it with the service grains customized, otherwise remove it. Finally, return the service composition list which meet user demands.

(5) As there are so many service compositions which contains mass number and varying quality of services, the Skyline algorithm is adopted to eliminate those redundant candidate services which are dominated by other services, in order to reduce the search space when service composition.

The major research contents is the creating of SGS instead of neither the skyline algorithm nor the course of reasoning Non-Dominated Solution Sets, whose related contents are available in the group's previous study [16].

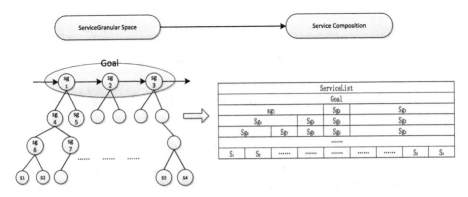

Fig. 5. The illustration of Service Composition Algorithm Based on SGS

Figures 3, 4, and 5 show the flow chart of the whole process based on SGS. As is shown in the pictures, the Algorithm 1 corresponds to the evolution course from services to service clusters and then to service granularity. Algorithm 2 and Algorithm 3 correspond to the process of how to build service granular space from service grain. Figure 5 shows the process of service composition algorithm which corresponds to how to get service composition.

6   Simulation

The experiments were done on a laptop which has Windows 10 x64 operating system, Inter Core i3-5005U CPU@2.00 GHz, and 8 GB RAM. The codes were running in the Java programming environment. The dataset was stored in the MYSQL database. User needs are the keywords used to describe the service. Although there are a lot of real data sets, such as WSDL and Mashup, the Web service WSDL data sets are messy and have no relationship, and Mashup API services has no semantic description after viewing the WSDL and Mashup statics crawled from the web. So they are not suitable for the experiment.

The test used simulated data sets SD (Simulated Data). Simulated dataset SD was mainly generated by imitating the real Web service features, including service id, service input, service output, type and QoS. The description of services inputs and outputs were used of the semantic description in semantic tree from China HowNet [17] randomly. QoS value was assigned by the random function of JAVA. The size of SD was controlled by the size parameters of JAVA algorithm artificially.

6.1   Parameter

The Optimal Granular. To reflect how the granular have an impact on the performance of service composition, a size of 1000 services are simulated. Change the granular and number of services grain by changing the similarity parameter between the services. Get five service compositions for each degree of similarity. Use the average response time and the average number of granular as the final result. Take the service response time as the metrics to determine the optimal granular.

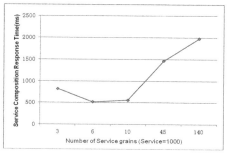
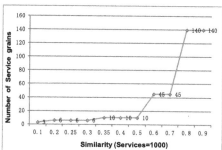

Fig. 6. Service composition response time changes with the number of service grains

Fig. 7. Number of service grains changes with similarity

As the number of services is fixed, when we change the parameter of similarity, the number of service grains is varied. The higher the degree of similarity, the smaller the number of atomic services in each service grain contained. The larger the number of services grain, the smaller service granularity. Limited by the experimental data, the changing of amplitude is subtle in the second decimal place of similarity parameter, and the experimental results did not change much as well. From Figs. 6 and 7, it is obvious that response time is the least when the service grains number is in the range of 6–10. And when the number of the service grain is not in this range, service composition response time increased significantly. So it can be confirmed that there is a range of service grain number that can significantly shorten the response time of service composition.

Optimal Degree of Polymerization. The degree of polymerization between service grains is the basis of SGS' building. Different degrees of polymerization parameters are set to observe the number of layers of SGS and service response time. The optimal threshold of degree of polymerization also can be confirmed according to the observation. The test set is randomly generated, which consist of 1000 services. Generate service compositions in five times for each degree of polymerization and calculate the average time of 5 services composition response time each group.

Limited by the experimental data, the experimental results did not change much as well when the changing of amplitude is subtle in the second decimal place. This test only compares a degree of polymerization of the decimal point. Figure 6 shows that the optimal degree of polymerization is 0.4.

Since the degree of polymerization affects the SGS construction, in order to observe the changes of the SGS layers, 500,1000,1500 services are generated respectively. For each degree, 5 service compositions are generated. This experiment uses the average number of layers of service granular space as metrics. Figures 8 and 9 shows that: the number of layers is almost identical, and the number of layers is 4 when the degree of polymerization is optimal. From the result it can be inferred that when the degree of polymerization is optimal, no matter how big the size of the services, there is always a range of number of SGS layers, which is consistent with a general point of service composition: the more layers of services grains, the more complex of the SGS, the longer of searching time.

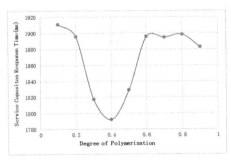 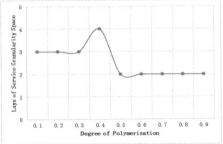

Fig. 8. Service composition response time changes with the degree of polymerization

Fig. 9. The number of layers changes with the degree of polymerization

6.2 Performance Test

From the Figs. 8 and 9, it is easy to find that when the similarity is between 0.2–0.5 the minimum response time of service composition. So this test takes the median value 0.35 as the value of similarity. And the follow experiment takes 0.4 as the value of degree of polymerization.

Comparison of Service Correlation Mining. This experiment randomly generates 100, 300, 500, 1000, 1500, 2000 size of services. Record the mean time of service

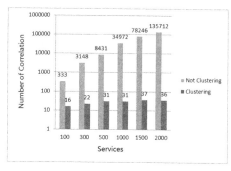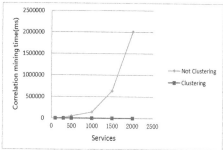

Fig. 10. Comparison of service correlation mining number

Fig. 11. Comparison of service correlation mining time

correlation mining (non-clustered and clustered) of each group to compare the time efficiency.

Seen from Fig. 10, after using a cluster algorithm, the number of service correlation excavated is far less than not using cluster algorithm. This may due to the inherent functionality similar phenomena among atomic services, after a cluster processing, a large number of non-affiliated service was filtered out. At the same time, it can be seen from Fig. 11: Time efficiency has been greatly improved, and the more of services number, the more obviously of the effect.

Comparison on Service Granular Space SGS using Skyline or not. This test uses different sizes of services as test sets. Execute algorithm several times on the case of before pruning and after pruning. Record the mean service composition response time to compare.

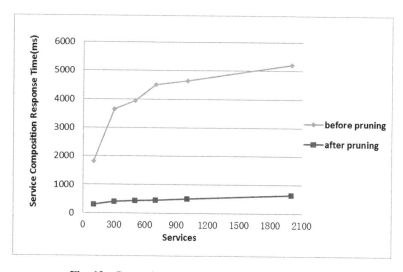

Fig. 12. Comparison on pruning of SGS using Skyline

From Fig. 12, it can be seen that the response time of service composition dramatically increased with the services number increasing in the case of not using skyline algorithm. On the contrary, the response time increased slowly with the increasing of services number after using skyline algorithm. This experiment demonstrates the effectiveness of the skyline pruning algorithm.

Multi-granularity Service Composition Algorithm based on SGS Testing. To test the efficiency of SGS model, traditional method Graph [18, 19] SGS-Type methods were chosen respectively. SGS-Type is a combination of SGS algorithm and Zhang Wei's [20] thoughts: First, get the Web service grain. Next is to find the relationships between the Web service grains. Then build SGS-Type model based on the type property. As a result, the Web service grains in the same field are divided into the same category, thus a "Field - Web service grain -Web service" three-layer service space model was formed. To get the service composition, the first step was determining the needs of users to its corresponding field, and then mapped the user need into corresponding type field. The last step was to find the service composition in the model. We still use service composition time to compare among SGS, SGS-Type and graph-planning.

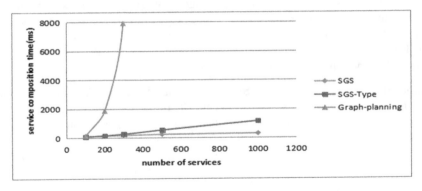

Fig. 13. Comparison on SGS, SGS-Type and Graph-planing

As shown in Fig. 13, when number of services is small, response time of service composition based on graph-planning is relatively similar to response time of SGS. This is because when you start a service granularity space construction, the difference between the various atomic services is relatively large, and the effect of clustering services is not obvious. Furthermore, the number of service cluster is small, correlation between services is not high, and the number of service grain in each layer is also small, so the response time of service composition is increased. With the increasing of number of atoms services, graph-planning methods involving large semantic calculations, son the time greatly increased in correspondence. Compared to SGS, SGS-Type is too simple and tough when using SGS-Type to do hierarchical classification and less flexible than SGS algorithm, so the efficiency is worse than SGS. While in the case of SGS model, the degree of similarity and correlation between services is increased, service clustering effect becomes strong, number of services also increased in each layer, the size of service granular space is bigger, the response time of service composition increases slowly. When the service composition is sufficient to meet the specific needs of users, service response time gradually stabilized, which shows service granularity space has the character of stabilizing from unstable and self-organization.

Scalability Testing. To further verify the validity of service granular space, we used bigger size of services for testing. The results are shown in Fig. 14 and Table 2 below.

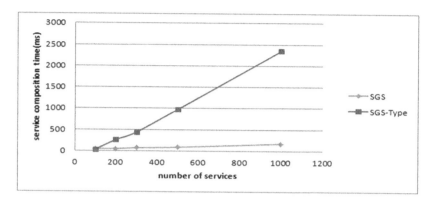

Fig. 14. Response time of service composition changes with the number of services

Table 2. Results of scalability Testing

Services	SGS (ms)	SGS-Type (ms)	Gragh planning (ms)
1000	296	1147	158542
2000	352	1689	— —
5000	756	3620	— —
10000	2065	10284	— —
15000	3882	21532	— —

Figure 14 and Table 2 show that, when the number of services is large, service composition response time based on SGS is relatively stable, and the response time of SGS-Type increases more fast than SGS, even the response time of graph-planing increases sharply. The comparison showed SGS stability and adaptability.

7 Conclusions

A service granular space (SGS) is proposed by using granular computing to order the large number of disordered services from different vendors so as to achieve the goal of getting multi-granularity service composition. First, clustering and correlation mining algorithm is invoked to order the atomic services in order to get the service grain which has correlation, hierarchical relationships and inheritance relationship. Then get the optimal service composition in the service granular space. Simulation results show that it is more efficient for service composition using SGS than using the graph-planning. At the same time the method can provide users with multi-granular service composition to meet the different granularity of needs of service users.

Acknowledgments. This work was partially supported by the National Natural Science Foundation of China (Nos. 61602536, 61309029 and 61273293), the Fundamental Research Funds for the Central Universities, and the Discipline Construction Foundation of the Central University of Finance and Economics.

References

1. Deng, S.G., Huang, L.T., Wu, J., et al.: Trust-based personalized service recommendation: a network perspective. J. Comput. Sci. Technol. **29**(1), 69–80 (2014)
2. Liu, J.-X., He, K.-Q., Wang, J., Yu, D.-H., Feng, Z.-W., Ning, D., Zhang, X.-W.: An approach of RGPS-Guided on-demand service organization and recommendation. Chin. J. Comput. **36**(2), 238–252 (2013)
3. Wang, G., Zhang, S., Liu, C., Han, Y.: A dataflow-pattern-based recommendation approach for data service mashups. In: Proceedings of the 2014 IEEE International Conference on Services Computing, SCC 2014, pp. 163–170. IEEE Computer Society, Washington (2014)
4. Wang, X., Cheng, Z., Zhou, Z., Ning, K., Zhang, L.J.: Geospatial web service sub-chain ranking and recommendation. In: Proceedings of the 2014 IEEE International Conference on Services Computing, SCC 2014, pp. 91–98. IEEE Computer Society, Washington (2014)
5. Xu, S., Shi, Q., Qiao, X., Zhu, L., Jung, H., Lee, S., Choi, S.-P.: Author-topic over time (AToT): a dynamic users' interest model. In: (Jong Hyuk) Park, J.J., et al. (eds.) Mobile, Ubiquitous, and Intelligent Computing. LNEE, vol. 274, pp. 239–245. Springer, Heidelberg (2014). doi:10.1007/978-3-642-40675-1_37
6. Liu, X., Turtle, H.: Real-time user interest modeling for real-time ranking. J. Am. Soc. Inform. Sci. Technol. **64**(8), 1557–1576 (2013)
7. Chen, G., Zhong, N.: Granular structures in graphs. In: Yao, J., Ramanna, S., Wang, G., Suraj, Z. (eds.) RSKT 2011. LNCS (LNAI), vol. 6954, pp. 649–658. Springer, Heidelberg (2011). doi:10.1007/978-3-642-24425-4_82
8. Chen, G., Zhong, N.: Three granular structure models in graphs. In: Li, T., Nguyen, H.S., Wang, G., G-B, J., Janicki, R., Hassanien, A.E., Yu, H. (eds.) RSKT 2012. LNCS (LNAI), vol. 7414, pp. 351–358. Springer, Heidelberg (2012). doi:10.1007/978-3-642-31900-6_44
9. Kalasapur, S., Kumar, M., Shirazi, B.A.: Dynamic service composition in pervasive computing. IEEE Trans. Parallel Distrib. Syst. **18**(18), 907–918 (2007)
10. Shen, L.F., Qi, Y.: A novel end-user Oriented Service Composition Model Based on Quotient Space Theory. In: International Conference on Service Sciences, pp. 180–184 (2010)
11. Cai, H.: Research on multi-tenant service composition approach based service granular space. Thesis for Master Degree, Shandong University (2014)
12. Romano, D., Pinzger, M.: A genetic algorithm to find the adequate granularity for service interfaces. In: 2014 IEEE World Congress on Services (SERVICES), pp. 478–485 (2014)
13. Zeng, C., Lu, Z., et al.: Variable granularity index on massive service processes. In: 2013 IEEE 20th International Conference on Web Services (ICWS), pp. 18–25 (2013)
14. Yu, Q., Bouguettaya, A.: Computing service skyline from uncertain QoWS. IEEE Trans. Serv. Comput. **3**, 16–29 (2010)

15. Alrifai, M., Skoutas, D., Risse, T.: Selecting skyline services for QoS-based web service composition. In: 19th International World Wide Web Conference (WWW 2010), Raleigh, pp. 11–20 (2010)
16. Zhang, Y., Cao, H., Jia, H., Mao, G.: Multi-objective service composition and optimization algorithms based on user preference. J. Chin. Comput. Syst. **37**(1), 38–42 (2016)
17. Ge, B., Li, F., Guo, S., Tang, D.: Word's semantic similarity computation method based on Hownet. Appl. Res. Comput. **1**, 101–103 (2016)
18. Xu, M., Cui, L.Z., Li, Q.Z.: An extended graph-planning based top-k service composition method. Acta Electronica Sin. **40**(7), 1404–1409 (2012)
19. Hatzi, O., Vrakas, D., Nikolaidou, M., Bassiliades, N., Anagnostopoulos, D., Ylahavas, L.: An integrated approach to automated semantic web service composition through planning. IEEE Trans. Serv. Comput. **5**(3), 319–332 (2012)
20. Zhang, M., Zhang, B., Zhang, X., Zhu, Z.: A division based composite service selection approach. J. Comput. Res. Dev. **5**, 1005–1017 (2012)

Exploring Body Constitution in Traditional Chinese Medicine with K-Means Clustering

Yinglong Dai[1], Yinong Long[1], Xiaofei Xing[2], and Guojun Wang[2(✉)]

[1] School of Information Science and Engineering,
Central South University, Changsha 410083, China
[2] School of Computer Science and Educational Software,
Guangzhou University, Guangzhou 510006, China
csgjwang@gmail.com

Abstract. Health states, which are the abstract concepts for body recognition, represent a set of body conditions. Forming the accurate concepts, which are constantly tuning as the growth of human experiences, may be a long-term process in the human history. Nowadays, advances in technology have made monitoring the various data of body condition available. As the explosion of the data, it goes far beyond the ability of our brain to handle. But the computer can help us discover the patterns from the big data. In order to discover new representative health states, we propose forming them based on clustering. We use K-means clustering algorithm to discover the nine body constitution (BC) types in traditional Chinese medicine (TCM) according to the items in *Constitution in Chinese Medicine Questionnaire* (CCMQ). The results illustrate the ability of computer system to discover human health states.

Keywords: Unsupervised learning · Clustering analysis · Health state · Body constitution · Traditional Chinese medicine · K-means

1 Introduction

Human body is a kind of complex dynamical systems, which can be described by numerous features, such as height, weight, temperature, heart rate, and even the abstract personality. The mechanism of human body is too complicated to recognize meticulously. Although it is difficult to look through the human body and model the system precisely, we could use some abstract concepts of health states to generalize the complicated human body phenotypes. In the long-term history of human society, the abstract health state concepts were gradually formed by observations, records and analyses. With the development of computer technology and bioinformatics, human beings hugely extend their abilities in data acquiring, memory capacity and operational capability. It means that we can obtain more comprehensive human body data and record all of them for retrieval and analysis under the assistance of computer.

Traditional Chinese medicine (TCM) is built on a foundation of more than 2,500 years of Chinese medical practice. TCM formes many abstract concepts

ⓒ Springer International Publishing AG 2016
G. Wang et al. (Eds.): APSCC 2016, LNCS 10065, pp. 52–64, 2016.
DOI: 10.1007/978-3-319-49178-3_4

to explain the mechanism of human body. Body constitution (BC), an ancient core concept in TCM, is widely applied in daily practice by Chinese medicine practitioners [19]. The most common BC instruments are the *Constitution in Chinese Medicine Questionnaire* (CCMQ) developed by Wang et al. in Mainland China for measuring BC type [16] and the *Body Constitutions Questionnaire* (BCQ) developed by Su et al. in Taiwan [8,12,13]. The CCMQ was developed by expert panel discussion, validity, and reliability on 2,854 subjects in Mainland China of these questionnaires in populations [17].

The contributions of this paper are: (1) Giving an insight into BC types based on the facts of CCMQ; (2) Illustrating the forming process of the BC concepts from the view of the computer. The clustering algorithms are the methods of data analysis in computer. The efficient K-means clustering algorithm is used to illustrate the mapping process from the human body features to the BC types. We provide a view of the clustering method for human body recognition, which has potential to assist the analysis of manpower.

The rest of this paper is organized as follows. To begin with, Sect. 2 introduces the diagnostic methods and the Body Constitution (BC) types in TCM. Then, the information process and the clustering method for classes discovery are introduced in Sect. 3. After that, Sect. 4 shows some experiments to illustrate how to use the clustering method to discover the BC types. Section 5 is the overview of the related works. Finally, we have conclusions in Sect. 6.

2 Body Constitution Types in TCM

2.1 The Four Diagnostic Methods of TCM

There are four well known diagnostic methods of TCM: inspection, auscultation (listening) & olfaction (smelling), interrogation, and palpation.

Inspection. Inspection is one kind of examining method which is applied to knowing the condition of disease by means of doctor's visual sense to look over the vitality, color, figure, posture of patient's whole or partial body and the changes of the figuration, color, texture and quality of the patient's discharges.

Auscultation & Olfaction. Auscultation is to find the abnormal sound of speech, respiration and cough etc. by means of auditognosis (listening). Olfaction is to know the smell of the patient's body, the secretion and excreta by means of osphresis (smelling).

Interrogation. Interrogation is to know the onset, development, treatment, present symptoms and other information of disease by questioning patient or the accompanying people for diagnosis.

Palpation. Palpation includes pulse examination and body pressing-touching. They are diagnostic methods that doctor uses his tactile sensation of fingers and palm to touch patient's body to get diagnostic data. Pulse examination is to feel the pulse while body pressing-touching is to touch and press the different parts of patient's body such as skin, hands and feet, chest and abdomen and so on.

Chinese medicine practitioners assess a person's state of health by collecting and analyzing clinical information on the basis of the four diagnostic methods. They just use their sensory perceptions without resorting to any apparatus. They can diagnose internal pathological (disease) changes through observation and analysis of external signs.

2.2   Classification Based on the Diagnostic Methods

Chinese medicine practitioners built their analytical theory on the basis of the clinical information collected from the four diagnostic methods. Wang [15] built the constitutional theory to classify body constitution (BC) types. The *Constitution in Chinese Medicine Questionnaire* (CCMQ), which synthesized the traditional diagnostic methods, was developed by Wang et al. in Mainland China [16]. It has 60 items measuring the 9 BC types, see Table 1.

Table 1. BC types

BC type	Brief description
Gentleness	Strong physique, stable emotional state and feel optimistic
Qi-deficiency	Flabby muscles, introvert and timid in personality
Yang-deficiency	Flabby muscles, quiet and introvert in personality
Yin-deficiency	Thin physique, outgoing and impatient in personality
Phlegm-wetness	Overweight, a mild temper, steady and patient
Wetness-heat	Normal or thin physique, irritable and short-tempered
Blood-stasis	Impatient and forgetful, a dull complexion, spots on the face, et al.
Qi-depression	Thin, emotional unstable, melancholy or suspicious
Special diathesis	Inborn weakness, allergy

The items could correspond to the four diagnostic methods respectively. Its reliability and construct validity were proven in 2500 people from five different geographical districts in China [23]. It has used in China nationwide campaigns mainly in epidemiological studies on the prevalence of BC types [18]. We have provided a webpage to evaluate the BC types based on CCMQ, see www.tizhiceshi.cn/EN.

3   The Clustering Method for Classes Discovery

It is worthwhile to have an intuition of the information process at the beginning. We provide a general view, see Fig. 1. Every entity will generate information to its external environment. In order to recognize an entity, we have to acquire its emission information into data as much as possible. Then we should transform the raw data to the reduced features that contain the information. Finally we use codes or classes to represent them. When the process runs in reverse, the codes could restore an image of the original entity.

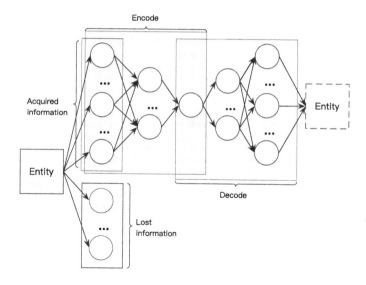

Fig. 1. The process of entity information encoding and decoding

To some degree, there are similarities between the human analysis and the computer process. Next, we specify the process of discovering the nine BC types from the view of computer. Among the unsupervised learning methods, the clustering technique can be used to encode different features into classes. We exhibit a classic clustering algorithm, K-means, to handle the data here.

3.1   K-Means Clustering Algorithm

K-means is one of the most popular clustering algorithms. It was elected as the top 10 algorithms in data mining by the *IEEE International Conference on Data Mining* (ICDM) [20]. Even though K-means has a history of over half a century, it is still famous for its simplicity and efficiency in clustering large data sets [5,11]. The algorithm is described as follows.

Let $X = \{x^{(1)}, ..., x^{(m)}\}$ be the set of m n-dimensional points to be clustered into a set of K clusters, $C = \{c^{(1)}, ..., c^{(K)}\}$. K-means algorithm finds a partition such that the 2-norm error between the mean of a cluster and the points in the cluster is minimized. Let $\mu^{(k)}$ be the mean of cluster $c^{(k)}$, and then it can be calculated as Eq. 1.

$$\mu^{(k)} = \frac{1}{|c^{(k)}|} \sum_{x^{(i)} \in c^{(k)}} x^{(i)} \tag{1}$$

The 2-norm error between $\mu^{(k)}$ and the points in cluster $c^{(k)}$ is defined as Eq. 2.

$$J(c^{(k)}) = \sum_{x^{(i)} \in c^{(k)}} \|x^{(i)} - \mu^{(k)}\|_2^2 \tag{2}$$

The goal of K-means is to minimize the sum of the 2-norm error over all K clusters. So the objective function is described as Eq. 3.

$$J(C) = \sum_{k=1}^{K} \sum_{\boldsymbol{x}^{(i)} \in \boldsymbol{c}^{(k)}} \|\boldsymbol{x}^{(i)} - \boldsymbol{\mu}^{(k)}\|_2^2 \tag{3}$$

When $K \geqslant 2$, minimizing this objective function is known to be an NP-hard problem [4]. Thus K-means can only converge to a local minimum. However, K-means often finds a near-optimal partition according to abundant empirical evidence through so many years. Meilă [10] has shown that with a large probability K-means could converge to the global optimum when clusters have low distortions. The steps of K-means algorithm are showed as Algorithm 1.

Algorithm 1. K-means

Input:
    The set of instances, $X = \{\boldsymbol{x}^{(1)}, ..., \boldsymbol{x}^{(m)}\}$;
    The number of clusters, K;
Output:
    The clusters, $C = \{\boldsymbol{c}^{(1)}, ..., \boldsymbol{c}^{(K)}\}$;
1: Random select K centroids: $\boldsymbol{\mu}^{(1)}, ..., \boldsymbol{\mu}^{(K)} \in \mathbb{R}^n$;
2: Repeat until centers are fixed
3:    For all $\boldsymbol{x}$,
4:       $k := \arg\min_j \|\boldsymbol{x}^{(i)} - \boldsymbol{\mu}^{(j)}\|_2^2$
5:      $\boldsymbol{c}^{(k)} := \{\boldsymbol{c}^{(k)}\} \cup \{\boldsymbol{x}_i\}$;
6:    For all $\boldsymbol{\mu}$,
7:      $\boldsymbol{\mu}_k := \sum_{\boldsymbol{x}^{(i)} \in \boldsymbol{c}^{(k)}} \boldsymbol{x}^{(i)} / |\boldsymbol{c}^{(k)}|$;
8: **return** C;

The input data are the samples of n-dimensional features and an argument of cluster number, K. K-means will partition the points into K clusters. At start, it selects K centroids arbitrarily in step 1. Then it goes to repeat updating clusters until convergence. Step 2–7 are the main iteration. There are two inner iterations, step 3–5 and step 6–7. Step 3–5 assign each point to the nearest centers. Step 6–7 recalculate the mean coordinates of each cluster.

The process of K-means algorithm is illustrated by Fig. 2. The input data, which are generated by three 20-point Gaussian distributions, are scattered in the two-dimension plane, as Fig. 2(a). The distance of points are measured by Euclidean distance. At first, K-means has randomly produced three centroids, as Fig. 2(b). Then, the points and centroids of each cluster are changing by each iteration, as Figs. 2(c)–(e). After several iterations, the centroids are fixed finally, as Fig. 2(f).

It is worth noting that K-means is sensitive to the starting centers. Indeed, the algorithm can generate arbitrarily bad clusters when the centers are chosen uniformly at random from the data points. In this case, we choose the starting

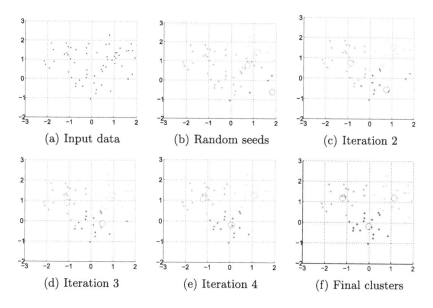

Fig. 2. The process of K-means algorithm.

centers using the strategy similar to K-means++ [1], see Algorithm 2. First, it takes one center $\mu^{(1)}$ chosen uniformly at random from X. Then, it repeatedly chooses $x^{(i)}$, which has the furthest distance to the nearest center that has already chosen, as the next center $\mu^{(j)}$, until to the Kth center. Finally we use the chosen K centers as the starting centers that substitute the random selected K centers chosen in the step 1 of Algorithm 1.

Algorithm 2. Select Initial Centroids

Input:
 The set of instances, $X = \{x^{(1)}, ..., x^{(m)}\}$;
 The number of clusters, K;
Output:
 The seeds, $\mu^{(1)}, ..., \mu^{(K)} \in \mathbb{R}^n$;
1: Choose $\mu^{(1)}$ uniformly at random from X;
2: For k=2:K
3: $\mu^{(k)} := \text{argmax}_{x^{(i)}} \min \|x^{(i)} - \mu^{(j)}\|_2^2, j \in \{1, ..., k-1\}$;
4: **return** $\mu^{(1)}, ..., \mu^{(K)}$;

3.2   The Body Data Generation

Without loss of generality, we assume that the body features of a community are similarly distributed as concluded in the *Constitution in Chinese Medicine Questionnaire* (CCMQ). So we can generate our experiment data set using a generative model.

We form 60 features according to 61 questions, in which two questions only for male or female form a feature, in the CCMQ. Each question corresponds to a score from 1 to 5 points. So we can use a 60-dimensional vector p represents the conditions of a body, and each value corresponds to a question in the CCMQ. Different body constitution (BC) type has a different Gaussian distribution of its values in the vector. In this case, each dimension has a zero covariance to other dimensions that the covariance matrix is diagonal matrix. The generative model of the i BC type can be written as

$$p^{(i)} \sim N(\mu^{(i)}, \Sigma^{(i)}) \tag{4}$$

where $\mu^{(i)}$ is a 60-dimensional vector of Gaussian means, and $\Sigma^{(i)}$ is a 60×60 matrix of covariances. For instance, the group people of the first BC type, gentleness, are generated from the model as

$$p^{(1)} \sim N(\mu^{(1)}, \Sigma^{(1)}) \tag{5}$$

where the $\mu^{(1)}$ and the $\Sigma^{(1)}$ are set by

$$\mu^{(1)} = (1,1,1,1,1,1,1,1,1,1,\quad 1,1,1,1,1,1,1,1,1,1,$$
$$1,1,1,1,1,1,1,1,1,1,\quad 1,1,1,1,1,1,1,1,1,1,$$
$$1,1,1,1,1,4,1,1,4,1,\quad 1,1,1,1,1,1,1,1,1,1)$$

$$\Sigma^{(1)} = \begin{pmatrix} 1 & & \mathbf{O} \\ & \ddots & \\ \mathbf{O} & & 1 \end{pmatrix} = I$$

where I is a 60×60 identity matrix.

We use the parallel coordinate to visualize the data set, as Fig. 3. The data set is generated from 9 Gaussian generative models, in which there are 20% of gentleness BC type and 10% of other 8 types respectively. The covariance matrix is set to $0.3I$ for observable convenience. The horizontal axis represents the dimensions of a vector, and the vertical axis represents the value of each dimension. Each line connecting the points from dimension 1 to 60 is a sample of the data set.

4   Experiments

4.1   Discover the BC Types

Then we use K-means algorithm to gain an insight into the data set. At start, we take a look into a data set containing 100 samples as Fig. 4 shows.

Given the data set without the labels, we use the K-means algorithm to cluster it and set K=9. The clustering result as Fig. 5 shows. The means of the clusters are illustrated as Fig. 6.

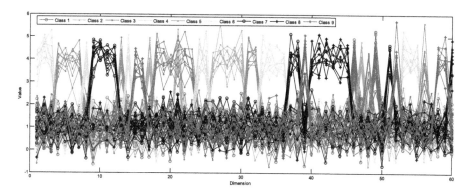

Fig. 3. Visualization of the sampled 60-dimension data of 9 classes ($\Sigma = 0.3I$)

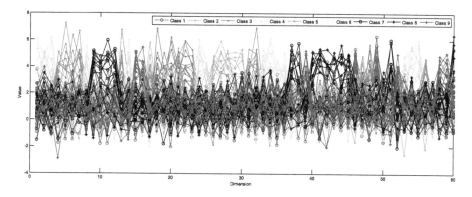

Fig. 4. The input data set of 100 samples ($\Sigma = I$)

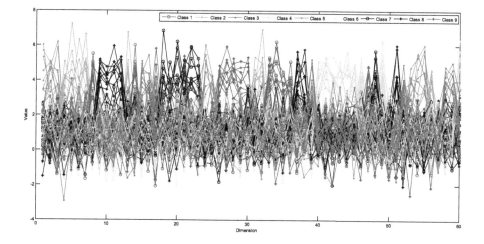

Fig. 5. The clustering result of the 100 samples

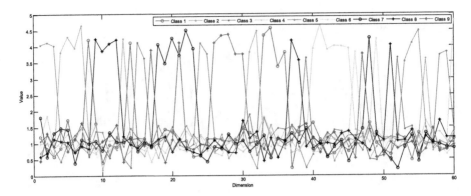

Fig. 6. The means of the clusters of the 100 samples ($\Sigma = I$)

After the clustering, we can regard the means of the clusters as the representations of different body conditions, that is the discovered BC types. For example, the first type (Class 1 in Fig. 6) acquired from the cluster mean as

$$\boldsymbol{\mu}^{(1)} = (1.20, 0.84, 0.60, 0.86, 1.72, 0.76, 1.00, 4.21, 1.610.40,$$
$$0.95, 0.89, 1.12, 4.11, 0.90, 1.14, 0.87, 1.11, 1.43, 1.36,$$
$$1.04, 1.07, 0.58, 0.62, 1.13, 1.13, 1.12, 0.73, 1.10, 1.45,$$
$$1.31, 1.18, 4.34, 4.56, 3.36, 3.81, 0.23, 1.34, 1.39, 1.62,$$
$$1.10, 0.60, 0.68, 0.92, 0.74, 0.97, 0.96, 1.61, 0.99, 0.77,$$
$$0.64, 1.22, 1.13, 0.47, 1.31, 0.96, 0.98, 0.78, 0.80, 1.11)$$

This type have bigger values in 8th, 14th, 42nd, 43rd, 44th, 45th dimension of the features around 4, and other features have smaller values around 1. We know that it is the Wetness-heat BC type. For instance, the 8th feature dimension corresponding to the 8th question, *"Did your nose or your face feel greasyoilyor shiny?"*, located in www.tizhiceshi.cn/EN.

4.2   Count More Data

Even though the data set contains some noises, the inferred distribution will be more and more approximate to the latent distribution as the growing of the data. In order to illustrate this point, we use a data set of 1000 samples to repeat the experiment. The means of the clusters as the Fig. 7 shows. We can see the results are closer to the latent means of 4 or 1 comparing to Fig. 6.

4.3   Exploring More Types

As the data set becomes rich enough, it is possible to detect more fine-grained classes. With the convenience of the computer, we can analyze the hyperparameter easily. Assume there is a BC type hidden in the gentleness BC type

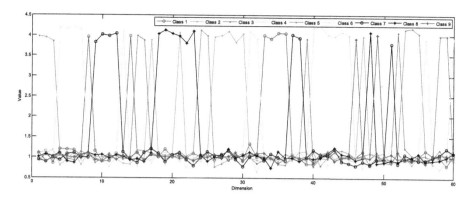

Fig. 7. The means of the clusters of the 1000 samples ($\Sigma = I$)

that we have not discovered. So we had better choose a bigger number of categories for clustering to discover the small group. Let the hidden type is called sub-yin-deficiency that is a Gaussian distribution with mean given by

$$
\begin{aligned}
\boldsymbol{\mu}^{(2)} = (&2.5, 2.5, 2.5, 1, 1, 1, 1, 1, 1, 1, \quad 1, 1, 1, 1, 1, 1, 1, 1, 1, 1, \\
&1, 1, 1, 2.5, 2.5, 1, 1, 1, 1, 1, \quad 1, 1, 1, 1, 1, 1, 1, 1, 1, 1, \\
&1, 1, 1, 1, 1, 3.4, 1, 1, 3.4, 1, \quad 1, 1, 2.5, 2.5, 2.5, 1, 1, 1, 1, 1)
\end{aligned}
$$

Again we produce the data set according to the generative models. At first, we set $K = 9$ when running the K-means algorithm. Figure 8 visualize the result of the means.

We can see the type 1 ("Class 1" in Fig. 8) has a little big values around 1.7 in the 1st, 2nd, 3rd, 24th, 25th, 53rd, 54th and 55th dimension respectively, while the values of 46th and 49th dimension are around 3.7. It is a mix distribution of two Gaussian generative models. Then we set $K = 10$ while running the K-means algorithm. The result is as Fig. 9 revealed.

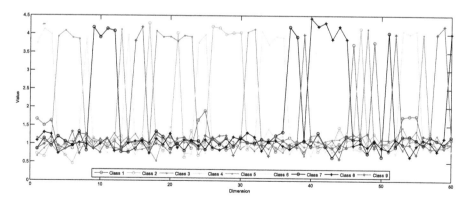

Fig. 8. Using K=9 to cluster samples of 10 classes ($\Sigma = I$)

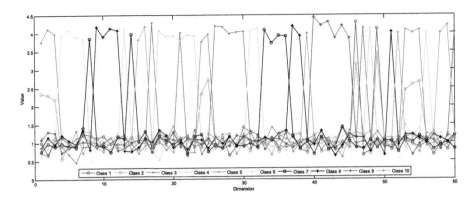

Fig. 9. Using K=10 to cluster samples of 10 classes ($\Sigma = I$)

At this moment, "Class 1" in Fig. 8 has been recognized as two types ("Class 1" and "Class 2" in Fig. 9). "Class 2" in Fig. 9 has values around 2.5 in the 1st, 2nd, 3rd, 24th, 25th, 53rd, 54th and 55th dimension respectively, while the values of 46th and 49th dimension are around 3.4. So this type is the sub-yin-deficiency type that we want to distinguish.

5   Related Works

In artificial intelligence of medical diagnosis, most of attentions are handling the supervised learning task, which is usually using labeled data set to train a model for classification or prediction. There are models like logistic regression (LR), support vector machine (SVM), decision tree, and artificial neural networks [3,7]. Caruana et al. [2] propose an intelligible and accurate model for predicting pneumonia risk and hospital 30-day readmission. Zhao et al. [22] provide an overview of machine learning algorithms in patient classification for Traditional Chinese Medicine (TCM), especially in the four diagnosis methods of TCM. However, only a very few unsupervised learning works are mentioned in their literatures.

In the researches of body constitution (BC) types of TCM, Wang et al. [14] review the establishment of the standard for classifying 9 BC types. Lu et al. [9] have explored the relationship between TCM patterns and the diagnosis in biomedical. Jiang et al. [6] use LR model to the research on the association between TCM constitution and maternal symptoms related to pregnancy, and find that women with unbalanced constitutions in early pregnancy have a greater likelihood of severe nausea and vomiting and poor sleep during pregnancy. In order to determine the relationship between TCM classification and genetic classification, Yu et al. [21] use the SVM model to classify the genetic samples. To the best of our knowledge, there is still no detailed work of using unsupervised learning methods for BC types discovery and validation.

6   Conclusion

Human body is a kind of complex dynamical systems that are somewhat difficult to be described from the micro perspective. An alternative approach is to analyze from the macro perspective. TCM provides a macro perspective for us. According to the CCMQ, we illustrate the process of discovering the 9 types of body constitution in TCM based on K-means algorithm. Furthermore, we demonstrate its flexibility to distinguish more fine-grained types. It shows that machine learning algorithms provide efficient and effective tools that can extend medical practitioners' data analysis ability to reveal interesting relationships in their data.

Acknowledgments. This work is supported in part by the National Natural Science Foundation of China under Grant Numbers 61632009, 61472451 and 61272151, and the High Level Talents Program of Higher Education in Guangdong Province under Funding Support Number 2016ZJ01.

References

1. Arthur, D., Vassilvitskii, S.: K-means++: the advantages of careful seeding. In: Proceedings of the Eighteenth Annual ACM-SIAM Symposium on Discrete Algorithms, pp. 1027–1035. Society for Industrial and Applied Mathematics (2007)
2. Caruana, R., Lou, Y., Gehrke, J., Koch, P., Sturm, M., Elhadad, N.: Intelligible models for healthcare: predicting pneumonia risk and hospital 30-day readmission. In: Proceedings of the 21st ACM SIGKDD International Conference on Knowledge Discovery and Data Mining, pp. 1721–1730. ACM (2015)
3. Delen, D., Walker, G., Kadam, A.: Predicting breast cancer survivability: a comparison of three data mining methods. Artif. Intell. Med. **34**(2), 113–127 (2005)
4. Drineas, P., Frieze, A., Kannan, R., Vempala, S., Vinay, V.: Clustering large graphs via the singular value decomposition. Mach. Learn. **56**(1), 9–33 (2004)
5. Gan, G., Ng, M.K.P.: Subspace clustering with automatic feature grouping. Pattern Recogn. **48**(11), 3703–3713 (2015)
6. Jiang, Q., Li, J., Wang, G., Wang, J.: The relationship between constitution of traditional Chinese medicine in the first trimester and pregnancy symptoms: a longitudinal observational study. Evid.-Based Complement. Altern. Med. **2016**(Article ID 3901485), 1–8 (2016)
7. Kononenko, I.: Machine learning for medical diagnosis: history, state of the art and perspective. Artif. Intell. Med. **23**(1), 89–109 (2001)
8. Lin, J.D., Lin, J.S., Chen, L.L., Chang, C.H., Huang, Y.C., Su, Y.C.: BCQs: a body constitution questionnaire to assess stasis in traditional Chinese medicine. Eur. J. Integr. Med. **4**(4), e379–e391 (2012)
9. Lu, A., Jiang, M., Zhang, C., Chan, K.: An integrative approach of linking traditional Chinese medicine pattern classification and biomedicine diagnosis. J. Ethnopharmacol. **141**(2), 549–556 (2012)
10. Meilă, M.: The uniqueness of a good optimum for k-means. In: Proceedings of the 23rd International Conference on Machine Learning, pp. 625–632. ACM, New York (2006)

11. Naldi, M., Campello, R.: Comparison of distributed evolutionary k-means clustering algorithms. Neurocomputing **163**(1), 78–93 (2015)
12. Su, Y.C.: Establishment of traditional Chinese medical constitutional scale and classificatory index (2–1). Yearbook Chin. Med. Pharm. **25**(5), 45–144 (2007)
13. Su, Y.C.: The creation of traditional Chinese medical constitutional scale and classification index (2–2). Yearbook Chin. Med. Pharm. **26**(5), 65–152 (2008)
14. Wang, J., Li, Y., Ni, C., Zhang, H., Li, L., Wang, Q.: Cognition research and constitutional classification in Chinese medicine. Am. J. Chin. Med. **39**(04), 651–660 (2011)
15. Wang, Q.: Status and prospect of constitutional theory in traditional Chinese medicine. Chin. J. Basic Med. Tradit. Chin. Med. **8**(2), 6–17 (2002)
16. Wang, Q.: Classification and diagnosis basis of nine basic constitutions in Chinese medicine. J. Beijing Univ. Tradit. Chin. Med. **28**(4), 1–8 (2005)
17. Wang, Q., Zhu, Y.B., Xue, H.S., Li, S.: Primary compiling of constitution in Chinese medicine questionnaire. Chin. J. Clin. Rehabil. **10**(3), 12–14 (2006)
18. Wang, Q., Zhu, Y.: Epidemiological investigation of constitutional types of Chinese medicine in general population: based on 21,948 epidemiological investigation data of nine provinces in china. China J. Tradit. Chin. Med. Pharm. **24**(1), 7–12 (2009)
19. Wong, W., Lam, C.L.K., Wong, V.T., Yang, Z.M., Ziea, E.T., Kwan, A.K.L.: Validation of the constitution in chinese medicine questionnaire: does the traditional Chinese medicine concept of body constitution exist? Evid.-Based Complement. Altern. Med. **2013**(Article ID 481491), 1–14 (2013)
20. Wu, X., Kumar, V., Quinlan, J.R., Ghosh, J., Yang, Q., Motoda, H., McLachlan, G.J., Ng, A., Liu, B., Philip, S.Y., et al.: Top 10 algorithms in data mining. Knowl. Inf. Syst. **14**(1), 1–37 (2008)
21. Yu, R., Zhao, X., Li, L., Ni, C., Yang, Y., Han, Y., Wang, J., Zhang, Y., Wang, Q.: Consistency between traditional Chinese medicine constitution-based classification and genetic classification. J. Trad. Chin. Med. Sci. **2**(4), 248–257 (2015)
22. Zhao, C., Li, G.Z., Wang, C., Niu, J.: Advances in patient classification for traditional Chinese medicine: a machine learning perspective. Evid.-Based Complement. Altern. Med. **2015**(Article ID 376716), 1–18 (2015)
23. Zhu, Y.B., Wang, Q., Origasa, H.: Evaluation on reliability and validity of the constitution in Chinese medicine questionnaire (CCMQ). Chin. J. Behav. Med. Sci. **16**(7), 651–654 (2007)

A Calibration-Free Crowdsourcing-Based Indoor Localization Solution

Jie Yin, Ying Wu[✉], Xinxin Zhang, and Miao Lu

College of Computer and Control Engineering, Nankai University,
Tianjin 300350, China
wuying@nankai.edu.cn

Abstract. Researches on crowdsourcing-based localization systems have been attracting much attention. It is a main problem that device diversity and short-duration signal strength measurement significantly degrade the localization accuracy in crowdsourcing-based systems. In this paper, we analyze underlying relationships between detected wireless Access Points (AP) and received signal strength (RSS), which are relatively invariable over devices and measurement times. Then we present a novel solution which uses these underlying relationships as key values for location determination. We use the first publicly available database in this field to evaluate this solution. The experimental results confirm that this solution provides high success rate and acceptable localization accuracy.

Keywords: Crowdsourcing-based indoor localization · Device diversity · Short-duration RSS measurement · Dependency of detected APs · RSS dependency

1 Introduction

There is a demand for more accurate location information along with the growth of mobile devices. As a result, many indoor localization systems have been proposed using wireless signals such as radio frequency identification, infrared, Bluetooth, ultrasonic and WiFi. Among these signals, WiFi is the most widely used. It does not require the installation of any additional hardware since it uses the existing WLAN infrastructures and most mobile devices like smartphones are already equipped with a WiFi module. In the last decade, a number of researchers have proposed their research related to fingerprint-based indoor localization. A fingerprint is a set of pairs: the MAC address and signal strength of a wireless Access Point. They build a radio map in "Offline Training Phase" and then estimate users' location in "Online Localization Phase". Most of these methods use collected RSS values in their localization solutions which are easy and intuitive.

Indoor localization systems can be classified into two categories according to professional literacy of the person who collects fingerprint data in the offline training phase. The initial model is named "Expert Surveyor". All the required

© Springer International Publishing AG 2016
G. Wang et al. (Eds.): APSCC 2016, LNCS 10065, pp. 65–76, 2016.
DOI: 10.1007/978-3-319-49178-3_5

jobs must be done by trained experts in this model. Taking into account the existing obstacles introduced by the indoor environment, the spread of radio signal in indoor environments is very hard to predict [3]. In addition, the device type is an important factor affecting collected RSS values. Experts have to prolong measurement times and carry the same type of devices. This model involves intensive costs on manpower and time, which limits the applicable building of wireless localization worldwide. In order to solve this problem, researchers have started applying the idea of crowdsourcing in their systems [7,9,11]. The crowdsourcing-based model recruits untrained people as volunteers who are active to share sensor data of their mobile devices. Untrained volunteers are allowed to participate in the training phase. UJIIndoorLoc [5] is a model like this. Data are collected by more than 20 users using 25 different models of mobile devices. This model can significantly reduce the map-building and maintenance cost, but it also introduces a new set of challenges:

- *Device Diversity*: As there is no constraint on type and number of devices, a radio map is built with RSS values which are collected by diverse devices.
- *Short-duration RSS Measurements*: Every volunteer should not be forced to sacrifice their time or their device's resources. And they could not afford long-enough measurement times for building a robust fingerprint database.

Measurement and calibration methods of RSS vary with different chipset and antenna business organizations, which led to different devices report apparently distinct RSS and distinct sets of APs even in the same location. So, it is necessary for localization techniques to tolerate device diversity.

Due to multipath effect, shadowing, fading and delay distortion [6], RSS is susceptible to environmental changes. A short period of times is incapable of depicting the true characteristics of the RSS distribution at a specific location. In order to solve this problem, experts prolong measurement times and use the average RSS value for each AP in the "Expert Surveyor" model. But all volunteers have no obligation to sacrifice their time or their device's resources. They are free to fill their own time according to their own choice with participating the training phase. And they could not afford long-enough measurement times for building a robust fingerprint database. So, average RSS values are not the representative values of detected APs in a crowdsourcing-based model. Therefore, crowdsourcing-based localization system need a novel method that extracts a reliable single value per AP from a short-duration RSS measurement. And these systems should insure that their radio maps provide accurate fingerprints even though they are built based on short-duration RSS measurement.

The rest of the paper has been organized as follows. Section 2 presents the related works. These works include some indoor localization systems which handle device diversity and short-duration measurement. Section 3 analyzes the underlying relationships of detected APs and collected RSS. And then we present our solution which uses these underlying relationships as key values for location estimation. Section 4 shows our experiment results. Finally, in Sect. 5 some conclusions are given.

2   Related Work

There are many indoor localization systems which can deal with diverse devices. RSS values reported by different devices reflect the same relationship indicating the distance to APs: the strongest RSS from the nearest AP and the weakest RSS from the farthest AP. The signal strength patterns are almost the same for different devices at a fixed location. So, some systems employ a calibration step which creates a linear mapping between the RSS collected with diverse devices. These calibration data need to be collected in advance [4]. Considering the huge amount of different IEEE 802.11 clients in the market, these methods are unpractical to use worldwide. [2] proposes a method named Hyperbolic Location Fingerprinting (HLF). HLF uses signal strength ratios between pairs of APs instead of absolute RSS in its estimate method. [1] proposes a method named DIFF. DIFF uses signal strength differences between pairs of APs in its estimate method. HLF and DIFF do not need a learning period to find a linear mapping between pairs of devices. The key idea of these two methods is that relationships of pairs of APs are less effected by device diversity than collected RSS values. As these relationships are expressed by RSS, [1,2,4] still need a prolong-enough measurement times to extract a reliable single fingerprint value per AP.

RSS varies over time due to moving objects, or prolonged dynamics like light, temperature and weather changes in an indoor environment. A short period of times is incapable of depicting the true characteristics of the RSS distribution at a specific location [8]. FreeLoc [10] observes that the most-recorded RSS in the case of the short-duration measurements is very close to the most-recorded RSS in the long-duration measurement case. And it presents a method that extracts a reliable single value pre AP from the short-duration RSS measurements. FreeLoc find that there is a certain underlying overall relationship of RSS. This relationship remains relatively stable in each sampling position, even though collected RSS values greatly change in every individual location. Radio map building and localization techniques are based on this overall relationship in FreeLoc. Its location accuracy becomes less reliant on measurement times and collected RSS. [1,2,8,10] show that traditional fingerprint is not the key distinguishing feature among different locations. The key distinguishing feature is hidden in traditional fingerprint and irrelevant to device attributes or measurement times. Following issues are token into account in the rest of this paper.

– The area covered by WLAN infrastructures is limited. Within the coverage area of a AP, all devices can detect this AP in each WiFi scan.
– Neighboring positions have a similar indoor environment including distribution of obstacles and relative distance to each AP. As a result, signal jitter scope of each AP is relatively stable in a small scale.
– RSS variations can be caused by prolonged dynamics like light, temperature and humidity changes in the environment. Considering such dynamics are similar for neighbor locations, the relationship of how RSS depends on its neighbors may exist.

3   Methodology

We use UJIIndoorLoc database in our experiment, which is the first public accessible database in indoor localization. There are 520 different APs and 933 sampling positions in UJIIndoorLoc database. As shown in Table 1, 21049 sampled points have been captured: 19938 for training and 1111 for validation. Each record is directly related to a single WiFi capture and it contains the 529 numeric elements: 001–520 RSS levels, 521–523 real world coordinates of the sample points, 524 building label, 525 space label, 526 relative position with respect to space label, 527 user label, 528 phone label and 529 timestamp. The 520-element vector from each record contains the raw intensity levels of the detected APs from a single WiFi scan. Not all the APs are detected in each scan and the RSS values of undetected APs use the artificial value +100dBm by default. Real-world coordinates of sampling position are represented by means of three values in each record, the longitude and latitude coordinates and the floor of a building. There is another value that indicates the building of sampling positions. Building label is an integer value that corresponds to the building. A good localization system should correctly locate validation fingerprints inside the corresponding building and floor. And the average error in meters should be as low as possible.

Table 1. Basic features of the training and validation data set in the UJIIndoorLoc database.

	Training date set	Validation date set
Captures	19938	1111
APs	465	367
RSS range (dBm)	$[-104,0]$	$[-102,-34]$
Sampling points	933	Unknown
Users	18	Unknown
Devices	16	11

In this section, the underlying relationship of detected APs and RSS dependency is completely described. Section 3.1 shows the relationship of detected APs. Section 3.2 shows the relationship of signal's jitter scope in a small scale. Section 3.3 analyzes the underlying relationship of RSS depending on its neighbors. At the end, Sect. 3.4 shows our estimate method in details.

3.1   Detected APs

Training records are collected with diverse devices in UJIInoodLoc database. Measurement and calibration methods of RSS vary with different chipsets and antennas. Each chipset and antenna organization has its own minimum standard of WiFi signal strength. A device can detect an AP only if the signal strength is greater than the device's minimum standard. This is why different devices may report apparently distinct list of detected APs in a specific position. This difference between detected APs obviously degrade localization accuracy. Figure 1 shows the details about the number of detected APs in a single capture. It is obviously that the main factors affecting to the number of APs reported by a WiFi scan are the location and the phone model.

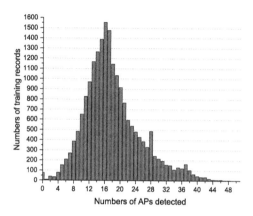

Fig. 1. Frequency distribution of the Number of APs which are detected on a single WiFi scan.

Considering the continuity of WiFi infrastructures' limited coverage, neighboring positions have quite similar set of detected APs. The intersection of detected APs sets is a reflection of the correlation of the distance between two sampling positions.

There are slightly differences between set of detected APs in each training record which is collected in position $(-7541.2642999999225, 4864920.7782000005, 2)$. The number of simultaneously detected APs are over 80 % of total detected APs in each record even through they are collected by different devices. Signal strengths of simultaneously detected APs are usually strong-enough and are higher than most devices' own minimum standard of wireless signal strength. This set of simultaneously detected APs is more stable and more representative in this sampling location. And it is marked as the key detected AP set of this sample position. The key detected APs of this position is expressed as $keyFp_i = \{keyAP_1, keyAP_2, ..., keyAP_k\}$.

We compare $keyFp_i$ with other key sets and get the similarity degree (the number of APs in intersection/the number of APs in $keyFp_i$) and the results are grouped according to Euclidean distance between real world coordinates of two records. As shown in Table 2, sampling records from the same floor have a higher similarity degree than others. In addition, the max value of similarity degree is generally higher when the Euclidean Distance is lower than 45 m.

Table 2. The relationship between the key detected APs set and physical distance.

Floor	Max value of similarity degree(0,45 m]	Max value of similarity degree(45 m,90 m]	Max value of similarity degree(90 m,200 m]
0	0.4	0.2	0
1	0.8	0.2	0
2	1	0.2	0
3	0.4	0.2	0
4	0	0	0

When the Euclidean distance is greater than 90 m, similarity degree is 0 which means that the intersection is empty.

We can use this similarity degree between key AP sets for rough location estimating. This underlying relationship of detected APs is relatively stable over devices. The higher similarity degree is, the smaller the physical distance between two positions is. When the similarity degree is greater than 0.5, we add this position to a candidate set of the estimate location. The estimate location of a localization request will be selected from this candidate set. Considering limited coverage of each AP, this rough estimating can reduce the possibility of locating the error building. A key detected AP set only includes these APs whose signal strength is strong-enough. Most devices can detect all these APs in a sampling position. This key set is relatively stable over devices. So, device diversity has a negligible effect on this step.

3.2 Signal's Jitter Scope

As reported RSS values are clearly affected by device diversity and complicated indoor environment, devices report apparently distinct RSS even in the same location and over any small time period. But RSS values reported by different devices reflect the same relationship indicating the distance to APs. The relative RSS value between pairs of APs is much more stable. And each position has similar indoor environmental impacts with its neighbors. The signal jitter scope of each AP is relatively stable in smaller range. When each WiFi scan is collected using different devices in a specific position, signal's jitter scope of these records have a positive correlation to each other and the correlation coefficients are theoretically closer to the ideal value. We use a vector as a digital representation of this feature. We define this vector as $scope_i = (AP_1: \min(RSS_1, RSS_2, ...), AP_1: \max(RSS_1, RSS_2, ...), ...)(AP_j \in keyFp_i)$ in position i. We can use this relationship between $scope_i$ and its neighbors to further localization. We compute the liner correlation coefficient of this relationship between $scope_i$ and fingerprints in the candidate set, as shown in Table 3. When records are collected at same building and floor, they have a positively correlation with $scope_i$. Positive correlation means that two positions exist similar signal jitter scope characteristics. And minor differences are manifested as a numerical value of linear correlation

Table 3. The relationship of signal's jitter scope.

Floor	The number of fingerprints in candidate set	Positive correlation(%)	Range of correlation coefficient
0	NA	NA	NA
1	17	11 %	[−0.698303, 0.0769472]
2	18	100 %	[0.268661, 0.971561]
3	NA	NA	NA
4	NA	NA	NA

coefficient. The higher this numerical value is, the smaller the physical distance between two positions is.

It is a feasible solution that the relationship of signal's jitter scope is used for further rough location estimate. Neighboring positions have a similar indoor environment including distribution of obstacles and relative distance to each AP. The digital representations of this relationship in neighboring positions are little different and they have a positive correlation with each other. Hence, When the liner correlation coefficient is lower than 0, this position should be removed from the candidate position set.

3.3   RSS Depending on Its Neighbors

Training records are divided into groups according to their sampling position and collected device. We use *(LONGITUDE, LATITUDE, FLOOR, PHONEID)* as the key value of each group in remainder of this article. So do validation records. More than 88.17 % training groups have no more than 10 scan records. More than 98.7 % validation groups only have 1 scan record. Obviously, using average RSS values or most-recorded RSS are not applicable in this situation. We need a novel method that extracts a reliable single fingerprint value per AP with the high tolerance of the RSS variation over short-duration measurements.

RSS varies over time due to moving objects, or prolonged dynamics like light, temperature and weather changes in an indoor environment. The dynamics are similar and have a similar effect in a small scale. In addition, neighboring positions have a similar indoor environment including distribution of obstacles and relative distance to each AP. The underlying relationship of RSS depending on its neighbors is relatively stable over time. This relationship is relatively stable in each WiFi scan. Each scan record is a digital representation of this relationship in a sampling position. As each AP has its own jitter scope and jitter rule, a WiFi scan record is a combination data of each AP's signal strength which falls within the AP's signal jitter scope. Short-during measurement make we only collect few records in each position. We only get few possible combinations and these combinations are not always representative. During online estimating phase, we generate a virtual WiFi scan record and use this virtual record to find an estimate location. This virtual record meets the following requirements:

- The virtual RSS value of an AP falls within the RSS value range of this AP.
- The virtual RSS value vector from this virtual record maximizes the liner correlation coefficient between this vector and the validation vector among all possible combinations.

This virtual record satisfies a fingerprint's all basic features including the relationship of detected APs, signal jitter scope, and RSS depending on its neighbors. And it is the most typical representative of how RSS depends on its neighbors in this position, when we use a validation record as a baseline. If these two records are sampled in the same position, the liner correlation coefficient between this virtual record and this validation record is theoretically closer to the ideal value.

After rough location estimate, we get a candidate position set. Then we generate a virtual scan record for each fingerprint in this candidate set. The liner correlation between each virtual records and a validation record is calculated to find the estimate position which maximizes this liner correlation coefficient.

3.4   Estimate Technique

We simulate that all training records are collected by volunteers and a radio map is built with these records before online localization phase. All training records in UJIIndoorLoc are grouped based on collected devices and sampling positions. The uniquely identify of a fingerprint is *(LONGITUDE, LATITUDE, FLOOR, PHONEID)* and the structure of fingerprints is mentioned in Sect. 3.1. Each validation record is used as a localization request data.

The online localization phase is divided into two steps: rough location estimating step and precise location estimating step in this paper.

As WLAN infrastructures have limited coverage, we firstly use this similarity degree between key detected AP sets for rough location estimate. And device diversity has a negligible effect on this step. Considering RSS reflect the relationship indicating the distance to APs, the relative signal jitter scope between pairs of APs is much stable in a sampling position. We use this relationship for future location estimate. After this rough location estimate, we get a candidate set of positions which have a higher likelihood being chosen as the estimate position.

The underlying relationship of RSS depending on its neighbors is relatively stable in each WiFi scan. Each scan record is used as a whole for location estimating in our method and single RSS value no longer has any significance in precise location estimate step. We generate a virtual WiFi scan record which satisfies a training fingerprint's all basic features including the relationship of detected APs, signal jitter scope, and RSS depending on its neighbors. It is the most typical representative of how RSS depends on its neighbors in this position, when we use a validation record as a baseline. Then we calculate the liner correlation to find the winner virtual fingerprint which maximizes this liner correlation coefficient between this training fingerprint and a validation fingerprint. The real world coordinates of the winner fingerprint is marked as the estimate location which will be sent to requester.

The key idea of our method is that these underlying relationships are used as key values for location estimating. And these relationships are more stable than absolute RSS values.

4   Performance Evaluation

We analyze system performance in two aspects: success rate and localization accuracy. The success rate corresponds to the percentage of validation records correctly located inside the corresponding building and floor. Localization accuracy is the average error in meters of the validation fingerprints which are correctly located inside the corresponding building and floor. We compare our method with Euclidean distance, DIFF, HLF and FreeLoc. Average RSS values are used in radio maps of Euclidean distance, DIFF and HLF. We have developed the Nearest Neighbor in conjunction to the Euclidean distance, DIF and DIFF as basic systems. Most-record RSS values are used in the radio map of FreeLoc.

Table 4 shows simulation results. Euclidean Distance accumulates RSS difference between each AP. Localization accuracy of this method completely relies on collected RSS values. Both short-duration measurement and devices diversity have a serious effect on absolute RSS values. The success rate and localization accuracy of this method are worst. So, Euclidean distance is not suitable for UJI-IndoorLoc database. DIFF and HLF use average RSS values in their radio maps. DIFF uses signal strength differences between pairs of APs instead of absolute RSS values. HLF uses signal strength ratios between pairs of APs instead of absolute RSS values. They rely on correlation between pairs of APs. This correlation is expressed as difference or ratio between RSS values of two APs. So, both these two methods need a robust radio map. But short-duration measurement could not satisfy this demand. Compared to Euclidean Distance, DIFF and HLF rely more on differences between pairs of APs which are more stable over devices. The success rate and localization accuracy of both methods are much better than Euclidean Distance.

FreeLoc extracts a reliable single fingerprint value pre AP from the short-duration RSS measurements. In FreeLoc, radio map building and localization techniques are based on the overall relationship among RSS of detected APs. The relationship is underlying RSS values and much stable over devices and measurement times. FreeLoc can handle device diversity and short-duration measurement. And success rate and localization accuracy of it are much better than methods mentioned above. But this method is not suitable for UJI-IndoorLoc as most validation data contains only one WiFi scan for each location request. The single fingerprint value per AP is calculated by a single WiFi scan which inject uncertainty of validation fingerprints. Our method uses the relationship of detected APs for rough estimating at first. This underlying relationship is relatively stable over devices. Then characteristics of signal jitter scope are used to narrow the candidate set. This relationship is little influenced by device diversity as the result of comparison between RSS values is device-independent. This rough location estimate step relies on two common senses:

WLAN infrastructures have limited coverage and RSS reflect the same relationship indicating the distance to APs for diverse devices. These two relationships are more stable over devices. Then we generate a digital representation of the relationship of RSS depending on its neighbors in the precise location estimate step. This representation satisfies all characteristics described in a fingerprint and is not limited to detected RSS values. It is the most typical representative of how RSS depends on its neighbors in this position, when we use a validation record as a baseline. As shown in Table 4, our method has better success rate and localization accuracy. And this result has verified the three relationships mentioned above.

As shown in Table 5, there are 2 out of 1111 requests (0.18 %) in which the building is not correctly predicted and 54 errors (5.4 %) in locating the correct floor in our method. In online estimate phase, detected APs are much more important than undetected APs. And a set of detected APs can be used for rough estimating which can decrease the possibility of located at error buildings. Then the relationship of signal jitter scope is used to narrow the candidate position set, which can decrease the possibility of located at error floors. Compared with other methods, our method has lower positioning error rate. This result confirms that the relationships of detected APs and signal jitter scope are existing and remain relatively stable. Device diversity and short-duration measurement have less effects in these two relationships. The rough estimate step has high localization success rate.

Table 4. Simulation results of success rate and localization accuracy.

Method	Success rate(%)	Min error(m)	Average error(m)	Max error(m)
Euclidean distance	89.7 %	0	8.2	121.5
DIFF	90.6 %	0	7.9	117.4
HLF	90.7 %	0	7.9	117.4
FreeLoc	94.2 %	0	7.1	99.2
Our method	94.4 %	0	7.0	102.8

Table 5. Simulation results of error rate including located in error building and error floor.

Method	Located in error building(%)	Located in error floor(%)
Euclidean distance	0.36 %	9.9 %
DIFF	0.27 %	9.1 %
HLF	0.27 %	9.0 %
FreeLoc	0.18 %	5.6 %
Our method	0.18 %	5.4 %

5 Conclusion

In this paper, we propose a calibration-free solution for handling device diversity and short-duration measurement in crowdsourcing-based indoor localization systems. This solution has two basic steps: rough estimate and precise estimate. It is clear that WLAN infrastructures have limited coverage. If the signal strength of an AP is strong-enough in a fixed location, all devices can detect this AP in each WiFi capture. Considering the continuity of each AP's limited coverage, neighbors have quite similar set of detected APs. This underlying relationship of detected APs is relatively stable over devices or measurement times. We use this similarity degree between detected AP sets for rough estimating. The higher similarity degree is, the smaller the physical distance between two positions is. RSS values reported by different devices reflect the same relationship indicating the distance to APs. The relative signal jitter scope between pairs of APs is stable in neighboring positions. This relationship is little influenced by device diversity as the result of comparison between RSS values is device-independent. We use this relationship for future rough estimate. Neighboring positions have a similar indoor environment including distribution of obstacles and relative distance to each AP. In addition, RSS varies over time due to prolonged dynamics which are similar for neighboring positions and have a similar effect on a small scale. The underlying relationship of RSS depending on its neighbors is relatively stable over time. Each scan record is a digital representation of this relationship. We generate a virtual WiFi scan record in precise estimate step. This virtual record satisfies a fingerprint's all basic features. And then we find the estimate position which maximizes this liner correlation coefficient. We compare our method with 4 methods, the simulation result confirms that these three relationships do exist and our method is reliable and feasible.

References

1. Dong, F., Chen, Y., Liu, J., Ning, Q., Piao, S.: A calibration-free localization solution for handling signal strength variance. In: Mobile Entity Localization and Tracking in GPS-less Environnments, pp. 79–90 (2009)
2. Kjaergaard, M.B.: Indoor location fingerprinting with heterogeneous clients. Pervasive Mob. Comput. **7**(1), 31–43 (2011)
3. Marques, N., Meneses, F., Moreira, A.: Combining similarity functions and majority rules for multi-building, multi-floor, wifi positioning. In: International Conference on Indoor Positioning and Indoor Navigation, pp. 1–9 (2012)
4. Park, J., Curtis, D., Teller, S., Ledlie, J.: Implications of device diversity for organic localization. Proc. IEEE INFOCOM **2**(3), 3182–3190 (2011)
5. Torres-Sospedra, J., Montoliu, R., Martinez-Uso, A., Avariento, J.P.: UJIIndoorLoc: a new multi-building and multi-floor database for WLAN fingerprint-based indoor localization problems. In: International Conference on Indoor Positioning and Indoor Navigation (2014)
6. Wang, X., Mao, S., Pandey, S., Agrawal, P.: CA^{2}T: cooperative antenna arrays technique for pinpoint indoor localization. Procedia Comput. Sci. **34**, 392–399 (2014)

7. Wu, C., Yang, Z., Liu, Y.: Smartphones based crowdsourcing for indoor localization. IEEE Trans. Mob. Comput. **14**(2), 444–457 (2015)
8. Wu, C., Yang, Z., Xiao, C., Yang, C.: Static power of mobile devices: self-updating radio maps for wireless indoor localization. In: IEEE Conference on Computer Communications (INFOCOM), pp. 2497–2505 (2015)
9. Wu, F.J., Luo, T.: Infrastructureless signal source localization using crowdsourced data for smart-city applications. In: IEEE International Conference on Communications (ICC), pp. 586–591 (2015)
10. Yang, S., Dessai, P., Verma, M., Gerla, M.: FreeLoc: calibration-free crowdsourced indoor localization. Proc. IEEE INFOCOM **12**(11), 2481–2489 (2013)
11. Zhang, L., Valaee, S., Zhang, L., Xu, Y., Ma, L.: Signal propagation-based outlier reduction technique (SPORT) for crowdsourcing in indoor localization using fingerprints. In: IEEE International Symposium on Personal, Indoor, and Mobile Radio Communications, pp. 2008–2013 (2015)

Comparison and Improvement of Hadoop MapReduce Performance Prediction Models in the Private Cloud

Nini Wang[1], Jian Yang[1], Zhihui Lu[1(✉)], Xiaoyan Li[1], and Jie Wu[2]

[1] School of Computer Science, Fudan University, Shanghai 200433, China
{14210240052, 12307130290, lzh, xylil4}@fudan.edu.cn
[2] Engineering Research Center of Cyber Security, Auditing and Monitoring,
Ministry of Education, Shanghai 200433, China
jwu@fudan.edu.cn

Abstract. Performance modeling for MapReduce applications with large-scale data is a very important issue in the study of optimization, evaluation, prediction and resource scheduling of the jobs over big data and cloud computing platforms. In this paper, we study the Hadoop distributed computing framework, which is the current trend of Big Data solutions. We use the locally weighted linear regression (LWLR) algorithm and linear regression (LR) algorithm to establish three kinds of computing models based on different characteristics to estimate the execution time of the applications that have large-scale data and run on the Hadoop framework, and at the same time we make comparison and improvement to the three models. By building different types of experimental environments, and running different types of jobs, we can draw a conclusion that all the three models have very good results in predicting the execution time and evaluating the performance of large-scale data applications with small-scale data.

Keywords: Big data · Hadoop · Private cloud · Mapreduce · Performance prediction model · Job estimation

1 Introduction

With the development and popularity of many applications and services, the amount of user data increases with exponential growth. The term "Big data" [1] is created to describe this situation. MapReduce [2] provides an efficient and easy way to deal with big data. Users specify the computation in terms of a map and a reduce function, and the underlying runtime system automatically parallelizes the computation and handles resource management and fault tolerance issues regardless of the system characteristics or scale [2]. Hadoop is an open source implementation of MapReduce, providing easy access to parallel computing. A lot of internet companies have deployed Hadoop clusters for data processing.

Although the jobs have been transferred from traditional IT systems to the cloud for running, how to save resources and time and how to reduce the cost of development and maintenance are still the most concerning problems for users [3]. Meanwhile, they are also the key indicators to evaluate the rationality of a system's architecture. When

© Springer International Publishing AG 2016
G. Wang et al. (Eds.): APSCC 2016, LNCS 10065, pp. 77–91, 2016.
DOI: 10.1007/978-3-319-49178-3_6

the input data is large, the application execution time will become very long, and can reach a few hours or even days. In this paper, we build models to predict overall job execution time before the job starts to run and see whether the Hadoop job can meet a deadline. Hadoop parameters tuning, scheduling policy and job performance optimization are important issues which are closely related to job performance prediction. Previous research on MapReduce performance prediction are on Hadoop 1. It is challenging to build the performance prediction model for Hadoop 2 since the resource allocation is different. Hadoop 2 uses YARN as the resource management system, which allocates resource based on real demand instead of fixed slots. Here Hadoop 1 refers to the versions of Hadoop 0.20.x, Hadoop 1.x or Hadoop CDH3 series. Hadoop 2 refers to the versions of Hadoop 0.23.x, Hadoop 2.x or Hadoop CDH4 series.

In this paper, we use the locally weighted linear regression algorithm [4] and linear regression algorithm to establish three kinds of computing models based on different characteristics to estimate the execution time of the applications that have large-scale data and run on the Hadoop framework, and at the same time we make comparison and improvement to the three models. By building different types of experimental environments, and running different types of jobs, we can validate the accuracy of the improved models.

The main contributions of this paper are as follows:

- The performance prediction model used in Hadoop 1 is not suitable for Hadoop 2, since Hadoop 2 allocates resource as containers instead of slots used in Hadoop 1. This paper modifies the prediction model used in Hadoop 1 to adapt to Hadoop 2.
- Previous research on MapReduce performance prediction are based on HDFS. Ceph is a unified, distributed storage system designed for excellent performance, reliability and scalability. It has received more and more support and attention. This paper validates the accuracy of the proposed models in Hadoop 2 which is deployed on both Ceph and HDFS.
- Based on different algorithms and different perspectives, many MapReduce performance prediction models were proposed. We make comparison and improvement to several representative models, including LWLR model, LR model and CRESP model. According to the specific needs of the user and provided conditions, the cloud platform managers can select different features and models to achieve the best performance prediction results.
- We build the Hadoop cluster in the private cloud to run the experiments. By changing the VM cluster scale, VM specification, types of benchmarks and input data size, we can validate the accuracy of the improved models thoroughly.

The rest of the paper is organized as follows. Section 2 gives related work. Section 3 gives the verification architecture of the improved models. Section 4 analyzes MapReduce job process in Hadoop 2. Section 5 presents and compares the improved job execution prediction models. Section 6 evaluates the accuracy and effectiveness of the proposed approach. Section 7 concludes the paper and points out some future work.

2   Related Work

A number of models were proposed to predict the MapReduce performance. Herodotou [5] built up a very expensive and comprehensive mathematical model of each phase of MapReduce. Lin et al. [6] divided the job processing from the perspective of resources dimension instead of the perspective of the execution order and proposed a cost vector. However, no predictions on reduce tasks were presented. Song et al. [7] presented a dynamic light-weight Hadoop job analyzer and a prediction module using locally weighted regression methods. Tian and Chen [8, 9] proposed a cost model that showed the relationship among the amount of input data, the available system resources (map and reduce slots) and the complexity of the reduce function for the target MapReduce job. Carrera [10] developed a simple model to predict execution time. It built a function of the number of machines in the cluster and the input size workload. Verma et al. proposed a framework ARIA [11], for a Hadoop deadline-based scheduler which extracted and utilized the job profiles from the past executions. These job profiles were used to compute the lower and upper bounds on the job completion time. Based on ARIA model, the HP model [12] added scaling factors and used a simple linear regression to predict the job execution for processing larger datasets. The work presented in [13] used a set of microbenchmarks to profile generic phases of the MapReduce processing pipeline of a given Hadoop cluster. Zhang et al. divided the map phase and reduce phase into six generic sub-phases and used a regression technique to predict the durations of these sub-phases. Then the overall job execution time can be computed as [11]. Building on the HP model [12], Khan et al. [14] presented an improved HP model for Hadoop job execution prediction. The improved HP model employed Locally Weighted Linear Regression (LWLR) instead of a simple regression technique to predict the execution time of a Hadoop job with a varied number of reduce tasks. Further, it took multiple waves into consideration.

However, previous models on MapReduce performance prediction are all based on Hadoop 1 which is very different from Hadoop 2. Hadoop 2 allocates resource as containers instead of slots used in Hadoop 1. Moreover, previous models lack the parameter of the cluster scale, which limits the use of the models.

In this paper, we use the locally weighted linear regression algorithm and linear regression algorithm to establish three kinds of computing models based on different characteristics to estimate the execution time of large-scale data applications running on the Hadoop framework, and at the same time we compare and improve the three models. By building different types of experimental environments, and running different types of jobs, we can verify the accuracy of the improved models.

3   Verification Architecture of Hadoop Performance Prediction Model

3.1   Benchmark Programs

We employ two typical MapReduce applications [3]. First, the TestDFSIO benchmark is a read and write test for file system. It is helpful for tasks to discover performance bottlenecks in network. Map tasks of TestDFSIO perform parallel read and write jobs respectively and the reduce task processes statistical information to get the throughput and average IO speed. Next, the Sort benchmark simply uses the MapReduce framework to sort the input data. The inputs and outputs must be sequence files where the keys and values are bytes writable.

3.2   Test Case Design

To validate the accuracy of the improved models thoroughly and study the effects of different cluster configurations on the performance of the MapReduce application, and to figure out how to enable applications to maintain high performance and low time and resource cost, several types of test cases are designed as follows. A specific test case will be a combination of the following options: benchmark in Sort and TestDFSIO, storage mode in HDFS and Ceph, experimental type in scalability and specification tests, the number of virtual machines and scale of data.

Performance comparison of different storage systems. By using HDFS and Ceph respectively, the objective is to see the performance difference of the HDFS and Ceph. When using HDFS, each computing node is also a storage node. If the data used in the computation task just is stored in this computing node, there won't be throughput among the nodes. If the cluster uses Ceph, then the computing nodes will be separated from the storage nodes. This experiment will use several fixed physical machines as the Ceph nodes. Thus the data for computing nodes to read or write must be transmitted across nodes and network throughput among nodes will increase. It can be expected that the storage systems have great influence on the performance of I/O intensive applications, and HDFS will have a relatively large impact on the I/O performance with the increasing scale of the virtual machines. However, Ceph will have little impact on the I/O performance with the cluster scale.

VM specification change test. In the specification tests, the number of total VCPUs and the total memory are fixed to 96 cores and 384 GB. We set 4 clusters and the node configurations of each cluster are shown as below (Table 1).

The purpose of this test case is to see the performance of less VMs with large resources and more VMs with small resources. For CPU intensive jobs, the total computing resource is fixed. If the number of VCPUs does not exceed the number of physical cores, the performance does not make difference. The storage system has larger impact on I/O intensive applications and the performance remains unchanged when the Ceph is used.

Table 1. Node configuration in the VM specification change test

Node	CPU	Memory	Disk
Master	4 cores	10 G	100 G
Slave in cluster1	6 cores	24 G	240 G
Slave in cluster2	4 cores	16 G	160 G
Slave in cluster3	3 cores	12 G	120 G
Slave in cluster4	2 cores	8 G	80 G

VM scalability change test. In the scalability tests, slave nodes have the same VM specification (2 VCPUs, 5 GB memory, 80 GB disk) and the same VM placement (6VMs/PM). The only difference is the cluster scale. The number of VMs that compose the clusters is 12, 24, 36 and 48. The purpose of this test case is to see whether cluster performance linearly scale. When the number of VMs increases, the number of physical machines increases at the same time. The performance of I/O intensive applications will not show linear growth due to the influence of the disk I/O of the physical machines. As for CPU intensive jobs, by adding VMs of the same specifications to the cluster, the performance shows linear growth, since it is less sensitive to disk I/O and the number of VCPUs does not exceed the number of physical cores.

3.3   Target Environment Design

In the experiment, we use OpenStack in our lab as our virtualization platform, which is made up of 9 physical machines, 8 of which are compute nodes which can hold VMs. Each compute node has an Intel 2.4 GHz CPU with twelve cores, 64 GB memory, 10Gbps network bandwidth and 2T disk capacity, and runs CentOS 7.1. The VM runs Ubuntu 12.04 64bit. Each compute node holds 6 VMs on it. We use Hadoop-2.7.1, and the replication level of data block is set to 3.

HDFS environment design. We use Ambari to deploy Hadoop on every VM in the Hadoop clusters as shown in Fig. 1.

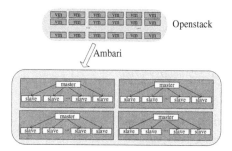

Fig. 1. Deployment architecture of Hadoop with HDFS

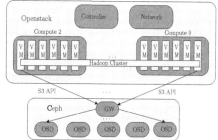

Fig. 2. Deployment architecture of Hadoop with Ceph

Ceph environment design. In this experiment, Hadoop directly uses Ceph instead of HDFS as the storage as shown in Fig. 2. When deploying Hadoop, we manually configure the components to access Ceph osds by S3 API. Ceph osd configuration is 1.8 TB disk (every pm has one disk) and we have 5 Ceph nodes and 1 admin node.

4   MapReduce Process Analysis

4.1   Resource Allocation of Hadoop 2

The MapReduce job consists of 3 parts in Hadoop 1: programming model, runtime environment (JobTracker and TaskTracker) and data processing engines (MapTask and ReduceTask). The resource model of Hadoop 1 mainly uses slots to organize the resource on each node. A slot is a unit of resources (CPU, physical memory) that can be assigned to a task. The maximum number of parallel map (reduce) tasks is the total number of map (reduce) slots in the cluster.

There exists obvious defects in the resource management of Hadoop 1. Firstly, Hadoop 1 uses a static resource allocation strategy. Once the slot has been set, it can't be changed dynamically. Secondly, the resources of map slots and reduce slots cannot be shared. In addition, Hadoop 1 divides the resources of CPU and memory equally, which leads that the granularity of the resource partition is too large and will cause the performance degradation.

Hadoop 2 uses YARN as the resource management system, which allocates resource based on real demand instead of slots. Each node provides the YARN scheduler with all the available memory and CPU resource, and then the YARN scheduler allocates these fine-grained resource to the applications. We build the following expression to get the maximum number of parallel map tasks Pm and the maximum number of parallel reduce tasks Pr. The prediction models on Hadoop 1 use the map and reduce slots. We find we can replace the number of map slot with Pm and replace the number of reduce slot with Pr to build the improved prediction models.

$$M = \left\lceil \frac{D}{Blocksize} \right\rceil \tag{1}$$

$$P_m = \min \left\{ \frac{yarn.nodemanager.resource.memory - mb}{mapredurce.map.memory.mb} \times V, M \right\} \tag{2}$$

$$P_r = \min \left\{ \frac{yarn.nodemanager.resource.memory - mb}{mapredurce.reduce.memory.mb} \times V, R \right\} \tag{3}$$

In these expressions, D is the size of input data. Blocksize is the size of a file block and is usually the amount of data processed by a map task. V is the number of nodes in the cluster. R is the reduce number. Usually Pr is equal to R. Yarn.nodemanager. resource.memory-mb is the total physical memory of the node that is available to YARN. mapreduce.map (reduce).memory.mb is the amount of memory required by each map (reduce) task and the default value is set to 1 GB.

4.2   Analysis of MapReduce Process

Typical execution of a MapReduce job is characterized below. We trace the start and finish time of every task in the MapReduce job, which can be extracted from the

Hadoop log. Some obviously unreasonable job records due to the unstable running environment (network delay, frequent task fail, etc) are eliminated. We select two experimental scenarios from Sort and TestDFSIO respectively to analyze the MapReduce process.

Sort. The experiments of Sort jobs in the "VM scalability change test" under HDFS are carried out. The data size changes from 1 GB to 200 GB. The number of VMs is 36. We set $Pr = R = 2 \times 36 = 72$. Figure 3 shows the progress of the map and reduce tasks over time (on the x-axis) vs the tasks (on the y-axis). Each line represents the life cycle of task from the beginning to the end. The job execution results in a single map and reduce wave with the 1 GB input dataset. As shown in Fig. 3(a) with the 50 GB input dataset, since the number of map tasks is greater than the maximum number of provided parallel tasks, the map phase proceeds in multiple rounds while the reduce phase will be still completed in a single wave. Figure 3(b) shows that with the increase of the data size, the execution time of each test presents an approximately linear growth, which indicates that the linear model can be used to predict the execution time of the MapReduce job.

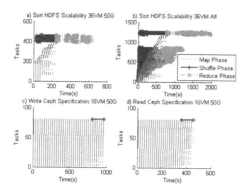

Fig. 3. The process of a sort job and a TestDFSIO read and write job

TestDFSIO. We analyze the process of the read job of the TestDFSIO in the "VM specification change test" under Ceph as shown in Fig. 3(d). The data size is 50 GB. The number of VMs is 16. Figure 3(d) shows $Pm = M = 80$, $Pr = R = 1$. The reduce task of TestDFSIO processes statistical information, so the number of reduce tasks is always set to 1. Due to the characteristics of Ceph, the input file is not in the computing node. In the read phase of map, the data is transferred from the Ceph node to the computing node, which is influenced by the performance of network I/O. The launch of tasks is affected by the network delay and the network I/O, so the parallel map tasks may not start at the same time and there exists a little delay. The execution process of the TestDFSIO write job is basically the same to the TestDFSIO read job, which is shown in Fig. 3(c).

5 Comparison and Improvement of Hadoop Performance Prediction Models

5.1 The Framework of Hadoop Linear Performance Prediction Model

Feature sets. The performance model relies on a set of parameters to predict the total job execution time. Hadoop parameter configurations, job settings, cluster scale, application types and its workload, all of these factors will influence the job execution time. We select some typical parameters from them to build the performance prediction model. These parameters serve as the feature set to describe different jobs in different Hadoop clusters.

Historical job profiles. The performance prediction model employs historical job execution records as training samples to get the relationship among variables.

Job profiles to be predicted. The feature sets of the query jobs need to be the input of the prediction model.

Algorithm. The performance prediction model mainly includes the regression algorithm and the prediction result calculation algorithm.

The process of MapReduce performance prediction is divided into 3 steps:

Step 1: select appropriate algorithms and feature set.

$$CV = \{P, S, A, C, D\} \tag{4}$$

where CV represents the feature set, P represents the Hadoop parameter configuration, S represents the job setting, C represents the cluster scale, A represents the application type and D represents its data scale.

Step 2: extract the data of the feature set from historical job profiles, and use the expression below to calculate the coefficients of the features.

$$B = regress(HisInp(T, CV)) \tag{5}$$

where B are the coefficients, *regress* is the regression algorithm, HisInp(T, CV) are the execution time and feature sets of the historical jobs.

Step 3: input the feature sets of the query jobs to the prediction model.

$$T = f_B(EstInp(CV)) \tag{6}$$

where T is the predicted completion time of the job, f is the prediction result calculation algorithm, and EstInp(CV) are the feature sets of the query jobs.

A lot of settings and their different values affect much of the job performance. For simplicity, we set Hadoop parameters as default or constant values. Different MapReduce applications have different logic and time complexity, so the training samples are all from the historical job profiles with the same application type. As for the job setting, we choose the most important ones to build the model and set other parameters as default or constant values. The simplified feature set is CV={S, V, D}. The specific feature set is determined by the selected model and actual situation.

5.2   LR Model

Linear regression is an approach for modeling the relationship between one or more independent variables and a dependent variable. It is the simplest one among the regression functions. In linear regression, the relationships are modeled using linear predictor functions whose unknown model parameters are estimated from the data. The least squares approach is often used to fit the linear regression models [5].

Ivan Carrera proposed a linear regression performance prediction model [12]. In this paper, this model is denominated for LR model. In such way, the feature set is simplified to CV = {V, D} where V is the number of VMs and D is the input workload size. The number of map tasks depends on the input data size and the reduce number is set to a recommended value [3].

The following expression can be used to construct the performance prediction model:

$$T = b_0 + b_1 V + b_2 D + b_3 \frac{1}{V} + b_4 DV + b_5 \frac{D}{V} \tag{7}$$

The coefficients $B = \{b_1, b_2, \cdots, b_5\}$ can be obtained through the following expression.

$$B = regress(T, [1, V, D, \frac{1}{V}, DV, \frac{D}{V}]) \tag{8}$$

Here $T = \{T_1, T_2, \cdots, T_N\}$ are the completion time of the historical jobs, $V = \{V_1, V_2, \cdots, V_N\}$ are the number of VMs for historical jobs, $D = \{D_1, D_2, \cdots, D_N\}$ are the input size for historical jobs, and *regress* is the linear regression function.

5.3   An Improved CRESP Model

Keke Chen et al. also proposed a performance prediction model using linear regression [11] called the CRESP model. LR model uses cluster scale and data size as the feature set without deep analysis on the MapReduce process. However, CRESP model uses map and reduce number as the feature set from a different angle. CRESP model is applied to Hadoop 1. This paper modifies the CRESP model to apply it to Hadoop 2. The improved CRESP model employs Pm, M and R as the feature set:

$$CV = \{P_m, M, R\}, \tag{9}$$

where Pm is the maximum number of parallel map tasks, M is the number of map tasks and R is the number of reduce tasks. These values are related to the number of VMs and usually Pr = R, so Pr is not considered in this model.

By analyzing the MapReduce job process, we model T with Pm, M and R:

$$T = b_0 + b_1 M + b_2 R + b_3 \frac{M}{P_m} + b_4 \frac{M}{R} + b_5 \frac{P_m}{R} + b_6 \frac{MR}{P_m} + b_7 \frac{M\log M}{R} \qquad (10)$$

Similarly, using historical job execution records, the coefficients B of the linear regression can be calculated and then the completion time of a new job can be predicted.

5.4   An Improved LWLR Model

Khan M et al. employed the LWLR to predict the execution time of a Hadoop job [16]. As the equation shows below, the LWLR model assigns a weight coefficient to each sample point. The rule is that points are weighted by proximity to the predicted x using a kernel.

$$w_i = \exp(-\frac{dis(x_i, x_p)}{2\tau^2}) \qquad (11)$$

where x_i is the i th sample point, x_p is the predicted point, w_i is the i th weight coefficient for x_i, and τ is the scope of neighbors which is a smoothing parameter.

We extend the LWLR model with a cluster scale parameter. The feature set of the sample point x_i in the improved LWLR consists of the input file size D_i, the reduce number R_i and the number of working machines in the cluster C_i. It can be expressed in the following mathematical equation:

$$x_i = [D_i, C_i, R_i]^T (i = 1, 2, \cdots, m) \qquad (12)$$

where m is the number of sample points.

Different features in each variable x_i are standardized in the same range, which makes different dimensions comparable. In this paper, we use the min-max algorithm to normalize the samples.

Next we define a matrix $X = [x_1, x_2, \cdots, x_m]$ to contain all the training dataset and a vector $Y = [y_1, y_2, \cdots, y_m]^T$ to express the time that corresponds to the sample point x_i. For example, if you want to predict the average execution time of the shuffle task in a new job, then y_i represents the actual average execution time of the shuffle task in the i th sample point. Y can be extracted from the past job execution records.

For the prediction of T_{phase}, we calculate the weight for each sample point to find the most similar jobs. Then we use a distance as the following expression shows.

$$dis(x_i, x_p) = \sqrt{(D_i - D_p)^2 + (C_i - C_p)^2 + (R_i - R_p)^2} \qquad (13)$$

Finally, using standard weighted least-squares theory, we can get T_{phase}, which is the prediction time of different phases of the new instance x_p. Further, we should take the practical meaning of T_{phase} into consideration to ensure its value is positive.

$$T_{phase} = e^T \left(X_x^T W X_x \right)^{-1} X_x^T W Y$$
$$\text{subject to } T_{phase} > 0 \tag{14}$$

Here $W = diag(w_i)$ is the diagonal matrix where all the non-diagonal cells are 0.

$$e = (1,0,0,0)^T \tag{15}$$

$$X_x = \begin{bmatrix} 1 & (X_1 - x_p)^T \\ \vdots & \vdots \\ 1 & (X_n - x_p)^T \end{bmatrix} \tag{16}$$

5.5   Comparison and Improvement of the Three Models

In this paper, the common points of the three Hadoop performance prediction models are extracted as a framework of the Hadoop linear performance prediction model. Moreover, we extend these models by applying them to Ceph. In order to be applied to Hadoop 2, the improved prediction models replace the number of map slot with Pm and replace the number of reduce slot with Pr. The mechanism of Ceph is very different from HDFS, but when using the same YARN scheduler, the built model can be applied to Ceph and the prediction accuracy is also very high.

While the linear regression model is very simple and doesn't need to retain the historical data, it also has high accuracy. It is a very good choice among all the candidate models. The improved LWLR model relies on historical data. When the amount of the historical data is large, the improved LWLR model costs more storage and is relatively low in computation speed but the accuracy will be improved. However, the linear regression function between the feature set and job execution time is hard to construct. It is very complex to form the characteristic polynomial and it needs a lot of arithmetic reasoning and experiments to determine a more accurate function. The improved LWLR model is relaxed on feature sets and it performs a regression around a point of interest using only training data that are "local" to that point.

The improved CRESP model estimates the execution time of the map, shuffle, and reduce phases. It is worth noting that since there exists overlap between the shuffle phase and map phase, we need to divide the shuffle phase into two parts: the overlapping portion with map phase and the non-overlapping part. We characterize the two shuffle parts respectively. Based on the improved CRESP model, the improved LWLR model considers multiple waves in the shuffle phase. Then we utilize the bounds-based model [13] to compute the upper bound and lower bound of execution time for different phases in the job which are completed in multiple waves.

6 Evaluation of the Improved Performance Prediction Models

6.1 Evaluation Method

Cross Validation. We perform a leave-one-out cross validation [9] to study the prediction accuracy of the improved models. That is, if there are N samples, each sample is used as a validation set separately and the remaining N − 1 samples are used as the training set. We utilize average relative errors (ARE) and R^2 over the N rounds of testing to formally assess the accuracy of performance model. ARE can be computed using the following equation.

$$ARE = \frac{1}{N} \sum_{i=1}^{N} \frac{|t_i^e - t_i^a|}{t_i^a} \tag{17}$$

where t_i^a represents the measured job execution time in the i th round of testing and t_i^e represents the predicted job execution time.

R^2 is a measure for evaluating the goodness of fit in regression modeling. $R^2 = 1$ means a perfect fit, while $R^2 > 90\%$ indicates a very good fit.

6.2 Evaluation Result

Typical evaluation results from different scenarios are shown here. We extract historical job records to get the completion time of jobs and corresponding feature sets which can be used to fit the model. Then we use these improved models to predict the new job's execution time.

We implement and evaluate these three performance models in the specification and scalability scenarios on Ceph and HDFS as shown in Figs. 4 and 5. The data size changes from 1 GB to 200 GB. Due to the characteristics of Ceph, the number of map tasks is fixed with different input data in TestDFSIO jobs. In the specification changing

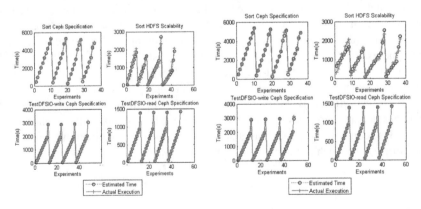

Fig. 4. Prediction of job execution time of Sort and TestDFSIO jobs using LR model (left) and the improved LWLR model (right)

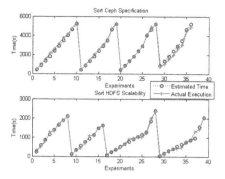

Fig. 5. Prediction of job execution time of Sort jobs using the improved CRESP model

tests, the number of total resources are the same among the clusters and thus the Pm and Pr of different clusters is equal. Then, in the improved CRESP model, TestDFSIO jobs have the same feature set, so the improved CRESP model can't predict the performance of TestDFSIO jobs in the specification changing tests under Ceph. The blue dots on the graph represent predicted job execution time and the red dots represent the actual measured values. The closer the two, the better quality the model has. All of the 3 graphs show good fitting results.

6.3 Analysis and Comparison

Table 2 shows the ARE and R^2 of these three models with leave-one-out cross validation under different scenarios. In the scenario of scalability test on HDFS, the accuracy of performance prediction relatively decreases but R^2 is still above 97 %. In these three models, all of them perform well in execution time prediction of MapReduce jobs. The LR model shows the best prediction while the improved CRESP model performs less accurately than others. However, both the LR model and the improved CRESP model ignore the impact of the number of reduce tasks on job performance. If the reduce number changes, the improved LWLR model is a good choice to predict the

Table 2. ARE and R^2 in leave-one-out cross validation

Scenarios	LR model		The improved CRESP model		The improved LWLR model	
	ARE	R^2	ARE	R^2	ARE	R^2
Sort Ceph specification	0.048	0.996	0.083	0.982	0.0483	0.995
Sort HDFS scale 12VM	0.066	0.986	0.119	0.988	0.124	0.979
Sort HDFS scale 36VM	0.112	0.985	0.151	0.986	0.119	0.970
TestDFSIO-write Ceph specification	0.030	0.999	\	\	0.046	0.998
TestDFSIO-read Ceph specification	0.025	0.999	\	\	0.029	0.999

performance. According to the specific needs of the user and provided conditions, the cloud platform managers can select different features and models to achieve the best performance prediction results. In the experiments, it is found that the results of the performance prediction are not only related to the model itself, but also have a great relationship with the experimental environment, application properties and parameter settings. The job execution time and feature set have a good linear correlation and the accuracy of these models can reach more than 95 % in a stable environment. However, in an unstable cluster (with network delay, frequent task fail, etc), the results are not so satisfactory and the accuracy only can reach 90 %.

7 Conclusion and Future Work

By building the performance model, we can predict job execution time, allocate resources for jobs reasonably, improve performance and cut costs. In this paper, we use the LWLR algorithm and LR algorithm to establish three kinds of computing models based on different characteristics to estimate the execution time of the applications that have large-scale data and run on Hadoop 2, and at the same time we make comparison and improvement to the three models. By building different types of experimental environments, and running different types of jobs, the accuracy of the improved models can be validated. We can draw a conclusion from the validation that all the three models have very good results in predicting the execution time.

As a next step, we will focus on whether the current model can be migrated or extended to other frameworks. Furthermore, the enhanced performance prediction model is utilized to estimate the amount of resources for Hadoop jobs with deadline requirements.

Acknowledgments. This work is supported by Shanghai 2016 Innovation Action Project under Grant 16DZ1100200-Data-trade-supporting Big data Testbed. This work is also supported by 2016–2019 National Natural Science Foundation of China under Grant No. 61572137-Multiple Clouds based CDN as a Service Key Technology Research, Shanghai 2015 Innovation Action Project under Grant No.1551110700- New media-oriented Big data analysis and content delivery key technology and application, and Fudan-Hitachi Innovative Software Technology Joint Project-"Cloud Platform Design for Big data".

References

1. Snijders, C., Matzat, U., Reips, U.D.: "Big Data": big gaps of knowledge in the field of internet science. Intl. J. Internet Sci. 7(1), 1–5 (2012)
2. Dean, J., Ghemawat, S.: MapReduce: simplified data processing on large clusters. Commun. ACM 51(1), 107–113 (2008)
3. Wang, X., Lu, Z., Wu, J., et al.: In: STechAH: an autoscaling scheme for hadoop in the private cloud. In: 2015 IEEE International Conference on Services Computing (SCC), pp. 395–402. IEEE (2015)

4. Ruppert, D., Wand, M.P.: Multivariate locally weighted least squares regression. Ann. Stat. **22**(3), 1346–1370 (1994)
5. Herodotou, H.: Hadoop performance models. arXiv preprint arXiv:1106.0940 (2011)
6. Lin, X., Meng, Z., Xu, C., et al.: A practical performance model for hadoop mapreduce. In: 2012 IEEE International Conference on Cluster Computing Workshops (Cluster Workshops), pp. 231–239. IEEE (2012)
7. Song, G., Meng, Z., Huet, F., et al.: A hadoop mapreduce performance prediction method. In: High Performance Computing and Communications. IEEE (2013)
8. Tian, F., Chen, K.: Towards optimal resource provisioning for running mapreduce programs in public clouds. In: 2011 IEEE International Conference on Cloud Computing (CLOUD), pp. 155–162. IEEE (2011)
9. Chen, K., Powers, J., Guo, S., et al.: Cresp: towards optimal resource provisioning for mapreduce computing in public clouds. IEEE Trans. Parallel Distrib. Syst. **25**(6), 1403–1412 (2014)
10. Carrera, I.: Performance modeling of mapreduce applications for the cloud. The Federal University of Rio Grande do Sul (2014)
11. Verma, A., Cherkasova, L., Campbell, R.H.: ARIA: automatic resource inference and allocation for mapreduce environments. In: Proceedings of the 8th ACM International Conference on Autonomic Computing, pp. 235–244. ACM (2011)
12. Verma, A., Cherkasova, L., Campbell, Roy, H.: Resource provisioning framework for mapreduce jobs with performance goals. In: Kon, F., Kermarrec, A.-M. (eds.) Middleware 2011. LNCS, vol. 7049, pp. 165–186. Springer, Heidelberg (2011). doi:10.1007/978-3-642-25821-3_9
13. Zhang, Z., Cherkasova, L., Loo, B.T.: Benchmarking approach for designing a mapreduce performance model. In: Proceedings of the 4th ACM/SPEC International Conference on Performance Engineering, pp. 253–258. ACM (2013)
14. Khan, M., Jin, Y., Li, M., et al.: Hadoop performance modeling for job estimation and resource provisioning. IEEE Trans. Parallel Distrib. Syst. **27**(2), 441–454 (2016)

Cross-Domain Tourist Service Recommendation Through Combinations of Explicit and Latent Features

Mingliang Qi[1], Jian Cao[1(✉)], and Yudong Tan[2]

[1] Department of Computer Science and Engineering,
Shanghai Jiao Tong University, Shanghai 200240, China
{qml_moon,cao-jian}@sjtu.edu.cn
[2] Air Ticketing B.U., Ctrip.com International, Ltd., Shanghai, China
ydtan@Ctrip.com

Abstract. Nowadays, Online Travel Agents (OTA) can provide massive amount of travel services (such as flights, hotels), which also bring selection dilemma to users. Thus, it is critical to apply recommendation technology to help users. However, tourist service recommendation such as hotel recommendation is challenging because of the data sparsity problem. Moreover, generally, only implicit feedbacks (e.g. booking records) are available. In this paper, we propose to combine latent factors and explicit features across multiple domains for tourist service recommendation. Specifically, we extend Heterogeneous Matrix Factorization (HeteroMF) with explicit features, e.g. price of the tourist product. We also learn users' preferences in different service domains with a transfer matrix to convert users' preferences from one service domain to another. Furthermore, we train our model with respect to Bayesian Personalized Ranking (BPR) optimization criterion. Experiments on a real-world dataset show that our proposed model significantly outperforms HeteroMF and other baseline methods.

Keywords: Tourist service recommendation · Cross domain · Explicit feature · Latent feature · Matrix factorization

1 Introduction

With the rapid growth of Online Travel Agents (OTA) in the last decades, people could get more and more travel product information and booking services from companies like Ctrip. However, the overloaded information costs user a lot of time searching for the proper products. For instance, searching hotels in Shanghai on ctrip.com will return approximately 2,000 results. To improve the service quality, it is necessary to develop a tool to help users select the appropriate products from massive candidates.

Recommender systems [1] have been widely applied to address this problem. In general, a recommender system could be designed with content-based [3] or collaborative filtering based [6,8,12,13] methods. Content-based methods rely on the

© Springer International Publishing AG 2016
G. Wang et al. (Eds.): APSCC 2016, LNCS 10065, pp. 92–105, 2016.
DOI: 10.1007/978-3-319-49178-3_7

users' profiles and context information while collaborative filtering based methods exploit explicit user-item ratings to calculate the missing ones. Some recommender systems [4,14] try to improve the recommendation quality by combing both content-based and collaborative filtering based approaches and obtain better results. Recently, Matrix Factorization (MF) [10,11,16] based collaborative filtering models have emerged and proved efficient in many cases. MF based methods decompose the rating matrix into the product of two low rank latent matrices U and V, where U stands for user latent factors and V stands for item latent factors.

However, unlike traditional recommendation tasks such as movie recommendation, tourist service recommendation is much harder because of its severer data sparsity problem. There are so many flights and hotels so that it is very rare that a user takes the same flight or book the same hotel for many times. In addition, most users don't leave a rating to the tourist service and only implicit data is available, i.e., booking records. In this case, recommender systems usually suffer from the over-fitting problem. In order to alleviate data sparsity problem, we introduce auxiliary data from another travel service domain to help complete the target travel service domain recommendation task. For instance, we can learn users' tastes from flight service domain for hotel recommendation.

Another characteristic in tourist service recommendation is it has explicit features that are known as important factors to support decision makings of users. For instance, price has a strong impact on users' decisions. The cost of a standard room in Shanghai can vary a lot. For example, one night stay in a luxury hotel may cost more than \$500 while \$20 is also enough to find a cheap hotel. In most cases, price has the highest priority among users' decision factors. Besides price information, features like flight class and hotel star may also affect users' choices. Moreover, these features have latent relationships. For example, a 5 star hotel's regular guest probably won't consider any 2 star hotels or economic class flights.

In this paper, we propose a personalized tourist service recommendation approach called ExHMF, which exploits the combination of explicit features and latent factors over auxiliary service domain and target service domain in order to ease the sparsity problem. The main goal of our approach is to introduce users' preferences over items' attributes to the heterogeneous latent model. In ExHMF, items are associated with explicit features, represented by a multi-dimensional vector C_j. Users' preferences over these attributes are represented by a Gaussian prior $\mathcal{N}(\mu_i, \sigma_i^2 \mathbf{I})$. Instead of a fixed value, Gaussian distribution can better reflect users' uncertain interests. Also, due to the fact that users' preferences to the auxiliary service domain may differ from the target service domain, a transform matrix will be learned to map the users' preferences between these two domains. Finally, rating of the user-item entry can be modeled as: $\mathcal{N}(C_j | \mu_i, \sigma_i^2 \mathbf{I}) \cdot U_i^T \cdot V_j$.

The main contributions of this paper are summarized as follows:

- We develop a personalized tourist service recommendation approach, which uses a transfer matrix to convert users' preferences over both explicit features and latent factors from auxiliary service domain into the target service domain.
- We learn our model with respect to Bayesian Personalized Ranking (BPR) [15] optimization criterion.

– We evaluate our approach on the real-world data. Experiments show that our approach outperforms state-of-the-art HeteroMF and other baseline approaches.

The rest of the paper is organized as follows: In Sect. 2 we briefly discuss related work. In Sect. 3 we present our proposed ExHMF model. In Sect. 4 we describe the experiment settings and results on a real-world dataset. Finally, We conclude the paper in Sect. 5.

2   Related Work

Matrix Factorization (MF) [10,11,16] has been considered the state-of-the-art approach for recommendation system. In general, MF approaches decompose the rating matrix into the product of two low rank latent matrices: the user latent factor and the item latent factor. A user often involves in multiple domains and thus knowledge can be transferred from one domain to another. Traditional MF approaches cannot take advantage of the data correlations between multiple domains. Collective Matrix Factorization (CMF) [17] is proposed to work on multiple domains. CMF also decomposes rating matrices in different domains into the product of two low rank latent matrices. The user latent factors are shared across different domains in CMF, so that a user's tastes in one domain can be transfered into those of another domain. However, Moshen J. and Laks V.S.L. [9] points out that CMF is problematic in two aspects. First, the user latent factors will be mainly learned from the domain that is not cold-start. Second, when the rating data in one domain is much more than another, this domain will dominate the learning process. Therefore, in both cases, the latent factors cannot be properly learned. Moreover, they suggest that the user latent factors should not be identical across different domains and further propose Heterogeneous Matrix Factorization (HeteroMF) to address these issues. HeteroMF introduces a transfer matrix on top of CMF in order to map the user latent factors between different domains.

Several works [2,5,7,18] related to travel product recommendation has been done before. For example, CARD [5] is a composite travel service recommendation framework on top of relational database that supports composite metrics definition, top-k recommendation, and preference learning. [2] aims to find the top-k tuples of travel services by searching keywords in the document. The tuples are of fixed size, i.e. one city, one hotel, and one flight. [18] further allows package to have variable size and proposes several approximate algorithms for top-k packages of composite travel services. [7] proposes a cost aware latent factor model, which uses a 2-dimensional vector to represent tourist's cost as well as a Gaussian prior to express the uncertainty of the travel cost.

Comparing with exisiting work, our model considers users' preferences over items' attributes. The closest work to us is [7], where users' preferences over cost are learned with Probabilistic Matrix Factorization (PMF). However, their model is designed on top of PMF, which doesn't take advantage of the correlations between multiple service domains. Moreover, we propose a transfer matrix to learn the relations between users' preferences over different domains.

3   The ExHMF Model

3.1   Design of ExHMF

In this section we introduce our ExHMF model that extends HeteroMF with explicit features and users' preferences.

As we have mentioned, we introduce additional data from an auxiliary service domain to target service recommendation in order to learn more knowledge. In the following paper, we use superscripts a and t to distinguish between these two domains. For example, we use C_j^t to denote the explicit attributes for item j in target service domain, C_j^a to denote the explicit attributes for item j in auxiliary service domain. Since attributes have different scales, we use Min-Max Normalization method to fit the values into $[0,1]$:

$$C_{j,k} = \frac{A_{j,k} - \min_j A_{j,k}}{\max_j A_{j,k} - \min_j A_{j,k}} \tag{1}$$

where $A_{j,k}$ denotes the value of k-th attributes of item j.

To better represent a user's preferences, it is necessary to include uncertainties instead of only using fixed values. Thus we choose Gaussian distribution $\mathcal{G}_i = \mathcal{N}(\mu_i, \sigma_i^2 \mathbf{I})$ to indicate a user's interests. Then the similarity between a user's preferences and an item's attributes can be modeled as:

$$S(C_j^a, \mathcal{G}_i^a) = \mathcal{N}(C_j^a | \mu_i, \sigma_i^2 \mathbf{I}) \tag{2}$$

$$S(C_j^t, \mathcal{G}_i^t) = \mathcal{N}(C_j^t | \mu_i M, \sigma_i^2 \mathbf{I}) \tag{3}$$

where M is the transfer matrix that maps a user's preferences from auxiliary service domain into target service domain. The reason why we don't use same preferences for both services is similar to the idea of HeteroMF. Assuming a user's preferences are identical for both services is problematic. It is obviously true that a user could have different preferences for two services.

Finally, the rating of user i to item j is designed to be the product of latent factors and similarity of the user's preferences over explicit features, which can be calculated by:

$$\hat{r}_{ij}^a = S(C_j^a, \mathcal{G}_i^a) \cdot U_i^T V_j^a \tag{4}$$

$$\hat{r}_{ij}^t = S(C_j^t, \mathcal{G}_i^t) \cdot U_i^T B V_j^t \tag{5}$$

where B is the transfer matrix that maps user latent factors from auxiliary service domain into target service domain, which is proposed in HeteroMF. Figure 1(b) shows the graphic model of ExHMF. From the figure, we can see that the main difference between our model and HeteroMF is the impact of explicit features on the final rating.

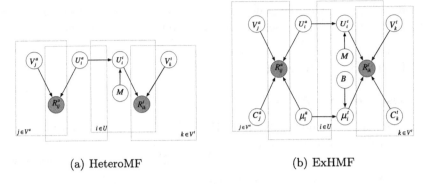

(a) HeteroMF   (b) ExHMF

Fig. 1. Graphic models of HeteroMF and ExHMF.

3.2   Optimize with Sum-of-Squared-Errors

Usually, the optimization problem is to minimize the sum-of-squared-errors. In our case, the sum-of-squared-errors in auxiliary service domain and target service domain are:

$$E^a = \sum_{i,j} I_{ij}^a (r_{ij}^a - \mathcal{N}(C_j^a|\mu_i, \sigma_i^2 \mathbf{I}) \cdot U_i^T V_j^a)^2 \tag{6}$$

$$E^t = \sum_{i,j} I_{ij}^t (r_{ij}^t - \mathcal{N}(C_j^t|\mu_i M, \sigma_i^2 \mathbf{I}) \cdot U_i^T B V_j^t)^2 \tag{7}$$

In the above functions, I_{ij} is an indicate matrix, $I_{ij} = 1$ means user i rated item j or 0 otherwise. The objective of collective matrix factorization is to minimize the weighted sum of the sum-of-squared-errors over two domains with respect to U, V^a, V^t, B, μ, and M:

$$E = \alpha E^a + (1 - \alpha)E^t \tag{8}$$

where α is the parameter that balances the influences of domains in the learning process.

In addition, we introduce several regularization terms to alleviate the overfitting problem, and the final objective function can be written as:

$$E = \alpha \sum_{i,j} I_{ij}^a (r_{ij}^a - \mathcal{N}(C_j^a|\mu_i, \sigma_i^2 \mathbf{I}) \cdot U_i^T V_j^a)^2$$
$$+ (1 - \alpha) \sum_{i,j} I_{ij}^t (r_{ij}^t - \mathcal{N}(C_j^t|\mu_i M, \sigma_i^2 \mathbf{I}) \cdot U_i^T B V_j^t)^2$$
$$+ \lambda_U ||U||_F^2 + \lambda_V (||V^a||_F^2 + ||V^t||_F^2) + \lambda_B ||B||_F^2 + \lambda_M Z ||M||_F^2 \tag{9}$$

where $\lambda_U, \lambda_V, \lambda_B, \lambda_M$ are regularization factors, $|| \cdot ||_F^2$ denotes the Frobenius norm.

A local minimum of the objective function can be found by gradient decent algorithm:

$$\frac{\partial E}{\partial U_i} \propto \alpha \sum_j I^a_{ij}(\mathcal{N}(C^a_j|\mu_i, \sigma^2_i\mathbf{I}) \cdot U^T_i V^a_j - r^a_{ij}) \cdot \mathcal{N}(C^a_j|\mu_i, \sigma^2_i\mathbf{I})V^a_j$$

$$+ (1-\alpha) \sum_j I^t_{ij}(\mathcal{N}(C^t_j|\mu_i M, \sigma^2_i\mathbf{I}) \cdot U^T_i BV^t_j - r^t_{ij})$$

$$\cdot \mathcal{N}(C^t_j|\mu_i M, \sigma^2_i\mathbf{I})BV^t_j + \lambda_u U_i \tag{10}$$

$$\frac{\partial E}{\partial V^a_j} \propto \alpha \sum_i I^a_{ij}(\mathcal{N}(C^a_j|\mu_i, \sigma^2_i\mathbf{I}) \cdot U^T_i V^a_j - r^a_{ij})$$

$$\cdot \mathcal{N}(C^a_j|\mu_i, \sigma^2_i\mathbf{I})U^T_i + \lambda_V V^a_j \tag{11}$$

$$\frac{\partial E}{\partial V^t_j} \propto (1-\alpha) \sum_i I^t_{ij}(\mathcal{N}(C^t_j|\mu_i M, \sigma^2_i\mathbf{I}) \cdot U^T_i BV^t_j - r^t_{ij})$$

$$\cdot \mathcal{N}(C^t_j|\mu_i M, \sigma^2_i\mathbf{I})U^T_i B + \lambda_V V^t_j \tag{12}$$

$$\frac{\partial E}{\partial B} \propto (1-\alpha) \sum_{i,j} I^t_{ij}(\mathcal{N}(C^t_j|\mu_i M, \sigma^2_i\mathbf{I}) \cdot U^T_i BV^t_j - r^t_{ij})$$

$$\cdot \mathcal{N}(C^t_j|\mu_i M, \sigma^2_i\mathbf{I})U_i(V^t_j)^T + \lambda_B B \tag{13}$$

$$\frac{\partial E}{\partial \mu_i} \propto \alpha \sum_j I^a_{ij}(\mathcal{N}(C^a_j|\mu_i, \sigma^2_i\mathbf{I}) \cdot U^T_i V^t_j - r^a_{ij}) \cdot U^T_i V^t_j \mathcal{N}'(C^t_j|\mu_i, \sigma^2_i\mathbf{I})$$

$$+ (1-\alpha) \sum_j I_{ij}(\mathcal{N}(C^t_j|\mu_i M, \sigma^2_i\mathbf{I}) \cdot U^T_i BV^t_j - r^t_{ij})$$

$$\cdot U^T_i BV^t_j \mathcal{N}'(C^t_j|\mu_i M, \sigma^2_i\mathbf{I})M \tag{14}$$

$$\frac{\partial E}{\partial M} \propto (1-\alpha) \sum_{i,j} I^t_{ij}(\mathcal{N}(C^t_j|\mu_i M, \sigma^2_i\mathbf{I}) \cdot U^T_i BV^t_j - r^t_{ij})$$

$$\cdot U^T_i BV^t_j (\mathcal{N}'(C^t_j|\mu_i M, \sigma^2_i\mathbf{I}))^T \mu_i + \lambda_M M \tag{15}$$

where $\mathcal{N}'(x|\mu, \sigma^2)$ is the derivative of Gaussian function with respect to μ.

3.3 Optimization with Bayesian Personalized Ranking

As is known to all, implicit feedbacks only indicate positive information and miss-ing values represent either positive or negative information. The most common approach is to ignore all the missing values and use only positive feedbacks to train the model. [15] proposed a novel approach by choosing item pairs as train-ing data and optimizing the ranks between every item pairs, named Bayesian Personalized Ranking (BPR). In BPR, items with positive feedbacks are assumed to be preferred over that with none feedback. For each domain d, items V^d and user u, BPR aims to find a total ranking $>_{d,u} \subset V^d \times V^d$, in the meantime, $>_{d,u}$ has to meet the following properties of total order:

$$\forall i, j \in V^d : i \neq j \Rightarrow i >_{d,u} j \vee j >_{d,u} i \qquad (totality)$$

$$\forall i, j \in V^d : i >_{d,u} j \wedge j >_{d,u} i \Rightarrow i = j \qquad (antisymmetry)$$

$$\forall i, j, k \in V^d : i >_{d,u} j \wedge j >_{d,u} k \Rightarrow i >_{d,u} k \qquad (transitivity)$$

For convenience, we also define:

$$P_u^d = \{i | i \in V^d : r_{ui}^d > 0\} \qquad (16)$$

From the user-item matrix of implicit feedbacks, BPR first construct user specific item pairs as training data. User that has positive feedbacks for item i but none for item j indicates user prefers i to j. Hence, we generate training data of user u in domain d by:

$$T = \{(d, u, i, j) | i \in P_u^d \wedge j \in V^d \backslash P_u^d\} \qquad (17)$$

In order to find such a total order, BPR tries to maximize the following posterior probability:

$$p(\Theta | >_{d,u}) \propto p(>_{d,u} | \Theta) p(\Theta) \qquad (18)$$

where Θ stands for the model parameters. By assuming users are independent with each other in each domain and users act independently in different domains, $p(>_{d,u} | \Theta)$ can be rewritten as:

$$p(>_{d,u} | \Theta) = \prod_{(d,u,i,j) \in T_u^d} p(i >_{d,u} j | \Theta) \qquad (19)$$

Furthermore, we define the probability that a user prefers item i to j as:

$$p(i >_{d,u} j | \Theta) = \sigma(\hat{r}_{uij}^d(\Theta)) \qquad (20)$$

where σ is the logistic function $\sigma(x) = 1/(1 + e^{-x})$, $\hat{r}_{uij}^d(\Theta)$ is a real-valued function of model parameters Θ that indicates the relation between user u, item i, and item j.

Finally, we assume Θ follows a multivariate Gaussian distribution $\Theta \sim N(0, \lambda_\Theta \mathbf{I})$ and the BPR optimization criterion can be formulated as:

$$
\begin{aligned}
\text{BPR-OPT} :&= \ln p(\Theta| >_{d,u}) \\
&= \ln p(>_{d,u} |\Theta) + \ln p(\Theta) \\
&= \sum_{(d,u,i,j) \in T_u^d} \ln \sigma(\hat{r}_{uij}^d) - \lambda_\Theta ||\Theta||^2
\end{aligned}
\tag{21}
$$

where λ_Θ is the regularization terms for model parameters.

To solve the optimization problem, gradient descent based algorithms are usually the first choice:

$$
\begin{aligned}
\frac{\partial \text{BPR-OPT}}{\partial \Theta} &= \sum_{(d,u,i,j) \in T_u^d} \frac{\partial}{\partial \Theta} \ln \sigma(\hat{r}_{uij}^d) - \lambda_\Theta \frac{\partial}{\partial \Theta} ||\Theta||^2 \\
&\propto \sum_{(d,u,i,j) \in T_u^d} (1 - \sigma(\hat{r}_{uij}^d)) \frac{\partial}{\partial \Theta} \hat{r}_{uij}^d - \lambda_\Theta \Theta
\end{aligned}
\tag{22}
$$

And the parameters Θ can be updated with:

$$
\Theta \leftarrow \Theta + \eta((1 - \sigma(\hat{r}_{uij}^d)) \frac{\partial}{\partial \Theta} \hat{r}_{uij}^d - \lambda_\Theta \Theta)
\tag{23}
$$

where η is the learning rate.

In order to learn our proposed model with BPR optimization criterion, we have to define the real-valued function that indicates the probability that user u prefer item i to j, so we first define:

$$
\hat{r}_{uij}^d = \hat{r}_{ui}^d - \hat{r}_{uj}^d
\tag{24}
$$

where $\hat{r}_{ui}^d$ is the predicted score for user u to item i in domain d, and $d = \{$auxiliary service, target service$\}$.

Then we can calculate the gradients with respect to the model parameters $\Theta = \{U_u, V_i^d, B^d, \mu_u, M^d\}$. The gradients in auxiliary service domain are as follows:

$$
\frac{\partial \hat{r}_{ui}^t}{\partial U_u} = \mathcal{N}(C_i^t|\mu_u M, \sigma_u^2 \mathbf{I}) B V_i^t
\tag{25}
$$

$$
\frac{\partial \hat{r}_{ui}^t}{\partial V_i^t} = \mathcal{N}(C_i^t|\mu_u M, \sigma_u^2 \mathbf{I}) U_u^T B
\tag{26}
$$

$$
\frac{\partial \hat{r}_{ui}^t}{\partial B} = \mathcal{N}(C_i^t|\mu_u M, \sigma_u^2 \mathbf{I}) U_u (V_i^t)^T
\tag{27}
$$

$$
\frac{\partial \hat{r}_{ui}^t}{\partial \mu_u} = U_u^T B V_i^t \mathcal{N}'(C_i^t|\mu_u M, \sigma_u^2 \mathbf{I}) M^t
\tag{28}
$$

$$\frac{\partial \hat{r}_{ui}^t}{\partial M} = U_u^T B V_i^t (\mathcal{N}'(C_i^t | \mu_u M, \sigma_u^2 \mathbf{I}))^T \mu_u \tag{29}$$

and the gradients in target service domain are as follows:

$$\frac{\partial \hat{r}_{ui}^a}{\partial U_u} = \mathcal{N}(C_i^a | \mu_u, \sigma_u^2 \mathbf{I}) V_i^a \tag{30}$$

$$\frac{\partial \hat{r}_{ui}^a}{\partial V_i^a} = \mathcal{N}(C_i^a | \mu_u, \sigma_u^2 \mathbf{I}) U_u^T \tag{31}$$

$$\frac{\partial \hat{r}_{ui}^a}{\partial \mu_u} = U_u^T V_i^a \mathcal{N}'(C_i^a | \mu_u, \sigma_u^2 \mathbf{I}) \tag{32}$$

In the experiments, we apply bootstraping based stochastic gradient descent algorithm to learn our model with BPR optimization criterion, which randomly selects (d, u, i, j) tuples from the training data to update the model parameters. Simply transversing the training data in a user-wise or item-wise way could lead to a poor convergence process as pointed in [15].

4 Experiments

In this section, we first describe the datasets and experiment settings. Then we present the experiment results of our proposed model.

4.1 Datasets

The experiments are based on a real-world dataset. We choose hotel recommendation as our target service recommendation task. In the meantime, flight service domain is used as auxiliary data source. We've selected hotel booking records in Shanghai and flight booking records from Peking to Shanghai starting from March 2014 to March 2016. In the flight booking records, explicit features such as price, flight class, takeoff time and arrival time are available. And in the hotel booking records, we can also extract price, hotel star, location and check-in time, etc. In the experiment, we use a 2-dimensional vector <price, flight class> as the explicit features of a flight and <price, hotel star> as the explicit features of a hotel. However, explicit ratings for these booking records are not available. Thus, instead of using explicit ratings, we use implicit ratings in our experiments, i.e. the number of booking records. Although more than 70% of the implicit ratings are 1, there are still a lot of implicit ratings larger than 1 and the maximum is even larger than 20. Thus, to constrain the implicit ratings into interval [0,1], we map the ratings using following function:

$$R(u_i, v_j) = \frac{N(u_i, v_j)}{\max_j N(u_i, v_j)} \tag{33}$$

where $N(u_i, v_j)$ means the number that user i has booked item j.

Unlike the famous Movielens dataset, the hotel dataset is yet too sparse. In order to reduce the challenge, we simply ignore users who ordered either flight or hotel less than 5 times. After that, we finally get our hotel dataset with sparseness of 1.004 %. And the flight dataset is a little bit denser, i.e. with sparseness of 3.831 %. More statistics of the datasets are listed in Table 1.

Table 1. General statistics of the dataset

Statistics	Flight	Hotel
Number of users	1367	1367
Number of items	234	711
Number of rating pairs	12253	9756
Min number of rating	5	5
Max number of rating	27	24
Average number of rating	8.96	7.14

4.2 Experiment Settings

In Sect. 3, we've presented two optimizations for our proposed model. Hence, here we use two kinds of evaluation metrics to measure the prediction quality. For optimization with sum-of-squared-errors, we use Root Mean Square Error (RMSE), defined as:

$$RMSE = \sqrt{\frac{\sum_{(uv) \in R_{Test}} r_{uv} - \hat{r}_{uv}}{|R_{Test}|}} \tag{34}$$

where r_{uv} denotes the true rating of user u to item v, $\hat{r}_{uv}$ denotes the predicted rating of user u to item v, and R_{Test} is the set of (u, v) pairs in test dataset.

On the other hand, the AUC metric is used to evaluate the performance with BPR optimization criterion. As done in [15], we apply the leave-one-out strategy to construct the test set, i.e., we randomly remove one observed rating from P_u^d per user. The models are then learned from the remaining ratings S_{train} and the predicted personalized ranking is evaluated on the test set S_{test} by the average AUC:

$$AUC = \frac{1}{|U|} \sum_u \frac{1}{|E(u)|} \sum_{(i,j) \in E(u)} \delta(\hat{r}_{ui} > \hat{r}_{uj}) \tag{35}$$

where $E(u)$ is the evaluation pairs in the test set for user u:

$$E(u) = \{(i,j)|(u,i) \in S_{test} \wedge (u,j) \notin S_{test} \cup S_{train}\} \tag{36}$$

In the experiments, we compare our proposed ExHMF with following baselines:

- CMF [17]: The collective matrix factorization method.
- HeteroMF [9]: The heterogeneous matrix factorization method that extends CMF with a transfer matrix for user latent factors.
- GcPMF [7]: The cost-aware probabilistic matrix factorization on single domain.

4.3   Experiment Results

First, we evaluate the performance of ExHMF with sum-of-squared-errors optimization criterion. Two important parameters need to be set in our model, i.e. the latent dimension k and the domain weight α. Figure 2(a) shows the effect of latent dimension on the RMSE performance of ExHMF. We can see that the performance doesn't increase after $k > 10$. In order to alleviate the over-fitting problem and save the computational cost, we set $k = 10$ in the following experiments. Figure 2(b) shows the effect of domain weight on the RMSE performance of ExHMF, which demonstrates the tradeoff between learning from single service domain and introducing another service domain. We also set $\alpha = 0.2$ in the following experiments for better performance.

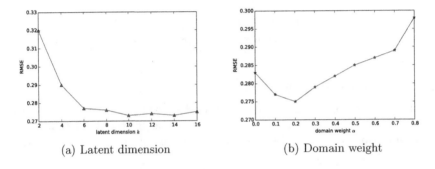

(a) Latent dimension   (b) Domain weight

Fig. 2. The effect of latent dimension and domain weight.

In the experiments, we have 1,3,5 and 7 hotel ratings per user that are given as training data while the remaining ratings are used as testing data. Flight ratings are always given fully. Results are shown in Fig. 3. From the figure, we can see that our proposed ExHMF model outperforms other baseline methods on all the four datasets. GcPMF performs slight better than HeteroMF on the datasets with 3,5 and 7 observed ratings, which indicates the benefit of combining matrix factorization with explicit features. However, GcPMF suffers a significant performance loss on the dataset with 1 observed ratings. The reason is clear: GcPMF works on single domain and no additional knowledge can be learned from the flight matrix when the hotel matrix is extremely sparse. On the contrast, ExHMF combines HeteroMF with explicit features, which improves the performance on all the four datasets.

Second, we test the performance of ExHMF with BPR optimization criterion. Figure 4 depicts the average AUC scores of the compared models. All the models are trained on the whole dataset, where one item entry per user is reserved for testing and others for training. From the figure, it is clear that our proposed ExHMF model gives the best result. GcPMF and HeteroMF perform slightly better than CMF, which implies that both explicit features and transfer matrix for user latent factors can improve the performance. Meanwhile, we find that

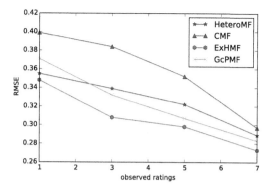

Fig. 3. RMSE performances of compared models on different observed rating sizes.

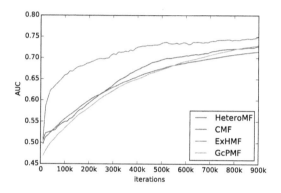

Fig. 4. Performance comparison in terms of AUC.

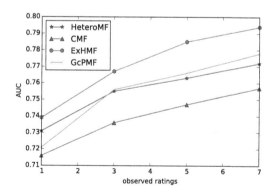

Fig. 5. AUC performances of compared models on different observed rating sizes.

ExHMF converges much faster than the other three baselines and finally gives the highest AUC score.

We also investigate the performance of compared models with BPR optimization criterion with different data sparseness. Figure 5 presents the performance comparison where the models are trained with different numbers of observed ratings. Result clearly shows that our ExHMF method outperforms other baseline methods no matter how sparse the dataset is. GcHMF still performs similar as HeteroMF method except for the case that only 1 observed rating is available.

The overall experimental results validate that our proposed ExHMF model can gain significant improvements by extending HeteroMF with explicit features.

5   Conclusion

In this paper, we have presented ExHMF that extended heterogeneous matrix factorization with combinations of explicit and latent features for tourist service recommendation. Due to the data sparseness in online tourism area, we propose to integrate knowledge learned across multiple domains. Users' preferences over features in each domain are linked via a transfer matrix. We further extend ExHMF with BPR optimization criterion that aims to find a total ranking order. Experiments on hotel recommendation task show that our proposed model outperforms the baselines with a significant margin.

Acknowledgments. This work is partially supported by China National Science Foundation (Granted Number 61272438, 61472253), Research Funds of Science and Technology Commission of Shanghai Municipality (Granted Number 15411952502, 14511107702) and Cross Research Fund of Biomedical Engineering of Shanghai Jiaotong University (YG2015MS61).

References

1. Adomavicius, G., Tuzhilin, A.: Toward the next generation of recommender systems: a survey of the state-of-the-art and possible extensions. IEEE Trans. Knowl. Data Eng. **17**(6), 734–749 (2005)
2. Angel, A., Chaudhuri, S., Das, G., Koudas, N.: Ranking objects based on relationships and fixed associations. In: EDBT 2009, 12th International Conference on Extending Database Technology, pp. 910–921 (2009)
3. Balabanovic, M., Shoham, Y.: Fab: content-based, collaborative recommendation. Commun. ACM **40**, 66–72 (1997)
4. Basu, C., Hirsh, H., Cohen, W.W.: Recommendation as classification: using social and content-based information in recommendation. In: Proceedings of the Fifteenth National Conference on Artificial Intelligence and Tenth Innovative Applications of Artificial Intelligence Conference, pp. 714–720 (1998)
5. Brodsky, A., Henshaw, S.M., Whittle, J.: CARD: a decision-guidance framework and application for recommending composite alternatives. In: Proceedings of the 2008 ACM Conference on Recommender Systems, pp. 171–178 (2008)
6. Deshpande, M., Karypis, G.: Item-based top-N recommendation algorithms. ACM Trans. Inf. Syst. **22**(1), 143–177 (2004)

7. Ge, Y., Liu, Q., Xiong, H., Tuzhilin, A., Chen, J.: Cost-aware travel tour recommendation. In: Proceedings of the 17th ACM SIGKDD International Conference on Knowledge Discovery and Data Mining, pp. 983–991 (2011)
8. Hofmann, T.: Latent semantic models for collaborative filtering. ACM Trans. Inf. Syst. **22**(1), 89–115 (2004)
9. Jamali, M., Lakshmanan, L.V.S.: Heteromf: recommendation in heterogeneous information networks using context dependent factor models. In: 22nd International World Wide Web Conference, pp. 643–654 (2013)
10. Koren, Y., Bell, R.M., Volinsky, C.: Matrix factorization techniques for recommender systems. IEEE Comput. **42**(8), 30–37 (2009)
11. Lee, D.D., Seung, H.S.: Algorithms for non-negative matrix factorization. Adv. Neural Inf. Process. Syst. **13**, 556–562 (2000)
12. Linden, G., Smith, B., York, J.: Amazon.com recommendations: Item-to-item collaborative filtering. IEEE Internet Comput. **7**(1), 76–80 (2003)
13. Marlin, B.M.: Modeling user rating profiles for collaborative filtering. In: Advances in Neural Information Processing Systems, vol. 16, pp. 627–634 (2003). [Neural Information Processing Systems]
14. Pazzani, M.J.: A framework for collaborative, content-based and demographic filtering. Artif. Intell. Rev. **13**(5–6), 393–408 (1999)
15. Rendle, S., Freudenthaler, C., Gantner, Z., Schmidt-Thieme, L.: BPR: Bayesian personalized ranking from implicit feedback. In: UAI 2009, Proceedings of the Twenty-Fifth Conference on Uncertainty in Artificial Intelligence, pp. 452–461 (2009)
16. Salakhutdinov, R., Mnih, A.: Probabilistic matrix factorization. In: Twenty-First Annual Conference on Neural Information Processing Systems, pp. 1257–1264 (2007)
17. Singh, A.P., Gordon, G.J.: Relational learning via collective matrix factorization. In: Proceedings of the 14th ACM SIGKDD International Conference on Knowledge Discovery and Data Mining, pp. 650–658 (2008)
18. Xie, M., Lakshmanan, L.V.S., Wood, P.T.: Breaking out of the box of recommendations: from items to packages. In: Proceedings of the 2010 ACM Conference on Recommender Systems, pp. 151–158 (2010)

An Event Grouping Approach for Infinite Stream with Differential Privacy

Mian Cheng[1]([✉]), Yipin Sun[1], Baokang Zhao[1], and Jinshu Su[1,2]

[1] College of Computer, National University of Defense Technology,
Changsha 410073, China
{cm,yipin_sun,bkzhao,sjs}@nudt.edu.cn
[2] National Laboratory for Parallel and Distribution Processing,
National University of Defense Technology, Changsha 410073, China

Abstract. With the rapid advances in Internet technology, publishing real-time statistics data, in a privacy-preserving way, has led to a large body of research. The current state-of-the-art paradigm for privacy preserving with differential privacy on data stream is w-event privacy. But it neglects if only a few part of the elements of dataset change over time and others are substantially stabilize, then processing all the user data in specified timestamps will bring additional noise and reduce the utility of data. In this paper, a novel privacy preserving approach called G-event which follow the conventional use of w-event differential privacy is proposed. We group the statistics result at each timestamp based on difference calculation. Then the high difference group will publish more often than the similar group. We guarantee that all result with greater change will publish by adding noise, and the result with smaller change will be approximate with the corresponding lastly published statistics. Experiment using real-life dataset show that our approach improves the utility of data.

Keywords: Differential privacy · Infinite stream release · Event grouping · Privacy preserving · Dynamic data

1 Introduction

The past decade has witnessed a huge growth in volumes of data from organizations and individuals has created. Numerous organizations maintain large collections of personal information. Examples include Web application, public health surveillance, traffic monitor, sense network, call detail records(CDRs), etc. These data can either be used for science research or business valuation, and brings significant research value to every area. Consider the example below:

Website statistic. An Internet service provider gathers dynamic data from each website at regular intervals. For instance, the number of visits to the website. More visitors always stand for more effective promotion of the website generalization. First, to understand the characteristics of the target population of the

G. Wang et al. (Eds.): APSCC 2016, LNCS 10065, pp. 106–116, 2016.
DOI: 10.1007/978-3-319-49178-3_8

site, it provides an important basis for product design. Second, it analyzes the coincidence degree of website visits between competitors. It is known as the most convincing evaluation.

In the data publishing paradigm, a data collector gathers data from thousands individuals and publish the statistics result on a web site once, then multiple queries extract any desired information from the published data (eg., a subset of counts). However, due to the original data may contain sensitive information about individuals, sharing user dataset can lead to serious privacy breaches, such as the notorious scandal, the privacy leakage of American On Line (AOL). Many previous research only for static data privacy preserving, i.e., Data publisher only responsible for the privacy of current results. But with the rapid development of network technology, increasing number of data information present in the form of data streams, many applications benefit from continuously detection of statistical data. In real life, user data stream arrive continuously over with time, the size is unpredictable, and its length may be infinite. So the major problem is how can data publisher continually release updated statistics, and meanwhile preserve each individual's privacy and utility?

There are already have been a few existing works on privacy preserving of data streams [10]. But releasing anonymized information is not safe because of unexpectable background knowledge. It is hard to model the attacker's background knowledge in big data. The current state-of-the-art paradigm against background knowledge is differential privacy [6], which requires a randomized algorithm K to perturb the aggregate statistics, and the output of K remains approximately the same if any single tuple in the input data is arbitrarily modified. Even an adversary can hardly infer much information about any individual in the input by analysing the output of K. It guarantee that privacy is protected.

In the past, there have been a series of techniques proposed for differential privacy data publication. In 2010, Dwork et al. proposed two privacy definitions for data stream publishing called *event-level* and *user-level* [4], in which the former can protect any single time series data point and the latter protect the entire data history of any user. In terms of application, Fan and Xiong [7] proposed a filtering and adaptive sampling method for releasing time series data with user-level privacy. Bolot et al. [1] proposed a differential privacy algorithm for delayed sums, also adopted the idea of event-level privacy.

However, those concept both have limited application. The scenario of event-level privacy is not sufficiently responsible for individual because of each time stamp may have background knowledge correlation which can be cause attack, and user-level privacy also is unsuitable to application because most of real streams are infinite. Hence, Kellaris et al. [9] presented a novel streaming data privacy model called *w-event* which protect data points in every w contiguous timestamps. This model successfully strike a nice balance between *event-level* and *user-level* privacy. The problem is that *w-event* neglects if a small amount of elements of the dataset change over time and the remaining stabilize. Moreover, processing all the user data from a specific timestamp will bring additional noise and reduce the utility of data.

In this paper, we propose a novel approach which follow the conventional use of w-event differential privacy mainly due to its ability to ensure the sum of privacy budget in sliding window less than total budget and support private analysis of infinite data streams with reasonable accuracy. We group the statistics result at each timestamp based on difference calculation. Then the high difference group will publish more often than the similar group. We guarantee that all result with greater change will publish by adding noise, and the result with smaller change will be approximate with the corresponding lastly published statistics. The advantage is all budget can be used as much as possible on the high discrepancy.

The rest of this paper is organized as follows: In Sect. 2 we provide the preliminary definitions which are necessary for the rest of the paper. Section 3 we give a detailed introduction on entire framework and two components of G-event differential privacy publishing. Section 4, we include detailed experimental evaluation of our G-event algorithm. Finally, Sect. 5 concludes our work.

2   Preliminaries

In this section, we introduce definitions on differential privacy and w-event privacy. For convenience, we summarize all frequently used notations in Table 1.

Table 1. Frequently used notation

Notation	Description
D	Original dynamic datasets
D^*	Released DP datasets for $\mathbf{D}$
D_i	Released DP datasets at timestamp i
D_j	Last released DP datasets at timestamp j
w	Sliding window size
ϵ	Overall privacy budget
ϵ_1	Privacy budget for the difference calculation step
ϵ_2	Privacy budget for the data publishing step

2.1   Data Stream Model

Traditional method of privacy protection is mostly for the static data. In contrast, we consider an infinite real-time data stream consisting of an infinite number of events. Each event belongs to a user which has an attribute value.

Definition 1 (neighbouring data stream [4]). *If data stream s_1 and s_2 only different in one timestamp t_0, that is $s_1(t_0) \neq s_2(t_0)$. Then for $\forall t \neq t_0$, $s_1(t) = s_2(t)$, we call data stream s_1 and s_2 are neighbouring data stream.*

2.2 Differential Privacy

Differential privacy is first introduced by Dwork and has recently emerged as the de facto standard for private data release. It uses to publish statistics computed on dataset D and without compromising the privacy of the respondents. Its biggest advantage is that the amount of noise is irrelevant to the size of dataset. This makes it possible to provide strong theoretical guarantees on the privacy and utility of released data. More specifically, irrespective of whether or not an individual is present in the data set, differential privacy guarantee privacy against intrusion by any adversary when all the entities in the database are independent.

Definition 2 (Differential Privacy) [6]. Privacy mechanism A gives ε-differential privacy if for any database D and D* differing on at most one record, and for any possible output O ∈ Range(A)

$$Pr[A(Q(D)) \in S] \le e^{\varepsilon} \cdot Pr[A(Q(D^{'})) \in S] \tag{1}$$

Then we call mechanism A achieves ε-DP, ε is a given positive parameter, called privacy budget, used to control unitary privacy level. In general, the lower value of ε indicates stronger privacy guarantee with lower utilization and a higher value indicates a weaker guarantee but provide better utilization.

Laplace Mechanism. The first and most widely used method for achieving differential privacy is the Laplace mechanism [8], which adds random noise following the Laplace distribution to the true answers to the query functions. ε-differential privacy can be achieved by adding independent Laplace random noise x to the answer of query Q. In the following, $Q^{*}(D)$ and $Q(D)$ denote the noisy data and a given original data, respectively.

$$Q^{*}(D) = Q(D) + x \tag{2}$$

Definition 3 (Laplace Mechanism) [3].

$$x \sim (x|\lambda) = \frac{1}{2\lambda} * exp(-|x|/\lambda) \tag{3}$$

where λ is a scale parameter of Laplace distribution, which equals to divide the *Global sensitivity* of query Q by ϵ. Global sensitivity is the maximum L_1 distance between the query results for any two neighboring databases.

Synthetic Theory. This theorem allows us to view ϵ as a privacy budget that is distributed among the r mechanism.

Theorem 1 [9]. Let $S_1, ..., S_r$ be a set of sub-components, where S_i provides ϵ_i-differential privacy. Let S be another mechanism that executes $S_1(D), ..., S_r(D)$ using independent randomness for each S_i, and returns the vector of the outputs of these mechanisms. Then, S satisfies $(\sum_{n=1}^{r} \epsilon_i)$-differential privacy.

2.3 *w*-event Privacy

Since the differential privacy is proposed, various mechanisms have been presented to enhance the accuracy of DP data publishing. In order to process the data stream efficiently, Dwork et al. [4] further propose the definition of event-level and user-level privacy, in which the former can protect any single time series data point and the latter protect the entire data history of any user. To solve the limitation, Kellaris et al. [9] propose a novel approach to merge event-level and user-level privacy called w-event privacy.

*Definition 4 (w-event privacy) [9]. Let A be a mechanism that takes as input a stream prefix of arbitrary size. Also let S be the set of all possible outputs of A. We say that A satisfies **w-event differential privacy** if for all sets $S \subseteq S^*$, all w-neighboring stream prefixes S_t, S_t, and all t, it holds that*

$$Pr[A(Q(D)) \in S] \leq e^{\varepsilon} \cdot Pr[A(Q(D^{'})) \in S] \tag{4}$$

2.4 Utility Metrics

Following the convention in [2], We quantitatively evaluate the data utility by Mean of Absolute Error (MAE) and Mean of Relative Error (MRE). The MAE measures the average magnitude of the errors in a set of forecasts, without considering their direction. It measures accuracy for continuous variables. Expressed in words, the MAE is the average over the verification sample of the absolute values of the differences between forecast and the corresponding observation. It is a linear score which means that all the individual differences are weighted equally in the average. We adopt the classical statistical metric of Mean Absolute Error and Mean Relative Error as shown below:

$$MAE = \frac{1}{M} \sum_{i=0}^{M-1} |p_i - q_i| \tag{5}$$

$$MRE = \frac{1}{M} \sum_{i=0}^{M-1} |p_i - q_i| / max\{q_i, \mu\} \tag{6}$$

where μ is a user-specified constant to mitigate the effect of excessively small query results (e.g., zero). We set $\mu = 1$ throughout the entire stream for count data [8].

3 Proposed Methods

In this section, we propose *G*-event privacy, a event grouping optimization algorithm for infinite data stream with differential privacy inspired by *w*-event privacy scheme. First, we provide an overview of our data stream perturbation algorithm and then elaborate its two key components: event-grouping component and data publishing component.

3.1   Overview

As shown in Fig. 1, we present the framework of G-event privacy. Event-grouping component is responsible for anonymizing all the samples in the data sequence with differential privacy. It prevents the background knowledge of user from privacy of dataset. To achieve this goal, We consider scenario of a trust server collects dynamic data streams if user's spatiotemporal data points continuously at each timestamp $i \in [1,t]$ and assume that a user only appear at most once at each timestamp. When the incoming database D_i arrived, we specify a variable ϵ for privacy level, namely the privacy budget. We let M to indicate the total amount of sampling result (i.e., the size of sliding window). Previous researches show that a lower value of ϵ can achieve a strong privacy protection, but cause higher noise. Our approach first distributes ϵ/M parts of privacy budget to each sample (e.g. the count) based on the synthetic theory. Then we perform a difference calculation between two neighboring elements of D_i and the last private release D_j and divide the calculation result into two groups. One is released by adding Laplace noise, and the other is approximated with the corresponding lastly released result. We develop an approximation strategy cooperating with dynamic budget allocation component to raise data utility. Algorithm 1 presents the pseudocode of our G-event privacy data publishing.

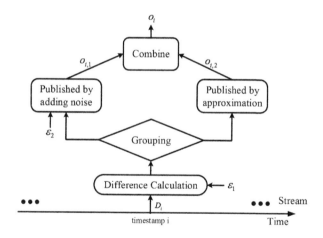

Fig. 1. Overview of G-event mechanism.

3.2   Event Grouping

This component is the main innovation of this paper, we group elements at each timestamp according to the difference comparison. Results with bigger difference will be released by adding noise and others will approximate them with the corresponding lastly released statistics.

In previous research, such as w-event privacy, they perform the calculation of the average difference between all the elements of each column to determine

---
Algorithm 1. Private publication by G-event privacy

Require: $\mathbf{D} = \{D_i | 1 \leq i \leq N, i \in Z\}$, ϵ and w

Ensure: $\tilde{\mathbf{D}} = \left\{ \tilde{D}_i \mid 1 \leq i \leq N, i \in Z \right\}$

1: Set $\epsilon_1 = \epsilon / kw, \epsilon_2 = \epsilon - \epsilon_1$;
2: Computer $c_i = Q(D_i)$;
3: For D_1, release a DP dataset $\tilde{D}_1$ with ϵ_2 / w privacy budget;
4: **for** each timestamp t_i with $i > 1$ **do**
5:    Identify last noise-added release o_l from $(o_1, \cdots, o_{i-1})$;
6:    **for** each element e_i in c_i and e_l in o_l **do**
7:      $dis = |e_i - e_l|$;
8:      **if** $dis > (w/\epsilon_2)$ **then**
9:        add $\{e_i, e_l\}$ to $Group1$;
10:      **else**
11:        add $\{e_i, e_l\}$ to $Group2$;
12:      **end if**
13:    **end for**
14: **end for**
15: **for** each element $\{e_i, e_l\}$ in $Group2$ **do**
16:    **Return** $o_i = o_l$;
17: **end for**
18: **for** each element $\{e_i, e_l\}$ in $Group1$ **do**
19:    Inject Laplace Noise by **Mechanism BA**;
20: **end for**

---

whether add random noise to the released data or approximate them. It helps data publisher to improve data validation. However, this approach ignores the difference between the individual element of each column. In many cases, only a small part of statistics in a column are changed. Based on average calculation, if we release all the elements in column, it will lead to most of the elements which should be chosen to approximate but adding noise to release. That will affect the availability of the entire dataset. Therefore, we propose a novel grouping approach to compare each pair of element $\{e_i, e_l\}$ in timestamp $\{t_i, t_l\}$ and segment every D_i into two groups. Formally, our approach first distributes ϵ/M parts of privacy budget to each sample (e.g. the count) based on the synthetic theory. If the original node x_k which appears in timestamp k, with privacy budget ϵ/M, then a ϵ/M-differentially privacy value r_k will be generated by adding a Laplace noise ν to the original value:

$$z_k = x_k + \nu, \quad p(\nu) \sim Lap(0, M/\epsilon) \tag{7}$$

If mechanism decide to release data on the timestamp i, it indicates the statistical results in i is different from the last released data. Thus, it is advantageous to invest a high privacy budget to the statistics at i for avoiding reducing the difference between the current result and last released data. In the next session, we will introduce the Data publishing method.

3.3   Data Publishing

In this session, data publishing component decides how to release each element of data stream in a sliding window. The key challenge is to improve the utility of the mechanism while preserving privacy level. i.e., How to measure whether spending privacy budget is a worthwhile investment or not?

Algorithm 2. Mechanism BA

Require: $dis, e_i , e_l , \epsilon_{i,2}$ and $\epsilon_{l,2}$
Ensure: e_i
1: $num\_null = \dfrac{\epsilon_{l,2}}{\epsilon/(2 * \omega)} - 1$;
2: **if** $i - l \leqslant num\_null$ **then**
3:     $e_i = null$;
4: **else**
5:     Set $num\_absorb = i - (l + num\_null)$;
6:     Set $\epsilon_{i,2} = \epsilon/(2 * \omega)$ and $\lambda_{i,2} = 1/\epsilon_{i,2}$;
7:     **if** $dis > \lambda_{i,2}$ **then**
8:         $e_i = e_i + Lap(\lambda_{i,2})$;
9:     **else**
10:         $e_i = null$;
11:     **end if**
12: **end if**

---

when receiving the grouping result, data publishing component release data in timestamp i with privacy budget ϵ_2. In this paper, we divide the privacy budget into two parts, one for calculating the difference, and the other for adding noise when data is decided to publish. To further increasing the validity of the released data, we learn that when the number of column d is much larger than the sliding window size w, the amount of noise which is allocated to the difference calculation mechanism becomes small. Hence, we may define a smaller value λ from the beginning, thus data publishing component receive more privacy budget for data release. Paper [5] propose that the scale value of $1/\epsilon$ can provide high accuracy. We set the ϵ_1 and ϵ_2 as below:

$$\epsilon_1 = \epsilon/d, \quad \epsilon_2 = \epsilon - \epsilon_1 \tag{8}$$

Moreover, we employ *Mechanism BA* to effectively release data stream via sliding window methodology. This method is proposed in paper [9]. In the algorithm, we first obtain the number of timestamps which has the null budget after l. If $i - l \leq num\_null$, we output $e_i = null$, it means e_i is approximated with the corresponding lastly released result. Otherwise, after absorbing the budget, mechanism calculates ϵ_2 and decides on whether to release the element by adding noise or just approximate them. Algorithm 2 presents the pseudocode of *Mechanism BA*.

4   Experimental Evaluation

We have implemented G-event privacy in Java, and used Java Statistical Classes (JSC) for simulating the Laplace distribution. All the experiments are performed on a PC with a 2.8 GHz CPU and 16 GB memory. We experimented with a real time-series datasets as below. And in order to compare the average case, each algorithm runs 10 times then outputs the average results.

– **WorldCup.** a well-known archived dataset which includes 1,352,804,107 Web server logs made to the FIFA 1998 Soccer World Cup website in 88 consecutive days. It contains 89997 unique URLs and the number of timestamps are 1320. The statistics result of this dataset shows that 92.18 % of the value recorded as zero.

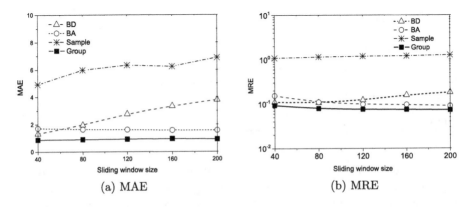

(a) MAE   (b) MRE

Fig. 2. Error vs. sliding window size

Benchmark methods. We compare our *Group* algorithm with benchmarks *BA*, *BD* and *Sample*. *BA* and *BD* algorithm is proposed in paper [9], adopting w-event privacy module and dynamically allocate the available privacy budget over time. *BD* algorithm optimistically assume that only a few data will be released in each sliding window, therefore we can allocate more privacy budget for each release. *BA* algorithm assume that there is not much difference between continuous neighbouring statistical results. the algorithm will allocate a larger privacy budget to the current data release, and hope it can obtain enough accurate approximate results in the next several release. *Sample* algorithm put the whole privacy budget ϵ into one timestamp in sliding window, so that the accuracy of this released data attain its maximum. However, it need to approximate the next $w - 1$ statistical results after releasing one. If these statistics much different from the prior release, the error may become excessive and lose the availability.

Figure 2 illustrates the MAE and MRE of our approach as a function of sliding window size w for the WorldCup dataset. We set up w from 40 to 200. With the increase of the sliding window size, G-event privacy method outperforms all competitors in all size. Its MAE (MRE) is 48.85 % (39.33 %) smaller than *BA*.

Figure 3 compares our approach with other methods under various privacy budget. With the change of privacy budget, we observe that our grouping method is more stable than *Sample* and *BD* algorithm and outperforms all competitors in all cases. According to calculations, G-event privacy method can improve the accuracy of *BA* by up to 39.45 %.

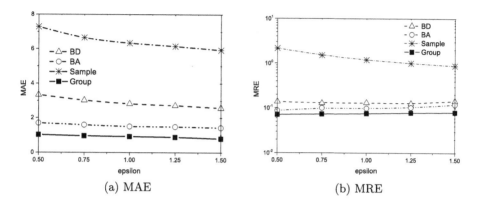

(a) MAE   (b) MRE

Fig. 3. Error vs. privacy budget

5   Conclusion

In this paper, we consider the problem of continuously publishing over an infinite data stream while satisfying differential privacy. We have proposed a novel sanitization framework G-event consisting of two components: event grouping component and data publishing component. Based on experimental, we guarantee that all result with greater change will publish by adding noise, and the result with smaller change will approximate them with the corresponding lastly published statistics. The advantage is all budget can be used as much as possible on the high discrepancy. However, we strongly believe that there are no "universal" sanitization solutions that fit all applications, i.e., provide good accuracy in all scenarios. We may change a different perspective to find out the research purpose in the next step.

References

1. Bolot, J., Fawaz, N., Muthukrishnan, S., Nikolov, A., Taft, N.: Private decayed predicate sums on streams. In: Proceedings of the 16th International Conference on Database Theory, pp. 284–295. ACM (2013)
2. Cao, Y., Yoshikawa, M.: Differentially private real-time data release over infinite trajectory streams. In: 2015 16th IEEE International Conference on Mobile Data Management, vol. 2, pp. 68–73. IEEE (2015)

3. Chen, R., Shen, Y., Jin, H.: Private analysis of infinite data streams via retroactive grouping. In: Proceedings of the 24th ACM International on Conference on Information and Knowledge Management, pp. 1061–1070. ACM (2015)
4. Dwork, C.: Differential privacy in new settings. In: SODA, pp. 174–183. SIAM (2010)
5. Dwork, C.: A firm foundation for private data analysis. Commun. ACM **54**(1), 86–95 (2011)
6. Dwork, C., McSherry, F., Nissim, K., Smith, A.: Calibrating noise to sensitivity in private data analysis. In: Halevi, S., Rabin, T. (eds.) TCC 2006. LNCS, vol. 3876, pp. 265–284. Springer, Heidelberg (2006). doi:10.1007/11681878_14
7. Fan, L., Xiong, L.: Real-time aggregate monitoring with differential privacy. In: Proceedings of the 21st ACM International Conference on Information and Knowledge Management, pp. 2169–2173. ACM (2012)
8. Fan, L., Xiong, L.: An adaptive approach to real-time aggregate monitoring with differential privacy. IEEE Trans. Knowl. Data Eng. **26**(9), 2094–2106 (2014)
9. Kellaris, G., Papadopoulos, S., Xiao, X., Papadias, D.: Differentially private event sequences over infinite streams. Proc. VLDB Endowment **7**(12), 1155–1166 (2014)
10. Riboni, D., Villani, A., Vitali, D., Bettini, C., Mancini, L.V.: Obfuscation of sensitive data for incremental release of network flows. IEEE/ACM Trans. Netw. **23**(2), 672–686 (2015)

Energy Optimization by Flow Routing Algorithm in Data Center Network Satisfying Deadline Requirement

Qianqian Zhang[1], Xiaoyong Zhang[1], Jun Peng[1], Yeru Zhao[1],
Kaiyang Liu[1], and Shuo Li[2(✉)]

[1] School of Information Science and Engineering,
Central South University, Changsha 410083, China
[2] College of Electrical and Information Engineering,
Changsha University of Science and Technology,
Changsha 410076, China
wqbzb@163.com

Abstract. Recently, the data center networks consume a large amount of energy, therefore, the energy saving is becoming increasingly important. Most previous works consolidate flows into as few switches as possible, which is not suitable for network-limited flows which require huge bandwidth to finish traffic transmission within deadline. To solve the challenge of energy-efficient path and deadline satisfied for network-limited flows, in this paper, we formulate the routing problem as a 0-1 integer programming problem, and propose a two-phase energy-efficient flow routing algorithm. Both energy saving and link utilization maximization are considered. Simulation results show that our algorithm achieves better performance in terms of energy saving, link utilization, as well as the active switch ratio.

Keywords: Data Center Network · Energy efficiency · Flow routing · Link utilization

1 Introduction

As the number and size of data centers grow explosively, huge amount of energy is being consumed to run data-intensive applications from cloud services such as search, web email. For example, US data centers are expected to consume about 140 billion kWh by 2020 [1]. The huge energy consumption of data centers has limited the sustainable development of cloud services and raised economic and environmental concerns. As a result, energy efficiency of data centers has attracted significant attention [2].

Energy efficiency can be improved from two aspects: infrastructure facilities (including cooling and power conditioning systems) and IT equipments (including servers, switches, storage, etc.), which are two main parts of energy consumption in a data center [3]. In the past years, the power efficiency of infrastructure facilities has been significantly improved. For example, the cooling power in Google data center is less

© Springer International Publishing AG 2016
G. Wang et al. (Eds.): APSCC 2016, LNCS 10065, pp. 117–129, 2016.
DOI: 10.1007/978-3-319-49178-3_9

than 6 % [4]. Hence, more progress will be obtained by focusing on the energy saving on IT equipments rather than on cooling or power distribution.

As for energy saving on IT equipments, most past efforts studying the IT equipments focused on servers. However, the fact is that the network (including switches and communication links) accounts for 10-20 % of the overall power consumption in typical data centers [5]. Recently, researchers pay more attention to data center network (DCN) to save energy of the data center [6–9].

In order to achieve higher network capacity, many advanced network architectures, such as Fat-Tree [10], Bcube [11], are proposed to replace the traditional tree topology. These new architectures employ abundant switches and links to achieve a 1:1 over-subscription ratio for traffic peak workload. The traffic in data center fluctuates heavily, which results in low link utilization ranging between 5 % and 25 % [12]. Therefore, a great number of network devices work in idle state in these richly-connected networks. What's more, because switches have the fixed overheads such as fans, switching fabric and line-cards, the energy consumption of switches is not proportional to the traffic workload, with the idle switch consuming up to 90 % of the peak power consumption [13]. Thus a large number of idle network devices waste significant amounts of energy.

To save energy consumed by DCN, some energy efficient flow routing approaches are proposed [14, 15]. The general idea is to consolidate the network flows into a subset of switches, and let the idle switches go into sleep mode for energy saving. The above methods may work well for application-limited flows, but they are not suitable for network-limited flows which require huge bandwidth to finish traffic transmission within deadline [7]. As we know, when selecting path, it's important to meet the flow's deadline, otherwise the transmission of the flow is useless [16]. However, all the above problems will bring a huge challenge for routing the network-limited flows. On one hand, many switches are expected to provide enough bandwidth for network-limited flows. On the other hand, many switches may lead to much energy consumption. Therefore, it's necessary to design an energy-efficient routing algorithm for the network-limited flows.

In this paper, we design a two-phase energy-efficient routing algorithm for network-limited flows in the data center. In the first phase, we allocate an energy-efficient path and expected bandwidth to each flow, and the expected bandwidth just satisfies the deadline of each flow. Besides, the flow can share links with others for energy saving. In the second phase, we allocate the available bandwidth of bottleneck links along with its expected bandwidth to flow, which maximizes the link utilization and reduces the completion time of network-limited flows at the same time. As we know, it's the first time to maximize the link utilization by adjusting bandwidth assigned to network-limited flows.

The rest of this paper is organized as follows. Section 2 discusses the related work. Section 3 formulates the path selection problem as a 0-1 integer programming problem. Section 4 introduces the two-phase flow routing algorithm. Section 5 evaluates the performance of our proposed algorithm and Sect. 6 concludes this paper.

2 Related Work

Most of flows are TCP packets in the data center, and TCP's performance is significantly reduced when packets need reordering, therefore, only one path is assigned to each flow to make its packets all take the same path [17]. Equal cost multi-path (ECMP), a traditional flow routing algorithm, is often used to forward packets in the data center network [17, 18]. However, this algorithm focuses on load balance rather than flow consolidation, wasting energy.

To consolidate flows into a subset of switches, in [19], Wang et al. propose a correlation-aware power optimization algorithm based on the discovery that the bandwidth demands of different flows do not peak at the same time. This algorithm greedily consolidates as many weak-correlation flows as possible into one path and further adjusts the data rate of each link to fully utilize the link and save energy. However, this algorithm is not suitable for data-intensive data centers which have highly correlated flows.

To maximize the energy saving in the data center, virtual machine (VM) placement and network flow routing are jointly considered in [20]. In particular, it uses depth-fast search to quickly traverse between different switch layers and best-fit criterion to consolidate flows. The bandwidth each flow occupies is its required bandwidth which can be obtained from the flow's information. Besides, flows can share the link bandwidth with all occupied bandwidth less than the link capacity, which is very likely to result in low link utilization.

Fairly sharing routing approach is proposed in both [7, 14] to improve the link utilization. In [7], Li et al. design a greedy approximate algorithm (named Willow) to schedule flows in an online manner. In [14], Heller et al. present a power-efficient manager namely elastic tree, by dynamically adjusting the set of active network elements-links and switches to satisfy changing data center traffic loads. The power manager also considers the tradeoff between energy efficiency, performance and robust. However, both in [7, 14], the flows get their bandwidth by fairly sharing the bandwidth of the bottleneck links, which obtains full utilization of the bottleneck links. However, this approach results in low utilization of some non-bottleneck links, wasting energy on them.

To further improve the utilization of more links, a new solution to energy-aware flow routing is explored in [8], in which flows always exclusively utilize the bandwidth of links in its routing path. Simulation results show that this approach is more energy efficient than regular fair-sharing routing approach in both Fat-Tree and BCube networks. The key is that exclusive occupation of link resources usually brings higher link utilization in high-radix data center networks. However, this flow routing method is not suitable for flows which may often compete with others for bandwidth to finish flow transmission within deadline.

In this paper, we design a two-phase energy-efficient flow routing algorithm. In our algorithm, flows can share links with others to make more network-limited flows finish traffic transmission within deadline. To save energy, flows are consolidated to as few switches as possible. Besides, link utilization is improved as much as possible by allocating the available bandwidth of the bottleneck links along with expected bandwidth to flows.

3   Problem Formulation

3.1   Energy Consumption Model

The switch in data center network has two states: idle and active. The idle switch consumes up to 90 % of the peak power consumption, so the idle switch is often put into sleep mode or powered off for energy saving. The power consumption of an active switch is composed of two parts: the fixed part (including chassis, switch fabric, etc.) and dynamic part (including ports in the switch). The fixed part is a constant when the switch is on, while the dynamic part is proportional to the number of active ports. The idle port can also be put into sleep mode to save energy. In this paper, the power consumption of an idle switch and an idle port is assumed to be 0. In particular, only when one switch is on, can the ports in it be on.

The energy consumption of communication links is ignored in this paper. According to [8], we use Eq. (1) to denote the energy consumed by the data center network.

$$E = \sum_{i=1}^{M} \left(\sigma_i \cdot P_i \cdot t_i + \sum_{i'=1}^{M_i'} \rho_{i,i'} \cdot Q_{i,i'} \cdot t'_{i,i'} \right) \tag{1}$$

Where the two elements in the bracket denote the fixed and dynamic part of energy consumption in switch i, respectively. We assume that there are M switches in the network and M_i' ports in switch i. P_i is the fixed power consumption in switch i, and $Q_{i,i'}$ is the power consumption by port i' in switch i. Here, both σ_i and $\rho_{i,i'}$ are 0-1 variables. σ_i is 1 if switch i is active; 0, otherwise. $\rho_{i,i'}$ is 1 if port i' in switch i is active; 0, otherwise. In particular, only when σ_i is 1, can $\rho_{i,i'}$ be 1. Otherwise, $\rho_{i,i'}$ is always 0. t_i denotes the working time of switch i, and $t'_{i,i'}$ denotes the working time of port i' in switch i. Switch i must keep active if any port in it is active, therefore, t_i is the maximum value of $t'_{i,i'}$.

Since many data center networks employ homogenous switches, P_i, $Q_{i,i'}$ and M_i' are same for all switches. We use P_0, Q_0 to stand for the fixed power consumption of any switch and power consumption of any port in the switch, respectively. M' is used to stand for the number of ports in each switch. Therefore, Eq. (1) can be further simplified as

$$E = \sum_{i=1}^{M} \left(\sigma_i \cdot P_0 \cdot t_i + Q_0 \cdot \sum_{i'=1}^{M'} \rho_{i,i'} \cdot t'_{i,i'} \right) \tag{2}$$

3.2   Problem Description

Figure 1 is the architecture of a partial 4-ary Fat-Tree. There are two main elements named switch and server in the data center. According to functionality, switches are classified to three kinds: core switch, aggregation switch and edge switch. Core switches are at the root of the tree, and the aggregation switches are responsible for routing, and the edge switches hold the pool of servers. For simplicity, it is assumed that all switches are same and the bandwidth capacity of all links in the topology is same.

In a k-ary Fat-Tree DCN, there are k pods, each of which has $k/2$ aggregation switches and $k/2$ edge switches. In a pod, each k-port edge switch is directly connected to $k/2$ servers and $k/2$ aggregation switches. Besides, each k-port aggregation switch is directly connected to $k/2$ edge switches and $k/2$ core switches. Obviously, the DCN has $k^2/4$ core switches and can hold $k^3/4$ servers. From Fig. 1, it is observed that between any given source and destination server pair connected to different pods, there are $k^2/4$ equal-cost paths, each corresponding to a core switch.

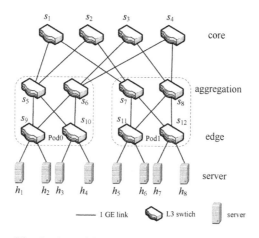

Fig. 1. A partial Fat-Tree network architecture

Although the link capacity is high in modern network, for network-limited flows with deadline demand, it's unavoidable to share and compete for the same resources, such as bandwidth. Our goal is to design a feasible routing algorithm for network-limited flows to save energy consumption of the data center network.

There are M switches and N servers in the data center network. s_i is the ith $i \in \{1, 2 \ldots M\}$ switch, and h_j is the $j^{th} j \in \{1, 2 \ldots N\}$ server. $l(x, y)$ is the link connecting two elements, such as a switch and a server or two switches. C is the link bandwidth capacity, which is a constant in the Fat-Tree DCN. As mentioned above, σ_i denotes whether s_i is active, and $\rho_{i,i'}$ denotes whether the port i' in switch s_i is active.

There are K network-limited flows in the data center network, where f_k is the $k^{th} k \in \{1, 2 \ldots K\}$ flow. f_k is defined as following: $f_k = (src_k, des_k, z_k, d_k)$, which denotes the source server, the destination server, the traffic size and the deadline, respectively. Assume that the traffic size and deadline of flow f_k is obtained when the flow arrives. P is the set of paths in the DCN. $\varepsilon_{p,k}$ denotes whether path p is assigned to flow f_k, where $p \in P$. $\delta_{p, l(x,y)}$ denotes whether path p includes link $l(x, y)$. src_k and des_k are connected to their dedicated edge switches, respectively, so the link connecting the servers and their edge switches are certainly in the assigned path. Therefore, we pay more attention to $\delta_{p,l(i,i_-)}$, where $l(i,i_-)$ is the link connecting two different switches, $i_- \in \{1,2...M\}$ and $i_- \neq i$. b_k is the expected bandwidth by flow f_k to finish traffic transmission within deadline. b'_k is the final bandwidth allocated to flow f_k.

To save energy consumption in the DCN, multiple network-limited flows may share the same link bandwidth. Make sure that the bandwidth occupied by flows in the same link is no more than the link capacity.

Table 1. Symbols and their meanings in problem formulation

Symbol	Meaning
P	the set of paths in the data center network
P_0	the fixed power consumption of each switch
Q_0	the power consumption of a port in each switch
C	the bandwidth capacity of each link
M	the number of switches in the data center network
M'	the number of ports in each switch
N	the number of servers in the data center network
K	the number of flows in the data center network
s_i	the ith switch in the data center network
h_j	the jth server in the data center network
t_i	the working time of switch i
$t'_{i,i'}$	the working time of port i' in switch i
f_k	the kth flow
src_k	the source server of flow f_k
des_k	the destination server of flow f_k
z_k	the traffic size of flow f_k
d_k	the deadline of flow f_k
b_k	the bandwidth expected by flow f_k
b'_k	the bandwidth allocated to flow f_k
$l(x,y)$	the link between a switch and a server or two switches
$l(i,i_-)$	the link between switch i and switch i_-
σ_i	**decision variable:** 1 if switch i is active, 0 otherwise
$\rho_{i,i'}$	**decision variable:** 1 if port i' in switch i is active, 0 otherwise
$\varepsilon_{p,k}$	**decision variable:** 1 if path p is assigned to flow f_k, 0 otherwise
$\delta_{p,l(i,i_-)}$	the relationship between path p and link $l(i,i_-)$: 1 if path p includes link $l(i,i_-)$, 0 otherwise

With the above notations(summarized in Table 1), the optimization problem is formulated as the following 0-1 integer programming problem.

$$\text{Min} \sum_{i=1}^{M} \left(\sigma_i \cdot P_0 \cdot t_i + Q_0 \cdot \sum_{i'=1}^{M'} \rho_{i,i'} \cdot t'_{i,i'} \right) \tag{3}$$

$$s.t. \forall k, \quad \sum_{p \in P} \varepsilon(p, k) = 1 \tag{4}$$

$$\forall i, \ k, \quad \sigma_i = \varepsilon_{p,k} \cdot \delta_{p,l(i,i\_)} \tag{5}$$

$$\forall i\_, \ k, \quad \sigma_{i\_} = \varepsilon_{p,k} \cdot \delta_{p,l(i,i\_)} \tag{6}$$

$$\forall k, \quad b_k = \frac{z_k}{d_k} \tag{7}$$

$$\forall k, \quad b'_k \geq b_k \tag{8}$$

$$\forall l(i, i\_), \quad \sum_{k=1}^{K} \sum_{p \in P} \varepsilon_{p,k} \cdot \delta_{p,l(i,i\_)} \cdot b_k \leq C \tag{9}$$

Equation (3) is the objective function to minimize the energy consumption of the data center network. Constraint (4) ensures that just one path is assigned to each flow, because TCP's performance is significantly reduced when packets need reordering. Thus all packets of each flow take the same path. Equations (5) and (6) ensures that the switch is active when there is flow passing it. Equation (7) is the bandwidth expected by each flow, which just satisfies the flow's deadline. Constraint (8) ensures that the final bandwidth assigned to each flow is more than its expected bandwidth to satisfy the flow's deadline. Constrains (9) satisfies that the total bandwidth assigned to flows sharing the same link cannot exceed its link capacity.

As above, there are $k^2/4$ different paths for each flow whose source and destination servers are connected to edge switches in different pods. Since the formulation covers all possible flow routing solutions, the solution space is very large when the network becomes large and the output solution is considered to be optimal on energy consumption. Therefore, it's a 0-1 integer programming problem and NP-hard problem.

4 Flow Routing Algorithm

To find the optimal allocation solution and improve the link utilization, we propose a two-phase energy-efficient routing algorithm, as shown in Algorithm 1. We find path for flows one by one. In phase 1, allocate one path and expected bandwidth to each flow. To save energy, the selected path is the one with the least number of increased switches and the least energy increment. In phase 2, adjust bandwidth allocated to each flow, that is, the available bandwidth of bottleneck links along with its expected bandwidth is allocated to flows, to improve the link utilization.

In phase 1, first, sort all flows in descending order of their expected bandwidth, to route flows with the larger expected bandwidths first (line 1). Next, select paths satisfying the flow's expected bandwidth from all its available paths (line 3–4). There will be two cases for P'_k: empty or not. If P'_k is empty, that is, none path satisfies flow f_k, it will be suspended, not transmitting traffic (line 5–7). Otherwise, we select paths with the least number of increased switches (line 9–12). Then, assign path with the least incremental energy p_k to flow f_k, and update the decision variable $\varepsilon_{p,k}$ as 1 (line 13–14). Finally, update the available bandwidth of links in path p_k, that is, subtract the expected bandwidth of flow f_k (line 15–16).

Algorithm 1. Flow Routing Algorithm

Input: flow f_k, P the set of paths in the data center network

Output: p_k the path allocated to flow f_k, b_k' the bandwidth allocated to flow f_k

Phase 1: allocate one path and expected bandwidth to each flow

1: sort f_k in descending order of the expected bandwidth b_k

2: **for** each f_k **do**

3:   $P_k \leftarrow$ select all available paths for flow f_k;

4:   $P_k' \leftarrow$ select paths satisfying the bandwidth expected by flow f_k from P_k

5:   **if** $P_k' = \varnothing$ **then**

6:     $p\_k \leftarrow \varnothing$

7:     $\sum_{p \in P} \varepsilon(p,k) = 0$

8:   **else**

9:     **for** each $p_k' \in P_k'$ **do**

10:       calculate the number of increased switches n_k, effected by new path p_k'

11:     **end for**

12:     $P_k \leftarrow \arg\min_{p_k' \in P_k'}(n_k)$

13:     $p\_k \leftarrow \arg\min_{p\_k \in P\_k}(\Delta E)$

14:     $\varepsilon_{p\_k,k} = 1$

15:     **for** all links in path p_k **do**

16:       $b_{(i,i\_L)} \leftarrow b_{(i,i\_L)} - b_k$

17:     **end for**

18:   **end if**

19: **end for**

Phase 2: adjust bandwidth allocated to each flow

20: sort f_k in descending order of deadline d_k

21: **for** each f_k **do**

22:   calculate the available bandwidth of bottleneck link $b(p\_k)$ in path p_k

23:   **if** $b(p\_k) = 0$

24:     continue

25:   **else**

26:     $b_k' = b_k + b(p\_k)$

27:     **for** all links in path p_k **do**

28:       $b_{(i,i\_L)} = b_{(i,i\_L)} - b(p\_k)$

29:     **end for**

30:   **end if**

31: **end for**

In phase 2, first, sort all flows in descending order of their deadlines, to adjust bandwidth for flows with longer deadline first and let them finish transmission more quickly (line 20). Second, calculate the available bandwidth of the bottleneck link in path p_k. If it is 0, jump to the next flow; else, allocate the available bandwidth along with the expected bandwidth to flow f_k, and update the available bandwidth of all links in p_k (line 21–28).

5   Simulation

In this section, we carry out simulations to evaluate the effectiveness of our proposed algorithm by comparing with ECMP. Simulation results illustrate that our proposed algorithm has advantages in saving the data center network energy consumption, improving the link average utilization and reducing active switch ratio.

5.1   Simulation Setup

Network topology. Fat-tree is a popular advanced network architecture, and it is chosen as the data center network topology in our simulations. The bandwidth capacity of each link is 1 Gbps. We simulate the impact of data center size on the network energy consumption by using switches with 4-port, 8-port, 12-port, 16-port and 20-port, respectively. Hence, the number of servers supported by the data center is 16, 128, 432, 1024 and 2000, respectively. For each network, it is assumed that there are half of servers having traffic flows to transmit. Every server pair has a flow, the number of flows in the simulation is as shown in Table 2. Without loss of generality, servers having flows are randomly selected.

Traffic flows. The flows used in our simulations follow an exponential distribution with the expected size of 64 MB, which is the typical size in distributed system in data centers [21]. Besides, the source and destination servers of each flow are chosen randomly. In particular, we remove the source and destination servers connected by the same edge switch, because the energy-efficient path is undoubtedly the one which passes the connected edge switch. The number of flows in the data center is half of servers having flows. Besides, we assume the completion time of each flow is proportional to its traffic size. The deadlines of flows are satisfied by allocated expected bandwidth to flows.

Power parameters. In simulation, we use the power parameter of Cisco Nexus 2224TP switch, whose fixed power consumption is 24 W and the power consumption of each port is 2 W [22]. The idle switch or port is assumed to enter sleeping immediately, that is, the transmission time between active state and sleeping state is ignored. The energy consumption of the data center network is calculated according to Eq. (2).

Table 2. Flow set used in our simulation

Number of switch ports in Fat-Tree	4	8	12	16	20
Number of flows in Fat-Tree		4	32	108	256	500

5.2   Simulation Results

We simulate the impact of different network topology on the total energy consumption, the link average utilization and the active switch ratio of our proposed algorithm and ECMP algorithm. The active switch ratio is the ratio of active switches to all switches in the data center network. The flow set in our simulation is shown in Table 2. The simulation results are shown in Figs. 2, 3 and 4, respectively.

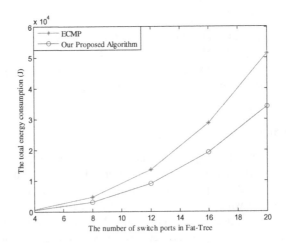

Fig. 2. The total energy consumption in the data enter of our proposed algorithm and ECMP algorithm

Figure 2 shows that the energy consumption of the data center in both algorithms increases quickly in larger networks, because more switches will become active to support more flows. Compared to ECMP algorithm, our proposed algorithm achieves about 30 % less energy consumption, because ECMP tends to use all switches all the time to balance the core switches' traffic, while our algorithm tries its best to save energy in two aspects. On one hand, it tries to consolidate flows into minimum number of switches to save energy. On the other hand, it reduces the running time of switches and ports as much as possible by assigning more bandwidth to flows, to reduce the completion time of flow.

Figure 3 shows that the average link utilization in each algorithm increases slowly as the data center become larger. In particular, the link utilization in ECMP algorithm is always below 50 %, while our proposed algorithm is greater than 70 %. Thus our proposed algorithm is about 70 % higher link average utilization than that of ECMP algorithm. Because our proposed algorithm assigns additional bandwidth to the flow as long as the bottleneck links in the selected path have available bandwidth, to make full use of the bottleneck links' bandwidth and maximize the non-bottleneck links' utilization as much as possible.

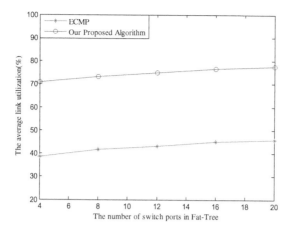

Fig. 3. The average link utilization in data center of our proposed algorithm and ECMP algorithm

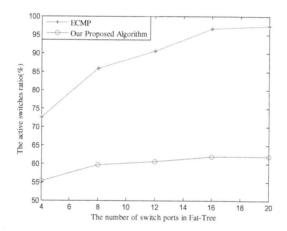

Fig. 4. The active switch ratio in data center of our proposed algorithm and ECMP algorithm

Figure 4 shows the active switch ratio in two algorithms, that is, the ratio of active switches to all switches in the data center network. It is observed that the active switch ratio in ECMP algorithm increases quickly as the data center becomes larger, while our proposed algorithm increase less than 10 % in total. Furthermore, the number of active switches in our algorithm is about 30 % less than that of ECMP algorithm. Because our proposed algorithm selects paths having the least number of increased switches for each flow and then selects the path with the least incremental energy consumption, while ECMP algorithm ignores the number of switches increased by the selected path.

6 Conclusion

The data center network has become an important part of energy consumption in the data center. In this paper, we design a two-phase energy-efficient flow routing algorithm to optimize energy consumption in the data center network. We first allocate an energy-efficient path and expected bandwidth to the flow, to make the flow finish transmission within deadline. Then, we adjust bandwidth allocated to the flow by allocating the available bandwidth of the bottleneck links in the selected path along with its expected bandwidth to the flow. Finally, we conduct simulations to evaluate the performance of our scheduling algorithm in energy consumption, link utilization and active switch ratio, respectively. Simulation results show that our algorithm saves about 30 % network energy, improves more than 70 % average link utilization and reduces about 30 % active switch ratio compared with ECMP algorithm.

Acknowledgments. The authors would like to acknowledge that this work was partially supported by the National Natural Science Foundation of China (Grant No. 61672537, 61672539, 61602529, 61502055, 61402538, 61403424, 61379111 and 61202342).

References

1. Delforge, P.: America's data centers consuming and wasting growing amounts of energy, Natural Resources Defense Council (2015). https://www.nrdc.org/resources/americas-data-centers-consuming-and-wasting-growing-amounts-energy
2. Patel, C. D., Bash, C. E., Sharma, R., Beitelmal, M. Friedrich, R.: Smart cooling of data centers. In: ASME 2003 International Electronic Packaging Technical Conference and Exhibition, pp. 129–137 (2003)
3. Energy efficiency policy options for Australian and New Zealand data centres, The Equipment Energy Efficiency (E3) Program (2014)
4. Data center efficiency: How we do it (2012). http://www.google.com/about/datacenters/efficiency/internal/
5. Greenberg, A., Hamilton, J., Maltz, D.A., Patel, P.: The cost of a cloud: research problems in data center networks. Proc. ACM SIGCOMM Comput. Commun. Rev. 39, 68–73 (2009)
6. Kliazovich, D., Bouvry, P., Khan, S.U.: DENS: data center energy-efficient network-aware scheduling. Cluster Comput. 16(1), 65–75 (2013)
7. Li, D., Yu, Y., He, W., Zheng, K., He, B.: Willow: saving data center network energy for network-limited flows. IEEE Trans. Parallel Distrib. Syst. 26(9), 2610–2620 (2015)
8. Li, D., Shang, Y., He, W., Chen, C.: EXR: greening data center network with software defined exclusive routing. IEEE Trans. Comput. 64(9), 1743–1751 (2015)
9. Zheng, K., Wang, X., Li, L., Wang, X.: Joint power optimization of data center network and servers with correlation analysis. In: Proceedings of INFOCOM, pp. 2598–2606 (2014)
10. Al-Fares, M., Loukissas, A., Vahdat, A.: A scalable, commodity data center network architecture. Proc. ACM SIGCOMM Comput. Commun. Rev. 38(4), 63–74 (2008)
11. Guo, C., Lu, G., Li, D., Wu, H., Zhang, X., Shi, Y., Tian, C., Zhang, Y., Lu, S.: BCube: a high performance, server-centric network architecture for modular data centers. Proc. ACM SIGCOMM Comput. Commun. Rev. 39(4), 63–74 (2009)

12. Carrega, A., Singh, S., Bolla, R., Bruschi, R.: Applying traffic merging to datacenter networks. In: Proceedings of the 3rd International Conference on Future Energy Systems: Where Energy, Computing and Communication Meet (e-Energy 2012), pp. 1–9 (2012)
13. Mahadevan, P., Banerjee, S., Sharma, P., Shah, A.: On energy efficiency for enterprise and data center networks. IEEE Commun. Mag. **49**(8), 94–100 (2011)
14. Heller, B., Seetharaman, S., Mahadevan, P., Yiakoumis, Y., Sharma, P., Banerjee, S., McKeown, N.: ElasticTree: saving energy in data center networks. In: Proceedings of 7th USENIX Conference on Networked Systems Design and Implementation (NSDI 2010), p. 17 (2010)
15. Shang, Y., Li, D., Xu, M.: Energy-aware routing in data center network. In: Proceedings of ACM SIGCOMM Workshop Green Networking, pp. 1–8 (2010)
16. Wilson, C., Ballani, H., Karagiannis, T., Rowtron, A.: Better never than late: meeting deadlines in datacenter networks. In: Proceedings of ACM SIGCOMM Computer Communication Review, vol. 41(4), pp. 50–61 (2011)
17. Al-Fares, M., Radhakrishnan, S., Raghavan, B., Huang, N., Vahdat, A.: Hedera: dynamic flow scheduling for data center networks. In: Proceedings of 7th Usenix Conference on Networked Systems Design and Implementation (NSDI 2010), p. 19 (2010)
18. Hopps, C.: Analysis of an equal-cost multipath algorithm. J. Allergy Clin. Immunol. **109**(1), 1–8 (2000)
19. Wang, X., Yao, Y., Wang, X., Lu, K., Cao, Q.: CARPO: correlation-aware power optimization in data center networks. In: Proceedings of IEEE INFOCOM, vol. 131(5), pp. 1125–1133 (2012)
20. Jin, H., Cheocherngngarn, T., Levy, D., Smith, A.: Joint host-network optimization for energy-efficient data center networking. Alzheimers Dement. **9**(4), 623–634 (2013)
21. Ghemawat, S., Gobioff, H., Leung, S.: The Google file system. In: Proceedings of 19th ACM Symposium on Operating Systems Principles, pp. 29–43 (2003)
22. Cisco Nexus 2200 series data sheet (2013). http://www.cisco.com/en/US/prod/collateral/switches/ps9441/ps10110/datasheet_c78-507093.html

Efficient Data Collection in Sensor-Cloud System with Multiple Mobile Sinks

Yang Li[1], Tian Wang[1(✉)], Guojun Wang[2], Junbin Liang[3],
and Hongyu Chen[4]

[1] College of Computer Science and Technology, Huaqiao University,
Xiamen 361021, China
wangtian@hqu.edu.cn
[2] School of Computer Science and Educational Software,
Guangzhou University, Guangzhou 510006, China
[3] School of Computer and Electronics Information, Guangxi University,
Nanning 530004, China
[4] Shijiazhuang Kelin Electric Co., Ltd., Shijiazhuang 050000, China

Abstract. Cloud computing extends the data processing ability and storage ability of wireless sensor networks (WSNs). However, due to the weak communication ability of WSNs, how to upload the sensed data to the Cloud within the limited time becomes a bottleneck of sensor-cloud system. To solve this problem, we propose to use multiple mobile sinks to help with data uploading from WSNs to Cloud. An efficient algorithm is designed to schedule the multiple mobile sinks, with several provable properties. We conduct extensive simulations to evaluate the performance of proposed algorithm. The results show that our algorithm can upload the data from WSNs to Cloud within the limited latency and minimize the energy consumption as well.

Keywords: Sensor-cloud · Multiple mobile sinks · Latency · Energy

1 Introduction

Nowadays the WSNs have been widely deployed in various applications including health monitoring [1], forest fire detection [2], etc. The WSNs in these applications frequently produce intensive data which need to be collected and processed under urgent delay constraint. Beyond that, sensors have limited battery, computing ability and storage ability to support vast data transmission and processing, which often leads to a short lifetime of networks. Fortunately, cloud computing extends the data processing ability and storage ability of WSNs. Moreover, inherited from cloud computing, the performance of WSNs can be enhanced, such as energy consumption, computing latency, service quality, etc. Therefore, combining WSNs and cloud computing is an inevitable trend and sensor-cloud was born [3, 4].

However, due to the weak communication ability of WSNs [5, 6], how to upload the sensed data to Cloud within limited latency becomes a bottleneck of sensor-cloud system. For example, a larger number of dispersed sensors are deployed to continuously monitor the temperature, humidity and gases of forest. If the sensed data are not

© Springer International Publishing AG 2016
G. Wang et al. (Eds.): APSCC 2016, LNCS 10065, pp. 130–143, 2016.
DOI: 10.1007/978-3-319-49178-3_10

transmitted to managers in time, the best rescue time for putting out fires would be missed. In [5], Zhang J. et al. proposed a novel variable width tiered structure routing scheme named variable width tiered structure routing to address delay and reliability of data collection. On the other hand, with the development of WSNs, mobile elements have been deployed for data gathering in WSNs in recent work [7, 8]. For one thing, the network lifetime could be prolonged by balancing the load of each sensor and avoiding the cost of multiple hops transmission. For another, the energy consumption of sensors could be reduced since mobile sinks can supplement their energy by recharging or replacement. However, when mobile sinks are applied to collect sensory data, a problem that cannot be neglected is the high delivery latency. Due to the limited velocity of mobile sinks, it usually costs hours to tour a large sensing field, which cannot meet the requirements of many delay-sensitive applications [9].

In this paper, we propose an efficient scheduling algorithm for gathering data from WSNs to Cloud with multiple mobile sinks. The multiple sinks move to cooperatively collect the sensory data in WSNs layer and upload the data to Cloud. When delivery delay is controlled within limited time, we focus on minimizing the network energy consumption to prolong the network lifetime. The main contributions of this paper are listed as follows:

1. We propose the data collection problem form WSNs to Cloud with multiple mobile sinks, while traditional data collection problem with mobile sensors focus on data collection from sensors to the sink.
2. We design an efficient algorithm aiming at uploading data from WSNs to Cloud within a limited time constrain and minimizing energy consumption. The algorithm is with several provable properties.
3. We conduct experiments to evaluate the performance of the proposed algorithm and the experimental results validate its effectiveness.

The remainder of this article is organized as follows: Sect. 2 reviews research related to the work presented herein. Section 3 discusses modeling of our study. The implementation details for our proposed MMSA algorithm is described in Sect. 4. Then Sect. 5 presents the analysis of our proposed algorithm. Section 6 shows simulation results, and the last section concludes our work.

2   Related Work

The proliferation of the implementation for low-cost, low-latency, multiple functional sensors has made WSNs a prominent data collection paradigm for extracting local measures of interests. In the traditional WSNs, sensors are generally densely deployed and randomly scattered over a sensing field and they form into autonomous organizations to collect or relay data to static sink [10, 11]. However, most of sensors send data to static sink through multiple-hop wireless communication, which highly increases the energy consumption. Furthermore, the sensors that close to the sink representatively deplete their energy due to more data transmission quantity. This phenomenon results in a bad connectivity and coverage of network. Accordingly, to mitigate these problems, the usage of mobile sinks is proposed in recent research.

Tunc C. et al. [12] propose Ring Routing a novel, distributed, energy-efficient mobile sink routing protocol, suitable for time-sensitive applications, which make use of mobile sink to provide load-balanced data delivery and achieve uniform-energy consumption across the network. Arquam M. et al. [13] propose a routing algorithm with sink mobility in hierarchical WSNs to improve network lifetime by eliminating energy holes. In their proposal, they consider upper and lower bound on delay while optimizing sojourn locations and sojourn time. Hou G. et al. [14] design an efficient path algorithm VG-AFSA based on Virtual Grids to meet most applications' requirements for data latency, which divides nodes into groups with virtual grids to scale down the space of searching optimal set of visited-nodes. However, these methods are based on single mobile sink, which are not applicable for the networks with large number of sensors and stringent time constrain.

In order to address these problems, methods with multiple mobile sinks are designed, which focuses on the issue of multiple mobile sink scheduling [15–17]. For example, Yi-Fan Hu et al. [15] design an efficient routing recovery protocol with endocrine cooperative particle swarm optimization algorithm (ECPSOA) to establish and optimize the alternative path, which improves the routing protocol robustness and efficiently. Meanwhile, the method reduces the communication overhead and the energy consumption. Using multiple mobile sinks to assist in data collection can increase the network connectivity and reliability, reduce cost, and decrease energy consumption at individual nodes, which is shown in [18]. To get the maximum benefit with the minimum cost, it is essential to design a schedule scheme for multiple mobile sinks to collect data in efficient manner. Wichmann et al. [19] focus on using faster mobile sinks to reduce the physical collection delay. However, such mobile sinks are often motion-constrained and require smooth path which cannot fits all kinds of application. Moreover, current methods merely consider the data collection from sensors to Cloud and cannot be applied to the sensor-cloud environment.

3   Problem Definition

In this paper, we assume the WSN consists of N sensors, denoted by a set $S = \{S_1, S_2, \ldots, S_N\}$. The set $K = \{MS_1, MS_2, \ldots, MS_M\}$ represents M mobile sinks (MSs). For any $S_i \in$ S, the sensing data rate is C byte/s, the single hop latency is t s and communication radius is R m. Any $MS_i \in K$ can collect data from sensors and upload data to Cloud. The throughput from sensors to MS is D byte/s, and the uploading rate from MS to cloud is Q byte/s. The velocity of MS is denoted by v m/s. We focus on the problem that multiple mobile sinks cooperate to Collect sensed data from WSNs to Cloud within a limited latency T_{spe} (hereafter referred to as CWC problem). The target is to minimize the network energy consumption while guaranteeing the delivery latency.

A simple example is illustrated in Fig. 1, where circles and small cars stand for fixed sensors and mobile sinks, respectively. Figure 1a shows the initial plan of data collection with two mobile sinks. The route of mobile sink M_1 is shown as solid arrows and the dotted arrows represent the route of mobile sink M_2. Both M_1 and M_2 can collect the data from sensors and then upload to Cloud. In Fig. 1b, the dark nodes

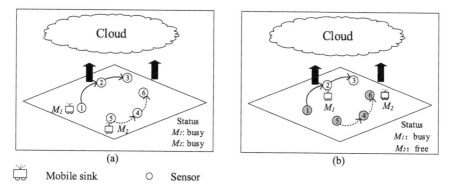

Fig. 1. An example of data collection from WSNs to Cloud with multiple mobile sinks

represent the sensors that have been visited. When M_1 is busy for collecting data of sensor 2, the M_2 has finished its job and becomes free. When there is a sensor 3 waiting for M_1, it leads to a longer collection time. In this situation, M_2 can be dispatched to help M_1 collect the data of sensor 3. Obviously, it is essential to design a schedule algorithm to efficiently collect data from WSNs to Cloud.

We have the following theorem regarding to the complexity of the CWC problem:

Theorem 1: For the CWC problem, designing the optimal method is a NP-hard problem.

Proof: We prove this theorem by showing a special case of SD-MSS, in which $M = 1$, the sensor transmission radius is zero and uploading time is zero. In this case, the CWC is equivalent to find a shortest path visiting all of the given sensors. Note that in order to minimize the path length, any optimal solution would not visit the same sensor twice, otherwise we can make it shorter by using triangular inequality. Therefore finding an optimal solution of this special case of SD-MSS is equivalent to find an optimal solution of Hamiltonian path problem (i.e., finding a path to visit all sensors with the minimum length), which is a well-known NP-hard problem.

3.1 Network Model

We model the WSN as an unoriented-weighted graph $G = \{V_{se}, E_{se}\}$, where $V_{se} = S$, $E_{se} \in \{V_{se} \times V_{se}\}$ is a set of edges, where $E_{i,j} \in E_{se}$ is the edge if the distance $d_{i,j}$ between S_i and S_j is small than R. Then we transform the G to a Minimum Cost Spanning Tree $MST = \{T_{node}, T_{edge}\}$, where $T_{node} = V_{se}$ and $T_{edge} \subseteq E_{se}$. The mobile sink will be controlled to visit portion of sensors called Polling Point (PP), denoted by $\{PP \subseteq S | P_1, P_2, \ldots, P_k\}$.

3.2   Delay Model

With multiple mobile sinks synchronously working, the network delivery delay can be estimated as follow:

$$T_{net} = Max\{T_{MS_1}, T_{MS_2}, \ldots, T_{MS_M}\} \tag{1}$$

where T_{MS_i} is the delivery time of MS_i. Each T_{MS_i} consists of four parts formulated as follows: transmission time T_t:

$$T_t = \frac{\sum_{j=1}^{s} C}{D} \tag{2}$$

uploading time T_d:

$$T_d = \frac{\sum_{j=1}^{s} C}{Q} \tag{3}$$

Multi-hops delay T_h:

$$T_h = \sum_{j=1}^{s} h_j * t \tag{4}$$

and MS_i travel time T_m:

$$T_m = \frac{L_{tsp}}{V} \tag{5}$$

Where s is the number of sensors assigned to MS_i. The variable h_j is the amount of hops from sensor S_j to MS_i and L_{tsp} is the routing length MS_i traveled. We assume $MS_i \in K$ can upload data to Cloud at any time. Therefore, the T_{MS_i} can be calculated as formula (6):

$$T_{MS_i} = \frac{\sum_{j=1}^{s} C}{D} + \sum_{j=1}^{s} h_j * t + Max\left(\frac{L_{tsp}}{V}, \frac{\sum_{j=1}^{s} C}{Q}\right) \tag{6}$$

Based on formula (6), we can conclude that h_j, L_{tsp} and the amount of sensors assigned to MS_i are the main factors affecting T_{MS_i}, which motivates us to design the algorithm in next section.

4   Multiple MS Scheduling Algorithm (MMSA)

4.1   Overview of the Algorithm

The MMSA consists of three stages: first, dividing the coverage area into M Sectors and generating the Minimum Cost spanning Tree MST (MS-MST); second, selecting

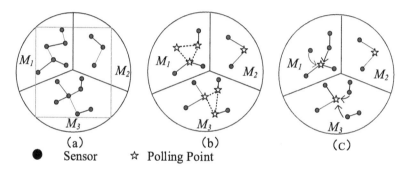

Fig. 2. The basic idea of MMSA algorithm

the polling points (PPs) in each sectors (S-PPA); last, based on the limited latency T_{spe}, designing the Schedule Scheme (SSA).

Figure 2 shows the main process of MMSA. The gray rectangle represents the coverage area of sensors, and the black circle is the circumscribed circle of rectangle in Fig. 2a. We divide the circle into M sectors equally with degree $\frac{2\pi}{M}$ such as M_1, M_2 and M_3. A minimum cost spanning tree (MST) is generated in each sector to provide delivery routes. Second, parts of sensors are selected as PPs like the star nodes in the Fig. 2b. The MS can gather the whole sensory data via dotted lines among the star nodes, and the remaining sensors send data to MS when MS stays at star nodes. However, due to the limited speed of MS, the delivery time may become larger than the limited latency T_{spe}. So we have to reduce delivery time by decreasing displacement distance of MS. Our method is to change part of PPs to the general sensors so that MS can visit less PPs to save moving time. Until there is only one PP in each sector, MS stays at a fixed sensor and serves as a static sink. As shown in Fig. 2c, the black nodes are sensors that parts of them deliver data to MS directly like the solid arrows and the remaining sensors send their data to MS through multiple hops transmission.

4.2 MS-MST: Partition and Generating MST

This stage is the first part of MMSA. It can be divided into two steps. First, the circumscribed circle of coverage area is equally divided into M sectors with central angle $\frac{2\pi}{M}$. Second, the sensors in each sector constitute M weighted graphs $\{G_{MS_i}(V_{sec_i}, E_{sec_i})|i = 1, 2, \ldots, M\}$, where $V_{se} = \sum\limits_{i=1}^{M} V_{sec_i}$. Besides, the weight of edge can be calculated by formula $E_{i,j} = \sqrt[2]{(S_i.x - S_j.x)^2 + (S_i.y - S_j.y)^2}$, where $S_i.x$, $S_i.y$ represent the abscissa and ordinate of sensor, respectively. If the edge $E_{i,j}$ is larger than radius R, the weight of this edge would be set as infinity. Then based on the sub graph $G_{MS_i}(i = 1, 2, \ldots, M)$ in each sector, we generate M minimum cost spanning trees by Prim algorithm, denoted as $\{Mst_i(Vt_i, Et_i)|i = 1, 2, \ldots, M\}$. According to the properties of MST, when delivery time of each mobile sink T_{MS_i} is smaller than the limited latency T_{spe}, the communication cost of network is the minimum.

Algorithm 1 MS-MST: Partition and Generating MST

Input: each sensors location $(S_i.x, S_i.y)$, the number of sensors N. Two sets
$T_{node} = \{\emptyset\}$, $T_{edge} = \{\emptyset\}$, represent the nodes and edge of MST,
respectively;
Output: M graphs $G(V_G, E_G)$ and MSTs, $T(V_T, E_T)$;
1: **while** i, j are smaller than N, **do**
2:     $E_{i,j} = \infty$
3:     $E_{i,j} = sqrt\left(\left(S_i.x - S_j.x\right)^2 + \left(S_i.y - S_j.y\right)^2\right)$;
4:     **if** $E_{i,j} > R$, **then** $E_{i,j} = \infty$;
5:     **end if**
6: **end while**
7: **while** $T_{node} \neq V_{sec}$ **do**
8:     edge= $Min\{E_{u,v} | u \in T_{node}, v \in S\}$;
9:     **if** $v \notin T_{node}$ **then**
10:        $T_{node} = \{T_{node} \cup v\}$ and $T_{edge} = \{T_{edge} \cup E_{i,j}\}$;
11:    **end if**
12: **end while**

4.3 S-PPA: Selecting Polling Points in Each Sector

This stage focuses on the selection of polling points. A basic principle can be described
as follow. When S_j is within the transmission range of S_i, MS can stay at S_i to collect
data of S_i and S_j. Consequently, MS can visit polling points to complete data collection.
A reasonable selection of PP can reduce the trajectory length of MS. It inspires us to
design a trajectory to visit less PP but access to all sensors. In the MS-MST we
proposed, the sensors that construct a MST can be classified into three types: root node,
potential PP node, leaf node. Root node is the start point of MS. Potential PP node is
kind of sensors that connected with more than one sensor directly. Leaf node is the
sensor connected with only one sensor. Figure 3a gives a physical storage structure of
MST called children linked list, which shows a clear relationship of sensors in MST.

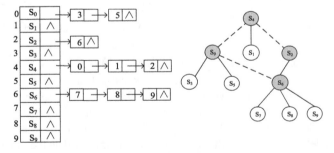

Fig. 3. (a) The physical structure of MST (b) The logic structure of MST

S_4 is the root node. S_6, S_0, S_2 are the potential PP nodes. S_1, S_3, S_5, S_7, S_8, S_9 are the leaf nodes.

It's easy known that MS can through visiting S_6, S_2, S_0 and S_4 to gather the whole sector sensed data. Then we set S_6, S_2, S_0, and S_4 as PPs like the gray nodes in Fig. 3b. On one hand, the trajectory of MS can be optimized by TSP algorithm. On the other hand, when MS stays at PP, the leaf nodes deliver data to MS through single hop to realize the energy consumption minimum.

Algorithm 2 S-PPA: The strategy of selecting PP and TSP algorithm

Input: T_{node} **&** T_{edge} Vt_i respect the sensors in sector i , $Path \{S_i\}$ stores the visiting order;

Output: the set of PP $S = \{P_1, P_2, ..., P_k\}$ and the trajectory of each MS;

1: u = start sensor;

2: Vis is the set to store the sensors which had been visited, Vis = u;

3: **while** Vis $\neq$ Vt_i **do**

4:    **if** $E_{u,v} \in T_{edge}$ && $v \notin Vis$ **then**

5:       Vis = {Vis $\cup$ v}

6:       **if** $v.degree > 1$ **then**

7:          $P_{MS_i} = \{P_{MS_i} \cup v\}$

8:       **end if**

9:    **end if**

10: **end while**

11: **while** the set *Path* not include all the sensor in P_{MS_i} **do**

12:    $next\ PP = S_u \xrightarrow{Min\ dis_{k,w}} S_w$

13:    $Path = \{Path \cup S_w\}$ and start sensor = w;

14: **end while**

4.4 SSA: Multiple-MS Scheduling Algorithm

From the above stages, we have designed an initial trajectory of MS in each sector. As we known, employing mobile sinks in WSNs can balance the load of sensors to prolong network lifetime. However, due to limited speed of MS, this method always has a high latency for data collection. In this stage, we make a multiple mobile sinks schedule scheme to ensure the delivery time $T_{MS_i} \leq T_{spe}$ and minimize energy consumption of network. In the initial phase, all sensors deliver data through single hop like white nodes in Fig. 4a.The gray nodes are PPs. Then we calculate collection time T_{MS_i} by formula (6). If T_{MS_i} is greater than T_{spe}, the algorithm would execute the schedule strategy. As shown in Fig. 4a, the orders of dotted arrows represent the order that PP becomes general sensor until just one PP is left. The strategy can be concluded that the PP who has less child nodes becomes general sensor node earlier.

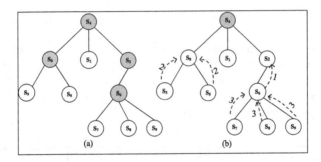

Fig. 4. The schedule of multiple mobile sinks

Algorithm 3 SSA: Multiple-MS Scheduling Algorithm

Input: the latency requirement T_{spe}, the actual delivery time
   $\{T_{MS_1}, T_{MS_2}, T_{MS_3}, ..., T_{MS_M}\}$, the set of PP, $\phi = \{PP_1, PP_2, ..., PP_w\}$;
Output: the route tree in each sector;
1: **for** i from 1 to the number of mobile sinks M ;
2:   **while** $T_{MS_i} > T_{spe}$ **do**
3:     PP$_s$=Min(PP$_1$.degree, PP$_2$.degree,..., PP$_w$.degree);
4:     $\phi = \phi - PP_s$
5:     $T_{MS_i} = Tsp(\phi)$;
6:   **end while**
7: **end for**

---

5   Analyses

Assuming that sensor coverage area is a rectangle ($L{\times}H$) and the number of MSs is M. The following properties of MMSA algorithm have been proved.

Property 1: The trajectory length of each MS L_{tsp} is smaller than $(1 + \frac{\pi}{M}) \times \sqrt{L^2 + H^2}$.

Proof: The sensor coverage area is a rectangle $L*H$ and its circumscribed circle is shown in Fig. 5. The circle radius is $R = \frac{\sqrt{L^2 + H^2}}{2}$. Then the circle is divided into M sectors equally and the central angle of each sector is $\theta = \frac{2\pi}{M}$. The arc of each sector is $\tau = \theta * R$. The maximum path of MS is $Dist_L = 2 * R + \tau$. Consequently, $L_{tsp} \leq (1 + \frac{\pi}{M}) \sqrt{L^2 + H^2}$.

Property 2: The time complexity of MMSA in the worst case is $O(n^3)$, where n is the number of sensors.

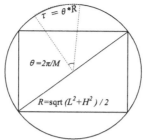

R: radius θ: degree τ: arc length

Fig. 5. M sectors in circumscribed circle of coverage area

Proof: The MMSA can be divided into three stages. In the first stage, the coverage area is divided into M sectors and time complexity of this stage is $O(1)$. In the second stage, MST is generated by Prim algorithm in M sectors and the complexity of each sector is $O(n^2)$, denoted by $M*O(n^2)$. When M is equal to n, the complexity is $O(n^3)$. In the last stage, the complexity of nearest neighbor heuristics TSP is $O(n^2)$. Consequently, the time complexity of MMSA in the worst case is $O(n^3)$.

Property 3: For the general value of T_{spe}, the delivery time T_{net} is smaller than T_{spe}. For the extreme value of T_{spe}, the delivery time T_{net} is minimized.

Proof: Assume sensors $S = \{\mu_1 \cup \mu_2 \cup \ldots \cup \mu_M\}$, where $\mu_i (1 \leq i \leq M)$ represents the set of sensors in sector δ_i. Each $\vartheta_i \in \mu_i$ is a set of the polling points and $\gamma_i = \mu_i - \vartheta_i$ is set of left sensors in δ_i which send sensory data to MS through hops. Based on the delay model in formula (6), the situation can be analyzed as follow in Fig. 4a. Where $\gamma_i * C = \sum_{j=1}^{s} C$, $h_j = 1 (j = 1, 2, \ldots, N)$ and L_{tsp} is the total distance to visit all PPs in ϑ_i, and we assume that MS can upload data to Cloud when MS is moving. Therefore, the delivery time of MS can be shown as formula (7).

$$T_{MS_i} = \frac{\gamma_i * C}{D} + \gamma_i * t + Max\left(\frac{L_{tsp}}{V}, \frac{\gamma_i * C}{Q}\right) \tag{7}$$

However, in this occasion, due to the limited speed of MS, the move time may occupy integral part of delivery time. Consequently, removing the sensors in ϑ_i and adding it to γ_i can reduce length of route that MS has to travel until $T_{MS_i} \leq T$. Furthermore, with the decreasing of ϑ_i and the increasing of γ_i, each MS stays at fixed sensor like the static sink and another sensors in γ_i send data to MS through multiple hop such as Fig. 4b, $L_{tsp} = 0$. Therefore, in the general value of limited T_{spe}, the network delivery time $Max\{T_{MS_1}, T_{MS_2}, \ldots, T_{MS_M}\}$ can meet the requirement. Even though the value of delay requirement is extreme small, our proposed algorithm can minimize the delivery time. It can be concluded in math description as follows, where T_{ideal} represents the ideal delivery time of network.

(1) If $T_{spe} \gg T_{ideal}$, $\begin{cases} \frac{\gamma_i * C}{D} + \gamma_i * t + Max(\frac{L_{tsp}}{V}, \frac{\gamma_i * C}{Q}) \le T_{spe} \\ h_j = 1 \end{cases}$

(2) If $T_{spe} \approx T_{ideal}$,

$$\begin{cases} \frac{\gamma_i * C}{D} + \gamma_i * t + Max(\frac{L_{tsp}}{V}, \frac{\gamma_i * C}{Q}) \\ h_j = 1 \end{cases} \le T_{spe} \&\& T_{spe} \le \begin{cases} \frac{\gamma_i * C}{D} + \frac{\gamma_i * C}{Q} + \sum_{j=1}^{\gamma_i} h_j * t \\ \gamma_1 = \gamma_2 = \ldots = \gamma_M \end{cases}$$

(3) If $T_{spe} \le T_{ideal}$, $\begin{cases} \frac{\gamma_i * C}{D} + \frac{\gamma_i * C}{Q} + \sum_{j=1}^{\gamma_i} h_j * t \approx T_{ideal} \\ \gamma_1 = \gamma_2 = \ldots = \gamma_M \end{cases}$

6   Evaluations

6.1   Experimental Environment Setting

We consider a wireless sensor network consisting of 100 sensors deployed in a 100 m × 100 m rectangle region. The data generating rate of each sensor is 5 byte/s. The transmission range of each sensor is 30 m and its initial energy capacity is 30 J. Energy consuming rate of sensor node of transmitting is 6×10^{-7} (J/bit) and receiving is 3×10^{-7} (J/bit). The speed of the mobile sink is 3 m/s. The data uploading rate from the mobile sink to Cloud is 5 byte/s. In the general case, there are 5 mobile sinks deployed in the WSNs.

To evaluate the effectiveness of proposed algorithm, we also implement two existing algorithms, EMMS [20] and SG-MIP [21] as benchmarks. The delivery delay T_{ms} is the max delivery time among all mobile sinks. The energy consumption represents the max energy consumption among all sensors. The energy consumption of each sensor is calculated based on the energy model in [22].

6.2   Performance Test

Figure 6 demonstrates the delivery delay and energy consumption under the scenarios with different number of sensors. As shown in Fig. 6a, when the number of sensor increases from 100 to 500, the delivery delay shows a rising trend. Due to the stringent deadline, when T_{spe} is smaller than 400 s, the delay requirement cannot be guaranteed. As the T_{spe} increases, our algorithm performs well on different number of sensors, which fitly proofs the third property of MSSA. Figure 6b shows the energy consumption for data collection. No matter the value of latency requirement is, as the number of sensors increases, the energy consumption decreases gradually since more sensors can deliver data to MS through the less hops. Moreover, the lower value of latency requirement is, the higher energy consumption is. This is because the number of PPs will be cut down to shorten the travel time of MS, which means more sensors will deliver data via multiple hops.

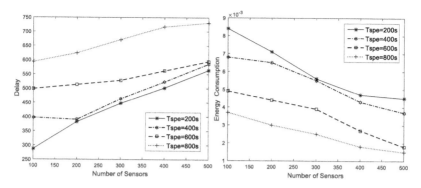

Fig. 6. (a) Number of sensors vs. delay (b) Number of sensor vs. energy consumption

We now evaluate the algorithms on delay. As shown in Fig. 7a, with the increase of the number of sensors, our proposed algorithm MMSA achieves the best performance among these three algorithms. Specifically, the delay achieved by SG-MIP is about twice than that of out algorithm. When the number of sensors is 250, the delay generated by EMMS is extreme high. In Fig. 7b, when the number of MSs increases, all algorithms perform better, but MMSA performs the best.

We now evaluate the effectiveness of algorithm on energy consumption and network lifetime. In Fig. 8a, the energy consumption achieved by EMMS stays steady due to single hop transmission of all the sensors. Beyond that, the energy consumption in MMSA and SG-MIP decrease when the number of MS is added, and MMSA realize the lower energy consumption. Figure 8b shows the trend of network lifetime with the variance of number of MS. As more MSs are employed in WSNs, the lifetime becomes longer. This is because sensors have more opportunities to communicate with MS directly. In contrast, the lifetime achieved by SG-MIP is shorter than our algorithm.

From the above figures, we can conclude that the MMSA we proposed performs well on uploading the data from WSNs to Cloud within the limited latency, meanwhile, the energy consumption is reduced as well.

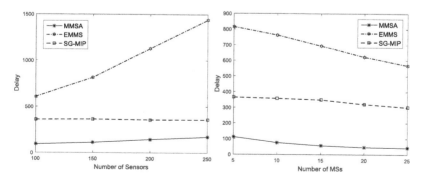

Fig. 7. (a) Number of sensor vs. delay (b) Number of MSs vs. delay

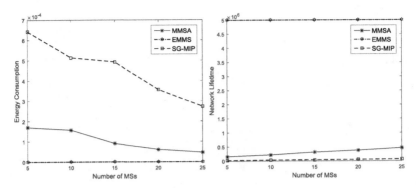

Fig. 8. (a) Number of MS vs. energy consumption (b) Number of MS on network lifetime

7 Conclusion

Due to the weak communication ability of WSNs, how to upload the sensed data to the Cloud within the limited time becomes a bottleneck of sensor-cloud system. In this paper, we have studied the data collection problem from WSNs to Cloud with multiple mobile sinks and formulated it as a constrained optimization problem. We designed MMSA algorithm for the problem with several provable properties. The performance of the proposed method is validated through simulations. Simulation results demonstrate that the proposed algorithm can reduce the delivery delay and energy consumption significantly.

Acknowledgments. Above work was supported in part by grants from the National Natural Science Foundation (NSF) of China under Grant Nos. 61572206 and the Natural Science Foundation of Fujian Province of China (Nos. 2014J01240 and 2016J01302) and Information Technology Integration and Innovation Alliance of Internet and Industry Pilot Project: Internet+ Distributed Photovoltaic Power Generation Monitoring and Operation Platform and the Foster Project for Graduate Student in Research and Innovation of Huaqiao University (No. 1511414005).

References

1. Cammarano, A., Spenza, D., Petrioli, C.: Energy-harvesting WSNs for structural health monitoring of underground train tunnels. In: Computer Communications Workshops (INFOCOM WKSHPS), pp. 75–76. IEEE (2013)
2. Harrison, D.C., Seah, W.K., Rayudu, R.: Rare event detection and propagation in wireless sensor networks. ACM Comput. Surv. (CSUR) **48**(4), 58–81 (2016)
3. Gupta A., Mukherjee N.: Implementation of virtual sensors for building a sensor-cloud environment. In: 2016 8th International Conference on Communication Systems and Networks (COMSNETS), pp. 1–8. IEEE (2016)
4. Guezguez, M.J., Rekhis, S., Boudriga, N.: A sensor cloud architecture for healthcare applications. In: Proceedings of the 31st Annual ACM Symposium on Applied Computing, pp. 612–617. ACM (2016)

5. Zhang, J., Long, J., Zhao, G., Zhang, H.: Minimized delay with reliability guaranteed by using variable width tiered structure routing in WSNs. Int. J. Distrib. Sensor Netw. **2015**(4), 1–12 (2015)

6. Kim, D., Uma, R., Abay, B.H., Wu, W., Wang, W., Tokuta, A.O.: Minimum latency multiple data mule trajectory planning in wireless sensor networks. IEEE Trans. Mob. Comput. **13**(4), 838–851 (2014)

7. Zhao, M., Yang, Y., Wang, C.: Mobile data gathering with load balanced clustering and dual data uploading in wireless sensor networks. IEEE Trans. Mob. Comput. **14**(4), 770–785 (2015)

8. Wang, T., Peng, Z., Wang, C., Wang, C., Cai, Y.Q., Chen, Y.H., Tian, H., Liang, J.B., Zhong, B.N.: Extracting target detection knowledge based on spatiotemporal information in wireless sensor networks. Int. J. Distrib. Sensor Netw. **2016**(1), 1–11 (2016)

9. Wang, T., Peng, Z., Chen, Y., Cai, Y.Q., Tian, H.: Continuous tracking for mobile targets with mobility nodes in WSNs. In: 2014 International Conference on Smart Computing (SMARTCOMP), pp. 261–268. IEEE (2014)

10. Wang, T., Jia, W., Wang, G., Guo, M.: Hole avoiding in advance routing with hole recovery mechanism in wireless sensor networks. Adhoc Sensor Wirel. Netw. **16**(1), 191–213 (2012)

11. Jose, D.V., Sadashivappa, G.: A novel scheme for energy enhancement in wireless sensor networks. In: 2015 International Conference on Computation of Power, Energy Information and Communication (ICCPEIC), pp. 0104–0109. IEEE (2015)

12. Tunca, C., Isik, S., Donmez, M.Y., Ersoy, C.: Ring routing: An energy-efficient routing protocol for wireless sensor networks with a mobile sink. IEEE Trans. Mob. Comput. **14**(9), 1947–1960 (2015)

13. Arquam, M., Gupta, C., Amjad, M.: Delay constrained routing algorithm for WSN with mobile sink. In: 2014 IEEE 17th International Conference on Computational Science and Engineering (CSE), pp. 1449–1454. IEEE (2014)

14. Hou, G., Wu, X., Huang, C., Xu, Z.: A new efficient path design algorithm for wireless sensor networks with a mobile sink. In: 2015 27th Chinese Control and Decision Conference (CCDC), pp. 5972–5977. IEEE (2015)

15. Hu, Y.F., Ding, Y.S., Ren, L.H., Hao, K.R., Han, H.: An endocrine cooperative particle swarm optimization algorithm for routing recovery problem of wireless sensor networks with multiple mobile sinks. Inf. Sci. **300**(10), 100–113 (2015)

16. Madhumathy, P., Sivakumar, D.: Enabling energy efficient sensory data collection using multiple mobile sink. Communications **11**(10), 29–37 (2014). China

17. Krishnan, A.M., Kumar, P.G.: An effective clustering approach with data aggregation using multiple mobile sinks for heterogeneous WSN. Wirel. Pers. Commun. **2015**(1), 1–12 (2015)

18. Di, F.M., Das, S.K., Anastasi, G.: Data collection in wireless sensor networks with mobile elements: a survey. ACM Trans. Sensor Netw. (TOSN) **8**(1), 1–31 (2011)

19. Wichmann, A., Korkmaz, T.: Smooth path construction and adjustment for multiple mobile sinks in wireless sensor networks. Comput. Commun. **72**(1), 93–106 (2015)

20. Shi, J., Wei, X., Zhu, W.: An efficient algorithm for energy management in wireless sensor networks via employing multiple mobile sinks. Int. J. Distrib. Sensor Netw. **2016**(9), 1–9 (2016)

21. Wang, J., Zhang, Y., Cheng, Z., Zhu, X.: EMIP: energy-efficient itinerary planning for multiple mobile agents in wireless sensor network. Telecommun. Syst. **62**(1), 93–100 (2015)

22. Zhu, C., Leung, V., Yang, L.T., Shu, L.: Collaborative location-based sleep scheduling for wireless sensor networks integrated with mobile cloud computing. IEEE Trans. Comput. **64**(7), 1844–1856 (2015)

Selecting Contract-Oriented Skyline Services for Service Composition

Haifang Wang, Pengfei Liu, Zhongjie Wang, and Xiaofei Xu$^{(\boxtimes)}$

School of Computer Science and Technology,
Harbin Institute of Technology, Harbin 150001, China
{wanghaifang, andy_lpf, rainy, xiaofei}@hit.edu.cn

Abstract. Facing massive services with different non-functional properties, obtaining the optimal composite service consumes considerable time. In order to reduce the search space and shorten the time of looking for the approximately optimal composite service, several methods based on skyline have been raised. However, these methods mainly focus on Quality of Service (QoS), which cannot describe non-functional properties adequately. Thus, service contracts are widely researched to make up for the deficiencies of QoS. Therefore, how to define the skyline services based on QoS and service contracts is becoming a critical challenge. To attach this issue, this paper proposes contract-oriented skyline services, including non-personalized skyline services and personalized skyline services. In addition, we discuss the natures of personalized skyline services. Besides, to deal with excessive skyline services, a method based on hierarchical clustering is presented, which contributes to the algorithm for contract-oriented service composition. Eventually, the verification experiments have been conducted, which illustrate the effectiveness of our methods.

Keywords: Service contract · Customer expectations · Service composition · Skyline services · Quality of service

1 Introduction

Nowadays customers' demands become so diversified and personalized that single service cannot meet the needs of customers. As a result, a mass of coarse-grained composite services are generated by mashup technology in both business and IT levels. How to acquire an optimal composite service that maximizes the overall utility value and satisfies global constraints has been a critical issue. Therefore, massive researchers have concerned service composition problems and achieved good results.

Zeng et al. [1, 2] focus on dynamic and quality-driven selection of services. Global planning is used to find the optimal service components for the composition. They adopt the mixed linear programming techniques to find the optimal selection of component services, which can meet the customers' needs in theory. And using linear programming to solve the global optimization problem has become a classic method of service composition. Similar to this approach, in [3], the authors extend the linear programming model to contain local constraints. Linear programming methods are

© Springer International Publishing AG 2016
G. Wang et al. (Eds.): APSCC 2016, LNCS 10065, pp. 144–158, 2016.
DOI: 10.1007/978-3-319-49178-3_11

quite effective for small-scale problem, but have poor scalability due to the exponential time complexity of the applied search algorithms [4].

However, facing an increasing number of services with the same functional and different non-functional properties in the market, it is time-consuming to achieve the optimal service composition, based on the number of subtasks comprising the service process and the number of alternative services for each subtask [5]. Here, integer programming algorithm cannot be adaptive. To acquire an appropriate composite service effectively and quickly, heuristic algorithms have been widely used to efficiently find an approximately optimal solution [6], including the Genetic Algorithm [7], the artificial bee colony algorithm [8], etc. Besides, several researchers observe that those services that belong to the skyline [9] have more contributions to the service composition. Therefore, in order to reduce the search space, the service selection method based on skyline has been raised. And several efficient algorithms have been proposed for skyline computation [10]. However, because of the distributions of QoS, the scale of skyline services may still be large. The literature [5] presents a method for further reducing the search space by examining only subsets of the candidate services.

Nevertheless, most researches pay more attentions to the optimization of service composition based on QoS(Quality of Service) [11] which cannot adequately describe the personalized customer's demand as well as the characteristics of the service offered by the broker. Therefore, service contracts have been introduced to make up for the deficiencies of QoS in [12], where we have built novel formal models for atomic and composite service contract. Based on the previous work, in this paper, we define the contract-oriented skyline service model and propose a new method to resolve the excessive skyline services. Besides, a novel algorithm to solve the contract-oriented service composition problem efficiently has been presented. Eventually, several experiments have been conducted, which illustrate the effectiveness of our methods.

The main contributions of this paper can be summarized as follow:

- We define two types of contract-oriented skyline services for service composition, including non-personalized skyline services and personalized skyline services.
- We discuss the natures of these two types of contract-oriented skyline services.
- We use a method based on hierarchical clustering to address the problem that arises when the amount of skyline services is quite large.
- We propose a novel algorithm to solve the contract-oriented service composition.

The remainder of the paper is organized as follows. Section 2 presents the contract-based service composition. Section 3 introduces contract-oriented skyline services and its natures. Section 4 describes the representative contract-oriented skyline services. Section 5 discusses the verification experiments. Finally, Sects. 6 offers some concluding remarks and overviews the future work.

2 Contract-Based Service Composition

2.1 Service Contract

In our previous work [12], we extend QoS by introducing the service contract, which contains three types of terms, including (1) numeric terms (i.e., traditional qos, e.g., *response time, reliability, price*), (2) non-numeric enumeration type terms (e.g., *payment method, service coverage, information offering method*), (3) non-numeric 0-1 type terms (e.g., *certification, payment security*). We employ the vector $V_s = \{v_1(s),\ldots, v_k(s), \ldots, v_r(s)\}$ to represent the values of the contract terms of service s, which are published by the service provider or the broker.

The global contract term values of a composite service are determined by the corresponding contract term values of its component services and the composition structures (e.g., sequence, parallel and selective structures). The service contract composition is performed by applying composition rules [12] on comparable contractual terms available in the compatible contracts. The values vector of contract terms of a composite service $CS = \{s_1,\ldots,s_i,\ldots,s_n\}$ is defined as $V_{CS} = \{v_1(CS), \ldots, v_k(CS), \ldots, v_r(CS)\}$, $1 \leq k \leq r$, in which $v_k(CS)$ is the aggregated value of the k-th contract term $term_k$ (CS) and $v_k(CS)$ can be computed by aggregating the corresponding values of the component services using composition rules.

2.2   Customer Expectations and Utility Function of Composite Service

We assume that the customer proposes one or more constraints on the aggregated values of contract terms of the requested composite service. These constraints are regarded as global expectations of contract terms, which are denoted by a vector $E = \{E_1,\ldots,E_k,\ldots, E_r\}$, $1 \leq k \leq r$, E_k represents the expectation of the k-th global contract term.

Given an abstract service process $SP = \{A_1,\ldots, A_i, \ldots, A_n\}$ constituted of n activities and a set of directed flows between activities and a vector of one customer's global expectations $E = \{E_1,\ldots, E_k,\ldots, E_r\}$, a feasible solution for service composition expressed as $CS = \{s_1,\ldots,s_i,\ldots,s_n\}$ consists of exactly one service selected from the corresponding candidate service set of each activity in the SP, and its aggregated values of contract terms satisfy the customer expectations of contract, i.e., $v_k(CS)$ is not worse than E_k, $\forall k \in [1, r]$.

For a given composite service $CS = \{s_1,\ldots,s_i,\ldots,s_n\}$, we can get its composite contract. We use the degree of the composite contract satisfying customer's expectations to measure the *utility* of CS. The larger the degree, the higher the *utility* of CS, in other words, the CS with higher *utility* is better. The *utility* computation of CS needs to scale the aggregated contract attributes' values to define a uniform measurement of the multi-dimensional service qualities, which is independent of their units and ranges.

Different contract terms correspond to different scaling criterions. For numeric contract terms, the value of each term is unified into a value belonging [0, 1]. For negative numeric terms (e.g., *Price, Time*), values are scaled according to formula (1). For positive numeric terms (e.g., *Reliability*), values are unified based on formula (2).

$$V'_k(CS) = \begin{cases} \frac{v_k^{\max}(CS) - v_k(CS)}{v_k^{\max}(CS) - v_k^{\min}(CS)}, & v_k^{\max}(CS) \neq v_k^{\min}(CS) \\ 1, & v_k^{\max}(CS) = v_k^{\min}(CS) \end{cases} \tag{1}$$

$$V_k'(CS) = \begin{cases} \frac{v_k(CS) - v_k^{\min}(CS)}{v_k^{\max}(CS) - v_k^{\min}(CS)}, & v_k^{\max}(CS) \neq v_k^{\min}(CS) \\ 1, & v_k^{\max}(CS) = v_k^{\min}(CS) \end{cases} \tag{2}$$

In addition, those non-numeric contract terms should be quantified firstly. Here, we discuss how to quantize these non-numeric contract terms. For an enumerated type contract term $term_k$, when customer raises expectation on it, he can state preferences for its different values, denoted by $Favor\,(term_k) \in [0, 1]$. Then the quantization method is based on formula (3).

$$V_k'(CS) = Favor(term_k(CS)) \tag{3}$$

For instance, assuming that $term_k = payment\ method$, the customer puts forward expectation and offers preferences on $payment\ method$ of CS, i.e., $E_k = \{Favor\ (Apple\ Pay) = 1,\ Favor\ (WeChat\ Pay) = 0.9,\ Favor\ (AliPay) = 0.8,\ Favor\ (others) = 0\}$. IF $term_k(CS) = AliPay$, then $V_k'(CS) = Favor(AliPay) = 0.8$.

If $term_k$ is the 0-1 type term whose value is either equal or not equal to E_k, the quantization method is according to formula (4).

$$V_k'(CS) = \begin{cases} 1, & term_k(CS) = E_k \\ 0, & term_k(CS) \neq E_k \end{cases} \tag{4}$$

Now the overall *utility* of a composite service CS is computed by formula (5).

$$U(CS) = \sum_{k=1}^{r} (V_k'(CS) \cdot w_k) \tag{5}$$

where $w_k \in [0, 1]$ and $\sum_{k=1}^{r} w_k = 1$. w_k represents the weight of $term_k$, which represents customer's priorities.

3   Contract-Oriend Skyline Services

3.1   Contract-Oriented Non-personalized Skyline Services

Several researchers have proved that those services belonging to the skyline [9] contribute more for the service composition. Thus, in this paper, we propose contract-oriented skyline services. First, we define skyline services without considering customer expectations, which is called contract-oriented non-personalized skyline services. In other words, whether one candidate service is skyline service has no relation to customer expectations, but depends on the corresponding candidate service set.

Definition 1 (*Contract-based Dominate*). Given a candidate service set S, two services $x, y \in S$, are characterized by a set of attributes T, i.e., various contract terms. x dominate y can be denoted as $x \prec y$, only if x is as good as or better than y in all attributes of T and better in at least one attribute, i.e., $x \prec y \Leftrightarrow \forall k \in [1, |T|]$: $term_k(x)$ is *BetterThan* or as good as $term_k(y)$ and $\exists k \in [1,|T|]$: $term_k(x)$ is *BetterThan* $term_k(y)$. The *BetterThan* relations of different types of contract terms can be defined as follow.

- Numeric terms

  (1) $term_k$ is negative attribute (e.g., *price, response time*):
      $term_k(x)$ is *BetterThan* $term_k(y) \Leftrightarrow term_k(x) < term_k(y)$
  (2) $term_k$ is positive attribute(e.g., *reliability*):
      $term_k(x)$ is *BetterThan* $term_k(y) \Leftrightarrow term_k(x) > term_k(y)$

- Non-numeric terms

  (1) $term_k$ is enumerated type
      If there exists inclusion relation ($\supset$) between the values of $term_k(x)$ and $term_k(y)$, then $term_k(x)$ is *BetterThan* $term_k(y) \Leftrightarrow term_k(x) \supset term_k(y)$.
      For instance, if $term_k$ is *payment method*, and $term_k(x) = exactlyAll\{Apple\ Pay, WeChat\ Pay, AliPay, Cash\}$, $term_k(y) = exactlyAll\{Apple\ Pay, AliPay\}$, thus $term_k(x)$ is *BetterThan* $term_k(y)$.
  (2) $term_k$ is 0-1 type
      For the 0-1 type term, the term value is either equal or not equal to the customer expectation. Due to no considering the customer expectations, we cannot judge which one of the two is better than the other, which means that we cannot define the *BetterThan* relation for the 0-1 type term.

Definition 2 (*Non-Personalized Skyline Services*). For a set of candidate services S, the non-personalized skyline services of S denoted as *NPSLs* contain these services that are not dominated by any other services. i.e., $NPSL_S = \{x \in S | \neg \exists y \in S: y \prec x\}$.

3.2   Contract-Oriented Personalized Skyline Services

Based on the definitions of the general non-personalized skyline services in Sect. 3.1, the personalized skyline services for individuals considering customer expectations are defined. For the diverse customer expectations, the *Contract-based Dominate* relation between x and y may be different, thus, we may get diverse skyline services. As a result, the definition of *Contract-based Dominate* has to be changed, which says that the definition of *BetterThan* relation should be altered as well.

Contract-based Dominate is still described as above, yet the *BetterThan* relation of different types of terms needs to be redefined by considering customer expectations.

- Numeric terms

  (1) $term_k$ is negative attribute (e.g., *price, response time*):
      $term_k(x)$ is *BetterThan* $term_k(y) \Leftrightarrow term_k(x) < term_k(y)$
  (2) $term_k$ is positive attribute (e.g., *reliability*):
      $term_k(x)$ is *BetterThan* $term_k(y) \Leftrightarrow term_k(x) > term_k(y)$

- Non-numeric terms

  (1) $term_k$ is enumerated type

  These non-numeric enumeration type terms cannot compare their value directly like the numeric qos. However, when a customer raises expectation on the $term_k$, he can state preferences order on different values of the $term_k$, denoted as $Favor\ (term_k)$.

  $term_k(x)$ is BetterThan $term_k(y) \Leftrightarrow Favor(term_k(x)) > Favor(term_k(y))$

  For instance, the customer puts forward expectation on *payment method*, i.e., $E_k = \{Apple\ Pay = 1,\ WeChat\ Pay = 0.9,\ AliPay = 0.8,\ other\ methods = 0\}$, therefore, $Favor\ (Apple\ Pay) > Favor(WeChat\ Pay) > Favor(AliPay)$. Then, $term_k(x) = Apple\ Pay,\ term_k(y) = AliPay$, which also indicates that $term_k(x)$ is BetterThan $term_k(y)$.

  Besides, combined with Sect. 3.1, the BetterThan relation of enumeration type terms can be summarized as follows:

  $term_k(x)$ is BetterThan $term_k(y)$ $\Leftrightarrow Favor(term_k(x)) > Favor(term_k(y))$ or $term_k(x) \supset term_k(y)$

  (2) $term_k$ is 0-1 type

  The term value is either equal or not equal to the customer expectation. Thus, the customer expectation should be the selecting standard of deciding whether one service is included in the skyline services. Suppose that $term_k(x) \neq term_k(x)$.

  $term_k(x)$ is BetterThan $term_k(y) \Leftrightarrow term_k(x) = E_k$

  The services that are not dominated by others and can satisfy the customer expectations will be selected as skyline services. The customer expectations E are proposed for the composite service, however some global expectations E_k can break into local expectation as $AE_k\_S_i$ for A_i in the SP. For instance, one customer expects that the composite service should have authoritative certification, which means that each activity A_i in the SP should have authoritative certification, then $AE_k\_S_i = E_k,\ \forall i \in [1,\ n]$.

Definition 3 (*Personalized Skyline Services*). For a set of candidate services S, the personalized skyline services of S denoted as *PSLs* are comprised of these services that are not dominated by any other services and satisfy the customer expectations. i.e., $PSL_S = \{x \in S | \neg \exists y \in S:\ y \prec x \&\& \forall term_k(x):\ term_k(x)$ is *as good as* or *BetterThan* $E_k\}$.

The numeric terms (qos) which can compare their values directly are relatively simple. Then, we assume that for a candidate service set S, each service is described by five non-numeric enumeration type terms, as illustrated in the toy example of Fig. 1. Each term corresponds to a coordinate axis, and the values on each coordinate axis are discrete, which are arranged in order of customers' preferences. Therefore, each service can be expressed as a pentagon in five-dimensional space with the coordinates of each pentagon corresponding to the values of the service in these five terms. In the coordinate space, if one pentagon is completely covered by another one, in other words, all the five terms of the former pentagon are better than the later pentagon, then the former dominates the later. As Fig. 1 shows, s_2 dominates s_1 and s_5 while s_2 do not dominates

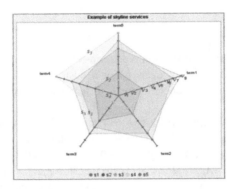

Fig. 1. A toy example of skyline services

s_3 and s_4. The pentagons corresponding to s_2, s_3 and s_4 cannot not be completely covered by any other pentagons, which means that s_2, s_3 and s_4 are not dominated by any other services. If their five terms all satisfy the customer expectations $AE_1\_S \sim AE_5\_S$, then they are personalized skyline services.

3.3 The Effect of Customer Expectations on Personalized Skyline Services

• The effect of customer expectations on the distribution of service contract terms

The scale of the skyline services has a significant difference for each dataset, as it strongly depends on the distributions of the contract terms and correlations between the different contract terms. And customer expectations may affect the distributions of some service contract terms. The numeric terms (qos) can compare their values directly, and their distributions are not affected by customer expectations. Therefore, we simply think about non-numeric enumeration type terms whose distributions are different for diverse customer expectations. Suppose that each service is described by five non-numeric enumeration type contract terms shown in Fig. 2. According to customer's preferences, the five terms may present different distributions in terms of different service sets. Besides, there may be anchoring relationship between the five terms. As a result, different service sets can form three types presented in Fig. 2.

We employ service contracts to redefine the three types of service sets proposed in [5] in the five-dimensional space:

(1) *Independent dataset*. The values of the five contract terms are independent to each other.
(2) *Correlated dataset*. A service that is good in one term is also good in the other terms.
(3) *Anti-correlated dataset*. There is a clear trade-off between the five terms, in other words, one term is bad while the other is good.

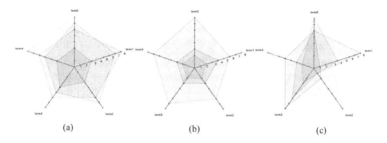

Fig. 2. Skyline of different service set types

For instance, customers would propose their own preferences on two terms, namely *payment method* and *buy way*. The preference order of *buy way* is *JingDong > TaoBao > VipShop*, thus the preference order of *payment method* is *WeChat Pay > Alipay > Online Banking*. Given that there exist anchoring relations between the two parameters in the candidate service set *S*, if *buy way = Jingdong*, then *payment method = WeChat Pay*; if *buy way = TaoBao*, then *payment method = Alipay*; if *buy way = VipShop*, then *payment method = Online Banking*. Thus, *S* belongs to the type (b).

If the preference orders are opposite to the above, then *S* is the type(c). If the values of the two parameters are independent to each other, then *S* belongs to the type (a).

The scale of skyline services is relatively small for correlated datasets, and it is large for anti-correlated datasets, meanwhile it is medium for independent datasets.

- The effect of strict degree level of customer expectations on the scale of personalized skyline services

Since numeric terms (qos) can compare their values barely, the strict degree level of them is relatively simple. Thus, we pay more attention to the non-numeric enumeration type terms. Strict degree level of them can be defined as follows: There are n values among all the values of $term_k$, which cannot satisfy the customer expectation, then, the strict degree level of $term_k$ is n. The customer expectation has different strict degree level for each term. If customer expectations ware too strict or outdated to adapt to the dynamic service market, the scale of skyline services would be quite small. For instance, customer A expects the term *information offering method* to be *Fetion* which has been outdated, however, there are no services whose *information providing method* is *Fetion* in the market.

Usually, customer expectations are fairly loose, which can be satisfied by most services from the candidate service set *S*, and result in plenty of skyline services. The overfull skyline services have not reduced the solution space significantly and cannot improve time complexity of service compositions. To further discuss the effect, several verification experiments have been conducted in Sect. 5.

- The effect of the term number in customer expectations on the scale of personalized skyline services

In addition, the scale of skyline services can be affected by the term number in customer expectations, namely the number of dimensions considered to distinguish skyline services. For instance, a service s_6 dominated originally by others is better than others in some new added dimensions, thus s_6 is no longer dominated by any other services and become a skyline service. Therefore, the scale of skyline services will increase. How will the term number in customer expectations affect the scale of skyline services? This will further studied in the experiments.

4 Representative Contract-Oriented Skyline Services

4.1 Representative Contract-Oriented Skyline Services

Based on the analysis above, it is easy to know that if the skyline services are massive, they cannot be applied practically. Therefore, several methods devoting to acquire smaller scale of representative services [5] have been proposed. Motivated by the ideas, we aim at selecting a set of representative contract-oriented personalized skyline services, which will be regarded as input of the BIP model. In order to reduce the scale of skyline services, a method for selecting representative contract-oriented skyline services has been proposed. The main difficulty is how to identify the representative skyline services that best represent all the various contract attributes and will contribute more to find an optimal solution that satisfies the customer expectations and also has a high *utility* score.

```
Algorithm 1. KReps-medoids(PSL, K)
Input: a set of personalized skyline services PSL, clusters`
number K
Output: K representative skyline services
1: K←Random(PSL)
2: while the cluster any one point belongs to is changed
3:    For each service in PSL
4:      For each cluster medoids
5:        calculate Similar(service, medoids)
6:      end for
7:      assign the service to the nearest cluster
8:    end for
9:    recalculate the medoids of each cluster
10: select a representative service with the best utility from
each cluster
11: output K representative skyline services
```

To address this challenge, a novel method based on hierarchical clustering [5] has been proposed. Here, we propose the similar method to select representative contract-oriented skyline services considering customer expectations, which is called *KReps-medoids*. The algorithm that is based on the well-known *k-medoids* algorithm divides contract-oriented skyline services into *k* clusters and selects one representative service with the best *utility* value from each cluster, which is presented in Algorithm 1.

For two given service *x* and *y*, the similarity between them is combination of the similarity of numeric terms and the similarity of non-numeric terms, which is expressed as formula (6). Suppose that the number of numeric terms is *q*, and the number of non-numeric terms is *t*. First, we measure the similarity between *x* and *y* in aspect of numeric terms (qos) which is based on Euclidean distance and calculated according to formula (7).

$$Similar(x, y) = \left(Similar_{terms} + Similar_{qos}\right)/2, \in [0, 1] \tag{6}$$

$$Similar_{qos} = 1 - \sqrt{\sum_{k=1}^{q} (V_k'(x) - V_k'(y))^2/q} \tag{7}$$

where $similar_{qos} \in [0,1]$. $V_k'(x)$ and $V_k'(y)$ are scaled values based on formula (1), (2).

Then we measure the similarity between *x* and *y* in terms of non-numeric terms, which is the text similarity in fact. Thus, it can be calculated based on cosine similarity. Through two steps of words segmentation and word frequency vector acquirement, we can calculate the cosine of two services' word frequency vectors $X(X_1,\ldots, X_i\ldots, X_{|terms|})$ and $Y(Y_1,\ldots, Y_i,\ldots, Y_{|terms|})$ according to formula (8).

$$\cos(\theta) = \frac{\sum_{i=1}^{|terms|} (X_i \times Y_i)}{\sqrt{\sum_{i=1}^{|terms|} (X_i)^2} \times \sqrt{\sum_{i=1}^{|terms|} (Y_i)^2}} \tag{8}$$

Where $|terms|$ is the number of all present non-numeric terms values of *x* and *y*, X_i stands for the frequency of the *i*-th word in service *x*. Thus, the similarity between *x* and *y* on non-numeric terms is $Similar_{terms} = \cos(\theta), \in [0,1]$.

4.2   Contract-Oriented Service Composition Based on *RepSkyline_BIP*

Based on the work in Algorithm 1, a tree structure of representatives can be built according to Algorithm 2. The tree structure is shown as an example in Fig. 3. The root and intermediate nodes of the tree correspond to the selected representatives of the clusters, while every leaf node corresponds to one of the skyline services in *PSL*.

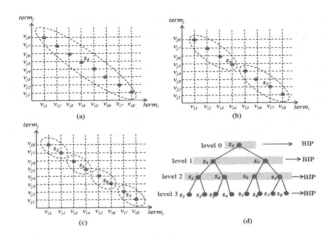

Fig. 3. Hierarchical clustering and tree structure of representatives

```
Algorithm 2. BuildTreeofRepresentatives(PSL)
Input: a set of skyline services PSL
Output: Tree_RepSkyline, a tree of representatives with service
s as a root
1: s←maxU(sᵢ), sᵢ∈PSL
2: CPLS←K-medoids(PSL,2)
3: For i=1 to 2
4:    If(CPLS[i].size>2) then
5:        C←BuildTreeofRepresentatives(CPLS[i])
6:    Else
7:        C←CPLS[i]
8:    End if
9:    s.addChildren(C)
10: end for
```

```
Algorithm 3: RepSkyline_BIP(Tree_RepSkyline)
Input: a tree of representatives with service s as a root
Output: CS = {s₁,…,sᵢ,…, sₙ}
1: LN ←number of total levels of Tree_RepSkyline
2: i = 0
3: CS = BIP←Tree_RepSkyline.root
3: while CS!= null &&i< LN
4:    i←i+1
5:    CS = BIP←Tree_RepSkyline.levelᵢ
```

Algorithm 2 takes the personalized skyline services set *PSL* of the candidate service set *S* as input and returns a binary tree built by representative services. It starts by the root s, which has the maximum *utility* value in *PSL*. Then, *PSL* is clustered into two sub-clusters *CPLS*[0] and *CPLS*[1], and then the method adds the representatives of the two sub-clusters to the child list of the root s. Repeat the process for each sub-cluster until no further clustering is available.

Based on the preparations above, a service composition algorithm named *RepSkyline_BIP* is proposed, which is shown in Algorithm 3. When it comes to a service composition request, we start to search the tree from its root, which means that we first take into account only the top representative service of each cluster (e.g. service s_4 for class S in the example). If we cannot get the composition solution based on the given representative skyline services, the next level of the tree will be searched, taking two representatives from each cluster (s_4 and s_7 for the candidate service set S in the example). Repeat this process until a solution is found or until reaching the lowest level of the tree, which contains all the skyline services. In the latter situation, the algorithm can guarantee that a solution will be found (if there exist one solution for the service composition problem), and it must be optimal.

5 Experiments

In this section, several experiments have been conducted to measure the efficiencies of our methods based on the execution time of these algorithms, including the effect of customer expectations on the scale of personalized skyline services and the experimental efficiency based on the number of services and contract constraints.

5.1 Experimental Settings

In the experiments, the service process contains 5 activities corresponding to 5 different candidate service set respectively. And each set consists of 1000 services, which are expressed as service contract vectors defined in Sect. 2.1. For simplicity, here we only consider negative attributes (positive attributes have been transformed into negative by multiplying their values by -1). Here, 5 service contract terms are considered, including *Time, Price, Reliability, Payment method*, and *Certification*, which are employed to build service contract vectors and customer expectation vectors.

Based on the analysis above, it is obvious that we try to find an optimal composite solution which maximizes the overall *utility* value and satisfy the specified customer expectations. Therefore, the customer expectations have been raised, which have been expressed as the following vector:

$$E = \{ <12\,\text{h}, <180\$, >0.9, \{Favor(Apple\,Pay) = 1, Favor(WeChat\,Pay) = 0.9,$$
$$Favor(AliPay) = 0.8, Favor(others) = 0\}, \text{Yes}\}.$$

In other words, the customer expects that *Time* is less than 12 h; *Price* is less than 180\$; *Reliability* is more than 0.9; his favor order of *Payment method* is Apple Pay = 1, *WeChat Pay* = 0.9, *AliPay* = 0.8, *others* = 0; he defines the value of *Certification* as *Yes*. Besides, he offers the weight vector $w = \{0.25, 0.2, 0.2, 0.2, 0.15\}$.

In addition, in the experiments we focus on the sequential structure, since other structures may be reduced or transformed into the sequential model [12].

The Algorithm 2 has been realized with Java. And the library function *bintprog* (*f,a,b,aeq,beq*) of *matlab* is adopted to contribute to the generated Binary Integer Programming (BIP) models. The input of the algorithm includes the customer expectation vector E and the weight vector w. Based on the following three methods, the contract-based service composition problem can be resolved. Besides, their efficiencies can be compared, which will illustrate the good performance of our methods.

> *Global_BIP*: it is the standard global optimization method with all candidate services represented in the BIP model.
> *Sykline_BIP*: this method is similar to the BIP method, except that only skyline services are taken into account.
> *RepSkyline_BIP*: it uses representative skyline services shown in Algorithm 3.

5.2   The Effect of the Strict Degree Level and the Term Number of Customer Expectations on the Scale of Personalized Skyline Services

To research the effect of the strict degree level and the term number of customer expectations on the scale of skyline services, firstly, we keep the number of terms fixed and change the strict degree level of each term to acquire the amount of skyline services, whose experimental results are shown in Fig. 4(a). Then, we simply change the term number of customer expectations and obtain the results shown in Fig. 4(b). In Fig. 4, "the scale of skyline services" is abbreviated to "*SSS*".

From Fig. 4(a), it is obvious that the scale of skyline services reduces significantly while the strict degree level increasing, especially for the term *Certification*. Based on the Fig. 4(b), it is easy to know that the scale of skyline services rises gradually as the term number increases.

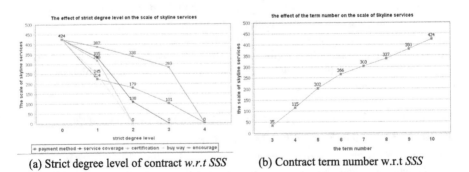

(a) Strict degree level of contract *w.r.t SSS*   (b) Contract term number w.r.t *SSS*

Fig. 4. Variations of the scale of skyline services based on contract constraints

5.3   Experimental Efficiency Based on the Number of Services and the Number of Contract Constraints

We measure the average execution time of the above three methods (*Global_BIP*, *Skyline_BIP* and *RepSkyline_BIP*) by solving the same contract-based service composition problem, varying the number of candidate services from 100 to 1000 for each candidate service set. The experimental results are presented in Fig. 5(a).

Compared with the performance of the three methods in Fig. 5(a), we can observe that the execution time of the *Global_BIP* method climes up significantly with the number of services increasing, while the execution time of the *Skyline_BIP* method grows up gradually. Meanwhile, the execution time of the *RepSkyline_BIP* method has barely grown with little influence by the number of services, which illustrates the effectiveness of our method adequately.

Based on the analysis above, it is easy to know the number of customer contract constraints may affect the performance of all methods. Thus, we measure the efficiency of the three methods by changing the number of contract constraints. Here, the fixed number of services in each candidate service set is 500, and the number of contract constraints varies from 1 to 5. The experimental results are shown in Fig. 5(b).

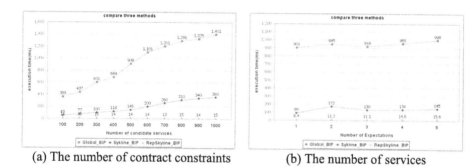

(a) The number of contract constraints   (b) The number of services

Fig. 5.   The experimental efficiency based on the number of services and contract constraints

From Fig. 5(b), it is easy to observe that the efficiencies of the three methods have not changed much with the variations of the number of contract constraints. Besides, it is obvious that the *RepSkyline_BIP* method outperforms other methods, which is followed by the *Skyline_BIP* method followed by the *Gloval_BIP* method. The experiments have provided more evidences to prove the effectiveness of our methods.

6   Conclusion

In this paper, we have defined contract-based dominance relations between services to select the candidates for contract-oriented service composition. Besides, two types of contract-oriented skyline services have been proposed, including non-personalized skyline services and personalized skyline services. For the latter, we consider customer's expectations. In addition, the natures of these two types of contract-oriented skyline services have been discussed. Then, a method based on hierarchical clustering is presented to deal with the excessive skyline services, based on which the algorithm for contract-oriented service composition has been put forward. Eventually, the verification experiments have been conducted compared with another two methods to solve the contract-based service composition problem, which illustrate the effectiveness of the methods proposed in our paper. Meanwhile, our experiments show that the performance of the skyline-based methods is affected by the scale of the candidate service set and the number of the contract constraints.

Acknowledgments. This work is supported by the Natural Science Foundation of China (No. 61272187, 61472106).

References

1. Zeng, L., Benatallah, B., Dumas, M., Kalagnanam, J., Sheng, Q.Z.: Quality driven web services composition. In: WWW, pp. 411–421 (2003)
2. Zeng, L., Benatallah, B., Ngu, A.H.H., Dumas, M., Kalagnanam, J., Chang, H.: Qos-aware middleware for web services composition. IEEE Trans. Softw. Eng. **30**(5), 311–327 (2004)
3. Ardagna, D., Pernici, B.: Adaptive service composition in flexible processes. IEEE Trans. Softw. Eng. **33**(6), 369–384 (2007)
4. Maros, I.: Computational Techniques of the Simplex Method. Springer, (2003)
5. Alrifai, M., Skoutas, D., Risse, T.: Selecting skyline services for QoS-based web service composition, p. 11 (2010)
6. Yu, T., Zhang, Y., Lin, K.-J.: Efficient algorithms for web services selection with end-to-end qos constraints. ACM Trans. Web **1**(1), 1–26 (2007)
7. Canfora, G., Di Penta, M., Esposito, R.: An approach for QoS-aware service composition based on genetic algorithms. In: Proceedings of the conference on Genetic and evolutionary computation, pp. 1069–1075. ACM (2005)
8. He, J., Chen, L., Wang, X., et al.: Web service composition optimization based on improved artificial bee colony algorithm. J. Netw. **8**(9), 2143–2149 (2013)
9. Borzsonyi, S., Kossmann, D., Stocker, K.: The skyline operator. In: ICDE, pp. 421–430 (2001)
10. Papadias, D., Tao, Y., Fu, G., Seeger, B.: Progressive skyline computation in database systems. ACM Trans. Database Syst. **30**(1), 41–82 (2005)
11. Cardoso, J., Sheth, A.P., Miller, J.A., Arnold, J., Kochut, K.: Quality of service for workflows and web service processes. J. Web Sem. **1**(3), 281–308 (2004)
12. Liu, P., Ma, C., Wang, Z., Comerio, M., Xu, X., Batini, C.: Generating global contract for composite services. In: ICSS (2015)

Passenger Prediction in Shared Accounts for Flight Service Recommendation

Yafeng Zhao[1], Jian Cao[1(✉)], and Yudong Tan[2]

[1] Department of Computer Science and Engineering,
Shanghai Jiao Tong University, Shanghai 200240, China
`zyfgs2012@163.com, cao-jian@sjtu.edu.cn`
[2] Air Ticketing B.U., Ctrip.com International, Ltd., Shanghai 200335, China
`ydtan@Ctrip.com`

Abstract. Personalized recommendation is needed for online flight booking service because it is a difficult task for a traveller to select the flight when the number of available flights is large. Traditionally, we can recommend flights to a user based on his historical orders collected from his account. However, people sometimes book tickets for his family members, friends or colleagues through his account. In this case, the preferences of other travellers should also be considered. Unfortunately, before placing the order, people will not provide passengers' information. Therefore, we propose a probabilistic method for passenger prediction based on historical behaviors and contextual knowledge. We then experimentally demonstrate its effectiveness on a real dataset. The result shows that our method outperforms conventional methods.

Keywords: Recommender system · Dirichlet distribution · Probabilistic topic model · Shared account · Gibbs sampling

1 Introduction

Recent years, with the rapid development of online travel agencies, there are more and more passengers booking flights through online travel service providers. Typically, an user may input his departure city, arrival city and departure time, then he will get a list of candidate flights. In general, there are dozens of flights within a list. We perform a search for flights from Beijing to Hong Kong at a website, there are total 156 matchable flights. The website only provides simple sorting strategies such as departure time, arrival time or price. Thus, it may take quite a long time for users to find the appropriate one. Therefore, a recommender system is necessary for better user experiences.

Essentially, a recommender system is used for generating a personalized ranking on a set of items [15]. Typical recommender systems assume that the preference model of an individual can be learned from each account. However, for online flight booking, it is quite common that a user books flights for his family members, friends or colleagues. Obviously, every passenger has his own preferences, which should be considered in flight recommendation. Unfortunately,

G. Wang et al. (Eds.): APSCC 2016, LNCS 10065, pp. 159–172, 2016.
DOI: 10.1007/978-3-319-49178-3_12

before placing the order, people will not provide passengers' information. Therefore, if we want to improve the accuracy of recommendation, we have to predict who are going to fly.

To predict who is using the account to place orders is regarded as the shared account problem. Some approaches have been proposed to extract implicit user information within an account. For example, in [2,3] the nonlinear latent factorization is applied to extract user information. However, these methods only rely on the analysis of relationships between products and users [1,5], and context information (such as time information, the query input) that can help differentiate users is neglected. Besides, current methods always assume an account represents a fixed number of implicit users, which are not always true in reality. Moreover, so far, the experiments have only been evaluated on artificial composite datasets.

The flight booking service providers can acquire passenger's personal information after he has submitted the order. Thus, our goal is to predict distributions of passengers in current session based on historical behaviors and contextual information so that we can make flight recommendations in a more precise way. To achieve this target, we adopt the probabilistic author-topic model to analyze passengers' behaviors. We regard all historical orders in an account as the corpus, all passengers appearing in the account as authors and orders together with context information as documents.

In experiment Section, we apply our method to a real flight order dataset. And the result shows that our method has higher identification accuracy and a better recommendation accuracy.

This paper has following contributions:

1. We provide a probabilistic passenger identification method for online flight booking service.
2. We apply the passenger prediction results to flight recommendation.
3. We evaluate our approach on a real flight order dataset, and the result shows that our approach can effectively improve the recommendation accuracy.

Paper organization. The rest of paper is structured as follows. We introduce related work in Sect. 2. In Sect. 3, we define the problem and describe the model. Besides, we also discuss how to do parameter inference. In Sect. 4, we propose a preference-based flight ticket recommendation approach, which also plays a role as a baseline method at evaluation stage. In Sect. 5, we introduce the experiment dataset, evaluation metrics, the experimental results of passenger prediction and flight recommendation. Finally, we conclude the paper in Sect. 6.

2   Related Work

Content based Recommendation. In online travel service industry such as airline tickets or hotel booking, the item (for example, an air ticket, a hotel booking order) information is usually highly structured, however, this information is quite mutable. Content-based recommender systems [7,9] are appropriate for highly structured items. The method needs proper representations of the attributes of items and the profile of user interests, then it tries to match the profile of user's interests with attributes of items.

Flight Ticket Recommendation. There is little work focusing on personalized flight recommendations. Many online flight booking agencies provide sorting and filtering strategies to improve users' experiences, such as sorting by price and filtering by airline etc. These methods do make sense in helping users find appropriate flights within less time. However, they can not provide personalized recommendations. Flight recommendation mainly bases on implicit feedback [8], which suffers from problems of data noises and lack of negative feedbacks. In 2004, Lorcan Coyle [17] proposed a Personal Travel Assistant(PTA). PTA is based on case-based reasoning, which takes users' historical orders as cases and recommends the most similar candidate flights to users' queries.

Probabilistic Topic Models. Topic models [10–12] are proposed for automated extraction of useful semantic information from corpus data. The main step is extracting latent factors from the corpus, named topics, which are commonly probabilistic distributions over words. Topic models provide a completely unsupervised approach to extract topics, thus requiring no document labels and no initialization. Besides, each document may consist of multiple topics and it can be considered as probabilistic distributions over topics. The author-topic model is a generative model that extends LDA to include authorship information for document modeling. In our approach, the topic model is innovatively applied to identify users.

Shared Account Recommendation. Some work aims at addressing the challenge of identifying users who share a single account. A top-N recommendation for shared account was proposed by Koen et al. [1]. It is an item-based top-N collaborative filtering recommender system on binary and positive-only feedbacks. Another method proposed by Santosh et al. [3] models users in an account with a much richer representation. It uses a nonlinear matrix factorization methods for predicting the recommendation score. Yutaka et al. [5] introduced an approach for modeling multiple users' purchase in a single account using an extended pLSA model. All above methods are applied in scenario that users' personal information can not be acquired explicitly.

3   Passenger Prediction Model

In this Section, we propose a generic model for predicting the probabilistic distribution of passengers, which can be used for recommendation. Figure 1 shows an overview of the recommendation process. At first, a dataset of orders is saved into the database, in which each account may correspond to several passengers. We use this dataset to train the passenger prediction model as well as to extract passengers' preferences. Before a recommendation process starts, we calculate

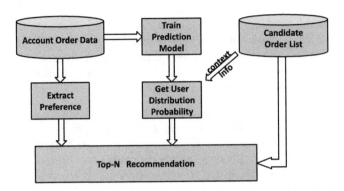

Fig. 1. Overview of flight recommendation based on passenger prediction

passenger distribution probability applying trained model and contextual information of current session. At the final step, we generate a ranked candidate list as the recommendation result based on passenger prediction and passengers' preference information.

3.1   Model Description and Notation

Topic models are widely used in recommender systems. For example, in pLSA model [16], a topic is a multinomial distribution over items and it represents a latent feature. An account is a multinomial distribution over topics and it can represent the preferences of an account. Each purchase can be regarded a sample that selects a topic z from account a, and takes an item from topic z.

When the topic model is applied to flight recommendation, there are some challenges. Firstly, the concepts behind flight tickets are quite difficult to be modeled. Conventional items only have static features, which means that the contents of an item are less likely to change in the future. For flight tickets, however, the price changes frequently even for the same flight number and class. Since the price factor plays a significant role in users' choice, we can not consider the tickets with different prices as different items. Secondly, the amount of tickets for a flight is limited, which leads to a very sparse user-item matrix so that we can not use a collaborative-filtering like method directly. Fortunately, the decisive factors of a flight ticket are quite fixed, such as airline, takeoff time, price and class etc. The number of alternatives for each factor is also quite limited.

Our notations are summarized in Table 1.

In author-topic model [13], a predefined vocabulary is generated containing discrete alternatives and intervals of all selected factors. We treat every order as a bag of words, thus deduce each order to a vector of word counts. Each passenger is associated with a multinomial distribution over topics and each topic is associated with a multinomial distribution over entries.

For an account M, we generate the observed passenger list P. We denote passengers' distribution over topics by a $|P| \times K$ matrix Θ. The multinomial distribution can be generated from Dirichlet prior distribution with hyper-parameter α.

Table 1. Notation

M	Number of accounts within the dataset
V	Number of words in vocabulary
O	Orders in an account
P	Passengers in an account
P_i	Passengers for order O_i
F	Selected factors
V	Size of vocabulary
K	Number of topics

Topics' distribution over words is denoted by a $K \times \sum_{i=1}^{|F|} |F_i|$ matrix Φ, also, distribution can be generated with hyper-parameter β. Generally, these hyper-parameters needn't be estimated, here, we fix α and β at 50/K and 0.01 respectively.

To generate a word, we need draw two latent variables, a passenger and a topic, respectively. First we draw a passenger uniformly from P, a topic Z from Θ_A and a word w from Φ_Z. The following process describes the generative model mathematically.

1. For each passenger $p = 1, \ldots, |P|$ draw $\Theta_p \sim Dirichlet(\alpha)$
2. For each topic $t = 1, \ldots, K$ draw $\Phi_t \sim Dirichlet(\beta)$
3. For each order $o = 1, \ldots, O$
   (a) given passengers P
   (b) For each word $i = 1, \ldots, N_o$
      (i) draw a passenger $X_{oi} \sim Uniform(P)$
      (ii) draw a topic $Z_{oi} \sim Discrete(\theta_{X_{oi}})$
      (iii) draw a word $w_{oi} \sim Discrete(\phi_{Z_{oi}})$

3.2 Parameter Inference

As mentioned above, the author-topic model includes two sets of unknown parameters, the P passenger-topic distributions θ and the K topic-word distributions ϕ. Generic EM algorithms are likely to face local maximum and computational inefficiency problems. Here we utilize Gibbs sampling [14] because it does not explicitly estimate parameters, instead, it evaluates posteriori distribution just based on drawn passengers X and topics Z. Thus it is simple for Dirichlet priors.

We can obtain the probability of every word $\mathbf{w}_o$ generated in each order, conditioned on Θ and Φ is:

$$P(\mathbf{w}_o|\Theta, \Phi, P) = \prod_{i=1}^{N_o} P(w_{oi}|\Theta, \Phi, \mathbf{p}_o)$$

$$= \prod_{i=1}^{N_o} \sum_{p=1}^{|P|} \sum_{t=1}^{K} P(w_{oi}|z_{oi} = t, \Phi) P(z_{oi} = t|x_{oi} = p, \Theta) P(x_{oi} = p|\mathbf{p}_o) \quad (1)$$

$$= \prod_{i=1}^{N_o} \frac{1}{|P|} \sum_{p \in p_o} \sum_{t=1}^{K} \phi_{w_{oi}t} \theta_{tp}$$

With the above generative model, $P(x_{oi} = p|\mathbf{p}_o)$ is assumed to be a uniform distribution over passenger list P. Each topic is drawn independently conditioned on Θ and p_o, and each word is drawn independently conditioned on Φ and z. Equation 1 can be applied as the likelihood of all orders in a single account. If we treat Θ and Φ as random variables, our target is to estimate the Maximum A Posteriori for the generative model.

In Gibbs sampling process, in order to draw a sample from the joint distribution $P(\mathbf{z}, \mathbf{x}|\alpha, \beta)$, we need to draw the assignment of passenger x_{di} and topic z_{di} for a word w_{di} conditioned on previous assignments for all other words in the whole corpus. In general, every word in the corpus should be sampled, and the batch sampling process will be performed for several iterations. A Markov chain [14] can be constructed that converges to the posteriori distribution on passenger x and topic z. $p(\Theta, \Phi|\mathbf{z}, \mathbf{x}, \alpha, \beta)$ can be calculated in terms of the property that Dirichlet distribution is conjugate to the multinomial distribution. Each pair of passenger and topic (z_i, x_i) is drawn according to the following equation:

$$P(x_{oi} = p, z_{oi} = t|w_{oi} = w, \mathbf{z}_{-oi}, \mathbf{x}_{-oi}, \mathbf{w}_{-oi}, \alpha, \beta, p_o)$$

$$\propto \frac{C_{tp}^{TP} + \alpha}{\sum_{t'} C_{t'p}^{TP} + T\alpha} \frac{C_{wt}^{WT} + \beta}{\sum_{w'} C_{w't}^{WT} + W\beta} \quad (2)$$

Equation 2 represents the probability of assigning topic t and passenger p for i-th word in order o. C^{WT} is the word-topic matrix, and C_{wt} is the times that word w is assigned to topic t except for the current word. C^{TP} represents the topic-passenger matrix, and C_{tp} indicates the times that passenger p is assigned to topic t except for the current word w_{oi}. Moreover, W is the size of vocabulary, T represents the number of topics and P is the number of passengers. From the sampling metric, we can estimate the topic-word distribution and passenger-topic distribution:

$$\theta_{tp} = \frac{C_{tp}^{TP} + \alpha}{\sum_{t'} C_{t'p}^{TP} + T\alpha} \quad (3)$$

$$\phi_{wt} = \frac{C_{wt}^{WT} + \beta}{\sum_{w'} C_{w't}^{WT} + W\beta} \quad (4)$$

where θ_{tp} is the probability of drawing topic t conditioned on passenger p and ϕ_{wt} is the probability of drawing word w conditioned on topic t. Thus in the process of parameter inference, we need to keep matrix C^{TP} and C^{WT}, besides, the sampled word-topic list T and sampled word-passenger list P should be updated after each sampling, where $T[o][i]$ represents the topic sampled for word i in order o and $P[o][i]$ represents the passenger sampled.

The algorithm performs in three steps, i.e., initialization, sampling and updating respectively. At the first step, we assign each word in the corpus with random passengers and topics. For every sampling operation, a word in corpus is chosen, the probability of topic distribution and passenger distribution is calculated conditioned on the rest words in corpus by applying Eq. 2, with these two probabilities, we can sample a new topic and passenger for the current word. After several batch iterations, the passenger-topic matrix Θ and topic-word matrix Φ can be updated by applying Eqs. 3 and 4. So the computational efficiency is the number of words multiplies number of topics, passengers and iteration times.

3.3   Passenger Prediction

Given the passenger topic probability matrix Θ and topic-word probability matrix Φ. We can predict passengers for an anonymous order. It's essentially a classification of an unlabeled order [6]. We perform the classification by choosing the passenger whose appearance can maximize the probability $p(p|o_n)$, represented in the following equation:

$$p(x = p|o_n, \Theta, \Phi) \propto p(p) \prod_{w \in o_n} \sum_t p(t|w)p(w|t, p) \qquad (5)$$

where $p(p) = |O_p|/|O|$, $|O_p|$ is the number of orders participated by passenger p. $p(w|t, p) = p(t|p) \times p(w|t)$ since the process of drawing topic from a passenger and drawing a word from a topic are independent of each other. $p(t|w)$ represents the probability that word w is assigned to topic t, which can be computed by: $\frac{C^{\bar{w}t}}{\sum_w C^{w't}}$.

In conclusion, the passenger prediction task can be partitioned into two steps. For the first step, a set of decisive factors are extracted based on domain knowledge to generate a vocabulary. And the parameter Θ and Φ are trained through several batches of Gibbs sampling. In the second step, passengers of an anonymous order can be predicted by applying Eq. 5. Algorithm 1 describes the predicting process mathematically.

4   The Preference-Based Recommendation Approach

There is little existing work aiming at providing flight recommendation. In this Section, we propose a user preference-based recommendation approach. In Sect. 5, we evaluate this method against some ranking strategies, such as price rank etc., to demonstrate that this method has a better accuracy. Then, we will apply the passenger prediction results to improve recommendation accuracy further.

Algorithm 1. passengerPrediction

Input: Account history order list O.
   Predefined discrete factor list F
   A test anonymous order o
Output: User's prediction list Pl
 1: List $Pl \leftarrow \emptyset$;
 2: stat word vector **W** for all orders;
 3: Model $M \leftarrow trainATM(W)$;
 4: calculate user's probability by Eq. 5;
 5: **for all** user : P **do**
 6:    **if** $user.probability > \frac{1}{|P|}$ **then**
 7:       $Pl.append(user, probability)$;
 8:    **end if**
 9: **end for**
10: normalize Pl;
11: **return** Pl;

4.1   Factor Selection and Frequency Statistic

A flight ticket contains a set of attributes. These attributes may be either discrete or continuous variables. We divide continuous attribute into a list of intervals, for example, takeoff time can be divided into morning, noon, afternoon, night etc. Thus, any factor can be represented by finite alternatives. Then, we count the distribution of alternatives from a user's historical orders to analyze user's preference on corresponding factor. In a word, the preference model can be described as a union of vectors, a vector indicates one factor and an element within one vector represents the frequency of corresponding alternative which the user has chosen.

We can also represent a candidate flight ticket as a vector, where each element is the corresponding alternative of each factor. So, for every ticket in candidate list, we compare the vector with users' preference model and get a score for every factor based on the frequency. We can sum up score of every factor to get a total score for that item, and rank all candidates according to the total score. We can then generate a top-N recommendation.

4.2   Weight of Factors

Since users may care different factors, we introduce personalized weight vector for each user. We estimate how much a user focuses on a factor through the information entropy, as mentioned in [18]. We believe that if a user focuses on a factor, his behavior will be more concentrated. The entropy H is a measure to describe the uncertainty for discrete random variable X and probability mass function $P(X)$. Here is the mathematical representation for entropy.

$$H(X) = E[-lnP(X)] = -\sum_{i-1}^{n} P(x_i)log_b P(X_i) \tag{6}$$

Algorithm 2. Preference-Based-Recommendation

Input: User's ID u

    User's history order list O

    Candidate item list C

Output: Ranked candidate list R

1: Define a factor list F;

2: $P \leftarrow extractUserPref(O, F)$;

3: initialize W by entropy;

4: $R \leftarrow \emptyset$;

5: **for all** $c : C$ **do**

6:     append $(c, weightedScore(c, W))$ to R;

7: **end for**

8: sort R by score;

9: **return** R;

The value b is the base of logarithm, and is usually 2. The entropy of every factor can be calculated and initialized as the weight value after normalization.

The preference based recommendation algorithm is described as Algorithm 2. First extracting a user's preference P and initializing weighted list W through entropy. Items in candidate list are ranked based on inner product of W and corresponding value of factor.

5 Experiments

In the following subsections, we introduce datasets and evaluation metrics. Then we evaluate the performance of passenger prediction and passenger prediction based recommendation respectively.

5.1 Dataset

In our experiments, we use a real flight ticket dataset, consisting of all submitted orders for two years. An order contains account id and all passengers' id. We use desensitized passenger id to distinguish individuals from each other. In our experiment, we select active users whose amount of historical orders reaches a threshold, thus passengers' preferences can be extracted with more confidence. In addition, many researches [4,5] on shared account recommendation generate an artificial dataset by composing single accounts' data. We also generate an artificial dataset combining single passengers' data from two different accounts. The overviews of these two datasets and the meta data of orders are summarized in Tables 2 and 3.

5.2 Settings and Evaluation Metrics

We take the latest order of a user as the test data and the rest ones as the training data. The test data also plays a role of providing contextual information for user prediction.

Table 2. Datasets

	# accounts	# passengers	# orders
Real	4632	7034	38907
Artificial	1604	3208	29759

Table 3. Meta data

Travel info	Airline, departure city, arrival city, departure airport, arrival airport, takeoff time, arrival time
Content info	Order time, login ip, geo location, other trace log information
Individual info	Account-id, passenger-id, age, gender
Order info	Flight number, price, craft type, class, rescheduling/canceling policy

One significant issue is that we can not know real candidates at the time when a user performs the search action. Fortunately, we can get an approximate set of candidates by collecting orders from all users in the dataset with the same order date, takeoff date, departure city and arrival city as the test order. In order to get a convincing evaluation result, we filter out test orders with the size of candidate list less than 20 and the average size of candidates is 45.

We apply two commonly used metrics MAP (Mean Average Precision) and top-N hit rate to evaluate the recommendation performance. The definition of MAP is described as follow:

$$MAP = \frac{\sum_{i=1}^{|M|} Acc(u_i)}{|M|} \tag{7}$$

$$Acc(u_i) = \begin{cases} 1 & \text{if N } = 1 \\ 1 - \frac{index-1}{N-1} & \text{if N } > 1 \end{cases} \tag{8}$$

$$top - N = \frac{\sum_{i=1}^{|M|} |top - N(u_i) \cap O_{u_i}|}{|M|} \tag{9}$$

where $|M|$ is the number of total test orders, $Acc(u_i)$ represents the accuracy of recommendation based on the rank percentages of test orders. The metric MAP is the average of each user's accuracy, and is a measurement for general performance. The top-N hit rate is the actual strategy for recommendation, we can stick up top-N candidates based on the ranked list. For each purchase, if top-N candidates hit the chosen order, we consider this recommendation has accuracy 1, else the accuracy is 0. We also calculate MAP for all accounts.

For passenger prediction, we propose the following metric to evaluate the accuracy:

$$Acc(u_i) = \frac{P' \cap A}{\sqrt{|P'| \times |A|}} \tag{10}$$

Since we treat every account as a corpus, a probabilistic distribution list is generated for all passengers contained in the account. At the first stage, we need to decide the passenger number for each test order. Assuming that there are total $|P|$ passengers in an account. So in average case, the probability of every passenger is $P_A = \frac{1}{|P|}$. We decide the passenger number by omitting passengers whose probability is not greater than P_A. We denote predicted passenger list as P', actual passenger list as A. Thus we can get the prediction accuracy by Eq. 10. The numerator is the number of hit passengers, the denominator is penalty item for the size of predicted passenger list and predicted passenger list.

5.3   Passenger Prediction

We train a probabilistic model for every account where topic number selected varying $5, 10, \ldots, 50$. We pick a test order for each account as a new document, then predict every passenger's probability of placing this order by Eq. 5. According to above evaluating metrics, the mean prediction accuracy rate of (a) real dataset and (b) artificial dataset is shown in Fig. 2. The left sub-figure is the evaluation result on the real dataset and the right one is on the artificial dataset. The figure's horizontal axis shows the number of trained topics and the vertical axis shows the prediction accuracy computed by applying above mentioned metrics. The Random method means assigning random probabilities to passengers, we also record 10 batch of random results as our approach does. For the artificial dataset, there are two passengers in every account and one passenger for every test order, so the accuracy of prediction is either 1.0 or 0. The results demonstrate that our model has a higher prediction precision than the random method on both datasets. Besides, when the topic number is 10 or 15, both datasets get the best performance while the performance goes down with the topic number increasing, which demonstrates that the size of corpus' vocabulary and number of words in each order also impact the optimal topic number. We will evaluate the recommendation performance with topic number fixed at 10.

5.4   Recommendation

After obtaining the predicted probabilistic distribution of passengers, we can extend preference based recommendation approach by extracting preferences of predicted passengers. If there are multiple predicted passengers for one test order, we generate a composite preference model that combines all involved passenger's preferences together.

We use MAP and top-N hit rate mentioned above to evaluate recommendation performance. We compare different recommendation approaches including preference based recommendation (shorted as Pre), transfered preference based

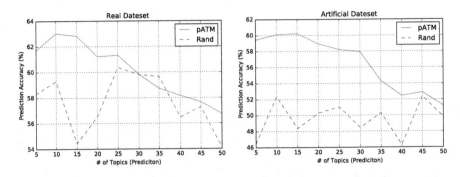

Fig. 2. MAP of user prediction

recommendation (tfPre), price rank (pRank), hot rank (hRank) and predicting preference based recommendation (pdPre). The transfered preference based method is the same as the previous one except it takes the difference between flight distribution of various air routes into consideration. This method groups training data by route, and evaluates similarity between routes by flight distribution on some attributes such as airline, class and price level. If a passenger isn't active on the target route, we transfer his preferences from most similar active routes with a transfer rate. In our experiment, the transfer rate is $\alpha = 0.5$. Price rank is a simple strategy that ranks candidates based on price in an ascending order. Hot rank is a strategy that ranks candidates according to the popularities, which is based on total order amount within a period of previous two weeks.

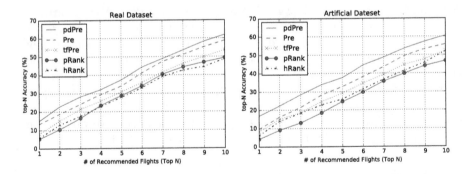

Fig. 3. Top-N accuracy of recommendation

Figure 3 shows recommendation accuracy on the real dataset and artificial dataset respectively. The figure's horizontal axis shows the number of top-N recommended flights. The accuracy increases linearly with the growth of recommended flights. Figure 4 shows MAP on two datasets. The results show that the baseline recommendation approach performs much better than price rank strategy. And content based recommendation combined with passenger prediction

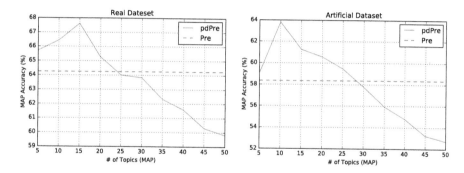

Fig. 4. MAP of recommendation

can achieve a higher accuracy than baseline method. We can also notice that the improvements on the artificial dataset is larger than on the real dataset. The reason may be that passengers in artificial dataset have more diversified preferences since they are randomly selected and composed.

6   Conclusion and Future Work

In this paper, we proposed a generic probabilistic model to predict passengers in a single flight booking account based on passengers' historical submitted orders. This model is appropriate for scenarios that individuals can not be explicitly identified before placing the order, such as online hotel booking. For specified contextual environment, we can make a prediction for passenger distribution. Then we integrate passenger prediction into recommendation process. For experiment evaluation, we propose a general preference based recommendation approach for implicit feedback, and verify the efficiency of proposed model on two datasets. The results suggest that both passenger prediction and recommendation approach achieve a higher accuracy.

In future work, we plan to do more research on how to determine the optimal amount of users in each session.

Acknowledgments. This work is partially supported by China National Science Foundation (Granted Number 61272438, 61472253), Research Funds of Science and Technology Commission of Shanghai Municipality (Granted Number 15411952502, 14511107702) and Cross Research Fund of Biomedical Engineering of Shanghai Jiaotong University (YG2015MS61).

References

1. Koen, V., Bart, G.: Top-N recommendation for shared accounts. In: Proceedings of ACM Conference on Recommender Systems, pp. 59–66 (2015)
2. Jason, W., Ron, J.: Nonlinear latent factorization by embedding multiple user interests. In: Proceedings of ACM Conference on Recommender Systems, pp. 65–68 (2013)

3. Santosh, K., George, K.: NLMF: nonlinear matrix factorization methods for Top-N recommender systems. In: International Conference on Data Mining Workshopp, pp. 167–174 (2014)

4. Amy, Z., Nadia, F., Stratis, I.: Guess who rated this movie: identifying users through subspace clustering. In: Proceedings of Conference on Uncertainty in Artificial Intelligence, pp. 944–953 (2012)

5. Yutaka, K., Tomoharu, I., Ko, F.: Modeling multiple users' purchase over a single account for collaborative filtering. In: Proceedings of International Conference on WISE, pp. 328–341 (2010)

6. Shanshan, F., Jian, C., Yuwen, C., Jing, Q.: A model for discovering unpopular research interests. In: Proceedings of International Conference KSEM, pp. 382–393 (2015)

7. Pasquale, L., Marco, G., Giovanni, S.: Content-based Recommender systems: state of the art and trends. In: Ricci, F., Rokach, L., Shapira, B., Kantor, P.B. (eds.) Recommender Systems Handbook, pp. 73–105. Springer, Heidelberg (2011)

8. Yan, S., Ping, Y.: Implicit feedback mining for recommendation. In: Proceedings of International Conference on Big Data Computing and Communication, pp. 373–385 (2015)

9. Deivendran, T., Shanmugasundaram, B.: Content based recommender systems. Int. J. Comput. Sci. Emerg. Technol. 382–393 (2011)

10. Dm, B., Ay, N., Mi, J.: Guess who rated this movie: identifying users through subspace clustering. J. Mach. Learn. Res. 993–1022 (2003)

11. Michal, R., Thomas, G., Mark, S., Padhraic, S.: The author-topic model for authors and documents. In: Proceedings of Conference on Uncertainty in Artificial Intelligence, pp. 487–494 (2012)

12. Mark, S., Padhraic, S., Michal, R., Thomas, G.: Probabilistic author topic models for information discovery. In: Proceedings of ACM SigKDD Conference Knowledge Discovery and Data Mining, pp. 306–315 (2004)

13. Rosen-Zvi, M., Thomas, G.: Learning author-topic models from text corpora. ACM Trans. Inf. Syst. **28**(1), 312–324 (2010)

14. Gregor, H.: Parameter estimation for text analysis. University of Leipzig (2009)

15. Lu, L., Matus, M.: Recommender systems. Hangzhou Normal University (2012)

16. Thomas, H.: Collaborative filtering via Gaussian probabilistic latent semantic analysis. In: Proceedings of International ACM Conference on Research and Development in Information Retrieval, pp. 259–266 (2004)

17. Lorcan, C.: Making personalised flight recommendations using implicit feedback. University of Dublin (2004)

18. Yang, F.: Personalized flight recommender. Shanghai Jiao Tong University (2016)

A Data Cleaning Method on Massive Spatio-Temporal Data

Weilong Ding[1,2(✉)] and Yaqi Cao[1,2]

[1] Data Engineering Institute, North China University of Technology,
Beijing 100144, China
dingweilong@ncut.edu.cn
[2] Beijing Key Laboratory on Integration and Analysis of Large-Scale
Stream Data, Beijing 100144, China

Abstract. In open conditions of Internet of Things, massive data would be rapidly accumulated from sensors in low quality. On huge size raw data, the correction for consistency is time-consuming and inaccurate to achieve, and the validation for legality is difficult to guarantee without prior knowledge. In this paper, time-based clustering and rule-based filtering for data cleaning is proposed on massive bus IC card data, which guarantees the consistency and legality among spatio-temporal attributes. Implemented through Hadoop MapReduce and evaluated on real data set, our method shows its efficiency and accuracy in extensive conditions.

Keywords: Data cleaning · Spatio-temporal data · Clustering · Filtering · Hadoop

1 Introduction

In the Internet of Things, massive data would be rapidly accumulated from sensors [1], which is the foundation for Big Data analysis. In Beijing until the end of 2015, more than 30 thousand buses on nearly one thousand lines have imported IC card readers, and 44 million IC cards have been released. It generates 15 thousand records with about 20 GB daily. The raw data from the open conditions is in low quality due to the variable sensor devices, network and storages, and impossible for directly usage. There are many kinds of errors in massive raw data, which makes it difficult to efficiently extract the valid records. Take the public transportation in Beijing for example again. About 5 % records of bus IC card data in 2013 contain errors: some misses the required attributes, some contains wrong timestamps, and some has the illegal interval between getting-on and getting-off timpstamp.

On massive data with typical spatio-temporal attributes, traditional data cleaning methods without extra prior knowledge would be time-consuming and inaccurate. That remains problems below to be solved. First, the consistency among records is hard to be corrected. For a record, its attributes may be inconsistent with that of others. In a record of bus IC card data, the date of getting-on is in 1990-01-01, but that of getting-off lie in 2015-05-31. It means records have inconsistent temporal attributes. However, this inconsistency cannot be corrected easily if there is no prior knowledge

G. Wang et al. (Eds.): APSCC 2016, LNCS 10065, pp. 173–182, 2016.
DOI: 10.1007/978-3-319-49178-3_13

about the real temporal range. Second, the legality of given records is hard to be validated. Because some records may be incomplete on the storage by whatever reasons, incomprehensible results would be deduced even on the consistent data. For example, for a passenger using a given IC card, it seems he takes 10 more hours on a bus if wrong timestamps are recorded. However, this illegality cannot be found at all if there is no prior knowledge about the validity. Additionally, the scalability of cleaning procedure on huge size data is not trivial either. For the metropolis as Beijing, larger data would be accumulated even faster in recent years. The traditional methods can do cleaning in parallel, but cannot scale linearly in performance due to the heavy IO among distributed machines.

In this paper, a data cleaning method on massive spatio-temporal data is proposed and includes these contributions. (1) The temporal range can be determined through time-based clustering without prior knowledge, which guarantees consistent timestamps. (2) The invalid records can be found through rule-based filtering, which guarantees legal spatio-temporal relationship. (3) Our method is implemented through Hadoop MapReduce, which shows the feasibility on real data through extensive experiments.

This paper is organized as follows. Section 2 shows the background including motivation and related works. Section 3 elaborates our method including time-based clustering and rule-based filtering. Section 4 quantitatively evaluates the performance and effects in various conditions. Section 5 summarizes the conclusion.

2   Background

2.1   Motivation

Our work originated from *Passenger Traffic Big Data Analysis Platform* in Beijing. The practical project is implemented with *eHualu*, one of the leader companies for smart cities and intelligent transportation in China. The goal here is to build public traffic system to relieve serious jams, improve air quality and develop coordinately with peripheral cities. eHualu had constructed the dispatch system for more than 30 new night-bus lines in 2014, and was eager to improve the service efficiency like reducing the departure intervals through the passenger traffic analysis the on bus IC card data. A record of bus IC card data as the unit contains 13 attributes as Table 1. Such a record is typical spatio-temporal data which contains three entity attributes, two temporal attributes and two spatial attribute-groups.

Through those multi-attributes, the passenger traffic can be analyzed in different perspectives. Big Data processing is required then, but the low data quality becomes the barrier for the further usage and user experience [2]. On the one hand, the timestamps among records are inconsistent. Raw data is organized as discrete files and no hints are about the covered temporal range. That makes it difficult to define the temporal correctness. For example, in a given data file, we cannot determine whether 2001-01-01 or 2015-05-31 is the factual date if both values appear in a record. On the other hand, the semantics is illegal of given records. The miss about records or attributes in a record are ordinary in the raw data. This agnostic of the integrity makes it difficult to illustrate the validity. For example, there may be a passenger using a card travelling on a bus so long without any getting-off behaviors when no factual traffic regulations or real conditions are considered. Additionally, parallel processing is focused in current methods but the heavy IO on GigaByte size data is main latency for data cleaning. That makes the method not scalable linearly when the data size grows. Therefore, a data cleaning method is required for massive spatio-temporal data. That is just our original motivation.

Table 1. The attributes in a record of bus IC card data.

Attribute	Notation	Type
card_ID	Identity of IC card	Entity
line_ID	Identity of bus line	
bus_ID	Identity of bus	
begin_time	Timestamp of getting-on	Time
end_time	Timestamp of getting-off	
from_station_ID	Identity of getting-on station	Space
from_station_name	Name of getting-on station	
from_station_longitude	Longitude of getting-on station	
from_station_latitude	Latitude of getting-on station	
to_station_ID	Identity of getting-off station	
to_station_name	Name of getting-off station	
to_station_longitude	Longitude of getting-off station	
to_station_latitude	Latitude of getting-off station	

2.2   Related Work

Data cleaning is the process of identifying unreasonable data and fixing possible errors [3] to improve data quality, which is important to keep the data consistency [4]. Generally, data cleaning includes multiple steps like defining error types, identifying errors and repairing data [5]. Here, we classify the related works in two perspectives as follows.

Identifying Error. The error of the raw data can be defined as several types including inconsistency, duplication, invalid and non-integrity. Correspondingly identifying error is the procedure to capture those violations according to predefined constraints [6]. Until now, so many technologies are applied to verify whether constraints were violated, like similarity join, clustering and parsing [5]. Traditionally, a violation may not explain which attributes are correct or wrong, but would guide dependable repair from those errors. Recently, the rule-based fixing [7] is proposed that can precisely identify the error during the validation when enough evidence is given. Nowadays, the sensory data with spatio-temporal attributes has been widely generated in Internet of Things, especially in some real-time scenarios [8]. However, the relationship among spatio-temporal attributes cannot be exploited in above technologies. In this paper our method focuses on temporal inconsistency error and spatio-temporal violation, which is urgent for further usage in practical requirements. A recent work [9] has concerned sensory data in wireless sensor network, but it only focuses on the error about redundant duplication.

Repairing Data. After errors were identified, repairing has to be done to correct the wrong records. Many heuristic methods are proposed based on functional dependency [10] or denial constraints [11]. Those works employ confidence values in repairing algorithms [12] to revise possible or missing attributes. In fact, the solution to repair data varies much in different domains [3], and requires consulting customers even in commodity cleaning system like NADEEF [13]. However, in public transportation domain, the business principle for data cleaning still lacks. In this paper, the rule to repair records for bus IC card data is employed, and is proved efficient and feasible in practice.

In brief, on massive spatio-temporal data, recent works still lack effective approaches to identify inconsistent errors and repair invalid records. Against the practical requirements of public transportation, we introduce our work through Hadoop MapReduce which is the de facto standard of parallel processing on massive data.

3   Data Cleaning on Massive Spatio-Temporal Data

3.1   Overview

We propose our data cleaning method as Fig. 1. The input here is multiple files containing massive raw data, and the output is one file with the clean data. The processing procedure includes two main steps, each of which can be implemented as a MapReduce job. The first step is time-based clustering. In this step, by once scanning the raw data, the most possible range of records' timestamp can be clustered by counting their appearances. After the temporal range is determined, the rule-based filtering in the second step would run. The spatio-temporal rules are defined to delete or modify the invalid records. That would be demonstrated in details next.

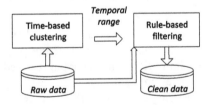

Fig. 1. The methodology

3.2   Time-Based Clustering

The raw data inevitably contains inconsistency especially in their temporal attributes. The temporal inconsistency cannot be determined easily on massive data if no prior

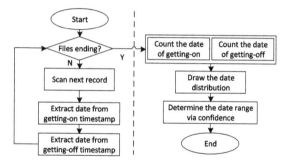

Fig. 2. The flow diagram of time-based clustering

knowledge exists. Here, take bus IC card data as an example, the procedure of time-based clustering is presented as Fig. 2.

The goal is to determine the factual date range of the raw data. An assumption here is that the singular values of timestamp, whether of getting-on or of getting-off, are far less than the correct ones. It is sound because in real world conditions, the count of such values is no more than 10 % compared with that of normal values. The procedure would be implemented as a MapReduce job, where the input is the raw data files and the output is the date distribution of two temporal attributes. The left part of Fig. 2 can be realized as a map task, and the right part as a reduce task. In the map task, each record is scanned once and its two timestamps are extracted. The intermediate key-value pair would be emitted to the reduce task, where the key is the date and the value is the composition of attribute name (0 for getting-on and 1 for getting-off) and a number one. In the reduce task, that intermediate key-value pairs would be gathered and counted by the key, which would generate the date distribution of the raw data for both attribute getting-on and getting-off. As the assumption above, we can found most dates, either of getting-on or of getting-off, lie in a certain interval. Therefore, the date range can be determined automatically by predefined confidence degree, or done manually. The confidence here is a threshold and implies the interval is considered as the factual one if the amount is the larger than it, and can be defined as 70 % ~ 80 % in practice.

3.3   Rule-Based Filtering

The illegal records are common in raw data and cannot be validated easily on massive data if no prior knowledge exists. After the consistent date range is determined in above step, the procedure of rule-based filtering on bus IC card is presented as Fig. 3.

The goal is to revise wrong records and collect the valid ones from the raw data. The procedure would be implemented as a MapReduce job without reduce task, where the input is the raw data files and the output is one clean date file. After scanned once, any record's timestamps (both getting-on and getting-off) are judged whether it is in the correct date range. If both are illegal, the record is considered as invalid one and not used further. If only one is illegal, the date of illegal date is substituted by that of the

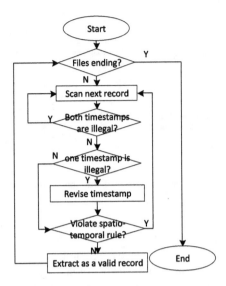

Fig. 3. The flow diagram of rule-based filtering

other legal one. Then the revised record would be judged whether it violates the spatio-temporal rule. If no violation, the record would be believed as the valid one and then written to the file of clean data.

The spatio-temporal rule is user-defined, and two key points are used here. (1) The timestamp of getting-on must be early than that of getting-off and their interval is no more than four hours. We considered these factors. According to Chinese traffic regulations, a driver cannot continue driving his vehicle more than four hours without a rest. Moreover, in the billing system of IC card in Beijing, a single trip cannot linger more than four hours. (2) The station of getting-on and getting-off must be different. It is possible that two successive stations in a record are presented as the same if the bus driver does not operates the IC reader timely. But such a record with the same stations is considered as invalid one because no hints would be deduced for passenger traffic analysis then.

4   Experiments and Evaluations

According to the requirements in Sect. 2.1, five virtual machines through Hadoop 1.0.4 are used to implement our method, each of which owns 4 cores CPU, 4 GB RAM and 1.2 TB storage with CentOS 6.6 x86_64 installed. Five Acer AR580 F2 rack servers were used via Citrix XenServer 6.2 for the virtualization in our private Cloud, each of which own 8 processors (Intel Xeon E5-4607 2.20 GHz), 48 GB RAM and 80 TB storage. As far as we know, no dedicated cleaning method exists for spatio-temporal data, which makes it impossible to compare with similar works. Instead, we evaluate the performance and effects in extensive conditions.

Raw data used here is the original bus IC card data which contains 25377417 records on 7349 buses of 233 lines. Like the description in Sect. 2.1, each record ought to contain 13 attributes depicting the behaviors of getting-on and getting-off (via attribute *begin_time, end_time, from_station_ID* and *to_station_ID*). In fact, two billing fashions for buses exist in Beijing due to IC card reader: one is charged by counts and a card is read only once when getting-on; the other is charged by distances and a card should be read twice when getting-on and getting-off. For convenience, all the data here was generated from the IC card readers in the latter type.

We had known the raw data generated in certain successive days, but did not know its exact temporal range in advance. Then the time-based clustering is used first and evaluated then.

Experiment 1. The whole raw data is used as the input of time-based clustering method. The temporal distribution drawn from the output is showed as Fig. 4 where (a) shows the timestamp distribution of getting-on and (b) presents that of getting-off.

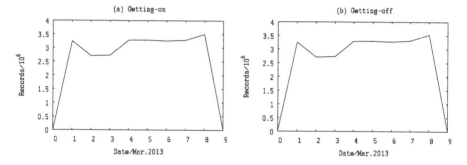

Fig. 4. Temporal distribution

In the result, the timestamp of getting-on or getting-off is respectively considered because some records may miss either or both attributes; more than 1000 distinct dates appear in the raw data including unreal 0-March-2013 or impossible 1-January-1990. We found 95.6 % timestamps, regardless of getting-on or getting-off, are evidently clustered round eight successive days of March 2013. Therefore, the temporal range of the raw data is manually determined as 1-March-2013 to 8-March-2013, which is proved consistent with the original documentation of the bus company. That is, our method shows its feasibility and correctness.

Moreover, we want to evaluate the performance of time-based clustering on different data size.

Experiment 2. The original raw data is divided into eight parts with identical size. We add a part into the input each time for time-based clustering and note the executive time under each input size. When input scales the result is showed as the solid line in Fig. 5(a), and the average executive time on 1 GB data could be deduced as the solid line in Fig. 5(b).

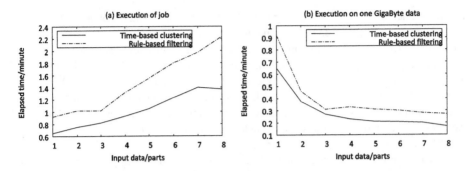

Fig. 5. Scalability of two steps for data cleaning

The performance of time-based clustering is proved scalable on data. When input scales, the increment of executive time of time-based clustering is better than linearity. The executive time on million records is not even doubled and is kept minute-level even when the input increases as eight folds. That trend can be clearly presented by Fig. 5(b) in another perspective, and that executive time on certain data size declines as input scales. It comes from the parallelism of count operation via the Hadoop. Either the initiation or the finish of the MapReduce job leads the latency, but their latency becomes relatively smaller proportion than that of counting operation when input scales.

Based on the two experiments above, our method can guarantee consistent temporal attribute in a scalable fashion. In the same way, we can evaluate the rule-based filtering then.

Experiment 3. The original raw data is divided into eight parts with identical size. We add a part into the input each time for rule-based filtering and note the executive time under each input size. When input scales the result is showed as the dotted line in Fig. 5(a), and the average executive time on 1 GB data could be deduced as the dotted line in Fig. 5(b).

The performance of rule-based filtering is also proved scalable on data. When input scales, the trend is the same as that of experiment 2: the executive time on million records is not even tripled and is kept minute-level even though the input increases as eight folds. It still comes from the parallelism via Hadoop MapReduce. Moreover, compared with experiment 2, the executive time here is larger on the same input size because more procedures are required for the validation.

Next, we generated artificial dirty records in the raw data and evaluate the effect of the validation.

Experiment 4. We select given records from the original raw data and produce the artificial dirty records by modifying their spatio-temporal attributes: in one half of the selected records, a decimal digit of a timestamp (*begin_time* or *end_time*) would be modified randomly; in the other half, a decimal number of both timestamps would be modified randomly. Analogously, spatial attributes are modified as follows: in one half of selected records, one station id (*from_station_ID* or *to_station_ID*) would be substituted to another existent one randomly; in the other half, both station ids would be substituted to other existent ones randomly. On the raw data with artificial dirty records, the rule-based filtering is executed. After the job finishes, we scan the clean data to distinguish whether all the artificial records are eliminated. The proportion of the selected records in the raw data is set as 5 %, 10 %, 15 %, 20 % or 25 % respectively in one test. In each test, we count the proportion of the correct records in the clean data. The result is showed as Fig. 6.

The accuracy of rule-based filtering is proved steady even when more artificial records are introduced. We find the proportion of correct records in clean data is more than 78 % and remains high even when artificial dirty record scales. In intuition, the result ought to decline because more illegal records are required to be judged as invalid ones. In fact, in our filtering method, the proportion of correct records in clean data has no relationship with the size of dirty records: any record would be scanned once and then judged once. Moreover, in this experiment, some artificial dirty records cannot be distinguished as illegality, because the modification in most of them does not violate the rule we have defined.

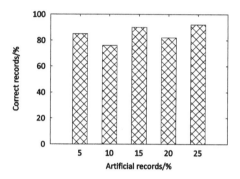

Fig. 6. Accuracy on the data including artificial dirty records

Based on two experiments above, our method can validate the legality of spatio-temporal data efficiently in a scalable fashion.

5 Conclusion

We propose a data cleaning method on massive spatio-temporal data: through time-based clustering, consistent temporal attribute can be determined; through rule-based filtering, legal records can be validated. The method shows its efficiency, accuracy and scalability on practical bus IC card data in extensive conditions. In the future, more illegal patterns like invalid duplication would be considered according to the business feedbacks and custom requirements.

Acknowledgments. This work was supported by the R&D General Program of Beijing Education Commission (No. KM2015_10009007), the Key Young Scholars Foundation for the Excellent Talents of Beijing (No. 2014000020124G011) and Foundation for the Excellent Youth Scholars of North China University of Technology.

References

1. Zheng, Y., Capra, L., Wolfson, O., Yang, H.: Urban computing: concepts, methodologies, and applications. ACM Trans. Intell. Syst. Technol. **5**, 1–55 (2014)
2. Carey, M.J., Jacobs, S., Tsotras, V.J.: Breaking BAD: a data serving vision for big active data. In: Proceedings of the 10th ACM International Conference on Distributed and Event-based Systems, pp. 181–186. ACM, Irvine (2016)
3. Tang, N.: Big data cleaning. In: Chen, L., Jia, Y., Sellis, T., Liu, G. (eds.) APWeb 2014. LNCS, vol. 8709, pp. 13–24. Springer, Heidelberg (2014). doi:10.1007/978-3-319-11116-2_2
4. Chen, M., Mao, S., Liu, Y.: Big data: a survey. Mobile Netw. Appl. **19**, 171–209 (2014)
5. Ganti, V., Sarma, A.D.: Data Cleaning: A Practical Perspective. Morgan & Claypool Publishers, Williston (2013)
6. Fan, W., Geerts, F., Tang, N., Yu, W.: Inferring data currency and consistency for conflict resolution. In: IEEE 29th International Conference on Data Engineering (ICDE 2013), pp. 470–481. IEEE (2013)
7. Wang, J., Tang, N.: Towards dependable data repairing with fixing rules. In: Proceedings of the 2014 ACM SIGMOD International Conference on Management of Data, pp. 457–468. ACM, Snowbird (2014)
8. Sun, D., Zhang, G., Zheng, W., Li, K.: Key Technologies for Big Data Stream Computing. Big Data: Algorithms, Analytics, and Applications. CRC Press, Taylor & Francis Group, USA (2014)
9. Wang, L., Xu, L.D., Bi, Z., Xu, Y.: Data Cleaning for RFID and WSN Integration. IEEE Trans. Industr. Inf. **10**, 408–418 (2014)
10. Beskales, G., Ilyas, I.F., Golab, L.: Sampling the repairs of functional dependency violations under hard constraints. Proc. VLDB Endow. **3**, 197–207 (2010)
11. Chu, X., Ilyas, I.F., Papotti, P.: Holistic data cleaning: Putting violations into context. In: 2013 IEEE 29th International Conference on Data Engineering (ICDE), pp. 458–469 (2013)
12. Fan, W., Li, J., Ma, S., Tang, N., Yu, W.: Towards certain fixes with editing rules and master data. VLDB J. **21**, 213–238 (2012)
13. Dallachiesa, M., Ebaid, A., Eldawy, A., Elmagarmid, A., Ilyas, I.F., Ouzzani, M., Tang, N.: NADEEF: a commodity data cleaning system. In: Proceedings of the 2013 ACM SIGMOD International Conference on Management of Data, pp. 541–552. ACM, New York (2013)

An Unsupervised Method for Linking Entity Mentions in Chinese Text

Jing Xu[✉], Liang Gan, Bin Zhou, and Quanyuan Wu

College of Computer, National University of Defense Technology,
Changsha 410073, China
{jing.xu,gl,binzh,qy.w}@nudt.edu.cn

Abstract. Entity linking is the process of linking entity mentions in text with the unambiguous entity objects in a knowledge base. The technology is a key step of expanding a knowledge base, and can improve the information filtering ability of online recommendation systems, search engines, and other practical applications. However, the large number of entities, the diversity and ambiguity of entity names bring huge challenges for entity linking research. In addition, the rare Chinese knowledge bases and the complex syntax of Chinese text restrict researching Chinese entity linking technologies. In order to meet the processing requirement of Chinese text, we propose an unsupervised Chinese entity linking method, namely un-CEML. This method uses Baidu encyclopedia as a knowledge base, exploits a similarity algorithm to obtain entries from Baidu encyclopedia, and combines the characteristics of this encyclopedia to obtain candidate entities, which can handle the abbreviation and wrongly segmenting entity mentions, ensuring the size of candidate entities and the probability of containing the target entity. In the ranking stage of candidate entities, we obtain the strongly relevant information of entity mentions based on the dependencies of components in a sentence as the context information, to reduce the noise of calculating the similarity with candidate entities. Because the nominal mentions are mostly common words, small correlation with the document knowledge, we deal with them separately. We conduct experiments on real data sets, and compare with some standard methods. The experimental results show that our method can solve the ambiguity problem of Chinese entity mentions, and achieve high accuracy of linking results.

Keywords: Entity linking · Baidu encyclopedia · Information extraction · Unsupervised · Chinese text

1 Introduction

With the development of information technology, there are vast amounts of unstructured text on the network, in which the diversity and ambiguity of entity names are widespread, reducing the utilization of text data. However, the entity disambiguation technology can solve these problems and have important influence for understanding the real meaning of natural language text. Entity linking is a method of entity disambiguation, and obtains the target entity by linking an entity mention to an unambiguous entity object in a knowledge base [1]. Specifically, entity mentions are some

G. Wang et al. (Eds.): APSCC 2016, LNCS 10065, pp. 183–195, 2016.
DOI: 10.1007/978-3-319-49178-3_14

strings pointing to some things in the world, and mainly include nominal mentions, such as concepts, technology items, and named mentions, such as person, location, etc. [2]. Entity linking is a disambiguation method of entity mentions, and is applied to the semantic search, question answering system, knowledge base expansion and heterogeneous knowledge fusion, etc.

In particular, the entity linking technologies can solve the diversity and ambiguity problem of entity names. The name diversity is that an entity has multiple names, such as alias, abbreviation. For example, the other names of the entity "peng li yuan" (In order to ensure that print format, we use pinyin instead of Chinese characters, and the other parts are the same), which is the wife of Chinese president, are "Liyuan Peng" and "peng ma ma" (Peng Mama). The name ambiguity is that an entity name is likely to point to different entities in different contexts. For example, Apple indicates a company in business documents, and indicates a fruit in health documents.

The key step of entity linking is calculating the similarity between an entity mention and its candidate entities. The traditional methods extracted the context information of entity mentions by setting the window size, which introduced a lot of noise, reducing the similarity. In addition, the large size of candidate entity size will bring a lot of time cost and storage cost, when calculating the similarity between entity mentions and candidate entities. Moreover, using the context similarity method to link the nominal mentions, is easy to produce some wrong results, because of the small correlation between the nominal mentions with document knowledge. To solve the above problems, we propose an unsupervised Chinese entity mention linking method, namely un-CEML. The main contributions of this method are as follows.

1. un-CEML needs no manual annotation data, comprehensively utilizing the entity type, population, name and context information, which can distinguish and identify the candidate entities accurately, and ensures the result accuracy and recall.
2. In the stage of generating candidate entities, un-CEML exploits a similarity algorithm to obtain entries from the knowledge base, which can process the abbreviation and wrongly segmenting entity mentions, ensuring the size of the candidate entities and the probability of containing the target entity.
3. In the stage of ranking candidate entities, un-CEML exploits the type consistency between an entity mention and its target entity, extracts the strongly relevant information of entity mentions based on the dependencies of components in a sentence, and links the nominal mentions separately, to reducing the time cost and improve the linking accuracy.
4. In order to verify the performance of un-CEML, we conduct some experiments on real data sets, and compare with some standard methods. The experimental results show that our method can solve the ambiguity problem of Chinese entity mentions, and achieve high accuracy of linking results.

The other parts are organized as follows. We describe the related works in Sect. 2 and the linking method of entity mentions in detail in Sect. 3. In Sect. 4, we report our experimental results and evaluation, and conclude our discussion in Sect. 5.

2   Related Works

The entity linking technologies have important research value for building and updating a knowledge base, which receives the extensive attention of the academic members in recent years. According to needing manual annotation data or not, the entity linking technologies are divided into supervised and unsupervised technologies, and we introduce the research status from the above two aspects. The supervised technologies include binary classification methods, learning to ranking methods, probabilistic graph based approaches. The idea of binary classification methods is using the pairs of entity mentions and candidate entities to train a binary classifier, such as SVM (support vector machine), binary logistic classifier, to determine whether the mention points to the candidate entity [3–6]. The idea of learning to ranking methods is studying a ranking model automatically with the training data to sort the candidate entities, whose different place with binary classification methods is considering the relationships between the candidate entities referring to the same entity mention. LINDEN exploited the max-margin method to get the target entity by combining the entity population, semantic correlation, semantic similarity and topic consistency [7]. Chen et al. exploited the listwise ranker ListNet to obtain the target entity [8]. The probabilistic graph based approaches are to simultaneously remove the ambiguity of multiple entity mentions by a collaborative linking method, based on the topic consistency of all entities in a document. Han et al. used a probabilistic graph to model the context similarity between entity mentions and candidate entities and the semantic correlation between the candidate entities referring to different entity mentions, and get the target entity by a collective linking method [9]. Hoffart et al. built a mention-entity graph, combining the entity population, context similarity and the coherence between entities, and calculated a subgraph containing a mention-entity edge for each mention, to obtain the target entity [10].

The unsupervised technologies need no manual annotation data to train models, including vector space model based methods (VSM) and information retrieval based methods. The idea of VSM is representing entity mentions and candidate entities into vector forms, and calculating their similarity, selecting the candidate entity with the highest value as the target entity. The other methods based on VSM are different on vector representation and similarity calculation [11–13]. The information retrieval based methods index every candidate entity into a document, and regard an entity mention and its context information as a query, to search the documents, and select the most relevant candidate entity as the target entity. Gottipat et al. studied a statistical language model based on the information retrieval method, and used the KL-divergence retrieval model to score candidate entities, and select the object with the highest value as the target entity [14].

Due to the richness and openness of English knowledge bases, such as English Wikipedia, Freebase, DBpedia, most entity linking technologies are processing English text. Relatively, the rare Chinese knowledge bases and the complex syntax of Chinese text restrict researching Chinese entity linking technologies. However, the massive Chinese resources and the demand of variety applications, urge researching Chinese entity linking technologies, which can make the machines understand and exploit these resource, and provide good services for human. In recent years, the Chinese entity linking technologies attract wide attention in academia and industry. For example, from 2015, TAC (Text Analysis Conference) issued a Tri-langual (English, Chinese, Spanish) entity discovery and linking task. Babelfy was an entity linking system based on graph, built with BabelNet, which is an open encyclopedia, and supported for the entity disambiguation task of multiple languages (English, Chinese, Russian, etc.). Babelfy exploited the restarting random walk algorithm to get the semantic relevance between entities, namely semantic signature, built the semantic relation graph based on semantic signature, and got the unambiguous entities by extracting the dense subgraph [15]. CASIA_EL regarded the wikipedia pages of words in the context of entity mentions as an external knowledge source, expanded the eigenvectors of the input text, and calculated the similarity between an entity mention and its candidate entities, selecting the object with the highest score as the target entity [16]. Liu et al. proposed a Chinese integrated entity linking method based on graph, which not only made full use of the structural relationship between entities in a knowledge base, but also acquired the external knowledge by the incremental mining algorithm, so as to collectively link multiple entity mentions in a document [17].

3   Approach

The proposed method, namely un-CEML, includes entity mentions extraction, candidate entities generation, candidate entities ranking, and NIL entity mentions clustering, whose process flow is shown in Fig. 1.

In the extraction stage of entity mentions, we use the method in the preliminary work to acquire the nominal and named mentions, as well as their categories. The detail method is described in "An Unsupervised Method for Entity Mentions Extraction in Chinese Text", which is waiting for publication. Particularly, the category of the nominal mentions is annotated as NOM, and the named mentions contain PER, LOC, GPE, and so on. The representation of the output information is $M = \{<m1, c1>, <m2, c2>, \ldots <mn, cn>\}$. m_i indicates an entity mention, and c_i indicates a category, $0 < i < n$.

3.1   Candidate Entities Generation

We use Baidu encyclopedia as a knowledge base. Baidu encyclopedia is the largest Chinese encyclopedia in the world, which adopts the crowdsourcing technology, allows all users to edit the entries, and has a professional team for review to ensure the correctness of all entries [18]. As of April 2016, Baidu encyclopedia has collected more than 13,000,000 entries, almost covering all known fields, which point to some things, and concepts in the real world. Each entry corresponds to a description page, mainly including the yixiang information, summary, infobox, content, and tag indicating the category of this entry. Particularly, the yixiang information contains some entries, which have the same name and different meanings with this entry. For example, the entry "Keqiang Li" corresponds to a premier of the state council, but also corresponds

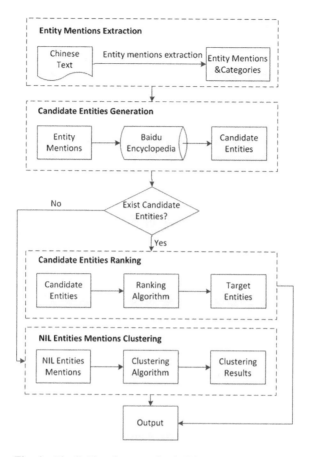

Fig. 1. The linking framework of Chinese entity mentions

to a professor, or other objects. Because Baidu encyclopedia does not provide the offline package, we use the online processing method. un-CEML puts entity mentions in Baidu search, and exploits a similarity method to filter the returned encyclopedia results, which can process the abbreviation and wrongly segmenting entity mentions. The similarity calculation method is shown in formula (1). For example, for the entity mention "shi wei zu zhi" (WHO), we can obtain the candidate entity "shi jie wei sheng zu zhi" (World Health Organization). For the entity mention "yan hua xiang hua gong you xian gong si" (Yan Hua Xiang Chemical Company), we can obtain the candidate entity "zhong yan hua xiang hua gong you xian gong si" (Zhong Yan Hua Xiang Chemical Company). Then un-CEML combines the filtered encyclopedia results and their yixiang information as the candidate entities. The output contains the encyclopedia term, tag and content, whose representation is $CE = \{CE_1, CE_2, \ldots CE_n\}$, and $CE_i = \{<term_1, tag_1, content_1>, \ldots, <term_j, tag_j, content_j>, \ldots\}$, $j = 1, 2\ldots$

$$\text{Sim}\big(m_i, term_j\big) = \begin{cases} \frac{Len\big(LCS\big(m_i, term_j\big)\big)}{Len(m_i)} & \big(ifLCS\big(m_i, term_j\big) \neq \emptyset\big) \\ \frac{Len\big(MCC\big(m_i, term_j\big)\big)}{Len(m_i)} & \big(ifLCS\big(m_i, term_j\big) = \emptyset\big) \end{cases} \tag{1}$$

In formula (1), m_i represents an entity mention, and $term_j$ indicates a candidate entity. The symbol "LCS" indicates acquiring the longest common substring of two elements, and "Len" indicates calculating the length of the element. "MCC" indicates acquiring the maximum common characters of two elements.

3.2 Candidate Entities Ranking

For the entity mentions owning candidate entities, we design a ranking algorithm, which exploits the entity category, population, names and context information, to rank the candidate entities and get the target entity. The output representation is E = {<m_1, e_1>, <m_2, e_2>, ...<m_n, e_n>}. The ranking algorithm is described as follows.

Algorithm 1 Candidate Entities Ranking Algorithm

Input: Entity Mention Set M, Candidate Entity Set CE
Output: Target Entity Set E
1: **for** $< m_i, c_i >\in$ M and $CE_i \in$ CE **do**
2:    **if** $c_i =$ 'NOM' **then**
3:       **for** $< term_j, tag_j, content_j >\in CE_i$ **do**
4:          **if** tag_j contains "ci yu" or "yu yan" **then**
5:             $< m_i, e_i >=< m_i, term_j >$;
6:             E $\leftarrow< m_i, e_i >$;
7:          **else**
8:             remove $< term_j, tag_j, content_j >$;
9:          **end if**
10:       **end for**
11:    **else**
12:       **for** $< term_j, tag_j, content_j >\in CE_i$ **do**
13:          **if** c_i and tag_j point to different categories **then**
14:             remove $< term_j, tag_j, content_j >$;
15:          **else**
16:             $p(term_j) = getPopulation(term_j)$;
17:             $c(m_i) = getRelInfo(m_i)$;
18:             $s_j = Sim(c(m_i), content_j)$;
19:             $< m_i, e_i >= arg_{e_i=term_j} max_{j=1,2,...}(p(term_j) \times s_j)$;
20:             E $\leftarrow< m_i, e_i >$;
21:          **end if**
22:       **end for**
23:    **end if**
24: **end for**
25: **return** E;

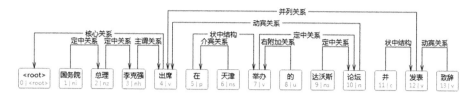

Fig. 2. The dependency parsing example of a Chinese sentence

Based on the observation, the nominal mentions generally refer to some common words, which have small relevance with the document knowledge. If we use the context similarity method to link them, we will get wrong target entities. Therefore, we get the target entity by judging the tags of candidate entities containing "词语" (term) or "语言" (language). For the named mentions, we use the context similarity method, which lowers the processing speed in case of the numerous candidate entities. To solve the above problem, we reduce the size of candidate entities based on the consistency between an entity mention and its target entity. In addition, because the entity is more popular, it is mentioned more frequently. We join the entity population in un-CEML, which helps ranking the candidate entities. The function is getPopulation($term_j$), which get the entity population by obtaining the editing number in the encyclopedia page.

The previous similarity methods obtain the context information of entity mentions by setting the window size, which cannot guarantee these information being related to entity mentions, and introducing a lot of noise, affecting the similarity between entity mentions and candidate entities. To solve this problem, we design a method of gaining the context information strongly related to entity mentions. Firstly, we gain the sentences including an entity mention. Secondly, according to dependency parsing, we get the relevant information of this entity mention, such as the attributive modifiers, other mentions related to this entity mention. For example, for the sentence "guo wu yuan zong li li ke qiang chu xi zai tian jin ju ban de da wo si lun tan bing fa biao zhi ci" (Keqiang Li, the premier of the state council, will attend davos BBS held in Tianjin, and make a speech.), the relevant information of "li ke qiang" (Keqiang Li) is "guo wu yuan zong li" (the premier of the state council), "chu xi da wo si lun tan" (attend davos BBS), "fa biao zhi ci" (make a speech), and "da wo si lun tan zai tian jin jv ban" (davos BBS is held in Tianjin). The dependency example of this sentence is shown in Fig. 2. In the ranking algorithm, getting the relevant information is represented by the function getRelInfo(m_i), which is described in Algorithm 2.

Particularly, the function Sim(c(m_i), $content_j$) is calculating the similarity between the context information of entity mentions and the description content of candidate entities, which is similar with formula (1).

Algorithm 2 $getRelInfo(m_i)$

Input: sentences containing EMs S, $m_i \in M$
Output: EMs and rele-mentions C
1: **for** $s_j \in$ S **do**
2:    set $L_j = \emptyset$;
3:    $L_j = parseDependency(s_j)$;
4:    **for** L_j **do**
5:       $C \leftarrow m_i$;
6:       **if** $L_j(m_i) = ($"ding zhong guan xi"$)$ **then**
7:          $C \leftarrow getATTcom(m_i)$;
8:       **else**
9:          **if** $L_j(m_i) = ($"zhu wei guan xi"$)$ **then**
10:             $C \leftarrow getPre(m_i)$;
11:          **else**
12:             **if** $L_j(m_i) = ($"dong bin guan xi"$)$ **then**
13:                $C \leftarrow getObj(m_i)$;
14:             **else**
15:                **if** $L_j(m_i) = ($"jie bin guan xi"$)$ **then**
16:                   $C \leftarrow getProObj(m_i)$;
17:                **else**
18:                   **if** $L_j(m_i) = ($"bin lie guan xi"$)$ **then**
19:                      $C \leftarrow getBL(m_i)$;
20:                   **end if**
21:                **end if**
22:             **end if**
23:          **end if**
24:       **end if**
25:    **end for**
26: **end for**
27: **return** C;

The function parseDependency(s_j) gets all components and their dependency tags by analyzing the dependency of components in the input sentence s_j. We use HanLP tool to analyze the dependency between components, which is a Chinese natural language processing tool [19]. The function getATTcom(m_i) gets the attributive modifiers of m_i by the dependency tag "ding zhong guan xi" (Attributive relation). The function getPre(m_i) gets the subject by the tag "zhu wei guan xi" (Subject-Predicate relation). The function getObj(m_i) gets the object by the tag "dong bin guan xi" (Verb-Object relation). The function getProObj(m_i) gets the adverbial modifiers by the tag "jie bin guan xi" (Preposition-Object relation). The function getBL(m_i) gets the adverbial modifiers by the tag "bing lie guan xi" (Parallel relation).

3.3   NIL Entity Mentions Clustering

For NIL entity mentions, which have no the corresponding entity object in knowledge base, we use a clustering algorithm to cluster them pointing the same entity. The clustering algorithm is described in Algorithm 3, which exploits the entity category, name and context similarity.

Algorithm 3 NIL Entity Clustering Algorithm

Input: NIL entity mentions M_{NIL}
Output: Clusters CL
1: **for** $< m_i, c_i, relInfo_i >, < m_j, c_j, relInfo_j > \in M_{NIL}$ **do**
2:     **if** c_i and c_j point the same category **then**
3:         $s(m_i, m_j) = Sim(m_i, m_j) \times Sim(relInfo_i, relInfo_j)$;
4:         **if** $s(m_i, m_j) > \delta$ **then**
5:             CL $=< m_i, m_j, ... >$;
6:         **end if**
7:     **end if**
8: **end for**
9: **return** CL;

The input element $relInfo_i$ is an entity mention and its relevant information. The similarity calculation is similar to formula (1), whose difference is choosing the object of smaller length as a denominator.

4   Experiment and Evaluation

We crawl 40 news texts in November 2013 from phoenix information news website as data sets, covering military affairs, politics, culture, society, etc. Using the method in the preliminary work, which has been introduced previously, we extract the entity mentions and categories, removing the wrong objects, and get 1852 entity mentions in total.

4.1   Evaluation Method

We use the evaluation method in the paper [17], but there is a little difference. Firstly, we link the entity mentions to the target entity in knowledge base artificially, and mark the entity mentions having no target entity as NIL. T_1 means the entity mentions linking to the knowledge base correctly, and T_2 means NIL entity mentions. Secondly, we process entity mentions by un-CEML. S_1 means the entity mentions, which are linked to the knowledge base by un-CEML. S_1' means the entity mentions linked correctly in S_1. S_2 means the NIL entity mentions by un-CEML, and S_2' means the correct NIL entity mentions in S_2.

We use Accuracy to evaluate the accuracy of the linking results by un-CEML. The formula is as follows.

$$Accuracy = \frac{|S_1'| + |S_2'|}{|T_1| + |T_2|} \times 100\% \tag{2}$$

We use Precision, Recall and F_1-value to evaluate the overall performance of un-CEML. The formula is as follows.

$$P = \frac{1}{2}\left(\frac{S_1'}{S_1} + \frac{S_2'}{S_2}\right) \times 100\% \tag{3}$$

$$R = \frac{1}{2}\left(\frac{S_1'}{T_1} + \frac{S_2'}{T_2}\right) \times 100\% \tag{4}$$

$$F_1 = \frac{2PR}{P+R} \times 100\% \tag{5}$$

4.2 Experimental Results

In the generation stage of candidate entities, we set the similarity threshold as 0.8 by several experiments, which means selecting the encyclopedia entries more than 0.8 as the candidate entities. If there is no encyclopedia entry, we mark the entity mention as NIL. In the clustering stage of NIL entity mentions, we set the similarity threshold δ as 0.65.

In order to verify the effectiveness of un-CEML, we choose a method with higher influence for experimental comparison. Babelfy is an entity linking system based on graph, which includes entity recognition, candidate entities selection and entity disambiguation [15]. Their linking results are shown in Table 1.

Table 1. Effectiveness of various entity linking systems (%)

System	Accuracy	Precision	Recall	F-measure
Babelfy	81.26	67.28	82.40	74.08
un-CEML	91.03	83.09	94.30	88.34

Table 1 shows that un-CEML is about 10 % higher on Accuracy and Precision than Babelfy. The main reason is that Babelfy depends on BabelNet greatly, which assigns an abstract entity for the entity mentions having no the target entity as a linking object, reducing the precision severely. However, Baidu encyclopedia is the most comprehensive Chinese encyclopedia, almost covering the knowledge of all areas, which improves the linking results.

To compare the effectiveness of extracting the relevant information of entity mentions based on the dependency, we regard the method extracting the context information by setting the window size as a contrast experiment, namely el-window, and the other modules is the same. The linking results are shown in Table 2, which shows that the method based on the dependency improves the linking performance obviously.

Table 2. Comparison of linking results using different extracting methods of content information (%)

System	Accuracy	Precision	Recall	F-measure
el-dp	91.03	83.09	94.30	88.34
el-window	82.72	77.90	77.15	77.52

To compare the effectiveness of linking the nominal mentions dividually, we set the contrast experiment of processing the nominal and named mentions together by calculating the context similarity, namely el-all. The other processing methods are the same. The linking results are shown in Table 3.

Table 3. Comparison of linking results linking the nominal mentions specially or not (%)

System	Accuracy	Precision	Recall	F-measure
el-dividually	91.03	83.09	94.30	88.34
el-all	62.69	67.13	78.37	72.31

Table 3 shows processing the nominal mentions dividually, has obvious influence for the linking results. The main reason is that the nominal mentions makes up large proportion in the entity mentions, and they have little correlation with the document. For example, for the nominal mention "zhu ti" (theme), its context text is "jin nian bei jing hui yi de zhu ti wei du dong zhong guo" (The theme of the meeting in Beijing is to understand China in this year). In Baidu encyclopedia, "zhu ti" (theme) is a Chinese term, whose description content is about literary works. Therefore, we cannot link the correct entity by calculating the context similarity.

4.3   Method Analysis

According to the experimental results, un-CEML is an effective method for linking Chinese entity mentions, which needs no manual annotation data, meeting the processing demand of massive network data. We analyze the wrong linking results, and sum up the following reasons. (1) the similarity method is comparing the similarity between characters, which cannot process the semantic information. For example, un-CEML cannot link the entity mention with the candidate entity, whose name is different but pointing to the same entity. (2) For the nominal entities, un-CEML use the rigid constraint to obtain their target entities, which is easy to produce some linking mistakes and NIL mentions for some special nominal entities.

5   Conclusion

We propose an unsupervised Chinese entity mention linking method, namely un-CMEL, which uses Baidu encyclopedia as a knowledge base, and exploits a similarity method and the encyclopedia features to ensure the size of candidate entities and the probability of containing the target entity. Moreover, un-CMEL mines and utilizes the relevant knowledge of entities (entity type, population, name and context similarity) to distinguish and identify the candidate entities, especailly extracting the context information of entity mentions by the dependency and linking the nominal mentions individually, which ensures the result accuracy and recall. In future, we will build a entity alias dictionary to improve the linking accuracy for various names, and add some semantic information to the similarity method, to improve the linking performance.

References

1. Shen, W., Wang, J., Han, J.: Entity linking with a knowledge base: Issues, techniques, and solutions. IEEE Trans. Knowl. Data Eng. **27**(2), 443–460 (2015)
2. Li, W., Qian, D., Lu, Q., et al.: Detecting, categorizing and clustering entity mentions in Chinese text. In: Proceedings of the 30th Annual International ACM SIGIR Conference on Research and Development in Information Retrieval, pp. 647–654. ACM (2007)
3. Varma, V., Bharat, V., Kovelamudi, S., Bysani, P., Santosh, G.S.K., Kiran Kumar, N., et al.: IIIT Hyderabad at TAC 2009, vol. 39, pp. 620–622 (2009)
4. Zhang, W., Su, J., Tan, C.L., et al.: Entity linking leveraging: automatically generated annotation. In: Proceedings of the 23rd International Conference on Computational Linguistics, pp. 1290–1298. Association for Computational Linguistics (2010)
5. Lehmann, J., Monahan, S., Nezda, L., et al.: LCC approaches to knowledge base population at TAC 2010. In: Proceedings of the TAC 2010 Workshop (2010)
6. Monahan, S., Lehmann, J., Nyberg, T., et al.: Cross-lingual cross-document coreference with entity linking. In: Proceedings of the Text Analysis Conference (2011)
7. Shen, W., Wang, J., Luo, P., et al.: Linden: linking named entities with knowledge base via semantic knowledge. In: Proceedings of the 21st International Conference on World Wide Web, pp. 449–458. ACM (2012)
8. Chen, Z., Ji, H.: Collaborative ranking: a case study on entity linking. In: Proceedings of the Conference on Empirical Methods in Natural Language Processing, pp. 771–781. Association for Computational Linguistics (2011)
9. Han, X., Sun, L., Zhao, J.: Collective entity linking in web text: a graph-based method. In: Proceedings of the 34th International ACM SIGIR Conference on Research and Development in Information Retrieval, pp. 765–774. ACM (2011)
10. Hoffart, J., Yosef, M.A., Bordino, I., et al.: Robust disambiguation of named entities in text. In: Proceedings of the Conference on Empirical Methods in Natural Language Processing, pp. 782–792. Association for Computational Linguistics (2011)
11. Cucerzan, S.: Large-scale named entity disambiguation based on Wikipedia data. In: EMNLP-CoNLL, vol. 7, pp. 708–716 (2007)
12. Han, X., Zhao, J.: NLPR_KBP in TAC 2009 KBP track: a two-stage method to entity linking. In: Proceedings of Test Analysis Conference 2009. TAC (2009)
13. Tamang, S., Chen, Z., Ji, H.: CUNY BLENDER TAC-KBP2012 entity linking system and slot filling validation system. In: Proceedings of the Text Analysis Conference (2012)
14. Gottipati, S., Jiang, J.: Linking entities to a knowledge base with query expansion. In: Proceedings of the Conference on Empirical Methods in Natural Language Processing, pp. 804–813. Association for Computational Linguistics (2011)
15. Moro, A., Raganato, A., Navigli, R.: Entity linking meets word sense disambiguation: a unified approach. Trans. Assoc. Comput. Linguist. **2**, 231–244 (2014)

16. Zeng, Y., Wang, D., Zhang, T., Wang, H., Hao, H.: Linking entities in short texts based on a Chinese semantic knowledge base. In: Zhou, G., Li, J., Zhao, D., Feng, Y. (eds.) NLPCC 2013. CCIS, vol. 400, pp. 266–276. Springer, Heidelberg (2013). doi:10.1007/978-3-642-41644-6_25
17. Liu, Q., Zhong, Y., Li, Y., et al.: Graph-based collective Chinese entity linking algorithm. J. Comput. Res. Dev. **53**(2), 270–283 (2016)
18. Baidu baike. http://baike.baidu.com/
19. Han Language Processing Toolkit. http://hanlp.linrunsoft.com/

A Fast Adaptive Frequency Hopping Scheme Mitigating the Effect of Interference in Bluetooth Low Energy Networks

Yongtak Yoon, Changsu Jung, Jihun Seo, Jilong Li, Jinbae Kim,
Seungpyo Jin, Nathali Silva, and Kijun Han$^{(\boxtimes)}$

School of Computer Science and Engineering, Kyungpook National University,
Daegu 702-701, Korea
{ytyoon, changsu, jhseo87, jllee, jbkim, spjin,
nathalis}@netopia.knu.ac.kr, kjhan@knu.ac.kr

Abstract. The speed and the efficiency of short range communication has increased with the evolution of wireless technologies i.e. Wireless Local Area Network (WLAN), ZigBee, and Bluetooth Low Energy (BLE). Especially, the BLE shows promising results in different fields such as Internet of Things (IoT), health-care, body area networks, etc. As a result of dramatic increase in the wireless device, the frequency interference in 2.4 GHz Industrial Scientific Medical (ISM) band has raised, resulting a higher packet loss. In this paper, we propose Fast Adaptive Frequency Hopping Scheme (FAFH) to mitigate the effects of interference in BLE. The proposed FAFH scheme immediately hops to a new channel without waiting for completion of the current connection event when the channel quality becomes worse by interference. The simulation results show that the FAFH performs better in dense wireless networks as well as improved performances comparing to AFH scheme.

Keywords: BLE · Bluetooth · Frequency hopping · Interference · Packet loss · 2.4 GHz

1 Introduction

Recently, the mobile user requirements i.e. data, speed, the internet, energy consumption, etc. has given the opportunity to introduce novel technologies. BLE is one of the prominent candidates to provide low power and low-cost communication. It was first introduced in version 4.0 of the Bluetooth Standard [1]. Since then it has become the leading wireless technology for a broad range of devices, including smartphones and household equipment, as well as automotive, medical, and wellness devices. It is expected that 35 % of wireless-enabled consumer medical devices shipped in 2016 will have BLE capabilities [2]. The ubiquitous presence of BLE makes it an excellent fit for short-range wireless communication i.e. Machine-to-Machine (M2M), Cyber-Physical System (CPS), and IoT [3]. Similarly, the BLE is equipped with several commercially available products such as Qualcomm 2netTM Hub wireless gateway, wellness trackers, etc. [4, 5].

© Springer International Publishing AG 2016
G. Wang et al. (Eds.): APSCC 2016, LNCS 10065, pp. 196–204, 2016.
DOI: 10.1007/978-3-319-49178-3_15

In order to achieve low power services, the Bluetooth standard made several changes in the architectural design of the BLE. For example, the 2.4 GHz ISM band is divided into 40 channels with 2 MHz spaces in between. Among these 40 channels, 3 channels (37, 38, 39) are dedicated as the advertising channels for the connection establishment. The remaining 37 channels are responsible for the data transfer among the devices, so that they are named as data channels. Unlike classical Bluetooth, the BLE switches to different modes in order to reduce the power consumption. Subsequently, it gives months of battery life. However, the power consumption is still not low enough for coin cells and energy harvesting applications. Moreover, a concise state machine is designed to facilitate the enhance device discovery with low power consumption. This unique low power functionality enables the BLE as a radio standard for the IoT and M2M communication. Since BLE does not support streaming services, it is not suitable for large data transfer. In general, a BLE device can operate in three communication modes i.e. advertising, scanning, and initiation. The advertising mechanism facilitates easy discovery and connection establishment [6].

As already stated, BLE operates in the unlicensed 2.4 GHz ISM band, which increase the chances of interference, congestion, and packet loss. The coexistence of other short-range communication technologies such as WIFI, ZigBee, etc. in the same environment overcrowd the 2.4 GHz ISM band. For instance, the IoT aware environments are greatly affected by installing a huge number of sensors in various environments such as smart homes, smart buildings, e-health services, etc. [7]. Therefore, controlling the communications of such sensors is challenging job to accomplish. Consequently, several research studies have been published concerning the co-existence issue of the BLE with other technologies [8–10]. However, there are still some challenges to be solved in this issue. In particular, the master continues data transmission during a connection event, even though it is aware that the channel quality is deteriorating due to interference caused by other wireless networks. In order to address the aforementioned problems in a congested IoT environment, this paper proposes Fast Adaptive Frequency Hopping (FAFH) scheme to mitigate the effects of interference, thereby enhances the performance of coexisting BLE networks in the crowded 2.4 GHz band. The rest of the paper is categorized as follows. An overview of the AFH scheme is presented in Sect. 2. Section 3 provides a detailed description of the proposed FAFH. The simulation and results are presented in Sect. 4 and finally, the conclusion is given in Sect. 5.

2   Standard AFH Overview

The AFH is one of well-known hopping mechanisms that provide environmental adapting properties by identifying and eliminating the fixed source of interference [11–13]. The AFH process starts when a slave device initiates an advertising process by sending an advertising request to the master device. The master device receives the advertising request and sends a connection request to the slave device. The connection request consists of a channel map and frequency hop increment. After receiving the response from the master device, the slave device establishes a connection in one of the channels from the channel map. After the connection is created between the master and slave, the channel is further divided into non-overlapping time units called connection events. However, each connection event always utilizes only a single data channel. The master always initiates the connection event, as it transmits a data packet to the slave. Consequently, the slave must send a response packet to the master, once it received the packet from the master. However, the master is not bound to respond to the slave after receiving a packet. The master always waits for at least T_{IFS} of 150 μs until the end of transmitting a packet and the start of the next packet transmission.

The master first measures condition of all channels and classifies them into two categories: used and unused channel sets. One of the used channels will be selected for data transmission between the master and the slave. We denote the used channel set by $\{C_0, C_1, C_2, \ldots C_N\}$. The connection request contains a hop increment and a channel map. The channel map consists of a sequence of 37 bits, each bit is used to indicate whether the channel belongs to used or unused data channel sets. For example, a channel map of 011011.... means that channel 1,2,4, and 5 belong to used data channel set while channel 0 and 3 belong to the unused data channel set [14]. The hop increment is a random value that ranges from 5 to 16. It is utilized for computation of hopping frequency for the next connection event. Once the master and slave device created a connection, the AFH algorithm selects a data channel to use throughout a connection event. A data channel for a connection event is selected by

$$f \leftarrow (f + hop) \bmod 37 \tag{1}$$

where f and hop represent the channel number and hop increment, respectively. The value of f is initially set to 0 for the first connection event and then sequentially changed depending on its value used in the previous connection event. If the chosen channel does not belong to the used channel set, it is remapped to one of the used channels by

$$i = f \bmod N \; ; f \leftarrow C_i \tag{2}$$

where N represents the total number of used channels. An example of the algorithm is shown in Fig. 1.

Let α denote the error rate of a data (or ACK) packet during a connection event. Considering that a BLE device retransmits its packet if it does not receive any response from the other until T_{IFS} is elapsed, the probability of packet retransmission is given by

$$\rho = 1 - (1 - \alpha)^2 \tag{3}$$

So, the channel utilization during the connection event is

$$U = 1 - \rho \tag{4}$$

Using a simple calculus, we get the average time until the successful transmission of a data packet by

$$E(T) = \sum_{k=1}^{\infty} k(1 - \rho) \rho^{k-1} = \frac{1}{1 - \rho} \tag{5}$$

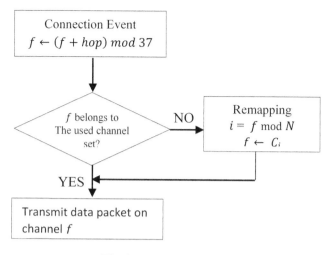

Fig. 1. Operation of AFH

3   Proposed Scheme

In this section, we provide a detailed description of the proposed FAFH. As previously stated, the AFH algorithm helps in avoiding interference. As a result, it cannot transmit the data packets at the occurrence of interference. The transmission of data packet fails due to two reasons, (1) when there is interference during transmission of a data packet from the master to the slave or (2) when there is interference during transmission of an acknowledgment from the slave to the master. In either situation, the transferred packet is garbled.

Consequently, the master retransmits the same data packet, which can be garbled again. The master continues data transmission until the end of current connection. Thus, it causes a severe wastage of channel capacity and takes a longer transmission time, since the master uses same channel when no more data packets are available. In AFH, the master continues data transmission until the completion of current connection event, even though it experiences interference during data transmission. Figure 2 illustrates a continuous interference scenario in AFH.

In order to overcome the drawback of AFH, we propose FAFH scheme. The FAFH scheme is enables the master to immediately hop to another channel when the interference occurrence is exceeding the predefined threshold.

Figure 3 shows the workflow of FAFH. FAFH closes the current connection event and start next connection event when INB reaches the threshold. Thus, FAFH scheme is capable of transmitting more data packets than AFH scheme within the same duration. In order to perform channel hopping, the current connection event requires to close the more data (MD) bit, which is included in data header. The MD bit is used to indicate that the master has more packets to send. The master sends a one-bit signal, MD bit, to the slave. If the MD bit received by the slave is 1, it indicates that master has more data packets to send, hence the connection event should be continued. Moreover, the slave should listen after sending an acknowledgement. On the other hand, if the

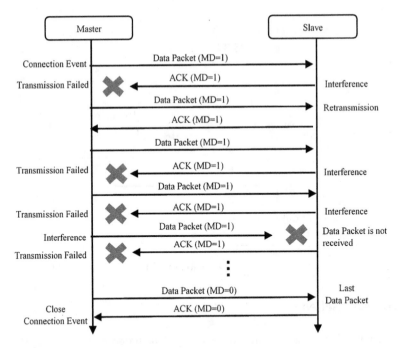

Fig. 2. Continuous interference in AFH

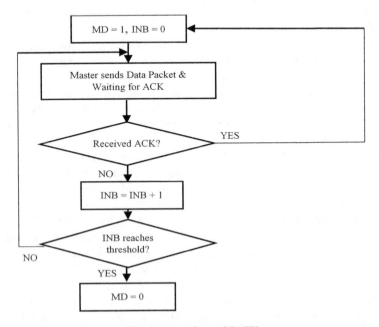

Fig. 3. Workflow of FAFH

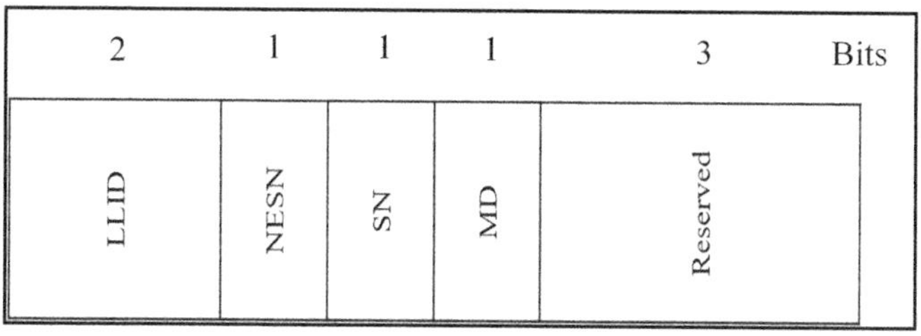

2	1	1	1	3	Bits
LLID	NESN	SN	MD	Reserved	

Fig. 4. A structure of data header

master sends "0" as the MD bit, it indicates that the master does not have more packets to send, thus the connection event can be ceased.

The proposed FAFH scheme uses 3 bits in the reserved field of data packet header to represent the interference as the Interference Notification Bit (INB). A structure of data header is shown Fig. 4.

INB bit uses a threshold about interference count, and it define from host at the creation of a connection. The initial INB value is set to 0. It increases when the master does not receive an ACK from the slave until the Inter Frame Space (TIFS) is elapsed after a data packet transmission. However, is the master receives an ACK in the next transmission, INB is assigned with the default value. If INB reaches the threshold, next data packet change MD bit 0 immediately. That means if current channel occur continuous interference, the master try to close current connection event immediately.

4   Simulation and Results

The proposed FAFH is tested through computer simulation using C language. The simulation environment is developed based on a BLE simulating program, which complies with the Bluetooth Low Energy 4.0 specifications. The simulation environment provided with random interference to simulate coexistence interference due to other wireless networks using 2.4 GHz ISM band like WLAN. For example, the interference caused in Unused channels from WLAN is considered in channel number 5–8, 14–16, 20–25, and 28–31. The rest of the twenty channels used the Used channels set. We simulate over 10 times for each scenario to get the average results, where parameter settings are selected with values listed in Table 1.

Figure 5 shows retransmit rate in FAFH and AFH. The retransmission rate directly depends on the interference. The result depicts a higher retransmission rate as the interference increases up to a certain level. The graph reveals that the AFH performance is deteriorated from high packet loss due to its single connection event when the transmission is failed between the master and slave. On the contrary, the proposed scheme has ensured less retransmission rate by closing current connection event and shifting to next connection event when transmission is failed between the master and a slave.

Table 1. Simulation parameters

Parameters	Values
Used channel set	0–4, 9–13, 17–19, 26, 27, and 32–36
Unused channel set	5–8, 14–16, 20–25, and 28–31
Number of used channels (N)	20
Packer error probability (α)	5 to 50 %
Inter frame space (T_{IFS})	150 μs
INB threshold (θ)	3

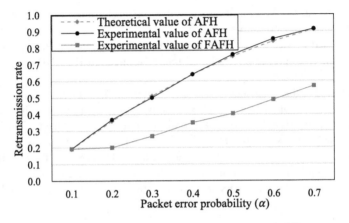

Fig. 5. Retransmission rate with packet error probability

We also compare the analytical results with those obtained via simulations. We can find that the theoretical results match with the simulative ones over the entire range of parameters.

The proposed scheme and AFH are compared in terms of average transmission time as shown in Fig. 6. Since AFH is retransmitting the packets in the same connection event, the average transmission time is significantly increased. In FAFH, the average transmission time is slightly increased with the packet error probability due to the switching time between connection events. However, FAFH offers a significantly less transmission time compared to AFH. We can also see that the theoretical result is well correlate with the simulation results.

As for the channel utilization shown in Fig. 7, we can see that FAFH is less affected by the packet error probability while AFH is severely suffered from low channel utilization with the increase of α. In fact, the high channel utilization of the proposed scheme is supported by switching into interference-free channels. It is also shown that the theoretical results are practically the same with simulation results.

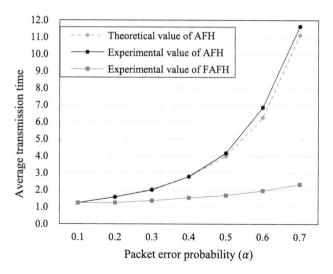

Fig. 6. Average transmission time with packet error probability

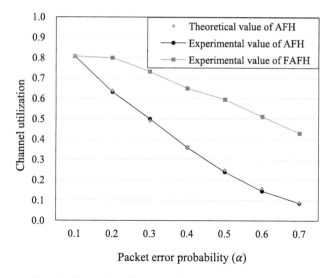

Fig. 7. Channel utilization with packet error probability

5 Conclusion

This paper presented Fast Adaptive Frequency Hopping (FAFH) scheme for coexistence of BLE networks in heterogeneous environments. FAFH immediately hops to a new channel without waiting for completion of the current connection event as is not case in the standard. The proposed scheme is tested through computer simulation in various interference scenarios. The simulation results have shown that the proposed FAFH offers a much shorter retransmission rate, average transmission time as well as higher channel utilization.

Acknowledgments. This work was supported by the Ministry of Education, Science Technology (MEST) and National Research Foundation of Korea (NRF) through the Creative Human Resource Training Project for Regional Innovation (2014). This work was supported by the IT R&D program of MSIP/IITP. [10041145, Self-Organized Software platform (SoSp) for Welfare Devices]. This study was supported by the BK21 Plus project (SW Human Resource Development Program for Supporting Smart Life) funded by the Ministry of Education, School of Computer Science and Engineering, Kyungpook National University, Korea (21A20131600005).

References

1. Group, B.S.I.: Specification of the Bluetooth System V4.0 (2010)
2. Arrowsmith, L.: Bluetooth smart to be the wireless technology most used in consumer medical devices by 2016. In: IMS Research (2016)
3. Bluetooth Smart Technology: Powering the Internet of Things (2016). http://www.bluetooth.com/Pages/Bluetoothsmart.aspx
4. http://www.fitbit.com/
5. QualcommLife. http://www.qualcommlife.com/wireless-health
6. Kalaa, M., Refai, H.: Bluetooth standard v4.1: simulating the Bluetooth low energy data channel selection algorithm. In: Globecom Workshops (2014)
7. Tong, J.-J., Huang, J., Zhang, H.-X.: The reform of three-dimensional to the practice of telecommunication system for the applications of internet of things. In: ICNDC (2012)
8. Taher, T.M., Rele, K., Roberson, D.: Development and quantitative analysis of an adaptive scheme for Bluetooth and Wi-Fi co-existence. In: CCNC, Las Vegas, NV (2009)
9. Gomez, C., Demirkol, I., Paradells, J.: Modeling the maximum throughput of Bluetooth low energy in an error-prone link. IEEE Commun. Lett. **15**(11), 1187–1189 (2011)
10. Tanbourgi, R., Elsner, J.P., Jäkel, H.: Optimizing practical adaptive frequency hopping and medium access control in ad hoc networks. In: WiOpt (2012)
11. Langhammer, N., Kays, R.: Enhanced frequency hopping for reliable interconnection of low power smart home devices. In: IWCMC, Limassol (2012)
12. Talarico, S., Valenti, M., Torrieri, D.: Otimization of an adaptive frequency-hopping network. In: MICOM (2015)
13. Zheng, M., Yang, B., Liang, W.: Adaptive frequency hopping in industrial wireless sensor networks: a decision-theoretic framework. In: CYBER (2015)
14. Kalaa, M.O.A., Refai, H.H.: Bluetooth standard v4.1: simulating the Bluetooth low energy data channel selection algorithm. In: Globecom Workshops, Austin (2014)

Mixed Reality with a Collaborative Information System

Charles Z. Liu[✉] and Manolya Kavakli

Department of Computing, Faculty of Science and Engineering, Macquarie
University, Sydney, NSW 2109, Australia
{charles.liu,manolya.kavakli}@mq.edu.au

Abstract. In this paper, we present a mixed reality environment
(MIXER) for immersive interactions. MIXER is an agent based collaborative information system displaying hybrid reality merging interactive
computer graphics and real objects. MIXER is an agent based collaborative information system displaying hybrid reality merging interactive computer graphics and real objects. The system comprises a sensor
subsystem, a network subsystem and an interaction subsystem. Related
issues to the concept of mixed interaction, including human aware computing, mixed reality fusion, agent based systems, collaborative scalable
learning in distributed systems, QoE-QoS balanced management and
information security, are discussed. We propose a system architecture
to perform networked mixed reality fusion for Ambient Interaction. The
components of the mixed reality suit to perform human aware interaction are Interaction Space, Motion Monitoring, Action and Scenario
Synthesisers, Script Generator, Knowledge Assistant Systems, Scenario
Display, and a Mixed Reality Module. Thus, MIXER as an integrated
system can provide a comprehensive human-centered mixed reality suite
for advanced Virtual Reality and Augmented Reality applications such
as therapy, training, and driving simulations.

Keywords: Mixed reality · Ambient interaction · Human aware computing · Mixed reality fusion · Collaborative scalable learning · QoE-QoS
management

1 Introduction

The firm demand for life like immersion inhuman-computer interaction (HCI)
for entertainment, education, military and healthcare [4, 12, 17, 18, 21, 22, 24, 26],
expedites the development of mixed reality and ambient interaction systems. A
mixed reality system refers to a computing system establishing a cyber environment, where physical and digital objects co-exist and interact in real time with
sensors, interactive subsystems,and immersive multimedia. Such a system merges
real and virtual worlds to reproduce virtualities and makes them ambient in the
environment, allowing individuals to navigate and interact with real and virtual

© Springer International Publishing AG 2016
G. Wang et al. (Eds.): APSCC 2016, LNCS 10065, pp. 205–219, 2016.
DOI: 10.1007/978-3-319-49178-3_16

objects. Correspondingly, the ambient interaction is reproduced using multimedia metaphors (related to senses of sight, hearing, smell, taste and touch) for work and private life scenarios in the cyber environment.

One of the emerging areas for research is immersive interaction to provide a realistic experience (e.g., [27, 28]). In order to perform immersive interactions, a number of sensors and actuators are required (as in [7]). Applications in military training is a typical example. Immersive training simulations combine real soldiers and physical environments with virtual soldiers and places to reproduce a lifelike battlefield with a series of metaphors. Interactive targets in the environment, including subjects (e.g. roles) and objects (e.g. weapons, cars) are either controlled by humans or by artificial intelligence. These simulations are used by the military to conduct training programs to perform tactical operations. Compared with real world scenarios, the reproduced environment can be built and modified in a more efficient way to adapt various scenarios. Thus, they provide a flexible and inexpensive environment for training. Advanced interactions would bring more lifelike experience but require human aware computing to support proactive interaction. This motivates us to develop a mixed reality suit to perform human aware interaction. Therefore, we design a mixed reality environment (MIXER). MIXER is an agent-based collaborative information system with hybrid reality merging interactive computer graphic. MIXER can provide a comprehensive human-centered mixed reality suite for advanced Virtual Reality (VR) and Augmented Reality (AR) applications such as therapy, training, and driving simulations.

In this paper, we present an interactive environment for tactical operations. Corresponding modules such as human aware computing, collaborative scalable learning in distributed systems, QoE-QoS balanced management and information security are discussed in the remaining sections.

2   Agent-Based System

MIXER is designed aiming at ambient interaction with visual computing support. The system comprises a sensor subsystem, a network subsystem and an interaction subsystem. For example, for military training, it requires an action sensor and a sensor shirt to capture motion, a weapon simulator, a smart helmet for interaction, and a smart gateway for network communication.

An ambient interaction system combining these technologies will not only bridge the gap between the real world and virtual environment, but also promote building increasingly complex virtual worlds for interactive artificial intelligence. In some cases, high level intelligent computing is needed to perform human-aware tasks for comprehensive interaction (e.g. support for decision making or assessment of fatigue state of the user, then a backend to support human-aware computation).

Considering the diversity of the devices and elements in MIXER, an agent based system [19] is designed based on an agent based model (ABM). Various hardware and software modules are abstracted as diverse agents according to

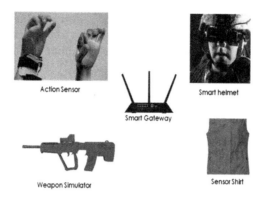

Fig. 1. Main devices of tactic training environment

Table 1. Intelligence classification

Class	Level	Functional capacity
A	Advanced	Perceive, apply complex inference and compute in complex data structures
B	Medium	Compute and process data with a medium data base
C	Simple	Store data and auto-react with string stack processing
D	Buffer	Use simple sensing and reaction, transmit data and store in a buffer

the roles they play. To simplify the management of the agents, we have divided intelligence level into four levels (A, B, C, D) as shown in Table 1. Some advanced functions can be implemented as the combinations of agents with different levels. The agents collaborate together under a specific structure to perform a certain functionality.

To enhance bodily interactions in VR, an agent based sensor network is used with a PPT camera system to address the localization problem in 3D VR [7]. Once the position of the subject in the virtual space is located, ambient interaction can be performed according to the motion of the subject. IEEE 1451.4 Transducers Electronic Data Sheets (TEDS) description model and Kullback-Leibler Divergence (KLD) method are used to identify the type of sensors and obtain the sensor data. Sensor networks can perform precise position tracking in a virtual world (e.g. [1]). Considering the possible heterogeneous data captured by hybrid devices in this type of hybrid systems, data fusion may be needed for the VR system before information processing.

To enable ambient interaction, system recognizes the target and judge the situation according to the human behavior. Cognitive differences between the novices and experts can be measured using psychophysiological feedback devices, such as EEG, ECG, EGG, etc., to understand human cognition and behavior. [11] revealed the possibility of applying the theory of mental imagery to read the mental state of participants and model human cognition. Further emotional states of user behaviors can be captured through speech and using a game pidgin language (GPL) and support vector machines (SVMs) to trigger the emotive response [10]. These studies support the use of human aware computation in interactive system design.

3   Mixed Interaction

The concept of mixed interaction refers to the interaction with different types of reality (VR and AR) and mixed reproduction of the objects. Both the subjects and objects in VR and AR can co-exist and be switched freely according to the demands of users, to perform human centered interaction adapting to the needs.

A military training simulation system with comprehensive interactions, as seen in Fig. 5, combines real soldiers and physical environments with virtual soldiers and reproduces a lifelike battle field with a series of metaphors. Interactive targets in the environment, including subjects (e.g. roles) and objects (e.g. weapons, cars) are either controlled by humans or by artificial intelligence. These simulations are used in military training programs to perform tactical operations. Compared with real world scenarios, the reproduced environment can be built and modified in a more efficient way to adapt various scenarios. This provides a flexible and inexpensive environment for training.

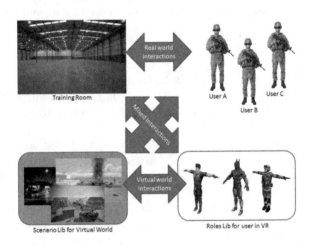

Fig. 2. Interactions in comprehensive reality world

During the interaction, mixed reality fusion (MRF) is required to perform reproduction of agents and objects and switching on the desired reality. This fusion is one of the technologies that plays an important role in the background research for MIXER development. With the support of the libraries of the roles and scenarios, as well as mixed interaction with data exchange between different reality environments, MRF can be performed. Figure 3 shows an example of

MRF. As shown in the figure, two subjects are not in the same scene in the real world but can be composed as if (a) they are in the same environment in MIXER and (b) partly appear to be in reality or VR in a specific scene (b). By switching the scene, real and virtual agents and objects we can provide a hybrid environment for co-existence of VR and AR agents.

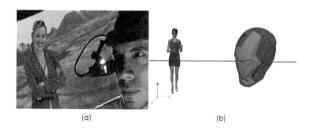

Fig. 3. Mixed reality fusion with the mixed interaction

Many existing researchers have been investigating the concept of interaction in VR and ambient intelligence. However, the issues about remote cooperation have not been addressed in detail. For example, if there is a group of the participants located in different places in different cities, training together members of this group is not possible since they are not co-located. This is an issue of remote cooperation in ambient interaction.

Figure 4 shows the design of a remote cooperation scheme with networked MRF. To implement mixed reality in the fusion of reality, action synthesizer and scenario synthesizer are used. Action synthesizer is used to detect and measure the behavior of human agents in the real world. Scenario synthesizer reproduces the virtual actions in the mixed reality world. Regarding the applications such as action movies and simulated training, script generator is used to adjust the virtual physical parameters in mixed reality, mapping the real behavior measurements to the values of actions with preset conditions and thresholds.

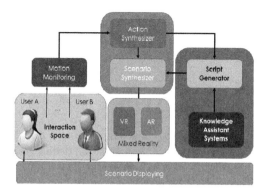

Fig. 4. Networked MRF for ambient interaction

This can reproduce a specific scene with a higher level of immersion for users to experience the real situation during interaction. The system logic can be built by the Knowledge Assistants network. Thus, MIXER can perform remote fusion providing the subjects with facilities to be either in real or virtual world.

4   Human Aware Computing

Another element that serves as an integral part in ambient interaction is human aware computing, where the agents act together as an autonomous entity of advanced intelligence with human-like awareness to perceive, feel, and be conscious of events, objects, or sensory patterns. To detect users intention and adapt to user and/or event on the scene, the system utilizes human aware computation. Thus, the system responds to preference-adaptive interaction by providing a proactive service. An anthropomorphic knowledge and a psychological expert system are included in human centered interaction. A logic system using perception-action cycle is modeled to compute interaction in MIXER. Subject perceives surroundings and then acts with a specific goal; actions affect the environment; the changes of the surrounding lead to further actions after being perceived by the human, which form a close cycle. With this logic model, MIXER is able to assess the behaviors of subject and support co-evolution. This also allows human like perception, recognition and reaction. Thus, a cyber-system serves not only human but as-if human.

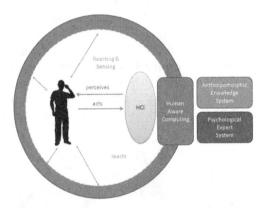

Fig. 5. Ambient intelligence for human aware computing

For the interaction in the mixed reality environment, positioning is an important issue to assess the quality of training. In some device based simulation systems, distance measurement is used to implement positioning task. For example, in latency training, the snaking interactions related to discovery or concealment depend on the distance between the receivers and transmitters of the devices.

In some cases, the device based systems could not simulate the real world situation since the physical measure (e.g. radiocommunication, electronicwave)for transmitter and receiver do not correspond to the real world sentry (e.g., vision, illumination). Usually the available distance of a typical distance detector is around 5 to 10 meters. The object further beyond this distance would not be detected by the detector.

To overcome the limitation of the distance measurement for the generalization of the system, stereo visual differentiating has been designed and integrated into the system. With visual sensing, recognition for human aware computing can be extended further using distance sensors.

An ambient interactive system requires to distinguish the target in the scenario from the trivial to implement human cognition. In many cases, human knowledge is expected to solve problems. For instance, in latency training or investigation, human knowledge to discover the target or ignore the trivial is needed. This can be also used for visual differentiation applications. With the knowledge system, stereo pattern analysis is used to obtain the stereo space mapping to recognize the objects in the environment [14]. As shown in Fig. 6, the system uses pattern context aware computing to differentiate the targeted object in the scenario.

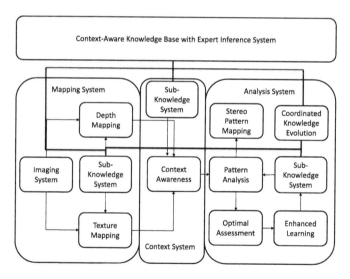

Fig. 6. The architecture of knowledge based context aware stereo pattern analysis

For transferring human knowledge, we design a knowledge system with adaptive fuzzy learning strategy for stereo differentiation. The uncertainty of data and solution are both taken into consideration. The measurement involved in the energy and the dimension of the anonymous pixels with estimated depth are objectives for optimization.

With the consideration of the uncertainties involved in texture condition, priori knowledge and solution, tail recursion and uniqueness of optimization guarantee the stability of the matting solution. Because of the adaptive learning strategy used in processing, the proposed scheme performs robust.

5   Collaborative Scalable Learning

Many works have addressed the questions about networking and communication in VR, AR and MR. Whereas, when it comes to the question with the consideration of networked data system, not much research is done on the issue of the scalability of dispersed knowledge architecture. In our work, we focus on the agent based collaborative scheme with a scalable learning strategy for knowledge evolution in dispersed knowledge systems.

With the consideration of the complexity of computation and the distribution of the agents, a scalable collaborative agents' framework is designed and used in the system. The agents are divided into groups according to the position and task orientation. The correlation among the groups are considered. Each group can be seen as a logical area and the whole system can be divided into many sub-areas for interactive computing. Because of the gradient nature of physical dynamics, there are overlaps among areas. As shown in Fig. 7, the logical overlap is modeled as correlations between the areas. Considering the uncertainties in the dynamical interaction in the overlap, we design a collaborative strategy using a distributed structure.

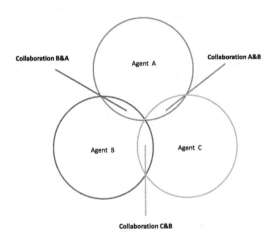

Fig. 7. The correlation of the collaborative agents

Figure 8 shows an overlapped exchange procedure between collaborative agents. The events regarding the patterns of interaction z are modeled as a series of states x of the agents i and j. Since the events are often distributed separately in space but correlated logically in operation, the strategy only uses the correlated states of agents to perform the process. This strategy reduces the consumption of the resources for computing, which enable the system filtering uncertainties with efficiency guarantee. The logically adjacent agents form a pair with dual direction links between each other that settled in different areas. The computation is dispatched in a dispersed structure and implemented by using the correlation information and interaction with agents.

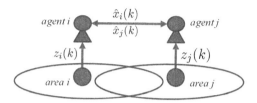

Fig. 8. Collaborative agents exchanging

After remote subsystems networked, the agents share the information and collaborate as a whole system to interact. To extend the system to support remote cooperation, we also design a network scheme for ambient interaction. In this case, the structure of the knowledge would be dispersed in the whole system. For many ubiquitous computing applications, both data and system are distributed, so is the knowledge system [5, 6, 16]. Correspondingly, the learning strategy should be proper for the systems in a distributed data structure. There have been many examples of distributed knowledge systems for intelligent applications (e.g. [2, 3, 9, 23, 25]). Mostly, they are established on a distributed database, in which the data processing is based on data dispatching via networked data organization, processing knowledge based on data dispatching via networked dataflow organization. Essentially, the organized dataflow in this type of systems serves to intergrade entire database in data processing. As shown in Fig. 10, they need to combine the new knowledge with obtained features to reorganize the knowledge as a whole to process data. Therefore, it still needs a medium to store whole updated knowledge, which is inflexible especially for the temporarily used knowledge or short term tasks. It is still needed for the tasks to obtain some information in the global data (e.g. calculating the covariance of the whole data space) before dispatching the workload into distributed computational structure, which renders the constraints on flexibility in applications of the scalable system. Thus, these methods still have some constraints on the flexibility and scalability, especially for the data system with heterogeneous knowledge obtained by various methods.

Considering the difficulty of the knowledge system updates in a distributed system, we design a scalable learning strategy for dispersed knowledge management. Here the issues to consider are data scalability and knowledge usability. A scalable learning scheme and ξ process are used to perform the scalable update [15]. As shown in Fig. 10, the updated parts of the knowledge can be distributed

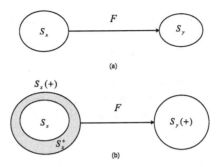

Fig. 9. Update learning

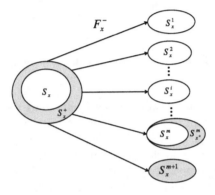

Fig. 10. Scalable learning for updating knowledge-base

to corresponding agents. Thus, the dispersed knowledge system can be used as a centralized system without knowing the overview of the global database with the proposed scheme.

6   QoE-QoS Management

In agent based interaction, the value of the facility must be ensured. Given network quality, Quality of Service (QoS) supplies a sound basis for a system to provide service. An ambient interactive system must consider both the Quality of Experience (QoE) for immersion experience and the QoS for system performance. However, it is difficult to arrange optimum levels of QoE and QoS at the same time since the resources for computation and communication are limited. How to manage QoE-QoS is a significant problem for next generation computational services, especially for those with a networked structure.

Besides the QoE-QoS balanced management, data-aware methods can be used to perform Quality of Experience (QoE) and Quality of Service (QoS) management [13]. With the data-aware scheme, the design and optimization of the agent-based interaction environment can be analytically simplified as data precision programming. Since the resolution of the level of precise data is more divided than the levels of MOS (Mean Opinion Score, usually only 5 levels), using the precise data can be more flexible. By the analysis of QoE-QoS, the level of QoE that the system capable of providing can also be assessed. Neither can the system keep working under low energy efficiency to pursuit QoE nor high-level QoS with low QoE. Therefore, the precision can be seen as an optimal reference to managing system under normal operating conditions (NOC), and QoE-QoS balance analysis can also be used to assess the optimal level of QoE that system is capable of providing under NOC.

7 Security

As one of the most significant factors in data communication for military applications, we take information security into consideration. We focus on the protection of the original data. Authentication and encryption are the issues to consider regarding access and attacks. While guaranteeing the performance of information security, the efficiency of processing big data is also taken into consideration in system design.

For the information security, we design a fast cryptosystem scheme with the consideration of both efficiency and performance. The scheme is designed with five main elements based on the public key cryptography (PKC) key management architecture as shown in Fig. 11, where the information agent (IA) refers to the user or the device, the element packing and unpacking serve for data encapsulation and decapsulation, and the security of the connection is guaranteed by the tunnel built with encryption and decryption subsystems.

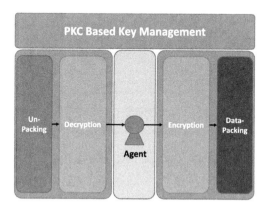

Fig. 11. PKC based scheme for confidential communication

Considering the delay in communication, these two series might be out of sync with each other at the beginning, even though the mechanism of the key generation is the same. We use the decrypted time stamps to synchronize the time slot for the communication. Chaotic cryptography is used here due to its quick encryption and decryption performance. Furthermore, the chaotic series for encryption can be generated by some simple circuits [20,29],which can save resources for cryptography. As shown in Fig. 12, customized parameter (CP) is set by IA to impact the chaos driven encryption (CDE). Authentication key (AK) is the key authorized by the key management with the certificate authority (CA) and registration authority (RA). This key is embedded into the chips with hardware security in the sensor before setting up the system, which guarantees that each node in the network is authenticated. As an authorized node, the sensor with AK is recognized as a legitimate object. To further guarantee the data integrity, a PKC based time stamp is used for tracking the creation and modification of the data with a digital signature. The information agent (IA) uses the PKC key to influence the chaotic series to encrypt time stamps for communication.

Let the CDE function be f_{CDE} and the chaotic series be X, the chaotic mapping in Fig. 12 can be modeled as:

$$X = f_{CDE}(CP, AK) \qquad (1)$$

where AK is known as embedded in the hardware and CP is shared by PKC authenticated handshaking with Diffie-Hellman protocol [8,30]. Each shared key has its lifetime period. When lifetime is expired, the PKC head will reset the keys distribution.

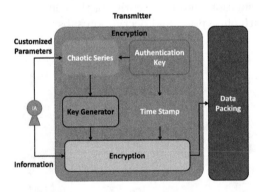

Fig. 12. Chaotic PKC transmitter

Correspondingly, the receiver is shown in Fig. 13, where the encrypted time stamps and message are unpacked from the received data pack. After decryption, time stamps will be used for the synchronization of the chaotic series for deciphering the messages. In the agents system implementation, the IA is an information process module (IPM), mainly responsible for capturing the information, coding and decoding. Anti-dismantle is used in the design of the devices.

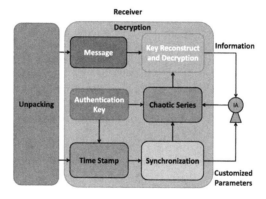

Fig. 13. Chaotic PKC receiver

Since the IPM is encapsulated with encryption and decryption module as one entity, both the AK and agent are integrated under the hardware protection.

8   Conclusion

In this brief paper, we mainly present a framework for a collaborative agent-based scheme for mixed reality. The framework uses mixed reality, ubiquitous computing, and human aware computing concepts. A scalable updating strategy for the knowledge system is introduced to make the system flexible. To perform mixed interaction, we investigate a human aware mixed reality technology using collaborative information processing strategies, and demonstrate a scheme to enhance security and authentication for the mixed reality application. We plan to implement this framework as a part of future work.

References

1. Aarabi, P.: Localization-based sensor validation using the kullback-leibler divergence. IEEE Trans. Syst. Man Cybern. Part B: Cybern. **34**(2), 1007–1016 (2004)
2. Aibat, H., Terano, T.: A computational model for distributed knowledge systems with learning mechanisms. Expert Syst. Appl. **10**(3), 417–427 (1996)
3. Angelopoulos, C.M., Nikoletseas, S., Raptis, T.P.: Wireless energy transfer in sensor networks with adaptive, limited knowledge protocols. Comput. Netw. **70**, 113–141 (2014)
4. Azuma, R.T.: A survey of augmented reality. Pres. Teleoper. Virtual Environ. **6**(4), 355–385 (1997)
5. Craenen, B.G.W., Theodoropoulos, G.K.: Ubiquitous computing and distributed agent-based simulation. In Fifth International Conference on Innovative Mobile and Internet Services in Ubiquitous Computing (IMIS), pp. 241–247. IEEE (2011)
6. Desruelle, H., Lyle, J., Isenberg, S., Gielen, F.: On the challenges of building a web-based ubiquitous application platform. In UbiComp 2012: Proceedings of the ACM Conference on Ubiquitous Computing, pp. 733–736. ACM (2012)

7. Gulrez, T., Kavakli, M.: Sensor relevance establishment problem in shared information gathering sensor networks. In: IEEE International Conference on Networking, Sensing and Control, pp. 650–655. IEEE (2007)
8. Hellman, M.E.: An overview of public key cryptography. IEEE Commun. Mag. **40**(5), 42–49 (2002)
9. Ho, C.-T., Chen, Y.-M., Chen, Y.-J., Wang, C.-B.: Developing a distributed knowledge model for knowledge management in collaborative development and implementation of an enterprise system. Rob. Comput.-Integr. Manuf. **20**(5), 439–456 (2004)
10. Kavakli, M.: Training simulations for crime risk assessment. In: 7th International Conference on Information Technology Based Higher Education and Training, ITHET 2006, pp. 203–210. IEEE (2006)
11. Kavakli, M., Gero, J.S.: Sketching as mental imagery processing. Des. Stud. **22**(4), 347–364 (2001)
12. Laver, K., George, S., Thomas, S., Deutsch, J.E., Crotty, M.: Virtual reality for stroke rehabilitation. Stroke **43**(2), e20–e21 (2012)
13. Liu, C.Z., Kavakli, M.: Data-aware qoe-qos management. In IEEE 11th Conference on Industrial Electronics and Applications (ICIEA), pp. 1823–1828. IEEE (2016)
14. Liu, C.Z., Kavakli, M.: Collaborative stereo pattern recognition for mixed reality based on context-aware analysis. In: IEEE ISMAR Workshop on Collaborative Mixed Reality Environments (COMIRE). IEEE (submitted, 2016)
15. Liu, C.Z., Kavakli, M.: Scalable learning for dispersed knowledge systems. In: 13th Annual International Conference on Mobile, Ubiquitous Systems: Computing, Networking and Services. EAI, submitted
16. Lopes, J., Gusmao, M., Souza, R., Davet, P., Souza, A., Costa, C., Barbosa, J., Pernas, A., Yamin, A., Geyer, C.: Towards a distributed architecture for context-aware mobile applications in ubicomp. In: Proceedings of the 19th Brazilian symposium on Multimedia and the Web, pp. 43–50. ACM (2013)
17. Mantovani, F., Castelnuovo, G., Gaggioli, A., Riva, G.: Virtual reality training for health-care professionals. CyberPsychol. Behav. **6**(4), 389–395 (2003)
18. Merchant, Z., Goetz, E.T., Cifuentes, L., Keeney-Kennicutt, W., Davis, T.J.: Effectiveness of virtual reality-based instruction on students' learning outcomes in k-12 and higher education: A meta-analysis. Comput. Educ. **70**, 29–40 (2014)
19. Minsky, M.: The Society of Mind. Simon & Schuster (1988)
20. Muthuswamy, B., Chua, L.O.: Simplest chaotic circuit. Int. J. Bifurc. Chaos **20**(05), 1567–1580 (2010)
21. Ohta, Y., Tamura, H.: Mixed Reality: Merging Real and Virtual Worlds. Springer Publishing Company, Incorporated, Heidelberg (2014)
22. Ong, S.K., Nee, A.Y.C.: Virtual and Augmented Reality Applications in Manufacturing. Springer Science & Business Media, London (2013)
23. Rinkus, S., Walji, M., Johnson-Throop, K.A., Malin, J.T., Turley, J.P., Smith, J.W., Zhang, J.: Human-centered design of a distributed knowledge management system. J. Biomed. Inf. **38**(1), 4–17 (2005)
24. Riva, G.: Ambient Intelligence: The Evolution of Technology, Communication and Cognition Towards the Future of Human-Computer Interaction, vol. 6. IOS Press, Amsterdam (2005)
25. Romero-Tris, C., Castellà-Roca, J., Viejo, A.: Distributed system for private web search with untrusted partners. Comput. Netw. **67**, 26–42 (2014)
26. Seitz, C.A., Poyrazli, S., Harrisson, M.A., Flickinger, T., Turkson, M.: Virtual reality exposure therapy for military veterans with posttraumatic stress disorder: a systematic review. New School Psychol. Bull. **11**(1), 15–29 (2014)

27. Sims, R.: Interactivity: A forgotten art? Comput. Hum. Behav. **13**(2), 157–180 (1997)
28. Spector, J.M.: Integrating, humanizing the process of automating instructional design. In: Tennyson, R.D., Barron, A.E. (eds.) Automating Instructional Design: Computer-Based Development and Delivery Tools, pp. 523–546. Springer, Heidelberg (1995)
29. Sprott, J.C.: A new class of chaotic circuit. Phys. Lett. A **266**(1), 19–23 (2000)
30. Steiner, M., Tsudik, G., Waidner, M.: Diffie-hellman key distribution extended to group communication. In: Proceedings of the 3rd ACM Conference on Computer and Communications Security, pp. 31–37. ACM (1996)

A Density Peak Cluster Model
of High-Dimensional Data

Cong Jin[✉], Xi Xie, and Fei Hu

Key Laboratory of Media Audio and Video, Ministry of Education,
Communication University of China, Beijing 100024, China
{jincong,cici.xie,hufei}@cuc.edu.cn

Abstract. Clustering is an important tool for data mining and analysis for massive data in big data. This paper proposes a clustering model of high-dimensional data based on the density peak cluster algorithm and accomplishes clustering for more than six-dimensional data with arbitrary shape simply and directly. This model achieves automatically pre-process and takes local points with larger density and far away from other local points as the clustering center followed by introducing the fine-tuning. Experimental results suggest that our model not only works for low-dimensional data, but also achieves promising performance for high-dimensional data.

Keywords: High-dimensional data · Density peak cluster · Clustering center · Data mining · Big data

1 Introduction

Clustering is a collection of physical or abstract objects into some subclasses that compose of some similar objects, and plays an important role in the field of data mining. What's more, clustering won the worldwide attention of scholars and research institutions. Predecessors in the field of clustering algorithm have made important contributions. For example, in the traditional clustering algorithm, K - means algorithm and K medoids algorithm [1] are easy to understand, convenient and quick to realize, but one major drawback is that the two algorithms are both sensitive to abnormal value; Hierarchical clustering algorithm [2] and partitioning clustering algorithm [3] is quick to cluster, but only can be applied to convex cluster; DBSCAN algorithm (Density-based Spatial Clustering of Applications with Noise) [6] and OPTICS algorithm (Ordering Points to identify the Clustering structure) [7], based on Density Clustering algorithm, have precisely solved some drawbacks of the above two kinds of algorithms. Compared with the commonly used distance sum of clustering center to continuously optimize algorithm [4, 5], the clustering algorithm based on density adopts a more ingenious way: in the whole sample points, all the target clusters are made up of a group of dense sample points, and these dense sample points are split by low density areas (noise), thus the purpose of the algorithm is to filter the low density areas, and to find the sample points with high density.

DBSCAN algorithm defines the clusters as the maximizing set of the connected density points, and is able to divide areas with high enough density into clusters, then

G. Wang et al. (Eds.): APSCC 2016, LNCS 10065, pp. 220–227, 2016.
DOI: 10.1007/978-3-319-49178-3_17

can find clusters with arbitrary shape in the spatial database of noise. However, the algorithm is also sensitive to initial parameters. OPTICS algorithm overcomes the problems of DBSCAN algorithm and achieves better results, but the problem of the algorithm is to implement is very complicated, and the interoperability in practical application is not strong. References [8] proposed density peak clustering (DPC) algorithm, which skillfully avoids the above problems and in a more direct and concise way completes the clustering. However, the proposed algorithm only has superior performance in the low-dimensional data, as with the increase of data's dimension, the clustering result falls sharply. Therefore, this article put forward an improved algorithm based on density peak clustering algorithm for clustering model of high- dimensional data, which can accomplish clustering with arbitrary shape of more than six dimensional data in the direct and simple way. This model implements the automatic pretreatment process, then puts larger local density points which are far away from other local density points as the clustering center, finally introduces the adjustment of parameters.

2 Density Peak Cluster

Density peak cluster (DPC) essentially belongs to the density algorithm. The basic idea is that we suppose some low local density points surround the center of each cluster, and these points are far away from other high local density points.

2.1 Density Clustering Algorithm

Suppose there are n sample points $\{1, 2, 3, \ldots n\}$, construct a distance matrix D,

$$D = \{d_{ij}\}_{\substack{1 \le i \le n \\ 1 \le j \le n}} \tag{1}$$

d_{ij} shows distance between point i and point j. Then, we define the local density of sample point i:

$$\rho_i = \sum_j \chi(d_{ij} - d_c) \tag{2}$$

$$\chi(x) = \begin{cases} 1; & x < 0 \\ 0; & other \end{cases} \tag{3}$$

Among them, d_c is a custom threshold (thresh), the local density of point i is the amount of all the points that distance to the point i less than the threshold. The selection of the threshold, directly determines the size of the local density.

In addition, we define the function δ of point i:

If i is the maximum density point, we define it as:

$$\delta_i = \min_{\rho_j > \rho_i} d_{ij} \tag{4}$$

Otherwise,

$$\delta_i = \max\{d_{ij}\} \tag{5}$$

At this time, δ is the minimum distance between all local density points greater than point i and point i. The selection of clustering center is based on a simple principle: the local density of the clustering center is large, and the clustering center is far away from others. Calculate the local density value ρ of all the sample points and δ, then select the points with larger δ and ρ as clustering centers. By the assumption of the algorithm, we can know, the local maximum density point is a central point. After confirming the clustering central point, other sample points should be in turn determined into their own clusters from near to far according to the collection of points in the distance with the judged points; Judgment criteria is each point's cluster is its own cluster of points which are the nearest in the neighborhood and local density are higher than that point.

2.2   Density Peak Cluster Model for High Dimension Data

The density peak cluster model we proposed for high-dimensional data includes three parts. First, we conduct automatic preprocessing to select the initial clustering center. The realization method is normalizing ρ, δ, computing $\mu = \rho * \delta$, and finding out the abnormal points of μ is higher than average a variance as the initial clustering centers; Then cluster, and finally adjust the parameters, correct the abnormal points. Specific steps are as shown in Fig. 1.

After data initialization, model begins to calculate the distance matrix and confirm the corresponding threshold. Then calculates ρ, δ of all the points and normalizes ρ, δ, to find out the point that $\delta * \rho$ is greater than the average one standard deviation as the initial clustering center; Again combines the near clustering centers, identifies classification; According to the distance from the classified point, identifies classification from near to far; Finally amends abnormal points with smaller ρ, larger δ, and mergers similar clusters.

Through the proposed model reasoning in this paper, the points of largest local density must satisfy δ is locally largest in this conclusion. The proof is as follows:

Proposition. Set r as the threshold value of neighborhood. For any $k \in \{k, d_{ik} < r\}$, meet $\rho_k < \rho_i$, then $k \in \{k, d_{ik} < r\}, \delta_k < \delta_i$.

Proof. Suppose $\delta_i < r$, that is $\delta_i = \min\limits_{\rho_j > \rho_i} d_{ij} < r$, then there is a point h, meet $d_{ih} < r$, and $\rho_h > \rho_i$, this is inconsistence with the condition, thus $\delta_i > r$. While k is not the maximum density point, as a result, there is

$$\delta_k = \min\limits_{\rho_j > \rho_k} d_{kj} < d_{ki} = d_{ik} < r \tag{6}$$

so $\delta_k < \delta_i$.

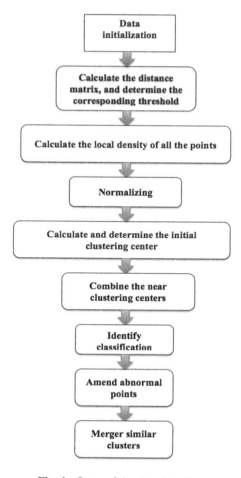

Fig. 1. Steps of density clustering

In fact, through the proof process of this proposition, we can find that δ of the biggest local density points are greater than δ of all the biggest nonlocal density points. So δ is enough to reflect the method of choosing the clustering center, thus the selection of clustering center, you just need to consider δ.

This article selects the clustering database given in the reference [8] using this model to simulate the two-dimensional data, and results are shown in Fig. 2. Among them, selection of threshold is according to the proposed condition: the average neighbor numbers for all points are 1 % to 2 % of the total numbers. The numbers in Fig. 2A respectively stands the local density of two-dimensional points from big to small. Figure 2B is the density - delta figure for all the points, the horizontal axis shows local density, the vertical axis shows δ. In Fig. 2B, δ of point 1 and point 10 is high, and also local density is high, so they are selected as the clustering centers. For undefined point 2, the point closest to the point 2 and the density higher than the point is point 1, so the point 2 marked as same as the 1 point.

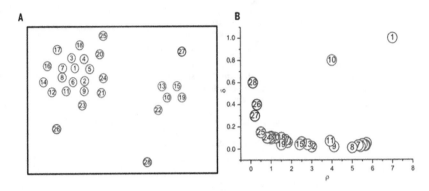

Fig. 2. Clustering for two-dimensional data

Defining the boundary area contains belonging to the class but the distance from other classes of points less than the threshold points. For another class of boundary area, the local density of the largest local density points is ρ_b, and in this class all the points of local density greater than ρ_b are considered as the reliable points, while the rest points are considered as abnormal points (noise).

3   The Experiment and Analysis

This article provides a method of data acquisition and the data settings; moreover, it expounds building the experimental environment and the experiment settings, and shows the result and analysis of the experiment.

3.1   Experiment Settings

In this paper, the experimental environment is in a Linux desktop computer platform based on Matlab. System configuration is 6 nuclear Intel Xeon Processor X4860, CPU 2.26 GHz 64 GB of memory. In the experiment, it also makes use of crawler technology, in the real network environment the creeper crawled a lot of consumption data by months based on website, to test the proposed model. The data contains more than one-dimensional data, through the analysis of the model for each-dimensional information can well guide practical application, such as accurate delivery for advertisements, customer recommendation system.

3.2   Result

The experiment is based on different data normalization methods for DPC clustering, which makes z - score normalization processing transform data into normal distribution of data. When the data is only processed by z - score normalization, the result is bad;

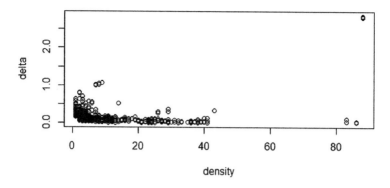

Fig. 3. The local density of six-dimensional data

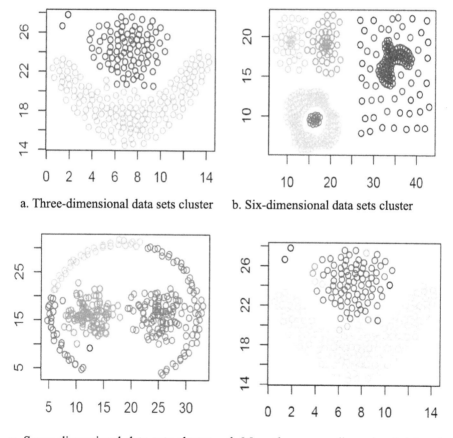

a. Three-dimensional data sets cluster   b. Six-dimensional data sets cluster

c. Seven-dimensional data sets cluster   d. More than seven-dimensional data sets
cluster

Fig. 4. Clustering effects for N-dimensional data sets

Processing the data only by linear normalization is not good; First use linear normalization and make z - score normalization, the effect is not good; Make log processing, and the effect is improved. Analyzing the data step by step, it appears a class of points, and in this class of points the local density are much higher than other local density. This leads although δ is less than others, μ is still larger, and μ in parts of the clustering centers is not a standard deviation from the mean value. The experiment expands our scope of looking for clustering centers, adjusts and reduces the lower limit of the initial clustering center in selection conditions, then clustering can get obvious change. But when relevant experiments process the source data and small-amplitude adjustment of weight, there is no effect on the clustering results. That is, adding a standard deviation into the average of partial data is enough to select the center point of the right points. Figure 3 is the local density of six- dimensional data. Moreover, the model for dealing with the data clustering in the convex hull types has remarkable effect. The clustering effects are as shown in Fig. 4.

4   Conclusion

This model's effect is good to deal with irregular graphical clustering in a variety of high-dimensional data, but must be paid attention to the premise of the proposed algorithm: each class of center is surrounded by some points of low local density, and the points are far from other high local density. What's more, the problem in the model that clustering effect is not ideal for different classes and big differences in order of magnitude, and needs further research and improvement.

References

1. Li, C.P., Li, J.H., He, M.: Concept lattice compression in incomplete contexts based on K-medoids clustering. Intl. J. Mach. Learn. Cybern. **7**(4), 539–552 (2016)
2. Gagolewski, M., Bartoszuk, M., Cena, A.: Genie: A new, fast, and outlier-resistant hierarchical clustering algorithm. Inf. Sci. **363**(3), 8–23 (2016)
3. Ying, W., Chung, F.-L., Wang, S.: Scaling up synchronization-inspired partitioning clustering. IEEE Trans. Knowl. Data Eng. **26**(8), 2045–2057 (2014)
4. Frey, B.J., Dueck, D.: Clustering by passing messages between data points. Science **315**(5814), 972–976 (2007)
5. Pereira, R., Fagundes, A., Melicio, R.: A fuzzy clustering approach to a demand response model. Intl. J. Electrical Power Energy Syst. **81**(10), 184–192 (2016)
6. Mahesh Kumar, K., Rama Mohan Reddy, A.: A fast DBSCAN clustering algorithm by accelerating neighbor searching using Groups method. Pattern Recogn. **58**(1), 39–48 (2016)
7. Ankerst, M., Breunig, M.M., Kriegel, H.P., Sander, J.: OPTICS: ordering points to identify the clustering structure. ACM Sigmod Rec. **28**(2), 49–60. ACM (1999)
8. Rodriguez, A., Laio, A.: Clustering by fast search and find of density peaks. Science **344**(6191), 1492–1496 (2014)
9. Fu, L., Medico, E.: FLAME, a novel fuzzy clustering method for the analysis of DNA microarray data. BMC Bioinform. **8**(1), 3 (2007)

10. Maza, S., Simon, C., Boukhobza, T.: Impact of the actuator failures on the structural controllability of linear systems: a graph theoretical approach. IET Control Theory Appl. **6**(3), 412–419 (2012)
11. Chang, H., Yeung, D.Y.: Robust path-based spectral clustering. Pattern Recogn. **41**(1), 191–203 (2008)

A Service Composition Method Through Multiple User-Centric Views

Huayong Luo[1], Weilong Ding[2,3(✉)], and Sheng Gui[1]

[1] Beijing China-Power Information Technology Company Limited,
Beijing 100085, China
{luohuayong, guisheng}@sgitg.sgcc.com.cn
[2] Data Engineering Institute, North China University of Technology,
Beijing 100144, China
dingweilong@ncut.edu.cn
[3] Beijing Key Laboratory on Integration and Analysis of Large-Scale
Stream Data, Beijing 100144, China

Abstract. User-centric service is wildly adopted in the Cloud environment, but its comprehensible composition is still challenge. On the one hand, intuitive programming perspective is required to hide low-level details with the reasonable abstract; on the other hand, effective guarantee is necessary to verify the application's legality. In this paper, we present a service composition method through multiple user-centric views in which different abstract is provided by orthogonal and orderly views. Domain applications can be synthesized and their consistency is guaranteed coordinately.

Keywords: User centric · Multiple views · Service · Service composition · Programming method

1 Introduction

Service has been widely adopted as the key component in the Cloud [1], and related technologies have experienced the procedure from *computer-centric* to *user-centric* [2]. User-centric service composition directly reflects the user demands to build applications in a cost-efficient way [3]. In our domain of Chinese *State Grid*, some business procedures have been modeled as the "micro-service [4]" and several applications have been built by business users' service compositions. In decision and policy-intensive domain, such as the finance and insurance sectors, business rules are especially useful to express, manage and update applications [5]. The business user in these domains who usually lacks the IT knowledge eagerly requires customized applications employing their familiar business rules. Nevertheless, there are still challenges to meet their business demands in a user-centric way. On the one hand, it is not convenient to modeling and organizing business rules through comprehensible programming elements like constraints; on the other hand, it lacks effective guarantee support to verify the correctness of applications built by users.

In this paper, we propose a user-centric multiple views service composition method, which contains declarative model for service composition, modeling operations and

G. Wang et al. (Eds.): APSCC 2016, LNCS 10065, pp. 228–238, 2016.
DOI: 10.1007/978-3-319-49178-3_18

system-aided support. The model declares the constraints through comprehensive *Specification Pattern* to express composition behavior i.e., the business rules. Meanwhile, according to the principle "separation of concerns" and rule characteristic, the constraints are declared and organized in two types of views: pattern view and scale view. In these orthogonal and orderly views, users declare constrains in different perspectives and our method guarantees the consistency of the constraints on-the-fly to synthesize the application from declarations in views.

The rest of the paper is organized as follows. Section 2 describes the application model for multi-view service composition. Section 3 elaborates the modeling approach. Section 4 presents a case study. Section 5 shows the related work, followed by conclusion in Sect. 6.

2   Multi-view Service Composition Model

2.1   Application Model Overview

There are two typical programming fashions for service composition: imperative and declarative [6]. The traditional imperative fashion strictly specifies how the process will be executed and yields well-formed structural processes. Its major drawback is the fact that users have to know well about the programming details, such as services' relations and the whole composition logic. On the contrary, declarative fashion specifies what the process is, such as the temporal logic demand among services' relations in composition, which supports loose structure at build time [6–8]. Although declarative fashion could build applications indirectly via constrains, some inevitable problems still cannot be ignored. That is, when constrains scale, the service composition cannot be expected to be comprehensive and controllable for the users.

Therefore, this paper proposes a programming model balancing availability and controllability above for business users.

Definition 1: Application model. Multi-view service composition model *App* is a two-tuple. *App* = *(P, V)*, in which *P* is the expression of process model for *APP* and *V* is the view set for constraints.

The process model *P* in *App* is synthesized from the constraints in views of *V* automatically.

Definition 2: Process model *P*. Process model describes the composite logic of the services, which is described as directed graph: *P* = *(activities, transitions)*. The *activities* refer to the set of *activity*, and *activity* = *(aId, type)*, consist of identifier and activity type. *type* = *{start, end, andSplit, andJoin, orsplit, orJoin, service}*, first six types are control-activity, and the last is service-activity. The service-activity *service* = *(sId, inputs, outputs)*, consist of identifier and its IO configuration. The *transitions* express a set of *transition. transition* = *(sourceId, targetId, data Mapping)*, describe the control flow between two activities, and the *dataMapping* is the transferred data.

2.2   Behavior Constraints of Service Composition

In our application model, behavior constraint (i.e., constraint in this paper) of service composition is declared through Specification Pattern System (SPS) [9], which is the abstracted pattern of the temporal logic CTL*. The constraints through SPS have strict formal foundations with high level comprehensible abstraction, which describes the behaviors in two parts *pattern* and *scope*. The *pattern* depicts the common behavior pattern, and *scope* describes the valid extent of the behavior pattern under certain metric. According to the characteristics of business user, only unary and binary constraints are concerned in this paper as Table 1 shown.

Definition 3: Behavior constraint of service composition. Constraint is expressed by SPS, and describes the behavior in service composition. Atomic constraint *bc* is the basic unit, and the constraints can be defined recursively: *constraint = bc|constraint∧constraint|constraint∨constraint*. Atomic constraint is constructed as *bc = pattern × scope*.

Table 1. Unary and binary atomic constraints

Pattern		Scope
P precedes Q	×	globally
P leads to Q		before S
P is absent		after R
P is universal		between R and S
P exists [at most / at least n times]		after R until S

Note: P, Q, R and S denote the behavior or state

(1) The *pattern* of behavior can be any one below.

P absent: under certain extent, service P cannot occur;

P universal: under certain extent, service P always occurs;

P exists [m..n]: under certain extent, service P could occurs (at least m times and at most n times);

P precedes Q: under certain extent, service P occurs ahead of service Q;

P response Q: under certain extent, once service P occurs, service Q must occur.

(2) The *scope* of behavior describes the valid extent via certain metric (such as KPI, key performance indicator), can be any one below.

globally: behavior is valid under whole metric extent;

before R: behavior is valid under the extent before the metric value R occurs;

after R: behavior is valid under the extent after the metric value R occurs;

R between S: behavior is valid under the extent between the metric value R occurs and metric value S occurs;

R until S: behavior is valid under the extent between the metric value R occurs and metric value S occurs (S could never occurs);

2.3   Views in View Set

Declared constraints construct the constraint set of application, and the scale of the constraint set could also influence the complexity of business user programming. So it is also necessary to provide rational organization of the constraints. Multi-view modeling approach describes different perspectives of the application, and it is a typical method to hide the complexity for the users. But the current workarounds always employ multi-view to manage, rather modeling the application. And the control flow based modeling method lack the support of the business rules. In order to reduce the complexity of the constraints scale, multi-view is proposed in our method to declare and organize the constraints. According to the structure of atomic constraint in Definition 3, the view set consists of several views in two types.

Definition 4: View set V in App. $V = \{patternView, scopeViews\}$, in which *patternView* is the behavior pattern view, and *scopeViews* is the set of metric scope view under orthogonal metric. That is, V consists of one pattern view and several scope views.

Pattern view organizes the declared constraints in the perspective of common behaviors in service composition.

Definition 5: Pattern view. Pattern view organizes subset of constraints in pattern perspective, which is consisted of the set of patterns. *pattern* = *uniPV|binPV*, in which unary pattern *uniPV* = *service uni-predicate*; binary pattern *binPV* = *service bi-predicate service*. Unary predicates *uni-predicate* = *{absent, universal, exist}*; binary predicates *bi-predicate* = *{precede, response}*. Service in patterns is determined by identifier *sId*.

Scope restricts the valid extend under certain metric, and scope view organizes the declared constraints in the perspective of metric extents. We assume the metrics among different scope view is orthogonal with each other.

Definition 6: Scope view. Scope view *scopeView* organizes subset of constraints in perspective of metric extents. *scopeView* = *(metricAxis, patternAxis, ps)*. The *metricAxis* is the axis of the scope metric, whose range is $(-\infty, +\infty)$ and the orientation is the partial order of the metric. The *patternAxis* is the axis of patterns, whose range is the enumeration of pattern defined in pattern view, and the orientation is time sequence defined. The *ps* is the set of binding from pattern to scope, *binding* = *(pattern, metricScopes)*. The *metricScopes* is the set of *metricScope*, which describes the valid extent of the pattern under this metric: *metricScope* = *(startMetric, endMetric)*, in which *startMetric, endMetric*$\in$*metricAxis* refer to the metric value of the extent boundary.

According to Definitions 4 and 6, there are several scope views under different metrics. The construction procedure of scope views under certain metric is called initiation of scope view. We have proved that scope view can be initiated if and only if there is partial ordered relation in the metric. Let's take time as the metric for example to initiate a scope view *timeView*. The sequence of time is naturally the partially ordered relation for time, and time period is the scope extend which could be determined by two time moments *startTime* and *endTime*. If we use the term $t1 < t2$ denotes *t1* occurs before *t2*, the timeView can be defined, and the semantic of *globally, before, after, between* and *until* for scope can be described either. We have implemented the *timeView* based on the time principle by Allen et al. [10]. Similarly, we could use region as metric to initiate the *spaceView* in an analogous way.

3   Multi-view Synthesized Application Building Procedure

3.1   Methodology

According to previous definitions, views' properties could be deduced.

Proposition 1: View is the subset of the orthogonal constraints.

Proposition 2: View is the subset of the orderly constraints.

Furthermore, the relationship among views is defined as follows.

Definition 7: Associations R among views. $R = (R_{pa}, R_{sa}, R_{sp})$. The association between pattern and process is R_{pa}, and its semantic is $\forall service \in patternView.\ pattern,\ \exists activity \in P.activities,$ and $service.sId = activity.aId$. The association between scope and process is R_{sa}, and its semantic is that $\forall service \in scopeView.ps.pattern,\ \exists activity \in P.activities,$ and $service.sId = activity.aId$. The association between pattern view and scope is R_{sp}, and its semantic is $\forall pattern \in scopeView.ps,\ pattern \in patternView$.

The associations depicts that operations on any view will coordinated to the other views and process model, which is the foundation of our synthesized method. Therefore, the rationale of user-centric multiple view service composition method can be illustrated as Fig. 1.

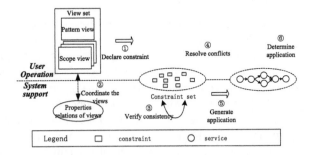

Fig. 1. Rationale of multi-view synthesized service composition

Application modeling procedure is illustrated as follows. (1) Users declare the behavior pattern of service composition in the pattern view, and declare the valid metric extents in scope views. (2) The effects of declarative operations above are coordinated to other views via the relations among views. The constraint set is constructed. (3) For each constraint user built is verified by the system to examine the consistency to the existed constraints in the view set. If there is any conflict, location the places in the constraint set. If not, go to set 5. (4) User resolves the conflicts until it is consistent among constraints set. (5) The constraint set is translated to executable process model. If the process is unique, the procedure ends. Otherwise, the candidate processes are returned to user in recommendatory order. Go to step 6. (6) User determines the process model. The procedure ends.

3.2   Operations in Multi-view

The first step of our method is to declare the constraints in the views as Fig. 2 showed. Views are user interface which consist of one pattern view and several scope views.

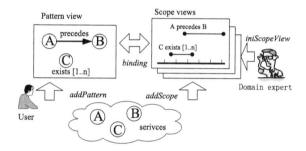

Fig. 2. Constraints declaration

There are some operations in these views for constraint declaration.

Operation 1: *addPattern(p).* This operation adds a new behavior pattern to the pattern view. The parameter p is the new pattern as Definition 5 defined. The services involved form the directed graph by certain pattern p. Pattern p and existed patterns $p_1, p_2 \ldots p_n$ in pattern view form the conjunction relation: $p_1 \wedge p_2 \wedge \ldots p_n \wedge p$. Meanwhile, the new pattern p could be referred in scope views.

Operation 2: *delPattern(p).* This operation deletes an existed pattern p in pattern view. Through the relations among the views, $\forall s\ binding_p(p,s) \in scopeView$, if $\neg \exists binding(p_i,s) \in scopeView$, $p_i \neq p$, the operation also deletes the metric scope s.

Operation 3: *iniScopeView(mAxis).* This operation is done by domain experts to initiate one scope view. The parameter *mAxis* is the user defined metric axis where the orientation is the partially ordered relation of the metric as Definition 6 defined. Such as, the time view is one dimension horizontal axis.

Operation 4: *addScope(s).* This operation adds a new metric scope s to the scope view. The *metricScope* in Definition 6 is determined by the value *startMetric* and *endMetric* on the metric axis. The relations among scopes are formed by operation *binding*.

Operation 5: *binding(p,s).* This operation binds one pattern p to one scope s, which also form one atomic constraint c. The default scope bind to one pattern is *globally*, which is rewritten by one *binding* operation. As a result, this operation always leads to one new constraint or modifies one existed constraint. Some explanations should be emphasized here. (1) In the same scope view, the scopes $s_1,s_2...s_n$ bound to certain pattern p form the disjunction relation: $p \times (s_1 \vee s_2 \vee ... \vee s_n) = c_1 \vee c_2 \vee ... \vee c_n$. (2) In the same scope view, the constraints $c_1,c_2...c_n$ form the conjunction relation: $c_1 \wedge c_2 \wedge ... \wedge c_n$. (3) In different scope view, constrains $c_1,c_2...c_n$ form the disjunction relation $c_1 \vee c_2 \vee ... \vee c_n$. The *binding(p,s)* could also be available in pattern view.

Operation 6: *delBinding(binding).* This operation deletes an existed *binding(p,s)* in the scope view. If *binding(p,s)* is the only binding s involved, the scope s is also deleted.

Therefore, these six operations we define here can construct the constraints in Definition 3.

3.3   Consistency Guarantee and Application Generation

User-centric building method transfers the controllability to the users, which improves the efficiency of building applications but also brought risks. Some severe problems may be introduced by business users who lack professional IT knowledge. If the problems are found later after the deployment, the cost of repair is always much higher. In this paper, each constraint c is verified with the existed ones in constraint set when c is formed by *binding* operation.

Definition 8: Consistency of application. The application is consistent if and only if in constraint set S, $\forall c1,c2 \in S$, $c1$ *SAT* $c2$. SAT here is the satisfaction relation between model and its properties.

A verification algorithm *cGuard* is designed in our work. The principle of this algorithm is explained here. The constraints are declared through SPS, which is high-level abstraction of temporal logic CTL*, thus the consistency verification could be transferred model satisfaction verification. Meanwhile, the temporal logic could be formally verified through the calculation of finite state automata, which could be verified automatically. Assume that there are constraint set S and new constraint c, the consistency could be determined whether there is intersection between the automata *FSAs* of S and automata *FSAc* of negated c. If the intersection is empty, S satisfies the constraint c, otherwise not. According to the complex calculation of automata, our algorithm *cGuard* pre-verified constraints in pattern view, and then confirm the found conflicts in scope views. The pre-verification is correct by the theorem: there is any conflict in constraints if and only if there are conflicts in behavior patterns. The proof and the details of algorithm *cGuard* could be found in our full page work. Only verification procedure is shown here as Fig. 3.

The consistent constraint set is then translated to process model of the application. The process model is executable XPDL-like workflow. The translation algorithm we designed referred to these works [6, 7, 11]. Considering the efficiency of verification, only sequence, switch and parallel structures are supported in current version of our prototype. If the process model is not unique from different declared constraints, the candidate process is returned visually to users ordered by recommendation. For example,

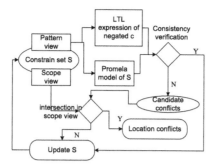

Fig. 3. The flow diagram of consistency verification

the recommendation can be determined by the size of least transitions in shortest path. After the process is determined by the user, the application could be executed in workflow engine. Therefore, the constraints generate application through these views.

4   Experiments and Evaluations

One prototype is implemented based on our software kit. The view set currently consist of one pattern view, one time scope view and one location scope view. The experiment designed here is to illustrate the effect of our work in user-centric service composition, which is run on the machine with 4 cores CPU, 4 GB RAM and 1.2 TB storage with CentOS 6.6 × 86_64 installed.

In this experiment, three simulated applications are constructed by employing 25 most popular services. Based on these services, more than one hundred constraints are generated by our simulation program. The constraint is divided into three groups to generate applications respectively. Count the size of programming elements according to the following two plans. In original plan, the constraints are generated to application by traditional method without multi-views in which the programming elements are the constraints itself. In multi-view plan, the constraints are synthesized to build application with three views, in which the programming elements are the patterns and scopes managed in respective views.

The statistical results are showed in Fig. 4. The multi-view plan has fewer elements than the original plan. The result could be explained as follows. The pattern and scope view manage the subset of the constraints. Assuming that there are m different patterns and n different scopes in the simulation, the upper limit of programming element in original plan (constraints size) is $m*n$; contrarily in multi-view plan (patterns and scopes) is m + n. Evidently, multi-view plan reduce the size of programming elements.

In the multi-view plan, we compare the response time of consistency verification between our cGuard algorithm and model checker tool without pre-verification. Figure 5 shows the result.

The result show that the response time increase as the constraint size grows. The pre-verification in pattern view of *cGuard* algorithm is separated the conflicts finding,

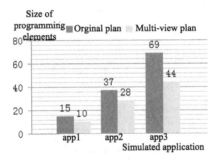

Fig. 4. The programming complexity

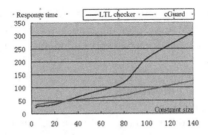

Fig. 5. Response time comparison in verification

which makes the incensement of response time more gently when the size grows larger. So *cGuard* provides more efficient verification support.

5 Related Works

On the one hand, traditional service composition model focus on depicting details of the control flow logic. One new trend is to describe composition by multiple perspectives. For example, Jablonski et al. [12] divided workflow into three profiles, van der Aalst [13] proposed three dimensional BPM model, and Frank [14] proposed modeling method through multi-view. Multi-view is a common technology to hide the complexity, and has been widely used in the management of bill of material (BOM) and enterprise integration. However, these early works lacks the formal method in views to model service characteristics. End-user programming is another trend for service composition. Yan et al. [15] and their subsequent work [16] improve the flexibility of service composition by user-defined goal and constrains, but high level professional knowledge is also required. Our work in this paper proposes comprehensive multi-views as a programing method to build service composition, which would reduce the barrier for the business users.

On the other hand, traditional rule-based modeling methods, such as like DECLARE [17] and PROPOLS [18], employ the temporal logic to model business logic. Although user would not disturbed by the structural details, the scale of constrains still aggravates the programming complexity. Our work in this paper divides business constrains in views and releases the burden to operate the programming elements. Moreover, through the model checker the consistency can be verified in an efficient way.

6 Conclusion

We propose multi-view modeling method for service composition in this paper. It reduces the programming complexity of business users through orthogonal and orderly views, and supports intelligent assistance by consistency verification. The evaluations demonstrate that our programming elements are reasonable with the correctness guarantee. In the future, we would apply our method in the business process management of State Grid to evaluate the practical effect.

Acknowledgments. This work was supported by the R&D General Program of Beijing Education Commission (No. KM2015_10009007), the Key Young Scholars Foundation for the Excellent Talents of Beijing (No. 2014000020124G011) and Foundation for the Excellent Youth Scholars of North China University of Technology.

References

1. Ding, W., Zhao, Z., Han, Y.: ePush: a streaming push service for mobile content delivery. Int. J. Embedded Syst. **8**, 135–145 (2016)
2. Sheng, Q.Z., Qiao, X., Vasilakosc, A.V., Szaboa, C., Bournea, S.: Web services composition: a decade's overview. Inf. Sci. **280**, 218–238 (2013)
3. Yu, J., Sheng, Q.Z., Falcarin, P.: A visual semantic service browser supporting user-centric service composition. In: IEEE International Conference on Advanced Information Networking and Applications (AINA 2010), pp. 244–251 (2010)
4. Ning, G., Ya-nan, W., Ming-yue, F., Feng-long, L., Feng-jiang, Y., Peng, W.: Research on the construction of standardized resource sharing service platform based on cloud computing (in Chinese). Standard Science, pp. 18–22 (2016)
5. Allen, B., Bresnahan, J., Childers, L., Foster, I., Kandaswamy, G., Kettimuthu, R., Kordas, J., Link, M., Martin, S., Pickett, K., Tuecke, S.: Software as a service for data scientists. Commun. ACM **55**, 81–88 (2012)
6. Pesic, M., Schonenberg, H., van der Aalst, W.: Declare: full support for loosely-structured processes. In: 11th IEEE International Enterprise Distributed Object Computing Conference (EDOC 2007), pp. 287–298. Citeseer (2007)
7. Aalst, W.M.P., Pesic, M.: DecSerFlow: towards a truly declarative service flow language. In: Bravetti, M., Núñez, M., Zavattaro, G. (eds.) WS-FM 2006. LNCS, vol. 4184, pp. 1–23. Springer, Heidelberg (2006). doi:10.1007/11841197_1
8. Ly, L.T., Maggi, F.M., Montali, M., Rinderle-Ma, S., van der Aalst, W.M.: A framework for the systematic comparison and evaluation of compliance monitoring approaches. In: 17th IEEE International EDOC Conference (EDOC 2013) (2013)

9. Dwyer, M.B., Avrunin, G.S., Corbett, J.C.: Property specification patterns for finite-state verification. In: Proceedings of the Second Workshop on Formal Methods in Software Practice in SIGSOFT, pp. 7–15. ACM (1998). 298598

10. Allen, J.F.: Maintaining knowledge about temporal intervals. Commun. ACM **26**, 832–843 (1983)

11. Esposito, C., Ficco, M., Palmieri, F., Castiglione, A.: A knowledge-based platform for Big Data analytics based on publish/subscribe services and stream processing. Knowl. Based Syst. **79**, 3–17 (2015)

12. Jablonski, S., Bussler, C.: Workflow management: modeling concepts, architecture and implementation. International Thomson Computer Press, London (1996)

13. Aalst, W.M.P.: Workflow verification: finding control-flow errors using petri-net-based techniques. In: Aalst, W., Desel, J., Oberweis, A. (eds.). LNCS, vol. 1806, pp. 161–183. Springer, Heidelberg (2000). doi:10.1007/3-540-45594-9_11

14. Frank, U.: Multi-perspective enterprise modeling (MEMO) - conceptual framework and modeling languages. In: Proceedings of the 35th Hawaii International Conference on System Sciences, pp. 72–81 (2002)

15. Yan, S., Han, Y., Wang, J., Liu, C., Wang, G.: A user-steering exploratory service composition approach. In: IEEE International Conference on Services Computing (SCC), pp. 309–316. IEEE Computer Society (2008)

16. Ding, W., Wang, J., Han, Y.: ViPen: a model supporting knowledge provenance for exploratory service composition. In: IEEE International Conference on Services Computing (SCC), pp. 265–272 (2010)

17. van der Aalst, W., Pesic, M., Schonenberg, H.: Declarative workflows: Balancing between flexibility and support. Comput. Sci. Res. Dev. **23**, 99–113 (2009)

18. Yu, J., Han, Y., Han, J., Jin, Y., Falcarin, P., Morisio, M.: Synthesizing service composition models on the basis of temporal business rules. J. Comput. Sci. Technol. **23**, 885–894 (2008)

Data Cost Optimization for Wireless Data Transmission Service Providers in Virtualized Wireless Networks

Yuansheng Luo[1,2](✉), Kun Yang[3], Qiang Tang[1,2], Jianming Zhang[1,2], Ping Li[1,2], and Shi Qiu[4,5]

[1] Hunan Provincial Key Laboratory of Intelligent Processing of Big Data on Transportation, Changsha 410114, China
luodyx@msn.com
[2] School of Computer and Communications Engineering, Changsha University of Science and Technology, Changsha 410114, China
[3] School of Computer Science and Electronic Engineering, University of Essex, Colchester, Essex CO4 3SQ, UK
[4] Department of Economy and Administration, Changsha University, Changsha 410000, China
[5] School of Business, Central South University, Changsha 410083, China

Abstract. Cellular communication has played an important role in current data transmission networks. Nevertheless, the price of cellular communication service is much higher than wired communication service. Thus each data transmission service provider has to make optimal decisions on cellular data plan to reduce the cost. This work put forward an optimal data cost scheme for the data transmission service in virtualized wireless networks. A formal cost model is put forward and the optimal algorithms have been used to approach the optimal solution. The simulation results show the efficiency and feasibility of proposed optimal algorithms.

Keywords: Cost optimization · Cellular communication · Virtual network operator · Virtualized wireless networks · Data transmission service

1 Introduction

Wireless data transmission and communication services are becoming increasingly indispensable in the state of the art of the emerging information techniques. One of the key deficiencies of cellular data transmission service is the expensive subscription fee for using this service. It is inevitable that the ISPs (Internet Service Providers) traffic increases with arising of the big data correlated techniques, such as the cloud storage [1], social network [2] and IoT [3]. With the growth in the volume of Internet traffic, ISPs have begun to pass some of their network costs on to consumers [4]. Thus the mobile data consumers monthly bill will increase inevitably. Although much work is conducted to study the optimal

© Springer International Publishing AG 2016
G. Wang et al. (Eds.): APSCC 2016, LNCS 10065, pp. 239–252, 2016.
DOI: 10.1007/978-3-319-49178-3_19

data pricing, their objective is mainly about the improvement of the economic efficiency of ISPs. There is little work on the optimizing data cost for the users of data transmission services.

In addition to the mobile network ISP, the mobile virtual network operators (MVNO) also can provide the cellular communication services. An MVNO is defined as a service provider that provides the mobile service to the user without its own frequency and government-issued license, which can be a mobile service provider or value-added service provider [5]. MVNOs can be categorized into three types: SP-MVNOs, Lite MVNOs and Full MVNOs [6]. SP-MVNOs provide the mobile communication service by relying on MNOs networks [5,6]. In this context, we only consider the SP-MVNOs who do not need to manage the underly infrastructures and resources.

Recently, network functions virtualization (NFV), is becoming a prevailing research area [7]. Since the efforts on NFV are beneficial to the telecommunications application infrastructure, the traditional MVNOs will also benefit from the NFV. The service networks will be created more conveniently with the NFV. The service networks created by the MVNOs with the support of the NFV are called as virtualized wireless networks in this context.

This work presents a formal model for data cost optimization with transmission time constraint. The system model is motivated on a real case scenario in transportation. The optimization formulation is deduced on queuing theory and real pricing model. The properties of the three-part tariff model are analyzed. The Fibonacci search algorithm is used to approach the optimal solution on the basis of the properties and the constraint. Marginal optimization is used to achieve the optimal solution at last. The simulation results show the efficiency and feasibility of proposed optimal algorithms.

2   Related Work

In mobile cloud computing environment, the cost can be split into two main parts, that is, the cost in data center and the cost in mobile communications. Albert Greenberg et al. [8] investigated the cost of the cloud and categorized the places where costs go into four types: Servers, Infrastructure, Power draw and Network. The proportion of the cost on Network in total cost is 15 %. Richard T. B. Ma [9] put forward a usage-based pricing in congestion-prone network service market. The impacts on price, such as the market structure, the users value on usage and sensitivity to congestion etc. were taken into account and the market equilibrium model was built. The above contributions are devoted to improve the operators cost efficiency but not the users. Junyi Wei et al. [7] proposed a pricing-based power allocation for virtual network operators (VNOs) in wireless networks. The pricing function is used as the cost function with power utility function to build the payoff function, which is used to formulate the non-cooperation game for VNOs users and to achieve the power efficiency among users.

As to the data dissemination in wireless networks, another emerging research area named opportunistic IoT is put forward by Bin Guo, et al. [10]. The opportunistic IoT is closely connected with the social mobile networking, IoT, mobile ad hoc networks and opportunistic networking etc. The research work of the opportunistic IoT aims to address the challenges on the information dissemination and sharing in the opportunistic communities. Though the research background of the opportunistic IoT is similar with that of the virtualized wireless network service computing, the differences between these two research areas are conspicuous: (1) the VNOs provide the data transmission services in a determined way while the users in the opportunistic IoT are usually intermittently connected with each other. (2) The relay nodes of a VNO are usually homogeneous especially with the support of the NFV while the network environment of the opportunistic IoT is usually heterogeneous. (3) The biggest difference between these two areas is the research objective. The VNOs operate at the level between the ISPs and the end users. Thus the objective of the VNOs is to optimize the network QoS of the data transmission, such as the delay and the price. On the other hand, the researches on the opportunistic IoT focus on the session level optimization, such as the collaboration of mobile users and brokers selection.

3 Motivation Scenario

In Hunan province, each highway toll station must transfer the collected information to Management Center located in Capital of Hunan. The Management Center (MC) plays a role as centralized data center for highway information computing and monitoring. A toll station can transfer the traffic information by private highway fiber network, or by VPN rented from China Telecom as a backup line. While in some areas, the wired channel to MC is very disruption-prone due to disrepair and aging of lines. Toll stations would have to subscribe the wireless broadband data transmission service from China Mobile when the wired channel failed and toll stations were disconnected from the MC. But in these areas, all stations aren't equipped with access points connecting cellular networks due to the limited budget. One of possible solutions under this condition is to select some toll stations as relay nodes. The nearby stations could transfer the traffic information to the relay node by wired channel or by wireless LAN. After that, the relay nodes would transfer the traffic information to MC by wireless broadband channel. The scenario is depicted in Fig. 1. There are two optimization questions to be answered:

(1) How many relay nodes should be deployed to meet the relay job requirements?
(2) Which data plan should be chosen to get the most out of each China dollar invested?

4 System Model

System model consists of Users, Virtual Network Operator (VNO), and Data Transmission Services. A VNO organizes a virtual wireless network in an Ad hoc way. The control node of VNO acts as a cluster head with the most computing

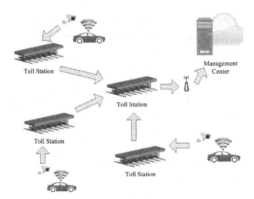

Fig. 1. Motivation Scenario: cellular relay node mode in transportation

resources. The users act as the member nodes joining in the virtual network. In the motivation scenario, the VNO and users are the operators of the toll stations. Relay nodes of VNO are used to connect to the Internet and visit the mobile cloud, in which the application services are deployed. The VNO provides the cloud service in the mobile cloud by subscribing the cellular service.

The Data Transmission Service has three attributes $< D, C, Q >$, where D is the collection of data plans, C is the corresponding monthly cost of each data plan, and Q is the QoS of the data transmission service. In this context, only the transmission delay and transmission rate are considered.

5   The Cost Optimization with Three-Part Data Plan Tariffs

5.1   Optimization Problem Formulation

As depicted in Fig. 2, the VNO need to transmit the user data to virtual server in SaaS cloud. User tasks arrive at the VNO according to the Poisson distribution, the arrival rate is $\lambda > 0$. Since the considered service is the data transmission service, it is reasonable to assume the task arrival process is a Poisson process. For example, in the motivation scenario, a task will be sent to the VNO when a car goes through a monitor camera. Hence the generation process of tasks is a Poisson process. The service time of the VNO before the user data reaches SaaS cloud obeys the Exponential distribution, the service rate is which approximates the number of transmitted jobs in a time unit through the cellular channel. The queuing service consists of dispatching jobs and user data transmitting. The dispatching time can be treated as a constant for simplicity. There may be a queuing duration before the user data can be transmitted.

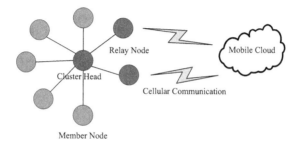

Fig. 2. System Model: Wireless virtualized network with cellular relay nodes

The formulation for the data plan cost optimization can be expressed as following formulas:

$$\min_{n_i} U(D) = \sum_{i=1}^{m} n_i \times C_1^i + \overline{C_2} \times E(O) \tag{1}$$

$$\text{subject to} : P(W > T) < \varepsilon \tag{2}$$

$$n_i = 0, 1, 2, \cdots \tag{3}$$

where $U(D)$ is the data plan total cost function. C_1 is the cost of data plan subscription, C_2 is the usage-based overage fee above the monthly data caps. The tariff of China Mobile data plan is listed in Table 1.

Table 1. Data plan monthly cost of China mobile

	Data package size	Price (¥)
Data plans	400 MB	40
	600 MB	50
	1 GB	70
	2 GB	100
	3 GB	130
	5 GB	180
	10 GB	280
Overage cost	¥0.29/Month	

As shown in Table 1, tiered data plans with usage-based overage fees are adopted by China Mobile. This kind of three-part tariff mode, which is defined by an access fee, a usage allowance, and an overage fee for exceeding the allowance, is prevailing in current cellular communication market [11]. Suppose there are m tiers data plans. n_i is the quantity of the ith tier subscribed data plans. $E(O)$ is the expect value of the overage data traffic volume. Thus (1) means choosing the optimal n_i to minimize the data plan monthly cost. W is the waiting time before a job arrives at the destination. T is the deadline of the job. The T can be specified in the SLA [12] file in service selection broker.

$P(*)$ is the cumulative probability distribution function (CDF). Thus (2) means the probability of violating the time constraint should be less than a threshold. The (3) means the n_i is an integer value.

5.2 Properties of the Monthly Costs

We summarize the properties of the data plan monthly costs in this section for the further analysis of the optimization problem.

Property 1. *A data plan i has three attributes as follows:*
C_1^i *- monthly cost of the ith tier data plan*
D^i *- data package size of the tier i*
$\overline{C_1^i}$ *- cost of per unit data of the tier i*
$C_1^i = \overline{C_1^i} \times D^i$

Property 2. *Let D^1 be the largest size of the data plan package, D^m is the smallest size of the data plan package, following inequalities hold:*
$D^1 > D^2 > \cdots > D^i > D^{i+1} > \cdots > D^m$
$C_1^1 > C_1^2 > \cdots > C_1^i > C_1^{i+1} > \cdots > C_1^m$
$\overline{C_1^1} > \overline{C_1^2} > \cdots > \overline{C_1^i} > \overline{C_1^{i+1}} > \cdots > \overline{C_1^m} > \overline{C_2}$
for any data plan index sequence:$1 \leq i1 \leq i2 \leq \cdots \leq is \leq im$
if $D^{i2} + D^{i3} + \cdots + D^{is} = D^{i1}$, there must be $C_1^{i2} + C_1^{i3} + \cdots + C_1^{is} > C_1^{i1}$ or if $C_1^{i2} + C_1^{i3} + \cdots + C_1^{is} = C_1^{i1}$, there must be $D^{i2} + D^{i3} + \cdots + D^{is} < D^{i1}$

Property 3. *Let the cost of each unit data be the data plan efficiency, the first tier data plan has the highest data plan efficiency. That is, the $\overline{C_1^1}$ is the highest data plan efficiency, which has the smallest cost of per unit data.*

Property 4. *The data plan efficiency of any mixed multi-tiers data plan would be not higher than $\overline{C_1^1}$. That is: $\frac{\sum_{i=1}^{m} n_i \times C_1^i}{\sum_{i=1}^{m} n_i \times D^i} \geq \overline{C_1^1}$*

These properties are intuitive and apparent for three-part tariff. We can use these properties to deduce the optimal solution of (1) in the next section.

5.3 Non-integer Optimal Solution for the Optimization Problem

The formulation (1) can be split to two parts U_1 and U_2:

$$U(D) = U_1 + U_2 \tag{4}$$

The first part can be rewritten as:

$$U_1 = \overline{C_1} \times \triangle \times K \tag{5}$$

where $\triangle$ is the average size of the job, K is the number of jobs can be sent within the data plans.

We only consider the situation that the VNO transmit the homogeneous tasks by the same relay nodes for the purpose of optimal task dispatching [13]. Thus each data job has the similar size and following equality holds:

$$\sum_{i=1}^{m} n_i \times D^i = \triangle \times K$$

The $\overline{C_1}$ is the data plan efficiency. According to the Property 4, the optimal U_1 should be:

$$U_1 = \overline{C_1^1} \times \triangle \times K \tag{6}$$

We cannot ensure the integer solution if we use (6) as part of the cost function. But we can still use it to calculate a non-integer solution at first, and then approach the integer solution.

The U_2 can be re-written as the same way:

$$U_2 = \overline{C_2} \times \triangle \times \sum_{i=k+1}^{\infty} (i - K) \frac{(\lambda t)^i}{i!} e^{-\lambda t}$$

$$= \overline{C_2} \times \triangle \times (\lambda t \sum_{i=k+1}^{\infty} (i - K) \frac{(\lambda t)^{(i-1)}}{(i-1)!} e^{-\lambda t})$$

$$= \overline{C_2} \times \triangle \times (\lambda t (1 - P(K-1)) - K(1 - P(K))) \tag{7}$$

where $P(*)$ is the CDF of Poisson distribution. Then the (1) can be re-written as:

$$\min_{K} U(K) = \overline{C_1^1} \times \triangle \times K$$

$$+ \overline{C_2} \times \triangle \times (\lambda t - K + K \times P(K) - \lambda t \times P(K-1)) \tag{8}$$

That is, it turns to calculate the optimal K to minimize the cost. The K can only be an integer value, so $U(K)$ is not a convex function. But the curve of $U(K)$ is approximate to a convex function and the derivative of $U(K)$ has no simple closed form, we choose the Fibonacci search algorithm [14] to get the non-integer optimal solution at first. The Fibonacci algorithm uses the Fibonacci number to approach the optimal solution.

The algorithm begins with the initial search interval $[a_1, b_1]$. In each iteration round, two tentative points α and β will be calculated to shrink the search interval.

$$\alpha_K = a_K + \frac{F_{n-K-1}}{F_{n-K+1}} (b_K - a_K), K = 1, 2, \cdots, n-1$$

$$\beta_K = a_K + \frac{F_{n-K}}{F_{n-K+1}} (b_K - a_K), K = 1, 2, \cdots, n-1$$

Algorithm 1. Fibonacci Search

---

1)Initialize $[a_1, b_1]$, L, $K = 1$, calculate the n satisfying:

$F_n \geq \frac{(b_1 - a_1)}{L}$

store the calculated Fibonacci numbers $F_1, F_2, \cdots, F_n$;

calculate the tentative points α_1 and β_1 as follows:

$\alpha_1 = a_1 + \frac{F_{n-2}}{F_n}(b_1 - a_1), \beta_1 = a_1 + \frac{F_{n-1}}{F_n}(b_1 - a_1)$

calculate $U(\alpha_1), U(\beta_1)$;

2)if $U(\alpha_K) > U(\beta_K)$ go to step 3, else go to 4;

3)$a_{K+1} = \alpha_K, b_{K+1} = b_K, \alpha_K = \beta_K$, calculate β_{K+1}

$\beta_{K+1} = a_{K+1} + \frac{F_{n-K-1}}{F_{n-K}}(b_{K+1} - a_{K+1})$ if $K = n - 2$ go to step 5,

else calculate $U(\beta_{K+1})$, $K = K + 1$, go to step 2;

4)$a_{K+1} = a_K, b_{K+1} = \beta_K, \beta_{K+1} = \alpha_K$, calculate α_{K+1}

$\alpha_{K+1} = a_{K+1} + \frac{F_{n-K-2}}{F_{n-K}}(b_{K+1} - a_{K+1})$ if $K = n - 2$ go to step 5,

else calculate $U(\alpha_{K+1})$, $K = K + 1$, go to step 2;

5)$\alpha_n = \alpha_{n-1}, \beta_n = \alpha_{n-1} + L$, calculate $U(\alpha_n), U(\beta_n)$

if $U(\alpha_n) > U(\beta_n)$ choose β_n as the optimal solution

else choose α_n as the optimal solution. Stop

---

where n is the number of the iterations. It should be ensured that the length of the final interval will not be bigger than L after n iterations. That is,

$$b_n - a_n \leq L$$

$$b_n - a_n = \frac{1}{F_n}(b_1 - a_1)$$

$$\Rightarrow F_n \geq \frac{(b_1 - a_1)}{L} \tag{9}$$

Thus the number of iterations n can be calculated by (9). The Fibonacci search algorithm is presented in Algorithm 1. After getting the optimal K^*, the optimal number of relay nodes n can be calculated using following formula:

$$n^* = \frac{\triangle \times K^*}{D^1} \tag{10}$$

But this result may not be the integer. To get the integer solution, we can use following formula:

$$n' = \lceil \frac{\triangle \times K^*}{D^1} \rceil \tag{11}$$

where $\lceil x \rceil$ means the nearest integer greater than or equal to x. That is, choose the nearest integer greater than or equal to n^*. Nevertheless, this result may not be the optimal integer solution. We will present the marginal optimization in the next sub-section.

Initial Search Interval. In the Fibonacci algorithm, it is important to choose the initial search interval because an appropriate initial interval can reduce the computing time and include the optimal solution properly. We can analyze the initial search interval with the median of the Poisson distribution [15]. Median is defined to be the least integer v such that $P(x \leq v) \geq \frac{1}{2}$.

The bounds for median of Poisson distribution are:

$$\lambda - \ln 2 \leq v < \lambda + \frac{1}{3} \tag{12}$$

For simplicity, we omit the time interval parameter t in (12). Suppose the λ is big enough, there is:

$$P(\lambda - \ln 2) \approx P(v) \approx P(\lambda + \frac{1}{3}) \approx 0.5$$

Let K be λ and $\lambda + \frac{1}{3}$ respectively, we have:

$$U(\lambda) \approx \overline{C_1^1} \times \triangle \times \lambda$$

$$U(\lambda + \frac{1}{3}) \approx \overline{C_1^1} \times \triangle \times (\lambda + \frac{1}{3}) - C_2 \times \triangle \times \frac{1}{6} \approx \overline{C_1^1} \times \triangle \times \lambda + \frac{\overline{C_1^1} \times \triangle}{3} - \frac{C_2 \times \triangle}{6}$$

case 1: if $\frac{\overline{C_1^1} \times \triangle}{3} - \frac{C_2 \times \triangle}{6} < 0 \Rightarrow \overline{C_1^1} < \frac{C_2}{2}$, $U(\lambda) > U(\lambda + \frac{1}{3})$

case 2: if $\overline{C_1^1} \geq \frac{C_2}{2} \Rightarrow U(\lambda) \leq U(\lambda + \frac{1}{3})$

According to the curve of the $U(K)$, as depicted in Figs. 3 and 4, in case 1, the minimum point is bigger than λ. In case 2, the minimum point is smaller than $\lambda + \frac{1}{3}$. Thus in case 2, we can get the initial search interval $[0, \lambda + \frac{1}{3}]$. In case 1, we still need to get the upper bound of the search interval. Since the variance of Poisson distribution is λ, we have $P(2\lambda - 1) \approx P(2\lambda) \approx 1$, then $U(2\lambda) \approx \overline{C_1^1} \times \triangle \times 2\lambda > U(\lambda)$

Hence we have the initial search interval $[\lambda, 2\lambda]$ in case 1 given the λ is big enough.

It should be noted that if the n^* is less than 1, which means the optimal number of relay nodes is less than the first tier data plan, our algorithm can start from the second tier data plan and so on.

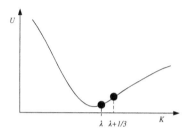

Fig. 3. Illustration of the case 2

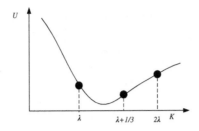

Fig. 4. Illustration of the case 1

5.4 Marginal Optimization

In previous section, we only get the integer solution, but it may not be the optimal solution. For example, suppose: $\triangle = 1\,\text{MB}, K = 15000, D^1 = 10\,\text{GB}, D^2 = 5\,\text{GB}, C_1^1 = 280, C_1^2 = 180$. These data plans are the first and second tier plans in the tariff of China Mobile as shown in Table 1. By (11), we can get the n=2, and $U(K) = 280 + 280 + U_2$. But the optimal solution should be $U(K) = 280 + 180 + U_2$. (The U_2 is same). Thus we should use the marginal optimization to approach the optimal solution. We give the following theorem of the marginal optimization exists.

Theorem 1. *Let* $K^i = \frac{D^i}{\triangle}, \varphi = mod(\frac{K^*}{K^1}), i = 1, 2, \cdots, m,$ *where* $mode(x)$ *means to get the modulus of* x. *The marginal optimization exists if and only if the following conditions hold:*
There exists an index sequences of data plans $i1 < i2 < \cdots < is, 1 < s \le m$ *so that,*

$$\varphi \le K^{i1} + K^{i2} + \cdots + K^{is} < K^1 \tag{13}$$

$$C_1^{i1} + C_1^{i2} + \cdots + C_1^{is} < C_1^1 \tag{14}$$

Proof. If the (13) and (14) hold, the data plan sequences $i1, i2, \cdots, is$ can be used as the optimal margin solution instead of the first tier data plan.

If the marginal optimization exists, the (14) must hold otherwise it is not optimal. There are two possible situations:

(1) there exists a data plan tier $i \ne 1, \varphi \le K^i < K^1, C_1^i < C_1^1$ which are the simplification of (13), (14);

(2) otherwise, for all $i \ne 1, K^i < \varphi$.

When in situation 2:

(1) if $\sum_{i=2}^{m} K^i < \varphi$, then there is no marginal optimization;

(2) otherwise, there is at least one data plan sequences, so that $\varphi \le K^{i1} + K^{i2} + \cdots + K^{is}$. For any sequence satisfies above condition, if $K^{i1} + K^{i2} + \cdots + K^{is} > K^1$, and there is no marginal optimization because according to Property 4, we will get $C_1^{i1} + C_1^{i2} + \cdots + C_1^{is} > C_1^1$. Thus $K^{i1} + K^{i2} + \cdots + K^{is} < K^1$ must hold.

For any index sequence satisfies (13), if $C_1^{i1} + C_1^{i2} + \cdots + C_1^{is} \ge C_1^1$ holds, there will be no marginal solution. Thus the (14) holds.

We can get the marginal optimization algorithm on the basis of the Theorem 1. The Algorithm 2 is used to get a marginal optimization solution. It should be noted that the Algorithm 2 can not ensure the best marginal solution to be found. The marginal optimization is a combination optimization problem with 2^{m-1} possible solutions. The Algorithm 2 is only used to find a near optimal solution for the marginal optimization.

Algorithm 2. Marginal Optimization

---

1)Initialize $C_1^1, \cdots, C_1^m, K^1, \cdots, K^m, \varphi$;
2)find a J satisfying: $K^J \geq \varphi, K^{J+1} < \varphi$;
3)if $J = 1$ or $K^J = \varphi$ go to (8);else go to (4)
4)let $l = m, sum = K^{J+1}$, go to (5);
5)if $l > (J + 1)$ $sum = sum + K^l$, go to (6);else go to (8);
6)if $sum \geq \varphi$ go to (7) else $l = l - 1$, go to (5);
7)if $(C_1^{J+1} + \sum_{h=l}^m C_1^h) < C_1^J$
choose data plans $J + 1, l, l + 1, \cdots, m$ as the marginal solution;Stop;
else go to (8);
8)choose data plan J as the marginal solution; Stop;

5.5 Constraint

At this section, we consider the constraint (2). Since the system model is an M/M/n queuing model [16], we have:

$$P(W > T) < \varepsilon \Rightarrow e^{-(n\mu-\lambda)T} < \varepsilon \Rightarrow n > \frac{-\ln \varepsilon}{\mu T} + \frac{\lambda}{\mu} \qquad (15)$$

where ε is a small probability value, such as 0.01. (15) is used to calculate the least number of necessary relay nodes. Thus if the solution of Sects. 5.3 and 5.4 does not satisfy the (15), we have to modify the solution.

Let n'' be the solution get by Algorithms 1 and 2. If $n'' \leq \frac{-\ln \varepsilon}{\mu T} + \frac{\lambda}{\mu}$,

$$n'' = n'' + \lceil \frac{-\ln \varepsilon}{\mu T} + \frac{\lambda}{\mu} - n'' \rceil + 1 \qquad (16)$$

To minimize the (1), we choose $\lceil \frac{-\ln \varepsilon}{\mu T} + \frac{\lambda}{\mu} - n'' \rceil + 1$ mth-tier data plans as the supplement relay nodes.

6 Simulation Study

6.1 Simulation Setup

We use the tariff of China Mobile listed in Table 1 as the experiment corpus. The λ varies from 10000 to 30000 with $step = 200$ in experiment 1. In experiment 2, the λ is 10000 and the time constraint will be changed. The other simulation parameters are as follows:

$$\triangle = 1\,\mathrm{MB}, \mu = 20000\ \text{packages}, T = 0.01\ \text{time unit}, \varepsilon = 0.01$$

6.2 Simulation Using the Tariff of China Mobile

As shown in Fig. 5, the marginal optimization will cause some more nodes to be selected in some cases. As shown in Fig. 6, the marginal optimization can make further cost reduction on the basis of Fibonacci search. The Fibonacci search result is ladder-like because the tariff of data plan is discrete and also is ladder-like.

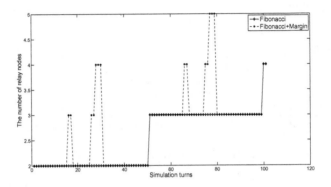

Fig. 5. The number of relay nodes in different arrival rates

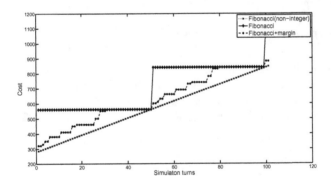

Fig. 6. The cost in different arrival rates

6.3 Impacts of the Constraint

In this simulation, we kept the arrival rate unchanged and varied the T from 0.001 to 0.0001 (we varied the reciprocal of T from 1000 to 10000 with step 100). As shown in Fig. 7, the number of the relay nodes required by the constraint will surpass the value got from the Fibonacci search and margin search after the T is less than $\frac{1}{6800}$ (the curves of Fibonacci search and margin search are overlapped). Thus as shown in Fig. 8, the cost will increase because of the additional relay

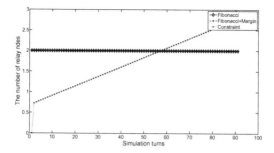

Fig. 7. The number of relay nodes with different time constraints

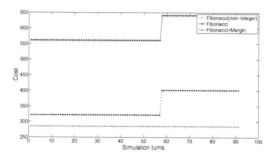

Fig. 8. The cost with different time constraints

nodes added. In this simulation, the Fibonacci+Margin search also perform better than pure Fibonacci search. The curve of the non-integer result is unchanged because we did not add the additional cost caused by additional relay nodes in the non-integer situation.

7   Conclusions

In this paper a data plan cost optimization strategy for data transmission service in virtualized networks is introduced. The cost model is established based on the real case scenario. The Fibonacci algorithm is used with the property analysis of data plan to approach the optimal solution. The marginal optimization algorithm is put forward to get the near optimal solution on the basis of Fibonacci algorithm. The simulation results show the efficiency and good performance of the proposed strategy.

Acknowledgments. This work is supported by the National Natural Science Foundation of China (Grant Nos. 61303043, 61502056, and 61572389), Hunan Provincial Natural Science Foundation of China, China (Grant Nos. 13JJ4052 and 2015JJ3010), Scientific Research Fund of Hunan Provincial Education Department (Grant Nos. 13C1022, 13C1023, and 15B009), EU FP7 Projects CLIMBER (GA-2012-318939), and UK EPSRC Project NIRVANA (EP/L026031/1). CROWN (GA-2013-610524), Key projects of Hunan Provincial Education Department(Grant No.14A004), the Scientific Research Fund of Hunan Provincial Transportation Department (Grant No. 201446).

References

1. Ren, Y., Shen, J., Wang, J., Han, J., Lee, S.: Mutual verifiable provable data auditing in public cloud storage. J. Internet Technol. **16**(2), 317–323 (2015)
2. Ma, T., Zhou, J., Tang, M., Tian, Y., Abdullah, A.-D., Al-Rodhaan, M., Lee, S.: Social network and tag sources based augmenting collaborative recommender system. IEICE Trans. Inf. Syst. **E98-D**(4), 902–910 (2015)
3. Bonomi, F., Milito, R., Natarajan, P., Zhu, J.: Fog computing: a platform for internet of things and analytics. In: Big Data and Internet of Things: A Roadmap for Smart Environments, pp. 169–186. Springer International Publishing (2014)
4. Sen, S., Joe-Wong, C., Ha, S., et al.: A survey of smart data pricing: past proposals, current plans, and future trends. ACM Comput. Surv. **46**(2), 1–37 (2012)
5. ITU.: Mobile Virtual Network Operators. Geneva:ITU. http://www.itu.int/osg/spu/ni/3G/resources/mvno
6. Kim, B.W., Seol, S.H.: Economic analysis of the introduction of the MVNO system and its major implications for optimal policy decisions in Korea. Telecommun. Policy **31**(5), 290–304 (2007)
7. Wei, J., Yang, K., et al.: Pricing-based power allocation in wireless network virtualization: a game approach. In: International Wireless Communications and Mobile Computing Conference (IWCMC). IEEE (2015)
8. Greenberg, A., et al.: The cost of a cloud: research problems in data center networks. ACM SIGCOMM Comput. Commun. Rev. **39**(1), 68–73 (2008)
9. Ma, R.T.B.: Usage-based pricing and competition in congestible network service markets. IEEE/ACM Trans. Netw. **24**(5), 3084–3097 (2016)
10. Guo, B., Zhang, D., Wang, Z., et al.: Opportunistic IoT: exploring the harmonious interaction between human and the internet of things. J. Netw. Comput. Appl. **6**(6), 1531–1539 (2013)
11. Bhargava, H.K., Gnagwar, M.: "Pay as You Go" or "All You Can Eat"? pricing methods for computing and information services. In: 49th Hawaii International Conference on System Sciences, pp. 5239–5248 (2016)
12. Ludwig, H., Keller, A., Dan, A., et al.: Web Service Level Agreement (WSLA) Language Specification. IBM Corporation (2003)
13. Hyytia, E., Righter, R., Aalto, S.: Energy-aware job assignment in server farms with setup delays under LCFS and PS. In: 26th International Teletraffic Congress (ITC). IEEE (2014)
14. Minoux, M.: Mathematical Programming: Theory and Algorithms. Wiley, New York (1986)
15. Choi, K.P.: On the medians of gamma distributions and an equation of Ramanujan. Proc. Am. Math. Soc. **121**(1), 245–251 (1994)
16. Iversen, V.B.: Teletraffic engineering handbook. ITU-D SG **2**, 16 (2005)

Genetic Based Data Placement
for Geo-Distributed Data-Intensive
Applications in Cloud Computing

Weifeng Fan, Jun Peng$^{(\boxtimes)}$, Xiaoyong Zhang, and Zhiwu Huang

School of Information Science and Engineering, Central South University,
Changsha 410083, China
pengj@csu.edu.cn

Abstract. Running data-intensive applications across the geo-distributed data centers in cloud computing needs to address the problem of how to place the data items to the appropriate data centers. The general methods are mainly hash-based which could be understood as random placement intuitively when the query needs distributed data items. In this paper, We propose an genetic based data placement (GBDP) scheme in which a tripartite graph based model is constructed to formulate the data replica placement problem by leveraging the genetic algorithm, and decompose the original problem into two simplified subproblems, which are solved alternately. Through extensive experiments with synthesized and realistic data items, the performance of the proposed scheme is proved validated.

Keywords: Cloud computing · Data placement · Data-intensive applications · Genetic algorithm

1 Introduction

Recent information technology developments encourage the emerging of data-intensive applications [1]. In scientific computing fields such as astronomy, high-energy physics, earth science, there are a huge amount of data stored in the geographically distributed data centers. The query from the users could request the data items across geo-distributed regions [2]. Hence, the user-experienced performance is determined by the storage location of the requested data items. Meanwhile, the optimized data placement can reduce resource consumption for service providers, consequently, lower the resource investment. Whereas for the users, lower resource consumption directly leads to lower monetary cost for using services [3]. Thus, for both the service providers and the users, it is an urgent problem of how to place the data items and replicas to the distributed datacenters in cloud computing efficiently, without compromising on service-level agreements.

Recently, the fault tolerance of data retrieving is an important issue attracting much attention. In traditional techniques, data has its fixed replica number, such as HDFS [4] and Cassandra [5], which are mainly hash-based and can be understood as random placement intuitively. As the cost of storage decreases, cloud service providers can

© Springer International Publishing AG 2016
G. Wang et al. (Eds.): APSCC 2016, LNCS 10065, pp. 253–265, 2016.
DOI: 10.1007/978-3-319-49178-3_20

adopt data distributed replication strategies to guarantee data reliability, i.e., storing several replicas (normally 2–4) for every data item in different data centers. If replicas of data items stored in data centers can be utilized effectively, it will significantly reduce resource consumption, and further reduce latency experienced by the users and improve the performance of the system.

The distributed data management systems today need to serve a range of different workloads, which include mainly analytical read-only workloads that need to handle large amounts of data in a resource-efficient manner, as well as transactional (OLTP [6]) workloads that need to support high throughputs with low latencies. When data items are distributed in multiple data centers, balancing the workload of distributed data centers becomes a critical factor to the placement problem. The unbalance workload of the data centers will lead to over-reliance on certain busy data centers. Therefore, it should be avoided as far as possible.

It is challenging to make the data placement solution that takes into account these different aspects. We will address the corresponding issues by two steps successively. Firstly, the placement problem is described by a tripartite graph model in which there are three kinds of vertexes representing query patterns, data replicas and distributed datacenters respectively, through which the optimization problem can be formulated. Secondly, we consider the scenario that each item can possess multiple replicas, which could be placed onto geo-distributed data centers. The existence of multiple replicas in different locations introduces the decision problem that which replica should be used to fulfill the query. Therefore a strategy based genetic algorithm is proposed to search the mapping from query patterns to data replicas and mapping from data replicas to data centers. We design a coding model which is constructed to represent the mappings, and an evaluation function is designed to evaluate the performance of the mappings. By using the genetic algorithm, mappings with excellent performance can be obtained as a near optimal solution to the data replica placement problem.

The state-of-the-art implementation in distributed storage systems today, is mainly hash-based which can be regarded as random placement, such as HDFS [4] and Cassandra [5]. Among the related work, some discussed the issues under the scenario of OSN [7, 8], which discussed the interconnection of social data among different objectives, which ignored the relationship between data items as well as the association that involves more than two entities. Literature [9] is the work most related to ours in the problem definition, but it didn't pay much attention to the group association in its early stage of the solution. To the best of our knowledge, data placement scheme makes the advancement of jointly improving the query span of resource consumption and the system time of associated data without compromising on the original objective. Besides, the developed genetic method to support replicas and to encode data replica placement problem are also novel and consequently, make the scheme more comprehensive.

The rest of this paper is structured as follows. Section 2 summarizes related works. Section 3 presents our modeling framework for the data replica placement problem. In Sect. 4, the genetic based location-aware data replica placement scheme is proposed. In Sect. 5, the scheme is evaluated through extensive experiments. Section 6 concludes the paper.

2 Related Work

It is discovered that using fewer nodes to fulfill a query is better in terms of the system efficiency. Therefore, a promising paradigm is to place the strongly associated data items, those who are often invoked together at the same location. In [7], Rochman et al. proposed a scheme of how to place the resources to distributed regions to reduce the cost of fulfilling requests locally. Literature [10] puts forward a workload-aware data placement and replication strategy, called SWORD, to minimize resource consumption. Whereas such work ignored that it is significant to fulfill the query locally, which results in that many queries might be served inefficiently, remotely.

Recent research has investigated the data placement in OSN, where the query involves not only the data items of a user itself but also that of its friends. In [8], Lei Jiao et al. studied multi-objective optimization for placing users' data over multiple clouds for socially aware services. They build a model framework that can accommodate a range of different objectives by leveraging graph cuts and solve them alternately in multiple rounds. In [11], Schism discussed a scheme based graph partition to minimize the number of distributed requests for an OLTP workload, without replicating data items with a high query frequency, which might affect the balance of load across multiple machines. On the contrary, we replicate each data items depending on the query frequencies.

There are many optimization algorithms can be used to solve the data placement problem for distributed data-intensive applications, such as Genetic Algorithm (GA), Particle swarm optimization (PSO), Ant Colony optimization (ACO) etc. These optimization algorithms have different characteristics, but the genetic has been demonstrated to achieve a better performance in many cases. In [12], Goyal et al. considered a performance comparative analysis in solving the traveling salesman problem by using ACO, GA and PSO respectively, which stated that the genetic can obtain a better performance than other algorithms in that case. Furthermore, the genetic algorithm has also been showed effectively in task scheduling problems in distributed systems. In [13], Xu et al. proposed a new grouping genetic algorithm for the mappers placement problem in cloud computing, which was not aware of the location difference among data centers and did not consider the necessity of fulfilling the request locally.

3 Modeling Framework

In this section, we propose a tripartite graph based model with definitions of important concepts, which formulate the data replica placement problem for distributed data-intensive applications in clouds. For the convenience of the readers, the major notations used in this paper are listed in Table 1.

3.1 Settings and Notations

As illustrated in Fig. 1, in the tripartite graph which is a example system representing the problem inputs of the distributed data centers, the data items are denoted by a set M,

Table 1. The major important notations

Symbol	Definition
M	The set of data items
d_{ij}	The jth replica of data d_i
L	The set of geographically distributed data centers
P	Initial replica placement leveraging the greedy
Q	The set of total query patterns
R_q	The query rate of each pattern $q \in Q$
S_r	The query span representing the number of data centers involved in the execution of a query
S_{ql}	The number of data items in query q that are fulfilled at node l
C^r	The abstract metric representing total system resource consumption of fulling all the queries
C^t	The necessary system time
R_{ql}	The query rate of pattern q to node l
$\mathbf{1}(q \in l)$	The 0–1 function $\mathbf{1}(q \in l)$ indicating whether the query q is executed at node l or not

which represents the data stored in the system. In the set M, a single data replica is defined as dij which is the jth replica of data di. Each data item has several distributed replicas according to its query frequency and other factors. The number of replicas is not the key point of this paper, so we suppose the number of replicas to each data item is known. And the data items may be files, segments or tables in practice depending on the actual type of data storage. Because the data items may be stored in geographically distributed data centers, the query of the users may need different items from different data centers, possibly remotely distributed, which can be denoted by a set L.

Compared with the centralized storage, the distributed storage can improve the access latency of most users and achieve a higher level of fault tolerance. We term a data center as a node in the following, so the data placement problem is about finding best nodes for each user's data items in order to minimize the total cost. Initially, we consider the scenario that every data item $d_{ij} \in M$ is placed at a data center $l \in L$, therefore our work focuses on designing the data placement scheme that provides a efficient solution of P, which is defined as $P \mid d_{ij} \to l$.

We denote the query patterns by a set Q, which is composed of all the queries. Here we use the q to indicate a query in a practical system, which may request at most x different items from the set M in each transaction. The query rate of each pattern $q \in Q$ can be denoted by Rq. In [14], J. S. Hunter conducted mature methods in predicting the rates which adopted as the input of our scheme to make the data placement decision, so the details of predicting the query rates are not included in this paper. The request rate set R is illustrated in the tripartite graph, where the edges between data centers and query patterns are weighted by the rate Rql, which indicates the query rate of pattern q to node l.

The state-of-the-art implementation in most distributed storage management systems, for fault tolerance, load balance, and availability, many data management systems

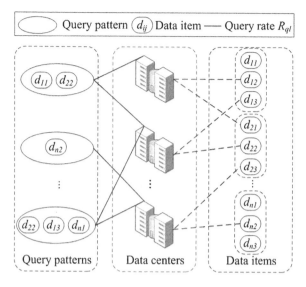

Fig. 1. Tripartite graph representing the problem inputs

usually adopt the hash-based method such as Hadoop Distributed File System (HDFS) [2], whose main concern was to achieve the load balance among nodes. Obviously the hash-based schemes did not pay enough attention to the system performance affected by the query rates between query patterns and data centers and ignored the potential performance improvement through the managed data placement. To attack this deficiency, we start with modeling the metrics of the resource consumption and system efficiency and then propose an efficient data placement scheme which fully exploits the benefits of the managed data placement.

3.2 Problem Analysis

(1) Metrics: Data placement can affect the system performance in both the resource consumption and system efficiency. We investigate the relationships between the placement and system performance and summarize them as two metrics.

Query Span: For both the service provider and the users, it is crucial to minimize the total resource consumption in executing the workload, without compromising on service-level agreements if any. However, it is difficult to directly model the resource consumption of a task, which depends not only on the characteristics of the task, but also on the overall status of the system including which other tasks are running simultaneously, which machines are being used to execute the task, and so on. Instead, we propose a more abstract metric called the query span, denoted by S_r, representing the number of data centers involved in the execution of a query q, so we have the relationship of

$$S_r = \sum_{l \in L} \mathbf{1}(q \in l) \tag{1}$$

where the 0–1 function $\mathbf{1}(q \in l)$ indicates whether the query q is executed at node l. Let λ be the average resource consumption of a data center node. We model the necessary resource consumption of fully fulfill a query q as

$$\lambda \sum_{l \in L} \mathbf{1}(q \in l) \tag{2}$$

With the query rates of different queries, the total system resource consumption of fulling all the queries can be denoted by C^r, which is denoted by $\sum_{q \in Q} R_q \sum_{l \in L} \lambda \cdot \mathbf{1}(q \in l)$, therefore, we can summarize the metric as

$$C^r = \sum_{q \in Q} \sum_{l \in L} R_q \lambda \cdot \mathbf{1}(q \in l) \tag{3}$$

System Time: The necessary system time to complete a given workload is an important feature of the cloud computing system. The average system time of a query involves not only the amount of information requested, but also the processing overhead at each node in a distributed data centers, cited in [4]. The number of data items invoked by a query denoted by S_q, and we denote the number of data items in a query q that are fulfilled at node l by S_{ql}. We model the necessary system time to fulfill a request q at node l as

$$S_{ql} + \varepsilon \cdot \mathbf{1}(q \in l) \tag{4}$$

It means that the system time consists of two parts, which one is the amount of information accessed, and another is the average constant overhead of handling the query, denoted by ε, therefore we can summarize the total system time as

$$C^t = \sum_{q \in Q} R_q \sum_{l \in L} [S_{ql} + \varepsilon \cdot \mathbf{1}(q \in l)] \tag{5}$$

(2) Optimization Problem: Our objective is to minimize the two metrics above, represented by

$$C = C^r + \beta C^t \tag{6}$$

where β is the trade-off parameter between the above two metrics. Minimizing (6) helps to lower the cost of the service provider, i.e., the amount of resource consumption and the monetary expense. Therefore the formulated problem can be generalized as: given the $\{Q, R\}$, find the optimal data placement of $P | d_{ij} \rightarrow l$ that minimizes the value of C.

4   Data Placement Strategy Based Genetic

We consider the scenario that a query accesses multiple data items, which are remotely distributed. Therefore the data replica placement problem would be decomposed into two subproblems: (1) data replica deployment problem, i.e., which replica of data items should be invoked by the query; (2) data replica allocation problem, i.e., where these data replicas should be stored. By combining these two subproblems, we can obtain a complete genetic scheme based location-aware data replica placement.

4.1   Encode Data Replica

Encode: Motivated by the genetic code technology, we decompose our data replica code strategy into two sub-strategies for the two subproblems above mentioned. The following sections are the coding methods of these two strategies.

Encode data replica deployment strategy: We consider the situation that there are m replicas of a data item, and one query can only access one replica of a data. Therefore the corresponding segment of the code can be used by a 0/1 code with the length of m to represent the case of every replica invoked by a query. If a query q requests a replica d_{ij}, which the jth replica of data item d_i, the bit corresponding to d_{ij} is 1, otherwise the bit is 0. The replica code of every single query consists of all data items' segments. Further, the replica deployment strategy code is made up of all queries' segment which is denoted as Pc. For example, we consider the scenario that if there are two queries q_1 and q_2, two data items d_1 and d_2. The replicas of d_1 are d_{11}, d_{12} and d_{13}, the replica of d_2 are d_{21}, d_{22} and d_{23}. When q_1 invokes d_{12} and d_{23}, the data replica deployment code of q_1 can be denoted by 010001, when q_2 invokes d_{11} and d_{22}, the data replica deployment code of q_2 can be denoted by 100010.

Encode data replica allocation strategy: We use the $|L|$ denote the number of the data centers, so a data node would be represented by $\delta(\log_2 |L|)$ binary bits, where $\delta(x)$ is a function that returns the smallest integer which greater than or equal to x. The code of node l_i is the binary number of i represented by $\delta(\log_2 |L|)$ bits. And the redundant binary bits which greater than L are not used. For a replica of data items, its storage location would be denoted by a binary code, whose length is $\delta(\log_2 |L|)$. The code of every data item consists of all its data replicas' segments. Further, the data replica allocation strategy code is made up of all data items' segments which is denoted as Pm. For example, if there are 5 data centers l_1, l_2, l_3, l_4, l_5, 3 data items d_1, d_2, d_3 and every data item has 2 replicas, when the replica d_{21} is located in l_4, d_{22} is located in l_2 the code segment of d_2 is 100010.

4.2   Criterion of Validation

The proposed genetic algorithm based heuristic scheme which incorporates mutation and crossover operations as sources of diversity, which will generate invalid placement. To eliminate the invalid placement, we proposed a criterion of validation.

(a) For a query pattern q which needs data item di, there is one and only one mapping from q to replicas of di, otherwise, it is an invalid mapping. On the contrary, if the q does not need di, but there is an mapping from q to replicas of di, it is an invalid mapping too.
(b) If there are more than one replicas of the same data item at the same data center, it is an invalid mapping from data replicas to data nodes.
(c) Besides, the load balance among nodes is another factor. The data items stored in different data centers should be balanced which would decrease the worst-case recovery time after a site failure. Therefore, we set the balance constraint that the load rate in each data center should be in a range of $[H - \mu, H + \mu]$, where H is the average number of items in all distributed nodes and μ is the balance parameter.

4.3   Over Procedure

To overcome the issues introduced by the replicas, we address the initial placement of data replicas by a greedy method, which is illustrated in Algorithm 1. Crossover and mutation operations are applied repeatedly which would generate new placement. Then put the new placement into the current placement solutions. The evaluation function C obtained from P is shown as Func in Algorithm 1. The general steps of the whole scheme are shown in Algorithm 1, which derives a relatively optimal solution to the data replica placement problem with genetic algorithm, and the time complexity of our scheme is no more than $O(|Q| * |L| * |M| * newSize * maxGen)$.

In every generation, there are newSize (the number of solutions created in every generation) new solutions being generated. After rounds of iterations of the crossover and mutation operations, the obtained performance tends to keep stable, and the iteration on the solutions will terminate if the improvement is less than 0.1 % in maxGen iterations (which means the iteration times of the genetic algorithm). Sort these solutions in the ascending order and pick the one with the minimum optimization objective to be the final data replica placement solution. With the deterministic replica allocation code Pc, Pm, we can obtain a hashing mapping function for each replica, whose input is a query pattern and output is the replica allocation destination of each replica in the pattern.

Algorithm 1. Data Placement with Replicas based Genetic

1: $P \leftarrow$ Initial replica placement leveraging the greedy;

2: Let $j = 0$;

3: **while** $j <= maxGen$

4:      **for** each placement in P **do**

5:          $(P'_c, P'_m) \leftarrow mutation(P_c, P_m)$;

6:          **while** P'_c, P'_m are invalid

7:          **end while**

8:      **end for**

9: Let $t = 0$;

10:     **while** $t <= newSize$ **do**

11:         $(P'_{c1}, P'_{c2}) \leftarrow crossover(P_{c1}, P_{c2})$;

12:         $(P'_{m1}, P'_{m2}) \leftarrow crossover(P_{m1}, P_{m2})$;

13:         **while** $P'_{c1}, P'_{c2}, P'_{m1}, P'_{m2}$ are invalid

14:         **end while**

15: Obtain new placement by integrating $P'_{c1}, P'_{c2}, P'_{m1}, P'_{m2}$;

16:     Add the new placement into P;

17:     $t++$;

18:     **end while**

19: $j++$;

20: **end while**

21: $C \leftarrow Func(P)$;

22: Sort the placement according to evaluation function;

23: **return** P_c, P_m

---

5   Performance Evaluation

5.1   Experiment Settings

With the proposed scheme implementation and conducted several studies, we run simulations in a realistic experiment settings. In the experiments, we consider there are $|L| = 20$ data centers, representing the geographically distributed data centers. The total number of data items is $|M| = 20,000$. The number of query patterns in the system is set to 40,000. In the simulation, at most 50 items from the set of $|M|$ items will be selected randomly for each query pattern. The mutation rate and the crossover rate are set to 0.1 and 0.9 respectively, which are determined empirically according to the literature [15]. The request rate for each query pattern can be considered as the Zipf distribution according to the literature [16], then the default values of other parameters are set as $\lambda = 3.0$, $\beta = 1.0$, and $\varepsilon = 4.0$, which concerns a small-size data item storing scenario. The initial generation of the genetic is set to 100, and there will be 1000 new placement solutions being generated and 1000 poor performance placement solutions will be eliminated in every generation.

In addition to the proposed scheme GBDP, the other schemes including Hash, Greedy and their variants which fit the replicas also implemented and being compared with. Hash places each replica randomly at data nodes, which is used in Hadoop Distributed File System (HDFS) [2]. Greedy places a data item to the node that is the closest location to that query.

5.2   Experiment Results

Performance of different replica numbers: In the experiment, we investigated the performance of different schemes under the scenario with different replicas. When the replica number is 6, the objective value of GBDP is superior to the others by more than about 40 %, as shown in Fig. 2. It achieves the near-optimal performance on the query span and obtains the best performance on the system time, by exploiting the advantage of replicas. As for the balance, the performance of the GBDP is better than other

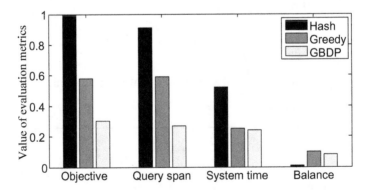

Fig. 2. Performance of different schemes under the scenario with 6 replicas

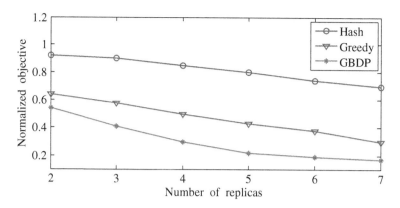

Fig. 3. The effect of changing the number of replicas

schemes. In fact, when compared with Greedy, which more relies on the workload from different locations to achieve the balance, in the GBDP, we can control the result of balance through adjusting the balance parameter of the genetic algorithm, initiatively, which will be shown later.

In order to show the effect of the number of replicas better, we conduct a simulation as shown in Fig. 3. To show the trend of performance change under the same scheme, the values are all normalized towards the objective value of Hash without replica. As the increase number of replicas, the system performance is expected to be improved, such as more requests can be fulfilled locally. As shown in Fig. 3, GBDP shows a better performance in all the cases implemented. In fact, the number of replicas cannot be too large which will increase the difficulty of consistency maintenance and the storage cost of the system.

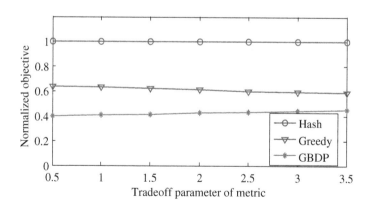

Fig. 4. The effect of tradeoff parameter β which used to tradeoff the resource consumption and system time

Effect of other parameters: As shown in Fig. 4, we have implemented the tradeoff parameter β which used to tradeoff the importance of the resource consumption and system time. It is obvious that when β increases, the improvement of GBDP over Greedy becomes lower, which is due to the weight of the associated data serving metric increases with β in the objective function so that the system time can give a better performance on that metric.

We further evaluate the balance in the heuristic genetic algorithm which takes the balance parameter μ as input. As shown in Fig. 5, when μ is larger, the normalized objective value becomes lower along with the balance among nodes becomes worse. So in our scheme, when given the reasonable level of balance, we can control the balance flexibly by tuning the parameter μ to improve the performance of the system while satisfying the balance constraint.

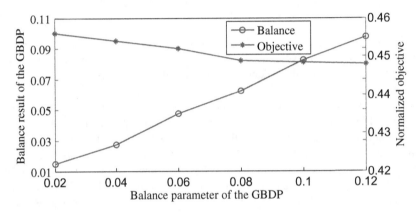

Fig. 5. The effect of balance parameter μ on the balance result and normalized objective

6   Conclusions

The data-intensive applications lead to a large amount of data stored in the geo-graphically distributed data centers and a high frequency of data access from the users of different regions. The unique features of data-intensive applications that distinguish themselves from other applications pose a new problem of optimizing data replica placement over multiple geographically distributed data centers.

In this paper, by formulating the scenario with replicas using a tripartite graph, we firstly studied the balanced data placement problem for geographically distributed data centers, which incorporated the query span and system time, and obtained the opti-mized solution. And then an optimization scheme based genetic was proposed which decomposed the original problem into two simplified subproblems. Finally, through extensive experiments with synthesized and realistic data items, the performance of proposed scheme was demonstrated validated.

Acknowledgments. The authors would like to acknowledge that this work was partially supported by NSERC, CFI and the National Natural Science Foundation of China (Grant No. 61379111, 61602529, 61672537, 61672539, 61402538, 61202342 and 61403424).

References

1. Expósito, R.R., Taboada, G.L., Ramos, S., et al.: Performance evaluation of data-intensive computing applications on a public IaaS cloud. Comput. J. **59**(3), 287–307 (2016)
2. Xu, H., Li, B.: Joint request mapping and response routing for geo-distributed cloud services. Proc. IEEE INFOCOM **12**(11), 854–862 (2013)
3. Le, K., Bilgir, O., Bianchini, R., Martonosi, M., Nguyen, T.: Managing the cost, energy consumption, and carbon footprint of internet services. Adv. Electron. Electron Phys. **38**(1), 487–499 (2008)
4. HDFS Architecture Guide (2008). http://hadoop.apache.org/docs/r1.2.1/hdfsdesign.html
5. About Replication in Cassandra. http://www.datastax.com/docs/1.0/clusterarchitecture/replication
6. Kumar, K.A., Quamar, A., Deshpande, A., et al.: SWORD: workload-aware data placement and replica selection for cloud data management systems. VLDB J. **23**(6), 845–870 (2014)
7. Rochman, Y., Levy, H., Brosh, E.: Resource placement and assignment in distributed network topologies. Proc. IEEE INFOCOM **12**(11), 1914–1922 (2013)
8. Jiao, L., Li, J., Du, W., Fu, X.: Multi-objective data placement for multi-cloud socially aware services. In: Proceedings-IEEE INFOCOM, pp. 28–36, April 2014
9. Agarwal, S., Dunagan, J., Jain, N., Saroiu, S., Wolman, A., Bhogan, H.: Volley: automated data placement for geo-distributed cloud services. In: USENIX NSDI, pp. 17–32 (2010)
10. Quamar, A., Kumar, K.A., Deshpande, A.: Sword: scalable workload-aware data placement for transactional workloads. In: Proceedings of the 16th International Conference on Extending Database Technology, pp. 430–441 (2013)
11. Curino, C., Jones, E., Zhang, Y., et al.: Schism: a workload-driven approach to database replication and partitioning. Proc. Vldb Endow. **3**(1–2), 48–57 (2010)
12. Goyal, N., Mittal, P.: Comparative analysis of genetic algorithm, particle swarm optimization and ant colony optimization for TSP. Artif. Intell. Syst. Mach. Learn. **4**(4), 202–206 (2012)
13. Xu, X., Tang, M.: A new grouping genetic algorithm for the MapReduce placement problem in cloud computing. In: 2014 IEEE Congress on Evolutionary Computation (CEC), pp. 1601–1608, July 2014
14. Hunter, J.S.: The exponentially weighted moving average. J. Qual. Technol. **18**(4), 203–210 (1986)
15. Grefenstette, J.J.: Optimization of control parameters for genetic algorithms. IEEE Trans. Syst. Man Cybern. **16**(1), 122–128 (1986)
16. Adamic, L.A., Huberman, B.A.: Zipf's law and the internet. Glottometrics **3**(1), 143–150 (2002)

Spectrum Allocation Based on Gaussian - Cauchy Mutation Shuffled Frog Leaping Algorithm

Zhe Qin, Jiaqi Liu$^{(\boxtimes)}$, Zhigang Chen, Lin Guo, and Ling Huang

School of Software, Central South University, Changsha 410083, China
liujiaqi@csu.edu.cn

Abstract. When solving the cognitive radio spectrum allocation problems, the traditional Shuffled Frog Leaping Algorithm (SFLA) will be trapped into the local optimal solution easily and search lack of population diversity at a later stage. To improve the solution performance of SFLA, this paper introduces the adaptive Gaussian and Cauchy mutation on the basis of the SFLA, and utilizes the dissimilarity to decide when population is falling into the local optimal solution. Jumping out of the local optimal solution in a timely manner and enhancing the population diversity with the stronger global searching ability of Cauchy mutation, or proceeding the local search with the stronger local searching ability of Gaussian mutation when groups trap into the local optimal solution. Finally, simulation results show that the algorithm in the 3 kinds of networks revenue is superior to the SFLA, Particle swarm optimization (PSO), Genetic algorithm (GA).

Keywords: Cognitive radio · Spectrum allocation · Shuffled Frog Leaping Algorithm · Gaussian mutation · Cauchy mutation · Dissimilarity

1 Introduction

Wireless spectrum resources are important non-renewable resource. With wireless communication technology developing rapidly, there will be users increasing with the result of growing conflicts. A large number of spectrum resources has been wasted because of unreasonable allocation [1]. Based on the background mentioned above, cognitive radio [2] is proposed, an effective method to relieve the crisis of spectrum resource scarcity. The core principle is that each secondary user can use free spectrum secondary without interfering with primary users [3–5]. Therefore, the key point is how to allocate free spectrum resources fairly, efficiently and reasonably [6].

At present, there are a lot of models for the spectrum allocation of cognitive radio, like the auction model [7], game theory model [8], the interference temperature model [9] and the graph theory model [10,15]. Graph theory model is preferred by many researchers because of its flexibility and applicability. In fact, it is convenient to deal with the problem by using graph theory model that

© Springer International Publishing AG 2016
G. Wang et al. (Eds.): APSCC 2016, LNCS 10065, pp. 266–277, 2016.
DOI: 10.1007/978-3-319-49178-3_21

describes vividly the problem of spectrum allocation in a graphical way. Meanwhile, many intelligent optimization algorithms are referenced to the spectrum allocation problem. In the literature [16], a spectrum allocation scheme based on genetic algorithm is proposed. Although the convergence rate is fast, it is more difficult to control because of too many existing parameters. In the literature [18], researchers proposed a new algorithm based on particle swarm optimization algorithm whose convergence rate is also fast, but it is easy to fall into local optimum. Shuffled frog leaping algorithm (SFLA), as a new intelligent optimization algorithm, has many advantages: simple design, less adjustable parameters, high calculation speed etc.

Focusing on the disadvantages in SFLA such as low convergence rate, easily falling into the local optimal solution, a new method that used Gaussian - Cauchy mutation operator improved SFLA (GCSFLA) was proposed. In this paper, based on the graph theory model and GCSFLA, we study the cognitive radio spectrum allocation. The mutation operator joined the update process. We use Cauchy mutation with strong global search capability, if falling into the local optimal solution judged by the dissimilarity, otherwise using Cauchy mutation with strong local search capability. The result shows that the better solutions produced by GCSFLA.

2 The Mathematical Model and Matrix of Cognitive Radio

2.1 Graph Theory Model of Spectrum Allocation

In the Fig. 1, it vividly described the structure model of cognitive wireless network. Each vertex represents one user, and the vertex in big circle is primary user (available spectrum), noted "PUi" and the vertex in small circle is secondary users, noted "SUi". The d^p and d^s represent the radius of their interference scope respectively. Interference would exist in the overlap of users. Take PU1 and SU1 for example, the secondary user SU1 can not use the spectrum I because of the interference. Although users SU2 and SU3 can use the spectrum II, it will produce interference when both of them use the spectrum II at the same time.

2.2 The Matrix of Spectrum Allocation

In order to deal with the spectrum allocation conveniently, we define 4 matrices for cognitive radio network spectrum allocation.

(1) The channel availability matrix:

$$L = \{l_{n,m} | l_{n,m} \in \{0,1\}\}_{N \times M}, 1 \leq n \leq N, 1 \leq m \leq M$$

L is a N by M binary matrix representing the channel availability; if channel m is available for user n, $l_{n,m} = 1$; otherwise, $l_{n,m} = 0$.

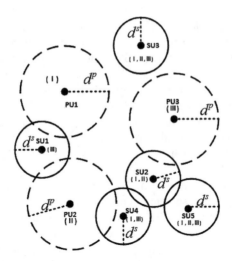

Fig. 1. An example of graph theory model.

(2) The interference constraint matrix:

$$C = \{c_{n,k,m}|c_{n,k,m} \in \{0,1\}\}_{N \times N \times M}, 1 \leq n, k \leq N, 1 \leq m \leq M$$

C is a N by N by M matrix representing the interference constraints among secondary users. If users n and k would interfere with each other if they use channel m simultaneously, $c_{n,k,m} = 1$. In fact, we can use the matrix L to study the matrix C. If $n = k$, $c_{n,k,m} = 1 - l_{n,m}$, because $c_{n,k,m}$ represents the interference constraints between a single secondary user n and the channel m at this time. If $n \neq k$, $c_{n,k,m} \leq l_{n,m} \times l_{k,m}$, because possible interference just in the case of channel m is available for the user n and user k simultaneously.

(3) The conflict free channel allocation matrix:

$$A = \{a_{n,m} \in \{0,1\}\}_{N \times M}$$

A is a N by M binary matrix representing the channel allocation. If $a_{n,m} = 1$, channel m is assigned to user n, otherwise $a_{n,m} = 0$. A should satisfy all the interference constraints defined by C, that is, $a_{n,m} + a_{k,m} \leq 1$, if and only if $c_{n,k,m} = 1$, $\forall 1 \leq n, k \leq N, 1 \leq m \leq M$.

(4) The channel reward matrix:

$$B = \{b_{n,m}|b_{n,m} \in (0, +\infty)\}, 1 \leq n, k \leq N, 1 \leq m \leq M$$

B is a N by M matrix representing the channel reward and $b_{n,m}$ is the reward generated by user n using channel m. $b_{n,m} > 0$ if $l_{n,m} = 1$.

2.3   The Efficiency of Spectrum Sharing

Obviously, the matrix that satisfies the above conditions is not unique. And the aim is the aim to get the optimal spectrum allocation. The matrix A which satisfies the conditions is defined as a set $A_{m,n}$, and the spectrum access problem becomes finding optimal spectrum allocation $A_{m,n}^*$. In this paper, we use three different efficiency functions to measure the performance of spectrum.

(1) Max-Sum-Reward-Mean (MSRM), which means the average of total network revenue.

$$U_{mean} = \frac{1}{N} \sum_{n=1}^{N} \sum_{m=1}^{M} a_{n,m} \times b_{n,m} \tag{1}$$

(2) Max-Min-Reward (MMR), which means the utilization of the limited spectrum. It is the minimum value for the benefit of a singer user.

$$U_{\min} = \min_{1 \leq n \leq N} \left(\sum_{m=1}^{M} a_{n,m} \times b_{n,m} \right) \tag{2}$$

(3) Max-Proportional-Fair (MPF), which means the largest proportion of fairness. it is the geometric mean of the reward of all secondary users.

$$U_{fair} = \left(\prod_{n=1}^{N} \sum_{m=1}^{M} a_{n,m} \times b_{n,m} + 10^{-4} \right)^{\frac{1}{N}} \tag{3}$$

3   Algorithm and Related Design

3.1   Shuffled Frog Leaping Algorithm

Shuffled Frog Leaping Algorithm (SFLA) is a swarm intelligent optimization algorithm proposed by Lansey and Eusuff in 2003 [11,12]. SFLA is inspired by Frogs (candidate solutions) foraging in wetlands (solution space), the frog population is divided into several subgroups to do a further local optimization (local information exchange). After the subgroups reach certain condition, mixing up the population (global information exchange) and searching for another time by regrouping until the termination condition was satisfied. Relatively speaking, SFLA is a high efficiency of optimization algorithm with higher degree of convergence, which enables tracking the optimal solution in complex space and solving some complex problems. Meanwhile, there are also some shortcomings, such as it will trap into local optimal solution easily, especially in the latter evolution period frogs tended to focus on one place that leads to a single searching direction and lacking of population diversity.

3.2   Gaussian-Cauchy Mutation Operator

It is easy to trap into local optimal solution and lead to a single searching direction by using SFLA in the latter evolution period. As a result, the difficulty of finding the optimal solution is increased. In this paper, we use the Gaussian - Cauchy mutation operator to deal with this problem.

It is showed in the Formula (4) that the one-dimensional probability distribution function of Gauss distribution is the normal distribution in the probability statistics. We call it the standard Gaussian distribution if $u = 0, \sigma^2 = 1$, noted $N(0,1)$. The mathematical expectation of Cauchy distribution does not exist, and the one-dimensional probability distribution function is showed in Formula (5). We call it the standard Cauchy distribution if $t = 1$, noted $C(0,1)$.

Compared to Gauss distribution in Fig. 2, Cauchy distribution changes faster around although both of the probability density curves are very similar. We can see that Gaussian distribution is narrower than Cauchy distribution. Most of Gaussian distribution concentrate on the middle so that Gaussian mutation has a strong local search capability [13,14] and it can improve the convergence rate. The scope of the Cauchy distribution is wide. If we using Cauchy mutation, the mutation step should be larger. To avoid the premature convergence of the algorithm, we use Cauchy mutation if population trapped into the local optimal solution.

$$f(x) = \frac{1}{\sqrt{2\pi}\sigma} e^{-\frac{(x-u)^2}{2\sigma^2}}, x \in R \tag{4}$$

$$f(x) = \frac{1}{\pi} \times \frac{t}{t^2 + x^2}, x \in R \tag{5}$$

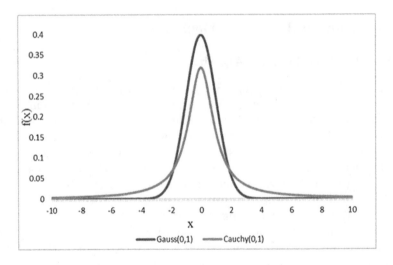

Fig. 2. Probability density distribution curve of Gaussian and Cauchy.

We can improve the way of updating frog's position so that the algorithm optimization capability can be enhanced greatly. For a frog $X_i = (x_{i1}, x_{i2}, x_{i3}, \cdots, x_{is})$(s represents dimension)

$$X_{i,j} = X_{i,j} \times (N(0,1) + 1) \tag{6}$$

if it is Gaussian mutation. $X_{i,j}$ represents the j-th dimension of X_i, $N(0,1)$ represents a Gaussian distribution of a group of numbers. if it is Cauchy mutation

$$X_{i,j} = X_{i,j} \times (C(0,1) + 1) \tag{7}$$

$C(0,1)$ represents a Cauchy distribution of a group of numbers.

3.3   Dissimilarity

In the process of optimization algorithm, SFLA overlooked the population when it began to trap into local optimal solution. In this paper, we made adjustments in time if the population traps into local optimal solution, so we need to study it. In order to reduce the computation complexity, we encoded each frogs. The dissimilarity is used to describe the dispersion degree of group which one frog as a center. It is easy to calculate dissimilarity after encoding them.

(a) Encoding. After initialization in this paper, each frog is a matrix (potential solution), and matrix is a multidimensional data object that is difficult to manipulate. Element 0 in Matrix L represents that channel m is unavailable for user n, which means that its series of operation of the data is meaningless. Based on the two points just said, not only operating data easily but also removing meaningless calculation, we will encode.

We can describe the process of encoding like this: put non-zero elements in the matrix into a vector, because only non-zero elements can be changed after several iterations of the algorithm. cl called encoded length, is the number of non-zero elements. Finally, the calculated results are mapped into a matrix. An example is given in Fig. 3.

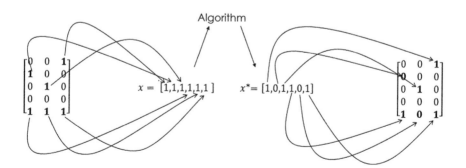

Fig. 3. Schematic of encode and decode (N = 5, M = 3).

(b) Calculation of Dissimilarity. $d(X_c, X_i)$ represents difference between X_c and X_i. The formula is $d(X_c, X_i) = \sum_{j=1}^{s} x_{cj} {}^{\wedge} x_{ij}$. $x_{cj} {}^{\wedge} x_{ij} = 0$, if $x_{cj} = x_{ij}$, otherwise $x_{cj} {}^{\wedge} x_{ij} = 1$. The formula for the dissimilarity is

$$p = \frac{\sum_{i=1}^{N} d(X_c, X_i)}{cl \times (Num - 1)} \tag{8}$$

cl is encoded length. Num is the size of populations. Molecular is the sum of dissimilarity. By testing many times, it is better for the result that threshold of p is 0.16. we consider that population trap into local optimal solution if $p \leq 0.16$.

3.4   Procedure of the GCSFLA

In summary, the spectrum allocation process based on improved SFLA in this paper are as follows:

Step 1: Initialization. There are some parameters, such as Population size Num, the number of subgroups n, dimension s, maximum moving step D_{max}, the max iteration of subgroups d, the max global iteration h and so on. $X_i = (x_{i1}, x_{i2}, x_{i3}, \cdots, x_{is})$ $(1 \leq i \leq N)$, represents the i-th frog. The whole population is expressed as $X = (X_1, X_2, X_3, \cdots, X_N)$. Generating L, B and C, and encoding each frog.

Step 2: Group. In this paper, (1), (2) and (3) are the fitness functions. We sort frog population from better to worse according to the results of the fitness function. Put the first frog into the first subgroup, the second frog into the second subgroup, and then the next frogs will be put into the next following subgroups $\cdots$ then the (n+1)-th frog is put into the first group. The frogs are all put into the subgroups in this way.

Step 3: Marking the best frog $X_g = (x_{g1}, x_{g2}, x_{g3}, \cdots, x_{gs})$ from all frogs, the best frog $X_b = (x_{b1}, x_{b2}, x_{b3}, \cdots, x_{bs})$ and the worst frog $X_w = (x_{w1}, x_{w2}, x_{w3}, \cdots, x_{ws})$ in each subgroup.

Step 4: The mutation step is calculated by the formula $D = rand \times (X_b - X_w)(-D_{max} \leq D \leq D_{max})$, $rand$ is a random number in the range $[0, 1]$. Calculate the dissimilarity by formula (8), and update it by Cauchy variation formula (7) if population trap into local optimal solution $(p \leq 0.16)$, otherwise update it by Gauss variation formula (6). $X_{w.new}$ is the new position. If $X_{w.new}$ is better than X_w, then use $X_{w.new}$ replace X_w, else X_g to replace X_w, do another updating. If $X_{w.new}$ is better than X_w, then $X_{w.new}$ replace X_w, otherwise random a position instead of X_w.

Step 5: Repeating step 4 until the max iteration of subgroups d, then go to step 6.

Step 6: Repeating step 2–5 until the max global iteration h, recording the best solution.

3.5 The Time Complexity Analysis of the Algorithm

It is easy to get the time complexity from procedure of algorithm. It is supposed some parameters, like population size Num, the number of subgroups n, dimension s, the max iteration of subgroups d, the max global iteration h. Finally, we need to terminate the algorithm. We can see the maximum time complexity is $O(s \bullet Num^2)$ from 1 to 5. So the maximum time complexity of GCSFLA is $O(h \bullet s \bullet Num^2)$ the same as SFLA. In this paper, we just change the update strategy which has not much impact on the complexity of the algorithm, but the performance of algorithm greatly improved (Table 1).

Table 1. The time complexity

Procedure	The time complexity
Initialization	$O(s \bullet Num)$
Sorting	$O(s \bullet Num^2)$
Grouping	$O(s \bullet Num)$
Marking x_b, x_w, x_g	$O(s \bullet (Num/n))$
Updating x_w	$O(s \bullet Num)$

4 Simulation Results and Discussions

4.1 Emulation Environment and Parameters Setting

In this paper, the simulation is based on the Matlab R2014a, the network topology generated by [15]. It makes a comparison among GCSFLA and SFLA, PSO, GA, according to these three different network efficiencies, MSRM, MMR, MPF. Different simulation network topologies are different, but it is the same in one experiment. The parameter of PSO and GA refers to [16]. The basic parameter of GCSFLA and SFLA refers to [17]. The threshold of dissimilarity $p = 16\%$. All algorithms will be terminated after 200 iterations generations. The average results of 30 experiments are as shown below.

4.2 The Discussions of Results

Experiment 1. As is shown in Fig. 4, if M = 15, N = 10, compared the convergent speed of GCSLFA, SFLA, PSO and GA. At first, the network revenue of GCSLFA, SFLA, PSO have increased relatively and quickly. PSO begin to

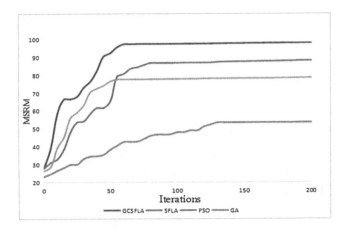

Fig. 4. The average revenues of system with increasing of iterations.

converge around 50 iterations rapidly, but the final revenue is not good because of the poor climbing ability. GA has the lowest rewards and converge to almost 130 iterations. SFLA reaches a peak about 80 iterations with a fast speed in the previous search, but the search ability greatly weakened by population trapping into the local optimal solution. After about 58 iterations, the GCSLFA begin to converge and grow rapidly because of the Gaussian mutation operator with strong local search capability used in the early time. The explanation for high profit is that jumping from the local optimal solution prevented the optimization from prematurity and fully searching in the final period of searching process.

Experiment 2. In practice, the number of the spectrum is limited, but the number of users is not under control. The experiment shows the changes of three kinds of network revenue with the increasing in the number of secondary users under the circumstances of constant number of spectrum. If $M = 19$, the results are shown in Figs. 5, 6 and 7. In each picture, the trend of the curve is roughly the same. the network revenue has decreased persistently with increasing of users, but not significantly, the reason of which is that the more users the more total network revenue but tiny increase in interference. With the further increasing of users, it leads to much more competition between users so that the network revenue rapidly declined. However, with the monitoring of the population state through the dissimilarity, the GCSFLA can adapt itself by adaptive Gaussian and Cauchy mutation once population trapped into the local optimal solution, which makes a higher returns and prove that the effectiveness of GCSFLA.

The relative difference between the rewards and the optimal values is given in the table. The optimal values are obtained by exhaustive method [15]. We set $M = N = 5$, taking into account the feasibility of computing because there is a NP problem with rapidly increasing in size. In an experiment, if the reward

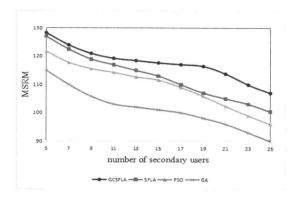

Fig. 5. MSRM changes when M = 19.

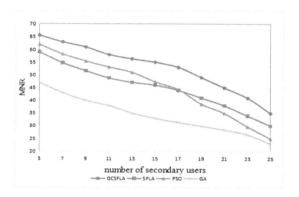

Fig. 6. MNR changes when M = 19.

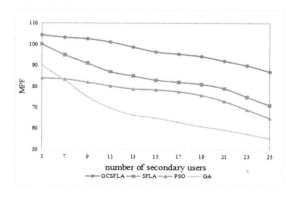

Fig. 7. MPF changes when M = 19.

Table 2. Comparison to optimal values

Iteration	Algorithm	Relative difference (%)		
		MSRM	MMR	MPF
30	GCSFLA	0.353	0.487	1.886
	SFLA	1.205	1.705	3.256
	PSO	0.338	1.238	1.897
	GA	1.094	2.764	3.241
100	GCSFLA	0	0	0.013
	SFLA	0	1.568	2.724
	PSO	0	1.433	0.961
	GA	0.434	2.431	3.173
200	GCSFLA	0	0	0.013
	SFLA	0	1.131	2.153
	PSO	0	0.57	0.579
	GA	0.057	2.247	2.781

is b and the optimal values is B, then the relative difference is $1 - b/B$. As is shown in the table, in the 100 iterations, the relative difference of GCSFLA is very small just in MPF. GCSFLA performs almost the same as the others under objectives MSRM after 200 iterations, but GCSFLA performs much better than others in MMR and MPF (Table 2).

5   Conclusion

In this paper, considering three kinds of network revenue based on spectrum allocation, a Gaussian - Cauchy mutation SFLA is proposed. SFLA traps into the local optimal solution easily. In this paper, we encode the mathematical model to reduce the computation complexity. GCSFLA not only can ensure the convergence speed, but also enhance the population diversity in late search by using adaptive Gaussian and Cauchy mutation and judging through the dissimilarity. Compared with SFLA, PSO and GA, the experimental results show that GCSFLA has better performance in the three kinds of network revenue, MSRM, MNR and MPF. Meanwhile, GCSFLA also has good performance in the relative difference.

Acknowledgements. This work is supported by the National Natural Science Foundation of China (Grant No. 61309001, Grant No. 61272149). This work is supported by the Research Fund for the Doctoral Program of Higher Education of China (Grant No. 20130162120080).

References

1. Cheng, X., Jiang, M.: Cognitive radio spectrum assignment based on artificial bee colony algorithm. In: 2011 IEEE 13th International Conference on Communication Technology (ICCT), pp. 161–164. IEEE (2011)
2. Jiang, T., Grace, D., Mitchell, P.D.: Efficient exploration in reinforcement learning-based cognitive radio spectrum sharing. IET Commun. **5**(10), 1309–1317 (2011)
3. Wang, B., Liu, K.J.R.: Advances in cognitive radio networks: a survey. IEEE J. Sel. Top. Sign. Proces. **5**(1), 5–23 (2013)
4. Yao, J., Zhang, H., Liu, S., et al.: Research on spectrum assignment in electric cognitive radio networks. In: 2014 International Conference on Power System Technology (POWERCON), pp. 1723–1729. IEEE (2014)
5. Boyd, S.W., Frye, J.M., Pursley, M.B., et al.: Spectrum monitoring during reception in dynamic spectrum access cognitive radio networks. IEEE Trans. Commun. **60**(2), 547–558 (2012)
6. Hua, N., Cao, Z.-G.: A research summary of studying cognitive radio network routing. Chin. J. Electron. **38**(4), 910–918 (2010)
7. Wang, X., Li, Z., Xu, P.: IEEE Trans. Syst. Man Cybern. B **40**, 587 (2010)
8. Wang, B.B., Wu, Y.L., Liu, K.J.: Comput. Netw. **54**, 2537 (2010)
9. Gozupek, D., Alagoz, F.: Int. J. Commun. Syst. **24**, 239 (2011)
10. Wu, J., Li, Y., Liu, G.: J. China Univ. Post Telecom. **21**, 9 (2014)
11. Zou, C.-R., Zhang, X.-D., Zhao, L.: Research summary of shuffled frog leaping algorithm. Inf. Res. **38**(5), 1–5 (2012)
12. Zhou, J., Dutkiewicz, E., Liu, R.P., et al.: A modified shuffled frog leaping algorithm for PAPR reduction in OFDM systems. IEEE Trans. Broadcast. **61**(4), 698–709 (2015)
13. Zhang, Y.-G., Quan, H.-Y.: Self-adaptive evolutionary algorithm for constrained optimization. Comput. Eng. Appl. **44**(33), 50–52 (2008)
14. Yang, X.S., Deb, S.: Engineering optimization by cuckoo search. Int. J. Math. Model. Num. Optim. **4**, 330–343 (2010)
15. Peng, C.-Y., Zheng, H.-T., Zhao, B.Y.: Utilization and fairness in spectrum assignment for opportunistic spectrum access. Mobile Netw. Appl. **11**(4), 555–576 (2006)
16. Zhao, Z.J., Peng, Z., Zheng, S.L., Shang, J.N.: Cognitive radio spectrum allocation using evolutionary algorithms. IEEE Trans. Wireless Commun. **8**(9), 4421–4425 (2009)
17. Peng, Z., Zhao, Z.J., Zheng, S.L.: Cognitive radio spectrum allocation using shuffled frog leaping algorithm. Comput. Eng. Appl. **36**(6), 210–217 (2010)
18. Zhang, L.Y., Zeng, Z.W., Chen, Z.G., et al.: Spectrum allocation algorithm based on constraint operator of binary particle swarm in the congnitive wireless networks. J. Chin. Comput. Syst. **34**(6), 1226–1229 (2013). in Chinese

Recommending a Personalized Sequence of Pick-Up Points

Yizhi Liu[1,2(✉)], Jianxun Liu[1,2], Jianjun Wang[1,2], Zhuhua Liao[1,2], and Mingdong Tang[1,2]

[1] School of Computer Science and Engineering,
Hunan University of Science and Technology, Xiangtan 411201, China
yizhi_liu@sina.cn
[2] Key Laboratory of Knowledge Processing and Networked Manufacturing,
Xiangtan 411201, China

Abstract. The value of GPS data has generated a group of location-based services. Pick-up points recommendation by mining taxis' trajectories can effectively both improve drivers' profits and reduce oil consumption. However, existing methods always ignore the spatial-temporal features and the drivers' preferences. Therefore, we propose to recommend a personalized sequence of pick-up points taking the two preceding factors into account. Firstly, we extract historical pick-up points from taxis' trajectories and use these points to generate candidate ones by a novel approach of spatial-temporal analysis. Secondly, we devise a collaborative filtering algorithm to choose candidate points again. According to the location and the time of historical pick-up points, our system can give taxi-drivers an optimal sequence of pick-up points. Experimental results show that our method can obviously improve both the accuracy and the preference of candidate pick-up points for taxi-drivers.

Keywords: Location-based services · Trajectory mining · Pick-up points recommendation · Spatial-temporal analysis · Personalized recommendation · Collaborative filtering

1 Introduction

The advances in location-acquisition, wireless communication, and mobile computing techniques have enabled us to collect massive spatial trajectory data of moving objects, such as people, vehicles and animals. Such a large number of trajectories provide us unprecedented opportunity to automatically discover useful knowledge, which in turn offer support for decision in various fields (e.g. taxi service). Taxicabs, frequently travelling in the city every day, have become an indispensable part of the intelligent transportation system. In order to facilitate residents' lives, lots of taxis traversing in urban areas. But vacant taxis cursing on roads not only waste gas and time of drivers but also generate additional traffic in a city.

There are many researchers have performed research on methods that can improve the utilization of vacant taxis and reduce the energy consumption effectively. These researches used some objective standards to calculate the corresponding optimal

© Springer International Publishing AG 2016
G. Wang et al. (Eds.): APSCC 2016, LNCS 10065, pp. 278–291, 2016.
DOI: 10.1007/978-3-319-49178-3_22

strategies, such as maximizing the drivers' profits, or maximizing the probability of finding passengers. In fact, every driver has his/her own driving habits and driving style. Thus, they usually made the decision according to their preferences and experiences to cruising roads and pick-up points).

In this paper, we provide a personalized sequence of pick-up points recommendation (PSPPR) method toward taxi drivers based on spatial trajectory data, and we present a probability optimization model (POM) for evaluating each candidate pick-up sequence. Our method is to satisfy the taxi drivers' maximize benefits as well as offer personalized services for fitting their preference. First of all, we extract historical pick-up points from taxis' trajectories, which are analyzed to generate candidate pick-up points by our method of spatial-temporal analysis, which can improve the probability of finding passengers for taxi driver. Then, according to the records of pick-up passengers of taxi, the request location and time, and using collaborative filtering algorithm to filter candidate points, the recommender system can recommend a sequence of probability optimization of pick-up points for drivers.

The remainder of this paper is organized as follows. Section 2 describes the related works. The framework of our approach is presented in Sect. 3. Next, we illustrate the two parts of our method in details: one is how to generate pick-up points in Sect. 4, another is how to recommend a personalized sequence of pick-up points in Sect. 5. Section 6 gives the experimental results. Finally, we state the concluding remarks and future directions in Sect. 7.

2 Related Works

Many researchers have focused on passengers-finding strategies which can both improve the profits of taxi-drivers and reduce oil consumption. Most of them proposed to recommend parking locations. Few of them focused on how to recommend a sequence of locations to maximize the probability of picking up passengers with less cruising time or less cruising distances. Others are focused on cruising route for the next passengers instead of fixed locations.

Chang et al. [1] extract hotspots from large amounts of historical data using clustering algorithm. Then, it would recommend a hotspot to taxi driver based on the hotness of the hotspot. Li et al. [2] study the passenger-finding strategies (hunting/waiting) of taxi drivers, and provide L1-norm support vector machine (SVM) to select features for classifying the passenger-finding strategies in terms of performance. In the literatures [3, 5], the authors propose an algorithm to extract parking places based on the distance between non-occupied trajectories' points. Then, it aims to provide the taxi driver with the best parking place and the best route to this parking place. Zhang et al. [4] propose a method to recommend top-5 passenger finding probability pick-up points for taxi drivers.

Ge et al. [6] present a novel model to recommend a taxi driver with a sequence of pick-up points or a sequence of potential parking positions so as to maximize the profit of a taxi driver. Hou et al. [7] envision a new cyber-technology enabled taxi dispatch system, different from the conventional operation mode, which can efficiently provide vacant taxis with cruising route suggestions that hop to find prospective customers.

Tang et al. [8] provide a Markov decision process (MDP) to model the problem of finding passenger, and compute a high-level profit-maximizing strategy for taxi drivers. In the literature [9], the authors present a system called HUNTS to solve the problem that formalizes the passenger-finding strategies into a new problem, global-optimal trajectory retrieving. Huang et al. [10] propose a mobile sequential recommendation using based on dynamic programming. They compute potential candidate sequences from a set of pick-up points mining from large amount of trajectories, propose a backward incremental sequence generation algorithm based on the identified iterative property of the cost function. Then adopt an incremental pruning policy to process the sequence and recommend a sequence of pick-up points. In the literature [11], the authors propose a recommender system by considering the distance between the current location and the recommendation location, waiting time for the next passengers, expected fare for the trip, and the experience of taxi drivers, recommending the next cruising location so as to improve the income of taxi-drivers.

In the literature [12], the authors construct a spatio-temporal profitability (STP) map based on historical data to guide the taxi drivers in terms of dividing a region into a grid of equally sized cells. Hu et al. [13] propose a pick-up tree based route recommender system to minimize the traveling distance of vacant taxis aiming to improve the efficiency of taxi drivers. Zhang et al. [14] propose a cruising system called p-Cruise for taxicab drivers to maximize their profits by finding the optimal route to pick up a passenger so as to reduce the cruising mile. Dong et al. [15] propose a system of linear equations to calculate the score of each road segment, and build a profitable cursing route to recommend cursing path for taxi. Wang et al. [16] propose a citywide and real-time model for estimating the travel time of any path in real time in a city by mining the trajectory data, which can provide real-time path planning. Qu et al. [17] propose a cost-effective recommender system aiming to maximize taxi-drivers' profits by recommending a potential profits driving route. Zhang et al. [18] intend to uncover the efficient and inefficient taxi service strategies aiming to predict the revenue of drivers based on a large-scale GPS historical database. Yang et al. [19] propose adaptive shortest expected cruising route (ASECR) algorithm to recommend a profitable route for taxi-drivers based on assigned potential profitable grids and then to update the profitable route constantly. Zheng et al. [20] propose a novel taxi-sharing system that accepts taxi-passengers' real-time requests from smart phones and schedules proper taxis to pick-up them via ridesharing, subject to time, capacity, and monetary constraints.

These researches are using some objective standard to calculate the corresponding optimal strategies, such as maximizing the drivers' profits, or maximizing the probability of finding passengers. Actually, every driver has his/her own driving habits or driving style. They made the decision according to their preferences and experiences to roads and pick-up points.

3   The Framework of Our Approach

Pick-up points are the locations where taxi-drivers find passengers. Its distribution can reflect drivers' behaviors to find passengers. If we discover the behavior rules of taxi-drivers, we could apply it to intelligent transport, urban planning, traffic management, etc. The framework of a personalized sequence of pick-up points recommendation is illustrated in Fig. 1. It consists of two parts: generating pick-up points and recommending a personalized sequence.

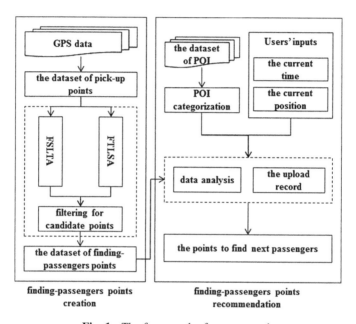

Fig. 1. The framework of our approach

First of all, extracted the locations where taxi drivers usually pick up passengers from a large number of GPS trajectory data, and using the spatial and temporal attribute of these locations by a novel approach of spatio-temporal analysis (STA), which can obtain some candidate points represent the region where taxi drivers often find passengers. We divided our STA into two steps. The first step is to do analysis using spatial and temporal attribute independent. The next step is to combine these candidate points, filtering them by voting mechanism. Then the candidate points' type is defined by POI (point of interest, e.g. hotel, hospital) in their regions. The drivers can find passengers quickly in these points, and reduce their vacant cruising time. After that, according to the records of pick-up passengers of taxi, the request location and time, and using collaborative filtering algorithm to filter candidate points, the recommender system can recommend a sequence of probability optimization of pick-up points for drivers. Our method is not only to satisfy the taxi drivers' maximize benefits, but also offer personalized services for fitting their preference.

4 Pick-Up Points Generation

In this section, we present the details of spatio-temporal analysis, which generate the candidate points, describe how we decide the type of these points, and compute the passenger finding probability in every point.

4.1 Spatio-Temporal Analysis (STA)

Taxi-drivers usually choose a place where they familiar with waiting for passengers, and in different time in different location. The GPS trajectory is a trace generated by taxicabs, usually represented by a series of chronologically ordered points, e.g. $P_1 \rightarrow P_2 \rightarrow \cdots \rightarrow P_N$, where each point consist of a geospatial coordinate set and a timestamp, which objectively record the information of the location and the time of finding passengers or drop off passengers, and the information of drivers' preference toward to the road characteristic and the type of passenger finding locations.

Extracting the historic finding-passengers locations from GPS trajectories by some characteristics (e.g. waiting or driving with a speed less than a threshold for a period of time, the taxi travel with a speed over one threshold for a long distance), such as shown in Fig. 2, and analyzing the distribution of these locations in space and time, can provide service for the taxi drivers and taxi management department.

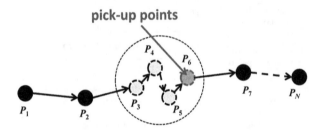

Fig. 2. Extracting Pick-up points

To analyze these passenger-finding locations, we put forward a STA model which is constructed by OPTICS algorithm, aiming to discover the essentially same pick up locations in space and time. The reason for using this method is that it outperforms other methods when dense regions in different time and in different place. The algorithm in this model described as "improve OPTICS algorithm" in Table 1, which considered the time as a parameter.

The property of extracted locations of historic passenger finding mark as p{tId, lat, lng, datetime, type}, p.tId describe the taxi id who find the passengers, p.lat and p.lng is the spatial attribute of location, p.datetime show that when the passenger was found, and p.type illustrate the type of the location, which decide by the nearest point of interest (e.g. restaurant, train station). Analyzing the data set P{p1, p2, ..., pn} of these extracted locations, we can find that the density of locations changed in different time slots. Figure 3 describe the density change features.

Table 1. Improved OPTICS algorithm

Input: Historic Pick-up Points Sets ppDatas[1...n], every
point has parameter latitude, longitude and timeslots
Output: Historic Pick-up Points Sets orderedDatas[1...m]

```
1 set ε and MinPts, create Nε(i) and cᵢ
2 vᵢ←0, rᵢ←Undefined, k←1, seedList←∅
3 while(i<n){
4   if(vᵢ==0){
5     vᵢ←1, pₖ←i, k←k+1;
6     if(|Nε(i)|>=MinPts){
          /* insert the key point into the seedlist*/
7         insertlist(Nε(i),{vₗ},{rₗ},cᵢ,seedlist); /* l=1...n, vⱼ=0 */
8         while(seedlist not empty){
9           get the first seed j from seedlist;
10          vⱼ←1, pₖ←j, k←k+1;
11          if(|Nε(i)|>=MinPts){
              /* insert the key point into the seedlist*/
12            insertlist(Nε(i),{vₗ},{rₗ},cᵢ,seedlist); // l=1...n, vⱼ=0
            }
14        }
15      }
16    }
17  i←i+1
18 }
19 for(i:n){
20   divideByTimeslots(i); //contain a threshold
21 }
22 return orderedDatas;
```

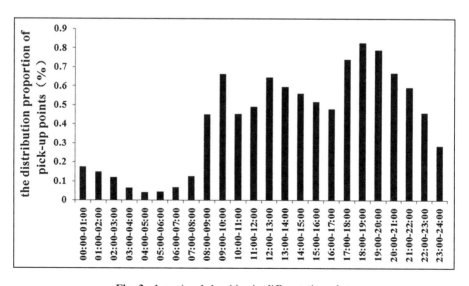

Fig. 3. Locations' densities in different time-slots

Based on the density-changing feature, we firstly consider spatial-temporal features in spatial-temporal analysis model. We divide one day into some time slots, which have 0.5 h, 1 h, 2 h, and 4 h independent. The spatial-temporal analysis model describe in detail as follows:

Step 1: Spatial-temporal analysis

(1) First space last time analysis (FSLTA). We firstly consider the space property of historic location points. We divided location points by regions, analyzing these points in every area, then, we process all areas comprehensive. After the space analysis, we can get the clusters contain time attribute. We process these historic location points further based on the time attribute. We can get a set of candidate points with temporal and spatial attribution, which relevant attribute describe as cp {id, lat, lng, timeslots, method}. cp.timeslots describe the slots of passenger finding, cp.lat and cp.lng show the location where the passenger finding, and cp. method illustrate the analysis type.

(2) First time last space analysis (FTLSA). This part is simple as we divide our pick-up points into every time-slots based on their time attribute, and process historic location points by spatial property in every time slots. Then we can get another set of candidate points with temporal and spatial property, which marked as cp{id, lat, lng, timeslots, method}.

The FSLTA better described the spatial gather phenomenon of historic location points than FTLSA, and compensate the problem of data sparseness of FTLSA in some extent. The FTLSA better described the temporal gather phenomenon of historic location points than FSLTA.

Step 2: Candidate-points filtering

It is obviously that the candidate points generated from step 1 and step 2 maybe in the same cluster, they represent the same region. So, we should delete one of them if they are in the same cluster. In the same time slots, if the distance $Dist_{i,j}$ between candidate point i generated by step 1 and candidate point j generated by step 2 less than a certain threshold d (e.g. 50 m).

We can use voting mechanism to generate one point replacing the adjacent candidate points. According to the distance of them to generate a buffer, then using historic location points (e.g. location point k) located in themselves respective buffer to voting themselves by the distance $Dist_{i,k}$ between historic location point k with candidate point i. The calculation method of voting described in (1).

$$Score_i = \sum_{k=1}^{n} (1 - \frac{Dist_{i,k}}{Dist_{i,j}}), Dist_{i,j} \in (0, d], Dist_{i,k} \in [0, Dist_{i,j}] \tag{1}$$

The $Score_j$ is calculated in the same way. Then, according to the score of candidate point i and j to calculate the position of new candidate point O. The position of O is described as

$$O_{lat, lng} = I_{lat, lng} \frac{Score_i * Dist_{i,j}}{Score_i + Score_j} \qquad (2)$$

or

$$O_{lat, lng} = J_{lat, lng} \frac{Score_j * Dist_{i,j}}{Score_j + Score_i} \qquad (3)$$

The O, I, J represent the position of candidate point respectively.

4.2   Candidate-Points' Types

Passenger finding usually occur nearby a particular POI (e.g. restaurant, station, etc.), and the region of the candidate point represented consist of POI. In this paper, we divide the POI sets of Beijing into eleven categories. They are health, food, travel, service, shopping, government, education, enterprise, entertainment, hotel and other. We can confirm the candidate point type by these categories based on the POI which contained. The candidate point type mark as Cp{id, lat, lng, type1, ..., type11, score}. The element Cp.lat and Cp.lng describe the location of the candidate point, Cp.type represents the proportion of a certain category POI, Cp.score shows the density of historic location points in the region of candidate point.

Figure 4 describe the proportion of a certain category POI in the region of candidate point 3 and 6 respectively. It obviously shows that the candidate point 3 contains two main POI categories, service and enterprise, but the candidate point 6 contains other main POI categories, service and education. In this paper, we select the top-5 proportion of category as the type label of those candidate points. For example, the mark of candidate point 3 is described as cp3.type{enterprise, service, education, travel, hotel}.

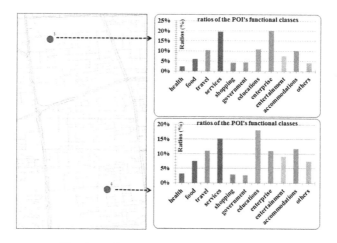

Fig. 4. Ratios of the POI's functional classes

When the passenger-finding location occur in candidate points, we can define a group of relations about the driver and the candidate point, marked as Pp{p.tId, p.datetime, Cp.id}. By analyzing these relationships we can describe the taxi drivers' preference about candidate points, and then recommend suitable points for drivers.

4.3 Probability Calculation

Whether a candidate-point is recommended to a taxi driver or not, not only depends on the driver's personal preference and historical experience, but also depends on the passenger-finding probability of the candidate-point per unit time. We can define the probability $P(C_i)$ of a candidate point C_i with Num_h, the number of historic location points contained, L_h, the perimeter of the cluster of historic location points, and TL_t, the length of the time slots. The passenger finding probability describe as follow:

$$P(C_i) = \frac{Num_h}{L_h * TL_t} \tag{4}$$

5 Constructing a Personalized Sequence of Pick-Up Points

Taxi drivers who drive in the city every day frequently have their driving habits and driving style, and the decision they decide relative to their preferences and historical experience, such as the features of cruising road and the type of pick-up point. Recommending suitable pick-up points to drivers based on the drivers' preferences and history experiences is a good choice.

5.1 Collaborative Filtering

Collaborative Filtering is one of the successful and widely-used recommendation methods. The core of Item-based collaborative filtering is to find the correlation between items, and using user's previous records to recommend similar item to user. In the view of computation, item based collaborative filtering is to search a vector to calculate the similarity of items, then predict some item that user have not touched recommend to user based on the records.

In this paper, we regard candidate points as the projects that will be filtered, and use item based collaborative filtering to filter the candidate point for taxi drivers based on their preference. Setting the candidate point as the n dimensional vector, the similarity of the candidate points can measure by the cosine of the angle between the vectors. Such as candidate point i and candidate point j are represented in n dimensional vector as vector $\vec{i}$ and $\vec{j}$. The similarity of vector $\vec{i}$ and $\vec{j}$ describe as follow.

$$Sim(i, j) = \cos(\vec{i}, \vec{j}) = \frac{\vec{i} \cdot \vec{j}}{|i||j|} \tag{5}$$

When a taxi driver u provides his/her location and time, the system will filter some candidate points near his/her location in the time slots. And the collaborative filtering will calculate the preference of u toward to these candidate points. Such as the degree of preference of taxi driver u toward to candidate point i describe as G(u, i), maybe the taxi driver never pick up a passenger in i previous.

$$G(u,i) = \frac{\sum\limits_{j \in S(i,k,u)} Sim(i,j)}{\sum\limits_{j \in N(u)} |Sim(i,j)|} \qquad (6)$$

The S(i, k, u) describe the set of candidate points where u has found passengers, and the size of the set is k, and these points similar with point i. N(u) is the set of candidate points where driver u ever pick up passengers.

5.2 Probability Optimization Model

The complexity and variability of urban environment lead a great deal of uncertainty to recommend a single result. It is obviously more meaningful to recommend top-k results, and there are strong spatial correlations among them. Choosing a route of sequence of candidate points with maximize passenger finding probability for taxi driver is very meaningful.

In this part, we select candidate-points around taxi drivers, conform their preference, within 5-minutes path, mark the length as d according to the collaborative filtering algorithm. Whether the taxi driver accept a candidate point or not is associated with the distance between the current location and the point, $Dist_{u,i}$. We describe the probability that the driver u accepts the candidate point i as P(u, i).

$$P(u,i) = 1 - \frac{Dist_{u,i}}{d} \qquad (7)$$

The passenger-finding probability of each candidate-points sequence can be seen as a full probability event. We can define the probability of a sequence r as

$$P(r) = \sum_i P(C_i)P(u,i), L(r) \leq L \qquad (8)$$

The L(r) describes the length of the sequence, and L is the maximum length of 5-minutes drive.

Choosing an optimal route for taxi driver is suitable for recommending. The optimal route described as

$$P(r) = \sum_i P(C_i)P(u,i), L(r) \leq L \qquad (9)$$

The sequence recommended not only conform the taxi drivers' preference, but also has the maximize passenger finding probability for the generation method of candidate points.

6 Experiments

Our data of experiments is public trajectory data set provided by Microsoft Research Asia, generated by GeoLife project. It contains 182 taxicabs' previous trajectory from April 2007 to August 2012 in Beijing. The data of POI come from datatang.com.

Our method is consisted of candidate-points generation and recommending a sequence of candidate-points. We evaluate the accuracy of the generation of candidate points in the first. Then, we compare the results of our approach with the classical Top-k recommendation.

6.1 Accuracy Evaluation

In Sect. 4, we divide a day using 4 ways. Candidate pick-up points are generated by two mechanisms: the voting mechanism generating candidate points, the intersection mechanism generating candidate points. We compare the voting mechanism with the intersection mechanism, and experimental results show that the voting mechanism is better. The intersection choice filter is that the new candidate point generated by the historic location points, which are the intersection of location points of adjacent candidate points.

Figure 5 describe the accuracy changed by four kind time slots. Obviously, the accuracy of voting mechanism is better than intersection choice in the 4 time-division way, and the accuracy improved when we extend the time slots. The accuracy of intersection choice can be easily affected by the sparse data distribution. Considering the Fig. 3, in this paper, we divide a day into six parts, every part has four hours, and it is the foundation of other experiments.

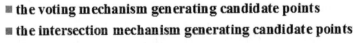

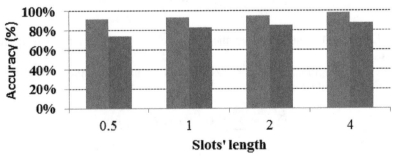

Fig. 5. The comparison between two mechanisms generating candidate points

In order to evaluate the accuracy of candidate points generated by voting mechanism, we reference the judgment method of parking place in literature [5]. They assume that the parking place is correct when a POI is within the scope of the parking place with 50 m. In this paper, we assume that every candidate point is a test point, and the point of interest in map, such as workplace, shop market, and the historic location point as the known point. We can judge the accuracy of candidate point by comparing the test point with the known point. If a known point located in the scope of the test point with a radius, the test point is correct. Figure 6 describes the accuracy with the changes of the detection radius.

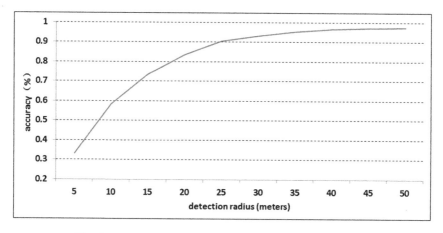

Fig. 6. The accuracy with the changes of the detection radius

The radius changes from 5 to 50 m. When we set 20 m as the radius, we can get a satisfactory result, the average accuracy is 87.6%, and recall is 85.0%. When we set 50 m as the radius, our average result is 98.7% of accuracy, and the recall is 95.4%. Next, we compare the accuracy of candidate points generated by STA with that of paper [5]. The result given in Table 2 shows that STA is obviously better than paper [5] (Table 3).

Table 2. The comparison of two methods

Method	The radius of buffer	Precision	Recall
MSRA	50	90.9%	88.9%
STA	50	98.7%	95.4%

Table 3. The comparison between the top-k recommendation and our PSPPR

Method	Precision	Recall
Top-K	70.5%	68.9%
PSPPR	87.3%	85.7%

7 Conclusions

The advances in location-acquisition and mobile computing techniques have generated massive spatial trajectory data of a diversity of moving objects, such as people, vehicles and animals. The value and conveniently collect of spatial trajectories have generated a group of location-based services. Pick-up points recommendation by mining taxi's trajectory can effectively improve drivers' profits and reduce consumption. However, the recommendation accuracy of existing approaches is not good enough owing to the ignorance of the spatial and temporal features of pick-up points and the preference of taxi drivers. In this article, we proposed a novel approach of personalized sequence of pick-up points recommendation. First, we extracted historical pick-up points from taxis' trajectories, which were analyzed to generate candidate pick-up points by our method of spatial-temporal analysis (STA). Second, according to the records of pick-up passengers of taxi, the request location and time, and using collaborative filtering algorithm to filter candidate points, the recommender system can recommend a sequence of probability optimization of pick-up points for drivers. Experimental results show that our approach was able to obviously improve the accuracy of candidate pick-up points, and the results were more in line with taxi drivers' preference.

In the future, we plan to predict the driving route and destination of taxi based on the road intersection of road network. We think that will be meaningful and interesting.

Acknowledgments. This work is supported by National Nature Science Foundation of China (61572187, 61370227, 61572186), Hunan Provincial Natural Science Foundation of China (2015JJ2056), Hunan Provincial University Innovation Platform Open Fund Project of China (14K037), General project of Hunan Provincial Education Department (16C0642).

References

1. Chang, H., Tai, Y., Hsu, J.Y.: Context-aware taxi demand hotspots prediction. Int. J. Bus. Intell. Data Min. **5**(1), 3–18 (2010)
2. Li, B., Zhang, D., Sun, L., Chen, C., Li, S.: Hunting or waiting? Discovering passenger-finding strategies from a large-scale real-world taxi dataset. In: Proceedings of the 8th IEEE International Workshop on Managing Ubiquitous Communications and Services, pp. 63–68 (2011)
3. Yuan, N.J., Zheng, Y., Zhang, L., Xie, X.: T-Finder: a recommender system for finding passengers and vacant taxis. IEEE Trans. Knowl. Data Eng. **25**(10), 2390–2403 (2013)
4. Zhang, M., Liu, J., Liu, Y., et al.: Recommending pick-up points for taxi-drivers based on spatio-temporal clustering. In: Proceedings of the 2nd IEEE International Conference on Cloud and Green Computing, pp. 67–72 (2012)
5. Yuan, J., Zheng, Y., Zhang, L., Xie, X., et al.: Where to find my next passenger. In: Proceedings of the 13th ACM International Conference on Ubiquitous Computing (2011)
6. Ge, Y., Xiong, H., Tu, A., et al.: An energy-efficient mobile recommender system. In: Proceedings of the 16th ACM SIGKDD International Conference on Knowledge Discovery and Data Mining, pp. 899–908 (2010)
7. Hou, Y., Li, X., Zhao, Y., et al.: Towards efficient vacant taxis cruising guidance. In: Proceedings of the IEEE Global Communications Conference, pp. 54–59 (2013)

8. Tang, H., Kerber, M., Huang, Q., et al.: Locating lucrative passengers for taxicab drivers. In: Proceedings of the 21st ACM SIGSPATIAL International Conference on Advances in Geographic Information Systems, pp. 504–507 (2013)

9. Ding, Y., Liu, S., Pu, J., et al.: HUNTS: a trajectory recommendation system for effective and efficient hunting of taxi passengers. In: Proceedings of the 14th IEEE International Conference on Mobile Data Management, pp. 107–116 (2013)

10. Huang, J., Huang, X., Sun, H., et al.: Backward path growth for efficient mobile sequential recommendation. IEEE Trans. Knowl. Data Eng. **27**(1), 46–60 (2015)

11. Hwang, R.H., Hsueh, Y.L., Chen, Y.T.: An effective taxi recommender system based on a spatio-temporal factor analysis model. Inf. Sci. **314**, 28–40 (2015)

12. Powell, J.W., Huang, Y., Bastani, F., Ji, M.: Towards reducing taxicab cruising time using spatio-temporal profitability maps. In: Pfoser, D., Tao, Y., Mouratidis, K., Nascimento, M. A., Mokbel, M., Shekhar, S., Huang, Y. (eds.) SSTD 2011. LNCS, vol. 6849, pp. 242–260. Springer, Heidelberg (2011). doi:10.1007/978-3-642-22922-0_15

13. Hu, H., Wu, Z., Mao, B., Zhuang, Y., Cao, J., Pan, J.: Pick-Up tree based route recommendation from taxi trajectories. In: Gao, H., Lim, L., Wang, W., Li, C., Chen, L. (eds.) WAIM 2012. LNCS, vol. 7418, pp. 471–483. Springer, Heidelberg (2012). doi:10. 1007/978-3-642-32281-5_45

14. Zhang, D., He, T.: P-Cruise: reducing cruising miles for taxicab networks. In: Proceedings of the 2012 IEEE 33rd Real-Time Systems Symposium, pp. 85–94 (2012)

15. Dong, H., Zhang, X., Dong, Y., et al.: Recommend a profitable cruising route for taxi drivers. In: Proceedings of the 17th International IEEE Conference on Intelligent Transportation Systems, pp. 2003–2008 (2014)

16. Wang, Y., Zheng, Y., Xue, Y.: Travel time estimation of a path using sparse trajectories. In: Proceedings of the 20th ACM SIGKDD International Conference on Knowledge Discovery and Data Mining, pp. 25–34 (2014)

17. Qu, M., Zhu, H., Liu, J., et al.: A cost-effective recommender system for taxi drivers. In: Proceedings of the 20th ACM SIGKDD International Conference on Knowledge Discovery and Data Mining, pp. 45–54 (2014)

18. Zhang, D., Sun, L., Li, B., et al.: Understanding taxi service strategies from taxi GPS traces. IEEE Trans. Intell. Transp. Syst. **16**(1), 123–135 (2015)

19. Yang, W., Wang, X., Rahimi, S.M., Luo, J.: Recommending profitable taxi travel routes based on big taxi trajectories data. In: Cao, T., Lim, E.-P., Zhou, Z.-H., Ho, T.-B., Cheung, D., Motoda, H. (eds.) PAKDD 2015. LNCS (LNAI), vol. 9078, pp. 370–382. Springer, Heidelberg (2015). doi:10.1007/978-3-319-18032-8_29

20. Ma, S., Zheng, Y., Wolfson, O.: Real-time city-scale taxi ridesharing. IEEE Trans. Knowl. Data Eng. **27**(7), 1782–1795 (2015)

Optimizational Methods for Index Construction on Big Graphs

Peiyang Li, Xia Xie$^{(\boxtimes)}$, Hai Jin, Hanhua Chen, and Xijiang Ke

Services Computing Technology and System Lab,
Big Data Technology and System Lab,
Cluster and Grid Computing Lab,
School of Computer Science and Technology,
Huazhong University of Science and Technology, Wuhan 430074, China
shelicy@hust.edu.cn

Abstract. Many indexes have been designed to solve the problem of the point-to-point distance query on big graphs. In this paper, we design an incremental updating method for the index construction on dynamic graphs. The results show that the method is much time-saving compared with the way of index reconstruction. We also propose an exact method for distance labeling focused on undirected unweighted dense graphs. A kind of tight substructure named clique commonly exists in some dense graphs, such as social networks and communication networks. We take advantage of the cliques to compress the index. The experiments show that the technique can save index space and bring about comparable query time.

Keywords: Big graphs · Distance queries · Index construction · Incremental updates · Cliques

1 Introduction

Computing the shortest distance or path between any two vertices is a basic problem. The problem is not only important to build many other algorithms, but also has numerous applications itself. For example, distance in social networks can reflect the closeness of two users and can be used to find more related users or content in the socially-sensitive search. In navigation, drivers want to take the optimal route with the least time or shortest distance. Distance can also indicates relevance in keyword search [11].

The sizes of the underlying graphs are often on the scale of millions of vertices and edges. The classical solutions for distance query are Dijkstra, *breadth-first search* (BFS) and Floyd-Warshall's algorithm. When facing the massive graphs, the long running time that classical algorithms result is unacceptable, especially for some online applications which require low latency for better user experience. On the other hand, the graphs are too large to fit into the memory. Since the classical algorithms are all memory-based solutions, none of the algorithms are practical

© Springer International Publishing AG 2016
G. Wang et al. (Eds.): APSCC 2016, LNCS 10065, pp. 292–305, 2016.
DOI: 10.1007/978-3-319-49178-3_23

on large graphs. To compute the shortest distance and answer the distance query in real time efficiently, many distance indexes have been proposed [7].

We revisit the problem of the shortest distance query and propose two optimizations for index construction in the paper. Most graphs in the real world are dynamic over time. That means that the index will be out-of-date over time. We propose an incremental updating method to make the index adapt for graph changes. In some dense graphs such as social networks, there exists dense core substructure such as cliques. When the distance to one vertex is known, the distances to other vertices within the same clique can be computed. Based on this observation, we can gather the distance information in the same clique together. This optimization allows us to compress the index and have a more efficient query process.

The paper is organized as follows. Section 2 shows the related work and Sect. 3 depicts the problem and introduces some basic knowledge. Section 4 presents our incremental updating methods and algorithms. Section 5 describes how to compress the index with cliques information. Section 6 reports our experiments and Sect. 7 concludes the paper.

2   Related Work

The existing distance query methods can be mainly divided into two groups, namely approximate ones and exact ones. Approximate methods obtain the approximate shortest distances as accurately as possible while exact methods always return exact shortest distances.

2.1   Approximate Methods

Approximate methods are more scalable than exact methods. The majority of approximate methods are landmark-based [4,15,16]. They focus on selecting a subset of vertices as landmarks to derive distance bounds as tight as possible [5]. Supposing that a subset LM of graph nodes are landmarks, these methods compute the distance $dist(l, v)$ between each landmark $l \in LM$ and each vertex v in graphs. Given two query vertices s and t, these methods apply triangle inequality on the top of distances from landmarks to vertices to estimate the approximate distance and return the tightest one. They return the minimum $dist(l, s) + dist(l, t)$ for $l \in LM$ as an estimate. These methods are easy to understand, but have one common shortcoming that the distance accuracy is hard to guarantee. The precision depends on whether the actual shortest path passes the nearby landmarks. For instance, two query vertices are closed to each other while the landmark is far away from them, the result is obviously unsatisfying.

2.2   Exact Methods

Most of the exact methods are based on 2-hop cover, which means that for any two vertices s and t, there exists at least one vertex w that included by the labels of s and t commonly if they are reachable. Finding the smallest 2-hop cover is very challenging and proves to be an NP-hard problem [6].

The *Highway Centric Labeling* (HCL) [13] was proposed to answer distance queries in large sparse road networks. It constructs a tree structured highway to connect the start and end vertices. That means, when computing $dist(s, t)$, the minimum value $dist(s, u_1) + dist_T(u_1, u_2) + dist(t, u_2)$ will be returned where $dist_T(u_1, u_2)$ is the shortest distance between u_1 and u_2 in the highway tree. *Arterial Hierarchy* (AH) was also designed to answer distance queries on road networks [17]. It constructs a vertex hierarchy and conducts a constrained version of Dijkstra algorithm for distance queries. *Contraction Hierarchies* (CH) [9] is a preprocessing algorithm and has been well studied for point-to-point distance queries in road networks. CH applies shortcut operations to each vertex in a particular order and insert additional edges into graphs to facilitate distance queries. *Hierarchical Hub Labeling* (HHL) [1] is another 2-hop labeling method which is based on CH. HHL builds a shortest path tree for each vertex to describe unmarked shortest paths beginning from the vertex. HHL is not scalable for its high computation and storage complexity when handling large graphs. The approach *Pruning Landmark Labeling* (PLL) [2] was proposed by Akiba et al. It conducts pruned BFS from each vertex. BFS is memory based and the pruning procedure demands the whole index to remain in the memory. Therefore, large memory is required and it limits PLL's scalability.

IS-Label [8] was proposed by Fu et al. It builds a vertex hierarchy for the given graph and constructs the labels from top to bottom. Jiang et al. designed *Hop Doubling Labeling* (HopDB) index with the assumption that the majority of long paths passing through some high degree vertices [12]. Their strategy is first ranking all the vertices in non-increasing order according to vertex degree and then generating label entries iteratively to cover the shortest paths with increasing numbers of hops.

All indexes introduced above are constructed for static graphs. In fact, the graphs may change over time, such as, users make new friends in the social network, new air routes open up in the transportation network. To avoid the reconstruction of indexes, Akiba et al. proposed an incremental updating method based on PLL [3]. When inserting a new edge into the origin graph, it re-conducts pruned BFS from the affected vertices and updates the distance information on the fly. Lin et al. proposed an patch-merge method to update indexes based on hopDB [14]. The method includes two steps, the first step is to generate patches for the indexes and the second step is to merge the patches into the indexes. Other methods are also proposed [10].

3   Preliminary

3.1   Problem Definition

We focus on undirected unweighted graphs. We study the following problem: given a disk-resident graph $G = (V, E)$ with a vertex set V and an edge set E, how to construct a disk-based index to answer point-to-point distance queries efficiently. The commonly used notations in this paper is shown in Table 1.

Table 1. Important notations

Notation	Description
$G = (V, E)$	A graph with vertex set V and edge set E
$dist(u, v)$	Shortest distance between u and v
$rank(v)$	Rank of v
S_i	Independent set after i-th iteration
G_i	Result graph after i-th iteration
$L(v)$	Plain label of vertex v
$V[L(v)]$	Vertices in the $L(v)$
C_x	Subset of vertices which in the same clique with x
$C_x^i(v)$	Subset of C_x where i denotes the distance difference
$CL(v)$	Label of vertex v with cliques

3.2   2-hop Labeling

The 2-hop labeling technique is an exact distance scheme proposed by Cohen et al. [6]. It preprocesses the given graph and constructs labels for each vertex. For each vertex $v \in G$, there is a label $L(v)$, which contains a set of entries (u, d) where $u \in V$ and d is the distance from u to v. If vertex s reaches t, there exist $(w, d_1) \in L(s)$ and $(w, d_2) \in L(t)$ such that $dist(s, t) = d_1 + d_2$. Then we say that vertex pair (s, t) is covered by entries (w, d_1) and (w, d_2). The distance query between vertices s and t can be answered by the labels $L(s)$ and $L(t)$ as follow:

$$dist(s, t) = min\{d_1 + d_2 | (u, d_1) \in L(s), (u, d_2) \in L(t)\} \tag{1}$$

If $L(s) \cap L(t) = \emptyset$, then $dist(s, t) = \infty$. We can compute $dist(s, t)$ by scanning the labels $L(s)$ and $L(t)$ in $O(|L(s)| + |L(t)|)$ time when $L(s)$ and $L(t)$ are sorted. Obviously the size of 2-hop labeling is important to the query efficiency. Let L denote the set of labels of all vertices. If the distance between any pair of vertices can be answered by L, the L is called a *2-hop cover* of G.

3.3   IS-Label

IS-Label is a variant of 2-hop labeling proposed by James et al. [8]. Since our work is based on this work, we briefly introduce it first. It builds a layered hierarchy for the vertices by removing sets of less important vertices recursively. The resulting graph of i-th iteration is also the input graph of $i + 1$ iteration procedure. The sets are called independent sets and the vertices in the same set do not connect to each other. Suppose the vertices removing in the i-th iteration is denoted as S_i, then the vertices are partitioned into several sets, namely $V = S_1 \cup S_2 ... \cup S_k$ and $S_i \cap S_j = \emptyset$ $(1 \leq i \neq j \leq k)$. Let the input graph to be G_0 and the i-th resulting graph is G_i. The graph $G_i(i \geq 1)$ is reduced from G_{i-1} by removing the vertices in S_{i-1}. To keep the connectivity and distances between vertices in the remaining graph when vertices are removed, additional edges are created. Finally, an augmented graph is obtained by inserting the additional edges into the original graph.

The $rank(v)$ of v is equal to i if and only if $v \in S_i$. A vertex u is an ancestor of v if there is one path from v to u in the augmented graph and the vertices on the path is in an ascending order of vertex rank. Each $L(v)$ records the distances to its ancestors by building the labels from higher ranks to lower ranks iteratively.

4   Incremental Updates

In this section, we will detail how to update the indexes based on IS-Label on dynamic graphs. More concretely, the dynamic graphs we focus on are those with new edge addition and no vertex addition.

4.1   Incremental Updating Procedure

The incremental updating procedure includes two steps, the first step is to generate the label patch, namely the new label entries which need to be merged into the indexes. The second step is to update the indexes with the patch generated in the first step. Note that although our update method also has two steps as the method proposed by Lin [14], they are based on totally different theory and have totally different realization. Lin's method is based on hopDB and generates patches by pruned BFS while our method is based on IS-Label and generates patches by the method we will discuss below.

We now discuss the patch generation step in two cases. When a new edge (u, v) is inserted into the graph, one case is that u and v have different ranks, that is to say they are in different independent sets. The other case is that u and v have the same rank, namely they are in the same sets after hierarchy building procedure. We first consider the first case. Supposing that $rank(u) < rank(v)$, if v is not an ancestor of u before adding edge (u, v), then v will become the ancestor of u and its descendants. Based on the rule of generating labels, new entries to v will be added to the labels of u and its descendants. The ancestors of v are also the ancestors of u and its descendants. For each ancestor w of v, if w is already the ancestor of u before the edge insertion, then the distance between w and u may change smaller and the label entries in u and its descendants to w should be updated. Otherwise, w is a new ancestor of u and its descendants, then new entries will be added to the labels of these vertices. Supposing that $rank(u) < rank(v)$ and v is an ancestor of u before adding edge (u, v). For this situation, no label entries will be added, but the distances from u and its

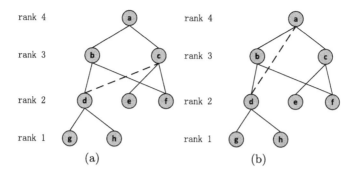

Fig. 1. Vertices with different ranks

descendants to v and its ancestors may change smaller, the distances in the labels need to be updated.

For example, in Fig. 1 the dotted line represents the adding edge. In Fig. 1(a), vertex c becomes the common ancestor of vertex d and its descendants g, h, then new label entries to c will be added into the indexes of d, g, and h. Vertex a is the ancestor of d before edge (c, d) insertion, the distances from d, g, h to a may change smaller, then the label entries to a need to be updated. In Fig. 1(b), since vertex a is already an ancestor of vertex d before inserting the edge (a, d), no new label entries will be added and the distances from d and its descendants to a need to be updated.

We now consider the second case. Supposing that $rank(u)$ equals to $rank(v)$ and $deg(u) < deg(v)$. When $rank(u)$ equals to $rank(v)$, it means u and v are in the same independent set before adding edge (u, v). According to the vertex hierarchy rule that one vertex and its neighbors should have different ranks, u and v will be divided into different sets after the edge addition. Usually the vertex with higher degree is more important than that with lower degree. We increase the rank of v by one, so does for vertices with a higher rank than v. Then v and its ancestors become the ancestors of u. Finally, the case is converted to the first case. For instance, in Fig. 2(a), vertex b and vertex c are in the same rank. Since

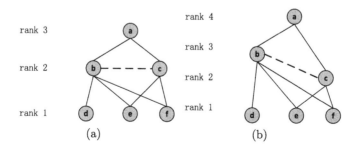

Fig. 2. Vertices with the same rank

$deg(b) > deg(c)$, we increase the ranks of b and a as shown in Fig. 2(b), then b becomes a new ancestor of c.

4.2   Update Algorithm

Algorithm 1 describes the pseudo code for generating patches. The algorithm first initializes P with $\emptyset$. Suppose that $rank(u) < rank(v)$. If $L(u)$ does not contain the label entry to vertex v or the edge weight $W(u,v)$ is smaller than $dist(u,v)$, then we add the new label entry $(v, W(u,v))$ into P. For each ancestor w of v, if $L(u)$ does not contain the label to w or the distance to w gets smaller via the new edge (u,v), then we add the new label entry $(w, W(u,v) + dist(w,v))$ into P. The procedure of generating patches is the same as mentioned above when $rank(u) = rank(v)$ and $deg(u) < deg(v)$.

Algorithm 1. Generate patches

Input:
     L , G and (u,v);
Output:
     P ;
1: let $P = \emptyset$;
2: **if** $rank(u) < rank(v)$ **then**
3:     **if** $(v, W(u,v)) \notin L(u) || W(u,v) < dist(u,v)$ **then**
4:         add $(v, W(u,v))$ into P;
5:     **for each** $(w, dist(w,v) \in L(v)$ **do**
6:         **if** $(w, W(u,v) + dist(w,v)) \notin L(u) || W(u,v) + dist(w,v) < dist(u,w)$ **then**
7:             add $(w, W(u,v) + dist(w,v))$ into P;

Algorithm 2 shows the pseudo code for updating the labeling with the label patch P. Suppose that u becomes a descendent of v after the insertion of edge (u,v). Let T_u stand for the vertex tree root at u in vertex hierarchy. Note that we do not really need to construct the tree T_u. If u is contained by $L(d)$, then d is a descendent of u and it must be in the tree T_u. For each $d \in T_u$ and for each entry $(w, dist(w, u))$ in P, if w is a new ancestor of d, then we add $(w, dist(d, u) + dist(u, w))$ to $L(d)$. If $L(d)$ contains the label entry to w but the distance between d and w gets smaller, then we update the $dist(d, w)$ with the smaller value $dist(d, u) + dist(u, w)$. If the label entries in $L(d)$ and P are sorted by vertex ID, the updating procedure is similar to a merging procedure. The total time complexity for update is $O(\sum_{d \in T_u}(|L(d)| + |P|))$.

5   Labeling with Cliques

A clique is a complete subgraph in which each vertex connects all other vertices. As we will show in the experiments in Sect. 6, the cliques commonly exist and cover a large portion of vertices in dense graphs, especially in strong connection

Algorithm 2. Update labeling

Input:
    L, P and T_u;
Output:
    $L(v), v \in V$;
1: **for each** $d \in T_u$ **do**
2:     **for each** $(w, dist(w, u)) \in P$ **do**
3:         **if** $(w, dist(d, u) + dist(u, w)) \notin L(d)$ **then**
4:             insert $(w, dist(d, u) + dist(u, w))$ into $L(d)$;
5:         **else if** $dist(d, u) + dist(u, w) < dist(d, w)$ **then**
6:             update $dist(d, w)$ with $dist(d, u) + dist(u, w)$;

graphs. When considering the cliques in the graph, the labels constructed by IS-Label can be extended. We will present how to compress labels and how to utilize the labels for distance query.

5.1   Label Compression

Let $V[L(v)]$ denote the vertices included by $L(v)$. Suppose that some vertices in $V[L(v)]$ form a clique and the maximum distance is $dist(v, x)$. Let the vertices set which form one clique with x be C_x. In other words, $x \cup C_x$ forms one clique and x has the largest distance to v. Based on triangle inequality, we can prove that for any vertex $v \in V$, vertex $u \in C_x$, then $dist(v, u) - dist(v, x) = 0$ or $dist(v, u) - dist(v, x) = -1$. Then the vertices in C_x can be divided into two subsets, namely $C_x^0(v)$ and $C_x^{-1}(v)$. Vertices in $C_x^0(v)$ have the same distance to v with x while vertices in $C_x^{-1}(v)$ have a shorter distance to v than x.

Akiba et al. proposed a bit-parallel BFS technique to speed up preprocessing and querying time in [2]. We define a similar structure but with a different aim. We can convert the ordinary label to a more compact form by gather the distance information of the vertices in the same clique together to save space. The label with cliques is called CLabel. The label of vertex v considering cliques is denoted by $CL(v)$, which is defined as following:

$$CL(v) = \{(x, dist(x, v), C_x^{-1}(v), C_x^0(v)) | v \in V\}.$$

5.2   Distance Queries

Similar to querying with ordinary labels, when processing the distance query between vertex s and vertex t with CLabel, we scan the $CL(s)$ and $CL(t)$. For each pair of labels in $CL(s)$ and $CL(t)$ sharing the same vertex x, the distance is the minimal value which can be computed via one vertex in $\{x\} \cup C_x$.

$$dist(s, t) = min\{dist(s, x) + dist(t, x) + \Delta\} \tag{2}$$

where:

$$(x, dist(x, s), C_x^{-1}(s), C_x^0(s)) \in CL(s), (x, dist(x, t), C_x^{-1}(t), C_x^0(t)) \in CL(t)$$

Δ is a variant which is equal to -2, -1, or 0. The value is decided by $C_x^{-1}(s)$, $C_x^0(s)$, $C_x^{-1}(t)$, and $C_x^0(t)$. If $C_x^{-1}(s) \cap C_x^{-1}(t) \neq \emptyset$, then s and t can both reach some vertices in C_x^{-1}. Suppose one common vertex is w, since $dist(s,w) + dist(t,w) = dist(s,x) - 1 + dist(t,x) - 1 = dist(s,x) + dist(t,x) - 2$, we can get the conclusion that $\Delta = -2$. Similarly we can prove that if $C_x^{-1}(s) \cap C_x^0(t) \neq \emptyset$ or $C_x^0(s) \cap C_x^{-1}(t) \neq \emptyset$, then $\Delta = -1$, otherwise $\Delta = 0$. The total time of each query is in $O(|CL(s)| + |CL(t)|)$ time.

5.3   Compressing Algorithm

Algorithm 3 describes the pseudo code for compressing labels with cliques. For all $L(v)$ and for each entry $(u, dist(u,v)) \in L(v)$, initialize $C_u^{-1}(v)$ and $C_u^0(v)$ with $\emptyset$. If there exists another entry $(w, dist(w,v)) \in L(v)$ that w is in the same clique with u, then we can add w into $C_u^{-1}(v)$ or $C_u^0(v)$ depending on the distance difference. We adopt a greedy strategy to calculate C_u. C_u is initialized with one element u. When scanning next label entry $(w, dist(w,v)) \in L(v)$, we judge whether w is a neighbor of each element in C_u. If so, we add u into C_u. K stands for the times of compressing labeling. Since there may exist more than one clique in the vertices set extracted from the normal labels, the compression procedure can be done more than once. As mentioned above, the distance $dist(w,v)$ can be derived from $dist(u,v)$ and $C_u^i(v)$, then we remove the entry $(w, dist(w,u))$ from $L(v)$.

6   Experimental Evaluation

We conduct experiments on real-world graphs. All algorithms are implemented in C++ and compiled by g++(version 4.8.3). All experiments are conducted on

---

Algorithm 3. Labeling with cliques

Input:
   L and G;
Output:
   $CL(v), v \in V$;
1: **for each** $v \in V$ **do**
2:     load the label $L(v)$ of v ;
3:     **for** i=1,2,3,...k **do**
4:        **for each** $(u, dist(u,v) \in L(v)$ **do**
5:           let $C_u^{-1}(v) = \emptyset, C_u^0(v) = \emptyset$;
6:           **for** $(w, dist(w,v)) \in L(v)$ **do**
7:              **if** $w \in C_u$ **then**
8:                 remove $(w, dist(w,v))$ from $L(v)$;
9:                 **if** $dist(w,v) + 1 = dist(u,v)$ **then**
10:                    add w into $C_u^{-1}(v)$;
11:                 **else**
12:                    add w into $C_u^0(v)$;
13:              insert $(u, dist(u,v), C_u^{-1}(v), C_u^0(v))$ into $CL(v)$

a 64-bit Linux server with an Intel 2.4 GHz CPU, 16 GB memory and one 7200 RPM SATA hard disk running CentOS 7.

6.1 Datasets

We choose various real-world graphs to conduct experiments, including social networks, web graphs, road networks, and communication networks. All the graphs are treated as unweighted undirected networks without duplicate edges and are gotten from the *Stanford Network Analysis Project* (SNAP). Table 2 summaries the types of the graphs, the number of edges, the number of vertices, and the average degree of vertices. The table also lists the average clique size and clique coverage of the graphs, we will discuss the two properties in Sect. 6.3.

Table 2. Datasets

Dataset	Type	$|V|$	$|E|$	Degree	CliqueSize	CliqueCoverage
Facebook	Social	4 k	176 k	86	10.65	61.13
Wiki-Vote	Trust	7 K	201 K	56	4.60	13.52
Email-Enron	Email	36 K	367 K	20	4.77	27.23
Epinions	Social	75 K	811 K	22	6.10	1.61
Twitter	Social	81 K	2.68 M	66	6.06	13.03
Gnutella	p2p	62 K	296 K	10	4.00	0.08
Amazon	Co-purchasing	335 K	1.85 M	12	4.31	0.19
RoadNet-PA	Roadnetwork	1.08 M	3.08 M	6	4.00	0.01

6.2 Performance of Incremental Updates

Update Time. We compare the time of reconstructing the whole labels with that of incrementally updating the labels. The labels are reconstructed with IS-Label. We randomly generate several groups of new edges and insert them into the original graphs. Let N denote the number of new edges inserted into the graphs and DLabel denote the incremental updating method. Table 3 shows the results. The update time is linear with the number of new edges N. When N is small, DLabel is much more time-saving than IS-Label, that is to say the incremental updating method is more efficient. With the increment of N, the time of DLabel increases, then at certain point, it exceeds the time of IS-Label.

Update Vertices. We count the numbers of update vertices per new edge on different datasets against N. Figure 3(a) shows the average numbers of vertices whose labels change when a new edge is added into the graphs. For the same dataset, the numbers of average update vertices do not be affected much by the number of new edges. For different datasets, the numbers of average update

Table 3. Time (in second)

Dataset	DLabel					IS-Label				
	N									
	1	10	10^2	10^3	10^4	1	10	10^2	10^3	10^4
Facebook	0.01	0.14	1.27	12.48	125.76	127.88	110.02	110.59	154.68	334.97
Wiki-Vote	0.03	0.28	2.57	25.58	257.00	83.25	77.77	94.63	151.69	142.23
Email-Enron	0.09	0.65	6.28	64.49	614.87	129.35	117.80	127.00	120.42	160.55
Epinions	0.66	4.66	54.03	472.50	4624.97	684.97	716.12	721.14	662.27	932.84
Twitter	1.97	20.59	192.45	1870.99	18888.80	1229.87	1142.12	1292.55	1414.56	3400.23

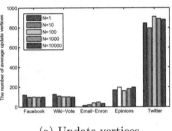

(a) Update vertices

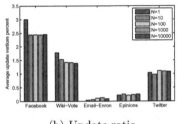

(b) Update ratio

Fig. 3. The incremental updates

vertices vary much. It is affected by the properties of the datasets, such as size and density. Larger, denser the datasets, larger the numbers of update vertices. Figure 3(b) shows the ratio between the numbers of update vertices and the vertex numbers of the graphs. The update vertices are only a small part of the whole vertices. It means that adding an edge only partially changes the topology of the graph and the incremental updates are carried on within a small part of the graphs. The result also proves the rationality of incremental updates.

6.3   Performance of Clique Labeling

Table 2 shows the properties of cliques of the datasets. Since computing the clique coverage is difficult, for large datasets, we only obtain a portion of them as samples. The average clique size is the number of vertices every clique contains on average. Moreover, we only consider cliques whose size are larger than three. Supposing that each vertex can only belong to one clique, the ratio that is equal to the number of vertices of all cliques divided by the total vertices number is defined as clique coverage. We can attain the following conclusions from Table 2: (1) the larger the average degree is, the higher the clique coverage is; and (2) social networks and communication networks have higher clique coverage. We also notice that the ratio of Twitter is lower than that of Facebook. The reason is that Facebook is a strongly connected graph while Twitter is a weakly connected graph. In Twitter, strangers may follow you while in Facebook the followers are all your friends.

Table 4. Index size and query time

Dataset	Index size (in MB)				Query time (in microsecond)			
	IS-Label	CLabel			IS-Label	CLabel		
		$k=5$	$k=10$	$k=20$		$k=5$	$k=10$	$k=20$
Facebook	8.5	7.7	7	6	0.045	0.325	0.313	0.287
Wiki-Vote	24	21	20	19	0.094	0.135	0.400	0.427
Email-Enron	137	127	119	115	0.725	0.500	0.527	0.470
Epinions	1034	999	972	919	6.822	3.146	2.920	2.785
Twitter	2532	2511	2489	2450	12.012	6.956	6.536	6.198
Gnutella	2051	2048	2044	2040	10.705	4.464	4.510	5.377
roadNet-PA	8328	8402	8499	8656	17.422	26.282	25.929	26.755
Amazon	23610	23616	23617	23637	16.069	14.762	17.862	27.011

Index Size. The left side of Table 4 shows the index sizes of different datasets. We compare the IS-Label with the CLabel with different parameters k. We let the IS-Label build a full 2-hop labeling. For social networks and communication networks, such as Facebook, Epinions, Wiki-Vote, and Email-Enron, the index size is smaller than that of IS-Label. This result is consistent with our consumptions mentioned above. On the contrary, for sparse networks, such as RoadNet-PA and Amazon, the connection is weak, and there are few cliques in these networks. The index size of CLabel is larger than that of IS-Label. Figure 4 reports the index compression ratio, which is equal to the index size difference between IS-Label and CLabel divided by that of IS-Label. The ratio is affected by the properties of graphs and the parameter k. We can find that for dense graphs, the compression ratio is positive. In other words, the effectiveness of the compression is obvious. Denser a graph is, higher the compression ratio is. For the sparse graphs, the compression is close to zero or even negative for its low clique coverage. This means that CLabel is not so effective.

Query Time. The right side of Table 4 shows the performance of query time between IS-Label and CLabel. The query time includes two parts, namely the time for loading labels and the time for computing the distance. We randomly obtain 10,000 pairs of vertices and calculate the average query time in microseconds. For small scale graphs, such as Facebook and Wiki-Vote, CLabel does not show advantage over IS-Label. Since the loading time is affected by the index size and the index size difference between IS-Label and CLabel on small dataset is small, the loading time difference between the two method is small.

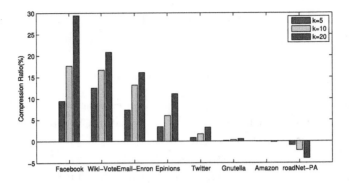

Fig. 4. The compress ratio

The computing time of CLabel is longer than that of IS-Label as CLabel is more complicated than IS-Label. It is the reason why CLabel is slower than IS-Label on small datasets. But for larger dense graphs, CLabel has better query performance. The size advantage of CLabel is demonstrated. For sparse graphs, the compression technique is ineffective and the index size generated by CLabel is larger than IS-Label. Since the query time is affected by label size, the query time of CLabel is longer than that of IS-Label.

7   Conclusions

In this paper, we revisit the problem of point-to-point distance query on big graphs. We propose an incremental updating method for index construction on dynamic graphs. This method avoids to reconstruct the whole index and the experiments prove its efficiency. When considering undirected unweighted graphs, we also propose a method to gather the distance information in the cliques together and compress the normal labels in a more compact style. Based on a set of experiments on real-world networks, we demonstrate that our labeling can effectively reduce the index size and bring about comparable query time for large dense graphs.

Acknowledgments. This paper is partly supported by the NSFC under grant No. 61433019.

References

1. Abraham, I., Delling, D., Goldberg, A.V., Werneck, R.F.: Hierarchical hub labelings for shortest paths. In: Epstein, L., Ferragina, P. (eds.) ESA 2012. LNCS, vol. 7501, pp. 24–35. Springer, Heidelberg (2012). doi:10.1007/978-3-642-33090-2_4
2. Akiba, T., Iwata, Y., Yoshida, Y.: Fast exact shortest-path distance queries on large networks by pruned landmark labeling. In: Proceedings of the 2013 ACM SIGMOD International Conference on Management of Data, pp. 349–360. ACM (2013)

3. Akiba, T., Iwata, Y., Yoshida, Y.: Dynamic and historical shortest-path distance queries on large evolving networks by pruned landmark labeling. In: Proceedings of the 23rd International Conference on World Wide Web, pp. 237–248. ACM (2014)
4. Chen, W., Sommer, C., Teng, S.H., Wang, Y.: A compact routing scheme and approximate distance oracle for power-law graphs. ACM Trans. Algorithms **9**(1), 615–630 (2012)
5. Christoforaki, M., Suel, T.: Estimating pairwise distances in large graphs. In: Proceedings of 2014 IEEE International Conference on Big Data, pp. 335–344. IEEE (2014)
6. Cohen, E., Halperin, E., Kaplan, H., Zwick, U.: Reachability and distance queries via 2-hop labels. In: Proceedings of the 13th Annual ACM-SIAM Symposium on Discrete Algorithms, pp. 1338–1355. SIAM (2003)
7. Dave, V.S., Hasan, M.A.: TopCom: index for shortest distance query in directed graph. In: Chen, Q., Hameurlain, A., Toumani, F., Wagner, R., Decker, H. (eds.) DEXA 2015. LNCS, vol. 9261, pp. 471–480. Springer, Heidelberg (2015). doi:10. 1007/978-3-319-22849-5_32
8. Fu, A.W.C., Wu, H., Cheng, J., Wong, R.C.W.: IS-LABEL: an independent-set based labeling scheme for point-to-point distance querying. PVLDB **6**(6), 457–468 (2013)
9. Geisberger, R., Sanders, P., Schultes, D., Delling, D.: Contraction hierarchies: faster and simpler hierarchical routing in road networks. In: McGeoch, C.C. (ed.) WEA 2008. LNCS, vol. 5038, pp. 319–333. Springer, Heidelberg (2008). doi:10.1007/978-3-540-68552-4_24
10. Greco, S., Molinaro, C., Pulice, C.: Efficient maintenance of all-pairs shortest distances. In: Proceedings of the 28th International Conference on Scientific and Statistical Database Management, pp. 95–106. ACM (2016)
11. Jiang, M., Fu, A.W.C., Wong, R.C.W.: Exact top-k nearest keyword search in large networks. In: Proceedings of the 2015 ACM SIGMOD International Conference on Management of Data, pp. 393–404. ACM (2015)
12. Jiang, M., Fu, A.W.C., Wong, R.C.W., Xu, Y.: Hop doubling label indexing for point-to-point distance querying on scale-free networks. PVLDB **7**(12), 1203–1214 (2014)
13. Jin, R., Ruan, N., Xiang, Y., Lee, V.: A highway-centric labeling approach for answering distance queries on large sparse graphs. In: Proceedings of the 2012 ACM SIGMOD International Conference on Management of Data, pp. 445–456. ACM (2012)
14. Lin, Y., Chen, X., Lui, J.: I/O efficient algorithms for exact distance queries on disk-resident dynamic graphs. In: Proceedings of the 2015 IEEE/ACM International Conference on Advances in Social Networks Analysis and Mining, pp. 440–447. ACM (2015)
15. Potamias, M., Bonchi, F., Castillo, C., Gionis, A.: Fast shortest path distance estimation in large networks. In: Proceedings of the 18th ACM Conference on Information and Knowledge Management, pp. 867–876. ACM (2009)
16. Qiao, M., Cheng, H., Chang, L., Yu, J.X.: Approximate shortest distance computing: a query-dependent local landmark scheme. TKDE **26**(1), 55–68 (2014)
17. Zhu, A.D., Ma, H., Xiao, X., Luo, S., Tang, Y., Zhou, S.: Shortest path and distance queries on road networks: towards bridging theory and practice. In: Proceedings of the 2013 ACM SIGMOD International Conference on Management of Data, pp. 857–868. ACM (2013)

Game Theory Based Interference Control Approach in 5G Ultra-Dense Heterogeneous Networks

Xin Gu, Xiaoyong Zhang$^{(\boxtimes)}$, Zhuofu Zhou, Yijun Cheng,
and Jun Peng

School of Information Science and Engineering, Central South University,
Changsha 410083, China
zhangxy@csu.edu.cn

Abstract. Considering the high-speed and low-latency communication requirements of future 5G networks, a Stackelberg game based interference suppression approach is proposed. We analyze the uplink interference of macrocell, which is located in ultra-dense heterogeneous cloud access networks. Dense deployment brings relief of traffic, but leads to new interference problems. A power pricing game model between macrocell user end (MUE) and RRH user ends (RUEs) is formulated and Nash equilibrium is analyzed. Different from traditional methods concentrating on power, our proposed approach can maintain the power and energy efficiency of different kinds of user ends, so as to increase the spectrum efficiency of the whole heterogeneous networks. Simulations validate the results and demonstrate the superiority of the approach.

Keywords: Heterogeneous networks · Interference control · Spectrum efficiency · Nash equilibrium

1 Introduction

The function of future networks is expected to be more diverse, integrated and intelligent. In recent years, with the rapid development of mobile networks and the emergence of Internet of things (IoT), a variety of intelligent terminals have been produced. As a result, more and more mobile devices access to networks, which brings explosive growth of mobile data traffic. Cisco forecast that mobile traffic will double every year before 2020 [1]. In order to meet future increasing demand of 1000 times higher mobile data volume per area, and accelerate the development of new services and new applications as well, fifth generation (5G) wireless communications systems have come into being. 5G system is developed for the new mobile communication requirements beyond 2020. Compared with 4G, 5G requests higher frequency spectrum and energy efficiency, and the transmission rate and resource utilization will also be significantly improved, providing faster data loading speed and lower network latency [2].

5G heterogeneous networks generally consist of macrocells and smallcells. Many new wireless transfer and access technologies are introduced so that the 5G terminal can intelligently choose the proper access network for a specified service [3]. Macro base

© Springer International Publishing AG 2016
G. Wang et al. (Eds.): APSCC 2016, LNCS 10065, pp. 306–319, 2016.
DOI: 10.1007/978-3-319-49178-3_24

stations are deployed to cover most areas, while many hotspots, which are usually some low-power small base stations such as Micro-BS, Pico-BS and Femto-BS are deployed to relieve the pressure of Macro base stations. New radio access technologies such as WiFi, 4G, LTE and UMTS are also integrated in future networks. As the number of connected devices grows fast, small-scale access networks are deployed in dense macrocell networks [4]. Due to the population mobility between business districts and residential areas day and night, the workload of networks will follow the fluctuation of population, similar to the tide effect. The load of networks in busy time is far lower than the average level, and different base stations cannot share processing capabilities, both of which make it hard to improve spectral efficiency.

Increasing signal bandwidth used to be one way to increase the transfer rate, but it's inefficient due to the scarcity of spectrum resources. In order to meet the increasing traffic demand, efficiently improve spectral efficiency and realize the high-speed, low-latency communication of 5G, Cloud Radio Access Network (C-RAN) is one of the key technologies to solve the problems above [5, 6]. As Fig. 1 shows, base stations consist of two parts, one is remote radio heads (RRHs) and the other is baseband units (BBUs). RRHs are responsible for transmitting and receiving RF signals. They are connected to a data center where baseband processing is performed. The processing is centralized by BBUs [7]. Different from hardware management architecture of traditional base stations, large numbers of BBUs are integrated into a cloud resource pool. This makes it easier to schedule resources by virtualization and centralized management and deployment, so as to achieve flexible and dynamic allocation. Simultaneously, RRHs densely deployed in various geographic areas can help achieve high-speed and low-latency data transmission.

Intensive network deployment not only brings the improvement of spectral efficiency and power efficiency, but also greatly improves system capacity, while it inevitably introduces some problems. In densely deployed networks, there may be interference between signals using the same frequency within the same wireless access technology, between different wireless access technologies due to spectrum sharing, between different levels of coverage. Therefore, it's import to slove the following problems: how to solve the interference caused performance deterioration, how to achieve the coexistence of varieties of wireless access technologies and coverage levels, and how to effectively improve the spectrum efficiency.

In recent years, game theory [8], a classic method in economics, has been introduced to solve all kinds of wireless communication problems concerning interference and power control. The downlink power allocation problem in a cellular network comprised of femtocells and macrocells has been studied in [9] and it was formulated as a Stackelberg game. In [10], the authors proposed a novel game theoretic model in WCDMA heterogeneous network deployments, and combined interference mitigation and unwanted mobility events in order to enhance quality of service in femtocells. As for cognitive networks containing lots of users, making full use of spectrum resources is very important. Considering the coexistence of primary users and secondary users, the authors in [11] built a relevant interference model by jointly considering the SINR and transmit power of secondary users and solved the problem based on a strategic non-cooperative game. The authors in [12] considered the competition between the users sharing the same interference channel, formulated a Stackelberg game model and used duality theory to simplify the solution process. As a result, the transmission strategy of users was optimized.

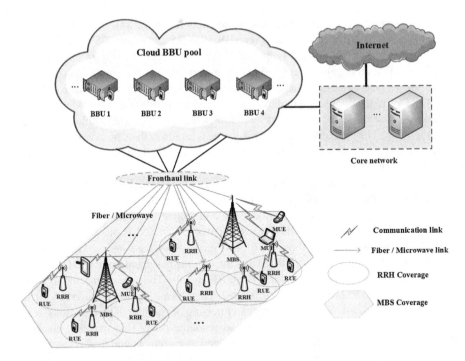

Fig. 1. C-RAN architecture in ultra-dense heterogeneous networks

All the researches above solve interference problems by formulating a game model and choosing proper power and channels. However, considering the complexity of 5G heterogeneous networks, we need to control not only the interference to macrocell users, but also the interference between smallcell users. The spectrum efficiency needs improving as well.

In the paper, a Stackelberg game is introduced to solve the uplink interference problem of macrocells. Considering the characteristics of ultra-dense heterogeneous networks based on C-RAN, we analyze MUE and RUEs, which act as the leader and followers respectively. We calculate the optimal utility through iteration and prove the existence and uniqueness of Nash equilibrium. Finally, the optimization of transmit power of user ends can be realized.

2 System Model

We address the problem of uplink interference control in densely deployed networks with one MBS and several RRHs, as depicted in Fig. 2.

According to Shannon theorem, the uplink spectrum efficiency of MUE is

$$R_{MUE} = \log_2 \left(1 + \frac{h_0 p_0}{\sum\limits_{i=1}^{N} h_{0,i} p_i + \sigma^2} \right) \tag{1}$$

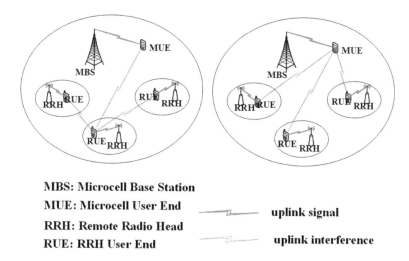

MBS: Microcell Base Station
MUE: Microcell User End
RRH: Remote Radio Head
RUE: RRH User End

————— uplink signal

·············· uplink interference

Fig. 2. Uplink communication and interference in macrocells

where h_0 is the channel gain between MUE and MBS and p_0 denotes the transmit power of MUE. Total interference to MUE from all RUEs is denoted by $\sum_{i=1}^{N} h_{0,i} p_i$, and $h_{0,i}$ is the channel gain between RUE i and MUE, and p_i is the transmit power of RUE i. The White Gaussian noise is denoted by σ^2 of zero mean value. Similarly, the uplink spectrum efficiency of RUE i is

$$R_{RUE_i} = \log_2 \left(1 + \frac{h_{i,i} p_i}{\sum_{j=0,j\neq i}^{N} h_{i,j} p_j + \sigma^2} \right) \tag{2}$$

where $h_{i,i}$ is the channel gain between RUE i and its corresponding RRH and p_i denotes the transmit power of RUE i. Total interference to RUE i from all other RUEs and MUE is denoted by $\sum_{j=0,j\neq i}^{N} h_{i,j} p_j$, and $h_{i,j}$ is channel gain between RUE i and RUE j.

Within the coverage of RRH, RUEs is supposed to adjust their transmit power to maximize energy efficiency, which is the rate of spectrum efficiency and energy consumption, with the power constraint for MUE. So the energy efficiency of RUE i is

$$U_{RUE_i}(\alpha_i, p_i, \mathbf{p}_{-i}) = \frac{R_{RUE_i}}{\alpha_i p_i} = \frac{\log_2 \left(1 + \frac{h_{i,i} p_i}{\sum_{j=0,j\neq i}^{N} h_{i,j} p_j + \sigma^2} \right)}{\alpha_i p_i} \tag{3}$$

where R_{RUE_i} can be calculated by (2). α_i denotes the power price MUE proposes to RUE i and p_i denotes the transmit power of RUE i. Then, the problem of maximizing energy efficiency of RUE can be formulated as

$$\text{max.} \quad U_{RUE_i}(\alpha_i, p_i, \mathbf{p}_{-i}) \tag{4}$$
$$\text{s.t.} \quad C1.$$

$$C1: \quad 0 \le p_i \le p_{\max}. \tag{5}$$

where $C1$ is the constraint of transmitted power of RUE, i.e., p_i can not be larger than $p_{\max}$.

Similarly, the energy efficiency of MUE can be denoted as

$$U_{MUE}(\boldsymbol{\alpha}, \mathbf{p}) = \beta R_{MUE} + \sum_{i=1}^{N} \alpha_i h_{0,i} p_i \tag{6}$$

where α and $\mathbf{p}$ denote the power pricing vector and power vector, respectively. R_{MUE} can be calculated by (1), and β is the profit related to spectrum efficiency. So the problem of maximizing the utility of MUE is formulated as

$$\text{max.} \quad U_{MUE}(\boldsymbol{\alpha}, \mathbf{p}) \tag{7}$$
$$\text{s.t.} \quad C2$$

$$C2: \quad SINR_{MUE} \ge \theta_0 \tag{8}$$

$C2$ shows the QoS constraint of MUE, i.e., SINR of MUE should be controlled below θ_0.

3   A Stackelberg Game Based Interference Control Approach

3.1   A Non-cooperative Game Model

As for heterogeneous networks, they differ in superiority and importance. MUE is defined as the leader in the Stackelberg game model, and RUE as the followers. MUE proposes the power price, which comes from interference of sharing the same frequency. The propose is to improve its own spectrum efficiency. When considering RUEs, we jointly optimize the spectrum efficiency and energy consumption by analyzing the rate of them. RUEs accepted the power price MUE proposes, and then adjust their transmit power to maximize their energy efficiency.

Definition 1. A non-cooperation game G is defined as a triple $G = \{I, (S_i)_{i \in I}, U_{RUE_i}(\alpha_i, p_i, \mathbf{p}_{-i})\}$, where I is the set of RUEs, $(S_i)_{i \in I}$ is the strategy set of followers and $U_{RUE_i}(\alpha_i, p_i, \mathbf{p}_{-i})$ is the energy efficiency set.

3.2 Nash Equilibrium and Function Transformation

A Nash equilibrium [13] exists in game G if for all $i \in I$, the strategy set $(S_i)_{i \in I}$ is a nonempty, convex and compact subset of Euclidean space, and in each strategy, the corresponding utility function $U_{RUE_i}(\alpha_i, p_i, \mathbf{p}_{-i})$ is continuous and concave. Obviously, strategy space meets the requirements.

However, the objective functions in (3) is non-convex because of the fractional form. So we convert it to a convex problem in subtractive form later. As shown in (9), ξ_i^* denotes the optimal efficiency of RUE i when the Nash equilibrium is achieved. And according to the power price charged by MUE, the strategies of RUE i is p_i^* given the others' strategies $\mathbf{p}_{-i}^*$.

$$\xi_i^* = U_{RUE_i}(\alpha_i, p_i^*, \mathbf{p}_{-i}^*) \tag{9}$$

Theorem 1. The transformed objective function $R_{RUE_i}(p_i, \mathbf{p}_{-i}) - \xi_i^* \alpha_i p_i$ is concave.

Proof. According to (2), we calculate the second order derivative with respect to pi to prove its concavity.

$$\frac{\partial \left(R_{RUE_i}(p_i, \mathbf{p}_{-i}) - \xi_i^* \alpha_i p_i \right)}{\partial p_i} = \frac{\frac{h_{i,i}}{\sum_{j=0, j \neq i}^{N} h_{i,j} p_j + \sigma^2}}{\ln 2 (1 + \frac{h_{i,i} p_i}{\sum_{j=0, j \neq i}^{N} h_{i,j} p_j + \sigma^2})} - \xi_i^* \alpha_i \tag{10}$$

$$\frac{\partial^2 (R_{RUE_i}(p_i, \mathbf{p}_{-i}) - \xi_i^* \alpha_i p_i)}{\partial p_i^2} = -\frac{\frac{h_{i,i}}{\sum_{j=0, j \neq i}^{N} h_{i,j} p_j + \sigma^2}}{\ln 2 (1 + \frac{h_{i,i} p_i}{\sum_{j=0, j \neq i}^{N} h_{i,j} p_j + \sigma^2})^2} < 0 \tag{11}$$

The first order derivative of $R_{RUE_i}(p_i, \mathbf{p}_{-i}) - \xi_i^* \alpha_i p_i$ is shown in (11), and the second shown in (12).

Theorem 2. The maximum energy efficiency ξ_i^* is achieved if and only if

$$\text{max. } R_{RUE_i}(p_i, \mathbf{p}_{-i}) - \xi_i^* \alpha_i p_i = R_{RUE_i}(p_i^*, \mathbf{p}_i^*) - \xi_i^* \alpha_i p_i^* = 0 \tag{12}$$

Proof. Similarly to [14], we prove the necessity proof first. For any ξ_i^*, we have

$$\xi_i^* = \frac{R_{RUE_i}(p_i^*, \mathbf{p}_i^*)}{\alpha_i p_i^*} \geq \frac{R_{RUE_i}(p_i, \mathbf{p}_{-i})}{\alpha_i p_i} \tag{13}$$

After rearranging it, we have

$$R_{RUE_i}(p_i^*, \mathbf{p}_i^*) - \xi_i^* \alpha_i p_i^* = 0 \tag{14}$$

$$R_{RUE_i}(p_i, \mathbf{p}_{-i}) - \xi_i^* \alpha_i p_i \leq 0 \tag{15}$$

Therefore, the maximum $R_{RUE_i}(p_i, \mathbf{p}_{-i}) - \xi_i^* \alpha_i p_i$ is 0 and it is obtained when $\mathbf{p}_i^*$ is achieved.

Then, we prove the sufficiency proof. We assume $\mathbf{p}_i^*$ is the optimal value, so we have

$$R_{RUE_i}(p_i, \mathbf{p}_{-i}) - \xi_i^* \alpha_i p_i \leq R_{RUE_i}(p_i^*, \mathbf{p}_i^*) - \xi_i^* \alpha_i p_i^* = 0 \tag{16}$$

By rearranging (16), we obtain (13). So the sufficiency proof is completed.

Lemma 1. max. $R_{RUE_i}(p_i, \mathbf{p}_{-i}) - \xi_i \alpha_i p_i$ is monotonically decreasing as p_i increases.

Proof. Define $\xi_i^* < \xi_i^{*'}$, p_i^* and $p_i^{*'}$ as their corresponding optimal solutions, respectively. We have

$$\text{max. } R_{RUE_i}(p_i, p_{-i}) - \xi_i \alpha_i p_i = R_{RUE_i}(p_i^{*'}, p_{-i}) - \xi_i^* \alpha_i p_i^* > R_{RUE_i}(p_i^{*'}, p_{-i}) - \xi_i^* \alpha_i p_i^{*'}$$

$$> R_{RUE_i}(p_i^{*'}, p_{-i}) - \xi_i^{*'} \alpha_i p_i^{*'} = \text{max. } R_{RUE_i}(p_i^{*'}, p_{-i}) - \xi_i^{*'} \alpha_i p_i^{*'}$$

So the lemma is proved.

Theorem 1. The solution of (12) is unique.

Proof. It's obvious to find

$$\lim_{\xi \to -\infty} \text{max. } R_{RUE_i}(p_i, \mathbf{p}_{-i}) - \xi_i^* \alpha_i p_i \to +\infty$$

$$\lim_{\xi \to +\infty} \text{max. } R_{RUE_i}(p_i, \mathbf{p}_{-i}) - \xi_i^* \alpha_i p_i \to -\infty$$

Since max. $R_{RUE_i}(p_i, \mathbf{p}_{-i}) - \xi_i \alpha_i p_i$ is monotonically decreasing as p_i increases, so max. $R_{RUE_i}(p_i, \mathbf{p}_{-i}) - \xi_i \alpha_i p_i = 0$ has the unique solution.

Overall, the problem of adaptively adjusting transmit power of RUEs can be solved by considering a new problem (17).

$$\text{max. } R_{RUE_i}(p_i, \mathbf{p}_{-i}) - \xi_i \alpha_i p_i$$
$$C: \ 0 \leq p_i \leq p_{max}. \tag{17}$$

3.3 Problem Analysis and Solution

Based on the proof above, the objective function of followers (RUEs) is convex, so there exists the maximum energy efficiency. According to the power price from MUE, all RUEs form a non-cooperative game which can achieve a Nash equilibrium through iteration. For any given ξ_i, problem (17) can be solved through the iterative water-filling algorithm. Then we have

$$
p_i = \left[\frac{\log_2 e}{\xi_i \alpha_i} - \frac{\sum\limits_{j=0, j\neq i}^{N} h_{i,j} p_j + \sigma^2}{h_{i,i}} \right]^+
\tag{18}
$$

where the value in $[\,]^+$ must be positive.

Therefore, the updated energy efficiency of RUE i at next iteration can be calculated by (13), assuming the current iteration is t.

$$
\xi_i(t+1) = \frac{R_{RUE_i}(p_i(t))}{\alpha_i p_i(t)}
\tag{19}
$$

The iteration process will not stop until iteration time used up or error is small enough.

After analyzing the followers, we turn to the optimization problem (7) of the leader MUE, which equals to the following two problems,

$$
\max. \ \sum\nolimits_{i=1}^{N} \alpha_i h_{0,i} p_i
\tag{20}
$$

$$
\max. \ \beta \log_2 \left(1 + \frac{h_0 p_0}{\sum\limits_{i=1}^{N} h_{0,i} p_i + \sigma^2} \right)
\tag{21}
$$

The profit of MUE comes from two parts, one is its own communication rate, the other is power pricing.

Intuitively, communication demand of MUE can be easily met with guaranteed SINR. But it's hard to ensure RUEs communicate normally if QoS of MUE is too large, so the profit from power pricing should be mainly considered. In addition, the previous problem (20) is much more important than the later one if the interference exceeds a certain threshold. So, we turn to solve (20) to gain the approximate optimal solution. According to (18), we have

$$
\max_{\alpha_i}. \ \sum\nolimits_{i=1}^{N} \alpha_i h_{0,i} \left(\frac{\log_2 e}{\xi_i \alpha_i} - \frac{\sum\limits_{j=0, j\neq i}^{N} h_{i,j} p_j + \sigma^2}{h_{i,i}} \right)
\tag{22}
$$

$$
s.t.\ C:\ \sum_{i=1}^{N} h_{0,i}\left(\frac{\log_2 e}{\xi_i \alpha_i} - \frac{\sum_{j=0,j\neq i}^{N} h_{i,j}P_j + \sigma^2}{h_{i,i}}\right) \leq \frac{h_0 p_0}{\theta_0} - \sigma^2. \tag{23}
$$

The corresponding QoS constraint is shown in (23).

Hence, the above optimization problem can be solved with Lagrange Multiplier. The Lagrangian associated with the problem (22) is given by

$$
L_{MUE}(\alpha_i, v_i) = \sum_{i=1}^{N} \alpha_i h_{0,i}\left(\frac{\log_2 e}{\xi_i \alpha_i} - \frac{\sum_{j=0,j\neq i}^{N} h_{i,j}P_j + \sigma^2}{h_{i,i}}\right)
$$
$$
- v_i\left[\sum_{i=1}^{N} h_{0,i}\left(\frac{\log_2 e}{\xi_i \alpha_i} - \frac{\sum_{j=0,j\neq i}^{N} h_{i,j}P_j + \sigma^2}{h_{i,i}}\right) - \frac{h_0 p_0}{\theta_0} + \sigma^2\right] \tag{24}
$$

where v_i is the Lagrange multiplier associated with the constraint C. Obviously, (24) is a differentiable convex function with constraints, so the optimal solution can be achieved according to KKT (Karush-Kuhn-Tucker) Conditions. The equivalent dual problem can be divided into two sub problems. One is a maximization problem solving the power pricing problem to find the best strategy, the other is a minimization problem solving the master dual problem to find the suitable Lagrange Multiplier. Overall, the dual problem in (18) is given by

$$
\min_{\mu_i, v_i \geq 0} \max_{\alpha_i}\ L_{MUE}(\alpha_i, v_i). \tag{25}
$$

The optimal solution of (25) can be achieved by

$$
\frac{\partial L_{MUE}(\alpha_i, v_i)}{\partial \alpha_i} = 0. \tag{26}
$$

So we obtain

$$
\alpha_i = \left(\frac{\log_2 e h_{0,i}}{\xi_i} v_i + \frac{h_{0,i}\left(\sum_{j=0,j\neq i}^{N} h_{i,j}P_j + \sigma^2\right)}{h_{i,i}}\right)^{-\frac{1}{2}} \tag{27}
$$

In order to solve the minimization problem in the dual problem, we update the Lagrange multipliers, using the gradient method. The updating formulation is as follow

$$v_i(t+1) = [v_i(t) + \kappa_{i,v}(t)(\sum_{i=1}^{N} h_{0,i} p_i^*(t) - \frac{h_0 p_0}{\theta_0} + \sigma^2)]^+ \qquad (28)$$

where t is the iteration index, and $\kappa_{i,v}(t)$ is the positive iteration step.

Therefore, the problem can be solved through the iterative method.

3.4   Proposed Algorithm

Based on the analysis above, we design Algorithm 1 to solve the interference control problem between MUE and RUEs.

Algorithm 1. Game based interference control algorithm

Inputs: $h_{i,j}$, p_i , ξ_i , α_i , v_i , Δ

Outputs: p_i^* , ξ_i^* , α_i^*

1. **for** $n=1$ to N **do**
2.   **if** RUE **then**
3.   *Optimal power adjusting strategy of RUE*
4.   solve (18) to calculate strategy set p_i

5.   **if** $|R_{RUE_i}(p_i,\mathbf{p}_{-i}) - \xi_i^* \alpha_i p_i| \le \Delta$, **then**

6. $p_i^* = p_i$, $\xi_i^* = \dfrac{R_{RUE_i}(p_i^*, \mathbf{p}_{-i}^*)}{\alpha_i p_i}$

7.   **break**
8.   **else**
9.   solve (19) to obtain $\xi_i(t+1)$, and $n=n+1$
10.   **end if**
11.   **else**
12.   *Optimal power pricing strategy of MUE*
13.   **if** $|\alpha_i(t+1) - \alpha_i(t)| \le \Delta$, **then**

14. $\alpha_i^* = \alpha_i$
15.   **else**
16.   solve (27) to obtain α_i ,
17.   solve (28) to obtain v_i ,
18.   and $n=n+1$
19.   **end if**
20.   **end if**
21. **end for**

---

4   Simulation

In order to validate our proposed approach, we consider one MBS and two RRHs located at certain coordinates. The MBS is located at (0, 0), and RRHs are deployed at (0, 20) and (−15, 0), respectively. Their corresponding users are not specially located but within the coverage of base stations. The initial transmit power of each RUE is set at 150 dBm, which is much higher than the realistic one. The noise variance is set to −30dBm. In this scenario, the signal intensity is inversely proportional to the square of the distance, i.e., hi, j is inversely proportional to the distance between RRH i (or MBS if i = 0) and RUE j (or MUE if j = 0).

In ultra-dense heterogeneous networks, different kinds of users communicate with each other, so uplink interference is inevitable when MUE and RUEs are close enough, as is depicted in the above scenario. So we use the power pricing approach. Figure 3 shows that MUE adjusts the power price to control the uplink interference from RUEs. And after about 10 times of iterations, the value of α turns to be stable. According to the scenario above, more interference between MUE and RUE 2 can be generated when they transmit signals to base stations, compared with that between MUE and RUE 1. So MUE charges higher power price to RUE 2 than RUE 1. Theoretically, when the price is set higher, RUEs will quickly decrease transmit power in next iteration to save cost.

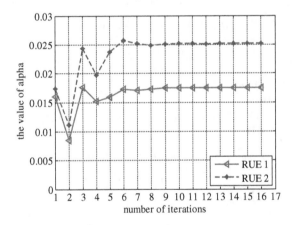

Fig. 3. Power price proposed by MUE

Figure 4 illustrates the general increase in energy efficiency of RUEs when the MUE and RUEs interact. Although the values of ξ of both RUEs are very high after 4th iteration, there is still server interference between MUE and RUEs, so it's necessary to decrease the transmit power of RUEs as shown in Fig. 5. In addition, the initial value of α is very low while the initial transmit power is very high, so they change rapidly at the beginning to bring interference under control. All these simulation results corroborate the earlier analysis and strongly prove that our proposed approach can quickly solve the interference problem.

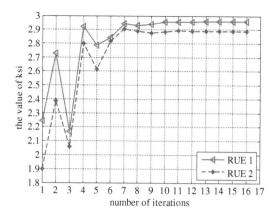

Fig. 4. Energy efficiency of RUEs

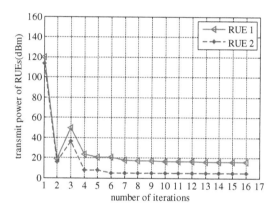

Fig. 5. Transmit power of RUEs

Figure 6 shows how the average energy efficiency varies when the number of RUEs increases. According to the analysis above, we know that deploying more RRHs means more RUEs will communicate with each other, which brings more interference, so it's sufficient to adjust the transmit power of RUEs in time. From Fig. 6, we clearly find that our proposed algorithm can well solve the interference problems as the average energy efficiency can be improved when the number of RUEs increases. Therefore, our proposed algorithm is suitable for complex and dense scenes of 5G networks.

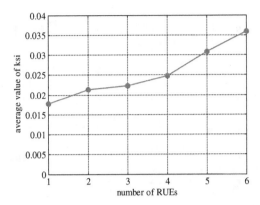

Fig. 6. Average energy efficiency of RUEs

5   Conclusion

In this paper, we have investigated the problem of interference control in 5G ultra-dense heterogeneous networks, where RRHs can share the traffic pressure of macrocell base station. We have formulated the interference problem as a two-stage Stackelberg game between end users of MBS and RRHs. Through analysis, we have proved Nash equilibrium in this game. Simulation results have demonstrated that our proposed algorithm can control the interference, as well as bring significant energy efficiency improvement, through adjustment of transmit power and power price.

Acknowledgments. The authors would like to acknowledge that this work was partially supported by the National Natural Science Foundation of China (Grant no. 61379111, 61402538, 61403424, 61502055, 61602529, 61672537, and 61672539).

References

1. Cisco Visual Networking Index: Global Mobile Data Traffic Forecast Update, 2013–2018, Cisco, San Jose, CA, USA, February 2013
2. Gupta, A., Jha, R.K.: A survey of 5G network: architecture and emerging technologies. IEEE Access **3**, 1206–1232 (2015)
3. Gohil, A., Modi, H., Patel, S.K.: 5G technology of mobile communication: a survey. In: IEEE International Conference on Intelligent Systems and Signal Processing, pp. 288–292 (2013)
4. Checko, A., Christiansen, H.L., Yan, Y., et al.: Cloud RAN for mobile networks—a technology overview. IEEE Commun. Surv. Tutorials **17**(1), 405–426 (2015)
5. Wu, J., Zhang, Z., Hong, Y., et al.: Cloud radio access network (C-RAN): a primer. IEEE Netw. **29**(1), 35–41 (2015)
6. Wang, R., Hu, H., Yang, X.: Potentials and challenges of C-RAN supporting multi-RATs toward 5G mobile networks. Access IEEE **2**, 1187–1195 (2014)

7. Wubben, D., Rost, P., Bartelt, J.S., Lalam, M., et al.: Benefits and impact of cloud computing on 5G signal processing: flexible centralization through cloud-ran. IEEE Sig. Process. Mag. **31**(6), 35–44 (2014)

8. Fudenberg, D., Tirole, J.: Game Theory, vol. 1(7), pp. 841–846. Mit Press Books, Cambridge (1991)

9. Guruacharya, S., Niyato, D., Hossain, E., et al.: Hierarchical competition in femtocell-based cellular networks. In: IEEE Global Telecommunications Conference, pp. 1–5 (2010)

10. Shyllon, H., Mohan, S.: A game theory-based distributed power control algorithm for Femtocells. In: IEEE International Conference on Advanced Networks and Telecommuncations Systems (ANTS), pp. 1–6 (2014)

11. Deng, X., Xia, W., Guan, Q., et al.: A novel distributed power control based on game theory in cognitive wireless network. In: 2014 IEEE/CIC International Conference on Communications in China (ICCC), pp. 59–63 (2015)

12. Shi, Y., Wang, J., Letaief, K.B., et al.: A game-theoretic approach for distributed power control in interference relay channels. IEEE Trans. Wirel. Commun. **8**(6), 3151–3161 (2009)

13. Gibbons, R.: A Primer in Game Theory. Harvester Wheatsheaf, New York (1992)

14. Dinkelbach, W.: On nonlinear fractional programming. Manage. Sci. **13**(7), 492–498 (1967)

An Unsupervised Method for Entity Mentions Extraction in Chinese Text

Jing Xu[✉], Liang Gan, Bin Zhou, and Quanyuan Wu

College of Computer, National University of Defense Technology,
Changsha 410073, China
{jing.xu,gl,binzh,qy.w}@nudt.edu.cn

Abstract. Entities play an important role in many natural language applications. Based on the Automatic content Extraction (ACE) conference, we study the extraction technologies of entity mentions in Chinese text. Compared to named entities, entity mentions have rich categories and complex structures, which bring great difficulty to the extraction task. To solve the above problems, we propose an unsupervised method to detect entity mentions and identify their categories in Chinese text, namely Un-MenEx. With the abundant data of Baidu Baike and Baidu search, Un-MenEx exploits a similarity calculation method to extract entity mentions in text, which solves the problem of identifying rare entity names difficultly and optimizes the mentions segmented wrongly. Moreover, Un-MenEx can meet the demand of processing massive data by reason of no manual annotation data. We conduct the experiments with the news text, and the experimental results show that this method has practical application value, and ensure the accuracy requirement.

Keywords: Entity mention extraction · Mention category recognition · Information extraction · Unsupervised · Chinese text

1 Introduction

Information extraction is a key step in understanding and processing the natural language text, whose goal is to detect and identify important information from the text, including the entities, relationships between entities and events, etc. The information extraction technologies provide data support for many applications, such as information retrieval, question answering system, knowledge base, text understanding, etc.

Entity mention extraction is the fundamental task for information extraction, which is originated from ACE conference. ACE conference is organized by the U.S. national standards and technology (NIST), aims to provide a standard of information extraction, so as to promote the development of the information extraction technologies. Entity mention extraction is similar to named entity recognition (NER). The main difference is that NER only focuses on the named references, but the entity mentions include the named, nounal, pronominal references. For example, a sentence "zhong guo guo jia zhu xi xi jin ping chu xi le hui yi, ta zhi chu liao dang qian jing ji gong zuo de zhong dian" (In order to ensure that print format, we use pinyin instead of Chinese characters, and the other parts are the same) (The Chinese Chairman Jinping Xi attended a meeting, he

G. Wang et al. (Eds.): APSCC 2016, LNCS 10065, pp. 320–328, 2016.
DOI: 10.1007/978-3-319-49178-3_25

pointed out that the key point of the current economic work), in which, "zhong guo" (Chinese) and "xi jin ping" (Jinping Xi) are named references, "guo jia zhu xi" (Chairman), "hui yi" (meeting) and "jing ji" (economy) are nominal references, and "ta" (he) is a pronominal reference. For each reference, we should not only get its string representation in the text, but also identify its category. Compared to the traditional NER, the named mentions are not restricted in person, location and organization, adding a lot of other categories, such as facilities, weapons, etc. The traditional NER methods creating a entity dictionary are not no longer applicable. In addition to the named mentions, entity mentions still include nominal mentions and pronominal mentions. Because of the changeable internal characteristics and the complex structures, the extraction task of entity mentions is more difficulty than named entities, which have simple structures and disciplinary naming rules. For example, "zhong guo guo jia zhu xi xi jin ping" (The Chinese Chairman Jinping Xi) is a nominal mention, containing a nominal mention and two named mentions nested within it. Entity mentions can be nested each other, but the nested size and depth are not uncertainty, lacking regularity. For example, a nominal mention can contain multiple named mentions and nominal mentions nested within it. In addition, we need solve the coreference resolution problems in extracting the pronominal mentions, which is clarifying their target entities. However, there exists a lot of ellipsis phenomenon in Chinese text for concise writing, which brings great difficulty to coreference resolution.

Entity mention extraction corresponds to the entity discovery and recognition (EDR) task in ACE conference, inspiring many scholars making a lot of researches. Later, the entity discovery and linking (EDL) competition and open information extraction (OIE) task push the entity mention extraction research to the climax. Ittycheriah et al. proposed a framework based on the maximum entropy model, combining with the analysis results of a natural language processing tool and a variety of features to recognize entity mentions [1]. Li et al. used the CRF model and SVM classifier, and combined local features to detect and classify entity mentions, then exploited the heuristic rules to gather the mentions referring to the same entity [2]. Chen and Hacioglu et al. converted the entity mention detection task to the classification problem, and used the maximum entropy model and SVM classifier respectively to detect the entity mentions, which achieved good results [3, 4]. Different from other methods, Daum et al. proposed a join model, which taked advantage of local features and global features to identify the entity mentions [5].

Li et al. used the semi-Markov chain and Bing search to extract entity mentions and the relationships between them, and exploited some global features to acquire their dependency relationship [6]. Lu et al. regarded entity mentions as a sequence of words, and used hypergraphs to detect and classify entity mentions with the position of each word and different combinations [7]. The above methods required manual annotation data and selected some appropriate features, which resulted into the extraction results depending on the training set and feature quality, not suitable for processing large-scale web text.

To process the problems of various mention categories, diverse internal characteristics and massive text processing requirement, we propose an unsupervised Chinese entity mention extraction method, namely Un-MenEx, which detects entity mentions from Chinese text and identifies their categories with the help of Baidu Baike (a Chinese encyclopedia) and Baidu search (a Chinese search engine). In this paper, the main contributions are as follows.

1. We propose an unsupervised Chinese entity mention extraction method, namely Un-MenEx, which can handle massive text without human intervention.
2. Un-MenEx optimizes the incorrect mentions by reason of segmenting wrongly and solves the problem of identifying the rare names with difficulty.
3. Un-MenEx improves the extraction recall and ensures the extracted entity mentions corresponding to the things and concepts in the real world.

The other parts are organized as follows. We describe the extraction method of entity mentions in detail in Sect. 2. In Sect. 3, we report our experimental results and evaluation, and conclude our discussion in Sect. 4.

2 Approach

Entity mentions are some character strings in natural language text pointing to some things or concepts in the real world. In general, the traditional methods select some features from the contexts of entity mentions, and train a model to extract mentions. However, compared to named entities, the structures of entity mentions are more complex and the various categories and the diverse characteristics make us discover regular patterns with huge difficulty, which has great effect on the precision and recall of the extraction results. In addition, the feature methods need large amount of manual annotation data, which makes them unable to meet the demand of processing massive network data.

To solve the above problem, we propose an unsupervised Chinese entity mention extraction method, namely Un-MenEx. Firstly, Un-MenEx selects the noun terms segmented by a natural language processing tool as the candidate named and nominal mentions, based on the observation of all entities being noun terms. However, not all nouns are entity mentions, and the wrong segmentation also introduces errors for entity mentions. Thus, we exploit Baidu Baike and Baidu search to select the true entity mentions, optimize the wrong entity mentions, and identify their categories. Finally, Un-MenEx clarifies the target entities of the pronominal mentions by mining their text features. The extraction process of Un-MenEx is as follows.

2.1 Baidu Baike

Baidu Baike established by Baidu Company is an open and free Chinese information collection platform covering all fields. Baidu Baike is the largest Chinese encyclopedia in the world, which adopts the crowdsourcing technology, allows all users to edit the entries, and has a professional team for review to ensure the correctness of all entries. The beta was launched in 2006, and the official version was released in 2008. As of April 2016, Baidu Baike has collected more than 13,000,000 entries, almost covering all known fields, which point to some things, concepts and terms in the real world.

Fig. 1. The extraction flow of entity mentions in Chinese text

Each entry corresponds to a description page, mainly including a summary, infobox, content, and tag indicating the category of this entry [8].

2.2 Baidu Search

Baidu Search is the largest Chinese search engine in the world, which is committed to meet the demand of the users' queries and let them access information conveniently. In Chinese search field, Baidu Search provides a number of search capabilities serving the ordinary users, including the relevant search, Chinese name recognition, the automatic conversion of Simplified and Traditional Chinese, Baidu snapshots, etc. Whether the query is an abbreviation, incomplete terms and emerging words, Baidu search can return the relevant results instantly by the Chinese web page database of more than billions [9].

中国国务院/nt，总理/nnt，李克强/nr，出席/v，21世纪理事会/nt，并/cc，发表/v，演讲/vn

Fig. 2. The word segmentation and POS tagging results of HanLP tool

2.3   Entity Mentions Extraction

Here, according to Fig. 1, we describe the extraction steps of entity mentions from Chinese text in detail.

1. We use HanLP tool to segment the text and tag POS, which is a Chinese natural language processing tool. The word segmentation model is trained by the People's Daily with 2014, and introduced a dictionary with 350,000 terms, covering the modern Chinese vocabulary and the network terms [10]. The word segmentation example is shown in Fig. 2. We select the nouns as the candidate named and nominal mentions, based on the observation of all entities being noun terms.

2. Because Baidu Baike does not provide an offline package, we use an online processing method. We treat each candidate mention as a query with Baidu search engine, and calculate the similarity between it and the returned Baike term, which also contains the alias in the infobox. If the similarity exceeds the threshold, we regard it as an entity mention and optimize its text representation with the Baike term, then output the complete representation as an entity mention. This method can solve the incorrect mentions caused by segmenting wrongly. Moreover, we reserve the tags of Baike terms, which are used to identify the categories of entity mentions in the subsequent steps. Because Baidu Baike cannot cover all entity mentions, especially the rare and distorted name mentions, we use Baidu search engine to cover the shortage.

3. For the candidate mentions without Baike terms or with low similarity, we treat them as queries with Baidu search engine, and extract the titles and summaries of the top 5 search results. Because the title not only contains entity mention but also contains other information, in order to remove the irrelevant information, we acquire the longest common substring between a title and a summary based on the idea of a summary being a brief description of a title. By observing the substring is an entity mention in the title, then we calculate the similarity between the substring and the candidate mention. If there is a similarity value exceeding the threshold among the 5 search results, we regard it as an entity mention, and optimize its text representation with the substring, then output the complete representation as an entity mention.

4. We created a pronoun dictionary to extract the pronominal mentions in texts. In addition, we clarify the target mention replaced by a pronominal mention with the pronominal categories, location restrains, distance constraints and occurrence numbers. For example, the target mention of a personal pronoun should be a personal name, and the target mention is front of the personal pronoun, and the distance between them do not exceed two sentences. Moreover, the more appearance of the object, the more important, and its description is more. Here we only process the personal pronouns.

5. The POS tagging set of HanLP tool is compatible with "ICTPOS 3.0 Chinese POS Tagging Set" and "Modern Chinese Corpus Processing Specification – Word Segmentation and POS Tagging". The POS granularity is small, especially the noun phrases, which are divided with various categories, including personal names, locations, bionts, food, diseases, etc. [10]. The sample is shown in Fig. 2. Firstly,

according to the POS tags, we identify the categories of entity mentions. Because there are two POS tags of "n" and "nz", which indicate a noun and a proper name respectively, no specific meaning, and the two POS tags are easy to be labeled wrongly. For the mentions with the above POS tags, we use the tags of Baike terms to identify the categories. If a mention has no a Baike term, we use NLPIR tool [11] to obtain the categories of 5 search results. If the categories are the same, we regard them as the category of the mention. If the categories are different, we use the meaning of its POS tag as the category of the mention.

The similarity calculation formulas used by the 2th step and 3th step in the above extraction steps are shown below.

$$
S(t_m, t_b) = \begin{cases} \frac{Len(LCS(t_m, t_b))}{Len(t_b)} & (t_m \cap t_b \neq \emptyset) \\ \frac{Len(MCC(t_m, t_b))}{Len(t_b)} & (t_m \cap t_b = \emptyset) \end{cases} \tag{1}
$$

$$
t_b = \begin{cases} t_b \,(t_b \text{ is a Baike term}) \\ r_t \cap r_s \,(t_b \text{ is not a Baike term}) \end{cases} \tag{2}
$$

In formula 1, t_m represents a candidate mention, t_b indicates a Baike term or a search result. Because the title of a search result not only contains entity mention but also contains other information, in order to remove the irrelevant information, we acquire the longest common substring between a title and a summary based on the idea of a summary being a brief description of a title, and assign the substring to t_b. The above calculation is shown in formula 2, and r_t indicates a title, and r_s represents a summary. $LCS(t_m, t_b)$ represents the longest common substring between t_m and t_b. The function Len indicates the length of a string. $MCC(t_m, t_b)$ represents the maximum common characters between t_m and t_b, which can process the similarity calculation between a full name and its abbreviation. For example, the abbreviation of "shi jie wei sheng zu zhi" (world health organization) is "shi wei zu zhi" (WHO), and their common substring is empty, but they point to the same entity. Therefore, we design the function MCC to solve the above problem.

3   Experiment and Evaluation

We crawl 40 news texts in November 2013 from phoenix information news website as data sets, covering military affairs, politics, culture, society, etc. We use HanLP tool to segment the text and tag POS, and select the nouns and the personal pronouns as the candidate mentions, acquiring 4027 candidate mentions in total.

3.1   Evaluation Method

Because we do not find an unsupervised Chinese entity mention extraction method, we use the precision, recall and F-value to evaluate the performance of this method proposed by us, namely Un-MenEx. The formula is as follow.

$$P = \frac{\text{the number of the correct entity mentions identified by Un-MenEx}}{\text{the number of all entity mentions identified by Un-MenEx}} \qquad (3)$$

$$R = \frac{\text{the number of the correct entity mentions identified by Un-MenEx}}{\text{the number of all entity mentions in texts}} \qquad (4)$$

$$F = \frac{2 \times P \times R}{P + R} \qquad (5)$$

3.2   Experimental Results

In this part, we show the detection results of mentions and the recognition results of their categories. We use the evaluation method in Section A to access the performance of our method.

Table 1. Mention detection results by Un-MenEx (%)

Mention	Method	Precision	Recall	F-measure
NAM NOM	Baidu Baike	91.16	84.20	87.54
	Baidu search	76.39	6.09	11.28
PRO	Dictionary+Rule	95.28	93.52	94.39
ALL	Un-MenEx	90.18	87.28	88.70

Table 1 shows the detection results of mentions extracted by Un-MenEx and its part modules. In view of the candidate mentions that have no corresponding entries in Baike, we use Baidu search to determine whether they are entities, so the recall of Baidu search is low. In addition, we can observe that Baidu Baike covers most entities from this table. Because we only deal with the personal pronouns, which have obvious regularity, their precision and recall are high.

Table 2. Categories and accuracy about true mentions (%)

Category	BIO	FOD	HED	ORG	MAT
Accuracy		100	87.50	86.90	100
Category	JOB	PER	LOC	PON	NOM
Accuracy	98.89	95.69	96.48	83.67	97.02

Table 2 shows the categories of true mentions and their accuracy. Specifically, BIO indicates the biont, such as animals, plants, whose accuracy is replaced by slash, on account of no mentions of this category. FOD indicates food, such fruits, vegetables.

HED indicates the entities about health, such as medicines, diseases. ORG indicates organizations or institutions, such as schools, companies. MAT indicates materials, such as farm tools. JOB indicates jobs, positions and the titles of technical posts. PER indicates personal names, and LOC indicates political locations, such as country, city, town. PON indicates other proper names, and NOM indicates the noun mentions, such as concepts and technology terms.

3.3   Method Analysis

Un-MenEx is an unsupervised Chinese entity mention extraction method, without manual annotation data, meeting the processing demand of massive network data. In addition, Un-MenEx can identify new names and aliases of entity mentions with the abundant of Baidu search, such as "ma shou fu" (Richest man Ma) as an alias of "ma yun" (Yun Ma). Because we select the segmentation results as the candidate mentions, the wrong segmentations impact the precision of entity mentions vastly. Un-MenEx can optimize the mentions based on the original meaning of the segmentation results. For example, the entity "zhong yan hua xiang hua gong you xian gong si" (Zhong Yan Hua Xiang Chemical Company) is segmented into "zhong" (Zhong) and "yan hua xiang hua gong you xian gong si" (Yan Hua Xiang Chemical Company), Un-MenEx can acquire its complete representation with the mention "yan hua xiang hua gong you xian gong si" (Yan Hua Xiang Chemical Company). However, Un-MenEx cannot modify the wrong mentions with independent meanings. For example, for the personal name "lin guang wen" (Guangwen Lin), the word segmentation tool segments it into "lin guang" (Guang Lin) and "wen" (wen). However, "lin guang" (Guang Lin) has the independent meaning and is also regarded a personal name. In addition, Un-MenEx identifies the categories of entity mentions based on the POS tags, whose correctness also impacts the precision of the extraction results.

4   Conclusion

In this paper, we propose a simple but efficient unsupervised Chinese entity mention extraction method. This method exploit the abundant information of Baidu Baike and Baidu search to detect and identify entity mentions in texts, which has good recognition effect, especially for the rare and new names of entity mentions. Exploiting the theory of this method, we can process English texts with Google search engine and Wikipedia. However, this method relies on the word segmentation tool heavily, which can optimize the mentions lacking complete semantic information, but not modify the wrong mentions with independent meanings. In addition, we do not process the nested mentions emphatically. In future, we will study a method to get rid of the impact of word segmentation, and extract the complex mentions emphatically. For the pronominal mentions, we will mine the deep text features to clarify their target entities.

References

1. Ittycheriah, A., Lita, L., Kambhatla, N., et al.: Identifying and tracking entity mentions in a maximum entropy framework. In: Proceedings of the 2003 Conference of the North American Chapter of the Association for Computational Linguistics on Human Language Technology: Companion Volume of the Proceedings of HLT-NAACL 2003–Short Papers-Volume 2, pp. 40–42. Association for Computational Linguistics (2003)
2. Li, W., Qian, D., Lu, Q., et al.: Detecting, categorizing and clustering entity mentions in Chinese text. In: Proceedings of the 30th Annual International ACM SIGIR Conference on Research and Development in Information Retrieval, pp. 647–654. ACM (2007)
3. Chen, J., Xue, N., Palmer, M.: Using a smoothing maximum entropy model for Chinese nominal entity tagging. In: Su, K.-Y., Tsujii, J., Lee, J.-H., Kwong, O.Y. (eds.) IJCNLP 2004. LNCS (LNAI), vol. 3248, pp. 493–499. Springer, Heidelberg (2005). doi:10.1007/978-3-540-30211-7_52
4. Hacioglu, K., Douglas, B., Chen, Y.: Detection of entity mentions occurring in English and Chinese text. In: Proceedings of the Conference on Human Language Technology and Empirical Methods in Natural Language Processing, pp. 379–386. Association for Computational Linguistics (2005)
5. Daumé III, H., Marcu, D.: A large-scale exploration of effective global features for a joint entity detection and tracking model. In: Proceedings of the Conference on Human Language Technology and Empirical Methods in Natural Language Processing, pp. 97–104. Association for Computational Linguistics (2005)
6. Li, Q., Ji, H.: Incremental joint extraction of entity mentions and relations. In: Meeting of the Association for Computational Linguistics (2014)
7. Lu, W., Roth, D.: Joint mention extraction and classification with mention hypergraphs. In: Proceedings of Conference on Empirical Methods in Natural Language Processing (2015)
8. Baidu baike: http://baike.baidu.com/
9. Baidu Search: www.baidu.com/
10. Han Language Processing Toolkit: http://hanlp.linrunsoft.com/
11. Natural Language Processing & Information Retrieval Sharing Platform: http://ictclas.nlpir.org/

A Lightweight Model for Stream Sensor Data Service

Shen Su[1,2], Chen Liu[1,2(✉)], Zhongmei Zhang[1,2,3], and Yanbo Han[1,2]

[1] Beijing Key Laboratory on Integration and Analysis of Large-Scale Stream Data,
North China University of Technology, Beijing 100144, China
liuchen@ncut.edu.cn
[2] Cloud Computing Research Center,
North China University of Technology, Beijing 100144, China
[3] School of Computer Science and Technology,
Tianjin University, Tianjin 300072, China

Abstract. The current Sensor Networks are generally domain-specific and task-oriented, tailored for particular applications with little possibility of sharing and reusing sensor data for different applications. The servitization of stream sensor data is an effective solution for sharing and reusing sensor data resources. Considering the limitations of existing methods on processing large-scale stream data and concurrent requests, this paper proposes a lightweight model for stream sensor data service, which processes sensor stream data with service modeling operations, and distributes data based on Pub/Sub mechanism. This paper fulfills the encapsulation by utilizing event-driven mechanism for stream data service processing, using SparkStreaming framework to process sensor events, and improving traditional matching-tree algorithm to distribute stream data efficiently. Finally, we evaluate our approach through experiments, and the stream data service can handle multiple requests and deliver data to corresponding applications in milliseconds level.

Keywords: Stream sensor data · Stream data service · Service modeling · Event-driven · Event matching

1 Introduction

With the rapid development of sensor network technology, an increasing number of sensors are deployed with access from Internet all over the world, and generate sustained, volumed, and high-speeded data stream. It is very valuable to share and fuse such sensor streaming data collected from multiple sources for further analysis and innovation. Unfortunately, most of the current sensor networks are domain specific or mission-oriented, which merely serve for settled private applications.

To share and reuse the stream sensor data for public applications are challenging. Among all the corresponding obstacles, there are mainly two concerns to stop it touching down. First, to transfer a volumed stream sensor data over

© Springer International Publishing AG 2016
G. Wang et al. (Eds.): APSCC 2016, LNCS 10065, pp. 329–342, 2016.
DOI: 10.1007/978-3-319-49178-3_26

Internet is quite expensive, especially when the stream data need to get across several ISPs (Internet Service Providers). Secondly, it is impractical to provide the raw sensor data directly to the client user. The raw sensor data may include privacy information, which sensor data owners don't want to expose, or worthless information, which the client users don't care.

To solve the above problem, a lot of efforts propose to encapsulate the stream sensor data as services. Sensor networks like USTL [1] and Homeport [5] provider sensor data by RESTful interfaces, however, such works consider no clients' demand. To fuse sensor data from multiple resources, a few research teams establish community-oriented platforms for stream sensor data, like SenseWeb from Mircosoft [6], Global Sensor Networks [7], and LiveWeb [8]. Such platforms enable coding the transferred stream data, but need to provide different interfaces for different users. Thus such platforms are not good choices to conduct large scale stream sensor data.

Towards a better solution, we propose to encapsulate the stream sensor data into service, which focuses on in-depth data processing and on-demand data distribution. Our contribution in this paper are mainly two-folded.

First, we propose a service model to encapsulate stream sensor data. The model provides in-depth data processing by defining integrating operations on streaming data, and distributes sensor data by sub/pub system. Secondly, we introduce a possible implementation for our service model. We realize the integrating operations on stream data based on Spark Stream operations, and realize event matching by our improved matching tree algorithm. With further evaluation, we prove the feasibility of our service model and corresponding implementation.

2   Related Works

One effective solution to share and reuse the sensor data resource is providing sensor stream data as a service. It can provide the ability to share data across organizations upon the Internet, and guarantee the security and privacy of data. Service needs to process and transform the original stream sensor data based on real-time processing. Works [2–4] implement data abstraction based on event-driven mechanism. In this paper, we regard data records produced by sensors as sensor events. A stream sensor data can be viewed as a sensor event stream, and multiple sensor events stream can generate event stream with richer semantic after processing, i.e. filter, aggregate, and join. In order to distribute stream data output by service to different users on demand, we use pub/sub system for event to realize the data distribution.

2.1   Stream Sensor Data as a Service

SenseWeb [6] provided a Web platform to assist users in mashing up shared sensor data and developing value-added applications. Global Sensor Networks [7] provided a flexible middleware which was able to integrate and manage different sensor data dynamically. The work [9] provided an abstract as Stream Feed for streaming data on the Web by extending the thoughts of Web feed. It provided filtering operation for stream data, and pushed stream data to users actively. However, the support of concurrency was limited by the resources of system itself.

[5,10,11] proposed the concept of "Web of Thing", and proposed two ways to integrate real-world devices into the existing Web by turning real objects into RESTful resources that can be used directly over HTTP. They also discussed the mashup in Web of Things. [11] discussed several ways of actively pushing messages to users. Because the sampling frequency of sensing devices was almost less than 1 HZ, it used Web Hooks to realize the data pushing. LiveWeb [8] presented a sensorweb portal with real-time search, monitor, and notification functions. It allowed the user to real time query, monitor the physical world at any time, and provide offline notifications.

There are researches sharing and obtaining sensor data as service for their sensor networks [1,5] or in concrete applications based on sensor streaming data [12,13]. Among them, [4,14] used the Server to Send Events (SSE) technology to implement the data actively pushing. These work shared sensor data or capacity of sensor data processing. However, when the third party applications acquired sensor data or processing capacity, they still needed to process sensor data further or improve the processing capacity according to the requirements.

2.2 Event Matching

From the data structure aspect, the event matching algorithm in content-based Pub/Sub system can be mainly classified two categories: tree-like structure and predicate indexing. In [14], Cough et al. proposed an event matching based on search tree, which can organize all the subscriptions into a tree structure. The event can obtain all the matching subscriptions through traversing the search tree from the root. However, the search tree is hard to change when adding or canceling subscriptions dynamically. Aguilera et al. proposed a tree-based content-matching method in [15]. However, it suffers from the large amount of content comparing, and only considers the correlation of part of predicates. Campailla et al. presented an approach for matching published events with subscriptions based on Binary Decision Diagrams, a compact data structure for representing Boolean functions [16]. It can integrate the Binary Decision Tree into Binary Decision Graph based on the same predicate in different subscriptions. Silvia et al. proposed an event matching algorithm based on R-tree [17]. It regards the subscription as a range and builds an R-tree based on overlay relationship of subscriptions. The R-tree is also used in articles [18,19], which build the tree based on the location constraints. The structure of subscription in this paper is more complex, and the relationship of the subscriptions is hard to represent, which means the R-tree is not suitable in our situation.

F. Fabret et al. [20] proposed a two-phase algorithm based on predicate indexing for high performance content-based matching. In the first phrase, satisfied constraints are computed. In the second phase, matched subscriptions are returned by utilizing counting algorithms. It achieves high throughput and low latency comparing with other methods in scenarios of a small number of subscriptions. [21–23] improved the two-phase algorithm in different phases respectively. [23] reduced the predicates matching through judging the equivalent relationship among event attributes and the equivalent and inclusive relationship among predicates, and increased the efficiency for event matching. The predicate indexing method avoids the repeat matching for equivalent predicate, but it needs to verify all the predicates.

3   Service Model

Basically, our idea is to provide the stream data generated by sensors as a service. Our principle is to merely transfer the necessary data. To that end, we drive our model on the granularity of event, and conduct event transformation and event matching in our model. In the following of this section, we first introduce the basic conceptions of our model, then we formulate our service model.

3.1   Basic Concept

Since our model is driven by events, we first need the concept of an event.

Definition 1. We define an event e as a list of attribute-value pairs.

$$e = \ <a_1, v_1>, <a_2, v_2>, \ldots, <a_n, v_n>$$

a_i is the attribute, and the v_i is the corresponding value. Based on the definition of **event**, we can formulate the original stream sensor data as a sequence of events, which could be used to describe both the input and output of our model.

With a certain event form, a service could define the topic of all input and output stream sensor data. However, a service may need just a part of certain topic data, thus our model describe the input and output of a service according to the events' content.

Definition 2. A service constrain $const$ describe the value range of each event's attribute.

$$const = \bigwedge C_{a_i}$$

a_i is the attribute, C_{a_i} represents the value range of attribute a_i. With **service constrains**, we can refine the description of the input and output of our service model.

Since our principle is to transfer as little unnecessary data as possible, we conduct operations on the input events to generate more valuable and compressed events as the output of the service.

Definition 3. An operation op could be represented by the following 3-tuple.

$$op = \ < func, in\_events, out\_event >$$

$func$ represents the processing logic of the operation; in_events represents the target event streams of the operation; out_event represents the generated events. It is noted that a service may have multiple operations.

Definition 4. We define a subscription r with a conjunctive predicates.

$$r = \wedge p_i$$

p_i describes the value range of the attribute a_i. Obviously, $C_{a_i} \rightarrow p_i$ is true.

3.2   Stream Sensor Data Service Model

With the above definitions, we now describe our stream sensor data service model. Our goal is to collect stream sensor data, and provider on demand service to the data consumers as a software defined "sensor".

Definition 5. We define a stream sensor data service as a 6-tuple as following:

$$< in\_events, out\_event, in\_const, out\_const, ops, rs >$$

in_events and out_event represent the input and output event streams of the service, in_const and out_const describe the service constrains of the input event stream and the output event stream. ops represents the processing logics on the input event streams, and rs represents the all subscriptions received from the data consumers.

4   Implementation

4.1   Conversion Operators

At present we design and realize three kinds of operators, which are transform operators for single stream data source, aggregation operators based on slide window, and fusion operators for multiple stream data sources. Since the size of stream data source accessed in the service can be huge, we mapping the operators into functions in Spark Streaming, and realize the operators in distributed framework. Table 1 shows the operators and its corresponding functions in SparkStreaming.

Transform Operator Filter: only event satisfied specific condition can be output through filter operator, the filter operator can be represented as:

$$filter(a, ro, v)$$

In which, a is an attribute included in the input events, $ro \in \{<, >, =, \neq, \leq, \geq\}$ is the relation operator, v is the value of a.

Project: specific attributes and corresponding values from source stream data can be mapped into a new stream data through project operator. The project operator can be represented as:

$$project(A, A, M, V)$$

Table 1. The service modeling operators and corresponding functions in SparkStreaming.

Type	Operator	Functions in SparkStreaming
transform	filter	filter(fun(a, rO, v))
transform	project	map(fun(A, V, M))map(fun(A, V, M))
transform	sort	window(wL,sI).sortByKey(o, [numTasks])
aggregation	Aggregator	reduceByWindow(fun(),wL,sI)
aggregation	IncAggregator	reduceByWindow(fun(),wL,sI).reduceByKey(sumfun())
fusion	merge	union(s)
fusion	join	join(s, [numTasks])

In which, A is the attributes selected from the source stream data, A is the new attribute set, $M = \{< a_1, a_1' >, < a_2, a_2' >, \ldots, < a_k, a_k' >\}$ is the mapping relationship between A and A, and $V = \{a_i', v_i\}$ is default values for attributes $A - A$.

Sort: sort operator can arrange the values of specific attributes within slide window. The sort operator can be represented as:

$$sort(a, o, wL, sI)$$

In which, a is one attribute included in the input events, $o \in \{asce, desc\}$ is used to specify the order is descending or ascending, wL means the size of slide window, and sI means the slide size of the slide window. The sort operator belongs block operation, which is different with the filter and project operator.

Aggregation Operator. The aggregation operator includes sum, counting, minimum, maximum, and average operation. Similar to the sort operator, aggregation operator also belongs block operation, and needs to specific parameter wL and sI. In this paper, we realized two kinds of aggregation operator:

$Aggregator = \{sum, count, min, max, avg\}$ only operate the data within the windows, and the new result has no relationship with result of the front windows. Take the maximum operation as an example, the maximum operation only output the max value in the window, it can be represented as:

$$max(a, wL, sI)$$

In which, a is one attribute included in the input events, wL means the size of slide window, and sI means the slide size of the slide window.

$incrAggregator = \{incrSum, incrCount, incrMin, incrMax, incrAvg\}$ is incremental operation, and can process results from multiple windows. Take incremental maximum operation as an example, the incremental maximum operation outputs the max value of all the windows, which can be represented as:

$$incrMax(a, wL, sI)$$

In which, a is one attribute included in the input events, wL means the size of slide window, and sI means the slide distance of the slide window.

Fusion Operators. The stream data service can utilize fusion operator to process multiple source stream data and outputs more valuable stream data.

Merge: the merge operator can merge two stream data with the same attribute set as one new stream data, which can be represented as:

$$merge(S)$$

In which, S is the second stream data which has the same attribute set with specific stream data.

Join: the join operator can join two stream data which are related to the same object or include same attribute into one stream data, which can be represented as:

$$join(S, a, wL, sI)$$

In which, S is the second stream data which is related to the same object of has same attributes with specific stream data, wL means the size of slide window, and sI means the slide distance of the slide window.

At present, the fusion operators are all dual operation, the stream data service can utilize multi-fusion operators to realize the fusion of more stream data.

4.2   The Event Matching Algorithm

Most of the existing event matching algorithm pre-process the set of subscriptions, and obtain the marched subscriptions based on specific data structure. [14,15] pre-process the subscriptions based on tree-based structure (event matching tree), to increase the efficiency of event matching. In this paper, we improve the matching tree to obtain the matched subscriptions more efficient.

The matching tree includes three kinds of nodes, which are virtual node, i.e. root node, predicate node, and leaf node. Specifically, the root node means the entrance of the matching tree, the predicate node include one predicate, and the leaf node represents one subscription.

One matching tree T can be represented by its root node t_r which has a set of child node of predicate node. The child nodes of one predicate node n can be constituted by predicate node n or leaf node l. The matching tree has the following characteristics:

(1) Given an event e, for any predicative node n, the children of n can be visited only when p is included by n is matched with e.
(2) Given an event e, assume L is all the leaf node in matching tree, and the matched subscriptions R are subscriptions represented by leaf nodes $L' \subseteq L$, which is all the leaf nodes visited by e.

(3) For any subscriptions $r_i = p_{i1} \wedge p_{i2} \wedge \cdots \wedge p_{in}$ and $r_j = p_{j1} \wedge p_{j2} \wedge \cdots \wedge p_{jm}$, assume $p_{i1} \wedge p_{i2} \wedge \cdots \wedge p_{ik}$ and $p_{j1} \wedge p_{j2} \wedge \ldots p_{jk}$ as the prefix-predicates of ri and rj respectively, in which $1 \leq k \leq min(n, m)$, if $(p_{i1} = p_{j1}) \wedge (p_{i2} = p_{j2}) \wedge \cdots \wedge (p_{ik} = p_{jk})$, then ri and rj can shared the same k predicate nodes in the matching tree.

(4) For the predicate nodes N in the child nodes of any node, the verify result of $N \subseteq N$ can be deduced by the result of specific predicate node $n \in N$.

Here is a simple example of the matching tree to explain the characteristics. Suppose subscriptions r_1, r_2, and r_3 as follows:

$$r_1 = p_1 \wedge p_2$$

$$r_2 = p_1 \wedge p_3$$

$$r_3 = p_4 \wedge p_5$$

In which, subscriptions r_1 and r_2 share the same predicate p_1, and predicates p_1 and p_4, along with p_2 and p_3 have inclusion relations $p_4 \prec p_1$ and $p_3 \prec p_2$. The matching tree constituted by the three subscriptions is showed as Fig. 1.

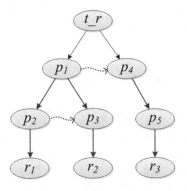

Fig. 1. Event matching tree example.

In Fig. 1, predicate p_2 and p_3 will be visited only when p_1 matched by given event (characteristic 1). For subscription r_1, the path: t_r, p_1, p_2, r_1 represents $r_1 = p_1 \wedge p_2$, and the visiting of r_1 indicates that r_1 is matched by given event (characteristic 2). Subscriptions r_1 and r_2 share the same predicate node in the matching tree (characteristic 3).

For decreasing the verify times of the predicate nodes, we utilize multi-level index structure to represent the relationship of the child predicate nodes for the root node and each predicate node. In figure *, for child predicate nodes p1 and p4 of root node, there is an index structure which indicate the relationship of them, and based on the index structure, the verify result of p_4 can be deduced by the result of p_1 (characteristic 4).

5   Evaluations

In this section, we firstly compare the performance of stream data service with different servitization methods. Then we evaluate our event matching algorithm with other existing algorithm.

5.1   Data Set and Environment

We evaluate the proposed methods on both real and synthetic traffic data sets. The ANPR data (S1) is collected from numerous traffic camera sites. The GPS data (S2) is come from one taxi enterprise. Meanwhile, we also generate two synthetic datasets (S3 and S4) based on the real GPS data. We regard one dataset as from one enterprise and another as from private drivers. Table 2 shows the detail information of the datasets.

Table 2. Dataset information.

Data set	Attributes	Origin	Size
ANPR(S1)	$cid, vid, time$	Traffic Administration Bureau	64G
GPS(S2)	$vid, time, \ldots$	Taxi Company	46G
GPS(S3)	$vid, time, \ldots$	Simulated	340M
GPS(S4)	$vid, time, \ldots$	Simulated	1.4M

Our method is implemented on a cluster consisting of 5 nodes, and the nodes are running in virtual machines with CentOS release 6.4 and java 1.70. The detailed configuration of the cluster is shown in Table 3. In which, master node and slave3 are utilized to realize the stream data service, slave4 is used to simulate the stream data source and slave5 is used to simulate different requests.

Table 3. Cluster configuration.

Role	CPU	Memory
master & slave1 Intel Xeon E312xx	6G	
master & slave2	Intel Xeon E312xx	6G
slave3	Intel Xeon E312xx	3G
slave4	Intel Xeon E312xx	3G
slave5	Intel Xeon E312xx	3G

As following are the main metrics we use in the experiments:

Service Latency: it is the interval form the moment when an event was generated from the stream data source to the moment when it was received by users. The service latency can be defined as:

$$SL_i = \frac{\sum(t_{ij\_rec} - t_{ij\_in})}{n}$$

In which, t_{ij_in} means the moment when the service receives the event e_j, t_{ij_rec} means the moment when user i receives the event e_j, and n is the total number of the events received by user i.

System Load: it is the load status of the system when users are invoking stream data services, the system load includes CPU load, memory load and net flow.

Event Matching Rate: it is the number of matched events per second.

5.2   Service Performance

In this subsection, we compared the performance of different methods. Firstly we realized stream data service with different methods, which are our method, method based on topic-based Pub/Sub mechanism, method based on contend-based Pub/Sub mechanism, and method based on traditional service model. And then we simulated 1000 subscriptions and required stream data with different methods. We set the rate of the stream data source as 10000 HZ, and set the subscriptions number as 100, 200, 400, 600, 800, and 1000. The experiment was executed three times and the average service latency and system load were calculated respectively. The experiment results are shown in Figs. 2, 3, 4 and 5.

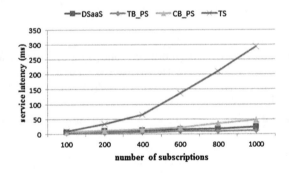

Fig. 2. The service latency in different numbers of subscriptions

As shown in Fig. 2, the method based topic-based Pub/Sub mechanism had the least service latency, it is because that this method didnt do any process for users subscription and send all the stream data to users directly. Figures 3 and 4 show the memory load and CPU load with different subscriptions numbers respectively, and since the net flows of method based on traditional service model and contend-based Pub/Sub mechanism are the same with our method, Fig. 5 only shows the net flow of out method and method based on topic-based Pub/Sub mechanism. As shown in Figs. 3 and 4, method based traditional service model had the highest memory load and CPU load, that is because it needs to execute one process for each subscription respectively, while other methods were based on the one-to-many mechanism. Furthermore, since our method adopt more

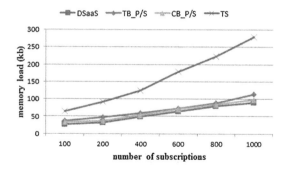

Fig. 3. The memory load in different numbers of subscriptions

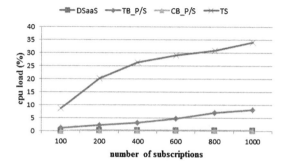

Fig. 4. The CPU load in different numbers of subscriptions

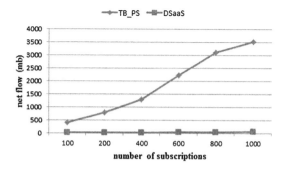

Fig. 5. The net flow in different numbers of subscriptions

efficient event matching mechanism and distributed process framework, it had higher efficiency and less service latency.

5.3   Event Matching Performance

The event matching algorithm is one of the key to guarantee the performance of service in our method. In this subsection we compare the efficiency of our event matching algorithm (Improved matching tree) with other event matching algorithms, which are normal matching tree, predicate index and brute force algorithm. We set the rate of stream data source as 10000 HZ, and firstly set the numbers of subscriptions as 100, 200, 400, 600, 800, and 1000, and evaluate the influence of subscriptions numbers for the event matching algorithm. Then we set the number of subscriptions as 100, and set the predicate numbers of subscription as 2, 4, 6, 8, and 10, and evaluate the influence of different predicate numbers.

As shown in Figs. 6 and 7, when with larger number of subscriptions and predicates, the brute force methods had lowest efficiency, and the normal matching tree had lower efficiency with large number of subscription and the predicate index algorithm had poorer performance with large number of predicates. Our method improved the matching tree with multi-level index structure, and

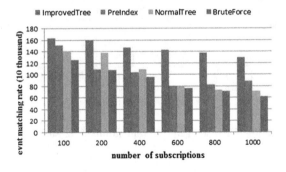

Fig. 6. The event matching efficiency in different number of subscriptions

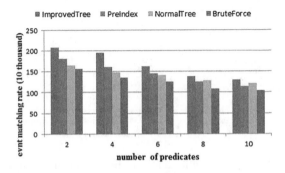

Fig. 7. The event matching efficiency in different number of predicates

decrease the unnecessary verifications based on the relationships between predicates. Therefore, our algorithm has higher efficiency with both lager number of subscriptions and predicates.

6   Conclusion

To share and reuse the sensor data among multiple applications, we describe a method to encapsulate service-oriented large-scale stream sensor data, and realize its on-demand distribution by a Pub/Sub system. To implement our service model, we realize several stream data processing operations based on the Spark Streaming package. We achieve efficient content-based data streaming distribution based on the improvement of traditional event matching algorithms. We further verify that our data streaming service can efficiently convert and distribute the raw data stream in a millisecond level.

Acknowledgments. This paper is supported by key program of Beijing municipal natural science foundation "Theory and Key Technologies of Data Space Towards Large Scale Stream Data Processing" (NO. 4131001).

References

1. Pinto, J., Martins, R., Sousa, J.B.: Towards a REST-style architecture for networked vehicles and sensors. In: IEEE International Conference on Pervasive Computing and Communications Workshops, pp. 745–750 (2010)
2. Gyllstrom, D., Wu, E., Chae, H.J., et al.: SASE: complex event processing over streams. In: Biennial Conference on Innovative Data Systems Research (2006)
3. Silberstein, A., Filpus, G., Munagala, K., et al.: Data-driven processing in sensor networks. In: Third Biennial Conference on Innovative Data Systems Research, Asilomar, CA, USA, 7–10 January 2007, Online Proceedings, pp. 325–333 (2007)
4. Wang, F., Zhou, C., Nie, Y.: Event processing in sensor streams. In: Aggarwal, C.C. (ed.) Managing and Mining Sensor Data, pp. 77–102. Springer, New York (2013)
5. Guilly, T.L., Olsen, P., Ravn, A.P., et al.: Homeport: middleware for heterogeneous home automation networks. In: IEEE International Conference on Pervasive Computing and Communications Workshops, pp. 627–633 (2013)
6. Grosky, W.I., Kansal, A., Nath, S., et al.: Senseweb: an infrastructure for shared sensing. IEEE Multimedia **14**(4), 8–13 (2007)
7. Aberer, K., Hauswirth, M., Salehi, A.: Infrastructure for data processing in large-scale interconnected sensor networks, Glasgow Caledonian University, pp. 198–205 (2007)
8. Yang, X., Song, W., Debraj, D.: LiveWeb: a sensorweb portal for sensing the world in real-time. Tsinghua Sci. Technol. **16**(5), 491–504 (2011)
9. Dickerson, R., Lu, J., Lu, J., Whitehouse, K.: Stream feeds - an abstraction for the world wide sensor web. In: Floerkemeier, C., Langheinrich, M., Fleisch, E., Mattern, F., Sarma, S.E. (eds.) IOT 2008. LNCS, vol. 4952, pp. 360–375. Springer, Heidelberg (2008). doi:10.1007/978-3-540-78731-0_23
10. Guinard, D., Trifa, V., Guinard, D.: Towards the web of things: web mashups for embedded devices, ResearchGate (2009)

11. Trifa, V., Guinard, D., Davidovski, V., Kamilaris, A., Delchev, I.: Web messaging for open and scalable distributed sensing applications. In: Benatallah, B., Casati, F., Kappel, G., Rossi, G. (eds.) ICWE 2010. LNCS, vol. 6189, pp. 129–143. Springer, Heidelberg (2010). doi:10.1007/978-3-642-13911-6_9

12. Han, Y., Wang, G., Yu, J., et al.: A service-based approach to traffic sensor data integration and analysis to support community-wide green commute in China. IEEE Trans. Intell. Transp. Syst., 1–10 (2015)

13. Sashima, A., Yoda, I., Kawamoto, M., et al.: A sensor data streaming service for visualizing urban public spaces. In: ACM Conference on Embedded Networked Sensor Systems, pp. 1–2 (2013)

14. Gough, J., Smith, G.: Efficient recognition of events in a distributed system. In: Australasian Computer Science Conference (2000)

15. Aguilera, M.K., Strom, R.E., Sturman, D.C., et al.: Matching events in a content-based subscription system. In: Proceedings of the Eighteenth Annual ACM Symposium on Principles of Distributed Computing (PODC) 1999, pp. 53–61. ACM (2003)

16. Campailla, A., Chaki, S., Clarke, E., et al.: Efficient filtering in publish-subscribe systems using binary decision diagrams. In: International Conference on Software Engineering, pp. 443–452 (2001)

17. Bianchi, S., Felber, P., Gradinariu, M.: Content-based publish/subscribe using distributed r-trees. In: Kermarrec, A.-M., Bougé, L., Priol, T. (eds.) Euro-Par 2007. LNCS, vol. 4641, pp. 537–548. Springer, Heidelberg (2007). doi:10.1007/978-3-540-74466-5_57

18. Hu, H., Liu, Y., Li, G., et al.: A location-aware publish/subscribe framework for parameterized spatio-textual subscriptions. In: IEEE International Conference on Data Engineering, pp. 711–722. IEEE (2015)

19. Guo, L., Chen, L., Zhang, D., et al.: Elaps: an efficient location-aware pub/sub system. In: IEEE International Conference on Data Engineering, pp. 1504–1507. IEEE (2015)

20. Fabret, F., Jacobsen, H.A., et al.: Filtering algorithms and implementation for very fast publish/subscribe systems. ACM SIGMOD Rec. **30**(2), 115–126 (2001)

21. Carzaniga, A., Wolf, A.L.: Forwarding in a content-based network. SIGCOMM **33**(4), 163–174 (2003)

22. Xue, T., Feng, B.-Q., Li, B.: Efficient matching for content-based publish-subscribe system. Mini-Micro Syst. **27**(3), 529–533 (2006). (in Chinese)

23. Liu, G., Zhou, Z., Wu, W.: Event matching algorithm based on the judgment of redundant attributes in publish/subscribe systems. J. Comput. Res. Dev. **47**(10), 1690–1699 (2010). (in chinese)

A Performance Study of Containers in Cloud Environment

Bowen Ruan, Hang Huang$^{(\boxtimes)}$, Song Wu$^{(\boxtimes)}$, and Hai Jin

Services Computing Technology and System Lab, Cluster and Grid Computing Lab,
School of Computer Science and Technology,
Huazhong University of Science and Technology, Wuhan 430074, China
{huanghang,wusong}@hust.edu.cn

Abstract. Container technology has gained great popularity since containers could provide near-native performance in cloud environment. According to different design purposes and underlying implementations, containers could be classified into application containers (e.g., Docker) and system containers (e.g., LXC). The diversity of containers may lead to a confusing choice about which kind of container is suitable for different usage scenarios. Meanwhile, the architectures of public container services are quite controversial because cloud platforms tend to run containers in virtual machines. From the perspective of performance, an extra virtual machine layer between the bare metal and containers probably brings in unnecessary performance overhead. In this paper, we carry out a performance study to explore the appropriate way to use containers from different perspectives. We first conduct a series of experiments to measure performance differences between application containers and system containers, then evaluate the overhead of extra virtual machine layer between the bare metal and containers, and finally inspect the service quality of ECS (*Amazon EC2 Container Service*) and GKE (*Google Container Engine*). Our results show that system containers are more suitable to sustain I/O-bound workload than application containers, because application containers will suffer high I/O latency due to layered filesystem. Running containers in virtual machine would result in severe disk I/O performance degradation up to 42.7 % and network latency up to 233 %. We also find out ECS offers better performance than GKE, and cloud platforms could acquire better performance by running containers directly on the bare metal.

Keywords: Container technology · Cloud platform · Performance comparison · Service quality · Virtualization overhead

1 Introduction

With lightweight design and near-native performance, container technology is emerging as a promising virtualization solution for developers to deploy applications, and has gained great popularity in the industry. Container technology

© Springer International Publishing AG 2016
G. Wang et al. (Eds.): APSCC 2016, LNCS 10065, pp. 343–356, 2016.
DOI: 10.1007/978-3-319-49178-3_27

is also called operating-system-level virtualization, which allows multiple iso-lated user-space instances sharing the same operating system kernel and applies CGroups to take control of resources in the host. So far, there have been a num-ber of container products released to the market, which include LXC (Linux Container), Docker, rkt (Rocket), and OpenVZ etc. Docker is the most preva-lent one among them and being widely used in startup companies like Uber and Groupon. Moreover, major cloud platforms include Amazon Web Service [3] and Google Compute Engine [7] are also beginning to provide public con-tainer services for developers to deploy applications in the cloud. Undoubtedly, the emergence of container technology has virtually changed the trend of cloud computing market.

According to different design purpose and underlying implementation, we can classify container products into application containers and system containers. Application containers (e.g., Docker and rkt) are designed to encapsulate a single task into a standard image to effectively distribute applications. To be more specific, application containers simplify a container as much as possible to a single process to run micro service. However, system containers (e.g., LXC and OpenVZ) are designed to provide fully functional operating system with the most frequently-used services. In a sense, system containers are like a virtual machine but with more lightweight design. Besides, another significant difference between application containers and system containers is filesystem. Application containers introduce a layered stack of filesystems [9], which allows different containers reusing these layers to diminish disk usage and simplify application deployment. But system containers originally support all sorts of filesystems and are not limited to one filesystem. In default, system containers directly bind the mount to the host. Because the diversity of containers may lead to a potential misuse in the cloud environment, the differences between application containers and system containers should be more clearly clarified.

At present, public container services, such as ECS (*Amazon EC2 Container Service*) and GKE (*Google Container Engine*), have a controversial issue that they tend to run containers in the virtual machines to acquire technical support from existing management tools [4]. It is obviously to understand that an extra virtual machine layer between the bare metal and containers probably brings in unnecessary performance overhead. In principle, the essence of public container service is to provide a generic running environment for developers, no matter what underlying infrastructure it is. Hence, it is worth a comprehensive inspec-tion for cloud platforms to evaluate the service quality. Then we are able to explore the most appropriate architecture to provide container services.

In this paper, we make the following contributions:

- We conduct a series of experiments to measure performance differences between application containers (Docker) and system containers (LXC). We find out Docker, compare to LXC, will suffer higher I/O latency due to AUFS's implementation. Besides, Docker's network latency is slightly higher than LXC because of port mapping.

- We evaluate the impact of adding an extra virtual machine layer between the bare metal and containers. By comparing the performance gap between Docker and Docker-Machine, we reveal that running containers in virtual machine will result in severe performance degradation in all aspects.
- We conduct an inspection of service quality of ECS and GKE. Our results show that ECS offers better performance than GKE, and cloud platforms could acquire better performance by running containers directly on the bare metal.

The rest of the paper is organized as follows. Section 2 provides necessary backgrounds for container technology. Section 3 describes experimental methodology, and we conduct the evaluation and analyze the experiment results in Sect. 4. We review related works in Sect. 5, and finally, Sect. 6 concludes the paper.

2   Background and Motivation

2.1   Container Background

Container technology is experiencing a rapidly development with the support from industry and being widely used in large scale production environment. Two outstanding features, speedy launching time and tiny memory footprint, make containers launch an application in less than a second and consume a very small amount of resources [2]. Relative to virtual machines, using containers not only improves the performance of applications, but it also allows the host to sustain multiple times more applications simultaneously.

Technically, we can classify containers as application containers and system containers. Application containers only contain a single process, and stop the container after this process finished. However, system containers contain a complete runtime environment, and run services like *init*, *sshd*, and *syslog* in the background. The idea behind application containers is to reduce a container as much as possible to a single process to provide micro service. Thus, an application is able to be deconstructed into many small parts, and every part will be executed in a container separately. On the contrary, the idea behind system containers is to provide fully functional operating system in a container. They are more like a lightweight virtual machine and mainly used for providing underlying infrastructure. To sum up, Table 1 demonstrates the comparisons between application containers and system containers.

One major feature of application containers is layered filesystem, which allows different containers reusing image layers to diminish disk usage and simplify application distribution. For instance, both MySQL image and Redis image could be built on top of Ubuntu image. They can share underlying system image and only store their own separate programs. Image registry is introduced as a database for developers to download existing images or submit their customized images. The ecosystem of application containers provides a convenient framework to build, ship, and run applications. In contrast, system containers support all sorts of filesystems and are not limited to one filesystem. Thus, system containers

Table 1. Comparison between application containers and system containers

	Application containers	System containers
Content	Contain a single process	Contain a complete runtime environment
Filesystem	Layered filesystem	Filesystem neutral
Design purpose	Run micro services	Provide a lightweight virtual machine
Usage scenario	Used for distributing applications	Used for providing underlying infrastructure

can not share images because they probably adopt completely different filesystems. Besides, operation system images like Ubuntu or CentOS are the only ones that originally supported by system containers. As a consequence, developers need to clone a container and then migrate to the other host to accomplish application distribution. With so many distinctions of implementation, we consider that application containers and system containers should be clarified more clearly and applied to different usage scenarios in the cloud environment.

2.2 Motivation

Due to the convenience of deploying applications, container technology triggers an overwhelming revolution for cloud platforms. Figure 1 demonstrates the architecture of mainstream container service. The CaaS (*Container as a Service*) layer is based on IaaS (*Infrastructure as a Service*) layer and provides container's running environment for developers to deploy their applications. At present, ECS and GKE have won the most shares of public container services in the industry. They allow developers to purchase virtual machines with pre-installed Docker running environment, and define their tasks and submit them to the cloud platform for execution. In contrast to the past, developers no longer need to take a long time to install softwares and tweak configurations. They could simply pull images from Docker hub and launch containers. Thus, public container service is a new solution for developers to build, deploy, and run their applications in an efficient method.

But one major deficiency of existing public container services is cloud platforms tend to run containers in the virtual machines to acquire mature support from existing management tools. Evidently, adding an extra virtual machine layer between the bare metal and container service probably generates unnecessary performance overhead. In principle, the essence of container service is to provide container running environment for developers, no matter what kind of underlying infrastructure it is. With the coming mature of container technology, the IaaS layer could be merged into CaaS layer. Nowadays container technology uses namespaces to isolate users, processes, and network between containers in the same host, and empower CGroups to control CPU, memory, and I/O usage for each container in fine-grained measure. Thus, the enhanced resource isolation and management mechanisms in containers could provide a

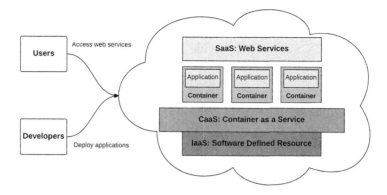

Fig. 1. The architecture of mainstream container service

sufficient virtual environment for tenants in shared resource environment. Based on current industry status, it is worth a comprehensive study to measure the exact overhead of the virtual machine layer and discuss how to provide container service appropriately.

3   Experimental Methodology

To systematically evaluate container performance in cloud environment, our experiments consist of two parts: evaluation for container technologies and evaluation for public container services.

3.1   Evaluation for Container Technologies

In this part, we will conduct a series of experiments on Docker and LXC to evaluate the performance differences between application container and system container. We use micro benchmarks to measure CPU performance, memory bandwidth, disk I/O, and network latency for our experimental objects. We also analyze the underlying implementation of different containers to figure out the fundamental reasons that lead to performance differences.

Meanwhile, in order to investigate the exact overhead introduced by extra virtual machine layer between the bare metal and container, we also measure the performance of Docker-Machine which is a virtualization tool to provide Docker environment by installing Docker in a virtual machine. We compare these three different forms of container to make an evaluation for container technologies.

3.2   Evaluation for Public Container Services

In this part, we will inspect the service quality of public container services. We choose ECS and GKE as our experimental objects because these two are most influential cloud platforms in the industry. So far, these two container services have gained a certain level of popularity and created several successful user cases.

Although both ECS and GKE provide highly scalable and high performance container management services, there also exist several differences between ECS and GKE. First, ECS is based on Amazon EC2, and GKE is based on Google Compute Engine. Amazon EC2 offers more options for developers to purchase instances with different hardware architectures for different usages, even for graphical calculation. In contrast, Google Compute Engine offers one unified hardware architecture that allows developers to customize the number of vCPUs and the capacity of memories. Second, ECS is tightly integrated with Amazon Web Services. Developers need to store their data in S3 (*Simple Storage Service*), and depend on web services including RDS (*Relational Database Service*) or EMR (*Elastic MapReduce*) to acquire a full range of support from AWS. However, GKE is more flexible because Kubernetes, the underlying management framework, permits GKE to access web services in other cloud platforms.

4   Performance Evaluation

4.1   Platform Setup

Local Platform. Our local testbed is a server with 32 cores Intel X5650 CPU and 64 GB memories. The operating system is Ubuntu 15.10, running with Linux 4.2 kernel. LXC is version of 1.1.3 and Docker is version of 1.9.1.

For different containers, we adjust CGroups control parameters to limit containers resource consumption to a same level. In other words, we only allow a container to occupy 2 vCPUs and 8 GB memories. For Docker-Machine, we create the virtual machine with 2 vCPUs and 8 GB memories as well. We conduct a series of experiments on a single container to measure performance differences between application containers and system containers. We also establish a container cluster that contains 8 computing nodes to evaluate the performance of distributed applications.

Cloud Platform. In order to unify the hardware specification, we choose m4.large instance on EC2 as standard computing node, which has 2 vCPUs and 8 GB memories. We purchase 8 m4.large instances to compose the container cluster. For GKE, we customize the instance for equivalent specification with EC2 for fair comparison.

4.2   Evaluation for Container Technologies

CPU Performance. In order to evaluate CPU performance [15], we adopt 473.astar and 450.soplex in SPEC CPU 2006 to test integer and floating computing capacity. SPEC CPU 2006 is an industry-standardized benchmark suite that test CPU performance. To be more specific, 473.astar is a path finding

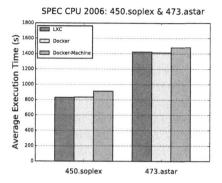

Fig. 2. Execution time of 450.soplex and 473.astar in SPEC CPU 2006. Lower is better

algorithm that derived from a portable game AI library, and 450.soplex solves a linear program using simplex algorithm and sparse linear algebra.

Figure 2 shows the result of SPEC CPU 2006. LXC and Docker have equivalent performance on CPU, and beat Docker-Machine by 8.4 % to 8.8 % in 450.soplex, 3.9 % to 4.6 % in 473.astar respectively. We can conclude that both LXC and Docker could utilize the CPU computing resource in a relatively high level, but extra virtualization layer will encumber the performance of containers. Although current hardware assisted virtualization technology allows virtual machine executing commands directly on CPU, a slightly delay is still exist for virtualization overhead.

Memory Bandwidth. We adopt STREAM [16] as memory benchmark, which is designed to measure sustainable memory bandwidth in high performance computers. At first, STREAM would allocate an array that is bigger than the machine's cache, then executes Copy, Scale, Add, and Triad operations in the memory. Since the program accesses memory with regular pattern, memory bandwidth is the main determinant of performance. At last, we collect the speed of each operation as the results. The version of STREAM is 5.10.

Table 2 shows the results of STREAM. No matter LXC, Docker, or Docker-Machine, they have similar memory bandwidth. We can conclude that there is no

Table 2. Memory bandwidth result

Stream operations	LXC	Docker	Docker-Machine
Copy (MB/s)	8420	8503	8311
Scale (MB/s)	8362	8564	8319
Add (MB/s)	9159	9085	8819
Triad (MB/s)	9199	9042	8964

significant difference on memory bandwidth for LXC and Docker. Even adding an extra virtualization layer only causes negligible overhead.

Disk I/O Performance. We adopt FIO [5] as the benchmark to test disk I/O performance. We collect IOPS of disk as the metric for evaluation. In FIO configuration file, we set *ioengine* to *libaio* (a Linux native asynchronous I/O library) in *O_DIRECT*, *iodepth* equals to 16 (number of I/O units to keep in flight), and *numjobs* equals to 8 (number of processes performing the same workload of this job). Besides, buffer size is 4KB and test file size is 1 GB. The version of FIO is 2.1.3.

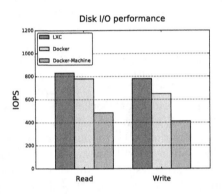

Fig. 3. Disk I/O performance of random read and random write. Higher is better

Figure 3 shows the results of FIO. We can observe that LXC has better disk I/O performance than Docker, and Docker-Machine suffers significant virtualization overhead and results in poor disk I/O performance. To be more specific, LXC advances Docker by 6.1 % in random read, and 16.6 % in random write. Docker-Machine falls behind Docker for 40.1 % in random read and 42.7 % in random write.

The disk I/O performance gap between LXC and Docker is caused by AUFS, the default filesystem in Docker container. Figure 4 illustrates the architecture of AUFS. AUFS is consists of image layers and container layer. Image layers are composed of multiple read-only AUFS branches. For each AUFS branch, it only saves differences relative to underlying branches to maximally support image reuse. Container layer is the writable layer to store modifications of a container. Eventually, a union mount point is introduced to provide a composite view of the filesystem for developers. In practice, AUFS could generate significant latency for write performance because the first time a container writes to any file, the file has to be located and copied into the container's top writable layer [1]. Latency will increase when file size is large or this file is saved in lower AUFS branch. Thus, file searches in AUFS branches and the requirement to copy files into top writable layer result in the extra disk I/O latency for Docker.

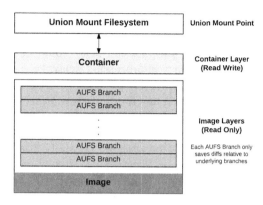

Fig. 4. The architecture of AUFS

For the reasons given above, we suggest developers prefer LXC to Docker when executing massive disk I/O requests. As for Docker-Machine, device emulation is the major source for poor disk I/O performance because every I/O operation in virtual machines must go through QEMU. Thus, we can conclude that adding an extra virtualization layer between the bare metal and container service will cause severe disk I/O latency.

Network Latency. For purpose of measuring network latency, we use Netperf's [12] request-response mode to test round trip latency. In request-response mode, client will send a 100 bytes packet to server, and server will reply it immediately after receiving the packet. This request-response action will repeat over and over again until being manually stopped. Thus, we can calculate network latency by counting the number of request/response in a specified period time. To avoid network congestion or other issues, we set up Netperf client in the host and communicate with Netperf server in the container.

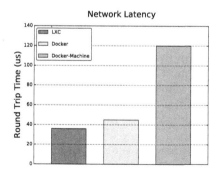

Fig. 5. Network latency of LXC, Docker and Docker-Machine. Lower is better

Figure 5 shows the result of Netperf. Docker's network latency is 1.25 times of LXC, and Docker-Machine greatly increases the network latency to 120 μs for each round trip. Considering propagation delay could be neglected in local network, the main source of latency is processing delay.

Both LXC and Docker use network namespace to create a virtual ethernet pair between the host and container, and every network packet should go through the bridge network. Comparing to LXC, Docker adds a NAT (*Network Address Translation*) mechanism to expose specific network ports. Only by port mapping, services in Docker containers could be accessed normally from the outside. As a result, the NAT mechanism increases the network latency and makes it difficult for service discovery across different hosts. However, LXC is much easier to use the full stack of Linux capabilities to manage container's network with no limitations.

In the case of Docker-Machine, network packets go through a virtual device created by virtio from guest OS to host OS. The combination of hardware emulation and NAT mechanism causes the severe network latency of Docker-Machine. Therefore, we can conclude that virtualization overhead for network latency is serious, and developers could prefer LXC to Docker for network-intensive applications in the perspective of low latency.

4.3 Evaluation for Public Container Services

In this part, we will inspect the service quality of public container services by using HiBench [10] to evaluate the performance of distributed data processing systems, Hadoop and Spark, on different container platforms. Nowadays, distributed data processing applications have been used extensively in cloud environment. We choose several typical workloads, including WordCount, TeraSort, PageRank, and Kmeans, as CPU-bound and I/O-bound workloads respectively to evaluate the performance. We briefly introduce these four workloads as follows:

- WordCount: WordCount is a classical MapReduce workload, which counts the number of occurrences for each word in input text. WordCount is a CPU-Bound workload. In our test, the input data is 10 GB and generated by RandomWriter and RandomTextWriter in Hadoop distribution.
- TeraSort: TeraSort is a classical workload, which sorts massive data as fast as possible. TeraSort is a CPU-Bound workload in map stage, but it turns into an I/O-Bound workload in reduce stage. In our test, the input data is 10 GB and generated by TeraGen in Hadoop distribution.
- PageRank: PageRank is a link analysis algorithm used widely in web search engines, which calculates the ranks of web pages according to the number of reference links. PageRank is a CPU-Bound workload. In our test, the input data is 0.5 GB.
- Kmeans: Kmeans is well-known clustering algorithm for data mining to partition input data into k clusters. In map stage, Kmeans is a CPU-Bound workload for data training. In reduce stage, Kmeans becomes an I/O-bound workload for data clustering. The input data is 4 GB and generated by DenseKmeans.

To carry out the experiment, we need to set up a cluster of 8 computing nodes. At first, we install required softwares and configure them properly in all computing nodes. Then we run HiBench, a benchmark developed by Intel to test Hadoop and Spark system, in the cluster to test aforementioned four workloads. For each workload, we run five times to eliminate performance deviation. At last, we collect each workload's execution time as the experiment results. The version of Hadoop is 2.7.2, and the version of Spark is 1.6.0.

Figures 6 and 7 show the results of Hadoop and Spark system in different container testbeds respectively. Due to the performance gap between underlying instances, ECS has better service quality than GKE in all workloads. To be more accurate, ECS takes the lead of GKE in a range from 1.4 % to 12.2 %. Although Docker-Machine in the local testbed is far surpassed by ECS and GKE, we find out both ECS and GKE have a certain degree of performance gap comparing to

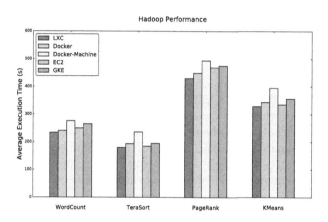

Fig. 6. Execution time of Hadoop in different container testbeds. Lower is better

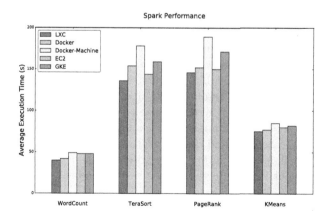

Fig. 7. Execution time of Spark in different container testbeds. Lower is better

LXC and Docker in the local testbed. That means running containers directly on the bare metal could gain more efficacy than running containers in virtual machines. Public container services still have enough room for improving their performance.

The experiment results also reveal that LXC has better performance than Docker in these scenarios in a range from 2.5 % to 11.6 %. According to previous experiment results, Docker has equivalent CPU performance comparing to LXC, but Docker would suffer severe network and disk I/O latencies when massive I/O requests arrive. Therefore, we recommend that users should carefully choose suitable container to execute I/O-Bound workload.

5   Related Works

Container technology is gradually gaining more and more attention from the research community, and comparisons between containers and virtual machines have been extensively conducted in many research works. Felter et al. [4] use a suite of workloads to measure the performance differences between Docker and KVM. They conclude that containers result in equal or better performance than virtual machines in almost all cases. Agarwal et al. [2] evaluate the density and start-up latency of LXC and KVM. They conclude that the overall density is highly dependent on the most demanded resource and the small memory footprint of containers could raise the density to a higher level. Morabito [11] measures power consumption of virtual machines and containers in different applications. Xavier et al. [17] measure the performance of containers when applying them into HPC environment. They conclude that containers could obtain a very low overhead leading to near-native performance, but performance isolation in containers is immature. However, these studies do not discuss the distinctions between different containers and the impact of adding an extra virtualization layer between the bare metal and containers.

Evaluation for cloud platform could provide a valuable guidance for developers to choose appropriate platform to deploy applications and save cost. Schad et al. [14] use established micro benchmarks to measure performance variance on EC2, and find out EC2's performance varies a lot and often falls into two bands having a large performance gap in-between. Taking performance variation and performance isolation [8,19] into account, studies [13] aim to propose QoS-aware frameworks to improve resource utilization in the cloud through diverse ideas and methods. Xu et al. [18] summarize the performance overhead of virtual machines in the cloud, and analyze the challenges of cloud platforms. Latest studies [6] review the benefits and requirements of container services and discuss the fitness of containers to facilitate applications in the cloud. On the basis of these studies, we make an inspection of the service quality of public container services including ECS and GKE.

6 Conclusion

Motivated by the increasing popularity of container technology in the industry, in this paper we conduct a performance study of containers in cloud environment. Our study focuses on two points: one is performance differences between application containers and system containers, and the other is performance overhead caused by extra virtual machine layer between the bare metal and containers. What's more, we make an inspection of service quality of public container services. To carry out experiments, we first conduct a series of experiments to measure CPU performance, memory bandwidth, disk I/O performance, and network latency among LXC, Docker, and Docker-Machine. Then we evaluate public container services by testing the performance of typical distributed data processing systems, Hadoop and Spark, on different container platforms.

Our experiments distinguish the differences between applications containers and system containers. We conclude that system containers have performance advantage on executing I/O-Bound workload and are more suitable to provide underlying infrastructure service. Our experiments also prove that running containers in virtual machine would result in severe disk I/O performance degradation up to 42.7 % and network latency up to 233 %. Our inspection for public container services reveal that the service quality of public container services are competitive, but their infrastructure architectures are quite controversial. Although both ECS and GKE keep updating their hardwares constantly, the performance of LXC and Docker in the local testbed could surpass these two public container services in most cases. Therefor, we learn that the performance overhead caused by extra virtual machine layer can not be neglected in public container services, and cloud platforms could acquire better performance by running containers directly on the bare metal.

To summarize, the performance study we present in this paper provides several suggestions for developers to choose appropriate containers in different usage scenarios. It also proposes several suggestions for the establishment of container services. With the coming mature of container technology, we believe containers could be extensively used and play a very significant role in the cloud environment.

Acknowledgments. This research is supported by National Science Foundation of China under grant No. 61232008, National Key Research and Development Program under grant 2016YFB1000500, National 863 Hi-Tech Research and Development Program under grant No. 2015AA01A203.

References

1. Docker and aufs in practice. https://docs.docker.com/engine/userguide/storage-driver/aufs-driver/
2. Agarwal, K., Jain, B., Porter, D.E.: Containing the hype. In: Proceedings of the 6th Asia-Pacific Workshop on Systems, pp. 8–16. ACM (2015)
3. Amazon web service. https://aws.amazon.com/

4. Felter, W., Ferreira, A., Rajamony, R., Rubio, J.: An updated performance comparison of virtual machines and linux containers. In: Proceedings of the 2015 IEEE International Symposium on Performance Analysis of Systems and Software, pp. 171–172. IEEE (2015)
5. Fio. https://github.com/axboe/fio
6. Fu, S., Liu, J., Chu, X., Hu, Y.: Toward a standard interface for cloud providers: the container as the narrow waist. IEEE Internet Comput. **20**(2), 66–71 (2016)
7. Google compute engine. https://cloud.google.com/
8. Govindan, S., Liu, J., Kansal, A., Sivasubramaniam, A.: Cuanta: quantifying effects of shared on-chip resource interference for consolidated virtual machines. In: Proceedings of the 2nd ACM Symposium on Cloud Computing, pp. 22–33. ACM (2011)
9. Harter, T., Salmon, B., Liu, R., Arpaci-Dusseau, A.C., Arpaci-Dusseau, R.H.: Slacker: fast distribution with lazy docker containers. In: Proceedings of the 14th USENIX Conference on File and Storage Technologies, pp. 181–195. USENIX (2016)
10. Huang, S., Huang, J., Dai, J., Xie, T., Huang, B.: The hibench benchmark suite: characterization of the mapreduce-based data analysis. In: Proceedings of the 26th IEEE International Conference on Data Engineering Workshops, pp. 41–51. IEEE (2010)
11. Morabito, R.: Power consumption of virtualization technologies: an empirical investigation. In: Proceedings of the 8th IEEE/ACM International Conference on Utility and Cloud Computing, pp. 522–527. IEEE (2015)
12. Netperf. http://www.netperf.org/netperf/
13. Novaković, D., Vasić, N., Novaković, S., Kostić, D., Bianchini, R.: Deepdive: transparently identifying and managing performance interference in virtualized environments. In: Proceedings of the 2013 USENIX Annual Technical Conference, pp. 219–230. USENIX (2013)
14. Schad, J., Dittrich, J., Quiané-Ruiz, J.A.: Runtime measurements in the cloud: observing, analyzing, and reducing variance. Proc. VLDB Endow. **3**(1–2), 460–471 (2010)
15. SPEC CPU 2006. http://www.spec.org/cpu2006/
16. Stream. https://www.cs.virginia.edu/stream/
17. Xavier, M.G., Neves, M.V., Rossi, F.D., Ferreto, T.C., Lange, T., De Rose, C.A.F.: Performance evaluation of container-based virtualization for high performance computing environments. In: Proceedings of the 21st Euromicro International Conference on Parallel, Distributed, and Network-Based Processing, pp. 233–240. IEEE (2013)
18. Xu, F., Liu, F., Jin, H., Vasilakos, A.V.: Managing performance overhead of virtual machines in cloud computing: a survey, state of the art, and future directions. Proc. IEEE **102**(1), 11–31 (2014)
19. Zhang, X., Tune, E., Hagmann, R., Jnagal, R., Gokhale, V., Wilkes, J.: Cpi 2: CPU performance isolation for shared compute clusters. In: Proceedings of the 8th ACM European Conference on Computer Systems, pp. 379–391. ACM (2013)

Combining Social Balance Theory and Collaborative Filtering for Service Recommendation in Sparse Environment

Lianyong Qi[1,2(✉)], Wanchun Dou[1], and Xuyun Zhang[1,3]

[1] State Key Laboratory for Novel Software Technology,
The Department of Computer Science and Technology,
Nanjing University, Nanjing 210023, China
lianyongqi@gmail.com, douwc@nju.edu.cn
[2] School of Information Science and Engineering,
Qufu Normal University, Rizhao 276826, China
[3] Department of Electrical and Computer Engineering,
University of Auckland, Auckland 1023, New Zealand
xuyun.zhang@auckland.ac.nz

Abstract. With the ever-increasing number of web services registered in service communities, many users are apt to find their interested web services, through various recommendation techniques, e.g., Collaborative Filtering (i.e., CF)-based recommendation. Generally, the CF-based recommendation approaches can work well, when the target user has similar friends or the target services (i.e., the services preferred by target user) have similar services. However, in certain situations when user-service rating data is sparse, it is possible that target user has no similar friends and target services have no similar services; in this situation, traditional CF-based recommendation approaches fail to generate a satisfying recommendation result, which brings a great challenge for accurate service recommendation. In view of this challenge, we combine Social Balance Theory (i.e., SBT) and CF to put forward a novel recommendation approach Rec_{SBT+CF}. Finally, the feasibility of our proposal is validated, through a set of simulation experiments deployed on MovieLens-1M dataset.

Keywords: Service recommendation · Sparse data · Friend user · Enemy user · Social Balance Theory · Collaborative Filtering

1 Introduction

With the ever-increasing popularity of SOA (Service Oriented Architecture), an increasing number of business processes from various domains are encapsulated into corresponding web services that are easy-to-access and further registered in various service communities [1–3]. Then users can browse, find and select their interested web services from service communities easily, which significantly facilitates the construction of various service-oriented business applications.

In a service community, there are often many candidate services that share same or similar functionality [4], which places a heavy burden on the service selection decision

© Springer International Publishing AG 2016
G. Wang et al. (Eds.): APSCC 2016, LNCS 10065, pp. 357–374, 2016.
DOI: 10.1007/978-3-319-49178-3_28

of a target user, as service evaluation and selection processes are often boring and time-consuming. In this situation, service recommendation technique provides a light-weight resolution that can alleviate the service selection burden on a target user. For example, the well-known Collaborative Filtering (abbreviated as CF, e.g., user-based CF, item-based CF and hybrid CF) recommendation technique [5] has been widely applied in various service recommendation applications. More concretely, (1) in user-based CF recommendation, the similar friends of target user are determined first; and afterwards, the services preferred by similar friends of target user are recommended to the target user. (2) In item-based CF recommendation, the similar services of target services (i.e., the services preferred by target user) are recommended to the target user. (3) In hybrid CF recommendation, both user-based and item-based CF recommendations are integrated.

Generally, the CF-based recommendation approaches can work very well, when (1) target user has one or more similar friends, or (2) target services have one or more similar services. However, due to the inherent sparsity of user-service rating data, it is possible that neither condition (1) nor condition (2) holds, when we recommend appropriate candidate services to the target user. In this situation, traditional CF-based recommendation approaches fail to output a pleasing recommendation result, which brings a great challenge for the service selection decision of target user. In view of this challenge, a novel service recommendation approach that combines Social Balance Theory (i.e., SBT) [6] and CF, i.e., Rec_{SBT+CF} (i.e., Recommendation based on SBT and CF) is put forward in this paper. Different from traditional CF-based recommendation approaches, we do not look for similar friends of target user directly in Rec_{SBT+CF}, instead, we first look for the "possible friends" of target user indirectly, based on "enemy(antonym of "friend")'s enemy is a friend" rule and "friend's friend is a friend" rule in Social Balance Theory. Afterwards, the services preferred by "possible friends" of target user are recommended to the target user.

The paper is structured as follows. In Sect. 2, the service recommendation problem is formalized, and then an example is presented to demonstrate our paper motivation. In Sect. 3, Social Balance Theory is introduced first and afterwards, a novel service recommendation approach Rec_{SBT+CF} is put forward. In Sect. 4, a set of experiments are deployed to validate the feasibility of our proposal. Related works and comparison analyses are presented in Sect. 5. Finally, in Sect. 6, we summarize the paper and point out the future research directions.

2   Formalization and Motivation

In this section, the service recommendation problem is specified more formally; and afterwards, an intuitive example is given to demonstrate the motivation of our paper.

2.1   Formalization

The CF-based service recommendation problem could be formalized with a four-tuple *Ser_Recommendation(USER, WS, R, user_{target})*, where

(1) $USER = \{user_1, \ldots, user_m\}$: user set in user-service invocation network. Here, m denotes the number of users.

(2) $WS = \{ws_1, \ldots, ws_n\}$: web service set in user-service invocation network. Here, n denotes the number of web services.

(3) $R = \{r_{i-j} \mid 1 \leq i \leq m, 1 \leq j \leq n\}$: historical user-service rating set. Here, r_{i-j} represents the rating value of web service ws_j by $user_i$. In this paper, for simplicity, we adopt the well-known $1* \sim 5*$ rating system to depict r_{i-j}.

(4) $user_{target}$: target user who requires service recommendation. And obviously, $user_{target} \in USER$ holds.

With the above formalization, the CF-based service recommendation problem could be specified more formally as below: recommend appropriate web services $ws_x (\in WS)$ to target user $user_{target} (\in USER)$, based on the historical user-service rating set R between users (in $USER$) and web services (in WS). In this paper, we focus on this CF-based recommendation problem.

2.2 Motivation

Next, an example is presented in Fig. 1 to demonstrate the paper motivation more intuitively. As Fig. 1 shows, there are totally three users, i.e., $USER = \{Jim, Lucy, Jack\}$ (Jim is the target user) and six web services, i.e., $WS = \{ws_1, \ldots, ws_6\}$ in the historical user-service invocation network (here, the services invoked and preferred by target user Jim, i.e., ws_1 and ws_2 are called "target services"). The user-service rating data is also presented in Fig. 1.

According to Adjusted Cosine Similarity [7] (as rating data is often discrete and the rating scales of different users are varied, Adjusted Cosine Similarity is more suitable here), the similarity between target user Jim and other users $user_i$ (i.e., $Lucy$ and $Jack$), i.e., $Sim(Jim, user_i)$ could be calculated. Concretely, $Sim(Jim, Lucy) = -0.27$, while $Sim(Jim, Jack) = Null$ (as Jim and $Jack$ have not rated common services). Therefore, target user Jim has no similar friends and hence, traditional user-based CF recommendation approaches fail to deliver a satisfying recommendation result.

Likewise, according to Adjusted Cosine Similarity, the similarity between target services (i.e., ws_1 and ws_2) and other services (i.e., ws_3, ws_4, ws_5, ws_6) could also be calculated. Concretely, $Sim(ws_1, ws_3) = Sim(ws_1, ws_4) = Sim(ws_2, ws_3) = Sim(ws_2, ws_4) = 0$, while $Sim(ws_1, ws_5) = Sim(ws_1, ws_6) = Sim(ws_2, ws_5) = Sim(ws_2, ws_6) = Null$. Therefore, a conclusion could be drawn that target services (i.e., ws_1 and ws_2) have no similar services and hence, traditional item-based CF recommendation approaches cannot generate an ideal recommendation result.

In this situation, traditional CF-based service recommendation approaches (e.g., user-based CF, item-based CF or hybrid CF) cannot give a satisfying recommendation result, as the user similarity or service similarity is either negative or null; which brings a great challenge for accurate service recommendation. In view of this challenge, a novel recommendation approach that combines SBT and CF, i.e., Rec_{SBT+CF} is put forward in the next section.

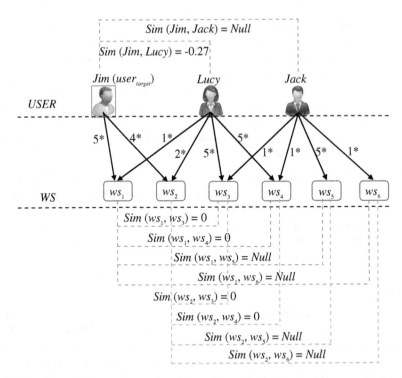

Fig. 1. An example where traditional CF-based service recommendation approaches fail

3 Service Recommendation Based on SBT and CF

First, in Subsect. 3.1, Social Balance Theory is introduced briefly. Afterwards, a novel approach Rec_{SBT+CF} is presented in Subsect. 3.2, to deal with the sparse recommendation situations where target user has no similar friends and target services have no similar services.

3.1 Social Balance Theory

Social Balance Theory was first put forward by F. Heider in 1958. The theory analyzed the stable and unstable social relationships among involved three parties (i.e., P, O and X) [6]. In this paper, only two stable social relationships shown in Fig. 2 are recruited for service recommendation. In Fig. 2, the dashed line and solid line denote the "enemy" relationship and "friend" relationship, respectively. Next, we introduce these two stable social relationships with more intuitive and easy-to-understand specifications, respectively.

(a) If O is a friend of P and X is a friend of O, then X is a possible friend of P (i.e., friend's friend is a friend).

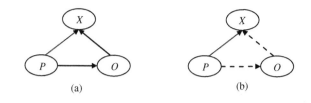

(a)   (b)

──────► Friend relationship   ─ ─ ─ ─► Enemy relationship   ┄┄┄┄┄► Inferred friend relationship

Fig. 2. Two stable social relationships among P, O and X according to Social Balance Theory

(b) If O is an enemy of P and X is an enemy of O, then X is a possible friend of P (i.e., enemy's enemy is a friend).

As Fig. 2(a) indicates, if target user P's "direct friend" (e.g., O) is present, we can infer the "possible friends" (e.g., X) of P based on "friend's friend is a friend" rule. Likewise, as Fig. 2(b) shows, if target user P's "direct friend" is absent while P's "enemy" (e.g., O) is present, we can infer the "possible friends" (e.g., X) of P based on "enemy's enemy is a friend" rule. With the above analyses, in the next subsection, we will introduce a novel approach Rec_{SBT+CF} based on Social Balance Theory and Collaborative Filtering, to deal with the service recommendation problems in sparse environment.

3.2 A Service Recommendation Approach: Rec_{SBT+CF}

In this subsection, a novel service recommendation approach named Rec_{SBT+CF} is put forward. The main idea of Rec_{SBT+CF} is: firstly, we look for the target user's "possible friends" based on Social Balance Theory and Collaborative Filtering; afterwards, the services preferred by "possible friends" of target user are recommended to the target user. Concretely, Rec_{SBT+CF} consists of the four steps in Fig. 3.

Step1: User similarity calculation. According to Adjusted Cosine Similarity, calculate similarity $Sim(user_i, user_j)$ between $user_i$ and $user_j$ ($user_i, user_j \in USER$ and $i \neq j$).

Step2: Judgment of friend or enemy. Set a similarity threshold P, and further judge the direct friend or direct enemy relationship between $user_i$ and $user_j$, based on the user similarity $Sim(user_i, user_j)$ derived in Step1.

Step3: Determining "possible friends" of $user_{target}$ based on Social Balance Theory. According to "friend's friend is a friend" rule and "enemy's enemy is a friend" rule in Social Balance Theory, determine target user $user_{target}$'s "possible friend" set $Possible\_friend\ (user_{target})$.

Step4: Service recommendation. Select the services preferred by "possible friends" in set $Possible\_friend\ (user_{target})$, and recommend them to $user_{target}$.

Fig. 3. Four steps of service recommendation approach Rec_{SBT+CF}

(1) Step 1: User similarity calculation.

In this step, we calculate the similarity between different users in set *USER*. Concretely, for any two users, i.e., $user_i$ and $user_j$($user_i$, $user_j \in USER$ and $i \neq j$), their similarity $Sim(user_i, user_j)$ could be calculated by (1) based on Adjusted Cosine Similarity.

In (1), I_i and I_j denote the service set rated by $user_i$ and $user_j$, respectively; I_{ij} denotes the common service set rated by both $user_i$ and $user_j$; r_{i-k} and r_{j-k} represent $user_i$'s and $user_j$'s ratings over service ws_k, respectively; while $\overline{r}_i$ and $\overline{r}_j$ denote $user_i$'s and $user_j$'s average ratings, respectively. Then according to (1), we can obtain the similarity between $user_i$ and $user_j$, i.e., $Sim(user_i, user_j)$. Please note that, if $user_i$ and $user_j$ do not have commonly rated web services (i.e., $I_{ij} = Null$), then their similarity $Sim(user_i, user_j) = Null$ holds. As can be seen from (1), $Sim(user_i, user_j) \in [-1, 1]$ holds, and a larger $Sim(user_i, user_j)$ means that $user_i$ and $user_j$ are more likely to be direct friends, vice versa.

$$Sim(user_i, user_j) = \frac{\sum\limits_{ws_k \in I_{ij}} (r_{i-k} - \overline{r}_i) * (r_{j-k} - \overline{r}_j)}{\sqrt{\sum\limits_{ws_k \in I_i} (r_{i-k} - \overline{r}_i)^2} * \sqrt{\sum\limits_{ws_k \in I_j} (r_{j-k} - \overline{r}_j)^2}} \tag{1}$$

(2) Step 2: Judgment of friend or enemy.

In this step, for any two users in set *USER*, i.e., $user_i$ and $user_j$($i \neq j$), we judge whether they are friends or enemies, based on their similarity derived in Step 1. Here, as our previous work [8] did, a similarity threshold $P(0.5 \leq P \leq 1)$ is introduced to aid the judgment process. Concretely, the judgment process is based on (2). In (2), *Friend_set* ($user_i$) and *Enemy_set*($user_i$) denote the direct friend set and direct enemy set of $user_i$, respectively; P and $-P$ are recruited as the similarity thresholds for friend relationship and enemy relationship, respectively. Here, please note that the friend relationship or enemy relationship is mutual. Namely, if $user_j \in Friend\_set(user_i)$, then $user_i \in Friend\_set(user_j)$ holds; likewise, if $user_j \in Enemy\_set(user_i)$, then $user_i \in Enemy\_set$ ($user_j$) also holds. Therefore, the time cost for judgment process could be reduced due to the mutual relationships. Then through Step 2, we can obtain the direct friend set and direct enemy set of each user.

$$user_j \begin{cases} \in Friend\_set(user_i) & \text{if } Sim(user_i, user_j) \geq P \\ \in Enemy\_set(user_i) & \text{if } Sim(user_i, user_j) \leq -P \end{cases} \tag{2}$$

(3) Step 3: Determining "possible friends" of $user_{target}$ based on Social Balance Theory.

In Step 2, we have obtained target user's direct enemy set $Enemy\_set(user_{target})$ and direct friend set $Friend\_set(user_{target})$ (As analyzed in Subsect. 2.2, this paper only focuses on the service recommendation problems where target user has no similar friends; therefore, $Friend\_set(user_{target}) = Null$ holds here). Next, in this step, we introduce how to indirectly determine the "possible friends" of $user_{target}$, i.e., *Possible_friend*($user_{target}$), based on the derived $Enemy\_set(user_{target})$ and Social Balance Theory. Concretely, Step 3 could be divided into the following two substeps.

Substep 3.1: For any $user_x \in Enemy\_set(user_{target})$, look for his/her enemy $user_y$ (i.e., $user_y \in Enemy\_set(user_x)$), based on the user similarity in (1) and judgment formula in (2). Then according to "enemy's enemy is a friend" rule in Social Balance Theory, we can infer that $user_y$ is a "possible friend" of target user, and the credibility that $user_y$ and $user_{target}$ are friends, i.e., $Credibility\_friend(user_{target}, user_y)$ could be calculated by (3). Please note that if $user_y$ is recommended by multiple enemies $\{user_{x1}, user_{x2...}\}$ of $user_{target}$ simultaneously, then their average credibility is adopted.

$$Credibility\_friend\left(user_{target}, user_y\right) = Sim\left(user_{target}, user_x\right) * Sim\left(user_x, user_y\right)$$

$$(3)$$

Then we put all $user_y$ into the "possible friend" set of target user, i.e., $Possible\_friend(user_{target})$, if $Credibility\_friend(user_{target}, user_y) \geq P$ holds (here, P is the similarity threshold defined in Step 2). To ease the understanding of readers, the relationships among $user_{target}, user_x$ and $user_y$ are shown in Fig. 4.

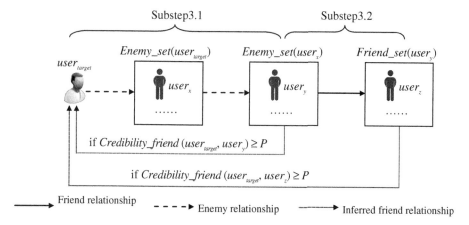

Fig. 4. Relationships among $user_{target}, user_x, user_y$ and $user_z$

Substep 3.2: For any $user_y \in Possible\_friend(user_{target})$, look for his/her direct friend $user_z$ (i.e., $user_z \in Friend\_set(user_y)$ as shown in Fig. 4), based on the user similarity in (1) and judgment formula in (2). Then according to "friend's friend is a friend" rule in Social Balance Theory, we can infer that $user_z$ is a "possible friend" of target user, and the credibility that $user_z$ and $user_{target}$ are friends, i.e., $Credibility\_friend(user_{target}, user_z)$ could be calculated by (4). Please note that if $user_z$ is recommended by multiple "possible friends" $\{user_{y1}, user_{y2...}\}$ of $user_{target}$ simultaneously, then their average credibility is adopted. Afterwards, if $Credibility\_friend(user_{target}, user_z) \geq P$ (here, P is the similarity threshold defined in Step 2), then we put $user_z$ into the "possible friend" set of target user, i.e., $Possible\_friend(user_{target})$.

$$Credibility\_friend\left(user_{target}, user_z\right) = Credibility\_friend\left(user_{target}, user_y\right) \\ * Sim\left(user_y, user_z\right) \tag{4}$$

Then through Step 3 (including Substeps 3.1 and 3.2), we can obtain all the "possible friends" of target user, i.e., $Possible\_friend(user_{target})$.

(4) Step 4: Service recommendation.

After Step 1–Step 3, we have derived the "possible friends" of target user, i.e., $Possible\_friend(user_{target})$. Next, we introduce how to recommend appropriate web services to $user_{target}$, by considering $user_{target}$'s "possible friends" in set $Possible\_friend(user_{target})$.

Concretely, for each $user_i \in Possible\_friend(user_{target})$, his/her preferred services (with 4* or 5* ratings) are put into set $WS\_recommended\_by(user_i)$. As $user_i$ is a "possible friend" of target user, we can infer that the services preferred by $user_i$, i.e., $ws_{i-j} \in WS\_recommended\_by(user_i)$ are also preferred by target user. However, the recommended services may not be unique, but multiple. Therefore, it becomes a necessity to discriminate and rank all the recommended services. Here, we introduce a novel concept of "Rec_Index" to depict the recommended degree of a web service. Concretely, for a recommended service $ws_{i-j} \in WS\_recommended\_by(user_i)$, its recommended degree $Rec\_Index(ws_{i-j})$ could be calculated by (5). In (5), $Credibility\_friend(user_{target}, user_i)$ is the credibility that $user_i$ and $user_{target}$ are friends, which has already been calculated by (3) or (4) in Step 3; $r_{i-(i-j)}$ denotes $user_i$'s rating value over service ws_{i-j}; the purpose of $(r_{i-(i-j)}/5)$ is to transform $r_{i-(i-j)}$ into range $[0, 1]$. Here, please note that if a service is recommended by multiple "possible friends" of target user simultaneously, then their average recommended degree is adopted. Finally, according to $Rec\_Index(ws_{i-j})$ in (5), we can rank all the services ws_{i-j} that are recommended to target user in descending order, and recommend them to $user_{target}$ respectively.

$$Rec\_Index\left(ws_{i-j}\right) = Credibility\_friend\left(user_{target}, user_i\right) * \left(r_{i-(i-j)}/5\right) \tag{5}$$

$$Final\_rec\_result = \{ \cup WS\_recommended\_by(user_i) \mid user_i \\ \in Possible\_friend\left(user_{target}\right)\} \tag{6}$$

With the above four steps of our proposed Rec_{SBT+CF} approach, a set of web services (denoted by final-recommendation-result set, i.e., union set $Final\_rec\_result$ in (6)) are recommended to the target user, to deal with the service recommendation problems in sparse environment. More formally, the pseudocode of our proposal is specified as below.

Algorithm: Rec_{SBT+CF} (*USER*, *WS*, *R*, $user_{target}$)

Inputs: (1) *USER* = {$user_1$, ..., $user_m$}: user set in user-service invocation network;
(2) *WS* = {ws_1, ..., ws_n}: web service set in user-service invocation network;
(3) $R = \{r_{i-j} \mid 1 \leq i \leq m, 1 \leq j \leq n\}$: a set of user-service rating records;
(4) $user_{target}$: target user that needs service recommendation.

Output: *Final_rec_result*: web service set that is recommended to $user_{target}$

1: Set user similarity threshold *P*
2: **for** each $user_i \in USER$ **do**   // Step1: calculate similarity between different users
3:       **for** each $user_j \in USER$ **do**
4:             calculate $Sim(user_i, user_j)$ by (1)
5:             **if** $Sim(user_i, user_j) \geq P$ // Step2: judgment of friend or enemy
6:                   **then** put $user_j$ into set $Friend\_set(user_i)$
7:                   **else if** $Sim(user_i, user_j) \leq -P$
8:                         **then** put $user_j$ into set $Enemy\_set(user_i)$
9:                   **end if**
10:             **end if**
11:       **end for**
12: **end for**
13: **for** each $user_x \in Enemy\_set(user_{target})$ **do** //Step3: determine possible friends of $user_{target}$
14:       determine $user_x$'s enemy $user_y$ by (2)
15:       calculate $Credibility\_friend (user_{target}, user_y)$ by (3)
16:       **if** $Credibility\_friend (user_{target}, user_y) \geq P$
17:       **then** put $user_y$ into set $Possible\_friend (user_{target})$
18:             determine $user_y$'s friend $user_z$ by (2)
19:             calculate $Credibility\_friend (user_{target}, user_z)$ by (4)
20:             **if** $Credibility\_friend (user_{target}, user_z) \geq P$
21:             **then** put $user_z$ into set $Possible\_friend (user_{target})$
22:             **end if**
23:       **end if**
24: **end for**
25: **for** each $user_i \in Possible\_friend (user_{target})$ **do**   // Step4: service recommendation
26:       determine $WS\_recommended\_by(user_i)$ by considering 4* and 5* ratings only
27:       **for** each $ws_{i-j} \in WS\_recommended\_by(user_i)$ **do**
28:             calculate $Rec\_Index(ws_{i-j})$ by (5)
29:       calculate *Final_rec_result* by (6)
30:       **end for**
31: **end for**
32: rank services ws_{i-j} in set *Final_rec_result* by $Rec\_Index(ws_{i-j})$ in descending order
33: **return** *Final_rec_result*

4   Experiment Analyses

In this section, we design a set of experiments to validate the feasibility of our proposed service recommendation approach Rec_{SBT+CF}, in terms of recommendation accuracy, recall and efficiency in sparse environment.

4.1   Experiment Dataset and Deployment

Our paper focuses on the service recommendation problem based on users' subjective ratings. However, to the best of our knowledge, the available user-service rating data is really rare today. Therefore, as works [9, 10] did, MovieLens-1M [11] dataset is employed in our experiments for the purpose of simulation. The dataset contains 1000209 user-movie ratings applied to 3952 movies by 6040 users. Besides, as our paper only concentrates on the service recommendation in sparse environment where target user has no similar friends and target services have no similar services, we select appropriate data from MovieLens-1M to simulate the specific service recommendation scenarios.

In order to test the recommendation effect of our Rec_{SBT+CF} approach, for each recruited target user in MovieLens-1M, we divide his/her ratings into two parts with the ratio of 9:1. In other words, 90 % ratings of a target user are employed for training and the remaining 10 % ratings for testing. In order to observe the recommendation effect of our proposal, recommendation accuracy, recall and efficiency are tested in the following experiments, respectively.

(1)   **Accuracy:** The well-known *Mean Absolute Error (MAE)* [12] is recruited to measure the service recommendation accuracy, which could be calculated by (7). In (7), *Final_rec_result* is the final recommendation result set, $| X |$ denotes the element number of set X, $r^{predict}_{target-j}$ and $r^{real}_{target-j}$ represent web service ws_j's predicted rating and real rating by $user_{target}$, respectively.

$$MAE = \sum_{ws_j \in Final\_rec\_result} \frac{| r^{predict}_{target-j} - r^{real}_{target-j} |}{|Final\_rec\_result|} \qquad (7)$$

(2)   **Recall:** The recommendation recall could be calculated by (8), where *Final_rec_result* is the final recommendation result set, $| X |$ denotes the element number of set X, *Preferred_ser_set* denotes $user_{target}$'s really preferred service set (i.e., with 4* or 5* rating) in the remaining 10 % test ratings.

$$Recall = \frac{|Preferred\_ser\_set \cap Final\_rec\_result|}{|Final\_rec\_result|} \qquad (8)$$

In the experiments, we compare our proposed Rec_{SBT+CF} approach with another two approaches, i.e., *WSRec* [13] and *SBT*-SR [8]. Concretely, in *WSRec*, *r_average* $(user_{target})$ (i.e., $user_{target}$'s average rating over all his/her invoked services) and *r_average*(ws_j) (i.e., ws_j's average rating from all the users who invoked ws_j) are considered, and their average value is adopted finally to predict *user*$_{target}$'s rating over ws_j. While in our previously proposed *SBT-SR* approach, only "enemy's enemy is a friend" rule is recruited for service recommendation.

The experiments were conducted on a HP laptop with 2.40 GHz processors and 4.0 GB RAM. The machine is running under Windows XP and JAVA 1.5. Each experiment was carried out 10 times and the average results were adopted.

4.2 Experiment Results

In our experiments, six profiles are tested and compared, which will be introduced respectively. Here, symbols m and n denote the number of users and number of web services in the user-service invocation network, and P represents the predefined user similarity threshold.

(1) *Profile*1: Recommendation accuracy comparison

In this profile, we test and compare the recommendation accuracy (i.e., *MAE*, the smaller the better) of different recommendation approaches. The concrete experiment parameter settings are as below: user similarity threshold $P = 0.5$ holds; number of users, i.e., m is varied from 200 to 1000; for each user, all his/her rating records are considered. The *MAE* values of three approaches are tested and compared, whose results are shown in Fig. 5.

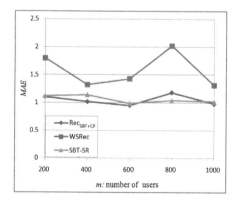
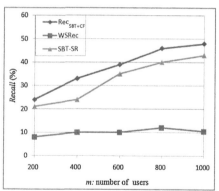

Fig. 5. Recommendation accuracy comparison   **Fig. 6.** Recommendation recall comparison

As Fig. 5 shows, the recommendation accuracy of *WSRec* is low (i.e., *MAE* is large), as *WSRec* only adopts the "average" rating from target user and target services, without considering the valuable social relationships hidden in user-service invocation network. Besides, as Fig. 5 shows, both *SBT-SR* and *Rec*$_{SBT+CF}$ outperforms *WSRec* in terms of recommendation accuracy, as the social relationships among different users are considered in both *SBT-SR* and *Rec*$_{SBT+CF}$. Furthermore, *SBT-SR* and *Rec*$_{SBT+CF}$ achieve approximate and stable recommendation accuracy, as "enemy's enemy is a friend" rule is considered in both approaches.

(2) *Profile2*: Recommendation recall comparison
In this profile, we test the recommendation recall of our *Rec*$_{SBT+CF}$ approach and compare it with *WSRec* and *SBT-SR*. Concretely, the user similarity threshold $P = 0.5$ holds; the number of users, i.e., m is varied from 200 to 1000. The *Recall* values of three approaches are tested respectively, whose results are shown in Fig. 6.

As Fig. 6 shows, the recommendation recall of *WSRec* is low; this is because the "average" idea is adopted in *WSRec*, while "average" idea often leads to a large prediction error and low recommendation hit rate. The recall of *SBT-SR* is improved by considering some social relationship (i.e., "enemy's enemy is a friend" rule) among different users. While our *Rec*$_{SBT+CF}$ outperforms *SBT-SR* in recommendation recall; this is because *Rec*$_{SBT+CF}$ considers not only "enemy's enemy is a friend" rule but also "friend's friend is a friend" rule, and hence, a higher recommendation hit rate is ensured. Besides, as Fig. 6 shows, the recall values of *SBT-SR* and *Rec*$_{SBT+CF}$ both increase with the growth of m (i.e., number of users); this is because more services (with 4* or 5* rating) would be recommended to the target user when more users as well as their respective rating records are taken into consideration, and hence, the recommendation hit rate is improved.

(3) *Profile3*: Failure rate of *Rec*$_{SBT+CF}$ w.r.t. m
As Sect. 3 indicates, our proposed *Rec*$_{SBT+CF}$ approach fails to generate any recommendation result to target user, if target user has no "enemies". While the number of users (i.e., m) is a key factor that determines whether target user has enemies, as it is difficult to find a qualified enemy of target user from few user-service ratings. Therefore, in this profile, we test the relationship between failure rate of *Rec*$_{SBT+CF}$ and the number of users (i.e., m). Concretely, the user similarity threshold $P = 0.5$ holds; m is varied from 100 to 500. The experiment result is presented in Fig. 7.

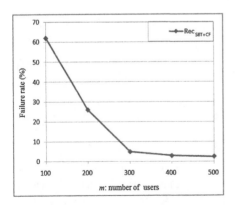

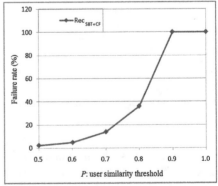

Fig. 7. Failure rate of Rec$_{SBT+CF}$ w.r.t. m   **Fig. 8.** Failure rate of Rec$_{SBT+CF}$ w.r.t. P

As Fig. 7 shows, when the number of users is small (e.g., $m = 100$), the failure rate of our recommendation approach Rec_{SBT+CF} is high (above 60 %), as it is a low-probability event to find the target user's qualified "enemy" from a small number of users. However, when m grows, the failure rate of our proposal drops sharply and stays relatively stable (around 4 %) when $m > 300$. This means that our proposed Rec_{SBT+CF} approach can often succeed in generating a recommendation result when many users are present in the user-service invocation network.

(4) *Profile4*: **Failure rate of Rec_{SBT+CF} w.r.t. P**

As formula (2) indicates, user similarity threshold, i.e., $P(0.5 \leq P \leq 1)$ is an important factor that determines whether target user has an enemy. Generally, a larger P often means a more strict filtering condition, as well as a smaller probability to find the qualified enemies of target user. Therefore, there is an indirect relationship between failure rate of Rec_{SBT+CF} and P, which will be tested in this profile. Concretely, P is varied from 0.5 to 1; the number of users, i.e., $m = 500$ holds. The experiment result is shown in Fig. 8.

As Fig. 8 shows, when P is small (e.g., $P = 0.5$), the failure rate of Rec_{SBT+CF} is low. While failure rate increases sharply with the growth of P; this is because a larger P often leads to less qualified enemies, as well as a lower recommendation hit rate. From Fig. 8, we can also observe that our proposed Rec_{SBT+CF} approach fails in recommendation (i.e., failure rate = 100 %) when $P \geq 0.9$; this is because the recruited experiment dataset MovieLens-1M is sparse, and hence, it is often difficult to find the "very dissimilar" enemies of target user.

(5) *Profile5*: **Execution efficiency of three approaches w.r.t. m**

Intuitively, it would take more time to obtain the service recommendation result from a user-service invocation network with more users. Therefore, in this profile, we test the relationships between execution efficiency of three approaches and number of users (i.e., m). The concrete experiment parameter configuration is as below: user similarity threshold $P = 0.5$ holds and the number of users, i.e., m is varied from 100 to 500; while the number of web services, i.e., $n = 1000$ holds. The experiment result is presented in Fig. 9.

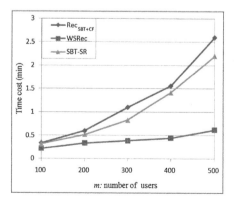
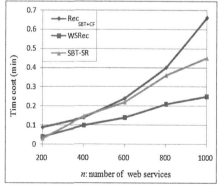

Fig. 9. Time cost comparison (w.r.t. m)   **Fig. 10.** Time cost comparison (w.r.t. n)

As Fig. 9 shows, the time cost of *WSRec* is the best and increases approximately linearly with the growth of m, as it only considers the easy-to-calculate average rating from target user and the average rating of target services. While the time costs of *SBT-SR* and Rec_{SBT+CF} both increase sharply when m grows, as more time is needed to calculate the user similarity when more users are present. Furthermore, Rec_{SBT+CF} generally requires more execution time than *SBT-SR*; this is because in *SBT-SR*, only the similarities between target user and other users, as well as the similarities between enemies of target user and other users need to be calculated; while in Rec_{SBT+CF}, the similarities between any two users would be considered. However, as Fig. 9 shows, the time cost of our proposed Rec_{SBT+CF} approach is still approximately polynomial with respect to m.

(6) *Profile6*: **Execution efficiency of** Rec_{SBT+CF} **w.r.t.** n
In this profile, we test the relationships between execution efficiency of three approaches and number of web services (i.e., n). Concretely, user similarity threshold $P = 0.5$ and number of users, i.e., $m = 200$ hold; while the number of web services, i.e., n is varied from 200 to 1000. The experiment result is presented in Fig. 10.

As Fig. 10 shows, *WSRec* performs the best in terms of execution efficiency and its time cost increases approximately linearly with the growth of n, as each service is considered only once in the average-rating calculation of *WSRec*. Similarly, *SBT-SR* also achieves linear increment of time cost when n grows, as a web service is considered only once (at most) in each user-similarity calculation process; furthermore, *SBT-SR* requires more time than *WSRec*, as the similarity calculation in *SBT-SR* often takes more computation time than the simple average-value calculation in *WSRec*. While the time cost of Rec_{SBT+CF} increases sharply when n grows, as a web service may be considered many times in the similarity-calculation process, if a web service was rated by multiple users simultaneously; besides, the recommended-degree ranking process would take more time if the number of services is large, as more recommended services would be probably returned to the target user when many web services are present in the historical user-service invocation network. However, as Fig. 10 shows, the time cost of Rec_{SBT+CF} is still approximately polynomial with respect to n.

5   Evaluation

In this section, we first analyze the time complexity of our proposed Rec_{SBT+CF}. Afterwards, related works and comparison analyses are presented, which is followed by discussions regarding the paper limitations and our future research directions.

5.1   Complexity Analyses

Suppose there are m users and n web services in user-service invocation network.

Step 1: User similarity calculation. In this step, for each user (totally m users), we calculate his/her similarity with the rest $(m - 1)$ users, based on the similarity formula in (1). While the time complexity of formula (1) is $O(n)$ as n web services are considered at most. Therefore, the time complexity of Step 1 is $O(m^2 *n)$.

Step 2: Judgment of friend or enemy. In this step, for each user (totally m users), we judge his/her relationships with the rest $(m - 1)$ users, based on judgment formula (2) and the obtained user similarity in Step 1. As the time complexity of judgment formula (2) is $O(1)$, the time complexity of Step 2 is $O(m^2)$.

Step 3: Determining "possible friends" of $user_{target}$ based on Social Balance Theory. According to Step 2, the target user $user_{target}$ has $(m - 1)$ enemies at most; likewise, each enemy has $(m - 1)$ enemies at most. Therefore, according to "enemy's enemy is friend" rule, we can obtain $(m - 1) * (m - 1)$ possible friends (here, friend repetition is considered) of $user_{target}$ in Substep 3.1. Then for each possible friend, we calculate his/her credibility by (3), whose time complexity is $O(1)$. Therefore, time complexity of Substep 3.1 is $O(m^2)$. Similarly, time complexity of Substep 3.2 is also O (m^2). With the above analyses, the time complexity of Step 3 is $O(m^2)$.

Step 4: Service recommendation. Target user $user_{target}$ has $(m - 1)$ possible friends at most, and for each possible friend, we select his/her preferred services with high ratings (at most n services) and recommend them to $user_{target}$. Therefore, we can obtain $(m - 1) * n$ recommended services (here, service repetition is considered). For each recommended service, its recommended degree could be calculated by formula (5), whose time complexity is $O(1)$. So $O(m*n)$ time complexity is necessary for determining all the recommended services (at most $n - 1$ services without considering service repetition) as well as their recommended degrees. Finally, all the recommended services (at most $n - 1$ services) are ranked in descending order based on their recommended degrees, whose time complexity is $O(n*log_2^n)$. Therefore, the time complexity of Step 4 is $O(m*n + n*log_2^n)$.

With the above analyses, a conclusion could be drawn that the total time complexity of our proposed Rec_{SBT+CF} approach is $O(m^2*n + n*log_2^n)$, which means that the service recommendation could be finished in polynomial time.

5.2   Related Works and Comparison Analyses

Collaborative Filtering is considered as an effective technique for finding the potential preference of target user, and nowadays is widely applied in service recommendation applications. In [3], a trustworthy web service discovery mechanism is brought forth, which realizes the service recommendation through the user-based Collaborative Filtering. A bidirectional service recommendation approach SD-HCF is introduced in [14], by integrating user-based and service-based collaborative filtering together, for high-quality service recommendation. However, the above recommendations approaches only consider the user similarity or service similarity, while omit other important recommendation information, e.g., trust among different users, user-service location and user interest. In view of this, user trust relationship is introduced in the recommendation models of [15] for better recommendation results, by considering not only similar but also trustable friends of target user. In [16], service recommendation is performed by considering user-service location information, where the "closest" web services would be recommended to the target user (as "closest" services often mean better service quality). While in [17], interest-aware service recommendation is put forward, by considering user interest and user-service invocation network simultaneously.

However, the above recommendation approaches often assume that (1) the target user has similar friends, or (2) the services preferred by target user own similar services, while neglecting the sparse data situation when neither (1) nor (2) holds. In view of this exceptional situation, an "average" idea is recruited in WSRec approach of [13], where r_average($user_{target}$) (i.e., $user_{target}$'s average rating over all his/her invoked web services) and r_average(ws_j) (i.e., ws_j's average rating from all the users who invoked ws_j) are considered, and the average of r_average($user_{target}$) and r_average(ws_j) is adopted finally to approximately predict $user_{target}$'s rating over ws_j. However, the "average" idea of WSRec leads to low recommendation accuracy and recall, which has been validated by the experiment results. In order to include more user-relationship information in service recommendation, we put forward an approach named SBT-SR in our previous work [8]. In SBT-SR, "enemy's enemy is a friend" rule of Social Balance Theory is recruited for recommendation, which is still not enough for exploring all the social relationships hidden in user-service invocation network. In view of this shortcoming, a novel service recommendation approach named Rec_{SBT+CF} is brought forth in this paper, which considers not only "enemy's enemy is a friend" rule but also "friend's friend is a friend" rule in Social Balance Theory. Finally, through a set of experiments deployed on MovieLens-1M dataset, we validate the feasibility and advantages of our proposal.

5.3 Further Discussions

(1) In our proposed Rec_{SBT+CF}, user similarity threshold P is an important parameter and its value is set manually (Actually, P's value is set based on our previous experiment result of user similarity based on MovieLens-1M. If P is set large (e.g., P = 0.9), then few friends or enemies of a user could be returned; while a small P (e.g., P = 0.3) does not make much sense for finding the real friends or enemies of a user), which cannot meet the personalized service recommendation requirements from various target users. In the future, we will investigate more personalized setting manner for parameter P.

(2) As Rec_{SBT+CF} is essentially a kind of CF-based recommendation approach, its time cost is still as large as other CF-based ones. In the future, we will investigate the parallel or distributed resolution to improve the recommendation efficiency.

6 Conclusions

In this paper, a novel service recommendation approach named Rec_{SBT+CF} is put forward, to deal with the service recommendation problems in sparse environment where the target user has no similar friends and the services preferred by target user have no similar services. Concretely, we first look for the "possible friends" of target user, by considering "enemy's enemy is a friend" rule and "friend's friend is a friend" rule in Social Balance Theory; afterwards, the services preferred by "possible friends" of target user are recommended to the target user. Finally, through a set of experiments deployed on MovieLens-1M dataset, we validate the feasibility and advantages of our proposal. In the future, we will improve the recommendation efficiency and investigate more personalized setting manner for similarity threshold P.

Acknowledgments. This paper is partially supported by Natural Science Foundation of China (No. 61402258), China Postdoctoral Science Foundation (No. 2015M571739), Open Project of State Key Laboratory for Novel Software Technology (No. KFKT2016B22).

References

1. Wang, J., Gao, P., Ma, Y., He, K.: Common topic group mining for web service discovery. In: Yao, L., Xie, X., Zhang, Q., Yang, L.T., Zomaya, A.Y., Jin, H. (eds.) APSCC 2015. LNCS, vol. 9464, pp. 92–107. Springer, Heidelberg (2015). doi:10.1007/978-3-319-26979-5_7

2. Fei, H., Mo, T., Wang, Y., Wu, Z., Liu, Y., Kuang, L.: The searching ranking model based on the sharing and recommending mechanism of social network. In: Yao, L., Xie, X., Zhang, Q., Yang, L.T., Zomaya, A.Y., Jin, H. (eds.) APSCC 2015. LNCS, vol. 9464, pp. 222–234. Springer, Heidelberg (2015). doi:10.1007/978-3-319-26979-5_16

3. Zapater, J.J.S., Escrivá, D.M.L., García, F.R.S., Durá, J.J.M.: Semantic web service discovery system for road traffic information services. Expert Syst. Appl. **42**(8), 3833–3842 (2015)

4. Qi, L., Dou, W., Chen, J.: Weighted principal component analysis-based service selection method for multimedia services in cloud. Computing **98**(1–2), 195–214 (2016)

5. Breese, J.S., Heckerman, D., Kadie, C.: Empirical analysis of predictive algorithms for collaborative filtering. In: Proceedings of the Fourteenth Conference on Uncertainty in Artificial Intelligence, pp. 43–52. Morgan Kaufmann Publishers, San Francisco (1998)

6. Cartwright, D., Harary, F.: Structural balance: a generalization of Heider's theory. Psychol. Rev. **63**(5), 277 (1956)

7. Sarwar, B., Karypis, G., Konstan J., et al.: Item-based collaborative filtering recommendation algorithms. In: 10th International Conference on World Wide Web, pp. 285–295. ACM Press, New York (2001)

8. Qi, L., Zhang, X., Wen, Y., Zhou, Y.: A social balance theory-based service recommendation approach. In: Yao, L., Xie, X., Zhang, Q., Yang, L.T., Zomaya, A.Y., Jin, H. (eds.) APSCC 2015. LNCS, vol. 9464, pp. 48–60. Springer, Heidelberg (2015). doi:10.1007/978-3-319-26979-5_4

9. Ma, Y., Wang, S., Hung, P.C., Hsu, C.H., Sun, Q., Yang, F.: A highly accurate prediction algorithm for unknown web service QoS values. IEEE T. Serv. Comput. **9**(4), 911–923 (2016)

10. Gong, M., Xu, Z., Xu, L., Li, Y., Chen, L.: Recommending web service based on user relationships and preferences. In: 20th IEEE International Conference on Web Services, pp. 380–386. IEEE Press, New York (2013)

11. MovieLens-1M Dataset. http://www.grouplens.org/datasets/movielens/

12. Mayer, D., Butler, D.: Statistical validation. Ecol. Model. **68**(1), 21–32 (1993)

13. Zheng, Z., Ma, H., Lyu, M.R., King, I.: QoS-aware web service recommendation by collaborative filtering. IEEE Trans. Serv. Comput. **4**(2), 140–152 (2011)

14. Cao, J., Wu, Z., Wang, Y., et al.: Hybrid collaborative filtering algorithm for bidirectional web service recommendation. Knowl. Inf. Syst. **36**(3), 607–627 (2013)

15. Tang, M., Xu, Y., Liu, J., Zheng, Z., Liu, F.: Combining global and local trust for service recommendation. In: 21st IEEE International Conference on Web Services, pp. 305–312. IEEE Press, New York (2014)

16. Jiang, D., Guo, X., Gao, Y., Liu, J., Li, H., Cheng, N.: Locations recommendation based on check-in data from location-based social network. In: 22nd International Conference on Geoinformatics, pp. 1–4. IEEE Press, New York (2014)

17. Cao, B., Liu, J., Tang, M., Zheng, Z., Wang, G.: mashup service recommendation based on user interest and social network. In: 20th IEEE International Conference on Web Services, pp. 99–106. IEEE Press, New York (2013)

Analysis of Big Data Platform with OpenStack and Hadoop

Xiaoyan Li[1], Zhihui Lu[1(✉)], Nini Wang[2], Jie Wu[2], and Shalin Huang[3]

[1] School of Computer Science, Fudan University, Shanghai 200433, China
{xyli14,lzh}@fudan.edu.cn
[2] Engineering Research Center of Cyber Security, Auditing and Monitoring, Ministry of Education, Shanghai 200433, China
{14210240052,jwu}@fudan.edu.cn
[3] Wangsu Science & Technology Co., Ltd., Shanghai 200433, China
sallyhuang@chinanetcenter.com

Abstract. In the era of big data, the cloud infrastructure needs to strongly support big data. As a distributed computational framework, Hadoop is one of the de facto leading software tools for solving big data problems. The cloud infrastructure has been proven to be a good support for three-tier architecture applications. In this paper, we construct a Hadoop big data platform based on OpenStack cloud. At the same time, we design three experimental scenarios, carry out a set of experiments using the standard Hadoop benchmarks TestDFSIO, TeraSort and PI, and examine the performance. Our experiments reveal that the disk read operation of physical servers can be a bottleneck for TestDFSIO and TeraSort. Wider allocation of VMs over physical servers achieves better performance for read jobs of TestDFSIO and TeraSort. For CPU-intensive job PI, the best practice is to centralize the allocation of VMs over physical machines.

Keywords: Hadoop · Benchmarks · Big data · HDFS · Cluster · Openstack · Cloud

1 Introduction

Big data [1] era is coming. Many definitions of big data are given by researchers such as big data [2] is the data that is massive, too fast or too hard for existing tools to handle and process. Here massive means the size of data can range from petabytes (PB) to exabytes (EB) or to zettabytes (ZB) [3]. It can be generated through many sources like business processes, transactions, social networking sites, web servers, etc. and remains in structured as well as unstructured form [4].

Big data refers to the technologies and architectures, which were developed to capture, store, process and run better quality volumes of data in lesser amount of time or even in real time [5]. It is a system that lets digitize massive amounts of information and amalgamating it with on hand databases.

Hadoop [6] (Apache) is one of these big data technologies and is one of the de facto leading software tools for solving big data problems. Hadoop provides a distributed

© Springer International Publishing AG 2016
G. Wang et al. (Eds.): APSCC 2016, LNCS 10065, pp. 375–390, 2016.
DOI: 10.1007/978-3-319-49178-3_29

computational framework Map-Reduce and a reliable scalable distributed file system HDFS(Hadoop Distributed File System) for the analysis and transformation of large amounts of data [7].

MapReduce [8] provides a computational framework for data processing. An MR program only consists of two functions, called Map and Reduce, which are supplied by the user and depend on the user's purposes.

A map function is used to process input key/value pairs and generate intermediate key/values, and a reduce function is used to merge all intermediate pairs associated with the same key and then generate outputs [9].

In recent years, the cloud infrastructure has been proven to be a good support for three-tier architecture applications, such as websites. But in the era of big data, the cloud infrastructure needs to strongly support big data application platform, such as Hadoop and Spark. In this paper, we propose a cloud-based framework based on OpenStack using Hadoop as a big data platform. At the same time, we design three experimental scenarios, carry out a set of experiments using the standard Hadoop benchmarks, namely TestDFSIO, TeraSort and PI, and examine the performance.

The rest of this paper is organized as follows: we review related work in Sect. 2. In Sect. 3, experimental setup is given. In Sect. 4, we design three experimental scenarios. Section 5 shows the results and the conclusions. Finally, we summarize the considerations and propose our future work in Sect. 6.

2   Related Work

To reduce the machine management difficulties, virtualization is used as a key technique for easy deployment, configuration, scheduling and efficient resource utilization. Xen [10], Kernel-based Virtual Machine (KVM) [11] and VMware [12] are well-known virtualization softwares. In [13], Jack Li et al. found that KVM was better for disk reading. So we examine the performance of VM Hadoop clusters on KVM from VM number, configuration and allocation.

Ishii M et al. built in [14] a Hadoop performance model and examined how the performance was affected by changing VM configuration, allocation of VMs over physical machines, and multiplicity of jobs. They found that performance of the I/O-intensive jobs was more sensitive to the virtualization overhead than that of CPU-intensive jobs. In our paper, we choose I/O-intensive job and CPU-intensive job to figure out the performance differences among different VM placements over physical servers and the influence of the number of VMs when the number of total VCPUs and total memory are fixed.

In [15], the authors proposed a simple big data workload differentiation, their results show that CPU intensive workloads consume more power and memory bandwidth while disk intensive workloads usually require more memory. But they didn't find out the bottlenecks of CPU intensive or disk intensive workloads.

In [16], Fan et al. designed a heuristic performance diagnostic tool which evaluates the validity and correctness of virtualized Hadoop by analyzing the job traces of popular big data benchmarks. With this tool, users could quickly identify the bottleneck according to hints provided by this tool. We find the bottlenecks of TestDFSIO and TeraSort in our paper.

The main contributions we make are listed below:

- Our experiments reveal that the disk read operation of physical servers can be a bottleneck for TestDFSIO and TeraSort.
- We find that if there is enough resource, the best practice is to increase the number of VMs and not to increase the number of VCPUs in a VM for I/O intensive job.
- Our experiments show that wider allocation over physical servers achieves better performance for read jobs of TestDFSIO and TeraSort. For CPU-intensive job PI, the best practice is to centralize the allocation of VMs over physical machines.

3 Experimental Setup

In this section, we describe the environment for our experiments. In Sects. 3.1 and 3.2, we give an overview of our experimental scenario and physical configurations, and in Sect. 3.3, we provide a brief overview of the benchmarks we adopt.

3.1 OpenStack Cloud-Based Hadoop

Figure 1 provides an overview of the environment for our experiments.

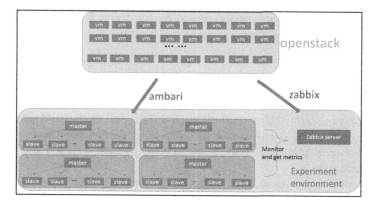

Fig. 1. Big data platform design

We use OpenStack as our cloud platform to launch the VM resource pool we need in the experiment, and we use Ambari to deploy Hadoop cluster into VM resource pool. And through installing one Zabbix server, we build a monitor system to retrieve metrics from the Hadoop clusters.

3.2   Physical Configurations

Table 1 provides an overview of physical configurations we use for our experiments.

Table 1. Hardware configuration

Physical machine	
Processor	Xeon E5-2603 v3
Memory	64 G
Operating System	CentOS 7.1
Disk	dell-10 k-2 TB

3.3   Benchmark

Several benchmarks are tested from Hadoop example applications: PI, TestDFSIO, and TeraSort.

- PI
  PI is a map/reduce program that estimates pi using a quasi-Monte Carlo method [17]. The map tasks are all independent and the single reduce task gathers very little data from the map tasks.
- TestDFSIO
  TestDFSIO is a map/reduce program that reads/writes random data from/to large files. It is mainly used to test the I/O speed of the cluster.
- TeraSort
  TeraSort is a standard benchmark created by Jim Gray. TeraSort is a two-phase Hadoop workload that performs in-place sort of all the words of a given data file.

4   Scenario Design

We design three experimental scenarios to examine the performance of Hadoop in this paper. We run the I/O intensive and CPU intensive experiments to see if there is difference between them. TestDFSIO is the I/O-intensive job, TeraSort and PI are the CPU-intensive jobs.

We get metrics such as memory usage, CPU utilization, read/write speed of disk, network input/output throughput along with other metrics by Zabbix. We select typical metrics to analyze their characteristics and achieve the purpose of each scenario.

4.1   Cluster Scalability Test

Target for Cluster Scalability Test: The purpose of this scenario is to figure out the bottleneck resource of VM/PM by adding VMs of same spec to the cluster.

Experiment Assumption for Cluster Scalability Test: The disk I/O of physical servers can be the bottleneck for I/O-intensive job, while CPU can be the bottleneck for CPU-intensive job. That is, in this scenario, disk write or read operation is the bottleneck for TestDFSIO, and CPU is the bottleneck for TeraSort.

Environment Brief Diagram: This environment makes some specific designs. All the VMs are in one cluster, which includes one master and several slaves. The slaves are all configured in the same way. But we use the cluster in three kinds of situations. Every job runs separately in one situation and the metrics are different. This allows us to compare results and draw conclusions. The total resources of three scenarios increase proportionately.

All the slaves are divided into three kinds of situations to do the test job. We launched VMs with proportional configuration and quantity. We rationally use the resources.

The Configuration and Distribution: There are totally 9 physical machines to deploy this environment. Every physical machine runs centOS 7.1 as operating system and all the virtual machines are Ubuntu 12.04. The Hadoop version is 2.6. We separate managing and monitoring nodes with job nodes. One master node, one Ambari server node and one Zabbix server node are on one physical machine. All the slave nodes are on the other 8 physical machines according to the arrangement as Fig. 2 shows. The configurations are shown in Table 2.

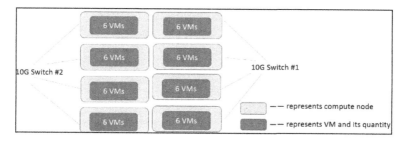

Fig. 2. Cluster scalability test environment diagram

Table 2. Configuration table of cluster scalability test

Node	CPU	Memory	Disk
Master	2 cores	8 G	100 G
Slave	1 cores	5 G	80 G
Ambari server	1 core	2 G	100 G
Zabbix server	8 cores	16 G	100 G

4.2 VM Specification Test

Target for VM Specification Test: The purpose of this scenario is to figure out the influence of the number of VMs when the number of total VCPUs and total memory are fixed.

Experiment Assumption for VM Specification Test: The disk I/O of physical servers can be bottlenecks for I/O-intensive job which we will prove in the cluster scalability scenario, while CPU intensive job is less sensitive to disk I/O if the number of VCPUs does not exceed the number of physical cores. That is, in this scenario, for I/O-intensive job, the cluster with more VMs will perform better. And for a CPU intensive job, the number of VMs in a cluster does not make a difference since the total number of VCPUs, in addition to being enough, are equal to or less than the total physical cores.

Environment Brief Diagram: For this environment, all the VMs are divided into two clusters as Fig. 3 shows, each including one master and several slaves. The slaves in the same cluster use the same configuration and differ from the slaves in the other cluster. Every job runs separately in two clusters and the metrics are different. This allows us to compare the results and draw conclusions. The total resources of two clusters are the same.

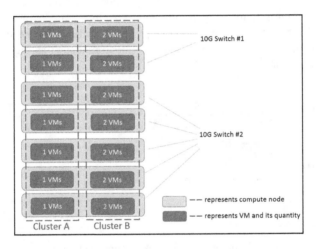

Fig. 3. VM Specification Test environment diagram

All the slaves are divided into two clusters to do the test job. We launch VMs with proportional configuration and quantity. We rationally use the resources.

The Configuration and Distribution: We use the same Hadoop version, operating systems and configurations for specification test as the ones for scalability test.

The configurations are shown in Table 3.

Table 3. Configuration table of VM specification test

Node	CPU	Memory	Disk
Master	2 cores	8 G	100 G
Slaves in cluster A	4 cores	10 G	100 G
Slaves in cluster B	2 cores	5 G	100 G
Ambari server	1 core	2 G	100 G
Zabbix server	8 cores	16 G	100 G

4.3 VM Placement Test

Target for VM Placement Test: The purpose of this scenario is to figure out the performance differences among different VM placements over physical servers with homogeneous VMs.

Experiment Assumption for VM Placement Test: In this scenario, for the I/O-intensive job, when the number of VMs in a physical server is changed, the centralized allocation needs more disk read and writes. Thus, the wider allocation over physical servers achieves a better performance.

Since the number of VCPUs used in VMs is less than the number of physical cores so that no context switch occurs, the VM allocation over physical servers does not affect the CPU-intensive job case.

Environment Brief Diagram: All the slaves are divided into three clusters to do the test job as Fig. 4 shows. We launched VMs which functioned as slaves with the same configuration.

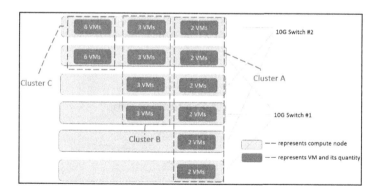

Fig. 4. VM placement test environment diagram

The Configuration and Distribution: We use the same Hadoop version, operating systems and configurations for VM placement test as the ones for the scalability test.

The configurations are shown in Table 4.

Table 4. Configuration table of VM placement test

Node	CPU	Memory	Disk
Master	2 cores	8 G	100 G
Slaves	1 core	5 G	80 G
Ambari server	1 core	2 G	100 G
Zabbix server	8 cores	16 G	100 G

5   Results and Discussion

5.1   Cluster Scalability Test

I/O-intensive Job-TestDFSIO: We set the VMs to 12, 24, 36, 48, set the map number to 8, 80, 800, 1600, 4000, set the reduce number to 1 and the file size to 128 M. The map number is equal to the total data size divided by the file size. As the reduce phase only need to collect and summarize all the statistical information of map tasks, we set the reduce number to 1. After we finish the write job of TestDFSIO, we record the total time of job printed in the Hadoop running console, the data size and calculate the total throughput as Fig. 5 shows.

$$< Total\,Throughput > \; = \; < Total\,data\,size > / < Job\,execution\,time >$$

When the data scale is set to 500 G, the hard disks volume of each task node is not enough during the process when VMs are 12 and 24, so the experiment of 500 G data can't be performed.

From Fig. 5 we can see that in most cases, when the data size is fixed, the total throughput is higher with a larger VM number. When the data size is more than 100 G with VMs at 48, the increment speed of total throughput is lower as the write job reaches the bottleneck.

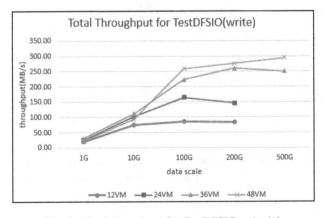

Fig. 5. Total throughput for TestDFSIO write job

So we get data from Zabbix when the data scale is 100 GB and draw the figures to find the bottleneck of TestDFSIO write job.

For the TestDFSIO write job, only map tasks execute actual workload. From Fig. 6 we can see 4 points as below:

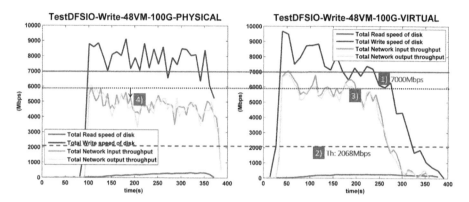

Fig. 6. Metrics for TestDFSIO write job

(1) *Disk throughput reaches above* 7000 *Mbps/8 PM (both in VM / PM layer.)*
(2) *Actual total throughput is* 2068 *Mbps. The disk throughput is much more than the actual total throughput as HDFS replica working during write job.*
(3) *Virtual environment: The network throughput is almost three times as much as the actual total throughput as HDFS replica working during write job and the HDFS replica is 3.*
(4) *Physical environment: Network transfer is less than virtual environment as local VM transfer within one PM is hidden from PM view.*

From Fig. 7 we can see CPU isn't fully utilized either in physical machines or in virtual machines, so CPU isn't the bottleneck.

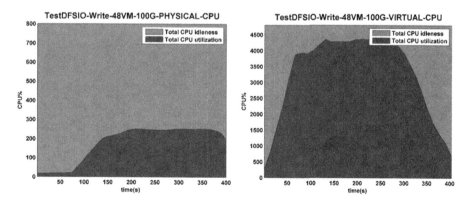

Fig. 7. Physical and Virtual CPU for TestDFSIO write job

We use the same configuration for read jobs as the one for writes. After we finish the read job of TestDFSIO, we record the relevant data as Fig. 8 shows.

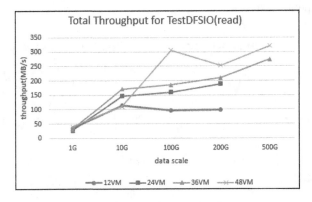

Fig. 8. Total throughput for TestDFSIO read job

When data scale is set to 500 G, the reason why the experiments can't be performed when VMs are 12 and 24 is the same as that for the write job.

From the Fig. 8 we can draw the same conclusion for read jobs as the one for writes.

So we get data from Zabbix and draw the figures to find the bottleneck of TestDFSIO read job. As the CPU utilization of read job is almost the same as that of the write job and CPU isn't fully utilized, we can conclude that CPU isn't the bottleneck.

For TestDFSIO read job, only map tasks execute actual workload. From Fig. 9 we can see 3 points as below:

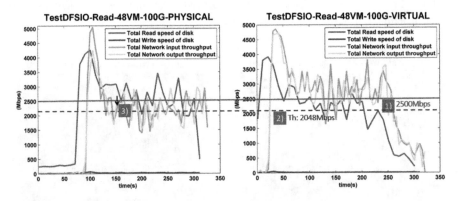

Fig. 9. Metrics for TestDFSIO read job

(1) *Disk throughput is* 2500–3000 Mbps/8 PM, *which is much lower than that of write.*

(2) *Actual Total Throughput is* 2048 Mbps, *which is almost the same as the disk read speed.*

(3) *Physical environment: The number of network transfer is less than the one in virtual environment as local VM transfer within one PM is hidden from PM view.*

Analysis and Conclusion of Cluster Scalability Test: For TestDFSIO write job, disk write is over 7000 Mbps/8 PM in TestDFSIO write. For the read job, disk read throughput is 1/3 of the disk write. Since network traffic throughput is higher in write test, disk read operation seems to be the bottleneck.

Using the same method we find that disk read operation, not the CPU is also the bottleneck of TeraSort, which doesn't bear out our assumption. The reason may be that TeraSort is not a particularly CPU-intensive job, and that it also needs a lot of writing and reading. So it is consistent with the assumption of the I/O-intensive job.

For the scalability test, we conclude that for TestDFSIO and TeraSort, the bottleneck is disk read operation.

5.2   VM Specification Test

I/O-intensive Job-TestDFSIO: We set the map number to 28, the reduce number to 1 and the file size to 1000 M. After we finish the write job of TestDFSIO, we record the relevant data as Fig. 10 shows.

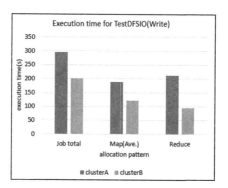

Fig. 10. Execution time for TestDFSIO write job

From Fig. 10 we can see that cluster B have better performance than cluster A. The total time of cluster B is 46 % less than cluster A.

CPU-intensive Job-PI: We change the map number to 28, set the reduce number to 1 and the execute number per map to $5*10^9$. By changing the number of map and the execute number per map, we can indicate the desired PI accuracy. The larger of the

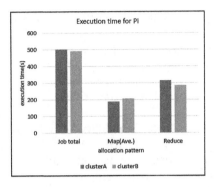

Fig. 11. Execution time for PI

multiplication of these two, the higher the accuracy. As the reduce phase only need to collect the statistical information of map tasks, we set the reduce number to 1. After we finish the job of PI, we record the relevant data as Fig. 11 shows.

VMs in cluster A and B are fully used when map number is 100. From Fig. 11 we can see that the performance of cluster B doesn't show much difference from that of cluster A. The performance degradation caused by the VM configuration change is 2 % for PI.

Analysis and Conclusion of VM Specification Test: We first set the map number to 28 for the write job of TestDFSIO. From the total execution time of the job we can see that for write, cluster B out-performs cluster A by 46 %. So we speculate that for I/O-intensive jobs, the best practice is to increase the number of VMs and not to increase the number of VCPUs in a VM.

Then we set the map number to 100 for PI, the performance of cluster B doesn't show much difference from that of cluster A. The performance degradation caused by the VM configuration change is 2 % for PI. So we conclude that for CPU-intensive job, the number of VMs in a cluster does not make much difference since the total number of VCPUs is enough and I/O utilization is small enough.

5.3   VM Placement Test

I/O-intensive Job-TestDFSIO: We set the map number to 48, the reduce number to 1 and the file size to 500 M. After we finish the read job of TestDFSIO, we record the relevant data as Fig. 12 shows.

VMs in cluster A, B and C are fully used when map number is 48. From Fig. 12 we can see that the total time of cluster A, B and C is increasing. The average time of map is increasing, too. We conclude that the wider allocation over physical servers achieves better performance for TestDFSIO.

CPU-intensive Job-TeraSort: We set the map number to 400, the reduce number to 12 and the sort size to 50 G. The map number is equal to the total data size divided by

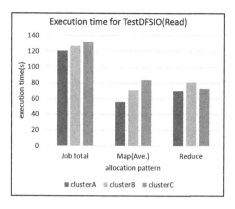

Fig. 12. Execution time for TestDFSIO read job

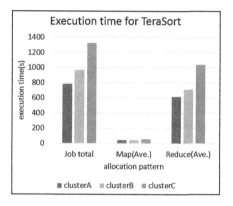

Fig. 13. Execution time for TeraSort

the file size. The reduce number is equal to the number of CPU cores. After we finish TeraSort job, we record the relevant data as Fig. 13 shows.

VMs in cluster A, B and C are fully utilized. From the Fig. 13 we can see that the total time difference among the three patterns is mainly caused by the cost of the reduce phase, and the total time of cluster A, B and C is increasing. We conclude that the wider allocation over physical servers achieves better performance for TeraSort.

CPU-intensive Job-PI: We set the map number to 48, the reduce number to 1 and the execute number per map to $1*10^9$. After we finish the job of PI, we record related data as Fig. 14 shows.

VMs in cluster A, B and C are fully utilized. From Fig. 14 we can see, the performance of cluster A and B doesn't show much difference. Cluster C achieves 21 % better performance than cluster A, achieves 26 % better performance than cluster B.

We conclude that the centralized allocation of VMs over physical machines can improve the efficiency of the CPU-intensive job-PI.

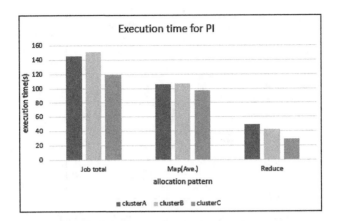

Fig. 14. Execution time for PI

Analysis and Conclusion of VM Placement Test: We set the map number to 48 for read jobs of TestDFSIO, set the map number to 400 for TeraSort jobs and we make full use of the VMs in 3 clusters for both of them. For TestDFSIO and TeraSort jobs, the total time of cluster A, B and C is increasing. So we conclude that the wider allocation over physical servers achieves better performance for TestDFSIO and TeraSort.

We set the map number to 48 for CPU-intensive job PI and we make full use of the VMs in this scenario in 3 clusters. Cluster C achieves 21 % better performance than cluster A, achieves 26 % better performance than cluster B. That is, the most centralized allocation of VMs over physical machines has the best performance.

For this scenario, we conclude that the wider allocation over physical servers achieves the better performance for TestDFSIO and TeraSort. The centralized allocation of VMs over physical machines can improve the efficiency of a CPU-intensive job-PI.

5.4   Summary

For scalability test, we conclude that for both TestDFSIO and TeraSort, the bottleneck is disk read operation.

For VM specification test, we conclude that for the I/O intensive job, the best practice is to increase the number of VMs and not to increase the number of VCPUs in a VM, for CPU intensive job-PI, the number of VMs in a cluster does not make big difference. The conclusion is the same as [14].

For the VM placement test, we conclude that the wider allocation over physical servers achieves the better performance for read job of TestDFSIO and TeraSort. TeraSort is not a typical CPU intensive job and it conforms to the assumption of the I/O intensive job. Centralized allocation of VMs over physical machines can improve the efficiency of a CPU-intensive job PI, which is not consistent with the conclusion of [14], possibly due to some context switch.

6 Conclusion and Prospect

In this paper, we have designed three experimental scenarios and compared their performances. Our experiments revealed that the disk read operation of physical servers can be bottlenecks for TestDFSIO and TeraSort. If the resource is enough, the best practice is to increase the number of VMs and not to increase the number of VCPUs in a VM for I/O intensive job. Wider allocation over physical servers achieves better performance for read job of TestDFSIO and TeraSort. For CPU-intensive job PI, the best practice is to centralize allocation of VMs over physical machines.

In our future work, the model of Hadoop will be studied and docker will be integrated into the big data system. We will test Hadoop performance by comparing HDFS and Ceph. Moreover, the rationality of parameter selection such as the number of map and reduce tasks and the influence of data size need to be further investigated.

Acknowledgments. This work is supported by Shanghai 2016 Innovation Action Project under Grant 16DZ1100200-Data-trade-supporting Big data Testbed. This work is also supported by 2016–2019 National Natural Science Foundation of China under Grant No. 61572137-Multiple Clouds based CDN as a Service Key Technology Research, Shanghai 2015 Innovation Action Project under Grant No. 1551110700 - New media-oriented Big data analysis and content delivery key technology and application, and Fudan-Hitachi Innovative Software Technology Joint Project-Cloud Platform Design for Big data.

References

1. Snijders, C., Matzat, U., Reips, U.D.: "Big Data": big gaps of knowledge in the field of internet science. Int. J. Internet Sci. **7**(1), 1–5 (2012)
2. Madden, S.: From databases to big data. IEEE Internet Comput. **16**(3), 4–6 (2012)
3. Kotiyal, B., Kumar, A., Pant, B., et al.: Big data: mining of log file through Hadoop. In: 2013 International Conference on Human Computer Interactions (ICHCI), pp. 1–7. IEEE (2013)
4. Patel, A.B., Birla, M., Nair, U.: Addressing big data problem using Hadoop and Map Reduce. In: 2012 Nirma University International Conference on Engineering (NUiCONE), pp. 1–5. IEEE (2012)
5. Nandimath, J., Banerjee, E., Patil, A., et al.: Big data analysis using Apache Hadoop. In: 2013 IEEE 14th International Conference on Information Reuse and Integration (IRI), pp. 700–703. IEEE (2013)
6. Hadoop. http://Hadoop.apache.org/Introduction
7. Song, G., Meng, Z., Huet, F., et al.: A Hadoop MapReduce performance prediction method. In: High Performance Computing and Communications, pp. 820–825. IEEE (2013)
8. Dean, J., Ghemawat, S.: MapReduce: simplified data processing on large clusters. Commun. ACM **51**(1), 107–113 (2008)
9. Yang, H., Dasdan, A., Hsiao, R.L., et al.: Map-reduce-merge: simplified relational data processing on large clusters. In: Proceedings of the 2007 ACM SIGMOD International Conference on Management of Data, pp. 1029–1040. ACM (2007)
10. Ko, B.M., Lee, J., Jo, H.: Toward enhancing block I/O performance for virtualized Hadoop cluster. In: Proceedings of the 2014 IEEE/ACM 7th International Conference on Utility and Cloud Computing, pp. 481–482. IEEE Computer Society (2014)

11. Vasconcelos, P.R.M., de Araújo Freitas, G.A.: Performance analysis of Hadoop MapReduce on an OpenNebula cloud with KVM and OpenVZ virtualizations. In: 2014 9th International Conference for Internet Technology and Secured Transactions (ICITST), pp. 471–476. IEEE (2014)

12. Kontagora, M., Gonzalez-Velez, H.: Benchmarking a MapReduce environment on a full virtualisation platform. In: 2010 International Conference on Complex, Intelligent and Software Intensive Systems (CISIS), pp. 433–438. IEEE (2010)

13. Li, J., Wang Q, Jayasinghe D, et al.: Performance overhead among three hypervisors: an experimental study using Hadoop benchmarks. In: 2013 IEEE International Congress on Big Data, pp. 9–16. IEEE (2013)

14. Ishii, M., Han, J., Makino, H.: Design and performance evaluation for Hadoop clusters on virtualized environment. In: The International Conference on Information Networking 2013 (ICOIN), pp. 244–249. IEEE (2013)

15. Aggarwal, S., Phadke, S., Bhandarkar, M.: Characterization of Hadoop jobs using unsupervised learning. In: 2010 IEEE Second International Conference on Cloud Computing Technology and Science (CloudCom), pp. 748–753. IEEE (2010)

16. Bortnikov, E., Frank, A., Hillel, E., et al.: Predicting execution bottlenecks in map-reduce clusters. Presented as part of the, p. 18 (2012)

17. Yin, J., Qiao, Y.: Performance modeling and optimization of MapReduce programs. In: 2014 IEEE 3rd International Conference on Cloud Computing and Intelligence Systems, pp. 180–186. IEEE (2014)

Using Relational Topic Model and Factorization Machines to Recommend Web APIs for Mashup Creation

Buqing Cao[1,2(✉)], Min Shi[1], Xiaoqing (Frank) Liu[3], Jianxun Liu[1], and Mingdong Tang[1]

[1] School of Computer Science and Engineering, Hunan University of Science and Technology, Xiangtan 411201, China
buqingcao@gmail.com, toshimin132@gmail.com,
ljx529@gmail.com, tangmingdong@gmail.com
[2] State Key Laboratory of Software Engineering, Wuhan University, Wuhan 430072, China
[3] Computer Science and Computer Engineering Department, University of Arkansas, Fayetteville 72701, USA
frankliu@uark.edu

Abstract. The rapid growth in the number of Web APIs, coupled with the myriad of functionally similar Web APIs, makes it difficult to find suitable Web APIs to develop Mashup applications. Even if the existing Web APIs recommendation methods show improvements in service discovery, the accuracy of them can be significantly improved due to overlooking the impact of sparsity and dimension of relationships between Mashup and Web APIs on recommendation accuracy. In this paper, we propose a Web APIs recommendation method for Mashup creation by combining relational topic model and factorization machines technique. This method firstly uses relational topic model to characterize the relationships among Mashup, Web APIs, and their links, and mine the latent topics derived by the relationships. Secondly, it exploits factorization machines to train the latent topics for predicting the link relationship among Mashup and Web APIs to recommend adequate relevant top-k Web APIs for target Mashup creation. Finally, we conduct a comprehensive evaluation to measure performance of our method. Compared with other existing recommendation approaches, experimental results show that our approach achieves a significant improvement in terms of precision, recall, and F-measure.

Keywords: Relational topic model · Factorization machines · Web APIs recommendation · Mashup creation · Service discovery

1 Introduction

Recently, Mashup technology, which allows software developers to compose existing Web APIs to create new or value-added composite RESTful Web services, has emerged as a promising software development method in a service-oriented environment [1]. Several online Mashups and Web APIs repositories have been established,

© Springer International Publishing AG 2016
G. Wang et al. (Eds.): APSCC 2016, LNCS 10065, pp. 391–407, 2016.
DOI: 10.1007/978-3-319-49178-3_30

such as ProgrammableWeb, myExperiment, and Biocatalogue. In these repositories, there are a large number of published Web APIs for providing external invocation, and users can compose various Web APIs with different functionality to create Mashup for completing users' complex requirement [1].

To fulfill Mashup development, selecting the most suitable Web APIs from the repositories for users is a very important task. However, it becomes a significant challenge due to the rapid growth in the number of available Web APIs, coupled with the myriad of functionally similar Web APIs. For example, ProgrammableWeb has published more than 13872 Web APIs as to November 2015. When a user wants to develop a Mashup application related to mobile, there are more than 1500 Web APIs found by the search engine of ProgrammableWeb site. It is difficult for the user to identify the most suitable Web APIs from so many Web APIs with the related functionality of mobile to complete users' Mashup development. Moreover, we observed that some Web APIs returned by the search engine do not meet users' Mashup development requirement.

To address the above problem, some researchers exploit service recommendation techniques to improve the accuracy of Web service discovery [2–5]. Their methods mainly include functionality-based, QoS-based, relationship-based, and hybrid service recommendations. Some of them explored similarity matching measurement between users' requirement and services to rank and recommend web services with high-matching [2]. Others focused on the issue of QoS-based service recommendation for predicting QoS (Quality of Service) of current user by collecting information from other similar users or items and recommend the optimal service to user [3]. Recently, several researchers considered correlation relationship among services and used service ecology network to achieve relationship-based service recommendation [4]. Especially, few works integrated two or manifold of functionality-based, QoS-based, and relationship-based service recommendations when recommending services [5, 6].

Even if the above existing methods show improvements in service recommendation, the accuracy of them can be significantly improved. To begin with, the sparsity problem of the historical links or invocations between Mashup and Web APIs, which result in poor recommendation accuracy. According to existing investigation [7], most Mashups only contain no more than 3 Web APIs, that is to say, it will be failed when a user wants to find more suitable Web APIs for a Mashup creation due to the huge sparsity of Web APIs in Mashups. Some researchers addressed on the issue [8, 9] and exploited topic model (e.g. Latent Dirichlet Allocation (LDA) [10]) to improve the accuracy of recommendation. The topic model technique was exploited to identify and derive latent topics of Mashup and Web APIs, and discover implicit semantic correlation between them [8, 9]. A limitation of these works is that only independent Mashup or Web APIs documents were used to derive document vector space or individual topics for calculating their similarity. Actually, the historical link relationships between Mashup and Web APIs can be identified and modeled to derive useful, latent topics for significantly improving recommendation accuracy [11]. Based on the LDA, J. Chang et al. developed relational topic model (RTM) [12] to model documents and the links between them. The RTM can be used to summarize a network of documents, predict links between them. In this paper, we use the RTM to characterize the relationships among Mashup, Web APIs, and their links for mining the latent topics, which served as a basis of similarity measurement between Mashup and Web APIs.

Moreover, some researchers exploit matrix factorization to decompose historical Mashup-Web API interactions (links) for Web APIs recommendations [13, 14]. Other research works considered matrix factorization rely on rich records of historical interactions, and incorporated users' social relations [15] or location similarity [16] into service recommendation. We observed that, some important multi-dimension relationships factors, such as co-occurrence and popularity of Web APIs in historical Mashup, can be incorporated into matrix factorization model to boost the accuracy of Web APIs recommendation. Matrix factorization can relieve the sparsity between Mashup and Web APIs, but it is not applicable for general prediction task but work only with special, single input data. When the sparsity and dimension of the input data (Mashup and Web APIs) for matrix factorization model increase, the performance of matrix factorization based Web APIs recommendation will decrease. S. Rendle et al. proposed factorization machines (FMs) [17, 18], a general predictor working with any real valued feature vector, which can model all interactions between input variables with multiple dimensions, using factorized parameters. It can estimate interactions even in problems with huge sparsity (like Mashup-Web APIs matrix). In this paper, we exploit the FMs instead of matrix factorization to train the multi-dimension relationships between Mashup and Web APIs for predicting the link relationship between them.

Inspired by above approaches, and our observation of impacts of sparsity and dimension of relationships between Mashup and Web APIs on recommendation accuracy, we propose to combine RTM and FMs for recommending Web APIs in Mashup creation. The contributions are summarized as follows:

- *We use the RTM to model the link relationship between Mashup and Web APIs, and derive the topics of Mashup and Web APIs to characterize the latent correlation relationship between them. In the RTM, the similarity between Mashup and Web APIs is measured by an improved cosine similarity computation method.*
- *We use the FMs to train the topics derived by RTM for predicting the link relationship among Mashup and Web APIs to recommend adequate relevant top-k Web APIs for target Mashup. In the FMs, multiple dimension information is considered as input data to improve the prediction accuracy.*
- *We develop a real-world dataset from ProgrammableWeb and conduct a set of experiments. Compared with other existing approaches, the experimental results show that our method achieves a significant improvement in recommendation accuracy.*

The rest of this paper is organized as follows: Sect. 2 presents the proposed method. Section 3 describes the experimental results. Section 4 discusses related works. Finally, we draw conclusions and discuss our future work in Sect. 5.

2 Method Overview

In this section, we firstly define the Web APIs recommendation problem for Mashup creation, and then model the relationships between Mashup and Web APIs via the RTM, to derive latent topics information of Mashup and Web APIs. Finally, we use the FMs to train the latent topics information to predict the probability distribution of Web APIs and recommend *top-k* Web APIs for target Mashup.

2.1 Problem Definition

Formally, a description document of a Mashup m is represented as $W^{(m)} = \{w_1, w_2, \ldots, w_{|W^{(m)}|}\}$, where w_i is the ith word of the document, and $|W^{(m)}|$ is the number of words the document contains. Analogously, a description document of an API a is denoted as $W^{(a)} = \{w_1, w_2, \ldots, w_{|W^{(a)}|}\}$, where w_i is the ith word of the document, and $|W^{(a)}|$ is the number of words the document contains. For a newly developed Mashup m' with a description document $w_{m'}$, our system aims to automatically recommend adequate relevant Web APIs to it.

2.2 The Relationships Modeling Between Mashup and Web APIs via RTM

The RTM [12], developed by J. Chang and D. M. Blei in 2009, is a hierarchical topic probabilistic model taking into account both the documents itself and the links between them. The RTM is based on LDA, which is a generative probabilistic model that documents are represented as random mixtures over latent topics and each topic is characterized by a distribution over words. In the RTM, each documents is first generated from topics as in LDA, the links between documents are then modeled as binary variable, one for each pair of documents. The links between documents depend on the distance between their topic proportions. In this paper, we use the RTM to model both the documents of Mashup and Web APIs, and their link relationship. The probabilistic graph of the RTM is shown in Fig. 1, in which the link relationships between Mashup and Web APIs, their words and latent topics are presented clearly.

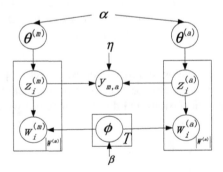

Fig. 1. The RTM model of generating latent topics

Here, as shown in the Fig. 1, T represents the number of topics, and W represents the number of words in document corpus of Mashups or Web APIs. $\theta^{(m)}$ and $\theta^{(a)}$ are respectively two vectors with a length T, indicating the proportions over all the topics for description document $W^{(m)}$ and $W^{(a)}$. ϕ is a vector with a length W, indicating the distributions over all words. What's more, $y_{m,a}$ is an observed binary variable, indicating whether Mashup and Web APIs documents are linked or not. The model contains the $y_{m,a}$ for each pair of description documents of Mashup and Web APIs, that generated on the topic assignments of all words from the corresponding documents $W^{(m)}$ and $W^{(a)}$, with a global regression parameter η. The generative process of our RTM model is as below:

- *For each topic that the description document of Mashup or Web APIs contains, draw a distribution over words $\phi \sim \text{Dirichlet}(\beta)$;*
- *For each description document of Mashup, draw a vector of topic proportions for the document $\theta^{(m)}|\alpha \sim \text{Dirichlet}(\alpha)$;*
- *For each description document of Web APIs, perform the same process as step (2);*
- *For each word $w_i^{(m)}$ in the description document of Mashup: Draw a topic assignment from those topic proportions for this document $z_i^{(m)}|\theta^{(m)} \sim \text{Multinomial}(\theta^{(m)})$; Draw a word from the corresponding topic distribution over words $w_i^{(m)}|z_i^{(m)}, \phi_{1:T} \sim \text{Multinomial}(\phi_{z_i^{(m)}})$;*
- *For each word $w_i^{(a)}$ in the description document of Web APIs, perform the same process as step (4);*
- *For each linked pair of description documents for Mashup m and Web API a, draw a binary link indicator: $y_{m,a}|z^{(m)}, z^{(a)} \sim \psi(\cdot|z^{(m)}, z^{(a)}, \lambda)$*

Here, $z^{(m)} = \{z_1^{(m)}, z_2^{(m)}, \ldots, z_T^{(m)}\}$, $z^{(a)} = \{z_1^{(a)}, z_2^{(a)}, \ldots, z_T^{(a)}\}$. The function ψ is the link (composition) probability function that defines a distribution over the link between m and a. This function is dependent on the topic assignments of $z^{(m)}$. and $z^{(a)}$ that generated their words. $y_{m,a} = 1$ means there is a link between m and a, and vice versa. In this paper, we improve cosine similarity [11] to measure the similarity (composition probability) between m and a as below:

$$\psi(y_{m,a} = 1) = \frac{\sum_{k=1}^{T} \frac{1}{e^{\lambda|z_k^{(m)} - z_k^{(a)}|}} Z_k^{(m)} \cdot Z_k^{(a)}}{\sqrt{(z_1^{(m)})^2 + \cdots + (z_T^{(m)})^2} \sqrt{(z_1^{(a)})^2 + \cdots + (z_T^{(a)})^2}} \tag{1}$$

In the above formula (1), a penalty factor $1/e^{\lambda|z_k^{(m)} - z_k^{(a)}|}$ is introduced to identify the dissimilarity between m and a, k is a topic variable. In other words, the more the difference between m and a, the greater the penalty for the difference. Parameter λ is a penalty severity degree of this dissimilarity. When $\lambda = 0$, the formula (1) reduces the normal cosine similarity.

Taking all words of description documents for Mashup and Web APIs and the link relationships between them as inputs, the posterior distribution of various latent variable $\theta^{(m)}$, $\theta^{(a)}$, ϕ, ϕ_t, $z^{(m)}$ and $z^{(a)}$ can be approximated by Gibbs sampling method. The sampling process takes the link relationship between Mashup and Web APIs into account. In our RTM, the topic assignment of a word not only originates from the topic distribution and topic proportions of Mashup document itself the word occurs, but also depends on the topic preference their linked Web APIs documents have. The update rule of description documents for Mashups is denoted as below:

$$p(z_i^{(m)} = j | z_{-i}^{(m)}, w, y) \propto \prod_{a \in A} \exp\left(\frac{\eta}{w^{(m)}} \cdot z_j^{(a)} \right) \cdot p(z_i^{(m)} = j | w, z_{-i}^{(m)}) \tag{2}$$

$$p(z_i^{(m)} = j | w, z_{-i}^{(m)}) \propto \frac{C_{j,-i}^{\left(w_i^{(m)}\right)} + \beta}{C_{j,-i}^{(\cdot)} + W\beta} * \frac{C_{j,-i}^{\left(w^{(m)}\right)} + \alpha}{C_{\cdot,-i}^{\left(w^{(m)}\right)} + T\alpha} \tag{3}$$

Here, w is a vector that represent all words, y is a vector that represents all link relationships between m and a, A is a Web APIs set in which all Web APIs have the link relationships with the Mashup m. $z_j^{(a)}$ is the probability value of topic j derived from a. η is a smoothing parameter, which characterize the importance of link relationship. Based on the topic assignments, the topic proportions of description documents for Mashups and topic distributions over words can be calculated as below:

$$p(z_i^{(m)} = j | w^{(m)}) = \frac{C_j^{\left(w^{(m)}\right)} + \alpha}{C_{\cdot}^{(w^{(m)})} + T\alpha} \tag{4}$$

$$p(w_i^{(m)} | z_i^{(m)} = j) = \frac{C_j^{\left(w_i^{(m)}\right)} + \beta}{C_j^{(\cdot)} + W\beta} \tag{5}$$

Similarly, the update rule of description documents for Web APIs is same as those of description documents for Mashup described from formulas (2) to (5).

2.3   The Link Relationship Prediction Between Mashup and Web APIs via FMs

FMs is a general predictor like Support Vector Machines (SVMs) but is also able to estimate reliable parameters under very high sparsity [17]. The FMs combines the advantages of SVMs with factorization models. On the one hand, FMs can work with any real valued feature vector like SVMs. On the other hand, different from SVMs, it models all interactions between feature variables using factorized parameters. Therefore, it can estimate interactions even in problems with huge sparsity (like recommender systems) where SVMs fail. It can be applied to many prediction tasks, for example, regression, binary classification and ranking [18]. In this paper, we use the

FMs to predict the link relationship between Mashup and Web APIs to recommend adequate relevant Web APIs for target Mashup.

The prediction task of FMs is to estimate a function $y : R^n \rightarrow T$ from a real valued feature vector $x \in R^n$ to a target domain T. In this paper, the prediction target is a typical classification problem, i.e. $y = \{0, 1\}$. The Web APIs prediction is defined as a task of ranking Web APIs and recommending adequate relevant Web APIs for the given Mashup. If there is a link between the target Mashup and active Web API, we set $y = 1$, otherwise $y = 0$. That is to say, when $y = 1$, the relevant Web API will be chosen as a member Web API of the given target Mashup. As we know, traditional recommendation system is a two-dimension model of user-item [3]. In our FMs modeling of Web APIs prediction, active Mashup can be regarded as user, and active Web APIs can be regarded as item. Besides the two-dimension features of active Mashup and active Web APIs, other multiple dimension features, such as similar Mashups, similar Web APIs, co-occurrence and the popularity of Web APIs, can be exploited as input features vector in FMs modeling to improve the accuracy of Web APIs prediction and recommendation for Mashup. Especially, we exploit the latent topics of both the documents of Mashup and Web APIs, and their link relationship between Mashup and Web

	Feature vector x																					Target y
x_1	1	0	0	...	0	1	0	...	0	0.3	0.7	...	0.3	0	0.7	...	0	0.5	0.5	...	12	1	y_1
x_2	1	0	0	...	1	0	0	...	0	0.5	0.5	...	0	0.5	0.5	...	0	1	0	...	3	1	y_2
x_3	0	1	0	...	0	1	0	...	0.7	0	0.3	...	0.5	0	0.5	...	0.5	0	0.5	...	7	1	y_3
x_4	0	1	0	...	0	0	1	...	0.6	0	0.4	...	0.4	0.6	0	...	0.5	0	0.5	...	21	1	y_4
x_5	0	0	1	...	0	0	1	...	0.3	0.7	0	...	0.1	0.9	0	...	0.5	0.5	0	...	5	1	y_5
x_6	0	0	1	...	1	0	0	...	0.4	0.1	0	...	0	0.8	0.2	...	0.5	0.5	0	...	3	1	y_6
x_7	0	1	0	...	0	1	0	...	0.4	0	0.6	...	0.4	0	0.6	...	0.5	0	0.5	...	8	1	y_7
x_8	1	0	0	...	0	0	1	...	0	0.8	0.2	...	0.7	0.3	0	...	0	1	0	...	1	1	y_8
	A_1	A_2	A_3		M_1	M_2	M_3		A_1	A_2	A_3		M_1	M_2	M_3		A_1	A_2	A_3		Freq		
	Box 1				Box 2				Box 3				Box 4				Box 5				Box 6		

Fig. 2. The FMs model of recommending web APIs for mashup

APIs, to support the model training of FMs, in which similar Mashups and similar Web APIs are derived from our RTM model in the Sect. 2.2.

The above Fig. 2 is the FMs model of recommending Web APIs for Mashup, in which the training data includes two parts (i.e. an input feature vector set and an output target set). Each row represents an input feature vector x_i with its corresponding output target y_i. The first binary indicator matrix (Box 1) represents the active Web APIs. For one example, the active Web APIs at the first row is A_1. The next binary indicator matrix (Box 2) represents the active Mashup. For another example, there is a link between M_2 and A_1 at the first row. The third indicator matrix (Box 3) indicates Top-A similar Web APIs of the active Web API in Box 1 according to their latent topic distribution similarity calculated by formula (1). In Box 3, the similarity between

A_1 and $A_2(A_3)$ is 0.3(0.7). The forth indicator matrix (Box 4) indicates *Top-M* similar Mashups of the active Mashup in Box 2 according to their latent topics distribution similarity calculated by formula (1). In Box 4, the similarity between M_2 and M_1 (M_3) is 0.3(0.7). The fifth indicator matrix (Box 5) shows all co-occurrence Web APIs of the active Web API in Box 1 that are invoked or composed in common historical Mashup. The sixth indicator matrix (Box 6) shows the popularity (i.e. invocation frequency or times) of the active Web API in Box1 in historical Mashup. The values in the Boxes 3, 4 and 5 are all normalized. Target y is the output result. If the active Mashup invokes the active Web API, we set $y = 1$, otherwise $y = 0$. Where, in the experiment section, we will investigate the effects of *top-A* and *top-M* on recommendation performance.

Given the input feature vector x and the output target variable y for Mashup and Web APIs, we define the 2-order FMs as below:

$$\hat{y}(x) := w_0 + \sum\nolimits_{i=1}^{n} w_i x_i + \sum\nolimits_{i=1}^{n} \sum\nolimits_{j=i+1}^{n} <v_i, v_j> x_i x_j \qquad (6)$$

Theoretically speaking, the value of y is o or 1, i.e. $y = \{0, 1\}$. But in practice, we can only obtain a predicted decimal value ranging from 0 to 1 derived from the formula (6) for each input feature vector. We rank these predicted decimal values and then classify them into positive value (+1, the Top-K results) and negative value (0). Those who have positive values will be recommended to the target Mashup. In the formula (6), the model parameters $\{w_0, w_1, \ldots, w_n, v_{1,1}, \ldots, v_{n,k}\}$ that need to be estimated are:

$$w_0 \in R, w \in R^n, V \in R^{n*k} \qquad (7)$$

And $<v_i, v_j>$ is the dot product of two vectors of size k:

$$<v_i, v_j> := \sum\nolimits_{f=1}^{k} v_{i,f} v_{j,f} \qquad (8)$$

Here,

- n—the length or number of feature vector x for Mashup and Web APIs, i.e. $x = \{x_1, x_2, \ldots, x_n\}$
- w_i—the strength of the ith feature vector x_i;
- $x_i x_j$—all the pairwise input feature variables of the training instances x_i and x_j for Mashup and Web APIs;
- $\hat{w}_{i,j} := <v_i, v_j>$ —all the pairwise interaction between feature vector x_i and x_j for Mashup and Web APIs;
- k—the dimensionality of the factorization.

It is worth noting that our FMs factorizes each pairwise interaction by a latent matrix $V \in R^{n*k}$, and project the mutual interaction into a latent space, which uses higher-order features to represent the mutual interaction among different features and thus is very suitable for training instance data training and recommendation of Web APIs for Mashup in huge sparsity and a variety of variables with multi-dimension scene. In our FMs, the model parameters w_0, w and V are learned from the training instances. To optimize these model parameters, like any kind of supervised learning model, it is necessary to define a loss function l for minimizing the sum of losses over the observed data S. The optimization function is as below:

$$Opt(S) = \arg\min_\Theta \sum_{i=1}^{N} l(\hat{y}(x_i), y) + \sum_{\theta \in \Theta} \lambda_{(\theta)} \theta^2 \qquad (9)$$

Here, parameter set $\Theta = (w_0, w, V)$ is final optimization object, which is obtained by minimizing the sum of error between the observed value y and predicted value $\hat{y}(x|\Theta)$ for each pairwise (x_i, x_j) in training instances of Mashup and Web APIs. N is the number of training instances, $\lambda_{(\theta)}$ is a regularization parameters. Especially, the loss function l can be defined as a logistic loss in Web APIs prediction for Mashup:

$$l(\hat{y}, y) = \log(1 + exp(-\hat{y}y)) \qquad (10)$$

To solve the optimization function $Opt(S)$ and obtain the corresponding optimal solution of parameters $\Theta = (w_0, w, V)$, some common optimization learning methods [18], for example Stochastic Gradient Descent (SGD), Markov Chain Monte Carlo (MCMC), Alternating Least Squares (ALS), can be used. Where, SGD algorithms are very popular for optimizing factorization models due to their simply, well-work with different loss functions and low computation cost and storage complexity, it can be found in literature [18]. The SGD algorithm iterates over each case $(x, y) \in S$ and performs below updates on the model parameters:

$$\theta \leftarrow \theta - \eta(\frac{\partial}{\partial \theta} l(\hat{y}(x), y) + 2\lambda_{(\theta)}\theta) \qquad (11)$$

Here, $\eta \in R^+$ is the learning rate or step size for gradient descent, $\theta \in \Theta$.

3   Experiments

In this section, we firstly describe experiment dataset, platform and settings, then present evaluation metrics and baseline methods, finally give experiment results.

3.1   Experiment Dataset, Platform and Settings

To evaluate the performance of different Web APIs recommendation methods, we crawled 6673 real Mashups 9121 Web APIs and 13613 links between these Mashups and Web APIs from the ProgrammableWeb site. For each Mashup or Web APIs, we firstly obtained their descriptive text and then performed a preprocessing process to get their standard description information. Figure 3 presents the statistics of Web APIs distribution in Mashups on the crawled dataset. From the Fig. 3, we can see that, 53.1 %/25.1 %/10.4 % Mashups respectively invoke 1/2/3 Web APIs. Totally, more than 99 % Mashups invoke 1–10 Web APIs. Therefore, we report experiment results obtained by recommending 1 to 10 Web APIs for target Mashup in this section.

Based on the crawled dataset and the link relationship between Mashup and Web APIs, we have developed a Mashup Service Network Platform (http://49.123.2.23: 8080/MashupNetwork2.0). In our experiment, we used the platform to identify the link relationship between Mashup and Web APIs, which served as a basis of latent topic similarity computation in the RTM. To enhance the effectiveness of our experiment, a five-fold cross-validation is performed. All the Mashups in the dataset have been divided into 5 equal subsets, and each fold in the subsets is used as a testing set (i.e. we manually removed all the linked Web APIs of these Mashups and used them as relevant Web APIs when evaluating), the other 4 subsets are combined to a training dataset. Then the results of each fold are summed up and their averages are reported. In the RTM, the optimal number of topics is set to 10, and the best α and β are set to 2.0, 0.1 respectively according to the experiment results. Furthermore, the smoothing parameter λ in formula (1) and η in formula (2) are set to 2 and 3, respectively.

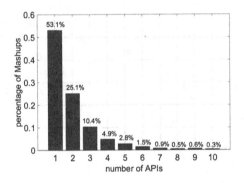

Fig. 3. Web APIs distribution of Mashups in the crawled dataset

3.2   Evaluation Metrics

In this paper, we choose the three metrics of precision, recall, and F-Measure from information retrieval to evaluate the accuracy of *top-k* Web APIs recommendation for Mashup, which are defined as:

$$Recall@k = \frac{|R(A_i) \cap RM(A_i)|}{RM(A_i)} \tag{13}$$

$$Precision@k = \frac{|R(A_i) \cap RM(A_i)|}{R(A_i)} \tag{14}$$

Here, $R(A_i)$ is a Web APIs recommendation result set, and $RM(A_i)$ is the relevant Web APIs set for a target Mashup. Integrating Precision and Recall, F-Measure represents an overall assessment of *top-k* Web APIs recommendation for Mashup. It is defined as:

$$F\text{-}Measure@k = \frac{2 * Recall * Precision}{Recall + Precision} \qquad (15)$$

In short, the bigger Recall, Precision, and F-Measure, imply that the accuracy of Web APIs recommendation for Mashup is the better.

3.3   Baseline Methods

We take six methods as baselines to evaluate our approach, which are shown as below.

- **TF-IDF.** It recommends Web APIs whose description documents are similar to those of target Mashup based on vector space model. The term frequency and inverse document frequency are used to calculate the similarity between Web APIs and target Mashup. Suppose the corresponding word vector space of target Mashup m as $V^{(m)}$, and those of the jth Web API as $V^{(a_j)}$. The similarity between $V^{(m)}$ and $V^{(a_j)}$, and the final Web APIs recommendation score are defined as formulas (16) and (17):

$$Sim(m, a_j) = \frac{V^{(m)} V^{(a_j)}}{||V^{(m)}|| ||V^{(a_j)}||} \qquad (16)$$

$$Score(m, a_j) = pop(a_j) \cdot Sim(m, a_j) \qquad (17)$$

Here, $pop(a_j)$ represents the popularity of Web API a_j, which is defined as:

$$pop(a_j) = \frac{U_{a_j} + c}{U_{a_j} + 1} \qquad (18)$$

In the formula (18), U_{a_j} is the invocation times of the Web API a_j in historical Mashup, the parameter c is set to 0.1 empirically.

- **Co-occurrence.** It recommends Web APIs with co-occurrence in historical Mash-ups. Suppose the true, relevant Web APIs set as $R^{(m)} = \{A_1, A_2, \ldots\}$ for target Mashup m. For each Web API A_i in the $R^{(m)}$, we firstly identify all those co-occurrence Web APIs with A_i from their historical Mashup records and build a co-occurrence Web APIs set $C^{(m)} = \{A_2, A_7, \ldots\}$. We calculate the similarity and popularity of each Web API in C^m via formulas (16) and (18) respectively, rec-ommending Web APIs with the higher recommendation score for target Mashup via formula (17).
- **E-LDA.** It firstly uses topic vector derived from LDA model to calculate the sim-ilarity between Mashup and Web APIs, and then integrates the popularity of Web APIs to recommend similar and popular Web APIs to target Mashup. Suppose the topic vectors of target Mashup m and the jth Web API a_j are respectively as

$Z^{(m)} = (Z_1^{(m)}, Z_2^{(m)}, \ldots, Z_T^{(m)}), Z^{(a_j)} = (Z_1^{(a_j)}, Z_2^{(a_j)}, \ldots, Z_T^{(a_j)})$, and T is the number of topics. Like the improved cosine similarity described in the formula (1), we also exploit it to calculate the similarity between m and a_j, which is as follows:

$$Sim(m, a_j) = \frac{\sum_{k=1}^{T} \frac{1}{e^{|Z_k^{(m)} - Z_k^{(a_j)}|}} Z_k^{(m)} \cdot Z_k^{(a_j)}}{\sqrt{(Z_1^{(m)})^2 + \ldots + (Z_T^{(m)})^2} \sqrt{(Z_1^{(a_j)})^2 + \ldots + (Z_T^{(a_j)})^2}} \tag{19}$$

Furthermore, the popularity factor is also integrated with the similarity to improve the recommendation by the formula (18). The final Web APIs with higher score are recommended for target Mashup.

- **E-RTM**. It is an enhanced version of RTM. This method not only takes the link relationship between Mashup and Web APIs into account, but also combines the popularity of Web APIs. The formula (1) is used to obtain the similarity between Mashup and Web APIs. It is also calculate Web APIs recommendation score by formula (17).
- **LDA-FM**. It firstly derives the topic distribution of document description for Mashup and Web APIs via LDA model, and then use the FMs to train these topic information to predict the probability distribution of Web APIs and recommend Web APIs for target Mashup. Similarly, the formula (1) is used to obtain the similarity between Mashup and Web APIs. Besides, it considers the co-occurrence and popularity of Web APIs. The final prediction value of Web APIs is ranked for recommendation.
- **RTM-FM**. The proposed method in this paper, which combines RTM and FMs to recommend Web APIs. Different from LDA-FM, it uses RTM to derive the topics of Mashup and Web APIs by modeling link relationships between Mashup and Web APIs. Similarly, it exploits the co-occurrence and popularity of Web APIs. A ranked Web APIs prediction result is recommended for target Mashup.

3.4   Experimental Results

In this section, we compare different approaches to evaluate their Web APIs recommendation performance in terms of recall, precision and F-measure. As for our RTM-FM approach, we investigate the impact of the parameters *top-A* and *top-M* on the recommendation result and choose their optimal values to achieve the best performance.

(1) *Recommendation Performance Comparison*

Figure 4 reports the comparisons of recommendation performance for different approaches when the number of Web APIs recommendation for target Mashup is ranging from 1 to 10 with a step 1 (i.e. *top-k = 1/2/3/.../10*). The comparisons show

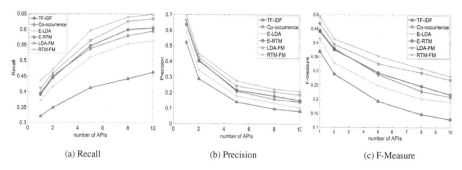

(a) Recall   (b) Precision   (c) F-Measure

Fig. 4. The recommendation performance comparison of multiple recommendation approaches

that our RTM-FM significantly improves the recommendation accuracy in terms of average Recall, Precision and F-measure, and outperforms all other baseline methods. Specifically, we have the following observations:

- The average F-measure of RTM-FM has 1.98 % improvement over LDA-FM, 5.53 % improvement over E-RTM, 6.04 % improvement over Co-occurrence, 9.33 % improvement over E-LDA and 14.49 % improvement over TF-IDF. The performance of TF-IDF is the worst in all cases. This is because TF-IDF only uses the term-based vector space model to represent the features of description document, without considering latent semantic correlation behind them. RTM-FM, LDA-FM, E-RTM and E-LDA all mine the latent topics of description document for Web APIs and target Mashup, to calculate their similarity with higher accuracy. The performance of Co-occurrence is superior to those of TF-IDF due to the popularity factor.

- E-RTM works better than E-LDA with all three metrics in all cases. E-RTM considers the historical link relationships between Mashup and Web APIs, which produces more similar topics between Mashup and its composable Web APIs. Thus E-RTM prefers to recommend more relevant Web APIs in similar latent topics for target Mashup.

- The performance of our RTM-FM surpasses to those of E-RTM. Compared to E-RTM, RTM-FM not only considers the link relationship between Mashup and Web APIs to derive their similar latent topics, but also exploits FMs to train these topics information to predict the probability distribution of Web APIs. The FMs in our RTM-FM, simultaneously takes multiple dimensions information into account, to recommend more relevant Web APIs for target Mashup. These multiple dimensions information includes the latent topics distribution of *Top-A* similar Web APIs and *Top-M* similar Mashups, the co-occurrence and the popularity of Web APIs in historical Mashups. The RTM-FM takes these dimensions information as inputs of FMs, to improve the accuracy of Web APIs recommendation.

- The performance of all methods consistently decreases with the increasing of the number of *top-k* Web APIs recommendation from 1 to 10. Since the number of Web APIs invoked by most Mashups is small in the experimental dataset, resulting in the accuracy of Web APIs recommendation drops with the increasing of k.

For example, according to the statistical results in the Fig. 3, 53.1 % Mashups invoke 1 Web API, 25.1 % Mashups invoke 2 Web APIs, and 10.4 % Mashups invoke 3 Web APIs.

(2) *Impacts of top-A and top-M*

In RTM-FM, we choose *top-A* similar Web APIs and *top-M* similar Mashups, to train the FMs for recommending *top-K* Web APIs for target Mashup.

We firstly investigate the impact of *top-A* on Web APIs recommendation. During the experiment, we select the best values of *top-M* for different *top-k* Web APIs recommendation results (*i.e. M = 20 for top-5 and top-10 web APIs recommendation*). We change the value of A from *10* to *50* with a step of *10*, and obtain the average values of F-measure in Fig. 5. The experimental results indicate that the F-measure of RTM-FM is the best when A = *10*. When A increases from 10 to 50, the F-measure of RTM-FM at all different values of *top-k* constantly decreases. Then, we can see that, Fig. 6 shows the impact of different *top-M* from *10* to *50* with a step of 10 on Web APIs recommendation in our RTM-FM. Similarly, we select the best values of *top-A* for different *top-k* Web APIs recommendation results (*i.e. A = 10 for top-5 and top-10 web APIs recommendation*). The experimental results indicate that the F-measure of RTM-FM reaches its peak value when M = *20*. With the decreasing (M <= *20*) or increasing (M >= *20*) of M, the F-measure of RTM-FM consistently drops. The observations indicate that it is important to choose appropriate values of *top-A* and *top-M* in Web APIs recommendation for Mashup creation.

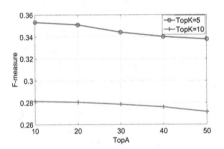

Fig. 5. Impact of top-A

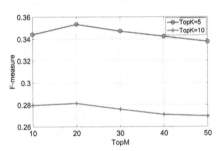

Fig. 6. Impact of top-M

4 Related Work

Web service recommendation technique plays an important role in service-oriented computing and effectively improves the quality of service discovery [1]. A number of research works have been done on Web service recommendation.

Currently, service documents are a main information sources for Web service recommendation [2, 11]. The similarity between users' requirement and services' document is measured to rank and recommend web services with high-matching [2]. Where, the functional feature vectors of services generally are characterized as a term-based vector space model by using TF-IDF technique to analyze service document (WSDL or Web APIs functional description) [11]. The matching degree between users' requirement and services' document were calculated by using similarity methods, such as cosine similarity. Only using a limited number of terms in service document for functional similarity measurement, it may result in unsatisfactory recommendation accuracy.

Some recent works show a promising advancement in terms of the accuracy of Web service recommendation through mining latent factors from service documents. Where, topic probability model [10] is an important technique for identifying the latent functional factors and discovering implicit semantic correlation among service documents. C. Li et al. [20] used LDA to extract functional features of Web services from their WSDL description. L. Chen et al. integrated WSDL documents with tagging data through augmented LDA for service discovery [8]. Even though topic probability model based methods improve the accuracy of Web service recommendation, it may be helpless when the historical invocation between Mashup and Web APIs is very sparse. To solve the data sparsity problem, some researchers exploit matrix factorization to decompose historical Mashup-Web API interactions for more accurate Web APIs recommendations [13]. Furthermore, considering matrix factorization rely on rich records of historical interactions, other research works incorporated users' social relations [15] or location similarity [16] into service recommendation. More importantly, several researchers combine topic probability model and matrix factorization to perform Web APIs recommendation [9, 14]. L. Yao et al. [14] explored both explicit textual similarity and implicit correlation of Web APIs, and proposed a probabilistic matrix factorization method to make Web API recommendation. X. Liu and I. Fulia [9] incorporated user, topic, and service related latent factors into Web APIs recommendation by combining topic model and matrix factorization.

The above existing latent factor based methods definitely boost performance of Web APIs recommendation. However, few of them perceive the historical link relationships between Mashup and Web APIs to derive the latent topics, and none of them use FMs to train these latent topics to predict the links between Mashup and Web APIs for recommending. Actually, the historical link relationships between Mashup and Web APIs can be identified and modeled to derive the latent topics. Based on the LDA, J. Chang et al. developed a RTM model [12], which considers not only the content of each item, but also the links between items. C. Li et al. [20] used the RTM model to characterize the relationship among Mashup, Web APIs, and their links, incorporated the popularity of Web APIs to the model, and performed prediction on the links between Mashup and Web APIs. In our prior work [11], we focused on the link relationships, and incorporated user interest derived from users' service usage history to build a service network for Mashup service recommendation. However, these works ignore the sparsity problem of the historical link between Mashup and Web APIs. As we know, even though matrix factorization can relieve the sparsity between Mashup and Web APIs, it is only work with special input data and not applicable for general prediction task. Due to the increasing of sparsity and dimension of the input data, the performance of matrix factorization based Web APIs recommendation may be decrease, FMs is a general predictor working with any real valued feature vector [17], which use factorized parameters to model all interactions between input variables with huge sparsity and multiple dimension. Moreover, different from SVMs, relying on support vectors, FMs can be optimized in the primal with linear complexity [18].

Motivated by above approaches, we focused on the sparsity and dimension problem of relationships between Mashup and Web APIs, and integrated RTM and FMs to recommend Web APIs for Mashup creation. We use the RTM model to characterize the relationships among Mashup and Web APIs, and their links, and derive the latent topics for measuring the similarity between Mashup and Web APIs. We exploit the FMs to predict the link relationship between Mashup and Web APIs to recommend adequate relevant Web APIs for target Mashup. The FMs model all interactions between multiple-dimension input variables with huge sparsity, including active Web APIs and Mashup, *Top-A* similar Web APIs, *Top-M* similar Mashups, the co-occurrence and popularity of the active Web API.

5   Conclusions and Future Work

This paper presents a Web APIs recommendation for Mashup creation via exploiting RTM and FMs. The relationships among Mashup and Web APIs, and their links are modeled by RTM to derive their latent topics. FMs is used to train the latent topics, model all interactions between input variables with huge sparsity and multiple dimension, and predict the link relationship between Mashup and Web APIs. The comparative experiments performed on ProgrammableWeb dataset demonstrate the effectiveness of the proposed method and show that our method significantly improves accuracy of Web APIs recommendation in terms of precision, recall and F-Measure. In the future work, we will investigate service providers, service users, and tags information of Mashup and Web APIs, and integrate them into our model for more accurate Web APIs recommendation.

Acknowledgments. The work was supported by the National Natural Science Foundation of China under grant No. 61572371, 61572186, 61572187, 61402167, 61402168, State Key Laboratory of Software Engineering (SKLSE) of China (Wuhan University) under grant No. SKLSE2014-10-10.

References

1. Xia, B., Fan, Y., Tan, W., Huang, K., Zhang, J., Wu, C.: Category-aware API clustering and distributed recommendation for automatic mashup creation. IEEE Trans. Serv. Comput. 8(5), 674–687 (2015)
2. Liu, L., Lecue, F., Mehandjiev, N.: Semantic content-based recommendation of software services using context. ACM Trans. Web 7(3), 17–20 (2013)
3. Zheng, Z., Ma, H., Lyu, M., King, I.: Qos-aware web service recommendation by collaborative filtering. IEEE Trans. Serv. Comput. 4(2), 140–152 (2011)

4. Wu, Q., Iyengar, A., Subramanian, R., Rouvellou, I., Silva-Lepe, I., Mikalsen, T.A.: Combining quality of service and social information for ranking services. In: ICOSC 2009, pp. 561–575 (2009)
5. Zhong, Y., Fan, Y., Huang, K., Tan, W., Zhang, J.: Time-aware service recommendation for mashup creation in an evolving service ecosystem. In: ICWS 2014, pp. 25–32 (2014)
6. Yao, L., Sheng, Q.Z., Ngu, H.H., Yu, Y., Segev, A., Yu, J.: Unified collaborative and content-based web service recommendation. IEEE Trans. Serv. Comput. **8**(3), 453–466 (2015)
7. Gao, W., Chen, L., Wu, J., Gao, H.: Manifold-learning based API recommendation for mashup creation. In: ICWS 2015 (2015)
8. Chen, L., Wang, Y., Yu, Q., Zheng, Z., Wu, J.: WT-LDA: User tagging augmented LDA for web service clustering. In: Basu, S., Pautasso, C., Zhang, L., Fu, X. (eds.) ICSOC 2013. LNCS, vol. 8274, pp. 162–176. Springer, Heidelberg (2013). doi:10.1007/978-3-642-45005-1_12
9. Liu, X., Fulia, I.: Incorporating user, topic, and service related latent factors into web service recommendation. In: ICWS 2015, pp. 185–192 (2015)
10. Blei, D., Ng, A., Jordan, M.: Latent Dirichlet Allocation. J. Mach. Learn. Res. **3**, 993–1022 (2003)
11. Cao, B., Liu, J., Tang, M., Zheng, Z.: Mashup service recommendation based on user interest and social network. In: ICWS 2013, pp. 99–106 (2013)
12. Chang, J., Blei, D.: Relational topic models for document networks. In: International Conference on Artificial Intelligence and Statistics, pp. 81–88 (2009)
13. Xu, W., Cao, J., Hu, L., Wang, J., Li, M.: A social-aware service recommendation approach for mashup creation. In: ICWS 2013, pp. 107–114 (2013)
14. Yao, L., Wang, X., Sheng, Q., Ruan, W., Zhang, W.: Service recommendation for mashup composition with implicit correlation regularization. In: ICWS 2015, pp. 217–224 (2015)
15. Ma, H., Zhou, D., Liu, C., Lyu, M.R., King, I.: Recommender systems with social regularization. In: Proceedings of the Fourth ACM International Conference on Web Search and Data Mining, pp. 287–296. ACM (2011)
16. Chen, X., Zheng, Z., Yu, Q., Lyu, M.: Web service recommendation via exploiting location and QoS information. IEEE Trans. Parallel Distrib. Syst. **25**(7), 1913–1924 (2014)
17. Rendle, S.: Factorization machines. In: ICDM 2010, pp. 995–1000 (2010)
18. Rendle, S.: Factorization machines with libFM. ACM Trans. Intell. Syst. Technol. (TIST) **3**(3), 57–78 (2012)
19. Li, C., Zhang, R., Huai, J., Guo, X, Sun, H.: A probabilistic approach for web service discovery. In: SCC 2013, pp. 49–56 (2013)
20. Li, C., Zhang, R., Huai, J., Sun, H.: A novel approach for API recommendation in mashup development. In: ICWS 2014, pp. 289–296 (2014)

A Sufficient and Necessary Condition to Decide Compatibility for Simple Circuit Inter-organization Workflow Nets

Leifeng He, Guanjun Liu$^{(\boxtimes)}$, and Mimi Wang

Department of Computer Science, Tongji University, Shanghai 201804, China
liuguanjun@tongji.edu.cn

Abstract. Inter-organization workflow nets (IWF-nets) can well model the interactions among multiple business processes by sending/receiving messages, and their compatibility is a very important property to guarantee that their logical behaviors are correct. Liu and Jiang introduce a class of IWF-nets named SCIWF-nets (simple circuit IWF-nets) to model inter-organizational business processes and this class can model many cases of interactions. In this paper, a necessary and sufficient condition is presented to decide compatibility for SCIWF-nets and it is dependent on the net structures only. This structure-based condition lays a foundation for designing an efficient algorithm to check compatibility of SCIWF-nets.

Keywords: Inter-organization Workflow nets · Compatibility · Business process model · Web services composition · Similar S-graph

1 Introduction

Petri nets are widely used to model concurrent/distributed systems because they can well characterize the processes of these systems and their relationships. For example of flexible manufacturing systems [6, 10], every product is manufactured in one or several manufacturing processes. Every process uses a group of resources (like machines or robots) by a fixed order. These processes are not required to interact or collaborate with each other but have to share common resources. S^{3}PRs [5], S^{4}PRs [8], S^{3}PMRs [17], and ERCN-merged nets [12] are some well-known Petri net classes of modeling these systems. Another famous application of Petri nets is to model and analyze such concurrent systems as web services. The execution process of each simple service is modeled by a simple Petri net. These simple Petri nets are combined via a group of common places that are the media of passing messages between services. Inter-organizational workflow nets (IWF-nets) [1, 4, 11, 14, 15], as a class of Petri nets, are used to model these concurrent systems. The model only considers the interaction among these processes but do not consider whether they share some common resources. This paper focuses on IWF-nets.

Compatibility [2] is a very important property for IWF-nets. It guarantees that the target state can always be reached, no deadlock or livelock takes place,

© Springer International Publishing AG 2016
G. Wang et al. (Eds.): APSCC 2016, LNCS 10065, pp. 408–422, 2016.
DOI: 10.1007/978-3-319-49178-3_31

and each task has a potential right to be executed. In fact, the compatibility of IWF-nets is equal to the soundness of workflow nets (WF-nets) [20,21]. In Sect. 2, it will be seen that WF-nets and IWF-nets may be viewed as two equivalent concepts.

Aalst et al. [11] proved that the soundness problem is decidable for general WF-nets. Therefore, the compatibility problem is also decidable. Alast el al. [3] gave a polynomial-time algorithm to solve the soundness problem for free-choice WF-nets. The algorithm is based on the rank theory proposed for free-choice WF-nets. It can also be used to solve the compatibility of free-choice IWF-nets. However, some concurrent systems [1] like web services composite must consider the interaction among different components/processes via sending/receiving messages, which makes the related models more and more complex so that free-choice WF-nets cannot model them. The general method to decide soundness or compatibility for these complex models is based on their reachability graphs which generally exist the space explosion problem. Except for free-choice nets and some other well-structured ones, there are not too many structure-based methods for these complex models. We also prove that the compatibility problem is PSPACE-hard [16,18]. Therefore, it is important and interesting to look for some structure-based methods to decide compatibility or soundness.

This paper proposes a necessary and sufficient condition to decide compatibility for a class of IWF-nets called *SCIWF-nets* that are defined by Liu and Jiang [19]. Necessary and sufficient conditions are proposed to decide compatibility in [19]. These conditions are based on two new net structures (*T-component* and *cap*) rather than some traditional net structures such as siphon or rank. This paper proposes a new decision condition based on some traditional structure concepts.

In fact, compatibility or soundness corresponds to two well-known properties: liveness and boundedness. An IWF-net is compatible or a WF-net is sound if and only if its trivial extension is live and bounded [20]. Therefore, the compatibility problem is equal to the liveness and boundedness problems. For liveness, there are many methods to check it. For example, a free-choice net is live if and only if its each minimal siphon is also a marked trap [9], and an asymmetric choice net is live if and only if its each minimal siphon is marked at each reachable marking [7,13]. This paper gives a new condition to decide the liveness for the trivial extension of SCIWF-nets and the ideas come from [22]. For boundedness, there are not too many methods about its decision. This paper gives a new condition to decide the boundedness for the trivial extension of SCIWF-nets. In a word, our work proposes a necessary and sufficient condition to decide liveness and boundedness so as to decide compatibility. The condition is based on the net structures only.

The paper is organized as follows. Section 2 introduces some basic terminologies. Section 3 introduces SCIWF-nets and some new concepts. Section 4 proposes conditions for compatibility of SCIWF-nets. Section 5 concludes this paper.

2   Petri Nets and IWF-nets

Petri nets and IWF-nets are recalled in this section. For more details, one may refer to [23,24]. Denote $\mathbb{N} = \{0, 1, 2, \cdots\}$. Given $m \in \mathbb{N}$ and $m > 0$, denote $\mathbb{N}_m = \{1, 2, \cdots, m\}$.

A *net* is a 3-tuple $N = (P, T, F)$, where P is a finite set of *places*, T a finite set of *transitions*, $F \subseteq (P \times T) \cup (T \times P)$ a set of *arcs*, and $P \cap T = \varnothing$.

A net may be seen as a directed bipartite graph. Generally, a transition is represented by a rectangle and a place by a circle in a net graph. A *path* of a net is a nonempty sequence $x_1 x_2 \cdots x_n$ of nodes such that $\forall j \in \mathbb{N}_{n-1}: (x_j, x_{j+1}) \in F$. A path $x_1 x_2 \cdots x_n$ is *elementary* if for any nodes x_j and $x_k: j \neq k \Rightarrow x_j \neq x_k$. An elementary path $x_1 x_2 \cdots x_n$ is a *circuit* if $(x_n, x_1) \in F$. A net is *acyclic* if it has no circuits. A net is *strongly connected* if for any nodes x and y there is a path from x to y. $N' = (P', T', F')$ is a *subnet* of $N = (P, T, F)$ if $P' \in P$, $T' \in T$, and $F' = F \cap ((T' \times P') \cup (P' \times T'))$. Sometime, we say that N contains N' if the latter is a subnet of the former.

A transition t is an *input transition* of a place p and p is an *output place* of t if $(t, p) \in F$. *Input place* and *output transition* can be defined accordingly. Given a net $N = (P, T, F)$ and a node $x \in P \cup T$, ${}^\bullet x = \{y \in P \cup T | (y, x) \in F\}$ and $x^\bullet = \{y \in P \cup T | (x, y) \in F\}$ are the *pre-set* and *post-set* of x, respectively. $N' = (P', T', F')$ is an *epitaxial subnet* w.r.t. P' if $P' \subseteq P$, $T' = \{t \in {}^\bullet p \cup p^\bullet | p \in P'\}$, and $F' = F \cap ((T' \times P') \cup (P' \times T'))$. An *epitaxial subnet* w.r.t. $T' \in T$ can be defined accordingly.

A *marking* of $N = (P, T, F)$ is a mapping $M: P \to \mathbb{N}$. A place $p \in P$ is *marked* at M if $M(p) > 0$. Notice that in this paper a marking is denoted as a multi-set of places. For example, the marking M such that place p_1 has one token, place p_2 has 3 tokens and other places have no tokens, is written as $M = p_1 + 3p_2$ or $M = (p_1, 3p_2)$. Transition t is *enabled* at M if $\forall p \in {}^\bullet t: M(p) > 0$, which is denoted as $M[t\rangle$. *Firing* an enabled transition t yields a new marking M', which is denoted as $M[t\rangle M'$, such that $M'(p) = M(p) - 1$ if $p \in {}^\bullet t \setminus t^\bullet$; $M'(p) = M(p) + 1$ if $p \in t^\bullet \setminus {}^\bullet t$; and $M'(p) = M(p)$ otherwise. A marking M_k is *reachable* from a marking M if there exists a transition sequence $\sigma = t_1 t_2 \cdots t_k$ such that $M[t_1\rangle M_1[t_2\rangle \cdots \rangle M_{k-1}[t_k\rangle M_k$. $M[\sigma\rangle M_k$ represents that M reaches M_k after firing transition σ. The set of all markings reachable from M in a net N is denoted as $R(N, M)$. A net N with an *initial marking* M_0 is a *Petri net* or *net system* and denoted as (N, M_0). In the net, a transition sequence σ is called a *T-invariant* if $M_0[\sigma\rangle M_0$.

A Petri net $(N, M_0) = (P, T, F, M_0)$ is *bounded* if $\exists k \in \mathbb{N}$, $\forall p \in P$, $\forall M \in R(N, M_0): M(p) \leq k$. A Petri net is *safe* if each place has at most one token at each reachable marking. A net N is *structurally bounded* if (N, M_0) is bounded for any initial marking M_0. A transition t is *dead* at a marking M if $\forall M' \in R(N, M_0): \neg M'[t\rangle$. A transition t is *live* at a marking M if for $\forall M' \in R(N, M)$, t is not dead at M'. (N, M_0) is *live* if each transition is live at M_0. A nonempty set S (resp. Q) of places is a *siphon* (resp. *trap*) if ${}^\bullet S \subseteq S^\bullet$ (resp. $Q^\bullet \subseteq {}^\bullet Q$). A siphon (resp. trap) is *minimal* if it does not contain other siphons (resp. trap). A nonempty set T_1 (resp. T_2) of transitions is a *generator* (resp. *absorber*) if ${}^\bullet T_1 \subseteq T_1^\bullet$ (resp. $T_2^\bullet \subseteq {}^\bullet T_2$). A generator (resp. absorber) is *minimal* if it does not contain other generator (resp. absorber).

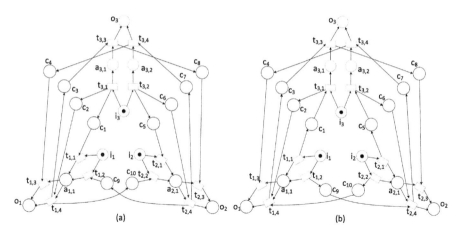

Fig. 1. (a) A compatible IWF-net and (b) an incompatible IWF-net [19]

Given a net $N = (P, T, F)$, it is a *marked graph* if $\forall p \in P$: $|{}^\bullet p| = |p^\bullet| = 1$; it is a *free-choice net* if $\forall p_1, p_2 \in P$: $(p_1^\bullet \cap p_2^\bullet \neq \varnothing \wedge p_1 \neq p_2) \Rightarrow |p_1^\bullet| = |p_2^\bullet| = 1$; it is an *asymmetric-choice net* if $\forall p_1, p_2 \in P$: $p_1^\bullet \cap p_2^\bullet \neq \varnothing \Rightarrow (p_1^\bullet \subseteq p_2^\bullet \vee p_2^\bullet \subseteq p_1^\bullet)$. A net $N = (P, T, F)$ is a *WF-net* if

1. N has two special places i and o, where $i \in P$ is *source place* if ${}^\bullet i = \varnothing$ and $o \in P$ is *sink place* if $o^\bullet = \varnothing$; and
2. the *trivial extension* $N^E = (P, T \cup \{b\}, F \cup \{(b, i), (o, b)\})$ of N is strongly connected where $b \notin T$.

Let $N = (P, T, F)$ is a WF-net, $M_0 = i$, and $M_d = o$. N is *sound* if

1. $\forall M \in R(N, M_0)$: $M_d \in R(N, M)$;
2. $\forall M \in R(N, M_0)$: $M \geq M_d \Rightarrow M = M_d$; and
3. $\forall t \in T, \exists M \in R(N, M_0)$: $M[t\rangle$.

The definition for soundness was given in the early work of Alast [2], and later he showed that the second requirement is implied by the first one. The first two requirements mean that a system can always terminate correctly and the third one means that each task has a potential chance to be executed. Generally, $M_0 = i$ and $M_d = o$ is called as the *initial* and *target* marking of a WF-net, respectively. Additionally, a safe (resp. bounded) WF-net means that the WF-net is safe (resp. bounded) at its initial marking.

A class of nets called *inter-organizational workflow nets* (IWF-nets) [1] are often used to model the composition of web services, inter-organizational business processes, or some other concurrent systems in which multiple processes interact via sending/receiving messages. An IWF-net describes the synchronous and/or asynchronous communication among multiple partners (each partner is modeled by a basic WF-net) [1]. The following definition considers the asynchronous communication only.

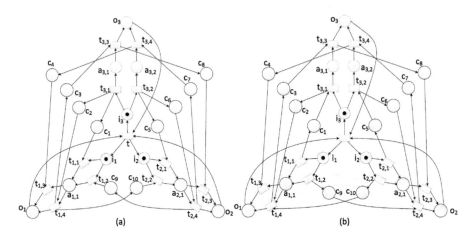

Fig. 2. (a) The EIWF-net of Fig. 1(a); (b) the EIWF-net of Fig. 1(b)

Definition 1 (IWF-net). *A net $N = (N_1, N_2, \cdots, N_m, P_C, F_C)$ is an IWF-net if*

1. $N_1 = (P_1, T_1, F_1)$, $\cdots$, *and* $N_m = (P_m, T_M, F_m)$ *are pairwise disjoint WF-nets where $m \geq 1$ and they are called basic WF-nets;*
2. P_C *is a finite set of channel places such that $P_C \cap P_j = \varnothing$ for each $j \in \mathbb{N}_m$;*
3. $F_C \subseteq (P_C \times \bigcup_{j=1}^{m} T_j) \cup (\bigcup_{j=1}^{m} T_j \times P_C)$ *is a set of arcs by which channel places are connected with the m basic WF-nets; and*
4. $\forall c \in P_C, \exists j, k \in \mathbb{N}_m: j \neq k \wedge {}^{\bullet}c \subseteq T_j \wedge c^{\bullet} \subseteq T_k \wedge {}^{\bullet}c \neq \varnothing \wedge c^{\bullet} \neq \varnothing.$

Figure 1(a) and (b) are two IWF-nets whose basic WF-nets are identical but interactions are different. From the fourth item of Definition 1 it is known that each channel place is used only by two fixed basic WF-nets. In other words, two different basic WF-nets cannot send messages into the same channel place; similarly, two different basic WF-nets cannot take messages from the same channel place either. Certainly, two different basic WF-nets may use multiple channel places to communicate.

Definition 2 (Compatibility of IWF-net). *Let $N = (N_1, N_2, \cdots, N_m, P_C, F_C)$ is an IWF-net, $M_0 = i_1 + i_2 + \cdots + i_m$, and $M_d = o_1 + o_2 + \cdots + o_m$. N is compatible if*

1. $\forall M \in R(N, M_0): M_d \in R(N, M)$;
2. $\forall M \in R(N, M_0): M \geq M_d \Rightarrow M = M_d$; *and*
3. $\forall t \in \bigcup_{j=1}^{m} T_j, \exists M \in R(N, M_0): M[t\rangle.$

For instance, Fig. 1(a) is compatible, but (b) is incompatible. Notice that, if we add two special places i, o, and two special transition t_i, t_o to an IWF-net such that ${}^{\bullet}t_i = \{i\} \wedge t_i^{\bullet} = \{i_1, i_2, \cdots, i_m\} \wedge {}^{\bullet}t_o = \{o_1, o_2, \cdots, o_m\} \wedge t_o^{\bullet} = \{o\}$, then the new net is a WF-net. Especially, the original IWF-net is compatible if and only if the new WF-net is sound. On the other hand, each IWF-net is composed of a group of basic WF-nets. Therefore, any WF-net is a special IWF-net since this IWF-net contains only one basic WF-net and has no channel place. Thus, the concepts of IWF-nets and WF-nets are equivalent.

In fact, the compatibility of IWF-nets is related to the liveness and boundedness of the trivial extension of IWF-nets whose definition is in the following.

Definition 3 (EIWF-nets). *A net* $N^E = (N_1, N_2, \cdots, N_m, P_C, F_C, t, F_t)$ *is the trivial extension of an IWF-net (EIWF-net for short) if*

1. $N = (N_1, N_2, \cdots, N_m, P_C, F_C)$ *is an IWF-net; and*
2. *t is a returned transition such that* $t \notin \bigcup_{j=1}^m T_j$ *and* $F_t = \bigcup_{j=1}^m \{(o_j, t) \cup (t, i_j)\}$.

IWF-nets are compatible if and only if the EIWF-nets of IWF-nets are live and bounded. For example, Fig. 2(a) shows the EIWF-net of the IWF-net in Fig. 1(a). Because Fig. 2(a) is live and bounded, Fig. 1(a) is compatible. But Fig. 2(b) which is the EIWF-net of the IWF-net in Fig. 1(b) is not live and thus Fig. 1(b) is incompatible. For convenience, M_0 and M_d in Definition 2 are called the *initial* and *target* markings of an IWF-net, respectively. If a WF-net is also a free-choice net, then it is called *free-choice WF-net* (FCWF-net for short). Similarly, *asymmetric-choice WF-net* (ACWF-net for short) can also be defined. If an IWF-net is also a free-choice net, then it is called *free-choice IWF-net* (FCIWF-net for short). Similarly, *asymmetric-choice IWF-net* (ACIWF-net for short) can also be defined. According to the structures of IWF-nets, the trivial extension of a FCIWF-net is also a free-choice net. Similarly, the trivial extension of an ACIWF-net is also an asymmetric-choice net. For instance, Fig. 1(a) and (b) are both ACIWF-nets, and their trivial extensions as shown in Fig. 2(a) and (b) are also asymmetric-choice nets.

3   SCIWF-nets

This section recalls the definition of SCIWF-nets [1], and then introduces some structural concepts for them.

Definition 4 (SCIWF-net). $N = (N_1, N_2, \cdots, N_m, P_C, F_C)$ *is a simple circuit IWF-net (SCIWF-net) if*

1. *N is an IWF-net;*
2. $\forall j \in \mathbb{N}_m$: N_j *is a sound acyclic FCWF-net; and*
3. $\forall c \in P_C$: $|{}^\bullet c| = |c^\bullet| = 1$.

In an SCIWF-net, each basic WF-net is acyclic but the entire net may permit circuits. This is also the reason why this class is named *simple circuit IWF-nets*. In fact, Fig. 1(a) and (b) are both SCIWF-nets, and they have the same basic FCWF-nets but their interactions are different. Each basic WF-net of an SCIWF-net is a free-choice net. FCWF-nets can not only model many basic structures of workflow such as AND-split, AND-join, OR-split, OR-join, but also own a nice property (i.e., their soundness is decided based on their structures). Additionally, an SCIWF-net considers the simplest case of using a message channel, i.e., for a fixed channel place, a message is sent into it by firing a unique transition and the message is taken away from it by firing another unique transition. Certainly, a transition may use multiple channel places.

Referring to the work in [22], we give the following concepts and properties by which we propose a necessary and sufficient condition to decide compatibility.

Definition 5 (Circled enabled transition sequence). *Let $N = (N_1, N_2, \cdots, N_m, P_C, F_C)$ be an SCIWF-net, and $\sigma_1, \sigma_2, \cdots, \sigma_n$ be all enabled transition sequences from M_0 to M where $M \geq M_d$. Then $\sigma_j t (1 \leq j \leq n)$ is called a circled enabled transition sequence of $N^E = (N_1, N_2, \cdots, N_m, P_C, F_C, t, F_t)$ where N^E is the trivial extension of N.*

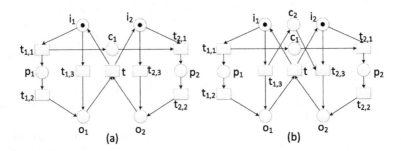

Fig. 3. (a) An unsafe ESCWF-net and (b) A safe ESCWF-net

In an SCIWF-net N, each basic WF-net is acyclic. Therefore, enabled transition sequences of N from M_0 to M ($M \geq M_d$) are finite. Then circled enable transition sequences are also finite. In N^E, circled enabled transition sequences can be fired infinitely.

Lemma 1. *Given a circled enabled transition sequence σt of N^E, then $\sigma_i t$ is a T-invariant of N_i^E where σ_i is the projection of σ over T_i.*

Proof: We assume that there are a circled enabled transition sequence σt of N^E and $i \in \mathbb{N}_m$ such that $\sigma_i t$ is not a T-invariant of N_i^E where σ_i is the projection of σ over T_i. Then N_i is not sound, which contradicts with the fact of N_i is sound. □

For example, Fig. 3(b) has two circled enabled transition sequences, that is $\sigma_1 = t_{1,1}t_{1,2}t_{2,1}t_{2,2}t$, $\sigma_2 = t_{1,3}t_{2,3}t$. The projections $\sigma_{1_1} = t_{1,1}t_{1,2}t$ and $\sigma_{2_1} = t_{1,3}t$ are both T-invariants of N_1^E, and the projections $\sigma_{1_2} = t_{2,1}t_{2,2}t$ and $\sigma_{2_2} = t_{2,3}t$ are both T-invariants of N_2^E.

Definition 6 (Live minimal generator). *Let $N^E = (N_1, N_2, \cdots, N_m, P_C, F_C, t, F_t)$ be the trivial extension of an SCIWF-net (ESCIWF-net for short) and N_i^E be the trivial extension of N_i ($1 \leq i \leq m$), then $T' \subseteq \bigcup_{j=1}^m T_j \cup \{t\}$ is a live minimal generator if*

1. T' is a minimal generator of N^E;
2. T_i' is a T-invariant of N_i^E where $T_i' = (T_i \cap T') \cup \{t\}$; and
3. each circuit of the epitaxial subnet w.r.t. T' includes t.

Lemma 2. *Any live minimal generator corresponds to a circled enabled transition sequence, and vice versa.*

Proof: In an ESCIWF-net, if there are a minimal generator T' and $i \in \mathbb{N}_m$ such that T_i' is not a T-invariant of N_i^E, T' is a dead transition sequence. Similarly, T' is also a dead transition sequence if the epitaxial subnet w.r.t. T' has a circuit that does not include t. Except the two classes of minimal generators, each of other minimal generator that is called live minimal generator T' can be fired in a proper order and firing T' yields a new marking M such that $M \geq M_0$. Therefore, each live minimal generator is also a circled enabled transition sequence according to Definition 5. A circled enabled transition sequence is also a live minimal generator because it meets conditions 1, 2 and 3 of Definition 6.   □

For example, Fig. 3(a) shows an ESIWF-net, and its live minimal generators are $T_1 = \{t_{1,1}, t_{1,2}, t_{2,1}, t_{2,2}, t\}$, $T_2 = \{t_{1,3}, t_{2,3}, t\}$, $T_3 = \{t_{1,1}, t_{1,2}, t_{2,3}, t\}$, which correspond to three circled enabled transition sequences $\sigma_1 t = t_{1,1} t_{1,2} t_{2,1} t_{2,2} t$, $\sigma_2 t = t_{1,3} t_{2,3} t$, $\sigma_3 t = t_{1,1} t_{1,2} t_{2,3} t$, and there are only three circled enabled transition sequences in Fig. 3(a).

Definition 7 (Strict siphon). *Let $N^E = (N_1, N_2, \cdots, N_m, P_C, F_C, t, F_t)$ be an ESCIWF-net, then $S \subseteq \bigcup_{j=1}^m P_j \cup P_C$ is a strict siphon if*

1. S is a siphon of N^E; and
2. S does not include any trap.

Definition 8 (Risky transition). *Let $N^E = (N_1, N_2, \cdots, N_m, P_C, F_C, t, F_t)$ be an ESCIWF-net, and $S \subseteq \bigcup_{j=1}^m P_j \cup P_C$ be a strict siphon, then $t' \in T'$ is a risky transition w.r.t. S if*

1. T' is the set of transitions of the epitaxial subnet of S; and
2. $t'^\bullet = \varnothing$ in the epitaxial subnet of S.

Siphon is an important structure for analyzing the liveness of Petri nets. Empty siphons are the reason for deadlocks of Petri nets, and risky transitions are the direct factor that causes a marked siphon to be an empty one.

For example, Fig. 4(a) is the epitaxial subnet w.r.t. minimal siphon $\{i_1, a_{1,1}, a_{2,1}, o_2, i_3, c_5, c_{10}\}$ of Fig. 2(a) and Fig. 4(b) is the epitaxial subnet w.r.t. minimal siphon $\{i_1, o_1, i_2, c_4, c_7, c_9, c_{10}\}$ of Fig. 2(b). They are marked and also strict. The siphon of Fig. 4(b) will eventually be empty if its risky transitions $t_{1,1}, t_{2,1}$ are fired. But the siphon of Fig. 4(a) will be marked at each reachable marking because its risky transition $t_{1,3}$ or $t_{3,1}$ has some special structure characters that are introduced in the following.

Definition 9 (Similar S-graph). *Let $N^E = (N_1, N_2, \cdots, N_m, P_C, F_C, t, F_t)$ be an ESCIWF-net, and $S \subseteq \bigcup_{j=1}^m P_j \cup P_C$ be a strict minimal siphon. Then the epitaxial subnet $N' = (S', T', F')$ w.r.t. $S' \subseteq S$ is a similar S-graph if*

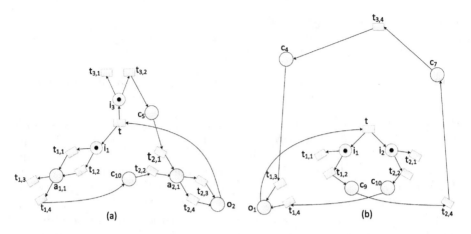

Fig. 4. (a) The epitaxial subnet w.r.t. minimal siphon $\{i_1, a_{1,1}, a_{2,1}, o_2, i_3, c_5, c_{10}\}$ of Fig. 2(a); (b) the epitaxial subnet w.r.t. minimal siphon $\{i_1, o_1, i_2, c_4, c_7, c_9, c_{10}\}$ of Fig. 2(b)

1. *there are one and only one source place and one and only one sink place in S';*
2. *$\exists t' \in T': t'^\bullet = \varnothing \Rightarrow t'$ is a risky transition of S; and*
3. *$\forall t' \in T': |^\bullet t'| \leq 1 \wedge |t'^\bullet| \leq 1$.*

In a live ESCIWF-net, every minimal siphon S includes at least one source place and only one sink place, and other places of S are in the path from one of the source places to the sink place in the epitaxial subnet w.r.t. S. Therefore, the epitaxial subnet is composed of a set of similar S-graphs.

For example, Fig. 4(a) has six similar S-graphs: $S_1' = \{i_1, a_{1,1}, c_{10}, a_{2,1}, o_2\}$, $S_2' = \{i_1, a_{1,1}, c_{10}, a_{2,1}, o_2, c_5\}$, $S_3' = \{i_1, a_{1,1}, c_{10}, a_{2,1}, o_2, c_5, i_3\}$, $S_4' = \{i_3, c_5, a_{2,1}, o_2\}$, $S_5' = \{i_3, c_5, a_{2,1}, o_2, c_{10}\}$ and $S_6' = \{i_3, c_5, a_{2,1}, o_2, c_{10}, a_{1,1}\}$. Figure 4(a) is obviously composed of them.

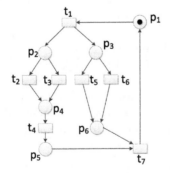

Fig. 5. A live Petri net

Definition 10 (Purely input and output transition). *Let $N^E = (N_1, N_2,$* *$\cdots, N_m, P_C, F_C, t, F_t)$ be an ESCIWF-net, $S \subseteq \bigcup_{j=1}^{m} P_j \cup P_C$ be a strict minimal siphon, and the epitaxial subnet $N' = (S', T', F')$ w.r.t. $S' \subseteq S$ be a similar S-graph. Then $t' \in T'$ is a purely input transition of N' if $^\bullet t' = \varnothing$ in N', and t' is a purely output transition of N' if $t'^\bullet = \varnothing$ in N'.*

For a strict minimal siphon, not all of its similar S-graphs have purely input transitions, but each similar S-graph of it must have purely output transitions, otherwise, the siphon must contain at least a trap and then it is not strict. For example, Fig. 4(a) itself is also a similar S-graph which has no purely input transition but has two purely output transitions $t_{1,3}$ and $t_{3,1}$.

Definition 11 (Control and strictly control). *In a net $N = (P, T, F)$, $t_2 \in T$ is controlled by $t_1 \in T$ if there is a path from t_1 to t_2 such that the pre-set of each place in the path are in the path; $t_2 \in T$ is strictly controlled by $t_1 \in T$ if there is a path from t_1 to t_2 such that the pre-set and post-set of each place in the path are also in the path.*

Control relation indicates that t_2 has a chance to be fired only if t_1 is fired under condition that the set of places of the path from t_1 to t_2 are empty. Strictly control relation indicates that t_2 will be fired only if t_1 is fired under condition that the set of places of the path from t_1 to t_2 are empty and the Petri net is live.

For example, Fig. 5 is a live Petri net, and t_2, t_3, t_5 and t_6 are all controlled by t_1 because they will not have a chance to be fired if t_1 is not fired. However, they are unnecessary to be fired after t_1 is fired since they have choice relationship. t_4 and t_7 both are strictly controlled by t_1 because they have to be fired and can be fired after t_1 is fired.

4   Deciding Compatibility of SCIWF-nets

Based on the concepts and properties in Sect. 3, we give a necessary and sufficient condition to decide compatibility of SCIWF-nets.

Theorem 1. *An SCIWF-nets $N = (N_1, N_2, \cdots, N_m, P_C, F_C)$ is compatible if and only if its trivial extension N^E is live and safe.*

Proof: *(Sufficiency)* This is obviously since safeness implies boundedness. *(Necessity)* Because N is compatible, N^E is live. For each N_i where $1 \leq i \leq m$, because N_i is a sound free-choice net, its trivial extension is a live and bounded free-choice net. Therefore $\forall p \in P_i$, there is a minimal siphon $S \subseteq P_i$ and $p \in S$, where S is also a S-invariant [13] and the token number in S is one forever. Therefore, p is safe and then the trivial extension of N_i is safe. Because N_i is acyclic, every transition in N can be fired at most once. Because $\forall p \in P_C$: $|^\bullet p| = |p^\bullet| = 1$, p is also safe in N^E.   □

Theorem 2. *An ESCIWF-nets $N^E = (N_1, N_2, \cdots, N_m, P_C, F_C, t, F_t)$ is safe if and only if each live minimal generator is also an absorber.*

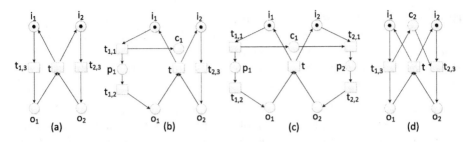

Fig. 6. (a)–(c) Three live minimal generators of Fig. 3(a); (c)–(d) two live minimal generators of Fig. 3(b)

Proof: *(Necessity)* We assume that there is a live minimal generator T' which is not an absorber. Therefore, there must exist $p \in P$ such that $p^\bullet = \varnothing$, where P is the set of places of the epitaxial subnet w.r.t. T'. Because each live minimal generator corresponds to a circled enabled transition sequence, T' corresponds to a circled enabled transition sequence that can be fired infinitely. Hence, p is not safe.

(Sufficiency) Because each live minimal generator is an absorber T', $\forall p \in P$: $p^\bullet \neq \varnothing$, where P is the set of places of the epitaxial subnet w.r.t. T'. Because T'_i is a T-invariant of N_i^E where T'_i is the projection of T' over T_i, and $\forall p \in P_C$: $|^\bullet p| = |p^\bullet| = 1$, T' is also a T-invariant. Because a live minimal generator corresponds to a circled enabled transition sequence, all circled enabled sequences are also T-invariants. From the proof of Theorem 1, we know that N_i^E is safe and every transition can be fired at most once for an SCIWF-net. Therefore, $\forall p \in P_C$ is also safe and thus N^E is safe.   □

Figure 3(a) shows an unsafe ESCIWF-net, and (b) shows a safe ESCIWF-net. Figure 6(a)–(c) show all live minimal generators of Fig. 3(a) in which (a) and (c) are also absorbers but (b) is not. This is the reason why Fig. 3(a) is not safe.

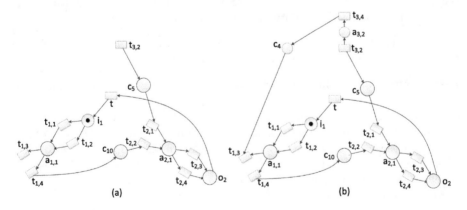

Fig. 7. (a) A similar S-graph of Fig. 4(a); (b) the control structure of (a)

Figure 6(c) and (d) show all live minimal generators of Fig. 3(b), and each of them is also an absorber. Therefore, Fig. 3(b) is safe.

Theorem 3. *An ESCIWF-nets $N^E = (N_1, N_2, \cdots, N_m, P_C, F_C, t, F_t)$ is live if each minimal siphon is a trap or a strict siphon and satisfies that (1) it includes at least one source place and (2) if it is a strict siphon, then it has a similar S-graph where its each purely output transition is strictly controlled by the corresponding purely input transition.*

Proof: Because each minimal siphon in N^E includes at least one source place, all minimal siphons are marked at the initial marking. For a minimal siphon which is a trap, it will not be empty forever. For a minimal siphon which is strict, there is a similar S-graph of it. Let S be the set of places of the similar S-graph. Then S is marked at the initial marking because S includes a source place. If all purely output transitions of the similar S-graph can not be fired, S will keep nonempty. If a purely output transition of the similar S-graph is fired, its corresponding purely input transition will be fired in advance because every purely output transition is strictly controlled by its corresponding purely input transition in N^E. Because N_i^E is safe and each transition of N can be fired at most once, the firing times of the purely output transition is less than or equal to the firing times of the corresponding purely input transition. Then S still keep nonempty even if there are some purely output transitions fired. In a word, all its minimal siphons will be marked at each reachable marking of N^E. We know that N^E is an asymmetric choice net. An asymmetric choice net is live if and only if its all minimal siphons are marked at each reachable marking [7,13]. Therefore, N^E is live.   □

Figure 7(a) shows a similar S-graph of Fig. 4(a), and it is called S'. Obviously, its purely output transition $t_{1,3}$ is strictly controlled by its purely input transition $t_{3,2}$ as shown in Fig. 7(b). Then S' is nonempty if $t_{1,3}$ is not fired, and $t_{3,2}$ will be fired in advance if $t_{1,3}$ is fired. Therefore, the token number of S' will add one and then subtract one, which means that S' is nonempty in the process. In other words, S' is marked at each reachable marking and thus the strict siphon of Fig. 4(a) is also marked at each reachable marking since S' is a subset of this siphon. Figure 2(a) shows the ESCIWF-net, and each minimal siphon includes at least one source place. Some minimal siphons are traps and others are strict siphons such as Fig. 4(a). Because a siphon is also marked at each reachable marking if the siphon is also a marked trap, each minimal siphon of Fig. 2(a) is marked at each reachable marking, and then Fig. 2(a) is live according to the well-known theorem that an asymmetric choice net is live if and only if its all minimal siphons are marked at each reachable marking [7,13].

Theorem 4. *An SCIWF-nets $N = (N_1, N_2, \cdots, N_m, P_C, F_C)$ is compatible if and only if $N^E = (N_1, N_2, \cdots, N_m, P_C, F_C, t, F_t)$ meets the following conditions:*

1. *each minimal siphon is a trap or a strict siphon and satisfies that (1) it includes at least one source place and (2) if it is a strict siphon, then it has*

a similar S-graph where its each purely output transition is strictly controlled by the corresponding purely input transition; and

2. *each live minimal generators is an absorber.*

Proof: *(Sufficiency)* It is derived directly from Theorems 1, 2 and 3.

(Necessity) From Theorem 1, we know that N^E is live and safe if N is compatible, and then condition 2 holds from Theorem 2. Because N^E is live and safe and is an asymmetric choice net, all its minimal siphons are marked at each reachable marking. We know that each minimal siphon either is a trap or a siphon that does not conclude any trap [13], and contains at least one source place. For a minimal siphon that does not contain any trap, it is obviously a strict one, and must include a similar S-graph where each purely output transition is controlled by its corresponding purely input transition. Otherwise, all its similar S-graphs will eventually become empty and then the siphon will eventually become empty, which contradicts with the fact of N^E is live. Because N^E is safe, a purely output transition must be fired if the corresponding input transition is fired and their firing times are equal. Otherwise, the sink place of the similar S-graph will eventually become unsafe. Therefore, for each strict minimal siphon, there is a similar S-graph where its each purely output transition is strictly controlled by its corresponding purely input transition. Therefore, condition 1 also holds. □

The ESCIWF-net in Fig. 2(b) has a strict minimal siphon as shown in Fig. 4(b), but the siphon does not have any similar S-graph such that each purely output transition is strictly controlled by the corresponding purely input transition. Therefore, the siphon can become empty(it will become empty if $t_{1,1}t_{2,1}$ are fired). Therefore, the ESCIWF-net in Fig. 2(b) is not live. The ESCIWF-net in Fig. 3(a) meets condition 1 and thus it is live, but it has a live minimal generator which is not an absorber and thus it is not safe. The ESCIWF-nets in Fig. 2(a) and Fig. 3(b) both meet conditions 1 and 2. Therefore, they are live and safe and thus the corresponding SCIWF-nets are compatible.

5   Conclusion

This paper proposes a necessary and sufficient condition to decide liveness and safeness for ESCIWF-net so as to decide compatibility for SCIWF-nets. The condition depends on the net structure only. Since SCIWF-nets only allow some simple cases of circuits, their modeling power is weaker than IWF-nets. In fact, SCIWF-nets are a particular class of asymmetric choice nets and their asymmetric structures are simpler than general asymmetric structures. The relation between SCIWF-nets and the famous FCWF-nets is that their intersection is not empty but they do not contain each other. Aalst et al. realized that the modeling power of FCWF-nets is limited and tried to explore the soundness of ACWF-nets. So far no one has proposed a universal net-structured-based condition to decide compatibility or soundness. Therefore, our work is helpful for exploring some bigger classes of IWF-nets, and this is our future work. We also plan to develop the related algorithms as well as a related tool.

Acknowledgments. This paper was supported in part by the National Nature Science Foundation of China (Grant No. 61572360) and in part by the Shanghai Education Development Foundation and Shanghai Municipal Education Commission (Shuguang Program).

References

1. Aalst, W.M.P.: Interorganizational workflows: an approach based on message sequence charts and Petri nets. Syst. Anal. Model. Simul. **34**, 335–367 (1999)
2. Aalst, W.M.P.: The application of Petri nets to workflow management. J. Circuit Syst. Comp. **8**, 21–66 (1998)
3. Aalst, W.M.P.: Workflow verification: finding control-flow errors using petri-net-based techniques. In: Aalst, W., Desel, J., Oberweis, A. (eds.) Business Process Management. LNCS, vol. 1806, pp. 161–183. Springer, Heidelberg (2000). doi:10.1007/3-540-45594-9_11
4. Aalst, W.M.P., Mooij, A.J., Stahl, C., Wolf, K.: Service interaction: patterns, formalization, and analysis. In: Bernardo, M., Padovani, L., Zavattaro, G. (eds.) SFM 2009. LNCS, vol. 5569, pp. 42–88. Springer, Heidelberg (2009). doi:10.1007/978-3-642-01918-0_2
5. Barkaoui, K., Ben Abdallah, I.: Structural liveness analysis of S^3PR nets. In: Symposium on Discrete Events and Manufacturing Systems, CESA 1996 IMACS Multiconference, pp. 438–443, January 1996
6. Chao, D., Li, Z.W.: Structural conditions of systems of simple sequential processes with resources nets without weakly dependent siphons. IET Control Theory Appl. **3**, 391–403 (2009)
7. Chu, F., Xie, X.: Deaklock analysis of Petri nets using siphons and mathematical programming. IEEE Trans. Robot. Autom. **13**(6), 793–804 (1997)
8. Colom, J.M.: The resource allocation problem in flexible manufacturing systems. In: Aalst, W.M.P., Best, E. (eds.) ICATPN 2003. LNCS, vol. 2679, pp. 23–35. Springer, Heidelberg (2003). doi:10.1007/3-540-44919-1_3
9. Desel, J., Esparza, J.: Free Choice Petri Nets. Cambridge University Press, Cambridge (1995)
10. Fanti, M.P., Zhou, M.C.: Deaklock control methods in automated manufacturing systems. IEEE Trans. Syst. Man Cybern. A. **34**, 5–22 (2004)
11. Hee, K., Sidorova, N., Voorhoeve, M.: Generalised soundness of workflow nets is decidable. In: Cortadella, J., Reisig, W. (eds.) ICATPN 2004. LNCS, vol. 3099, pp. 197–215. Springer, Heidelberg (2004). doi:10.1007/978-3-540-27793-4_12
12. Jeng, M.D., Xie, X.L., Chung, S.L.: $ERCN^*$ Merged nets for modeling degraded behavior and parallel processes in semiconductor manufacturing systems. IEEE Trans. Syst. Man. Cybern. Part A **34**, 102–112 (2004)
13. Jiao, L., Cheung, T., Lu, W.: On liveness and boundedness of asymmetric choice nets. Theoret. Comput. Sci. **311**, 165–197 (2004)
14. Kim, T.H., Chang, C.K., Mitra, S.: Design of service-oriented systems using SODA. IEEE Trans. Serv. Comput. **3**, 236–249 (2010)
15. Kindler, E.: The ePNK: an extensible Petri net tool for PNML. In: Kristensen, L.M., Petrucci, L. (eds.) PETRI NETS 2011. LNCS, vol. 6709, pp. 318–327. Springer, Heidelberg (2011). doi:10.1007/978-3-642-21834-7_18
16. Liu, G.J.: Some complexity results for the soundness problem of workflow nets. IEEE Trans. Serv. Comput. **7**(2), 322–328 (2014)

17. Liu, G.J., Chen, L.: Deciding the liveness for a subclass of weighed Petri nets based on structurally circular wait. Int. J. Syst. Sci. **47**, 1533–1542 (2016)
18. Liu, G.J., Jiang, C.J.: Co-NP-hardness of the soundness problem for asymmetric-choice workflow nets. IEEE Trans. Syst. Man Cybern. Syst. **45**(8), 1201–1204 (2015)
19. Liu, G.J., Jiang, C.J.: Net-structure-based conditions to decide compatibility and weak compatibility for a class of inter-organizational workflow nets. Sci. China Inf. Sci. **58**, 072103(16) (2015)
20. Liu, G.J., Jiang, C.J., Zhou, M.C., Xiong, P.C.: Interactive Petri nets. IEEE Trans. Syst. Man Cybern. Syst. **43**(2), 291–302 (2013)
21. Liu, G.J., Reisig, W., Jiang, C.J., Zhou, M.C.: A branching-process-based method to check soundness of workflow systems. IEEE Access **4**, 4104–4118 (2016)
22. Matshmoto, T., Tsuruta, Y.: Necessary and sufficient condition for liveness of asymmetric choice Petri nets. IEICE Trans. Fundam. **E80-A**, 521–533 (1997)
23. Murata, T.: Petri nets: properties, analysis and applications. Proc. IEEE **77**, 541–580 (1989)
24. Reisig, W.: Understanding Petri Nets: Modeling Techniques, Analysis Methods, Case Studies. Springer, Heidelberg (2013)

Prediction of Virtual Networks Substrata Failures

Baker Alrubaiey$^{(\boxtimes)}$ and Jemal Abawajy

Faculty of Science, Engineering and Built Environment, Deakin University,
Burwood, VIC 3125, Australia
{balrubai,jemal.abawajy}@deakin.edu.au

Abstract. In a Virtual Network Environment (VNE), a failure in the substrate network will affect the many virtual networks hosted by the substrate network. To minimize un-predicted failures, maximize system performance, efficiently use resources and determine how often failures may occur, we must be able to predict failure occurrence. In this paper, we present a prediction mechanism to forecast the Time-To-Failure (TTF) of the VNE components based on time series data. In addition, we use supervised learning based on a Support Victor Regression (SVR) model to predict future failures in the VNE. The prediction can be used to establish a tolerable maintenance plan in the event of substrate and virtual network failure. Failure prediction can be used to enhance virtual network (VN) dependability by forecasting the failure occurrences in the substrate network using runtime execution states of the system and the history of observed failures.

Keywords: Failure · Time-To-Failure · Virtual Network Environment · Substrate network · Support vector machine regression · Virtual network

1 Introduction

Because multiple virtual networks run on a shared physical network, failure in the physical network will cause failure in each of the virtual networks. Virtual network failure may cause a huge amount of data loss and it may not be possible to reactivate the virtual network after the failure. Failure prediction is used to forecast failure occurrences in the substrate network using runtime execution states of the system and the history of observed failures. The aim of a failure prediction model is to assess whether there is a risk that the virtual networks cannot operate as expected. The risk assessment depends on system characteristics such as the TTF for each component, whether each component in VNE operate with a backup or without backup in the event of failure and the current load of the system. In addition, failure prediction can be used to predict a critical situation and apply countermeasures to prevent the occurrence of a failure and reduce the time to repair for the upcoming failure. To identify a failure-prone situation in a virtual network, the output prediction is either a binary decision or a continuous measurement and can be used to judge the current situation as more or less failure-prone. In this paper, we propose failure prediction method to predict failure in more than one component in a VNE by adopting multiple regression

© Springer International Publishing AG 2016
G. Wang et al. (Eds.): APSCC 2016, LNCS 10065, pp. 423–434, 2016.
DOI: 10.1007/978-3-319-49178-3_32

model for time series data and the SVR model. As far as we know, this is the first time that such a modelling technique has been used for the prediction of failure in a VNE. Our contributions are as follows:

- We prepared a failure prediction method that accurately predicts failure of virtual infrastructure components (physical links, physical nodes and virtual networks) in a VNE
- We used TTF of the physical link, physical node and virtual network to forecasting failure in these components.
- We integrated a time series forecasting modelling technique with the SVR model to predict failure in virtual infrastructure components.
- We evaluated the accuracy of our prediction method by computing the percentage errors between the prediction values and actual values. Our method achieved very high accuracy.
- We evaluated the performance of the SVR model compared with multilayer perceptron (MLP) and Gaussian process. According to our results, the SVR model outperforms the MLP and Gaussian process.

For the remainder of the paper, problem formulation with the related work is presented in Sect. 2. In Sect. 3 we highlighted the proposed method for failure prediction, the time series with SVR prediction model. The performance evaluation such as experimental results and SVR model performance presented in Sect. 4. Finally, we conclude the paper with discussion and future works in Sect. 5.

2 Problem Overview and Related Works

In this section, we describe the failure problem in the virtual network environment (VNE) components. The process of instantiate virtual network by allocating substrate network resources to the virtual network is called virtual network mapping algorithm. Virtual network mapping is taking into account the processing and bandwidth capacity requirements of VN requests. Multiple virtual networks are mapped onto a shared substrate network with limited network resources such as bandwidth and CPU capacity as well as different configurations and requirements. Therefore, virtual network mapping is considering as an NP-hard problem [1, 2], and a variety of heuristics have been developed in the literature for efficient mapping. A single substrate entity failure will affect all virtual entities that are mapped onto it. Therefore, failure occurs in a virtual network when the critical physical node or link fails. There are different scenarios for failure in the virtual infrastructure components, such as maintenance [3, 4] or when the virtual network consumes all of the substrate network resources such as bandwidth and CPU capacity [5]. The main problem addressed in this paper is preventing failure before the failure occur in a VNE. Adopting preventive failure strategies in a VNE is a promising approach to further enhance system dependability. In addition, predicting failure is becoming an increasingly significant area of research on dependability to prevent maintenance or reducing time-to-repair. Recent research into the prediction of failures in cloud computing has focused on using the unsupervised learning with Bayesian models to deal with unlabeled datasets [6]. One prediction method is based on a Bayesian model for predicting the mean load over a long period to capture trends and pattern of host load in cloud computing [7]. A framework has been presented to predict demand and provide proactive resources for cloud computation dynamically by using autoregressive integrated moving average [8]. Prediction anomalies behaviors of virtual machines, unsupervised behavior learning looks for early deviations from normal system behavior by capturing the pattern of normal virtual machines operation [9]. Prediction methods have been used to forecast the future load demand profiles in cloud data center network by using auto-regressive linear prediction and neural network prediction [10]. Recent research in prediction the failure in virtual infrastructures component adopted by [11–15], in [11] using traces taken from distributed system for predicting node availability to capture the relationships between the availability of different nodes. Predicting failure in a virtual link has been achieved by checking the traffic rate of a user link and adapting the allocated bandwidth based on the predicted traffic [12]. A dynamic meta-learning prediction method adjusts its rules of failure patterns according to accuracy tracing and dynamic re-training with time [13]. Linear traffic predictors have been used to dynamically resize the bandwidth of virtual private network links [14]. Active virtual network management prediction mechanism has been used for active prediction in virtual network [15]. Failure prediction is essential for developing proactive fault-tolerance mechanisms and self-managing resource burdens for system-level dependability and productivity assurance [16]. Therefore, we develop a prediction mechanism solution to predict the TTF of the virtual infrastructure components based on time series and use SVR to forecast failure.

3   Prediction Failure in VNE

In this section, we propose a new approach for predicting failure in virtual infrastructures using the time series forecasting modelling technique and the support vector regression (SVR) model. Because multiple factors can produce failure in a VNE, we adopted a multiple regression model to predict the future failure of each component in VNE. Therefore, The SVR algorithm is adopted for solving multiple regression problems, it is used a kernel function can run any dimension of feature space and it can be used to solve a multiple regression problem, it is robust to very large numbers of attributes with small numbers of instances, it employs very sophisticated mathematical principals to avoid overfitting and gives greater experimental results compared with other models [17]. Time series data are a set of observation that occur over time or a collection of random variables indexed in time to represent samples of the system's behavior over time. The forecast of the system's behavior progression over time involves the forecast of the time series explaining the system's behavior. The architecture of the failure prediction model is illustrated in Fig. 1. The input data of our failure prediction model are the TTF for each component (physical links, physical nodes and virtual networks) in the VNE. The mean time to failure (MTTF) can be used to measure the probability of failure by integrating the probability distribution function (pdf), that is, $\mathrm{MTTF} = \int_{t_0}^{\infty} f_T(t)dt$. Therefore, TTF is chosen as a feature in our prediction model because it can be used to measure the probability of the physical network fail at or before time t_0. From the TTF input dataset we construct lagged variables. Lagged variables are the main mechanism to capture the relationship between the past and current values of a series by support vector machines learning algorithms. To create periodicity, we create a set of lagged input variables within a fixed-length window in the time series. In our model, we used variables lagged between 1 and 24 h, where 1 is the minimum previous time step to create a lagged variable that holds the target value at time t-1, and 24 is the maximum previous time step to create a lagged variable that holds the target value at time t-24. Thus, the period between the minimum and maximum lag will become the lagged variables. When the lagged variables have been constructed, the variable can be predicted from itself. We are interested in predicting failure in more than one component because multiple factors can produce failure in VNE, for example, physical link failure, physical node failure and virtual network failure. Therefore, we adopted a multiple regression model for the time series data to predict the future failure of each component in VNE. The lagged variables created from the TTF input dataset are used in multiple regression model. We used the lagged variables $x_{i,t-1}, x_{i,t-2}, \ldots, x_{i,t-p}$ in the multiple regression model to represent the TTF of the physical links, physical nodes and virtual networks. The aim of multiple regression model is to forecast each entry in the time series accurately by finding a formula that capture the autocorrelation between the lagged values and the current values of the series. Thus, the time-series forecasting modelled as follows:

$$Y_t = f(X_{i,t}) = f(x_{i,t-1}, x_{i,t-2}, \ldots, x_{i,t-p}) \qquad (1)$$

where Y_t is the output observation at time t of inputs $X_{i,t}$, and $X_{i,t}$ is the input vector of lagged variables $(x_{i,t-1}, x_{i,t-2}, \ldots, x_{i,t-p})$, i is a constant number i = 1, 2, 3, …., n (i = 1 represents a vector of lagged variables TTF of physical links, i = 2 represents a vector of lagged variables TTF physical nodes and i = 3 represents a vector of lagged variables TTF of virtual networks), t is the number of observation at time, p represent the number of past observations and f is a function to find autocorrelation between the time-lagged value and current value. Thus, (1) can be written as follows:

$$Y_t = f(x_{1,t-1}, x_{1,t-2}, \ldots, x_{1,t-p}), (x_{2,t-1}, x_{2,t-2}, \ldots, x_{2,t-p}), (x_{3,t-1}, x_{3,t-2}, \ldots, x_{3,t-p})$$

Thus, the training pattern can be constructed in the SVR model as shown in Table 1. Where t-p is the total number of training data, p is the number of lagged variables, Xi is the lagged variables vector for VNE components, such as (i = 1 for the lagged variables TTF of physical links, i = 2 for the lagged variables TTF of physical nodes and i = 3 for the lagged variables TTF of virtual networks) and Y is the predicted output. The multiple regression model is a complex and nonlinear problem because there are multiple predictor variables in the model. Therefore, we adopted the SVR model to solve nonlinearity problem and identify the correct time series model for forecasting a failure in VNE. The inputs used by SVR model are the lagged variables of the time series, and these variables are used to capture the unknown relationship between the lagged input variables and the output. In addition, to solve nonlinear problem in multiple regression model and to forecast future failure, the f function need to be approximated by an SVR model. The SVR model parameters C, σ and ε need to

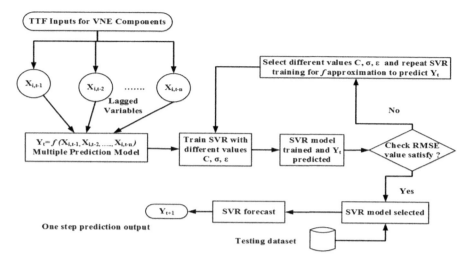

Fig. 1. Architecture of failure prediction model in VNE

be chosen by the user. Therefore, we train the SVR model with different value of C, σ and ε to find the optimal prediction model to capture the correlation between the time-lagged input and the output. The prediction quality of the SVR on the training dataset can be evaluated using the RMSE metric to measure the difference between the values predicted by the model and the real values of the modelled dataset. If the RMSE value is very low, the model is selected, otherwise we choose a different value for SVR parameters C, σ and ε.

$$RMSE = \sqrt{\frac{\sum_{i=1}^{n}(S_{p,i} - S_{r,i})^2}{N}} \qquad (2)$$

where $S_{r,i}$ are the actual values, $S_{p,i}$ are the predicted values at time i and N is the number of the forecasts.

Following successful training, the SVR model with the lowest error rate according to the RMSE metric can be selected. The selected SVR model can then be evaluated using the testing dataset to predict the future failure Y_{t+k} at different time steps k.

Table 1. Construction of training pattern

X_i				Y
$X_i, 1$	$X_i, 2$	...	X_i, p	$X_i, p + 1$
$X_i, 2$	$X_i, 3$	...	$X_i, p + 1$	$X_i, p + 2$
$X_i, 3$	$X_i, 4$	...	$X_i, p + 2$	$X_i, p + 3$
.	.	...	.	.
.	.	...	.	.
$X_i, t - p$	$X_i, t - p + 1$	...	$X_i, t - 1$	X_i, t

For example, if k = 1 uses the t-th TTF as input to forecast a one-step ahead t+1-th TTF as output. The second prediction is a two-step ahead when k = 2 and uses the same input as before and predict t+2-th TTF as output. The results of the SVR model performance was compared with MLP and Gaussian Process algorithms by calculating the normalized root mean square error (NRMSE) for each prediction model using the following equation:

$$NRMSE = \frac{RMSE}{S_{max} - S_{min}} \tag{3}$$

4 Performance Evaluation

In this section, we evaluate the performance of the proposed SVR prediction model and compare it with a variety of techniques such as MLP and Gaussian process.

4.1 Experimental Setup

We used a discrete-event Network Simulator 3 and Boston University Representative Internet Topology generator to generate a hierarchical topology to represent substrate network topology and virtual network topology. The substrate network consists of 50 physical nodes where each node is connected to two neighbor nodes. CPU and bandwidth resources are uniformly assigned to each node and link. The TTF is assigned to each physical node and link. The virtual network topology was generated using the virtual network mapping proposed in [18]. Up to four virtual nodes can be mapped onto each physical node with an average lifetime of 1,000 time units for each virtual network request through the simulation of 50,000 time units in a substrate network. In addition, Weka version 3.7.13 with forecast package was used to build an SVR model based on the training dataset to find optimal function f with given values of the SVR parameters C, ε, σ to capture the unknown relationship between the time-lagged input and the output.

4.2 Data Sets

We used Network Simulator 3 in our research as a platform to be used to analyses network features and collect interesting data (TTF). In our model, we assume that the component failure time decreases linearly according to the number of virtual networks sharing the substrate component. In addition, we assume the virtual network is mapped onto the physical network without redundancy. When the physical component fails, the virtual network fails. The TTF of the hardware and software components are shown in Table 2, which is based on factory specification and adopted from recent literatures [19–23]. Based on Table 2, random numbers were uniformly generated over the interval [35,100] to represent the TTF of the TTFs of the infrastructure components

Table 2. TTF for virtual infrastructure components

Node	XTTF (h)
Physical Switch/Router	320,000
Virtual Machine Monitor	2,880
Network Interface Card	6,200,000
CPU	2,500,000
Hard Disk	200,000
Operating Systems	1,440
Memory	480,000
Optical Link	19,996

adopted by mapping algorithm. The collected TTF data may be treated as a time series of failure times for components in a VNE.

4.3   Results and Discussions

From our experiment results, we found the optimal parameters that best fit our training dataset for building the SVR model to predict the failure in a VNE, as shown in Table 3. We used 9,702 instances for building the SVR model for one-step ahead and two-steps ahead forecasting the TTF in virtual network, physical link and physical node. To forecast failure in the VNE components, we built an SVR model using the TTF for virtual network, physical node and physical link as input to predict one step ahead (t + 1) TTF as output (future failure prediction). Figures 2, 3 and 4 show the actual and predicted TTF for one-step ahead for failure occurrences in virtual network, physical node and physical links respectively. The predicted values and the actual TTF values for virtual networks, physical nodes and physical link are identical. The SVR model achieved very accurate results because the difference between predicted values and actual values was very low.

Table 3. Training parameters for SVR

SVR parameters	One step ahead	Two steps ahead
C	1560	1560
σ	0.00001	0.00001
ε	0.00001	0.00001

4.4   Validation

The RMSE is used for evaluation of a numerical prediction and measures the average of the square of all the errors between the predicted values and the actual observed values. The RMSE gives a high weight to large errors. Therefore, the RMSE is useful to measure error rates when large errors are especially unwanted in evaluation a numerical prediction. To validate the prediction results from the SVR for virtual networks, physical nodes and physical links, we used a testing set method by splitting the

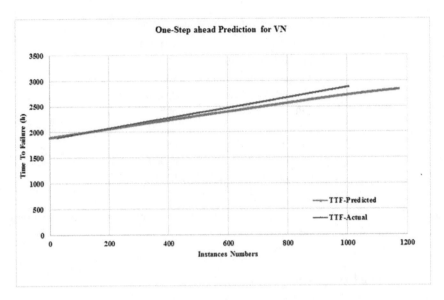

Fig. 2. Prediction of One Step ahead TTF of the Virtual Networks

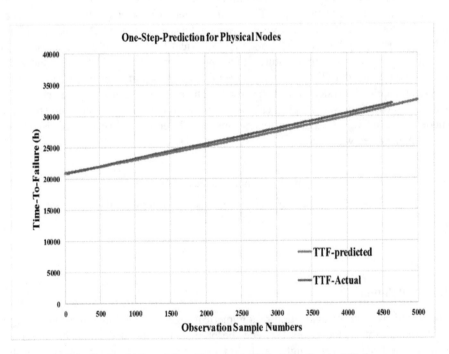

Fig. 3. Prediction of One Step ahead TTF of the Physical Nodes

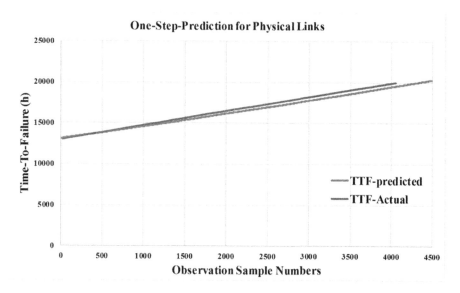

Fig. 4. Prediction of One Step ahead TTF of the Physical Links

dataset into a training dataset and a test dataset. The proportions used for the testing dataset were 10 %, 20 % and 30 % which means that the first experiment was run with 90 % of the data used for the training dataset and 10 % used for the test dataset. From the results of each run, we computed the RMSE, and then calculated the average RMSE for the three runs. The results in Table 4 show our SVR models achieved a very good accuracy because the RMSE, values are very low: 0.16 %, 3.13 % and 1.83 for the VN-SVR, physical node-SVR and physical link-SVR models respectively. The low value of the RMSE indicates that the RMSE achieved very high accuracy in forecasting failure in the VNE. Even with the most advanced learning algorithms, the prediction accuracy could not reach 100 %, and our predictions achieved high accuracy in forecasting the TTF of virtual networks, physical nodes and physical links.

4.5 Failure Prediction Performance

To maximize the performance of the SVR in forecasting the TTF in virtual infrastructure components, three parameters namely C, σ and ε need to be controlled in setting the SVR model. The SVR model's performance on the test dataset is measured by computing the NRMSE. The NRMSE provides an indication of how well the predictor is performing. Low values of the NRMSE indicate that the predictor performs well. Two different regression models - MLP and Gaussian process - were used to compare the performance of the SVR model. The performance comparison was based on 10 %, 20 %, and 30 % of the dataset set aside as a test dataset. The results in Table 5 show that the NRMSE values for both one-step ahead and two steps ahead prediction of failure in virtual network was 0.0008 for the SVR model. In addition, the NRMSE values for the MLP model were 0.0461 for one-step and 0.0893 for two steps

Table 4. RMSE for svr model for virtual network component

% Testing data	VN-SVR		Physical Node-SVR		Physical ink-SVR	
	1-Step	2-steps	1-Step	2-steps	1-Step	2-steps
10	0.092	0.093	2.42	2.76	1.74	1.94
20	0.102	0.112	2.96	3.26	1.67	1.84
30	0.279	0.285	4.01	4.23	2.08	2.21
Average RMSE	0.16	0.16	3.13	3.42	1.83	2.00

Table 5. NRMSE for virtual network SVR, MLP and Gaussian process models

% Testing data	VN-SVR		VN-MLP		VN-GP	
	1-Step	2-steps	1-Step	2-steps	1-Step	2-steps
10	0.0009	0.0009	0.0598	0.0600	0.3645	0.3658
20	0.0005	0.0006	0.0235	0.0236	0.3059	0.3066
30	0.0009	0.0009	0.0550	0.1843	0.3361	0.3367
Average NRMSE	0.0008	0.0008	0.0461	0.0893	0.3355	0.3363

prediction. For the Gaussian process model, the NRMSE values were 0.3355 for one-step ahead and 0.3363 for two steps ahead prediction. Because the NRMSE computed by SVR model is lower than the NRMSE values computed by the MLP and Gaussian process models, the SVR outperforms the Gaussian process and MLP models for forecasting the TTF in virtual networks. We conclude that SVR models achieved high performance with a big dataset or small dataset because the predictors depend on their parameters to fit the data into a model.

5   Conclusion and Future Work

In the VNE, multiple virtual networks run on a shared physical network, and therefore, a failure in a physical node or a physical link can affect many virtual networks. The consequence of a failure in physical network include the loss of critical data lost, the need for reconfiguration of the failed virtual networks and profit loss due to the failure. Therefore, we need a system to predict failure before it takes place. In this paper, we designed a prediction mechanism to forecast the failure of the virtual infrastructure components based on time series and SVR models. Each component in a VNE has a factory-specific feature such as TTF. We modelled the time series as a set of TTF observations ordered in time. To predict the TTF for each component, we used SVR based on the input time series as a one step ahead or two steps ahead. We evaluated the SVR model by using the dataset and comparing it with other technologies such as MLP and Gaussian process. The results show that the NRMSE for the SVR model is very low compared with the NRMSE of the other models. In other words, the SVR model achieved high performance in prediction of failure in a VNE because the predicted results are very close to the actual values. Our prediction mechanism based on time-to-failure feature of VNE components; in future, we will extend the features that include CPU, bandwidth and memory to predict the failure in VNE.

References

1. Maciel, P., Trivedi, K., Kim, D.: Dependability modeling. In: Performance and Dependability in Service Computing: Concepts, Techniques and Research Directions, vol. 13. IGI Global, Hershey (2010)
2. Callado, A., Kamienski, C., Szabo, G., Gero, B., Kelner, J., Fernandes, S., et al.: A survey on internet traffic identification. IEEE Commun. Surv. Tutorials **11**, 37–52 (2009)
3. Markopoulou, A., Iannaccone, G., Bhattacharyya, S., Chuah, C.-N., Diot, C.: Characterization of failures in an IP backbone. In: Twenty-Third Annual Joint Conference of the IEEE Computer and Communications Societies, INFOCOM 2004, pp. 2307–2317 (2004)
4. Markopoulou, A., Iannaccone, G., Bhattacharyya, S., Chuah, C.-N., Ganjali, Y., Diot, C.: Characterization of failures in an operational IP backbone network. IEEE/ACM Trans. Networking (TON) **16**, 749–762 (2008)
5. Gill, P., Jain, N., Nagappan, N.: Understanding network failures in data centers: measurement, analysis, and implications. In: Proceedings of the ACM SIGCOMM 2011 Conference, Toronto, Ontario, Canada, pp. 350–361 (2011)
6. Guan, Q., Zhang, Z., Fu, S.: Ensemble of Bayesian predictors for autonomic failure management in cloud computing. In: 2011 Proceedings of 20th International Conference on Computer Communications and Networks (ICCCN), pp. 1–6 (2011)
7. Di, S., Kondo, D., Cirne, W.: Host load prediction in a Google compute cloud with a Bayesian model. In: Proceedings of the International Conference on High Performance Computing, Networking, Storage and Analysis, p. 21 (2012)
8. Mickens, J.W., Noble, B.D.: Exploiting availability prediction in distributed systems, vol. 1001, p. 48103, Ann Arbor (2006)
9. Prevost, J.J., Nagothu, K., Kelley, B., Jamshidi, M.: Prediction of cloud data center networks loads using stochastic and neural models. In: 2011 6th International Conference on System of Systems Engineering (SoSE), pp. 276–281 (2011)
10. Fang, W., Lu, Z., Wu, J., Cao, Z.: RPPS: a novel resource prediction and provisioning scheme in cloud data center. In: 2012 IEEE Ninth International Conference on Services Computing (SCC), pp. 609–616 (2012)
11. Dean, D.J., Nguyen, H., Gu, X.: Ubl: unsupervised behavior learning for predicting performance anomalies in virtualized cloud systems. In: Proceedings of the 9th International Conference on Autonomic Computing, pp. 191–200 (2012)
12. Wei, Y., Wang, J., Wang, C., Wang, C.: Bandwidth allocation in virtual network based on traffic prediction. In: 2010 International Conference on Computer Design and Applications (ICCDA), pp. V5-304–V5-307 (2010)
13. Gu, J., Zheng, Z., Lan, Z., White, J., Hocks, E., Park, B.-H.: Dynamic meta-learning for failure prediction in large-scale systems: a case study. In: 37th International Conference on Parallel Processing, ICPP 2008, pp. 157–164 (2008)
14. Cui, W., Bassiouni, M.A.: Virtual private network bandwidth management with traffic prediction. Comput. Netw. **42**, 765–778 (2003)

15. Bush, S.F.: Active virtual network management prediction: complexity as a framework for prediction, optimization, and assurance. In: Proceedings of the DARPA Active NEtworks Conference and Exposition, pp. 534–553 (2002)
16. Guan, Q., Zhang, Z., Fu, S.: A failure detection and prediction mechanism for enhancing dependability of data centers. Int. J. Comput. Theor. Eng. **4**, 726–730 (2012)
17. Vapnik, V.: The Nature of Statistical Learning Theory. Springer, New York (2013)
18. Chowdhury, M., Rahman, M.R., Boutaba, R.: ViNEYard: virtual network embedding algorithms with coordinated node and link mapping. IEEE/ACM Trans. Networking **20**, 206–219 (2012)
19. Schroeder, B., Gibson, G.A.: Disk failures in the real world: what does an MTTF of 1, 000, 000 hours mean to you? In: FAST, pp. 1–16 (2007)
20. Vishwanath, K.V., Nagappan, N.: Characterizing cloud computing hardware reliability. In: Proceedings of the 1st ACM Symposium on Cloud Computing, pp. 193–204 (2010)
21. Longo, F., Ghosh, R., Naik, V.K., Trivedi, K.S.: A scalable availability model for infrastructure-as-a-service cloud. In: 2011 IEEE/IFIP 41st International Conference on Dependable Systems & Networks (DSN), pp. 335–346 (2011)
22. Saripalli, P., Walters, B.: Quirc: a quantitative impact and risk assessment framework for cloud security. In: 2010 IEEE 3rd International Conference on Cloud Computing (CLOUD), pp. 280–288 (2010)
23. Hu, X., Liu, S., Ma, L.: Research on dependability of virtual computing system based on stochastic petri nets. In: 2010 International Conference on Computer Application and System Modeling (ICCASM), pp. V8-239–V8-243 (2010)

Freshness-Aware Data Service Mashups

Guiling Wang[✉] and Shuo Zhang

Beijing Key Laboratory on Integration and Analysis of Large-Scale Stream Data,
Cloud Computing Research Center, North China University of Technology,
Beijing 100144, China
wangguiling@ict.ac.cn, 1761391019@qq.com

Abstract. Data mashups provide end-users with an opportunity to create situational applications which aggregate and manipulate data from multiple diverse data sources. A challenging problem is once the data sources are updated and propagate bottom-up to the top level, how to ensure the freshness of mashups. In this paper, an approach is proposed to generate a data mashup scheme and its corresponding synchronous policy guaranteeing the optimal data freshness quality. The paper firstly applies the heuristic transformation rules to select some optimal mashup schemes, and then selects an equivalence mashup by solving the 0-1 integer programming problem. Lastly the paper applies a heuristic algorithm on the mashup scheme to get the operation nodes needed to be materialized and then the synchronous policy. This paper also reports a number of experiments studying the benefits and costs of the proposed approach.

Keywords: Data services · Mashups · Data freshness · Quality-aware mashups

1 Introduction

Recently, with the booming of Web 2.0 and Cloud computing technology, data mashups has become a new form of application, which allows non-professional users to build Web applications by combining and processing data offered by more than one websites, APIs or backend databases to deal with situational and ad-hoc problems. Mashup platforms such as IBM Damia [1], Yahoo Pipes [2], Zapier [3], IFTTT [4] have emerged to support building this type of applications. Data mashups, while providing enhanced immediacy and personalization to explore, aggregate and enrich data from various heterogeneous sources, also pose distinct performance challenges. For data mashups, they often have no strict restriction for their data sources. So the data sources of mashups often have various characteristics such as update frequency, data volume and performance. Since data mashups are designed for non-professional users, there are often a large number of mashups hosted on one mashup platform. These make it quite necessary to ensure the quality of mashups. However, the quality assurance schemes used in traditional Web applications and traditional web service applications can't be directly used in mashups. Among various attributes of the mashup quality, data freshness has been identified as one of the most important attributes for data consumers [5].

This paper proposes an approach to address the issue of how to guarantee data freshness quality goal of mashups. The main contributions of this paper are that we

© Springer International Publishing AG 2016
G. Wang et al. (Eds.): APSCC 2016, LNCS 10065, pp. 435–449, 2016.
DOI: 10.1007/978-3-319-49178-3_33

presented and analyzed the algorithms for generating the optimal data service mashup scheme and determining the operational nodes to be materialized and the corresponding synchronous polices.

We have developed a real data service sharing and integration prototype. This paper reports the experimental evaluation studying the benefits and costs of the proposed approach.

2 Motivation

For some mashup applications such as monitoring application for emergency management, it is very important if the data is fresh enough for end users. Data freshness has been identified as one of the most important attributes of data quality for data consumers. However it has several definitions and metrics according to the different objectives of the applications [6, 7]. Mokrane Bouzeghoub and Verónika Peralta have presented the taxonomy of freshness metrics and their relations with the application types and synchronization policies. [8] In the following, we firstly analyze the freshness metrics for different kinds of mashups and then give a motivating example to illustrate the problem this paper tries to solve.

Michael has classified mashups into several patterns. [9] For the mashups of "Harvest Pattern", "Assemble Pattern" and "Manage Pattern" need to reflect the changes of the data sources. For these mashups, if the underlying data sources change frequently, we can use the currency metric that measures the time elapsed since the source data changed without being reflected in the mashup application to define the freshness metric. If the data sources are comparatively stable, the timeliness metric that measures the difference between query time and the last update time is more appropriate [10]. In this paper, we use the currency metric to measure the freshness factor of mashup applications because we focus on those mashups whose underlying data sources are changing frequently.

Consider the mashup which fetches the top 10 popular movies from mtime.com (the largest movie portal in China) and the popular movies from movie.hao123.com (a famous movie guide portal in China), combines the results, and fetches the movie reviews from douban.com (the most popular book & movie reviews portal in China) with the combined results as the input, as shown in Fig. 1. It is the mashup of "Assemble Pattern". In this mashup, the content from "mtime, hao123 and douban"

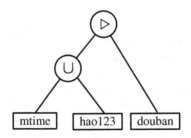

Fig. 1. A data service mashup example

may all change frequently. These changes should propagate to the results presented to users as soon as possible to ensure the users get the freshest results.

3 Background and Problem Definition

3.1 Data Service Mashup Model

We designed a set of operations for data service mashup building [11]. The mashup can be modeled as a *calculation dag* G in which the nodes of G are of three types: source nodes, target nodes and operation nodes. The source nodes represent the atomic data services and have no input edges, the target nodes represent the mashup results and have no output edges, the operation nodes represent the intermediate mashup results with both input and output edges. The edges of G represent the data flow where a node is calculated from another.

3.2 Freshness Evaluation

The currency metric that measures the time elapsed since the source data changed without being reflected in the mashup application is influenced by several factors. In the following, we will analyze these factors.

Synchronization policy

Synchronization policy describes the synchronization between a node and a successor node. There are four policies: *synchronous-pull*, *asynchronous-pull*, *synchronous-push* and *asynchronous-push*. For the synchronous-pull mode, the successor asks the node for data, the latter executes and answers with the produced data. For the asynchronous-pull mode, the successor asks the node for data and the latter answers with its materialized data. For the synchronous-push mode, the node executes and sends the produced data to the successor. For the asynchronous-push mode, the node sends its materialized data to the successor.

In the area of database research, there are often three approaches to such kind of data integration problem: virtual view, data warehousing and hybrid integrated view approach. Similar to such a classification, the implementation of a data service mashup system has three approaches. One is the mediation-based mashup system corresponding to the virtual view approach. One is materialization-based mashup system corresponding to the data warehousing approach. The other is the hybrid data service mashup system. The synchronization policy depends on the type of the mashup systems. For example, in a mediation system all the nodes have synchronous-pull/push policies. In a materialized mashup system, all the nodes that answer user queries from materialized data follow synchronous-pull/push policies between their successors, while the nodes that refresh the materialized data follow asynchronous-push/pull policies between their successors.

When there are asynchronous synchronization policies between two consecutive nodes, the data produced by the former must be materialized for being requested later by the latter, and could introduce synchronization delays. The synchronization delay measures the amount of time passed between the end of the execution of one operation and the start of the other. Synchronous delay is one of the most important factors that influence the freshness metric. In the example shown in Fig. 2, the data produced by A_4 can have been materialized for almost 10 h when read by A_5, then the delay will be 10 h in the worst case. However, when there is no materialization, the nodes execute immediately after its predecessors so there are no delays. Furthermore, nodes having the same execution frequencies (as A_2 and A_4) can be synchronized to execute one after the other without delay.

Access Constraints

Sometimes the data services are very expensive or don't allow users to access it very frequently. The access constraints measure the maximum access period of the data services. The access constraints can impact the freshness metric. For example, if there is the access constraint for a data source, the corresponding data service should periodically materialize data to assure the availability of the source data.

Processing Costs

The processing cost of an operation is the amount of time, in the worst case, necessary for reading input data and generating the result. It depends on the communication cost with the former nodes or data sources, the computing cost of the data and the materializing cost.

Execution Frequency

The execution frequency of the nodes is their execution period. If the execution frequencies of two consecutive nodes are the same, there may be no delay between them. If the execution frequency of the former is less than the latter, the delay may be zero too.

The above factors can all impact the freshness value. In the following, the accurate freshness definition is given:

Definition 1. The freshness of an operation or target node in a calculation dag G is the maximum sum of the freshness of a predecessor node, plus the synchronization delay between nodes, plus the processing cost of the node.

$$\text{Freshness}(A) = \max\{\text{Freshness}(B) + \text{delay}(B,A,G)/B \in \text{predecessor}(A,G)\} + \text{cost}(A,G)$$

Figure 2 shows the calculation dag of Fig. 1 labeled with the *ActualFreshness*, *Cost* (processing cost), *Materialization*, *Efrequency* (execution frequency), *AccessConstraint*, *Spolicy* (synchronization policy), and *Delay* (synchronization delay) properties. The Spolicy property has the values Spull (synchronous pull) and Apull (asynchronous pull). The Materialization property has the values V (virtual) and M (materialized). The *Cost* property value is expressed in minutes. The other property values are expressed in hours and minutes (for example, "10" means 10 h, "10h5m" means 10 h and 5 min).

The freshness of a source node (as S_1, S_2 and S_3) is its actual freshness. According to the Definition 1, the freshness of every node in a mashup can be calculated out from

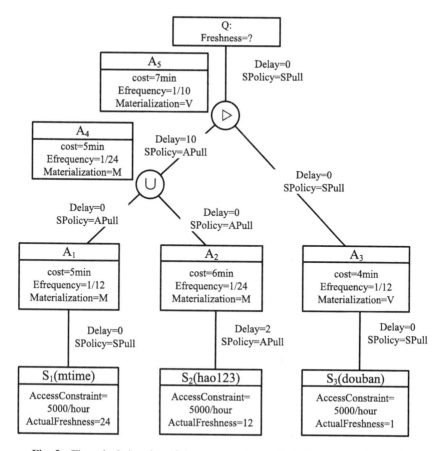

Fig. 2. The calculation dag of the same mashup with different execution modes

bottom to top. Figure 3 shows the freshness of every node in the mashups shown in Fig. 2. For example, for A_5, it has two predecessor nodes A_4 and A_3. The sum of the freshness of A_4 (24h10m), plus the synchronization delay between A_4 and A_5 (10), plus the processing cost of the node A_5 (7m) is 34h17m (24h10m + 10h + 7m). The calculated freshness value from the other predecessor node A_3 is 1h11m. So both the freshness values are compared. The maximum value (34h17m) is taken as the freshness of A_5 as shown in Fig. 3.

We observed that neither a mediation approach (for example, setting all the synchronization policy as *synchronous-pull*) nor a materialization approach (for example, setting all the synchronization policy as *asynchronous-pull*) can get the lowest freshness value. If we set some nodes materialized and some not, we can achieve the best freshness value. So what we should solve is to find the proper synchronization policy so that the best freshness can be achieved. Here firstly we give the problem definition:

3.3   Problem Definition

A data service mashup scheme is a *calculation dag* $G = (V, E, C_v, F_v, D_e)$, where:

- V and E are the set of nodes and edges of G.
- C_v is the processing cost of the node v.
- F_v is the freshness value of the node v.
- D_e is the synchronous delay value of the edge e.

Now the problem for freshness aware data service mashup building can be described as: determine the synchronous policies of all edges in E, such that the freshness value of the target node is the smallest possible.

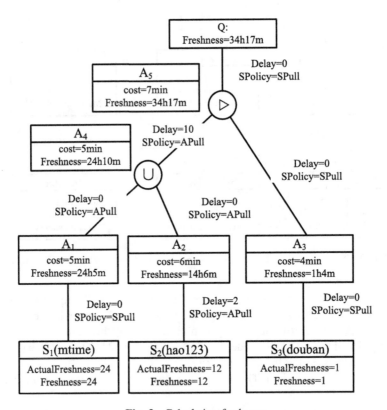

Fig. 3. Calculating freshness

4   Freshness-Aware Data Service Mashups

4.1   Synchronous Policy Determination

Given a mashup scheme, we shall find the optimal synchronous policies of the edges such that the freshness is minimal by comparing the freshness of every possible combination of edges. Suppose there are n edges in a mashup scheme G, then we have to try 4^n combinations. So we should use some heuristics to reduce the search space.

The above analysis shows that if and only if there are asynchronous synchronization policies between two consecutive nodes, there will be delay between these two nodes (the delay can be zero if the execution frequency are the same). So the nodes that should be materialized can be firstly selected and then generate the synchronous policy combinations of the edges.

The algorithm in Fig. 4 for determining M(nodes) is based on the following idea: whenever a new node is considered to be materialized, we calculate the saving it brings in freshness. If this value is positive, then this node can be considered to be materialized. For each node that can be considered to be materialized, we calculate the new freshness value by subtracting the old freshness value using the saving. Then we compare the new freshness value of this node's siblings to get the minimum new freshness value as the freshness value of the father node.

For a data service mashup scheme $G = (V, E, C_v, F_v, D_e)$, assume all the nodes are not materialized in the initial state. $w(v)$ denotes the cost of a node when it is materialized. $\text{Cost}(v)$ denotes the cost of a node when it is not materialized. $C_s(v)$ denotes the saving a node v brings in freshness if this node is materialized. It is calculated by $C_s(v) = \text{cost}(v) - w(v) - \text{delay}(v)$. The first part of this formula $(\text{cost}(v) - w(v))$ indicates the saving cost if node v is materialized. The second part indicates the delay for materialization. LV is the list of nodes traversing G in post-order.

```
begin
G= (V, E, Cv, Fv, De)
M := ∅
create list LV by traversing G in post-order;
pick up the first node v and its siblings from LV as SV;
calculate Cs(v) = cost(v) - w(v) - delay(v) for each v in
SV
remove v from LV and SV where Cs(v) <= 0
if SV ≠ ∅
for each Cs(v) > 0 in SV :
calculate the new freshness value of D(v) = freshness(v)
- Cs(v)
calculate the new freshness of the father node of v as :
freshness(father(v)) = minᵥ∈ₛᵥ(D(v)), denote the node whose new
freshness value is the smallest as u
insert u into M
repeat step 4 until LV = ∅
end;
```

Fig. 4. HAmashup algorithm to determine the materialized nodes

As soon as the nodes needed to be materialized have been determined, the synchronous policies of all the nodes can be generated.

At the extreme condition when the processing cost of the nodes is very small compared with the delay value, we can neglect the processing cost of the nodes and the best freshness value can be acquired if the nodes are not materialized.

We now demonstrate this algorithm with our example in Fig. 1. For G, $f(A_1) = 24h5m$, $f(A_2) = 14h7m$, $f(A_3) = 1h4m$, $f(A_4) = 24h14m$, $f(A_5) = 24h18m$. Initially $LV = <A_1, A_2, A_3, A_4, A_5>$, and $M = \emptyset$. Firstly we pick up A_1, A_2, A_3 from LV into SV and calculate $C_s(v)$ for each node in SV. So $C_s(A_2) = (7 - 6) - 10 < 0$; $C_s(A_1) = (8 - 5) - 0 = 3$, and $C_s(A_3) = 0$. Thus we calculate the new freshness value of $f(A_4) = 24h14m - 3m = 24h11m$. Because $C_s(A_3), C_s(A_4), C_s(A_5)$ are all <= 0, so they are removed from LV.

As a result, A_1 will be materialized and the new freshness of Q is $f(Q) = 24h11m + 7m = 24h18m$, which is consistent with our observations.

4.2   Mashup Scheme Generation

In fact, in order to get the same results, different users may use different mashup scheme. The right side of Fig. 5 shows the other mashup scheme. Their execution cost may not be the same. In this example, the join operation and the union operation has different cost and the total execution costs are different. So we should firstly select the optimal mashup scheme which has the smallest execution cost. After the optimal mashup scheme is generated, we can begin to determine the synchronous policies to get the smallest freshness value.

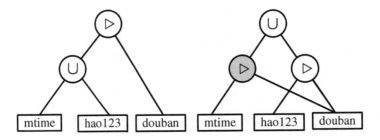

Fig. 5. Order of the operation nodes

In order to simplify the description, we use $\sum$, σ, s, μ, π, respectively to represent rowcount, rowfilter, rowsort, columndelete(projection), rowtruncate(or rowtail). We use $\cup$ and $\cap$ to represent the union and join operations of two tables. Based on the equivalence transformation rules for relational algebra, our equivalence transformation rules also mainly consist of commutative law, distributive law and concatenate law.

Learned from heuristic rules for relation algebra, we firstly use the heuristic transformation rules in order to get the optimal mashup scheme:

- To carry out filter as soon as possible. Generally, filter can reduce the intermediate results for computation. However, if truncate and tail are prior to filter, then the order of filter operator will not be changed.

- To execute filter and projection simultaneously. If there are some filter operators and projection operators, and all of them are applied to the same tuples, then all the operators will be executed simultaneously to avoid duplication of scanning of the tuples.
- To combine projection with union and join. This rule can reduce the scanning on tuples.

We can model the optimal mashup scheme selection problem as 0-1 integer programming (IP) problem. This IP problem formulation states that to select a subset of mashup schemes such that all nodes can be executed and the total mashup execution cost is the minimum. In the following, we shall first calculate the total mashup execution cost, and then present the IP formulation of the problem.

The basic idea to calculate the execution of a mashup is to accumulate the estimated cost of each operation nodes in this mashup. In the following we present all the equivalent mashups and their corresponding operation nodes using vectors and matrices, and then calculate their estimated execution cost.

$E(v_i)$ is the set of the mashups which are equivalent to the mashup m_i. $E(v_i)$ can be obtained by using equivalence transformation rules. E represents all mashups, each of which is equivalent to an element in the set V, and we call any element of E an equivalent mashup. In this example, $E(v_1) = \{(DS_1 \cup DS_2) \triangleright_{Ri} DS_3, (DS_2 \cup DS_1) \triangleright_{Ri} DS_3 \ (DS_1 \triangleright_{Ri} DS_3) \cup (DS_2 \triangleright_{Ri} DS_3), (DS_2 \triangleright_{Ri} DS_3) \cup (DS_1 \triangleright_{Ri} DS_3)\} = \{e_1, e_2, e_3, e_4\}, E(v_2) = \{DS_1 \triangleright_{Ri} DS_3\} = \{e_5\}, E = \{e_1, e_2, e_3, e_4, e_5\}$.

$O(e_i)$ is the set of all operation nodes of the equivalent mashup m_i. O represents the set of all operation nodes of all equivalent mashups in E, and we call any element of O intermediate result. In this example, $O = \{DS_1 \cup DS_2, DS_2 \cup DS_1, DS_1 \triangleright_{Ri} DS_3, DS_2 \triangleright_{Ri} DS_3, (DS_1 \cup DS_2) \triangleright_{Ri} DS_3, (DS_2 \cup DS_1) \triangleright_{Ri} DS_3, (DS_1 \triangleright_{Ri} DS_3) \cup (DS_2 \triangleright_{Ri} DS_3), (DS_2 \triangleright_{Ri} DS_3) \cup (DS_1 \triangleright_{Ri} DS_3)\}$.

After we get E and O, we can construct two matrices EV and OE. But we have to first introduce some symbols, of which the $\otimes$ represents the "multiplication" between two vectors with the same length respectively, and the $\times$ represents the "multiplication" between matrix and vector, and the "/" indicates matrix transpose or vector transpose.

EV is a 0-1 Boolean matrix with $|V| \times |E|$, and if and only if $E(v_i) = e_j$, the EV(i, j) = 1, else EV(i, j) = 0.

$$EV = \begin{pmatrix} 1 & 1 & 1 & 1 & 0 \\ 0 & 0 & 0 & 0 & 1 \end{pmatrix}$$

OE is a 0-1 Boolean matrix with $|E| \times |O|$, if and only if $O(e_j) = o_i$, the OE(i, j) = 1, otherwise OE(i, j) = 0. The following is OE in this example.

$$OE = \begin{pmatrix} 1 & 0 & 0 & 0 & 1 & 0 & 0 & 0 \\ 0 & 1 & 0 & 0 & 0 & 1 & 0 & 0 \\ 0 & 0 & 1 & 1 & 0 & 0 & 1 & 0 \\ 0 & 0 & 1 & 1 & 0 & 0 & 0 & 1 \\ 0 & 0 & 1 & 0 & 0 & 0 & 0 & 0 \end{pmatrix}$$

For every operation node o in the vector O, we introduce an Ecost(o) function to denote the estimated cost of a node which is calculated considering the benefit of sharing the materialized result among multiple mashups. Ecost(o) is defined as:

$$\text{Ecost(o)} = \left\{ \sum\nolimits_{q \in R} C^q(o) \right\} / n_v$$

where $q \in R$ is the set of mashups, $C^q(o)$ is the saving cost of mashup q accessing node o. n_v is the number of mashups which can share the materialized result of o. c^O is the Ecost vector of the operation nodes. For example, the Ecost of the single step computing of the $(DS_1 \cup DS_2) \triangleright_{Ri} DS_3$ is the Ecost of join operation between $DS_1 \cup DS_2$ and DS_3. It can be acquired by monitoring the execution of the nodes. Based on the assumption that there exists v_1 and v_2 on the same platform, we get the cost and estimated cost for each operation node as shown in Table 1 and $c^O = (7, 7, 9, 12, 7, 7, 8, 8)$.

Table 1. Cost of the operation node

Operation node	$DS_1 \cup DS_2$	$DS_2 \cup DS_1$	$DS_1 \triangleright_{Ri} DS_3$	$DS_2 \triangleright_{Ri} DS_3$	$(DS_1 \cup DS_2)$ $\triangleright_{Ri} DS_3$	$(DS_2 \cup DS_1)$ $\triangleright_{Ri} DS_3$	$(DS_1 \triangleright_{Ri} DS_3)$ $\cup (DS_2 \triangleright_{Ri} DS_3)$	$(DS_2 \triangleright_{Ri} DS_3)$ $\cup (DS_1 \triangleright_{Ri} DS_3)$
n_v	1	1	3	2	1	1	1	1
Cost = $\sum_1^{n_v} C^q(o)$	7m	7m	27m	24m	7m	7m	8m	8m
Ecost(o)	7 m	7 m	9 m	12 m	7 m	7 m	8 m	8 m

After we get the matrices EV, OE and the cost vector c^O, we can calculate the mashup execution cost:

Firstly, we calculate $O^S = (I^V \times EV) \otimes x^E$, which is a vector of the selected equivalent mashups, where I^V is a row vector with the length of $|V|$ and all the elements are 1, x^E is a 0-1 vector, and 0 indicates that the equivalent mashup is not selected and 1 indicates the equivalent mashup is selected.

After we get O^S, we multiply O^S with OE, which is $O^S \times OE$, and get the vector of the single step computing of the operation nodes of the selected equivalent mashups.

Then $O^S \times OE$ is multiplied by c^O, which is $(O^S \times OE) \otimes c^O$. We can get the vector of the execution cost of the operation nodes.

Lastly, we multiply the above result with $I^{o'}$ to calculate the total cost of the mashup execution. where $I^{o'}$ is a column vector with the length of $|O|$ and all the elements are 1.

Then the problem of selecting the optimal mashup scheme reduces to selecting a subset of l mashup scheme $\{e_1, e_2, ..., e_l\}$ where $l = |O|$, so as to:

minimize $C_R = (((I^V \times EV) \otimes X^E) \times OE) \otimes c^O \times I^{o'}$, subject to $X^E \times EV' = I^V$

The constraint $X^E \times EV' = I^V$ indicates that only one schema is selected for each mashup. The solution to the above 0-1 integer programming formulation gives the optimal mashup schemes. Thus the problem of selecting the optimal mashup schemes is solved by 0-1 integer programming.

Based on the formulation, we get the vector of the single step computing of the operation nodes and the total cost for every X^E where $X^E \times EV' = I^V$ as shown in Table 2.

Table 2. Total cost of the mashups

X^E	[1,0,0,0,1]	[0,1,0,0,1]	[0,0,1,0,1]	[0,0,0,1,1]
$O^s \times OE$	[1,0,1,0,1,0,0,0]	[0,1,1,0,0,1,0,0]	[0,0,2,1,0,0,1,0]	[0,0,2,1,0,0,0,1]
C_R	23	23	38	38

From this table, we can see that after we solve the 0-1 integer programming problem we get the optimal solution $X^E = [1,0,0,0,1]$ or $X^E = [0,1,0,0,1]$ namely $\{e_1, e_5\}$ or $\{e_2, e_5\}$ are selected to form the optimal mashup scheme.

4.3   Freshness-Aware Data Service Mashup Design Algorithm

In the following, we explain the algorithm for freshness-aware data service mashup design based on the above analysis. The algorithm includes 5 steps:

(1) Read a group of mashup scripts from database.
(2) For each mashup, first apply the heuristic transformation rules and then apply the distributive law of join and union.
(3) For each mashup in the group, select an equivalence mashup by solving the 0-1 integer programming problem. They constitute a new group g, so that the total mashup execution cost of the new group is the minimum.
(4) Apply the HA_{mashup} algorithm on the new group g to get the synchronous policy for each mashup in g.
(5) Output the materialized nodes M, the synchronous policy vector p^E and the mashup schema vector x^E.

In this example, $x^E = [1,0,0,0,1]$ or $[0,1,0,0,1]$. We take $x^E = [1,0,0,0,1]$ for an example. If we select $\{e_1, e_5\}$, after using the HA_{mashup} algorithm, the output $M = \{A_1\}$. If $M = \{A_1\}$, p^E can be all possible combinations as long as SPolicy(A_1, A_4) = APull, or SPolicy(A_1,A_4) = APush.

5   Experiments

Our experimental setup is based on our data service mashup platform DSS and simulates a group of data services spread out on the Internet based on TPC-H[1]. TPC-H describes a multi-part production and sales scenario, involving eight data tables, shown in Fig. 6, where the arrows indicate the dependencies.

---

[1] http://www.tpc.org/tpch/.

In our experiments, we encapsulated the tables into a group of Internet accessible data services. Then we constructed ten.

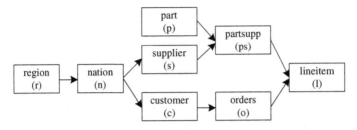

Fig. 6. The sample data source

In the following experiments, we build 10 mashups. To simulate the real data service mashups, the average number of operators in one data service mashup is limited to less than 8, which is similar to those mashups on Yahoo! Pipes [2]. To simulate the real large-scale scenario, we duplicate 1000 data service mashups according to the Zipfian distribution with $\alpha = 0.9$ based on the statistical observation from syndic8 [12], a popular repository for RSS and Atom feeds.

We use symbol f to denote the unitary operator such as *filter* and *projection* to simplify the expression and use JMeter[2] to simulate the stress testing on a single machine with 2 GB memory and 2.26 GHz CPU.

To study the effects of our algorithms, we compare the freshness of three mashup schemes. One is "Materialized All Nodes" scheme that all the operation nodes in the mashup are materialized. one is "No Materialized Node" scheme that none of the operation nodes are materialized. The other is "Selecting Materialized Nodes" scheme which is introduced in this paper.

In Fig. 7(a), we randomly select mashups, and compare the freshness of the three strategies as the number of the mashups increases from 50 to 1000. All the actual freshness of the sources is set to 5. As the results indicate, the freshness incurred by the DSS is lower than the other two schemes throughout the simulated range. The most important thing is DSS's curve shows $\log_2 x$ tendency with the growth of the number of the mashups rather than linear tendency, which shows the DSS has the lowest freshness value. The reason is that probability of reuse and reorder increases as the number of the operation nodes increases.

In Fig. 7(b), we study the effect of actual freshness of data sources on the freshness value of the three schemes. There are totally 30 mashups. The system is assumed to have enough storage to materialize the results of all mashups. The actual freshness of all data sources is varied from 1 to 10 h. As the results indicate, the freshness value incurred by the DSS's materialized nodes and execution mode selection is lower than the other two schemes throughout the simulated range. In "No Materialized" scheme, the increase of freshness value is mainly due to the actual freshness of the sources and

---

[2] http://jmeter.apache.org/.

the processing cost of the operation nodes. In "Materialized All" scheme, the increase of freshness value is due to not only the actual freshness of the data sources but also the delay between different operation nodes. Though the materialized results decrease the processing cost of the operation nodes, the decrease is too small compared with the actual freshness and its effect is not apparently.

We thus conclude that main freshness improvement of the DSS system is achieved when there are higher numbers of mashups and actual freshness of the data sources.

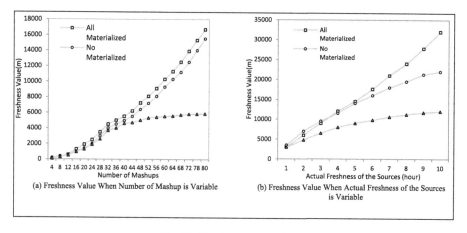

(a) Freshness Value When Number of Mashup is Variable

(b) Freshness Value When Actual Freshness of the Sources is Variable

Fig. 7. Freshness comparisons

6   Related Works

In recent years, many mashup tools and platforms have been developed to support just-in-time data integration such as Yahoo! Pipes [2], IBM Damia [1] and SpreadMash [13]. However, there are seldom works focusing on the performance. Though some research works has been done on proposing a quality model for mashups [14], proposing a caching mechanism to improve the efficiency of mashup execution [12], none work has been done on the freshness quality assurance for mashups as far as we know.

In the database research domain, there has been quite a lot of work on optimizing the performance of data integration systems. Materialized view selection is one of the important approaches. Since Harinarayan published the first paper about materialized view selection [15], the materialized view selection had been gradually warmed up, and attracted a growing number of researchers. Many research results continue to emerge, including the static selection [16], the dynamic selection [17] and the hybrid approach [18], but all of them focus on traditional data integration on the data warehouse. There are some research works on optimizing the freshness of data integration systems. For example, Verónika Peralta et al. have done some work on analyzing and evaluating data freshness in data integration systems [10]. A framework for analysis of data freshness has been proposed [5]. This paper is based on their work on evaluating data freshness.

Though data service mashup systems in essence provide an approach of integrated accessing to multiple, distributed, heterogeneous data sources, there are some important differences between data service mashups and traditional data integration systems in guaranteeing freshness. Firstly, the quality properties of the source services (for example, the actual freshness) can't be determined in advance and may be changed by some external conditions (for example, the service provider may change their access constraints). Secondly, there are many mashups hosted on a mashup platform so the intermediate results of the operation nodes may be shared among those many mashups. So the synchronous policy decisions are based upon dynamic freshness analysis and have taken into account all these special factors.

7   Conclusions

We have proposed an approach for designing freshness-aware data service mashup, e.g., how to determine the mashup scheme and its synchronous policies so that the update of the data sources can be propagated to the mashup as soon as possible and with minimum cost. Our approach relies on analyzing and evaluating the freshness of data service mashups so as to derive the optimal synchronous policies. The approach firstly applies the heuristic transformation rules to select some optimal mashup schemes, and then selects an equivalence mashup by solving the 0-1 integer programming problem. Lastly the approach applies a heuristic algorithm on the mashup scheme to get the operation nodes needed to be materialized and then the synchronous policy. Prototype has been developed applying this approach. Experiments show that our approach can achieve optimal freshness for a data service mashup system.

The work presented here is the outcome of the first stage of research on freshness-aware data service mashup design. We are currently extending our work towards a freshness-aware data service mashup approach in the Cloud computing environment where the data sources has large data volume and the operation nodes can be executed in a parallel way.

Acknowlegments. This work is supported in part by the Key Program of Natural Science Foundation of Beijing under Grant No. 4131001.

References

1. Simmen, D.E., Altinel, M., Markl, V., Padmanabhan, S., Singh, A.: Damia: data mashups for intranet applications. In: SIGMOD 2008: Proceedings of the 2008 ACM SIGMOD International Conference on Management of Data, pp. 1171–1182. ACM (2008)
2. Pruett, M.: Yahoo! Pipes. O'Reilly, Sebastopol (2007)
3. ZAPIER (2015). http://zapier.com
4. A, S., Pautasso, C.: End-user development of mashups with naturalmash. J. Vis. Lang. Comput. **25**(4), 414–432 (2014)

5. Peralta, V., Ruggia, R., Kedad, Z., Bouzeghoub, M.: A framework for data quality evaluation in a data integration system. In: 19th Brazilian symposium on databases (SBBD 2004), pp. 134–147. Universidade de Brasilia, Brasilia, Brazil (2004)
6. Takatsuka, Y., Nagao, H., Yaguchi, T., Hanai, M., Shudo, K.: A caching mechanism based on data freshness. In: 2016 International Conference on Big Data and Smart Computing (BigComp 2016), pp. 329–332 (2016)
7. Martins, P., Abbasi, M., Furtado, P.: AScale: big/small data ETL and real-time data freshness. In: Kozielski, S., Mrozek, D., Kasprowski, P., Małysiak-Mrozek, B., Kostrzewa, Daniel (eds.) BDAS 2016. CCIS, vol. 613, pp. 315–327. Springer, Heidelberg (2016). doi:10.1007/978-3-319-34099-9_25
8. Bouzeghoub, M., Peralta, V.: A framework for analysis of data freshness. In: International Workshop on Information Quality in Information Systems (IQIS 2004), France (2004)
9. Ogrinz, M.: Mashup Patterns: Designs and Examples for the Modern Enterprise, 1st edn. Addison-Wesley Professional, Reading (2009)
10. Peralta, V., Ruggia, R., Bouzeghoub, M.: Analyzing and evaluating data freshness in data integration systems. Ing. Syst. Inf. 9(5–6), 145–162 (2004)
11. Wang, G., Yang, S., Han, Y.: Mashroom: end-user mashup programming using nested tables. In: Proceedings of the 18th International Conference on World Wide Web, pp. 861–870 (2009)
12. Hassan, O.A., Ramaswarny, L., Miller, J.A.: The MACE approach for caching mashups. Int. J. Web Serv. Res. 7(4), 64–88 (2010)
13. Kongdenfha, W., Benatallah, B., Saint-Paul, R., Casati, F.: SpreadMash: a spreadsheet-based interactive browsing and analysis tool for data services. In: Bellahsène, Z., Léonard, M. (eds.) CAiSE 2008. LNCS, vol. 5074, pp. 343–358. Springer, Heidelberg (2008). doi:10.1007/978-3-540-69534-9_27
14. Cappiello, C., Daniel, F., Koschmider, A., Matera, M., Picozzi, M.: A quality model for Mashups. In: Auer, S., Díaz, O., Papadopoulos, G.A. (eds.) ICWE 2011. LNCS, vol. 6757, pp. 137–151. Springer, Heidelberg (2011). doi:10.1007/978-3-642-22233-7_10
15. Harinarayan, V., Rajaraman, A., Ullman, J.D.: Implementing data cubes efficiently. ACM SIGMOD Rec. 25(2), 205–216 (1996)
16. Yang, J., Karlapalem, K., Li, Q.: Algorithm for materialized view design in data warehousing environment. In: Jarke, M., Carey, M.J., Dittrich, K.R. (eds.) Proceedings of the 23rd International Conference on Very Large Data Bases (VLDB 1997), pp. 136–145. Morgan Kaufmann Publishers, Athens (1997)
17. Kotidis, Y., Roussopoulos, N.: A case for dynamic view management. ACM Trans. Database Syst. 26(4), 388–423 (2001)
18. Shah, B., Ramachandran, K., Raghavan, V., Gupta, H.: A hybrid approach for data warehouse view selection. Int. J. Data Warehouse. Min. 2(2), 1–37 (2006)

Maximizing the Spread of Positive Influence Under LT-MLA Model

Feng Wang[1], Guojun Wang[2(✉)], and Dongqing Xie[2]

[1] School of Information Science and Engineering,
Central South University, Changsha 410083, China
[2] School of Computer Science and Educational Software,
Guangzhou University, Guangzhou 510006, China
csgjwang@gmail.com

Abstract. Since the steady development of online social networks, it has resulted in wide-spread research works in the social network analytical areas, especially in the area of influence maximization. Previous works study the influence propagation process based on the social influence model. But traditional influence models ignore some important aspect of influence propagation. The drawbacks of the models are the simplistic influence diffusion process, and the models lack attitude states and capability to capture the interaction between users. To address these problems, we modify Linear Threshold model based on multi-level attitude and users' interaction, which is proposed modeling the positive and negative attitude towards an entity in the signed social network and the effect of interaction relationship between users. Then we propose the LT-MLA greedy algorithm to solve the positive influence maximization problem. Finally, we conducted experiments on three real-world data sets to select initial k seed with the positive attitude. The results show that the proposed solution in this paper performs better than other heuristic algorithms.

Keywords: Diffusion model · Influence maximization · Attitude · Signed social networks · Linear threshold model

1 Introduction

With the rapidly increasing popularity of Online Social Networks (OSNs), they have become an integral part of the every users' daily life. The wide spread researches of OSNs pave the way for a large amount of applications such as viral marketing, outbreak detection, community formation, evolution and detection, recommendations using social-media and many more [6–8,12]. In most existing work, previous information diffusion models only consider the possibility of positive influence, and the nodes in active state cannot turn to inactive or neutral state. However, it is not what happened in the OSNs. According to users' preference, product quality or other reasons, different people may have different

© Springer International Publishing AG 2016
G. Wang et al. (Eds.): APSCC 2016, LNCS 10065, pp. 450–463, 2016.
DOI: 10.1007/978-3-319-49178-3_34

attitudes. Thus, we need consider the different attitudes in the influence diffusion process. To this end, in the problem of influence maximization, we focus on maximizing the activated users with positive attitudes, rather than the overall activated users.

A signed social network contains a set of positive attitude and negative attitude nodes [1]. And it is denoted as a directed and signed graph $G = (V, E, \omega)$, where V is a node set that represent users in social networks, and E is an edge set that represent relationships between them. The parameter ω denotes the edge weight on each E, which ranges in [-1, 1]. In this paper, $\omega(u, v)$ denotes that the influence value from user u to v. $\omega(u, v)$ ranges in [0, 1] represents the positive influence between users, while [-1, 0] means the negative influence. Figure 1 provides a simple example of modeling a signed social network, and it shows that the different influence between users.

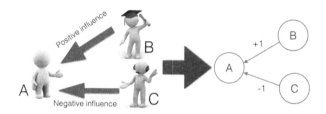

Fig. 1. An example of modeling a signed social network.

With its applicability in solving the mentioned problems above, the Influence Maximization (IM) problem has been one of the most widely studied problems over the past years. Kempe et al. [2] proposed the diffusion models, which are Independent Cascade (IC) model and Linear Threshold (LT) model. They also proved that influence maximization problem is NP-hard, and a natural greedy algorithm can obtain $1 - 1/e$ approximation ratio. Then for the purpose of improve the quality of select influential users, a lot of algorithms have been proposed in the previous works [5–8].

However, these previous works ignore some important aspects in the process of influence propagation. Previous models meet some problems as follows:

Simplistic influence diffusion process: Traditional models only considered active and inactive state. They only consider the possibility of positive influence in the influence diffusion process.

Lack of attitude states: Previous works lack the capability to incorporate the emergence and propagation of multi-level attitudes into the influence diffusion process.

Lack of capability to capture interaction: Previous models ignore to capture the way in which information is perceived between users' interaction.

The challenges in our paper is solving the problems above in a properly way. We extend the LT model to incorporate multi-level attitude (LT-MLA) in the influence diffusion process. We add a parameter which named attitude weight η, which represents the attitudes to each entity (news, product, event et.al). With respect to an entity, people may have different attitudes. We categorize these diverse attitudes into five Attitudes State (AS_i) in LT-MLA model. And we also define every edge in the signed social networks using another parameter, relationship weight ρ, which denotes the interaction relationships between nodes.

In the IM problem, by taking into account the existence of different attitudes in the influence diffusion model, we focus on maximizing the activated users with positive attitudes, rather than maximizing the number of overall activated users. We formulate the Positive Influence Maximization (PIM) problem, and we further prove that PIM problem is NP-hard. We also designed an efficient LT-MLA greedy algorithm, and the goal of scalability to large size networks can be achieved.

In this paper, we develop solutions to the Positive Influence Maximization problem under the LT-MLA model. More specifically, our contributions are summarized as follows:

- We are the first to combine multi-level attitudes and users' interactions in the Linear Threshold model. We propose a Linear Threshold with multi-level Attitude (LT-MLA) model and the PIM problem.
- We demonstrate the PIM problem under LT-MLA model is NP-hard. We also prove the influence function is monotonous and submodular. We propose the LT-MLA greedy algorithm to get an approximation optimal solution.
- We conduct experiments on three real-world datasets of Epinions, WikiVote, and NetHEPT. The experimental results show that the LT-MLA greedy algorithm perform better than several other heuristics, and it is suitable to solving the problem of maximizing the positive influence.

The rest of this paper is organized as follows. Section 2 discusses the related work. Section 3 gives the detailed description of the LT-MLA model. Section 4 shows the analysis of the PIM problem, and it proves its in approximate ability. Section 5 presents LT-MLA greedy algorithm. Section 6 presents the experiment results on three real-world data set. Section 7 concludes the paper.

2   Related Work

Domingos and Richardson [4] are the first to study influence maximization as an algorithmic problem, and their methods are probabilistic. But Kempe et al. [2] are the first to formulate the problem as a discrete optimization problem, and their work proposed Independent Cascade (IC) and Linear Threshold (LT) models. They proved that the influence maximization problem is NP-hard, and they proposed a greedy approximation algorithm.

Kempe et al. [2] shows the details of LT model which is shown in Fig. 2. We assume that only node A is active and the other four are inactive in step 1. When node A begins to propagate influence to nodes B and C through edges, nodes B and C will get the influence from node A as represented by the blue histograms.

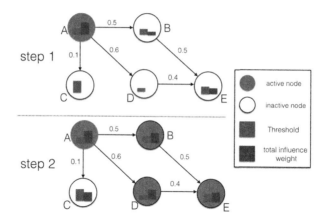

Fig. 2. Propagation of influence in LT model.

If a node receives a certain level of influence greater than its personal influence threshold, the node will be influenced successfully and be active state, such as node B and D in the step 1. In step 2, node B and D becomes active and starts to propagate its influence to node E. With the influence weight from node B and D, node E becomes active too. At last, nodes A, B, D, and E are active while node C remains inactive.

A number of works [5–8] aim at improving the efficiency of the greedy algorithm or providing alternative heuristics. Lappas et al. [9] study k-effectors problem, which contains influence maximization as a special case. They also use a tree structure to make the computation tractable, and then approximate the original graph with a tree structure. But they only considering the positive opinion. Leskovec et al. [12] proposed Cost Effective Lazy Forward (CELF) algorithm, which significantly shorten the execution time. Goyal et al. [13] extended the original CELF algorithm to CELF++. [5,7,14,15] also improved the efficiency of the greedy algorithm.

Chen et al. [10] extend the IC model with negative opinions, and the novel model named IC-N model. This work incorporated the model with negative opinions, and introduced a parameter q to model the behavior of people turning negative to a product. However, IC-N model does not consider the influential competition between positive and negative attitude during influence propagation. Li et al. [11] studied IM problem with an opinion in signed social networks, and each node has their own opinion and foes capable of doing the opposite. Another related work is influence maximization with the consideration of negative opinions. Hassan et al. [16] proposed the influence weight with trust threshold to determine if two nodes hold trust or distrust relationship. These previous works show that solving influence maximization problem with various opinions becomes more and more important.

3   Linear Threshold Model with Multi-level Attitude

In this section, first we extend Linear Threshold model with multi-level attitude (LT-MLA). Then we present the properties of our influence diffusion model.

3.1   Model Definition

The Linear Threshold model for solving influence maximization problem in online social networks is firstly proposed in [2]. In this model, each node is in the state of active or inactive, and the nodes can only change from inactive state to active state, but not vice versa. Besides, all nodes have an independent threshold θ_u that choose from [0, 1]. The diffusion process unfolds in discrete time steps. At $step = 0$, the seed set S_0 is activated while all other nodes are in the inactive state. The seed nodes try to activate their inactivate neighbors, only if the total weight of its active in-neighbors exceeds its threshold θ_u, that is $\sum_{v \in S_{t-1}} \omega_{uv} \geq \theta_u$, where S_{t-1} is the set of active nodes by step $t - 1$. The influence diffusion process will finish till no nodes can be activated.

Now we extend the LT model to incorporate multi-level attitude in the influence diffusion process. And we give several definitions in LT-MLA model as follows.

Definition 1 Attitude weight (η). We provide attitude weight η as a new parameter, and this parameter represents the attitudes to an entity (news, product, event et al.). With respect to an entity, people may hold different kinds of attitudes. We categorize these diverse attitudes (AS_i) into five state.

Positive attitude and Active state (PA): Users hold positive attitudes, and the users have influence power to affect others.
Positive attitude and Inactive state (PI): Users hold positive attitudes, but the users do not influence others.
Neutral state (N): Users hold neutral attitude, and they do not affect other users.
Negative attitude and Inactive state (NI): Users have negative attitudes, but they do not influence others.
Negative attitude and Active state (NA): Users have negative attitudes, and they have the influence ability to affect other users.

As the attitude maybe various states, a user's attitude can be quantified as a value. We distinguish the five different attitude states with the attitude weight range from -1 to 1. The attitude value can be different states according to the corresponding attitude value. The positive and negative attitude can cancel each other out in the influence diffusion process [3]. But their attitudes toward an entity can be strengthened when people receive positive influences. The value of attitude will be increased. On the other hand, the attitude value will in turn be decreased if people affect by negative influences.

Definition 2 State Transition Condition (STC). The attitude value is mapped to attitude states using a state transition condition, which contains four thresholds. $STC_i = [\theta_{PA_i}, \theta_{PI_i}, \theta_{NI_i}, \theta_{NA_i}]$. The corresponding relations of Attitude State (AS_i) and attitude weight as follows:

  PA – The Node i being at attitude state PA if the attitude weight $\eta_i \geq \theta_{PA_i}$;
  PI – The Node i being at attitude state PI if the attitude weight $\theta_{PA_i} > \eta_i \geq \theta_{PI_i}$;
  N – The Node i being at attitude state N if the attitude weight $\theta_{PI_i} > \eta_i > \theta_{NI_i}$;
  NI – The Node i being at attitude state NI if the attitude weight $\theta_{NI_i} > \eta_i > \theta_{NA_i}$;
  NA – The Node i being at attitude state NA if the attitude weight $\theta_{NA_i} \geq \eta_i$.

Each user have a personal state transition condition in LT-MLA model. When the users receive the influences from neighbors, they adjust their attitude values to the corresponding attitude states. But the LT-MLA should observe the basic rule of LA model, when user s_i attitude states change from inactive state to positive active state, their attitude state cannot be altered.

Definition 3 Relationship weight (ρ). We define relationship weight ρ in every edge, which denotes the interaction relationships between nodes. The relationship weight ρ_{ij} denotes the directed edge from node i to j. The value of relationship weight ρ ranges in $[-1, 1]$.

The relationship weight from user A to B ranges in $[0, 1]$ if user A has positive relationship with user B. And if user A has negative relationship with B, the relationship weight from user A to B ranges in $[-1, 0]$. Then if user A has frequent interaction with user B, user A could influence user B efficiently and easily, thus the value of relationship weight from user A to B may be higher.

From the introduction above, we know that classic LT model only focus on the positive influence. But in the LT-MLA model, we consider multi-level attitude states and its value in every node, and the interaction relationship weight for edges. Moreover, we consider the state transition condition with more specific in the influence diffusion process. Therefore, the process of influence diffusion can be simulated more properly than the existing works.

3.2 Influence Propagation

In the signed social network $G = (V, E, \omega, \rho)$, the influence diffusion process in the LT-MLA model is as follows. At the first step, the seed set $S \in V$ in which each node with positive attitude is active. At step $t > 0$, node $v \in (V - S)$ will change their attitude state when the total influence weights from its activated in-neighbors reach the state transition condition, and the node's attitude state will be changed. The process will be ended when no more positive attitude nodes activation happens.

In the LT-MLA model, each node has a parameter η which denotes users' attitude weight and a state transition table which contains four threshold θ_{PA_i},

θ_{PI_i}, θ_{NI_i}, and θ_{NA_i}. Each edge has two parameters, the influence weight ω denotes the influence power between users and the relationship weight ρ represents the interaction level between users. We should satisfy the following criteria in the LT-MLA model. Given node $v \in V$, the influence weight should satisfy $\omega(u, v) \in [0, 1]$, and $\sum_{u \in V \setminus v} \omega(u, v) \leq 1$.

In the process of influence diffusion, node v changes his attitude state if the parameter η satisfied the state transition condition. And the attitude weight η can be calculated by

$$\eta_v^t = \sum_{u \in A_v^t} \eta_u \times \rho(u, v) \times \omega(u, v) \tag{1}$$

where η_v^t denotes node v's attitude weight at step t. A_v^t is the set of activated neighbors of node v at step t. $\rho(u, v)$ is the weight of interaction relationship between user u to v.

4   Positive Influence Maximization

In this section, we formally state the Positive Influence Maximization (PIM) problem. We provide the definition of PIM problem, and the properties of this problem.

4.1   Problem Definition

In the LT-MLA model, we formally state the PIM problem using the concepts described in the previous sections.

Definition 4 PIM Problem. Provided a graph $G = (V, E, \omega, \rho)$ and the LT-MLA model with defined as in Sect. 3.1. And given a size k, which denotes the number of the seed set that holds positive attitude. The problem that maximizing the number of the positive influenced nodes in the social networks, it can be formalized as follows

$$S = max_{S \in V, |S| = k} \sigma(S) \tag{2}$$

where $\sigma(\cdot)$ denotes the social influence spread function, the value of $\sigma(S)$ means that the expected number of nodes which are positive active by the seed set S in the LT-MLA model.

4.2   Properties of PIM Under the LT-MLA Model

NP-hardness

Lemma 1. The PIM problem is NP-hard.

Proof 1. The Influence Maximization problem is reducible to an instance of the PIM problem based on the LT-MLA model, when the relationship weight of each node $\rho = 1$, the attitude state only contains the positive active and inactive, and only positive influence is propagated in the influence diffusion model. It is known that any generalization of a NP-hard problem is also NP-hard. As IM problem in the social networks is NP-hard [2], and we have argued that IM problem is a special case of PIM problem, thus the PIM problem is NP-hard as well.

Monotone and submodular

Lemma 2. For any influence graph $G = (V, E, \omega, \rho)$, the influence spread function $\sigma(S)$ on seed set S is monotonous and submodular.

Proof 2. In the graph, we can obtain a subgraph G'. $\varphi(G)$ means the set of all the subgraphs. And $Pro(G')$ denotes the probability of G' can be obtained. $d_{G'}(u, v)$ denotes the length of the shortest path between node u and v.

Notice that

$$\sigma_G(S) = \sum_{G' \in \varphi(G)} Pro(G')\sigma_{G'}(S).$$

Let $S \subseteq T \subseteq V$ and $u \in V \backslash T$, and it is clear that $d_{G'}(S, v) \geq d_{G'}(T, v)$. If $d_{G'}(u, v) \geq d_{G'}(S, v)$, then $\sigma_{G'}(S \bigcup \{u\}) - \sigma_{G'}(S) = \sigma_{G'}(T \bigcup \{u\}) - \sigma_{G'}(T) = 0$. If $d_{G'}(u, v) \leq d_{G'}(T, v)$, then $\sigma_{G'}(S \bigcup \{u\}) - \sigma_{G'}(S) = \sigma_{G'}(T \bigcup \{u\}) - \sigma_{G'}(S) \geq \sigma_{G'}(T \bigcup \{u\}) - \sigma_{G'}(T)$. So we know that $\sigma_{G'}(\cdot)$ is monotonically increasing. And if $d_{G'}(S, v) > d_{G'}(u, v) > d_{G'}(T, v)$, we have $\sigma_{G'}(S \bigcup \{u\}) - \sigma_{G'}(S) > 0 = \sigma_{G'}(T \bigcup \{u\}) - \sigma_{G'}(T)$. Therefore, $\sigma_G(S)$ is monotone and submodular.

5 Algorithm for the PIM Problem

In this section, we provide our algorithm to maximize the influenced users with positive attitude. First, we give the introduction of classic greedy algorithms. Then we present our enhancements to make greedy algorithm truly fit for the LT-MLA model in the social networks.

5.1 Greedy Algorithm

First we introduce the classic greedy algorithm. Note that in Algorithm 2. The greedy algorithm sequentially selects a node u into the seed set S that maximizes the following marginal gain $\sigma_u(S)$. The function $f(\cdot)$ denotes the total attitude of influenced nodes, and $f(\cdot)$ is a general submodular function.

We apply the greedy approximation algorithm that achieves $1 - 1/e$ approximation ratio for the influence maximization problem. And Algorithm 1 also shows the set function $f(\cdot)$ with generic monotonous and submodular. The algorithm iteratively selects a new seed u that maximizes the incremental change of $f(\cdot)$ in the seed set S until k seeds are all selected.

Algorithm 1. Greedy Algorithm

Require:
  Graph $G = (V, E, \omega)$, the size of seed set k, and the function $f(\cdot)$;
Ensure:
  A seed set S;
1: $S \leftarrow \emptyset$;
2: While the seed size $|S| < k$ do;
3:    $u \leftarrow argmax_{\omega \in V \backslash S}(f(S \bigcup \{\omega\}) - f(S))$;
4:    $S \leftarrow S \bigcup \{u\}$
5: **end for**
6: output S

5.2   LT-MLA Greedy Algorithm for PIM

Based on the definitions above, we propose a modified greedy algorithm to solve PIM problem under LT-MLA model. We use CELF optimization to improve the efficiency of our algorithm. The details of LT-MLA Greedy algorithm is as follows.

In the LT-MLA Greedy algorithm, the initialization of set S is null at first, and we select the first seed node through the following process. We set each node's attitude weight is 1, and then we respectively calculate their positive influence spread according to the influence propagation process of LT-MLA model. Meanwhile, we consider the effect of interaction relationship weight between users in the diffusion process. We select the node which has the maximum positive influence spread add into the seed set S. Secondly, we set the attitude weight of nodes in S as 1, and then we select a node which in $V \backslash S$ to add in S to calculate the influence spread based on LT-MLA model. This node which has the maximum positive influence spread in S as the second seed node. So we can select the k seed nodes until the size of seed set S is k in the similar approach.

6   Experiments

6.1   Dataset Description

We conduct the experiments on three real-world data sets, which are widely used for information diffusion and social influence analysis, and we summary their basic statistics in Table 1.

Epinions. This is a who-trust-whom online social network of a general consumer review site www.Epinions.com [20]. Members of the site can decide whether to trust each other. All the trust relationships interact and form the Web of Trust that is then combined with review ratings to determine which reviews are shown to the users.

WikiVote. This is a network for voting in Wikipedia, where nodes in the network represent Wikipedia users [18]. The network contains all the Wikipedia

---

Algorithm 2. LT-MLA Greedy Algorithm

Require:
    Graph $G = (V, E, \omega, \rho)$, the seed size of k, and the function $f(\cdot)$;
Ensure:
    A seed set S with positive attitudes;
 1: $S \leftarrow \emptyset$;
 2: While the seed size $|S| < k$ do;
 3:    for any $v \in (V \backslash S)$ and $\eta_v > \theta_{PI}$ do;
 4:        if $i = 1$, set $\eta_v > \theta_{PA}$;
 5:            $m = 0$
 6:            for each node $j = 1$ to R do;
 7:            $m = m + (\sigma(S \bigcup v) - \sigma(S))$
 8:            end for
 9:            $m = m/R$
10:        Update attitude state (v) using Eq. (1)
11:        Update interaction relationship weight (v, u)
12:        Select node $v \leftarrow arg\,max_{\omega \in V \backslash S}(f(S \bigcup \{\omega\}) - f(S))$;
13:        $S \leftarrow S \bigcup \{v\}, \eta_v > \theta_{PA}$
14:    end for
15: Return S

Table 1. Statistics of the three real-world networks

Network	Epinions	WikiVote	NetHEPT
Nodes	131828	7115	27770
Edges	841372	103689	352807
Avg. Degree	6	14	12
Max. Degree	3478	457	2414

voting data from the inception of Wikipedia till January 2008. Nodes in the network represent Wikipedia users and a directed edge from node i to node j represents that user i voted on user j.

NetHEPT. An academic collaboration network extracted from High Energy Physics - Theory section of the e-print arXiv, with nodes representing authors and edges representing co-authorship [19]. Arxiv HEP-PH citation graph is from the e-print arXiv and covers all the citations within a dataset of 34546 papers with 421578 edges. If a paper i cites j, the graph contains a directed edge from i to j. If a paper cites, or is cited by, a paper outside the dataset, the graph does not contain any information about this.

6.2 Experimental Setup

In the experiments, we assume each user's **attitude threshold** value of $\theta_{PA_i} = 0.75$, $\theta_{PI_i} = 0.25$, $\theta_{NI_i} = 0$, $NI = -0.25$, and $\theta_{NA_i} = -0.75$.

Table 2. The Algorithms

Algorithms	Descriptions
Random	Randomly select k nodes as the seed set in the graph
Greedy Algorithm	The greedy Algorithm 2 for PIM problem
CELF	Cost-Effective Lazy Forward selection optimization [12]
LT-MLA	The Algorithm presented in Sect. 5.2

To assign the **influence weight** on each edge, we use the method in [7], where we uniformly generate the influence weight of edges at random in the range [0, 1], and then normalize the weights of all incoming edges of a node v.

We use the following method to generate **user opinions** [17]: the normally distributed method, more precisely, it generates user opinions follow the normal distribution in three ways, $O \sim N(0, 1)$, where no bias on neither positive opinions nor negative opinions, and $O \sim N(0.5, 1)$, where positive opinions are dominating and $O \sim N(-0.5, 1)$, where negative opinions are dominating in the networks.

Having computed the attitude of each node, we calculate the **relationship weight** associated with an edge between two nodes (directed) as the fraction of the probability. They agree with each other across the sub-graphs corresponding to all the topics in the past and not just those corresponding to the related topics.

Algorithms Compared. In our experiments, we compare our algorithm with several other heuristics listed in Table 2.

6.3   Experiment Results

Figs. 3, 4 and 5 present the influence diffusion results for the three real-world data sets. For ease of reading, each figure lists the algorithms in the same order as their corresponding influence spread with the size of seeds from 5 to 55. All figures show that the LT-MLA greedy algorithm consistently perform better than the other algorithms in all three data sets. These Figures also show the influence spread using random algorithm is significantly worse than the LS-MLA greedy algorithm and other algorithms. These results are consistent with previous research results.

From these figures above, when the number of seed set is 55, positive influence by LT-MLA Greedy algorithm is about 50 % higher than by CELF. In Figs. 3 and 4, the trends are more obvious. In LS-MLA model, we add two parameters of attitude weight η and relationship weight ρ. Moreover, we incorporate multi-level and state transition conditions in the diffusion process, these improvements make the influence diffusion process closer to the actual. Therefore, we conclude that the LT-MLA greedy algorithm outperforms CELF and other heuristics regarding positive influence spread.

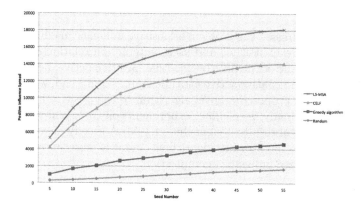

Fig. 3. Positive influence spread for Epinions.

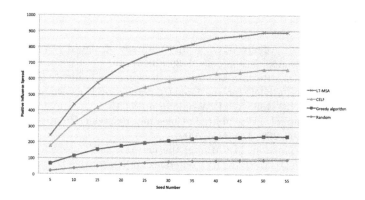

Fig. 4. Positive influence spread for Wikevote.

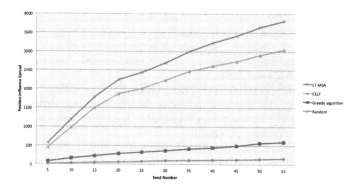

Fig. 5. Positive influence spread for NetHEPT.

7   Conclusion

In this paper, we addressed the problem of positive influence maximization under the setting of multi-level attitude and users' interaction relationship, where the nodes can hold any one of the positive inactive, positive active, neutral inactive, negative inactive and negative active attitude state. To this end, we provided the LT-MLA model and proposed a novel algorithm to the positive influence maximization problem. Finally, we conduct experiments on three real-world datasets. From the experimental results, we conclude LT-MLA greedy algorithm has better performance than the previous algorithms, and it is more suitable for solving the problem of positive influence maximization.

Acknowledgments. This work is supported in part by the National Natural Science Foundation of China under Grant Numbers 61632009, 61472451 and 61272151, and the High Level Talents Program of Higher Education in Guangdong Province under Funding Support Number 2016ZJ01.

References

1. Tang, J., Chang, Y., Aggarwal, C., et al.: A Survey of Signed Network Mining in Social Media. Computer Science, pp. 1–39 (2015)
2. Kempe, D., Eva, K.J.: Tardos.: Maximizing the spread of influence through a social network. In: ACM SIGKDD International Conference on Knowledge Discovery and Data Mining, pp. 137–146. ACM, Washington (2003)
3. Schiffman, L., Kanuk, L., Wisenblit, J.: Consumer Behavior. Prentice Hall, Pearson Schweiz Ag, pp. 260–268, 370–374 (2009)
4. Domingos, P., Richardson, M.: Mining the network value of customers. In: Proceedings of the 7th ACM SIGKDD Conference on Knowledge Discovery and Data Mining, pp. 57–66. ACM, San Francisco (2001)
5. Chen, W., Wang, C., Wang, Y.: Scalable influence maximization for prevalent viral marketing in large scale social networks. In: ACM SIGKDD International Conference on Knowledge Discovery and Data Mining, pp. 1029–1038. ACM, Washington (2010)
6. Chen, W., Wang, Y., Yang, S.: Efficient influence maximization in social networks. In: ACM SIGKDD International Conference on Knowledge Discovery and Data Mining, pp. 199–208. ACM, Paris (2009)
7. Chen, W., Yuan, Y., Zhang, L.: Scalable influence maximization in social networks under the linear threshold model. In: IEEE International Conference on ICDM, pp. 88–97. IEEE, Sydney (2010)
8. Wang, Y., Cong, G., Song, G., Xie, K.: Community-based greedy algorithm for mining top-k influential nodes in mobile social networks. In: Proceedings of the 16th ACM SIGKDD Conference on Knowledge Discovery and Data Mining, pp. 1039–1048. ACM, Washington (2010)
9. Lappas, T., Terzi, E., Gunopulos, D., Mannila, H.: Finding effectors in social networks. In: Proceedings of the 16th ACM SIGKDD Conference on Knowledge Discovery and Data Mining, pp. 1059–1068. ACM, Washington (2010)
10. Chen, W., Collins, A., Cummings, R., et al.: Influence maximization in social networks when negative opinions may emerge and propagate. In: 2010 SIAM International Conference on DATA MINING, pp. 379–390. SIAM, Columbus (2010)

11. Li, Y., Chen, W., Wang, Y., Zhang, Z.-L.: Influence diffusion dynamics and influence maximization in social networks with friend and foe relationships. In: Proceedings of the 6th ACM International Conference on Web Search and Data Mining, pp. 657–666. ACM, Rome (2013)
12. Leskovec, J., Krause, A., Guestrin, C., Faloutsos, C., VanBriesen, J., Glance, N.: Cost-effective outbreak detection in networks. In: Knowledge Discovery and Data Mining (KDD), pp. 420–429. ACM, California (2007)
13. Goyal, A., Lu, W., Lakshmanan, L.V.S.: CELF++: optimizing the greedy algorithm for influence maximization in social networks. In: International Conference Companion on World Wide Web, pp. 47–48. WWW 2011, Hyderabad (2011)
14. Lu, W., Lakshmanan, L.V.S.: SIMPATH: an efficient algorithm for influence maximization under the linear threshold model. In: IEEE International Conference on Data Mining, pp. 211–220. IEEE Computer Society, Vancouver (2011)
15. Lu, Z., Fan, L., Wu, W., Thuraisingham, B., Yang, K.: Efficient influence spread estimation for influence maximization under the linear threshold model. Comput. Soc. Netw. **1**(1), 1–19 (2014)
16. Hassan, A., Abu-Jbara, A., Radev, D.: Extracting signed social networks from text. In: Association for Computational Linguistics Workshop Proceedings of TextGraphs-7 on Graph-based Methods for Natural Language Processing, pp. 6–14. PA, USA (2012)
17. Zhang, H., Dinh, T.N., Thai, M.T.: Maximizing the spread of positive influence in online social networks. In: IEEE International Conference on Distributed Computing Systems, pp. 317–326. IEEE, Philadelphia (2013)
18. Leskovec, J., Huttenlocher, D., Kleinberg, J.: Predicting positive and negative links in online social networks. In: International Conference on World Wide Web, pp. 641–650. ACM, North Carolina (2010)
19. Leskovec J.: High energy physics theory collaboration network. http://snap.stanford.edu/data/ca-HepTh.html
20. Leskovec J, Huttenlocher D, Kleinberg J.: Signed networks in social media. In: Proceedings of Chi Conference on Human Factors in Computing Systems, pp. 1361–1370. ACM, Atlanta (2010). http://snap.stanford.edu/data/soc-sign-epinions.html

Frequent Subgraph Mining in Graph Databases Based on MapReduce

Kai Wang, Xia Xie$^{(\boxtimes)}$, Hai Jin, Pingpeng Yuan, Feng Lu, and Xijiang Ke

Services Computing Technology and System Lab,
Big Data Technology and System Lab,
Cluster and Grid Computing Lab,
School of Computer Science and Technology,
Huazhong University of Science and Technology, Wuhan 430074, China
shelicy@hust.edu.cn

Abstract. In recent years, graph mining has become a popular research direction in the area of data mining. Frequent subgraph mining is an important technology of graph mining that can be used in many fields such as chemical informatics, bioinformatics, and social sciences. The increasing size of graph database is challenging traditional methods of subgraph mining. In this paper, we propose a new approach based on MapReduce to mine frequent subgraph patterns from the vertex-classified graph databases in large sizes. There are two rounds operation to MapReduce. The first round is to mine the locally frequent subgraphs in each node and then we collect the results for all nodes and filter some redundant graphs to obtain a set of frequent subgraphs candidate in global view. The second round is to calculate the global frequency for each graph using the set of candidate generated by the first round. Some topical frequent subgraphs are filtered according to special requirement. The experimental results show that this approach reduces the execution time when dealing with large graph databases.

Keywords: Frequent subgraph mining · MapReduce · Graph database · Isomorphism test · Big data

1   Introduction

In the era of big data, how to extract desired information from a large amount of data is becoming more and more important. This is what the data mining needs to do. Graphs, with their powerful expressive ability, are widely applied in chemical informatics, bioinformatics, medicine, and social sciences. Frequent subgraph mining technologies are important research techniques in these fields. The goal of mining frequent subgraphs is to find patterns of subgraph whose occurrences are no less than a given support threshold. There are two different kinds of frequent subgraphs mining. The first category is to deal with a set of graphs [1,2]. Since it can help biologists to reduce the cost of protein structure matching experiments, finding frequent subgraphs plays a very important role

© Springer International Publishing AG 2016
G. Wang et al. (Eds.): APSCC 2016, LNCS 10065, pp. 464–476, 2016.
DOI: 10.1007/978-3-319-49178-3_35

in bioinformatics. The second category is to deal with a single large graph [3–5]. Such as in social network analysis, frequent subgraph mining can find some community in a social network, then predict users social behavior in the future [6].

Frequent subgraph mining is a classic issue in the area of graph mining. Usually, frequent subgraph mining is an iterative process. A typical algorithm is composed of two steps: (i) find the candidate subgraph [7]; (ii) calculate the frequency of the candidate subgraph [8]. Finding the candidate subgraph and calculating its frequency are both NP-hard problems.

Sometimes, vertices in the graph database will be divided into several classes according to certain attributes. For example, in a social network, people can be classified according to their jobs. In this case, the number of frequent subgraphs is much smaller than in a normal situation. This type of labeled database is known as a vertex-classified database.

In this paper, we propose a distributed method of mining frequent subgraph based on MapReduce in a vertex classified database. In this database, all the vertices are divided into several categories and each graph is in a medium size. The number of graphs in the database is in the order of millions.

Several subgraph mining algorithms have been developed, such as *Apriori-based Graph Mining* (AGM), Gaston, *Fast Frequent Subgraph Mining* (FFSM), *Frequent Subgraph* (FSG) and *Graph-Based Substructure Pattern* (gSpan) [9,10]. Most of these methods are used to solve the situation of database in medium size. But with the growth in size of the graph databases, it provides challenges to the above approaches. On the one hand, the size of graph database is always too large to fit in main memory. It may be interrupted several times through the whole mining process in a single machine. On the other hand, because both steps are NP-hard problems, the increments about the size of the graphs will lead to exponential growth in execution time.

As parallel processing and distributed computing have an advantage in dealing with large data, many researchers choose to use this way to solve the problem [11]. Many researchers choose to take advantage of parallel processing and distributed computing in order to handle the challenges of large data in subgraph mining. For instance, the *MapReduce-subgraph Mining* (MRSUB) [12] is a method of mining frequent subgraphs using the MapReduce framework.

The rest of this paper is organized as follows. In Sect. 2, we discuss related work and its advantages/disadvantages. In Sect. 3, we present our approach to the large-scale subgraph mining problem using MapReduce. We describe our experiments and make comparisons in Sect. 4. At last, we conclude the paper in Sect. 5.

2   Related Work

Previous frequent subgraph mining methods fall into the following three major categories [13].

2.1   Methods Based on Apriori Property

These methods, such as AGM and FSG [2,9], apply the Apriori property to enumerating the candidate subgraphs by expanding a vertex or an edge one step at a time to generate a candidate subgraph and then do subgraph isomorphism to calculate the candidate subgraph in each iterative step. Because of the Apriori property (if a graph is frequent, all of its subgraphs are frequent), we only need to find all of the biggest subgraphs. This kind of approach help to find all the frequent subgraphs in a very simple way. However, it will greatly increase time cost for calculating the support of the candidate graphs. It will scan the whole database each time so that these methods are inefficient when the graph size is large.

2.2   Methods Based on Pattern Growth

These methods such as gSpan, FFSM, and Gaston adopt the pattern growth methodology, which can avoid the overheads from candidate subgraph construction based on Apriori property [10]. These approaches extend patterns from a single pattern directly. For example, gSpan gives each graph one unique label and maps each graph for minimum DFS code. When generating a candidate subgraph, they use a depth first search strategy by adding an unused frequent edge. Furthermore, each graph are uniquely represented as the minimum sequence of the lower triangular of its adjacency matrix. It just tests the sequences of the graphs when do isomorphism test. These two strategies greatly reduce the costs with candidate subgraph construction and improves the efficiency of isomorphism testing, but it does require more memory.

2.3   Methods Based on MapReduce

These methods are always transplantations of approaches based Apriori property to generate the candidate subgraphs [1,5,6]. These approaches can be divided into two distinct steps: candidate generation and subgraph isomorphism. For example, MapReduce-FSG [12] uses the MapReduce framework to implement a distributed FSG. They enumerate all k-sized candidate subgraphs by the set of $(k-1)$-sized frequent subgraphs each time. Then they calculate the frequencies of these k-sized candidate subgraphs to find the set of k-sized frequent subgraphs. These methods have the advantage of being able to deal with big data, but the key is how to transpose the classic approaches to the MapReduce framework and how to solve the problem of communication overhead between nodes.

3   Method for Subgraph Mining

In this section, we present our approach for subgraph mining with MapReduce. Vertices are classified into several types in our database. As shown in Fig. 1, according to traditional definition, Graph 2 is a subgraph of Graph 1.

In this paper, it is not the subgraph of Graph 1, even though they have a same subgraph structure. This is the reason why the number of frequent subgraph drops in the case of vertices classified. Vertices of kind a, b and c are represented as ⊘ ◉ ⊗.

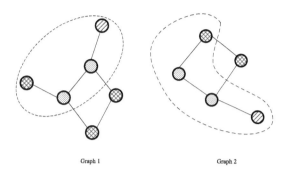

Graph 1   Graph 2

Fig. 1. Example of vertices-classificated graphs

3.1 Method Based on MapReduce

We propose an approach using the MapReduce framework [14]. The collection of graphs in the database are distributed into nodes according to the attribute of their vertices and each node just mines locally to find the frequent subgraph. We then collect all the results from the nodes and sort by the number of vertices. Finally, we take out the redundant part of the results. Some important definitions we used are given as follows.

Definition 1 (Subgraph support). *Given a graph database G, g_i is a graph of G and n is the number of graphs in it. The support of a subgraph g in G is defined by*

$$Support(g, G) = \frac{\sum_{i=1}^{n_i} \delta(g, g_i)}{n} \tag{1}$$

where:

$$\delta(g, g_i) = \begin{cases} 1, g \subseteq g_i \\ 0, otherwise \end{cases} \tag{2}$$

$f(g) = \sum_{i=1}^{n} \delta(g, g_i)$ *is the frequency of g in G.*

Definition 2 (Globally frequent subgraph). *For a given minimum support threshold $\theta \in [0, 1]$, g is globally frequent subgraph if $Support(g, G) \geq \theta$.*

Definition 3 (Locally frequent subgraph). *For a given minimum support threshold $\theta \in [0, 1]$, g is locally frequent subgraph in node i if $Support(g, G_i) \geq \theta$.*

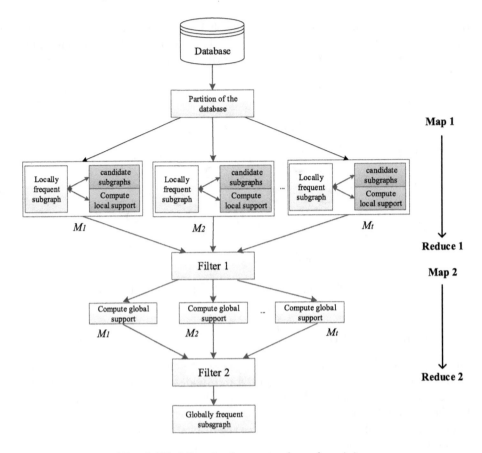

Fig. 2. Workflow for frequent subgraphs mining

The notations used in this paper are listed in Table 1. G is the graph set that needs to mine its frequent subgraphs. M_i is the i-th machine we use. G_i is the subset of G distributed to M_i. $f(g)$ and $s(g)$ are the global frequency and global support of a graph g in the graph set G. $f_i(g)$ and $s_i(g)$ are the local frequency and local support of a graph g in the graph set G_i.

Our distributed method to mine frequent subgraph in the case of vertex classification has at least following two advantages:

First, our method can find out all frequent subgraphs in a parallel way. If a graph g is not reported as a candidate by any machines, then its frequency must satisfy the following inequality:

$$f(g) = \sum_{i=1}^{m} f_i(g) \leq \sum_{i=1}^{m} (\theta \cdot n_i) = \theta \cdot n \tag{3}$$

the graph g cannot be a frequent subgraph of G [1].

Table 1. Summary of notions

Notations	Description
G	input set of graphs
n	number of graphs in G
θ	given support threshold
t	number of machines
M_i	i-th machine
G_i	subset of G that is distributed to M_i
n_i	number of graph in G_i
$f(g)$	frequency of g in G
$f_i(g)$	frequency of g in G_i
$s(g)$	occurrence percentage of graph g in set G
$s_i(g)$	occurrence percentage of graph g in G_i

Second, the graph database can be naturally divided into several categories, separate treatment can reduce the amount of isomorphism testing so as to improve the efficiency of the whole process of mining.

As shown in Fig. 2, in the first map phase, each machine M_i $(i = 1, ..., m)$ gets a subset G_i of G and mines all locally frequent subgraphs in $M(i)$, such that: (i) each frequent subgraph g in M_i whose local frequency must satisfy: $f_i(g) \geq \theta \cdot n_i$; (ii) g is likely to be a globally frequent subgraph in G. In the first reduced phase, we collect graphs into a set named $SummaryResults$ from $M(i)$ $(i = 1, ..., m)$. We then take measures (Filter 1) to remove some redundant graphs from it and get the set of candidate global subgraphs.

In the second map phase, each machine receives the candidate global subgraphs and calculates their local frequency. We can then get the global frequency by the equation $f(g) = f_1(g) + f_2(g).. + f_m(g)$. Finally, we remove the graphs whose global frequencies do not satisfy (3) and gain the set of globally frequent subgraphs (Filter 2).

3.2 Partitions of Graph Database

Due to the fact that the vertex contains information, we can use this information to distribute the graph within the database to the corresponding node. This can reduce the subgraph isomorphism testing in the next step when each node mines the frequent subgraph locally. We distribute the graph according to the number of each kind of vertices in the graphs, so that each division has as even a number of types of vertices as possible. Furthermore, we put each type of vertices in different nodes as far as possible to reduce the amount of isomorphism testing. For example, a candidate subgraph has five vertices of v_1, it therefore needs to do at least 5! isomorphism testings; if it has three vertices of v_1, and two vertices of v_2, it needs to do 3!*2! isomorphism testings at least.

3.3   Candidate Generation

The first step of our approach in frequent subgraph mining is to generate candidate subgraphs [7]. We form a candidate subgraph based on Apriori property in an iterative way by adding an edge step by step. Edges are represented as (a, b) and $(2, 3)$. First, we count the number of each type of edge and collect all frequent edges into *Edges*, our base case. We then construct size k-subgraphs from$(k-1)$-sized subgraphs by adding an unused frequent edge. In this step, we use the label of the two vertices of an edge to charge whether the edge is unused.

Let $Edges(i)$ be the set of frequent edges in g_i and subgraphs(i) be the set of $(k-1)$-sized subgraphs in g_i; *Subgraphs* is the set of the frequent subgraphs that have been mined in the node i; *newSubgraphs* is the set of constructed k-sized candidate subgraphs from $(k-1)$-sized subgraphs. Algorithm 1 is as follow:

Algorithm 1. Local candidate subgraphs generation in node i

Input:
    The set of graphs in node i: G_i;
    Sets of frequent edges in g_i, $Edges(i)$;
    The set of $(k-1)$-sized frequent subgraphs of g_i, subgraphs(i);
    The set of frequent subgraphs in node i that have been mined: *Subgraphs*.
Output:
    k-sized local candidate subgraphs in node i;
1: newSubgraphs $\in \emptyset$;
2: for each $g(i) \in G_i$, extract the set of frequent edges $Edges(i)$;
3: for each $(k-1)$-sized frequent subgraphs $s \in subgraphs(i)$, generate all k-sized candidate subgraphs that contain s by adding an unused frequent edge in $Edges(i)$;
4: add all k-sized candidate subgraphs in *newSubgraphs*;
5: **return** *newSubgraphs*;
6: END

3.4   Isomorphism Testing

Isomorphism testing is the most important operation in the process of frequent subgraph mining. For each of the candidate subgraphs, we will test if it is isomorphic to each of the other graphs in the database, and then count the number of occurrences of the candidate subgraph to calculate its frequency. How to reduce the cost of isomorphism testing is the key to improve the efficiency of frequent subgraph mining.

We adjust the isomorphism testing algorithm in order to adapt to the situation of vertex classification. Graph is defined as a form with its adjacency matrix in traditional isomorphism testing algorithm [9]. Since self-loop is forbidden in the graphs, elements on the main diagonal are valued 0 and they will be omitted when doing isomorphism testing [15] (Fig. 3). In the case of vertex classification, we give a value to each element on the main diagonal according to the kind of the vertex. When we do isomorphism testing, we will take the diagonal elements

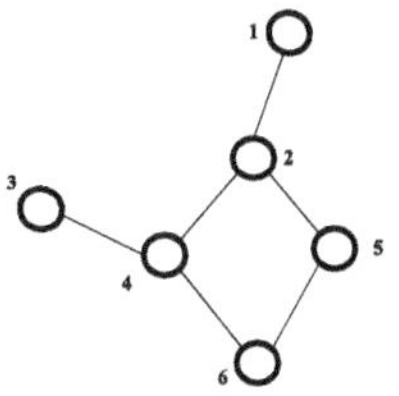

$$\begin{bmatrix} 0 & 1 & 0 & 0 & 0 & 0 \\ 1 & 0 & 0 & 1 & 1 & 0 \\ 0 & 0 & 0 & 1 & 0 & 0 \\ 0 & 1 & 1 & 0 & 0 & 1 \\ 0 & 1 & 0 & 0 & 0 & 1 \\ 0 & 0 & 0 & 1 & 1 & 0 \end{bmatrix}$$

Fig. 3. Adjacent matrix of traditional graph

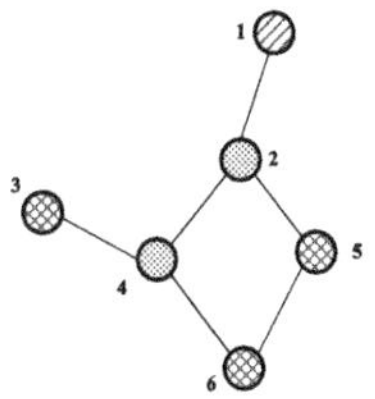

$$\begin{bmatrix} a & 1 & 0 & 0 & 0 & 0 \\ 1 & b & 0 & 1 & 1 & 0 \\ 0 & 0 & c & 1 & 0 & 0 \\ 0 & 1 & 1 & b & 0 & 1 \\ 0 & 1 & 0 & 0 & c & 1 \\ 0 & 0 & 0 & 1 & 1 & c \end{bmatrix}$$

Fig. 4. Adjacent matrix of vertices-classified graph

into account (Fig. 4). This method can guarantee that if two graphs are considered to be isomorphic, they not only have the same structure but also have the same kind vertices in the same place.

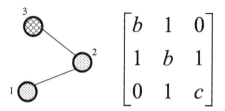

$$\begin{bmatrix} b & 1 & 0 \\ 1 & b & 1 \\ 0 & 1 & c \end{bmatrix}$$

Fig. 5. Example of a candidate subgraph

As a matrix is symmetrical to its main diagonal, we choose to use a lower triangular matrix to represent the matrix and flatten it into a sequence. For instance, we can represent the adjacency matrix for the Fig. 4 as (a1b00c011b0100c00011c). All we need to do is to test whether the sequences of candidate subgraphs exist in each graph in the database. For example, if we get a candidate subgraph (Fig. 5) and need to test whether it is a subgraph of Fig. 4, the detailed is as follow. First we get the sequence of Fig. 5 (b1b01c). Then; according to the three vertices of Fig. 5, we generate two kinds of relevant sequences from the sequence of Fig. 4: (b1b01c), (b1b10c). As long as the sequence of Fig. 5 is included in the two sequences, Fig. 5 is a subgraph of Fig. 4.

3.5 Computing Local Frequency

Another important task is to calculate the local frequency of candidate subgraph s to determine whether s is a frequent subgraph in the node. Let *Subgraphs* be the set of the frequent subgraphs that have been mined in a node. When we get a candidate subgraph, we first test whether it exists in the *Subgraphs*.

If $s \in Subgraphs$, we add s to $Subgraphs(i)$. This step not only reduces the cost of scanning all graphs in the node, but also guarantees all frequent subgraphs have no copies in *Subgraphs* in this node. If $s \notin Subgraphs$, we scan all graphs

---

Algorithm 2. Computing local frequency

Input:
    The set of graphs in node i: G_i;
    The set of k-sized candidate frequent subgraphs: $newSubgraphs$;
    The set of frequent subgraphs of g_i that have been mined: $Subgraphs$.
Output:
    k-sized local subgraphs in node i;
1: for each $s \in newSubgraphs$, if $s \in Subgraphs$, add s to $Subgraphs(i)$;
2: if $s \notin Subgraphs$, do isomorphism testing between s and each graph of G_i;
3: calculate the local frequency of s: $f_i(s)$;
4: if $f_i(s) \geq \theta \cdot n_i$, add s to $Subgraphs$ and $subgraphs(i)$;
5: delete all $(k\text{-}1)$-sized frequent subgraphs from $subgraphs(i)$;
6: **return** $newSubgraphs$;
7: END

---

in the node to calculate its local frequency. If the frequency of a k-sized subgraph s satisfies the equation: $f_i(s) \geq \theta \cdot n_i$, we add s to $Subgraphs$ and $Subgraphs(i)$, then delete the $(k\text{-}1)$-sized subgraph from $subgraphs(i)$. Algorithm 2 is as follow:

3.6 Removing Redundant Graphs

Since each node only does local mining, it means the method has a drawback [1]; it will produce many redundant graphs among the nodes. There are three kinds of redundant graphs: (i) some are subgraph of others; (ii) some are the copies of others; (iii) some are not the globally frequent subgraph. These redundant graphs must be removed from the summary of the results. In $SummaryResultes$, for graph g_i and graph g_j, if they has same node sets, we do the isomorphism testing. If $g_i = g_j$, delete g_i from $SummaryResults$. Filter 1 can remove the redundant graphs of (ii) from the result. Then in Filter 2, we calculate the global frequency of each candidate global subgraphs by the Eq. (1). Then, according to the inequality (2), we delete the graphs whose global frequency is less than $\theta \cdot n$ to remove the redundant graphs of (iii). Finally, for all graphs in globally frequent subgraphs, if g_i and g_j has same node sets, we do isomorphism testing between g_i and g_j. If $g_i \subseteq g_j$, delete g_i to remove the redundant graphs of (i) from the result and obtain the set of the biggest globally frequent subgraphs.

4   Experiments

Our experiment is tested on 4 nodes, each machine with 16 GB memory dual core processor. The algorithm is coded in Java so as to work with Hadoop [16]. The datasets used in experimental study are described in Table 2. The sizes of datasets range from 10M to 493M and the graph number range from 10,000 to 500,000. Each graph has 25-70 vertices and 50-180 edges. The synthetic datasets

Table 2. Experimental data

Datasets	Type	Number of graphs	Size on disk	Average vertices
DS1	Synthetic	10000	10MB	50-70
DS2	Synthetic	50000	49MB	40-60
DS3	Synthetic	100000	98MB	40-50
DS4	Real	27200	26MB	25-35
DS5	Synthetic	200000	200MB	25-45
DS6	Synthetic	500000	493MB	25-35

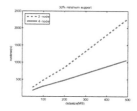 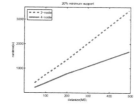 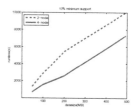

Fig. 6. Comparison with support of 30 %

Fig. 7. Comparison with support of 20 %

Fig. 8. Comparison with support of 10 %

Table 3. Experimental results

Datasets	θ	2-nodes (s)	4-nodes (s)
DS1	10 %	217	12
DS1	20 %	65	45
DS1	30 %	41	29
DS2	10 %	1347	712
DS2	20 %	407	214
DS2	30 %	264	178
DS3	10 %	2825	1536
DS3	20 %	724	389
DS3	30 %	473	296
DS4	10 %	542	298
DS4	20 %	184	94
DS4	30 %	102	77
DS5	10 %	5437	2589
DS5	20 %	1353	776
DS5	30 %	848	478
DS6	10 %	—	7283
DS6	20 %	3356	1687
DS6	30 %	2241	1060

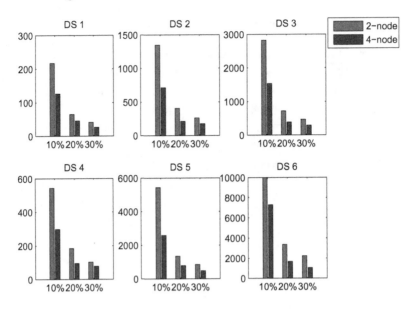

Fig. 9. Comparison in different datasets

are generated by the synthetic data generator from [17]. The real dataset we tested is available from [18].

We select the thresholds of 30 %, 20 %, and 10 %, and the runtimes of each kind of situation are listed in Table 3. The first column of Table 3 is the dataset used. The second column is the value of the given support threshold. The third column is the running time under the situation of 2-nodes. The fourth column is the running time under the situation of 4-nodes. It is observed that the runtimes of 10 % is much higher than the runtimes of 30 % in the same dataset. With the decrease of the threshold in every dataset, there are more subgraph patterns whose frequencies meet the inequality: $f(g_i) \geq \theta \cdot n$. This is the reason why the runtimes of smaller thresholds are higher than the bigger thresholds in a dataset.

As is shown in Figs. 6, 7 and 8, there is an almost linear relationship with runtime and the database size in each kind of threshold. Furthermore, the performance of our method in the case of 4-nodes is better than in the case of 2-nodes especially when the database is bigger. Because the slopes of the lines that represent 4-nodes cases are smaller than the 2-nodes cases. Adding machines can significantly improve the mining efficiency. When the number of graphs in datasets are less than 200,000, our approach is able to mine all the frequent subgraphs almost less than 1,000 s in both 20 % and 30 % cases.

In Fig. 9, we compare runtime in each dataset. Our method can significantly reduce the execution time by increasing the number of nodes. With the increase of the database, adding nodes to mine frequent subgraphs does not increase a lot of extra overhead.

5   Conclusion

We provide an approach based on MapReduce for frequent subgraph mining in large scale of graph databases. There are two rounds of MapReduce in our method. First round is to find the locally frequent subgraphs in each node; second round is to get the globally frequent subgraphs in this iteration. We use a sequence derived from lower triangular matrix to indicate an undirected graph. To improve the efficiency of the isomorphism testing, we transform the graph isomorphism testing into a limited number of string matching and take some measures to reduce the amount of isomorphism testing by scanning a set of subgraphs that have been mined, instead of scanning all the graphs in the node. In this paper, we make some optimizations for frequent subgraph mining, but there are also some problems: (i) how to further reduce the redundancy of frequent subgraph to reduce the time cost of the algorithm; (ii) how to improve the algorithm in order to adapt to the situations of larger graph databases and a super large graph.

Acknowledgments. This paper is supported by the NSFC under grant No.61433019 and Science and technology project of Guangdong Province (No. 2016B030306003 and 2016B030305002).

References

1. Lin, W., Xiao, X., Ghinita, G.: Large-scale frequent subgraph mining in mapreduce. In: Proceedings of IEEE International Conference on Data Engineering, pp. 844–855 (2014)
2. Xu, S., Su, S., Xiong, L., Cheng, X., Xiao, K.: Differentially private frequent subgraph mining. In: Proceedings of IEEE International Conference on Data Engineering, pp. 229–240 (2016)
3. Shahrivari, S., Jalili, S.: Distributed discovery of frequent subgraphs of a network using mapreduce. J. Comput. **97**(11), 1101–1120 (2015)
4. Elseidy, M., Abdelhamid, E., Skiadopoulos, S., Kalnis, P.: Grami: frequent subgraph and pattern mining in a single large graph. In: Proceedings of the VLDB Endowment, pp. 517–528 (2014)
5. Chen, Y., Zhao, X., Lin, X., Wang, Y.: Towards frequent subgraph mining on single large uncertain graphs. In: Proceedings of IEEE International Conference on Data Mining, pp. 41–50 (2015)
6. Zhao, Z., Wang, G., Butt, A.R., Khan, M., Kumar, V.S.A., Marathe, M.V.: Sahad: subgraph analysis in massive networks using hadoop. In: Proceedings of IEEE International Parallel and Distributed Processing Symposium, pp. 390–401 (2012)
7. Afrati, F., Fotakis, D., Ullman, J.: Enumerating subgraph instances using mapreduce. In: Proceedings of IEEE International Conference on Data Engineering, pp. 62–73 (2012)
8. Lee, J., Han, W.S., Kasperovics, R., Lee, J.H.: An in-depth comparison of subgraph isomorphism algorithms in graph databases. In: Proceedings of the VLDB Endowment, pp. 133–144 (2012)
9. Kuramochi, M., Karypis, G.: Frequent subgraph discovery. In: Proceedings of IEEE International Conference on Data Mining, pp. 313–320 (2001)

10. Yan, X., Han, J.: Gspan: Graph-based substructure pattern mining. In: Proceedings of IEEE International Conference on Data Mining, pp. 721–724 (2002)

11. Teixeira, C., Fonseca, A.J., Serafini, M., Siganos, G., Zaki, M.J., Aboulnaga, A.: Arabesque: a system for distributed graph mining. In: Proceedings of Symposium on Operating Systems Principles, pp. 425–440 (2015)

12. Hill, S., Srichandan, B., Sunderraman, R.: An iterative mapreduce approach to frequent subgraph mining in biological datasets. In: Proceedings of ACM Conference on Bioinformatics, Computational Biology and Biomedicine, pp. 661–666 (2012)

13. Han, J., Cheng, H., Xin, D., Yan, X.: Frequent pattern mining: current status and future directions. Data Min. Knowl. Discov. **15**(15), 55–86 (2007)

14. Dean, J., Ghemawat, S.: Mapreduce: a flexible data processing tool. Commun. ACM **53**(1), 72–77 (2010)

15. Inokuchi, A., Washio, T., Motoda, H.: Complete mining of frequent patterns from graphs: mining graph data. J. Mach. Learn. **50**(3), 321–354 (2003)

16. http://www.intsci.acxn/pdin/pdminer.html

17. http://www.cse.ust.hk/graphgen/

18. http://oldwww.comlab.ox.ac.uk/oucl/groups/machlearn/PTE

A Distributed Algorithm for Balanced Hypergraph Partitioning

Wenyin Yang[1,2], Guojun Wang[3(✉)], Li Ma[1], and Shiyang Wu[1]

[1] School of Electronic and Information Engineering,
Foshan University, Foshan 528000, China
cswyyang@163.com, molly_917@163.com, wooshiyoung@foxmail.com
[2] School of Information Science and Engineering, Central South University,
Changsha 410083, China
[3] School of Computer Science and Educational Software,
Guangzhou University, Guangzhou 510006, China
csgjwang@gmail.com

Abstract. Hypergraph is good at modeling multi-node relationships in complex networks. Balanced hypergraph partitioning helps to optimize storage of large sets of hypergraph-structured data over multi-hosts in the Cloud, and share the query loads. Several centralized vertex partitioning algorithms have been developed to address this problem. However, edge partitioning is proved more effective than vertex partitioning for graph processing. Aim of this paper is to explore a new approach based on hyperedge partitioning, in which hyperedges, rather than vertices, are partitioned into disjoint subsets. We propose a distributed hyperedge partition algorithm, HyperSwap, to partition the hypergraph into balanced sub-hypergraph as required, without global information and central coordination. We show the feasibility, evaluate it on Facebook dataset with various settings, and compare it against two alternative solutions. Experiment findings show that HyperSwap outperforms the other two partitioners because it obtains good partitions with low cut cost while conforming to any balance requirement.

Keywords: Hypergraph partitioning · Hyperedge partitioning · Distributed algorithm · Load balancing

1 Introduction

There are various ever expanding real-world applications spare no effort to the contribution of the Big Data era, including the info networks, online social networks, and biological networks, etc. [1]. It is a great challenge to exploit how to store and process these data and the complex data relationships efficiently. Generally, data are modeled as a graph beforehand before the graph being partitioned and deployed over multiple clusters, such as virtual machines in the cloud or distributed databases, in order to partition the query loads between these clusters [2], enabling the parallel processing as well. In this case, maintaining the

© Springer International Publishing AG 2016
G. Wang et al. (Eds.): APSCC 2016, LNCS 10065, pp. 477–490, 2016.
DOI: 10.1007/978-3-319-49178-3_36

locality of data based on their relationships could benefit the reduction of cross-server communication cost and speed up the context-based parallel processing. In addition, evenly distributing or uniform partitioning is also important to balance the computational working load between clusters, and optimize the usage of memory. Therefore, a good partitioning can be used to minimize communication cost, to balance, or to identify densely connected clusters [3].

While most of the researches focus on partitioning solutions based on usual graphs, namely dyadic graphs, there has been limited ones shed light on the partitioning of hypergraph. A hypergraph is a generalization of a graph, where a hyperedge can connect any number of vertices. Recent studies have showed that hypergraphs perform better than dyadic graphs at modeling groups in many fields [4–7]. Take social network as an example, users could be modeled via vertices in a hypergraph, and the multi-user interactions could be modeled as hyperedges. Placing and replicating social network users on suitable servers according to the multi-way operations could relieve the communication costs, especially the inter-server query cost, namely the cut cost of hypergraphs. Minimizing the cut cost is the main optimization target of the hypergraph partitioning problem, which is the main focus of this paper.

Although there are a few algorithms designed for hypergraph partitioning [5,6], none of them is tailored to address the partitioning problem in a distributed way, to the best of our knowledge. Since the hypergraph could be fully distributed on several separated hosts, we try to solve the hypergraph partitioning problem in a parallel way. In addition, balance constraint also matters in hypergraph partitioning. Traditionally, hypergraph partitioning refers to *vertex partitioning*, that is, dividing the vertex set into nearly equal sized partitions, with minimized cut hyperedges. However, dividing the vertex set in equal sized partitions does not imply that the corresponding subgraph have the same size and the workload is balanced, since the distribution of edges or hyperedges may not be balanced, especially in terms of the power-law graphs, leading to unbalanced workload [8]. We suggest a new hypergraph partitioning approach, named *hyperedge partitioning*, to achieve the real workload balance. Hyperedge partitioning refers to partitioning the hyperedge set into disjoint subsets, while vertices may have to be cut (replicated) since they may belong to several partitions. A good hyperedge partitioning requires minimum number of vertex replicas. Figure 1 depicts the difference between vertex partitioning and hyperedge partitioning. So far, there is very few researches shed light on hyperedge partitioning, in spite of some on *edge partitioning* schemes for dyadic graphs [8–12].

To address the challenges of balanced hypergraph partitioning in a distributed way, we introduce a heuristic algorithm, named *HyperSwap*, which exploits the local adjacency information to swap the hyperedges under certain balance constraints instead of vertices. As a consequence, HyperSwap exposes substantially greater parallelism, reduces network communication costs and necessary replicas, and provides a new highly effective approach to distributed hypergraph partitioning. We describe the design of HyperSwap and evaluate it using real-world dataset Facebook with variety of settings.

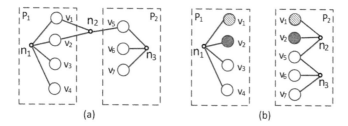

Fig. 1. Example of hypergraph partitioning using (a) *vertex partitioning*, i.e. each vertex locates in only one partition, while hyperedges may be cut and span more than one partition; and (b) *hyperedge partitioning*, i.e. each hyperedge appears in only one partition, while vertices may be cut and replicated in more than one partition.

In particular our key contributions are two-fold: First, we put forward the concept of hyperedge partition as a new kind of hypergraph partitioning method. Second, we propose a distributed balanced hyperedge partition algorithm, named HyperSwap, to partition hypergraphs based on hyperedge swapping operations.

Evaluation findings demonstrate that HyperSwap produces quality partitions and scales well with different number of partitions and balance constraints. Especially, HyperSwap outperforms khMETIS and random hyperedge partitioning solutions with respect to the trade-off between cut-vertex numbers, communication cost and balance level.

The rest of the paper is structured as follows. Related research works are discussed in Sect. 2. Section 3 introduces the definitions of hyperedge partitioning and the optimization problem. Next, we present the solutions for distributed hyperedge partitioning scheme in Sect. 4. Section 5 includes the experiment results and analysis. Finally, in Sect. 6, we give our conclusions and suggest future work.

2   Related Work

The problem of optimally partitioning a dyadic graph or a hypergraph is known to be NP-hard [13]. Graph partitioning algorithms can be classified as either vertex partitioning (a.k.a edge-cut partitioning) or edge partitioning (a.k.a. vertex-cut partitioning). So far, a significant number of heuristic algorithms with near-linear runtime has been developed.

2.1   Vertex Partitioning for Hypergraph

Fiduccia-Mattheyses (FM) algorithm [14] introduces single-vertex move rules and enables K-way partitioning based on recursively bi-partitioning. Later, a direct K-way partitioning based on FM algorithm is put forward [14]. Based on the FM algorithm, hypergraph partitioning tools named hMETIS [15] and khMETIS [16] are developed to implement the multi-level framework via recursive bisection and direct K-way approaches, respectively. These tools are effective in reducing both execution time and cut sizes. Lately, Yaros [17] proposed to use information-theoretic entropy as an imbalance constraint, and it enables the partitioner, named hyperpart, to find high quality solutions for given levels of imbalance. Inspired by hyperpart, Yang [18] proposed a hypergraph partitioner, named EQHyperpart, to partition the hypergraph based on information entropy modularity. The algorithms mentioned above are classified as vertex partitioning methods for hypergraph, because they divide vertices of a hypergraph into disjoint partitions, aiming to minimize the number of hyperedge that span separated partitions, that is, minimizing the cut hyperedges.

2.2   Hyperedge Partitioning for Hypergraph

Recently, there are several literatures casting efforts on edge partitioning. SBV-Cut [9] is a newly proposed edge partitioning tool running in centralized model. DFEP [10], PowerGraph [8], JA-BE-JA-VC [11], and VSEP [12] are state-of-the-art distributed approaches for edge partitioning. There are both theory and practice studies [8] prove that edge partitioning is more efficient than vertex partitioning in parallel processing of power-law graphs [11].

Likewise, corresponding to the vertex partitioning, there could be hyperedge partitioning for hypergraphs. rFM [19] is a hypergraph partitioning tool that considers the vertex replication and vertex moving at the same time. But the essential operation of rFM is single vertex move, and hyperedges are still cut and span across multi-partitions. Therefore, rFM is essentially a kind of vertex partitioning algorithm. Additionally, hypergraph partitioning also calls for distributed algorithms. To the best of our knowledge, HyperSwap is the first algorithm that fill in the gap of hyperedge partitioning and can produce balanced partition results in distributed model.

3   Problem Statement

We are given an undirected hypergraph $\mathcal{H} = (\mathcal{V}, \mathcal{N})$, where $\mathcal{V}$ is the set of vertices and $\mathcal{N}$ is the set of hyperedges (a.k.a. nets). Each net $n_j \in \mathcal{N}$ connects a subset of vertices. The set of vertices connected by net n_j is represented by Vertices(n_j). The set of nets that connect vertex v_i is denoted as Nets(v_i). The vertices v_i and v_j are said to be neighbors if they are connected by at least one common net, i.e., Nets(v_i) $\cap$ Nets(v_j)$\neq \varnothing$. A (n_j, v_i) tuple denotes a pin of n_j where $v_i \in$ Vertices(n_j). The nets n_i and n_j are said to be neighbors if they have at least one common pin, i.e., Vertices(n_i) $\cap$ Vertices(n_j) $\neq \varnothing$. The degree of a net n_j is equal to the number of vertices it connects, $|Vertices(n_j)|$. The total number of pins $P = \sum_{n_j \in \mathcal{N}} |Vertices(n_j)|$ denotes the size of a given hypergraph $\mathcal{H}$. A vertex weight value $w(v_i)$ is associated with each vertex v_i, and a hyperedge weight value $w(n_j)$ is the total weight of the connected vertices of net n_j, i.e. $w(n_j) = \sum_{v_i \in Vertices(n_j)} w(v_i)$.

$\Pi = \{\mathcal{N}_1, \ldots, \mathcal{N}_K\}$ is a K-way hyperedge partition of $\mathcal{H} = (\mathcal{V}, \mathcal{N})$ if each part $\mathcal{N}_K$ is a nonempty subset of $\mathcal{N}$, the parts are pair wise disjoint, and the union of K parts is equal to $\mathcal{N}$. The set of vertices located on partition $\mathcal{N}_k$ is represented by $Vertices(\mathcal{N}_k)$, and the set of nets that located on partition $\mathcal{N}_k$ is denoted as $Nets(\mathcal{N}_k)$. The weight $W(\mathcal{N}_k)$ of a part $\mathcal{N}_k$ is the sum of the weights of the hyperedges in that part, i.e., $W(\mathcal{N}_k) = \sum_{n_j \in \mathcal{N}_k} w(n_j)$. A partition Π is said to be balanced if each part $\mathcal{N}_k \in \Pi$ satisfies the *balance constraint*:

$$W(\mathcal{N}_k) \leq (1 + \epsilon)W_{avg} \quad for \quad k = 1, \ldots, K, \tag{1}$$

where $W_{avg} = W(\mathcal{N})/K$ and ϵ is the predetermined maximum imbalance ratio.

In a partition Π, a vertex is said to locate in a part if it is connected by at least one hyperedge in that part. The locality set $\Lambda(v_i)$ of vertex v_i is defined as the set of parts which v_i locates in. The cardinality of locality set $\Lambda(v_i)$ of vertex v_i is denoted by $\lambda(v_i) = |\Lambda(v_i)|$, or λ_i for short, which is equivalent to the number of required replicas for vertices v_i. A vertex is said to be *cut* or *frontier* if it locates in more than one part ($\lambda(v_i) > 1$), and *uncut* or *interior* if it locates in only one part ($\lambda(v_i) = 1$). The set of cut vertices in a partition Π is denoted as $\mathcal{V}_F$. Since the frontier vertices are the channels through which the partitions communicated, the communication cost is mainly related with these vertices. A cost value $c(v_i)$ is associated with each vertex v_i, and the cost function for a vertex set is denoted by $c(\mathcal{V}) = \sum_{v_i \in \mathcal{V}} c(v_i)$. The *cutsize* metrics to represent the cost of a partition Π of hypergraph $\mathcal{H}$ can be either (2) or (3).

$$C(\mathcal{H}, \Pi) = \sum_{v_i \in \mathcal{V}_F} c(v_i) \tag{2}$$

$$C(\mathcal{H}, \Pi) = \sum_{v_i \in \mathcal{V}_F} (\lambda(v_i) - 1)c(v_i) \tag{3}$$

We name the cost definitions in (2) and (3) as the *cut-vertex* metric and the *replication* metric, respectively. For example, the cut-vertex and replication metrics model the minimization of the communication volume in parallel sparse matrix vector multiplication utilizing collective and point-to-point communication schemes, respectively.

Now we can formulate the optimization problem as follows: find the optimal partitioning Π^* such that:

$$\Pi^* = \arg\min_{\Pi} \; C(\mathcal{H}, \Pi)$$
$$s.t. \quad W(\mathcal{N}_k) \leq (1 + \epsilon)W_{avg} \quad for \quad k = 1, \ldots, K \tag{4}$$

In other words, given a hypergraph $\mathcal{H} = (\mathcal{V}, \mathcal{N})$, balanced K-way hyperedge partitioning can be defined as finding a K-way partition $\Pi = \{\mathcal{N}_1, \ldots, \mathcal{N}_K\}$ that minimizes the cutsize (2) or (3) while maintaining the balance constraint (1).

4   Distributed Hyperedge Partitioning Solution

We propose HyperSwap, a heuristic distributed hyperedge partitioning algorithm to address the balanced K-way hypergraph partitioning problem. In this section, we will discuss the details of this algorithm.

4.1   Basic Steps of HyperSwap

Hyperedge partitioning algorithm HyperSwap performs after random initialization at certain balance level. Every partition carries out HyperSwap iteratively, and it maintains the states information of local vertices and hyperedges, including their neighbour relationships, but it should achieve information of other partitions through communications. The basic optimization steps of HyperSwap is illustrated in Algorithm 1.

Algorithm 1. Basic steps of HyperSwap.

1: //Swapping procedure at Partition P_k
2: $swapOutNet \leftarrow$ selectSwapOutNet () //see Algorithm 2.
3: $swapInNetCandidates \leftarrow$ selectSwapInCandidates ()
4: **if** $swapInNetCandidates \neq \varnothing$ **then**
5:    $swapInNet \leftarrow$ chooseNetfromCandidates($swapOutNet, swapInNetCandidates$) //see Algorithm 3
6:    swapLocation($swapOutNet, swapInNet$)
7: **end if**

In each iteration, a partition proceeds with the following three steps: (i) swap-out hyperedge selection (line 2), (ii) swap-in hyperedge selection (line 3–5), and (iii) hyperedge swap (line 6). There are various approaches for the realization of each step. In the remaining parts of this section, we introduce a few possible schemes for these steps.

4.2   Swap-Out Hyperedge Selection Scheme

In this step, a partition should choose a local hyperedge for swapping out. There are basically two schemes for selection: *random* and *greedy*. Random scheme is fair and straight forward by choosing a local hyperedge randomly, but it is difficult to lead to an optimal result. Worse still, it is possible to choose a hyperedge with pure interior vertices to swap out and increase the cut size instead. Greedy scheme always chooses a hyperedge $n^\star$ with the most cut vertices (see (5)) or most replication copies (see (6)) upon to the cut size metric. This scheme will have a higher chance of reducing the cut size, because there are more replicated vertices would have probability to find the same copy in the other partition. But there is a possibility that the same hyperedge is chosen all the time and could not be swapped out, where the algorithm may get stuck in endless loop.

On account of the above analysis, we combine the two schemes for swap-out hyperedge selection.

$$n^\star = \underset{n_j \in Nets(P_k)}{\arg\min} \; |\,\{v_i | v_i \in \{\mathcal{V}_F \cap Vertices(n_j)\}\}\,| \tag{5}$$

$$n^\star = \underset{n_j}{\arg\min} \sum_{v_i \in \{\mathcal{V}_F \cap Vertices(n_j)\}} \lambda(v_i) \tag{6}$$

Algorithm 2 illustrates the process of how to select a hyperedge for swapping out. We calculate the sum of cut vertices or replicated vertices of every net located on the same partition, up to the cut size metric (line 2–13). Then the hyperedges are sorted in descendant order, based on the assigned cut size metric (line 14). Finally, we choose a hyperedge randomly in the sorted net list within the top t elements as the net for swapping out (line 15).

Algorithm 2. Selection of swap-out hyperedge.

1: //Swap-out hyperedge selection procedure at Partition P_k
2: **for all** $n_j \in Nets(P_k)$ **do**
3:    **for all** $v_i \in Vertices(n_j)$ **do**
4:       **if** $\lambda(v_i) > 1$ **then**
5:          **if** $cutsizemetric == \text{"}cut - vertex\text{"}$ **then**
6:             $vcut\_num = vcut\_num + 1$
7:          **end if**
8:          **if** $cutsizemetric == \text{"}replication\text{"}$ **then**
9:             $replication\_num = replication\_num + \lambda(v_i) - 1$
10:          **end if**
11:       **end if**
12:    **end for**
13: **end for**
14: $netlist \leftarrow \text{sort}(Nets(P_k), cutsizemetric, desc)$
15: $swapOutNet \leftarrow \text{getRandomTopElement}(netlist, t)$
16: **return** $swapOutNet$

4.3 Swap-In Hyperedge Selection Scheme

In this step, a candidate set of hyperedges for swapping in should be chosen from the other partitions. We consider two sets of hyperedges for selection: *neighbour hyperedges* and *random hyperedges*. Hyperedges, which are both one-hop neighbours of the swap-out hyperedge and located on the other partitions, constitute the major part of the candidate set. One-hop neighbours, a.k.a. directed neighbours of a hyperedge n, constitute a set of hyperedges that every member has at lease one common pin vertex with n.

The rest part of swap-in hyperedge candidate set is a handful of random hyperedges in the hypergraph. Random nets, which are acquired by random walk, help to increase the chance of finding a proper swap partner for the optimization problem.

4.4   Hyperedge Swap Scheme

To choose a proper swap-in hyperedge within the candidate set, we explore a metric, named *swap benefit*, to measure the swap utility.

Swap benefit refers to the reduction amount of cut vertices or replication copies of them. The vertices sets of swap-in net n_{in}, swap-out net n_{out} and the two swap partner partitions P_{in} and P_{out}, should be employed to compute the swap benefit. We calculate the reduced replica set of two partitions by (7) and (8), and the increased replicas by (9) and (10). Take the replication metric as example, the *swap benefit* is calculated by (11). The higher the *swapBenefit* value is, the lower cutsize the exchange may cause.

$$reducedR(n_{out}, n_{in}, P_{out}) = Vertices(n_{out}) -$$
$$\cup_{n_i \in \{Nets(P_{out}) - \{n_{out}\}\}} Vertices(n_i) - Vertices(n_{in}) \tag{7}$$

$$reducedR(n_{out}, n_{in}, P_{in}) = Vertices(n_{in}) -$$
$$\cup_{n_i \in \{Nets(P_{in}) - \{n_{in}\}\}} Vertices(n_i) - Vertices(n_{out}) \tag{8}$$

$$increasedR(n_{out}, n_{in}, P_{out}) = Vertices(n_{in}) -$$
$$\cup_{n_i \in \{Nets(P_{out})\}} Vertices(n_i) \tag{9}$$

$$increasedR(n_{out}, n_{in}, P_{in}) = Vertices(n_{out}) -$$
$$\cup_{n_i \in \{Nets(P_{in})\}} Vertices(n_i) \tag{10}$$

$$swapBenefit = |reducedR(n_{out}, n_{in}, P_{out}) + reducedR(n_{out}, n_{in}, P_{in})| -$$
$$|increasedR(n_{out}, n_{in}, P_{out}) + increasedR(n_{out}, n_{in}, P_{in})| \tag{11}$$

Algorithm 3 describes the procedure of choosing the swap-in net from the candidate set. We first calculate the swap benefit for every pair of swap-in and swap-out nets (line 2–4), and sort the candidate swap-in nets according to the corresponding benefit values (line 5). Then the net with the highest swap benefit value in sorted list would be used to check the balance constraint (line 7–8). The first net in sorted list would be removed until find one that does not violate the balance constraint, and this one would be chosen as the final swap-in hyperedge (line 6–14).

5   Experiments

5.1   Metrics

We measure the following metrics to evaluate the quality of the hyperedge partitioning:

Algorithm 3. Choose Swap-in net from Candidate Set.

Input: $swapOutNet$, $swapInNetCandidates$
Output: $swapInNet$
1: //Swap-in hyperedge selection procedure at Partition P_k
2: **for all** $n_i \in swapInNetCandidates$ **do**
3:      $swapBenefitScore_i =$ calculateSwapBenefit $(swapOutNet, n_i)$
4: **end for**
5: $netlist \leftarrow$ sort $(swapInNetCandidates, swapBenefitScore, desc)$
6: **while** $netlist \neq \varnothing$ **do**
7:      $swapInNet \leftarrow$ getFirstElement$(netlist)$
8:      **if** breakbalance $(swapoutNet, swapInNet)$ is $true$ **then**
9:          $swapInNet \leftarrow NULL$
10:         removeFirstElement $(netlist)$
11:     **else**
12:         break
13:     **end if**
14: **end while**
15: **return** $swapInNet$

(i) **Communication cost (number of replicas):** This metric counts the number of times that vertices has to be cut. That is related to the total replicas of all the vertices in cut state, or the sum of frontier vertices of all the partitions, which is closely in connection with the cut size metric (3). Meanwhile, the replica numbers directly affects the required communication cost of the partitioned hypergraph. Because modification to a vertex should be propagated to all its replicas for consistency, or the distinct states of all replicas of each frontier vertex should be collected and computed to get a new state, which is then copied into the replicas in distributed framework. Therefore, the communication cost is computed as $CommCost = \sum_{i=1}^{K} |F_i|$. Here, F_i is the set of frontier vertices of partition i, and K is the number of partitions.

(ii) **Imbalance:** In the initialization stage, a predetermined imbalance ratio ϵ limits the maximum imbalance level of the partition result. According to the balancing constraint defined by (1), we define the imbalance degree θ by $(W_{max} - W_{avg})/W_{avg}$, where $W_{max} = max_{1 \leq k \leq K} W(\mathcal{N}_k)$, and judge whether the swap process breaks the balance constraint by comparing θ with ϵ.

(iii) **Normalized standard deviation of partition sizes:** Each partition should be as close as possible to the same size. Since imbalance metric ignores the sizes of non-max weight partitions, we utilize *normalized standard deviation of partition sizes (NSTDEV)* as a measurement of the balance level between partitions. We first normalize the sizes, so that a partition of size 1 represents a partition with exactly $|P|/K = \sum_{n_j \in \mathcal{N}} |Vertices(n_j)|/K$ pins. Then the standard deviation of the sizes is computed by $NSTDEV = \sqrt{\frac{\sum_{i=1}^{K}(\frac{|P_i|}{|P|/K}-1)^2}{K}}$. Here, K is the number of partitions and P_i denotes the pins set of partition i , i.e., $|P_i| = \sum_{n_j \in \mathcal{N}_i} |Vertices(n_j)|$.

5.2 Dataset

We evaluate the proposed method by performing algorithms on a Facebook dataset offered by SNAP (Stanford Network Analysis Project). It is an undirected type of social networks with 4039 nodes and 88234 edges, which reflects the earlier stage of a classical scale-free network. The dataset is modeled using hypergraph according to the inherent characteristic, before partitioning execution. In our evaluation experiment, hyperedges are formed by the friendship relationship.

5.3 Performance of HyperSwap

In this section, we observe how the HyperSwap performs under the three hyperedge partitioning performance metrics mentioned in Sect. 5.1, with two different cut size metrics: cut-vertex metric and replication metric. For this experiment, we perform HyperSwap and partition the dataset into 4, 8, 16, and 32 partitions, under different unbalance degree requirements (10 %, 30 %, 50 %, 80 % and 100 %), respectively. To simplify the experiment, every vertex weight value is assigned unit value.

Figure 2 depicts the number of replicas with different partition numbers under different unbalance degree requirements. We can observed that the cut sizes increase with the increase of partition amount under the same unbalance level, but decrease with the increase of imbalance degree when partitioning into the same number of parts. It implies that the number of times that vertices has to be cut are less, thus there are less communication costs even under different settings.

Figure 3 shows the relationship between the required imbalance degrees (ϵ) and the actual imbalance degrees (θ) with different partition numbers. As shown, HyperSwap never breaks the balance constraint, and it produces more balance partition results when the number of partitions is not so big, say 4. The two schemes perform neck and neck with respect to balanced partitioning ability. Figure 4 reveals that with the increase of partition numbers and the unbalance level, the deviation of partition sizes become further. The scheme aiming for cut-vertex metric achieves more balanced partitioning results in most situations.

5.4 Comparison to Other Partitioning Algorithms

In this section, we evaluate the partitioning performance of HyperSwap and two alternative partitioning solutions: khMETIS and random hyperedge partitioning.

Random hyperedge partitioning refers to allocating the hyperedges to a random partition under a predetermined balance constraint. khMETIS is a centralized K-way vertex partitioner for hypergraph. Since vertex partitioning algorithms,

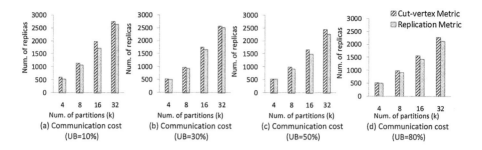

Fig. 2. Communication costs under different cut size metrics.

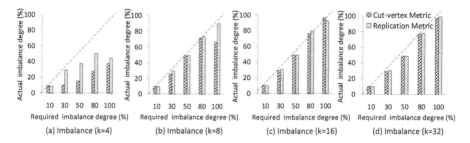

Fig. 3. Imbalance degrees under different cut size metrics.

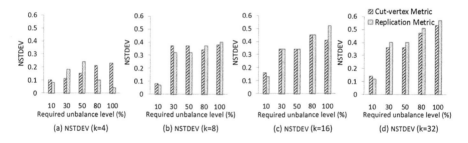

Fig. 4. Normalized standard deviation of partition sizes under different cut size metrics.

such as hMETIS and khMETIS, require vertex partitioning based measures, like edge-cut, whereas hyperedge partitioning algorithms should be evaluated using hyperedge partitioning based measures, like vertex-cut. We overcome this difficulty by conducting conversion between vertex partitioning and hyperedge partitioning. More precisely, we convert the vertex partitioning results that khMETIS returns into a hyperedge partitioning form, and use hyperedge partitioning based metrics to compare khMETIS with HyperSwap.

The evaluation experiment is also conducted on the hypergraph modeled Facebook dataset, and the three partitioners would be perform several times, aiming to partition the hypergraph into 4, 8, 16, and 32 partitions, under different imbalance degree requirements (10 %, 30 %, 50 %, 80 % and 100 %), respectively.

The partitioned hypergraph resulting from khMETIS would be converted under the same balance constraints as requirements. Similarly, every vertex weight value is assigned unit value.

Figure 5 shows that the number of replicas produced by khMETIS, HyperSwap and Random partitioners all increases with the partition amount. Random partitioner performs worst, and the performance of HyperSwap is modest. khMETIS always generate the minimum replica, however, this comes at the cost of high imbalance.

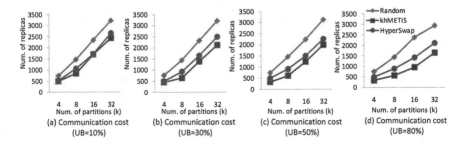

Fig. 5. Comparisons of communications cost.

Figure 6 demonstrates that when the imbalance constraint increases, the actual imbalance degrees of the three partitioners all increase, in general. Partitions resulting from HyperSwap are nearly as balanced as the required balance level. But the khMETIS is extremely unbalanced and always breaks the balance constraints. Figure 7 presents the same phenomenon. As to HyperSwap and random partitioners, they both perform well with the balance constraints. Synthesizing these two figures, we can observed that, HyperSwap produces more balance partitioning results than random partitioner when the balance requirement is strict, such as 10 % imbalance degree requirement.

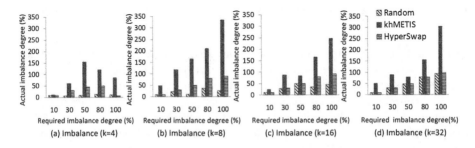

Fig. 6. Comparisons of imbalance level.

In summary, the findings show that HyperSwap outperforms the other two solutions because it produces balanced partitions while requiring a low cut size.

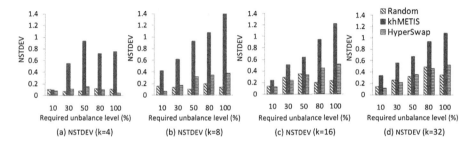

Fig. 7. Comparisons of normalized standard deviation of partition size.

6   Conclusion

In this paper, we introduced the concept of hyperedge partitioning for distributed hypergraph processing. In particular, we presented `HyperSwap`, a heuristic distributed hyperedge partitioning algorithm for balanced hypergraph partitioning. To compute the partitioning, nodes on every partition run `HyperSwap` in parallel and require only some local information and necessary communications with other partitions. Swapping hyperedges and replicating the cut vertices push the placement towards balanced while low cut size states. We compared `HyperSwap` with other two popular hypergraph partitioning algorithms, and the findings showed that `HyperSwap` not only guarantees to keep the partitions balanced as required, but also performs well with respect to cut size reduction. As future work, we plan to implement `HyperSwap` more efficiently and investigate which types of datasets and frameworks are solvable by it, and which ones need completely different heuristic schemes.

Acknowledgments. This work is supported in part by the National Natural Science Foundation of China under Grant Numbers 61632009, 61272151 and 61472451, the High Level Talents Program of Higher Education in Guangdong Province under Funding Support Number 2016ZJ01, the Natural Science Foundation of Guangdong Province in China under Grant Number 2015A030313638, and the Foundation for Distinguished Young Talents in Higher Education of Guangdong in China under Funding Support Number 2015KQNCX179.

References

1. Saleh, I., Wei, T., Blake, M.B.: Social-network-sourced big data analytics. Internet Comput. IEEE **17**(5), 62–69 (2013)
2. Pujol, J.M., Erramilli, V., Siganos, G., Yang, X., Laoutaris, N., Chhabra, P., Rodriguez, P.: The little engine(s) that could: scaling online social networks. ACM SigComm Comput. Commun. Rev. **40**(4), 1162–1175 (2010)
3. Rahimian, F., Payberah, A.H., Girdzijauskas, S., Jelasity, M., Haridi, S.: Ja-Be-Ja: a distributed algorithm for balanced graph partitioning. In: IEEE 7th International Conference on Self-Adaptive and Self-Organizing Systems (SASO), pp. 51–60 (2013)

4. Heintz, B.C.A.: Beyond graphs: toward scalable hypergraph analysis systems. ACM SIGMETRICS Perform. Eval. Rev. **41**, 94–97 (2014)
5. Yang, W., Wang, G.: Directed social hypergraph data allocation strategy in online socail networks. J. Chin. Comput. Syst. **36**, 1559–1564 (2015)
6. Turk, A., Selvitopi, R.O., Ferhatosmanoglu, H., Aykanat, C.: Temporal workload-aware replicated partitioning for social networks. IEEE Trans. Knowl. Data Eng. **26**(11), 2832–2845 (2014)
7. Guzzo, A., Pugliese, A., Rullo, A., Saccà, D.: Intrusion detection with hypergraph-based attack models. In: Croitoru, M., Rudolph, S., Woltran, S., Gonzales, C. (eds.) GKR 2013. LNCS (LNAI), vol. 8323, pp. 58–73. Springer, Heidelberg (2014). doi:10.1007/978-3-319-04534-4_5
8. Gonzalez, J.E., Low, Y., Gu, H., Bickson, D., Guestrin, C.: PowerGraph: distributed graph-parallel computation on natural graphs. In: Usenix Conference on Operating Systems Design and Implementation, pp. 17–30 (2012)
9. Kim, M., Candan, K.S.: SBV-Cut: vertex-cut based graph partitioning using structural balance vertices. Data Knowl. Eng. **72**(1), 285–303 (2012)
10. Guerrieri, A., Montresor, A.: Distributed edge partitioning for graph processing, CoRR abs/1403.6270
11. Rahimian, F., Payberah, A.H., Girdzijauskas, S., Haridi, S.: Distributed vertex-cut partitioning. In: Magoutis, K., Pietzuch, P. (eds.) DAIS 2014. LNCS, vol. 8460, pp. 186–200. Springer, Heidelberg (2014). doi:10.1007/978-3-662-43352-2_15
12. Zhang, Y., Liu, Y., Yu, J., Liu, P., Guo, L.: VSEP: a distributed algorithm for graph edge partitioning. In: Wang, G., Zomaya, A., Perez, G.M., Li, K. (eds.) ICA3PP 2015. LNCS, vol. 9532, pp. 71–84. Springer, Heidelberg (2015). doi:10.1007/978-3-319-27161-3_7
13. Borndörfer, R., Heismann, O.: The hypergraph assignment problem. Discrete Optim. **15**(4), 15–25 (2015)
14. Fiduccia, C.M., Mattheyses, R.M.: A linear-time heuristic for improving network partitions. In: Papers on Twenty-five Years of Electronic Design Automation, pp. 175–181. (1982)
15. Karypis, G., Aggarwal, R., Kumar, V., Shekhar, S.: Multilevel hypergraph partitioning: applications in VLSI domain. IEEE Trans. Very Large Scale Integr. Syst. **7**(1), 69–79 (1999)
16. Karypis, G., Kumar, V.: Multilevel k-way hypergraph partitioning. In: Proceedings of the 36th annual ACM/IEEE Design Automation Conference, pp. 343–348 (1999)
17. Yaros, J., Imielinski, T.: Imbalanced hypergraph partitioning, improvements for consensus clustering. In: The 25th IEEE International Conference on Tools with Artificial Intelligence (ICTAI). IEEE Press, pp. 358–365 (2013)
18. Yang, W., Wang, G., Bhuiyan, M.Z.A.: Partitioning of hypergraph modeled complex networks based on information entropy. In: Proceedings of the 15th International Conference on Algorithms and Architectures for Parallel Processing, pp. 678–690 (2015)
19. Selvitopi, R.O., Turk, A., Aykanat, C.: Replicated partitioning for undirected hypergraphs. J. Parallel Distrib. Comput. **72**(4), 547–563 (2012)

DHMRF: A Dynamic Hybrid Movie Recommender Framework

Xiangyong Liu[1], Guojun Wang[2](✉), Wenjun Jiang[3], and Yinong Long[1]

[1] School of Information Science and Engineering,
Central South University, Changsha 410083, China
[2] School of Computer Science and Educational Software,
Guangzhou University, Guangzhou 510006, China
csgjwang@gmail.com
[3] College of Computer Science and Electronic Engineering,
Hunan University, Changsha 410082, China

Abstract. Current movie recommender system is hard to capture user's preference due to the multidimensional and dynamic characteristics. Aiming at this problem, in this paper, we propose a dynamic hybrid movie recommender framework which models user's preference from four different aspects. The framework is organized according to the classic two-stage information retrieval dichotomy: first, we adopt a suitable recommender algorithm for each aspect respectively for candidate generation, and then a linear combination model is designed to produce the final recommendation list. In order to capture the dynamics of user's preference, We also constructe a feedback learning mechanism which utilize the utility function to compute the best weight vector for each recommender algorithm. Case study on our framework shows that our model can accurately capture user's current interest with acceptable cost.

Keywords: Hybrid algorithm · Recommender system · Feedback learning · Utility function · Multidimensionality

1 Introduction

Imagine that, in the near past, people can easily find what they really interested in through searching in the Internet. With the rapid growth of Internet information, they get confused when face up with so many choices. A tool which filters the unwanted information for users is needed, and recommendation system (RS) meets this demand [26]. RS makes use of user's preference information which is acquired by the system explicitly (typically by collecting user's ratings) or implicitly (typically by monitoring user's behavior, such as clicks, downloads) [17,21].

On one hand, RS helps users find valuable resource that they truly needed. On the other hand, it enables the resource be more likely presented to relevant users. RS acts both as the filter for users and the solver of Long Tail problem for resource provider. The main task of those system is mining users' preference and recommending the correct resource to them. However, the efficiency of current

© Springer International Publishing AG 2016
G. Wang et al. (Eds.): APSCC 2016, LNCS 10065, pp. 491–503, 2016.
DOI: 10.1007/978-3-319-49178-3_37

recommender algorithm is not satisfactory due to the difficult of capturing user's preference. There are mainly two reasons:

User's preference are multidimensional. Take movie, for example, suppose Bob watches a comedy movie. There are many reasons for visiting a particular resource. Maybe he is working on a comedy subject. It is possible that Bob's friend once told him in the past that it is interesting. It is very likely that Bob is boring at that time and randomly selects this movie to kill time. It is hard to make sure which is the real reason, all we can do is try our best to guess the most possible reason according to Bob's feedback within a period of time.

User's preference are dynamic. User's preference on resource, such as movie, changes by year, or month even day. Suppose an example which is showed in Table 1. Bob watched a lot of comedy movie at time t (t can be one day, one month or one year). At this time he was making research related to comedy. Then Bob watched many adventure movies at time $t+1$ because his friends loved adventure movie and recommended their favorite movies to Bob. At time $t + 2$, Bob cared about the famous movies so he watched a larger number of movies from the popular list. Bob was boring at time $t + 3$ and randomly selected a movie to watch from movie library during this period of time.

Table 1. Bob's dynamic preference on movie

Time	Interest	Reason
t	Comedy	Research requirement
t + 1	Adventure	Social requirement
t + 2	Top-N	Pursue popularity
t + 3	Randomization	Kill time

During the first period of time, Bob watched many comedy movie, the general way of recommending movies to Bob maybe among one of those: recommends more comedy movies to Bob, shows Bob more movies which his friends watched, presents the most popular movies to Bob, and randomly recommends some movies to Bob. We are not sure which is Bob's real preference according to the movies which Bob watched in the past, hence any independent algorithm may fail. It can be solved by putting two or more methods together. We know that Bob's preference is dynamic from the second period of time. At time t, It is suitable to recommend more comedy movies to Bob, but if we still recommend comedy movie to Bob at time $t + 1$, it won't be useful. It's also improper if we recommend to Bob more movies that his friends watched at time $t + 2$. The dynamics of Bob's preference can be learned from Bob's feedback. In other word, we can know how fast Bob changed his preference and how much he was changed from his clicks toward recommender list we provided.

The motivation of our work arises from the task of serving the most suitable movies to user. This involves a number of challenges ranging from modeling user's multidimensional interest to predicting user's current preference. With amount of user's activity history, it is easy to build an accurate algorithm which performs well on off-line experiment. However, It is non-trivial to capture user's multidimensional and dynamic preference. Traditionally, content-based recommender algorithm always show user the similar movies to which user has watched. While collaborative filtering recommenders user the movie which similar users have watched. Our method provides an extension of the existing recommender algorithm commonly used for recommendation, which is, combines four different algorithms and assigns a linear weight on them. Also, a learning algorithm on the weight is designed to solve the dynamic preference problem. Those four algorithms aim at the following four aspects:

Content Aspect. That is, Takes movie's features, such as genres, into consideration and presents to user the similar movies according to user's watching history recently.

Collaboration Aspect. Movies are watched by many users, and those users may have similar preference, though providing target user the movies which similar users have viewed would be helpful.

Popularity Aspect. The most popular movies get more attention, and user is easy to accept them when faced with so much information about the Top-N movies.

Randomization Aspect. It is possible that user is boring at that period of time. For example, user stays at home alone and randomly picks a movie to watch without caring about the content of this movie or whether his friends have watched it or not.

In this paper, we aim at solving the problem of multidimensional and dynamic preference in movie recommendation environment, and the recommender algorithm and learning mechanism have been researched accordingly. The key contribution in this paper are the following:

- We propose a fine-grained method to model user's preference from four different aspects, focusing on a particular subject, following the preference of friends, pursuiting the popularity and passing the time. For each aspect, a recommender algorithm is built for candidate generation, and the final recommendation list comes from the combination of those four algorithms.
- We construct a feedback learning mechanism to model the dynamics of user's preference. User's feedback (e.g. clicks) towards the recommendation list are recorded, and a four bytes memory space is used to connect the list with the above four aspects.
- We provide an useful case study to show that how our system works and indirectly prove that our framework can truly improves the recommender performance and captures user's real preference.

2   Related Work

Recommendation system are software agents that elicits the interests and preferences of individual consumers, and makes recommendation accordingly [29].

The most basic recommender methods are content-based recommendation [5], collaborative filtering [4] and knowledge-based recommendation [27]. However, a great volume of literature are focusing on proposing new methods in order to improve the accuracy, diversity and other metrics on recommendation system, this is out of the scope of this paper. We consider the recommendation from the perspective of user, that is to say, user's decision is affected by particular content, social relation and so on. Recommendation system is currently centered on, but not limited to, topics such as movies [8,12], books [19,20], documents [11,25] , music [10,28] and e-commerce [9,32]. The example used in this paper is movie, but our framework can also be applied to other fields such as topics mentioned above.

As we all know that one particular method is designed for one class of problems, and it is true that any one independent recommendation algorithm has its shortcomings. For instance, content-based method requires product features and textual description, collaborative filtering cannot work well when faced up with data sparsity and cold-start problems, and knowledge-based recommendation rely on the explicit knowledge models from the domain. Hence hybrid recommendation is often used [2], and the classification of hybrid algorithm is proposed by different methods [1,6,7]. At present, lots of works have been done on hybrid recommendation. Basu et al. proposed a hybrid approach which combines the collaborative features, such as likes and dislikes, with content features of items category [3]. Pazzani combined collaborative filtering with demographic user characteristics to bootstrap recommendation system even when not enough item ratings are known [23]. Another feature combination approach was proposed by Zanker and Jessenitschnig, who exploit different kinds of rating feedback based on their predictive accuracy and availability [31]. All these methods are feature combination hybrids, and differently in this paper, we combine four recommender algorithms and compute the weighted sum of generated list. Most closely related are the works done by Zanker and Jessenitschning [30], the key difference is that they identify the optimum weighting scheme, while in our mechanism the weight scheme changes over time.

The reliability of feedback (e.g. clicks) has been studied in a great volume of literature [13–15]. On one side, the feedback can be used to construct the rating data [18,22]. On the other side, user's feedback may be integrated into user's preference [16,24]. Unlike the traditional mechanism, the feedback (preferably implicit feedback) in this paper are recorded and used to acquire the improved weight vector. It cannot be sure whether the new weight vector after users feedback is the optimal result, but we can believe that this is improved from the direction of users feedback and also determined by the quality of users feedback.

3   System Model

3.1   Design of the System

As we explained before, user's preference is multidimensional and changes over time. A user visits a resource for many reasons, and the dynamics of users preference is affected by many factors such as personal preference on the resource, the recommendation from friends, and so on. In this paper, we model user's preference from 4 different aspects which is described in Fig. 1. The first aspect is **Content**, which means the user visits the resource because he or she likes it. Take movie for example, Bob watch Godfather because he likes gangster movies. The second aspect is **Collaboration**, we can easily acquire the status of friends owing to the great development of social network. The food they have eaten, the movies they have watched, the cloth they have bought, to name but a few. We all live in an inter-connected community, and our life is influenced by the people around us. The third aspect is **Randomization**, we take this aspect into consideration comes from the situation that sometimes we visit the resource without any particular purpose. Just like the commonly reply, whatever or I don't care, when we were asked which food we want to eat or which music we want to listen. The last aspect is **Popularity**, which can also be represented with the phenomenon Matthew Effect: the popular get more popular and the unpopular get more unpopular. When visiting the resource, the most popular resource have the higher probability to be visited compared to the unpopular resource.

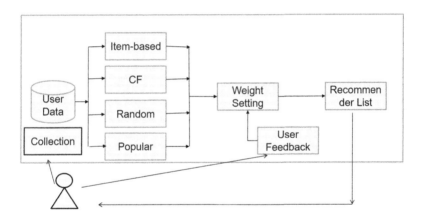

Fig. 1. Design of recommender system

For each aspect, a corresponding algorithm is designed to generate the recommendation list. We adopt the most common algorithm which has been widely used in recommendation field. The aspect of content is represented with content-based filtering, and its purpose is to find the similar resource and recommend them to the user. Very closely, we use collaborative filtering to model the aspect of collaboration. The target of this algorithm is to search for the most similar users and recommend the resources which they have visited. As for the randomization aspect, a random algorithm is constructed which randomly selects the resource from the resource space to do recommendation. For the last aspect, a popularity algorithm is proposed to recommend the most popular resource at a fixed period of time. A linear combination strategy is designed to build the final recommendation list from the sub recommendation lists generated by each of the algorithm, as showed in Eq. 1.

$$Result = w_1 * Content() + w_2 * CF() + w_3 * Random() + w_4 * Popular() \quad (1)$$

where w_1, w_2, w_3 and w_4 are four dimensions of the weight vector, and those four functions represent four aspects of user's preference. In order to get user's current preference, operations (e.g., clicks) are recorded and considered as the feedback for updating the weight vector. The details of the feedback mechanism will be explained later.

3.2   Algorithm of Each Aspect

User's preference is modeled from four different aspects: **Conent Aspect, Collaborative Aspect, Popularity Aspect**, and **Randomization Aspect**, and an recommender algorithm is constructed to represent each aspect, respectively. In this section, we will show the details of each algorithm which represents those four aspects mentioned before. All of the algorithms can be further improved, we take more focus on the improvement of the feedback mechanism instead of the precision of each independent algorithm. Also, they can be replaced by other algorithm for better representation of the preference of users.

Algorithm 1. Content-based Filtering.

Input: R, A, u, k;
Output: $Rank$;
1: $Rank, Visited = null$;
2: **for each** $item \in R[u]$ **do**
3:    $Visited.add(item)$;
4: **end for**
5: **for each** $item \in A$ **do**
6:    **if** $item \notin Visited$ **then**
7:       $sim = Jaccard_similarity(A[item], Visited)$;
8:       $Rank[item] = sim$;
9:    **end if**
10: **end for**
11: **return** $Rank[0 : k; reverse]$;

Content Aspect. The content-based algorithm is used to produce relevant resource as described in Algorithm 1. At first, a recommendation list is initialized to empty. Then, aiming at all the resources in the resource space which user have never visited, compute the Jaccard similarity between them and the visited resources. Finally, the Top-k most similar resources are added to the recommendation list. The Jaccard similarity is defined in Eq. 2.

$$Sim = \frac{A_{11}}{A_{10} + A_{01} + A_{11}} \tag{2}$$

where, A_{11} is the common attribute set that belongs to both resources, and A_{10}, A_{01} means the attribute set that belongs to only one resource. The Jaccard similarity measures the distance of two resources based on the characters of the resource.

Algorithm 2. Collaborative Filtering.

Input: R, u, m, k;
Output: $Rank$;
1: $Rank = null, Visited = null, User = null, C[n] = 0$;
2: **for each** $user \in R$ **do**
3:      **for each** $item \in R[user]$ **do**
4:          $Visited[user].add(item)$;
5:      **end for**
6: **end for**
7: **for each** $user \in Visited$ **do**
8:      $C[user] = Cosin_s imilarity(Visited[user], Visited[u])$;
9: **end for**
10: $User = C[0 : m; reverse]$;
11: **for each** $user \in User$ **do**
12:     **for each** $item \in Visited[user]$ **do**
13:         **if** $item \notin Visited[u]$ **then**
14:             **if** $item \notin Rank$ **then**
15:                 $Rank[item] = 1$;
16:             **else**
17:                 $Rank[item]+ = 1$;
18:             **end if**
19:         **end if**
20:     **end for**
21: **end for**
22: **return** $Rank[0 : k; reverse]$;

Collaborative Aspect. The collaborative filtering algorithm is showed in Algorithm 2. First, initial the rank to be empty. Second, for all users in user space, compute the cosine similarity between them and the target user. We view the similar users as friends, and it can be replaced by the real social relationship. Finally, the Top-n resources which are visited by the Top-k most similar users are added to the recommendation list. The cosine similarity is defined in Eq. 3.

$$S_{u,v} = \frac{N(u) \bigcap N(v)}{\sqrt{|N(u)| * |N(v)|}} \tag{3}$$

where, $N(u)$ is the resource set which user u has visited. We can see from the equation, the more resources two users both visited, the more similar they are.

Algorithm 3. Randomization Algorithm.
***
Input: R, u, A, k;
Output: $Rank$;
1: $Rank, Visited = null$;
2: **for** each $item \in R[u]$ **do**
3:     $Visited.add(item)$;
4: **end for**
5: **for** each $item \in A$ **do**
6:     **if** $item \notin Visited$ **then**
7:         $Rank.add(item)$;
8:     **end if**
9: **end for**
10: $Rank = Random(Rank)[0 : k]$;
11: **return** $Rank$;
***

Randomization Aspect. Randomization is a very simple algorithm which randomly selects k resources from the resource space. It's described in Algotithm 3.

Popularity Aspect. As described in Algorithm 4, on the beginning we initial the rank to be empty. Then, compute the popularity, that is, the number have been visited. Finally, the Top-k resources with higher visited number are added to the recommendation list.

Algorithm 4. Popularity Algorithm.
***
Input: R, u, k;
Output: $Rank$;
1: $Rank, Visited = null$;
2: **for** each $item \in R[u]$ **do**
3:     $Visited.add(item)$;
4: **end for**
5: **for** each $user \in R$ **do**
6:     **for** each $item \in R[user]$ **do**
7:         **if** $item \notin Visited[u]$ **then**
8:             **if** $item \notin Rank$ **then**
9:                 $Rank[item] = 1$;
10:            **else**
11:                $Rank[item]+ = 1$;
12:            **end if**
13:        **end if**
14:    **end for**
15: **end for**
16: **return** $Rank[0 : k; reverse]$;
***

3.3 Feedback Mechanism

The feedback mechanism is the most important part of the system for improving the efficiency of recommendation. In this section, we will give a clear introduction of how it works. We have acquired four recommendation lists from the aforementioned four aspects, and a linear combination through is applied to generate the final recommendation list. After be presented to the user, user's operations(e.g., clicks) on this list will be recorded and used for updating the weight vector. Before introducing the detail of the feedback, we introduce the concept of utility function firstly. An utility function is a function which measures the ability of something which satisfies the particular needs. In this paper, we use the utility function to evaluate the utility of weight vector as described in Eq. 4.

$$Utility = m^T * w \tag{4}$$

where m is a vector represents the direction of user's feedback, w is the weight vector, the purpose of utility function is to find the best weight vector, that is, fits user's feedback better. Algorithm 5 describes the procedure of feedback learning. At the beginning, a vector m is initialized to $(0,0,0,0)$ which represents the direction of user's feedback. For each step, a weight vector w_t with max utility to the user is presented to generate the recommendation list and the user's feedback on the list is recorded, in other words, user's feedback of weight vector w_t' is recorded. Then m is updated in the direction $w_t' - w_t$.

Algorithm 5. Feedback Algorithm.

1: $m_1 = (0,0,0,0)$;
2: **for** $t = 1$ to T **do**
3:    $Present\ w_t = argmax_{w \in W}(m_t{}^T * w)$;
4:    $Obtain\ feedback\ w_t'$;
5:    $Update\ m_{t+1} = m_t + w_t' - w_t$;
6: **end for**

Assume that we have generated the recommendation list, the next step is to obtain user's feedback and transform it into weight vector. We use a four bytes space to trace back the source of each item in the recommendation list. The space structure is showed in Table 2.

Table 2. Four bytes space structure

Content-based	Collaboration	Randomization	Popularity
8	4	2	1

For each item in the recommendation list, a number belongs to [1,15] is bound to it which indicates the source of this item before linear combination. We can easily distinguish which aspect the user prefer through the feedback he or she puts on the item. For instance, an item with a number 11, we can know that the user prefers content-based, randomization and popularity if he or she give feedback on that item. Because we can see 11 as 8+2+1, and they represent content-based, randomization and popularity, respectively.

4   Case Study

In this section, we will show how our system works through a simple case study. As showed in Fig. 2, we can see that there are mainly four parts and it is very similar to the figure of the design of the system.

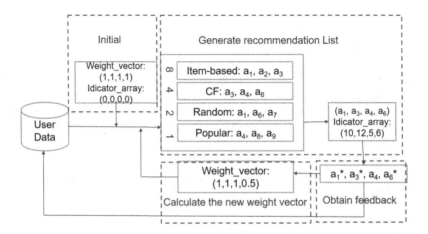

Fig. 2. Work flow of the system

Initial. In initial part, we first initial the idicator_array to (0,0,0,0) and the weight_vector to (1,1,1,1). The idicator_array stands for the variable m in Algorithm 5. The weight_vector is used for generating the original recommendation list.

Generate recommendation list. The recommendation list is generated from a linear combination of four basic recommender algorithms. For each recommender algorithm, a number is used to label the position. From this figure, we can see that item-based recommender is labeled with number 8, number 4 is set for CF recommender, number 2 is set for Random recommender and number 1 is set for Popular recommender. A initial recommendation list is generated by those four recommender algorithms. The length of the list is set to 3. Then a linear combination is used for generating the final recommendation list and the length is set to 4. With equal weight_vector, the final recommendation list is (a_1, a_3, a_4, a_6) because they have been recommended 2 times and the others are 1. After getting the final recommendation list, we can calculate the idicator_array. Take a_1 for example. a_1

comes from item-base engine and CF engine, and their labels are 8, 2 respectively. In total the label is 10. Other items can be calculated the same way.

Obtain feedback. After presenting the final recommendation list to user, the feedback (e.g. click) are collected. We can see that the user takes actions on a_1, a_3, and a_6. Those actions can be used for the calcualtion of new weight_vector.

Calculate the new weight vector. With the feedback information from previous part. The calculation is as following:

$1 + 1/2 + 0 + 1/2 = 2$;
$1 + 1/2 + 1/2 + 0 = 2$;
$1 + 1/2 + 0 + 1/2 = 2$;
$1 + 0 + 0 + 0 = 1$;

Then the new weight vector is $(2,2,2,1)$, divided by the max value we get the final weight_vector. The first number 1 is added for the purpose of diversity. The second to the fourth number represent the interest of each item in the recommender algorithm. For example, while calculating the weight of item-based recommender, we know that there are three items be recommender in initial recommendation list, a_1, a_2, and a_3. Only a_1 and a_3 get feedback by the user, and a_1 and a_3 are also recommender by CF recommender and Random recommender respectively. Hence the result is $1/2 + 0 + 1/2$, with the diversity number 1, the final result is 2. After getting the new weight_vector, we can calculate the best weight for the following recommendation as described before.

5   Conclusion

In this paper we proposed DHMRF which models user interest from four different aspects for the purpose of capturing user's multidimensional preference. Additionally, our model can still work well when user's preference changes over time. Our model works on four basic recommender algorithms and centers on the improvement of user's satisfaction through the feedback learning. Other recommender algorithm can also be integrated into our framework and our framework can easily be expanded. Future works includes fine-grained feedback algorithm on each recommender algorithm. Moreover, a fast and low cost recommender algorithm is required to further increase the performance of our framework.

Acknowledgments. This work is supported in part by the National Natural Science Foundation of China under Grant Numbers 61632009, 61472451 and 61272151, and the High Level Talents Program of Higher Education in Guangdong Province under Funding Support Number 2016ZJ01.

References

1. Adomavicius, G., Tuzhilin, A.: Toward the next generation of recommender systems: a survey of the state-of-the-art and possible extensions. IEEE Trans. Knowl. Data Eng. **17**(6), 734–749 (2005)

2. Balabanović, M., Shoham, Y.: Fab: content-based, collaborative recommendation. Commun. ACM **40**(3), 66–72 (1997)
3. Basu, C., Hirsh, H., Cohen, W.: Recommendation as classification : using social and content-based information in recommendation. In: Proceedings of AAAI-98 (1998)
4. Bobadilla, J., Hernando, A., Ortega, F., Bernal, J.: A framework for collaborative filtering recommender systems. In: The Adaptive Web, Methods and Strategies of Web Personalization, pp. 46–45 (2015)
5. Bogers, T., Koolen, M.: Report on recsys 2015 workshop on new trends in content-based recommender systems. ACM SIGIR Forum **49**(2), 141–146 (2016)
6. Burke, R.: Hybrid recommender systems: survey and experiments. User Model. User Adap. Inter. **12**(4), 331–370 (2002)
7. Burke, R.: Hybrid web recommender systems. In: Brusilovsky, P., Kobsa, A., Nejdl, W. (eds.) The Adaptive Web. LNCS, vol. 4321, pp. 377–408. Springer, Heidelberg (2007). doi:10.1007/978-3-540-72079-9_12
8. Carrer-Neto, W., Hernández-Alcaraz, M.L., Valencia-García, R., García-Sánchez, F.: Social knowledge-based recommender system. application to the movies domain. Expert Syst. Appl. **39**(12), 10990–11000 (2012)
9. Castro-Schez, J.J., Miguel, R., Vallejo, D., López-López, L.M.: A highly adaptive recommender system based on fuzzy logic for B2C e-commerce portals. Expert Syst. Appl. **38**(3), 2441–2454 (2011)
10. Cheng, Z., Shen, J.: On effective location-aware music recommendation. ACM Trans. Inf. Syst. **34**(2), 13 (2016)
11. Habibi, M., Popescu-Belis, A.: Keyword extraction and clustering for document recommendation in conversations. IEEE Trans. Audio Speech Lang. Process. **23**(4), 746–759 (2015)
12. Hayashi, T., Onai, R.: Movie recommendation using reviews on the web. Trans. J. Soc. Artif. Intell. **30**(1), 102–111 (2015)
13. Joachims, T., Granka, L., Pan, B., Hembrooke, H., Gay, G.: Accurately interpreting clickthrough data as implicit feedback. In: Proceedings of the 28th Annual International ACM SIGIR Conference on Research and Development in Information Retrieval, pp. 154–161. ACM (2005)
14. Joachims, T., Granka, L., Pan, B., Hembrooke, H., Radlinski, F., Gay, G.: Evaluating the accuracy of implicit feedback from clicks and query reformulations in web search. ACM Trans. Inf. Syst. (TOIS) **25**(2), 7 (2007)
15. Kelly, D., Teevan, J.: Implicit feedback for inferring user preference: a bibliography. ACM SIGIR Forum. **37**, 18–28 (2003)
16. Lee, D.H., Brusilovsky, P.: Reinforcing recommendation using implicit negative feedback. In: Houben, G.-J., McCalla, G., Pianesi, F., Zancanaro, M. (eds.) UMAP 2009. LNCS, vol. 5535, pp. 422–427. Springer, Heidelberg (2009). doi:10.1007/978-3-642-02247-0_47
17. Lee, S.K., Cho, Y.H., Kim, S.H.: Collaborative filtering with ordinal scale-based implicit ratings for mobile music recommendations. Inf. Sci. **180**(11), 2142–2155 (2010)
18. Lee, T.Q., Park, Y., Park, Y.T.: A time-based approach to effective recommender systems using implicit feedback. Expert Syst. Appl. **34**(4), 3055–3062 (2008)
19. Núñez-Valdéz, E.R., Lovelle, J.M.C., Martínez, O.S., García-Díaz, V., de Pablos, P.O., Marín, C.E.M.: Implicit feedback techniques on recommender systems applied to electronic books. Comput. Hum. Behav. **28**(4), 1186–1193 (2012)

20. Nez-Valdez, E.R., Lovelle, J.M.C., Hernndez, G.I., Fuente, A.J., Labra-Gayo, J.E.: Creating recommendations on electronic books: a collaborative learning implicit approach. Comput. Hum. Behav. **51**, 1320–1330 (2015)

21. Nez-Valdz, E.R., Lovelle, J.M.C., Martnez, O.S., Garca-Daz, V., Pablos, P.O.D., Marn, C.E.M.: Implicit feedback techniques on recommender systems applied to electronic books. Comput. Hum. Behav. **28**(4), 1186–1193 (2012)

22. Palanivel, K., Sivakumar, R.: A study on implicit feedback in multicriteria e-commerce recommender system. J. Electron. Commer. Res. **11**(2), 140–156 (2010)

23. Pazzani, M.J.: A framework for collaborative, content-based and demographic filtering. Artif. Intell. Rev. **13**(5–6), 393–408 (1999)

24. Peska, L.: User feedback and preferences mining. In: Masthoff, J., Mobasher, B., Desmarais, M.C., Nkambou, R. (eds.) UMAP 2012. LNCS, vol. 7379, pp. 382–386. Springer, Heidelberg (2012). doi:10.1007/978-3-642-31454-4_41

25. Porcel, C., Tejeda-Lorente, A., Martínez, M., Herrera-Viedma, E.: A hybrid recommender system for the selective dissemination of research resources in a technology transfer office. Inf. Sci. **184**(1), 1–19 (2012)

26. Ricci, F., Rokach, L., Shapira, B.: Introduction to recommender systems handbook. In: Ricci, F., Rokach, L., Shapira, B., Kantor, P.B. (eds.) Recommender Systems Handbook, pp. 1–35. Springer, Heidelberg (2011)

27. Sugumaran, V.: Knowledge-based recommendation systems: a survey. Int. J. Intell. Inf. Technol. **10**(2), 1–19 (2014)

28. Tan, S., Bu, J., Chen, C., He, X.: Using rich social media information for music recommendation via hypergraph model. In: Hoi, S.C.H., Luo, J., Boll, S., Xu, D., Jin, R., King, I. (eds.) Social Media Modeling and Computing, pp. 213–237. Springer, Heidelberg (2011)

29. Xiao, B., Benbasat, I.: E-commerce product recommendation agents: use, characteristics, and impact. Mis Q. **31**(1), 137–209 (2007)

30. Zanker, M., Jessenitschnig, M.: Case-studies on exploiting explicit customer requirements in recommender systems. User Model. User Adap. Inter. **19**(1–2), 133–166 (2009)

31. Zanker, M., Jessenitschnig, M.: Collaborative feature-combination recommender exploiting explicit and implicit user feedback. In: 2009 IEEE Conference on Commerce and Enterprise Computing, pp. 49–56. IEEE (2009)

32. Zhao, Q., Zhang, Y., Friedman, D., Tan, F.: E-commerce recommendation with personalized promotion. In: ACM Conference on Recommender Systems, pp. 219–226 (2015)

Appropriate Feature Selection and Post-processing for the Recognition of Artificial Pornographic Images in Social Networks

Fangfang Li[1], Siwei Luo[1], Xiyao Liu[1], and Jianbin Li[2(✉)]

[1] School of Information Science and Engineering, Central South University,
Changsha 410083, Hunan, China
lifangfang@csu.edu.cn
[2] Information Security and Big Data Research Institute, Central South University,
Changsha 410083, Hunan, China
lijianbin@csu.edu.cn

Abstract. Spreading and transmitting pornographic images over the Internet in the form of either real or artificial images is illegal and harmful to teenagers. Because traditional methods are primarily designed to identify real pornographic images, they are less efficient in dealing with artificial images. Therefore, a novel feature selection and post-processing method for the recognition of artificial pornographic images in social networks was proposed in the work. Firstly, features related to image size, skin color region, gray histogram, image color, edge density and direction, Gray Level Co-occurrence Matrix (GLCM) and Local Binary Patterns (LBP) were selected. Secondly, a post-processing process for these multiple feature was proposed, which includes two steps. The first step is feature expansion, which is aimed at improving the generalization ability of the recognition model. The other step is rapid feature extraction, which is aimed at reducing the time required for image recognition in social networks. Finally, experimental results demonstrate that the proposed method is effective for the recognition of artificial pornographic images in social networks.

Keywords: Feature selection · Image recognition · Artificial pornographic image · Post-processing · Social networks

1 Introduction

Pornographic images are harmful to physical and mental health, especially for teenagers. With the explosive growth of images on the Internet, recognizing pornographic images has recently attracted considerable attention. It is a meaningful and urgent task to protect people from accessing unexpected pornographic images. In recent years, several well-known social networks have developed the ability to automatically detect such images released by criminals who have bad intentions. Therefore, these criminals have begun to release artificial pornographic images instead in order to escape automatic detection.

© Springer International Publishing AG 2016
G. Wang et al. (Eds.): APSCC 2016, LNCS 10065, pp. 504–516, 2016.
DOI: 10.1007/978-3-319-49178-3_38

Artificial pornographic images, which are generated by computer software and contain many exaggerated erotic elements, are different from real pornographic images. Images in erotic games belong to this type. During the process of image release, criminals who have bad intentions often mingle normal information with artificial pornographic images to manipulate users into clicking on links and subsequently guide users to illegal websites and even induce them to commit crimes. Currently, the use of artificial pornographic images has become a new way for criminals to escape supervision. Therefore, the development of techniques for effectively identifying artificial pornographic images has become an important open issue.

Existing methods for the recognition of pornographic images can be divided into four categories: methods based on body structure, image retrieval, skin color region and visual words.

Methods based on body structure. A method based on body structure was proposed by Fleck and Forsyth in 1996 [1,2]. In this type of method, skin color regions are detected and prior body structure information is utilized to organize and combine the identified regions into a body. In this way, a pornographic image could be recognized. This type of method is straightforward and easy to implement. However, as human bodies are non-rigid objects and can assume a wide variety of postures, it is difficult to construct a complete database of body posture. Therefore, the recognition accuracy of these methods is not high [3,4].

Methods based on image retrieval. These methods try to find the best matching images in a pre-classified database, instead of analyzing a certain type of image directly [5,6]. However, the recognition effect of these methods relies heavily on the sample database. Because both the pornographic and non-pornographic images have various forms, the construction of a database with complete samples is very difficult. In order to ensure the recognition accuracy, large numbers of samples are required, which leads to a low recognition speed [4].

Methods based on skin color region. In this type of method, features that represent skin information, such as color and texture, are first extracted and then a pattern classifier is utilized to determine the recognition results [7–9]. Multi-agent neural and Bayesian learning methods are utilized to extract skin regions in Ref. [10] and the features from the skin are extracted to classify the images as either pornographic or non-pornographic [11]. The most challenging task of these methods is the extraction of effective features for distinguishing pornographic images. As mentioned above, pornographic images usually have various forms, therefore, it is hard to extract effective features for representing all of them [4].

Methods based on visual words. In recent years, image recognition based on visual words has attracted much attention and gained enormous popularity in object classification. Inspired by text content analysis, researchers realized the feasibility of considering an image as the combination of visual words. In this manner, methods for text content analysis could be applied to image semantic annotation, which provides a novel insight for the recognition of pornographic images [12]. In this type of method, the extracted visual words are used to describe the semantic content of images. Afterwards, the bag-of-words (BoW) model is introduced for the recognition of pornographic images [13]. Visual words and the semantic information of associated tags are used simultaneously in Ref. [14,15] to estimate the relevance scores of all user-tagged images. In addition, the BoW model has been developed for more accurate and efficient multimedia tagging, such as tag ranking, tag recommendation and tag refinement [16]. Bag-of-visual-words and text information are used in Ref. [17] to detect pornographic images. The SURF (Speeded Up Robust Features) descriptor was adopted in [18] to create a visual vocabulary, and then an SVM classifier was utilized to identify pornographic images.

However, the above methods are mainly intended for the recognition of real pornographic images, and currently there is no relevant research on the recognition of artificial pornographic images. Moreover, many problems are encountered when directly utilizing the above methods for the recognition of artificial images for the following two reasons. Firstly, features of artificial pornographic images are quite different from those of real pornographic images. Therefore, it is difficult to select features that are conducive to the recognition of artificial pornographic images. Secondly, because the number of artificial pornographic images on the Internet is relatively small and the proportion of these images relative to normal images is small, the unbalanced dataset will bring some difficulties to the subsequent processing.

To address the above problems, a novel feature selection and post-processing method for the recognition of artificial pornographic images in social networks is proposed in this paper. Our key contributions are as follows.

(1) Appropriate feature selection. Features that are conducive to the recognition of artificial pornographic images are first selected and extracted.

(2) Extracted feature post-processing. Because the longer existence of pornographic images in social networks will lead to wider spread and greater harm to people, especially to teenagers, it is important to recognize these images as quickly as possible. This puts forward a higher requirement on the speed of the recognition model. Therefore, a post-processing method for the extracted features is proposed in this paper. Firstly, a method for the rapid extraction of multiple features is designed, which aims to shorten the time required for image recognition in social networks. Then, a method for the expansion of multiple features is designed, which aims to improve the generalization ability of the image recognition method.

The rest of this paper is organized as follows. Section 2 gives a detailed description of the appropriate feature selection and feature post-processing. Section 3 presents the experimental results and analysis. Section 4 presents the papers conclusions and discusses future research.

2   Feature selection and post-processing

The workflow of the approach is shown in Fig. 1.

In the step of feature selection, seven types of features are selected, and each type of feature has the same length and represented meaning. In the step

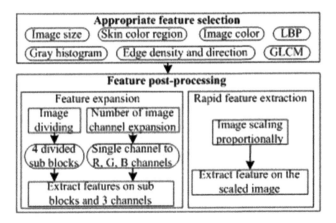

Fig. 1. Workflow of the method

of feature post-processing, the feature expansion and fast extraction methods are proposed, in order to improve the generalization ability of the recognition algorithm and increase the speed of image recognition, respectively, in social networks.

The following sections will describe each step in detail.

2.1 Appropriate Feature Selection

There is a wide range of image types and sizes on the Internet. An important problem is how to select appropriate features with the same length and represented meaning from different images. If the selected features have different lengths or represented meanings, there is no consistency in the feature representation and the subsequent recognition step can not be performed. Therefore, seven types of features are selected first in this paper, and each type of feature has the same length and represented meaning.

2.1.1 Image Size-Related Features

In social networks, artificial pornographic images that are too small in size cannot attract the attention of Internet users, while those too large in size cannot be released and spread quickly. Therefore, the sizes of artificial pornographic images are generally moderate. In view of this characteristic, image size can be used as a basic feature to distinguish between artificial pornographic images and normal images. The image size-related features selected in this paper are listed in Table 1.

As seen from Table 1, in addition to the basic image dimensions (height H and width W), some expanded features such as H*W, H/W, Max (H, W) and Min (H, W) are adopted in this paper. Through this expansion, higher-dimensional feature vectors with better ability to distinguish between different image sizes are obtained. Numerical values rather than Boolean values are adopted to represent

Table 1. Image size related features

Term	Interpretation
H	Image height
W	Image width
H*W	H multiplied by W
H/W	H divided by W
Max (H, W)	The maximum value in H and W
Min (H, W)	The minimum value in H and W

these features in this paper. For all the images, the six types of features have the same length and represented meaning.

2.1.2   Skin Color Region-Related Features

The skin color region has been widely used in the recognition of real pornographic images. Although the skin colors in artificial and real pornographic images are only slightly different, skin color is of some help for the recognition of artificial pornographic images. Therefore, the skin color region is selected as a feature and the method of J.A.M [19] is adopted to extract it in this paper. Specific steps are as follows. Firstly, the original RGB image is converted into the YCbCr image in the color space using formula (1). Secondly, if the value of a pixel satisfies a certain threshold, it is determined to be a skin color pixel. If an image does not contain any skin color pixel, it is assigned a feature vector of zeros. Finally, based on the extracted region, the five features listed in Table 2 are computed.

$$\begin{bmatrix} Y \\ C_b \\ C_r \end{bmatrix} = \begin{bmatrix} 16 \\ 128 \\ 128 \end{bmatrix} + \begin{bmatrix} 65.481 & 128.553 & 24.996 \\ -37.797 & -74.203 & 112 \\ 112 & -93.786 & -18.214 \end{bmatrix} \begin{bmatrix} R \\ G \\ B \end{bmatrix} \tag{1}$$

Table 2. Skin color region related features

Term	Interpretation
Pscs/Pi	Pixels of the skin color regions divided by pixels of the image
Psc/Pr	Pixels of the skin color region divided by pixels of the rectangle in which it is located
Ncr	Number of skin color pixel connected regions
Pmsc/Pscs	Pixels of the maximum skin color region divided by pixels of the total skin color regions
Pmsc/Pr	Pixels of the maximum skin color region divided by pixels of the rectangle in which it is located

2.1.3   Gray Histogram-Related Features

Because an artificial pornographic image is generated by computer software, its gray histogram is different from that of a real image. Therefore, the gray histogram can be used as an important feature in the recognition of artificial pornographic images. The eight features listed in Table 3 are computed on the basis of the gray histogram, where p(i) is the proportion of the pixels with gray value i relative to the set of all pixels of the image, which represents a normalized gray histogram.

Table 3. Gray histogram related features

Term	Interpretation
$mp = max_i p(i)$	The maximum value of p(i)
$gray = argmax_i p(i)$	The gray value of the pixel corresponding to the mp
$\mu = \sum_i i p(i)$	The average gray value of the histogram
$\sigma = \sqrt{\sum_i p(i)(i - \mu)^2}$	The standard deviation of the histogram
$med = \inf_j \{j : \sum_{i=0}^{j} p(i) \geq 0.5\}$	The median value of the histogram
$ent = -\sum_i p(i) log p(i)$	The entropy of the histogram
$skew = \sum_i p(i)\left(\frac{i-\mu}{\sigma}\right)^3$	The skewness of the histogram
$bias = \frac{\mu - med}{\sigma}$	The bias between μ and med

2.1.4   Image Color-Related Features

Color is the most direct visual feature of an image. Compared with other features, color is not sensitive to image translation, scaling, rotation and so on. It is very robust and easy to calculate. Because an artificial pornographic image is generated by computer software, its colors are different from those of a real natural image. Therefore, image color can be used as an important feature for the identification of artificial pornographic images. For each image in our dataset, firstly the image pixels are clustered by the K-means algorithm in RGB space, and then the features listed in Table 4 are extracted, where pi, j represents the pixel in row i and column j of the image, K is the number of the clustered classes, C_k represents the k-th clustered class and $|Ck|$ is the number of elements in C_k.

In order to make the above features of different images have the same represented meanings, the clustered classes are sorted in descending order according to the number of elements contained in each cluster. For different images, the features in the k-th clustered class all reflect the detailed information of the largest color block. Therefore, the features selected above all have the same represented meanings. Finally, the number of extracted features of each image is 3K + 3.

Table 4. Image color related features

Term	Interpretation
$m = \frac{1}{K}\sum_k m_k$	The average pixel value of all classes
$m_k = \frac{\sum_{i,j} p_{i,j} I\{p_{i,j} \in C_k\}}{\sum_{i,j} I\{p_{i,j} \in C_k\}}$	The average pixel value of Ck
$\sigma = \sqrt{\frac{1}{K}\sum_k (m_k - m)^2}$	the standard deviation of all classes
$\sigma_k = \sqrt{\frac{\sum_{i,j} I\{p_{i,j} \in C_k\}(p_{i,j}-m_k)^2}{\sum_{i,j} I\{p_{i,j} \in C_k\}}}$	The standard deviation of Ck
$r_k = \frac{|C_k|}{|\sum_k C_k|}$	The number of elements in Ck divided by the number in all classes
$e = \frac{\sum_{i,j}\sum_k I\{p_{i,j} \in C_k\}(p_{i,j}-m_k)^2}{\sum_k |C_k|}$	The average value of the squared errors which represents the closeness degree of all clustered classes

2.1.5 Edge Density and Direction

Texture features contain a large amount of image information and are commonly used for image classification and retrieval [20]. Different from a real image, the texture of an artificial pornographic image is more smooth and relatively simple. Therefore, texture can be used as an important feature for the identification of artificial pornographic images. Edge density and directional features are used to represent the textures of the images in this paper. Firstly, a gradient-based edge detection operator is applied to the original image to obtain a gradient image. Each pixel p of the gradient image contains two pieces of information: gradient magnitude Mag (p) and gradient direction Dir (p). Secondly, based on Mag (p), the edge density distribution of the unit area of the image [21] is calculated by formula (2), where N is the number of pixels in the image and T is the manually set threshold.

$$F_{edgeness} = \frac{|\{p|Mag(p) \geq T\}|}{N} \tag{2}$$

Thirdly, Mag (p) and Dir (p) are divided into a number of grades (10 in this paper). In this way, two normalized histograms Hmag and Hdir can be obtained from one image. Finally, these two histograms are combined together to form the edge density and directional feature as follows.

$$F_{magdir} = (H_{mag}, H_{dir}) \tag{3}$$

2.1.6 Gray Level Co-occurrence Matrix

Gray Level Co-occurrence Matrix (GLCM) [22] is used to describe the gray level distribution of an image. Given a direction vector d = (dr, dc), the GLCM of an image is defined as follows.

$$C_d(i,j) = |\{(r,c) : I(r,c) = i \text{ and } I(r+dr, c+dc) = j\}| \tag{4}$$

Table 5. GLCM-related features

Term	Interpretation
$ene = \sum_{i,j} N_d^2(i,j)$	The energy of N_d
$ent = -\sum_{i,j} N_d(i,j)\log_2 N_d(i,j)$	The entropy of N_d
$cont = \sum_{i,j} (i-j)^2 N_d(i,j)$	The contrast of N_d
$hom = \sum_{i,j} \frac{N_d(i,j)}{1+|i-j|}$	The homogeneity of N_d
$corr = \frac{\sum_{i,j}(i-\mu_i)(j-\mu_j)N_d(i,j)}{\sigma_i \sigma_j}$	The correlation of N_d

Generally, the GLCM is normalized:

$$N_d(i,j) = \frac{C_d(i,j)}{\sum_{i,j} C_d(i,j)} \tag{5}$$

For each image in our dataset, the features listed in Table 5 are extracted. where

$$\mu_i = \sum_i \sum_j i N_d(i,j), \mu_j = \sum_i \sum_j j N_d(i,j)$$
$$\sigma_i^2 = \sum_i \sum_j N_d(i,j)(i-\mu_i)^2, \sigma_j^2 = \sum_i \sum_j N_d(i,j)(j-\mu_j)^2 \tag{6}$$

Given a direction vector d, a GLCM can be obtained. For each image in our dataset, the five features listed in Table 5 are extracted. Finally, these features are combined together to form a feature vector which represents the image texture as follows.

$$Vector = [energy1, entropy1, contrast1, homogeneity1, correlation1, ...] \tag{7}$$

2.1.7   Local Binary Patterns

Local Binary Pattern (LBP) [23] is an effective and simple computed texture feature, which is widely used in face recognition. In this paper, the specific extraction steps of LBP are as follows. Firstly, the gray value of pixel p is compared with the gray values of its 8 neighboring pixels and an 8-bit binary number b1b2b3b4b5b6b7b8 is constructed, where bi is assigned a value of 0 or 1. If bi is assigned a value of 0, this indicates that the gray value of the i-th neighboring pixel is less than or equal to the gray value of p. Otherwise, it is assigned a value of 1. Secondly, an LBP image which has the same size as the original image is obtained. Finally, the histogram of the LBP image is calculated and normalized to obtain the LBP features of the image.

2.2   Feature Post-processing

Many types of features have been selected in the previous section. However, these features are still not sufficient for the recognition of artificial pornographic images. Therefore, these features need to be expanded. Moreover, it is important to recognize these images in social networks as quickly as possible, in order to prevent them from spreading widely and causing greater harm to people, especially to teenagers. Therefore, the rapid extraction of these multiple features is required.

2.2.1   Feature Expansion

Two methods of feature expansion are adopted in this paper. The first method involves dividing the image into sub blocks and later extracting the features of each sub block. Features of the sub blocks are combined together to constitute features of the image. For example, suppose an image is divided into 4 sub blocks: upper left, upper right, lower left and lower right. Features related to such factors as image size and skin color region are extracted from each of these four blocks. In this manner, not only is the set of features expanded. The distinguishing ability of the features is enhanced due to the addition of space distribution information of the features.

The other method involves expanding the number of image channels on which features are extracted, from a single channel to multiple channels. For example, histogram features can be extracted from R, G, and B channels separately, and then combined to constitute the final histogram features of the image. After applying the two expansion methods described in this section, the features extracted from each image ultimately constitute an 888-dimensional feature vector. The dimension of each type of feature is shown in Table 6.

Table 6. The ultimate feature vector

Feature	Dimension
Image size	6
Skin color region	5
Gray histogram	600
Image color	20
Edge density and direction	84
GLCM	45
LBP	128
Total	888

2.2.2   Rapid Feature Extraction

As with the image size related features, the extraction times of the other six types of features are proportional to the size of the image. Take the image color feature as an example. A clustering operation is performed during its extraction. If the size of the image is large, many pixels need to be clustered, and the feature extraction will be time consuming. Therefore, if the complete 888-dimensional feature vector is extracted from the original images, it will take considerable time, making it hard to meet the requirement of speed of the algorithm for the recognition of artificial pornographic images in social networks. To solve this problem, a fast feature extraction method is proposed in this paper.

Unlike the image size related features, which are fixed attributes of the image, the other features described above are invariant to image size. Consider the histogram feature, for example. If an image is scaled proportionally, the histogram shape of the scaled image is almost exactly the same as that of the original image. For the skin color region and image color related features because the five features of the former and the six features of the latter are calculated in a proportional way, they are invariant to image size. For features related to edge density and direction because Fedgeness is the marginal distribution density per unit area, it is invariant to image size. Also, because Fmagdir is the normalized histogram of gradients of magnitude and direction, if the image is scaled proportionally, it is also invariant. The same is true for the GLCM and LBP features. Table 7 shows the histogram comparison between the original image and the scaled image.

Table 7. Histogram comparison between the original image and the scaled image

Image	Size	Histogram
	536*362	
	150*101	

Therefore, unlike the features related to image size, if an image is scaled proportionally, the above features calculated on the scaled image are almost the same as those calculated on the original one. Therefore, in this paper, all original images are first scaled proportionally to a smaller size. Then the extraction of the above features, except the features related to image size, is implemented on the scaled images, which could significantly shorten the time required for the feature extraction.

3 Experimental Results and Analysis

Images from the worlds largest Chinese communication platform, Baidu post Bar, were used as the data resource. A total of 9808 images, released by users, were collected. Among the images, 7860 images were selected as the training dataset, of which 1191 were artificial pornographic images. For the testing dataset, 1948 images were selected, of which 308 were artificial pornographic images. The ratio of normal images to artificial pornographic images was approximately 6 to 1. Examples of selected images are shown in Table 8.

Table 8. Examples of artificial pornographic (first row) and non-pornographic (second row) images

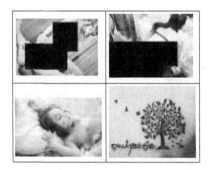

During the experiment, 1000 images of a variety of sizes were selected randomly. Two different methods were adopted to calculate the features: one method is based on the original images, and the other is based on the proportionally scaled images. Under the configuration of Core I5, RAM 4G, the results are shown in Table 9. During the experiment, we observed that if the above features are calculated directly on the original images, it will take too much time. For a large-sized image, the feature calculation will take almost one second. If the original image is scaled first, the time will be shortened greatly, to approximately 34 milliseconds per image. For 1000 images, the total time will be reduced more than 20-fold.

Table 9. Time cost comparison for feature extraction (1000 images)

Comparison	Total time (msec)	Mean time(msec)
Original images	588081	588.08
Scaled images	25939	25.94

4   Conclusions

In this study, appropriate feature selection and post-processing method for the recognition of artificial pornographic images in social networks is proposed. The method has the following merits.

(1) In the process of feature selection, seven appropriate types of features are selected for distinguishing artificial pornographic images, and each feature of each type has the same length and represented meaning.

(2) The feature expansion and fast extraction methods are proposed, in order to improve the generalization ability of the recognition algorithm and increase the speed of image recognition, respectively, in social networks.

The above selected features and post-processing method has made good foundation for the further recognition of artificial pornographic images. Therefore, in the near future, we will attempt to use tree models for the recognition of artificial pornographic images in social networks.

Acknowledgments. This study is supported by the China Postdoctoral Science Foundation (2016M592450), and the Hunan Provincial Natural Science Foundation of China (2016JJ4119).

References

1. Forsyth, D.A., Fleck, M.M.: Identifying nude pictures. In: Proceedings of the 3rd IEEE Workshop on Applications of Computer Vision, pp. 103–108, Sarasota. IEEE (1996)
2. Fleck, M.M., Forsyth, D.A., Bregler, C.: Finding naked people. In: Buxton, B., Cipolla, R. (eds.) ECCV 1996. LNCS, vol. 1065, pp. 593–602. Springer, Cambridge (1996). doi:10.1007/3-540-61123-1_173
3. Hu, W., Wu, O., Chen, Z., Fu, Z., Maybank, S.: Recognition of pornographic web pages by classifying texts and images. IEEE Trans. Pattern Anal. Mach. Intell. **29**(6), 1019–1034 (2007)
4. Zhou, L., Zhang, J., Zhao, Y., Zhao, S.: Compressed domain based pornographic image recognition using multi-cost sensitive decision trees. Sig. Process. **93**(8), 2126–2139 (2013)
5. Wang, J.Z., Li, J., Wiederhold, G., Firschein, O.: System for screening objectionable images. Comput. Commun. **21**(5), 1355–1360 (1998)
6. Wang, M., Hua, X.S.: Active learning in multimedia annotation and retrieval: a survey. ACM Trans. Intell. Syst. Technol. **2**(2), 10–31 (2011)
7. Wang, M., Hua, X.S., Tang, J.H., Hong, R.C.: Beyond distance measurement: constructing neighborhood similarity for video annotation. IEEE Trans. Multimed. **11**(3), 465–476 (2009)
8. Wang, M., Hua, X.S., Hong, R.C., Tang, J.H., Qi, G.J., Song, Y.: Unified video annotation via multi-graph learning. IEEE Trans. Circ. Syst. Video Technol. **19**(5), 733–746 (2009)
9. Meng, W.A.N.G., Xian-sheng, H.U.A., Tao, M.E.I., Ri-chang, H.O.N.G., Guo-jun, Q.I., Yan, S.O.N.G., Li-rong, D.A.I.: Semi-supervised kernel density estimation for video annotation. Comput. Vis. Image Underst. **113**(3), 384–396 (2009)
10. Zaidan, A.A., Ahmad, N.N., Karim, H.A., Larbani, M., Zaidan, B.B., Sali, A.: On the multi-agent learning neural and Bayesian methods in skin detector and pornography classifier: an automated anti-pornography system. Neurocomputing **131**, 397–418 (2014)
11. Zheng, H., Daoudi, M., Jedynak, B.: Blocking adult images based on statistical skin detection. Electron. Lett. Comput. Vis. Image Anal. **4**(2), 1–14 (2004)

12. Zhang, J., Sui, L., Zhuo, L., Li, Z., Yang, Y.: An approach of bag-of-words based on visual attention model for pornographic images recognition in compressed domain. Neurocomputing **110**, 145–152 (2013)

13. Wang, Y., Li, Y., Gao, W.: Detecting pornographic images with visual words. Trans. Beijing Inst. Technol. **28**(5), 410–413 (2008)

14. Gao, Y., Wang, M., Zha, Z., Shen, J., Li, X., Wu, X.: Visual-textual joint relevance learning for tag-based social image search. IEEE Trans. Image Process. **22**(1), 363–376 (2013)

15. Wang, M., Yang, K., Hua, X., Zhang, H.: Towards a relevant and diverse search of social images. IEEE Trans. Multimed. **12**(8), 829–842 (2010)

16. Meng, W.A.N.G., Bing-bing, N.I., Xian-sheng, H.U.A., Tat-seng, C.H.U.A.: Assistive tagging: a survey of multi-media tagging with human-computer joint exploration. ACM Comput. Surv. **44**(4), 1–24 (2012)

17. Dong, K., Guo, L., Fu, Q.: An adult image detection algorithm based on bag-of-visual-words, text information. In: 10th International Conference on Natural Computation, pp. 556–560. IEEE (2014)

18. Liu, Y.Z., Xie, H.T.: Constructing SURF visual-words for pornographic images detection. In: Proceedings of the 12th International Conference on Computers, Information Technology, pp. 404–407. IEEE (2009)

19. Marcial-Basilio, J.A., Aguilar-Torres, G., Snchez-Prez, G., et al.: Detection of pornographic digital images. Int. J. Comput. **2**, 298–305 (2010)

20. Manjunath, B.S., Ma, W.Y.: Texture features for browsing and retrieval of image data. IEEE Trans. Pattern Anal. Mach. Intell. **18**(8), 837–842 (1996)

21. Shapiro, L.G., Stockman, G.C.: Computer Vision. Prentice-Hall, Upper Saddle River (2011)

22. Haralick, R.M., Shanmugam, K., Dinstein, I.H.: Textural features for image classification. IEEE Trans. Syst. Man Cybern. **6**, 610–621 (1973)

23. Ahonen, T., Hadid, A., Pietikainen, M.: Face description with local binary patterns: application to face recognition. IEEE Trans. Pattern Anal. Mach. Intell. **28**(12), 2037–2041 (2006)

Author Index